ML
410
V4
T7
1972

74-3555

DATE DUE

WITHDRAWN FROM RCSJ LIBRARY

GLOUCESTER COUNTY COLLEGE
LIBRARY
SEWELL, NEW JERSEY 08080

PORTRAIT OF VERDI

by Boldini

GIUSEPPE Verdi

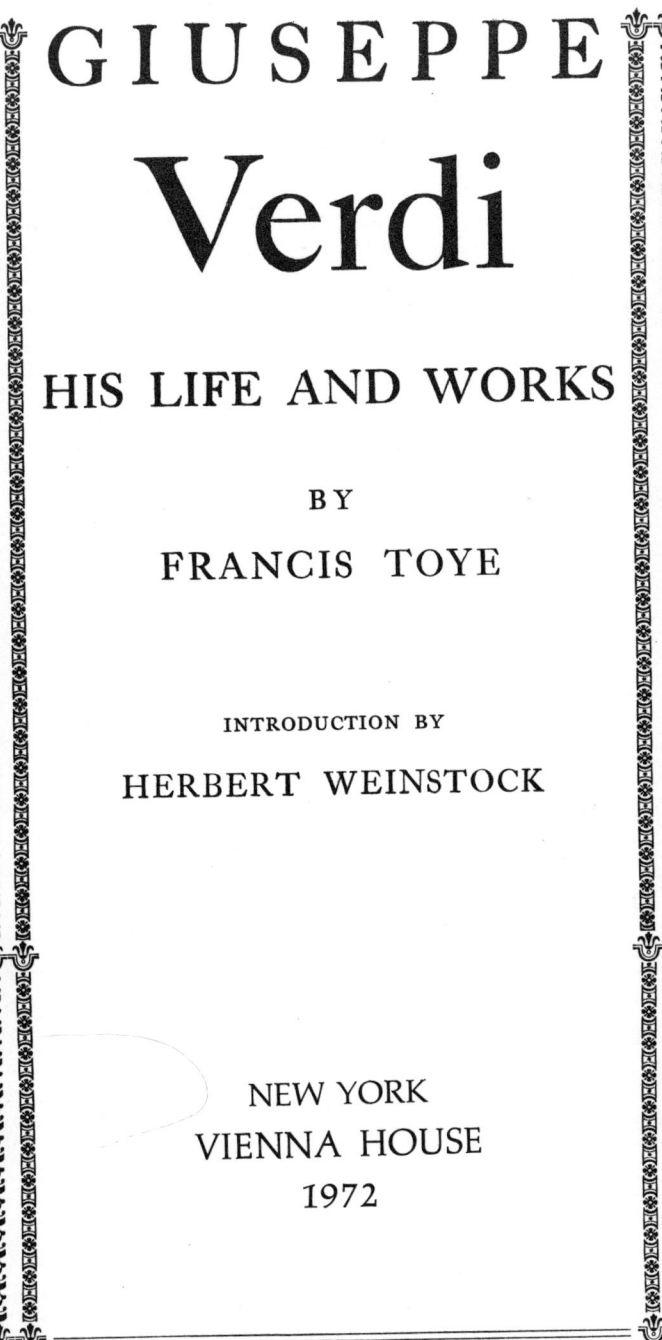

HIS LIFE AND WORKS

BY

FRANCIS TOYE

INTRODUCTION BY

HERBERT WEINSTOCK

NEW YORK
VIENNA HOUSE
1972

Introduction © *1946 by Alfred A. Knopf, Inc.*

*This 1972 VIENNA HOUSE edition is reprinted
by arrangement with Alfred A. Knopf, Inc.
International Standard Book Number: 0-8443-0067-5
Library of Congress Catalogue Number: 72-81577
Manufactured in the United States of America*

TO

MARY NEWCOMB

in admiration of her integrity as a woman

and an artist

INTRODUCTION

First-rate biographies of composers are astonishingly rare. Acquaintance with them by conductors, singers, and instrumentalists remains, to the misfortune of concert and opera, even rarer. The result is that in those places where we should discover men and women steeped in the periods, significances, and styles of the pieces of music they re-create from symbols on paper we discover instead virtuosos making use of the outlines of Bach and Mozart and Beethoven and Wagner for flaunting the pennants of their own periods and significances and styles. How can a man honestly re-create the B-minor Mass who does not know how it came to be, for what Bach intended it, how Masses were sung during the first half of the eighteenth century, or whether Bach approached the liturgy as a pious Catholic, a Lutheran, or an atheist? How can a soloist sing it without knowing how men and women were expected to sing when it was composed? Where would this background information exist in readier state than in a first-rate biography of Bach? In Bach's case, for that matter, full familiarity with his musical education, habits, and environment is essential even to a poor performance: his surviving scores are usually altogether devoid of the most rudimentary indications of tempo, volume, and color. And only a slothful interpreter will, without question or study, make use of markings "edited" into the score by someone other than the composer.

Those who assert that a musical layman cannot familiarize himself with a Mozart symphony simply by reading about Mozart the man — in Jahn, in Wyzewa and Saint-Foix, in Turner, in Emily Anderson's wonderful edition of Mozart's letters — are correct. They are correct if they mean that such reading is not by itself enough, and for the purpose must be superimposed on complete acquaintance with the score. But that a man thoroughly educated in the art and science of music and not at all educated in Mozart the man and composer is equipped to understand a Mozart symphony (really to understand it in the most complete sense) is a claim that this correct statement makes by indirection, and makes falsely. No man can comprehend everything to be understood about Köchel 543, the great E-flat Symphony, if he knows only how to parse its musical sentences, chart its formal design, and read its signposts of pitch, speed, volume, phrasing, and instrumentation. To become intimate with its inmost nature, even merely to be introduced to that nature, he must also know under what circumstances, at what stage in its creator's development, and in what sort of emotional weather it was composed. The most fastidi-

Introduction

ously written-out score is no more than an outline: it must be filled in with the life-giving element called style. More about the style required for adequate (not to mention luminous) performance of the E-flat Symphony is to be learned from the most scrupulous studies of Mozart than from however many hours spent with a score of the symphony itself but without sympathetic intimacy with the man who created that score. If music is a kind of golden mathematics, the adjective is surely as important as the noun; here, as everywhere, the gift without the giver is bare.

Perhaps the first really satisfactory modern biography of a great composer was Otto Jahn's *Life of Mozart* (1856-60). Then came Friedrich Chrysander's *G. F. Händel* (1858-67, incomplete), Philipp Spitta's *J. S. Bach* (1884-5), and Alexander Wheelock Thayer's *Beethoven* (1866-79 in German; completed by Riemann; English version, 1921). These were the first monuments of musicological biography; without knowledge of them and their successors, no conductor and no soloist should attempt to perform the music of the men they re-create. More recently there have been large-scale and essential works on Bach by André Pirro, Albert Schweitzer, and Charles Sanford Terry; on Mozart by Teodor de Wyzewa and Georges de Saint-Foix, and on Wagner by Ernest Newman. No reliable and satisfactory work on a comparable scale and of comparable quality has ever dealt with the lives and works of Gluck, Haydn, Weber, Schubert, Mendelssohn, Schumann, Chopin, Liszt, Berlioz, Brahms, Mussorgsky, or Debussy. About them, many essential facts and much detailed enlightenment must be pursued through dusty periodicals, old volumes half filled with fiction, incomplete but honest books written too soon, and wide expanses of writing of a badness that is excruciating.

Fully deserving place on the shelves beside the comprehensive, basic books are perhaps twenty-five volumes built to a smaller scale. To mind at once (to mention only books written in English) come W. J. Turner's *Mozart* and *Berlioz*, Ernest Newman's *The Man Liszt*, Tom S. Wotton's *Hector Berlioz*, and Francis Toye's *Rossini* and *Giuseppe Verdi*. These slighter books do not obviate the need for definitive volumes of biographical and critical treatment of the same subjects. They do fill a need that continues after such definitive volumes appear. For in addition to a good musical biography's value as one means of understanding the music, it has values in itself — as biography, as history, as fascinating reading, as a reference book. Not every reader will have need or time for Wyzewa and Saint-Foix, but everyone who loves Mozart can read Turner.

Of the expertly conceived, highly useful, and entertainingly written modern biographies of composers, none, it seems to me, is

Introduction

achieved with more aplomb, more apposite and yet objective nearness to its subject, than Francis Toye's *Giuseppe Verdi*. (Toye's *Rossini* also fits its subject like a glove, and therefore proceeds without the scope and profound seriousness of the *Verdi*.) Mr. Toye has the first virtue of a writer: he writes well, places words and ideas in good order and with an unflagging sense of their texture, hue, and influence on their surroundings. He has, too, the first virtue of a biographer: he knows his subject as thoroughly as research, familiarity with works, and long rumination allow. Nor does he lack the biographer's second virtue: objective sympathy with his subject. He can, as added tints, color his paragraphs with wit and humor. And he has avoided the probably impossible project of launching protracted discussions of Verdi's operas at the moments of their occurrence in the unfolding of Verdi's life story. Allowing his material to dictate its own form, he has in fact given us two books in one, the first a purely biographical sketch that tells as much about Verdi the man as any non-specialist wants to know, the second a history and analysis — again as detailed as the non-specialist could wish — of Verdi's twenty-six operas, Requiem Mass, E-minor String Quartet, and miscellaneous short works.

From the first section of Mr. Toye's book emerges the living figure of Giuseppe Verdi, peasant, musical genius, and master craftsman. The figure is clearly outlined: there is no mystery about Verdi, that being only one of many ways in which he is the opposite of his greatest contemporary among opera-composers, Richard Wagner. Seldom can a convincing portrait of a long-lived man (Verdi died at past eighty-seven) have been so well drawn at an average speed of something over one thousand words to each year. For Mr. Toye is a compact and allusive writer, no more wasteful of his materials than was the composer of *Falstaff*. The ninety thousand words of this section, let it be said, add up to the biography of a great composer, not to the biography of a man who happened, outside the pages of this book, to compose great music. It is a creation that time will alter in detail, but is unlikely to change in proportion or emphasis. It is, that is to say, artistically true.

From the second, slightly longer section of Mr. Toye's book emerge several valuable and related discussions: one on the gradual enrichment and purification of Verdi's one and only style, another on the flaws in his literary and theatrical judgment, a third on the genius of Arrigo Boïto. There are others. For Mr. Toye is not afraid to go beyond the limits of his design if fancy beckons. As a result, this second section is one to make an opera-goer sick with longing, if not with fury. He will be acquainted with four of the twenty-six Verdi operas if he has attended opera at all: *Rigoletto, Il Trovatore,*

La Traviata, and *Aïda*. Has he been persistent and fortunate, he may know six more (including two of the greatest operas ever composed): *Macbeth, Simon Boccanegra, Un Ballo in Maschera, La Forza del Destino, Otello*, and *Falstaff*. Old enough (or very widely traveled), he may conceivably have met with four more: *I Lombardi, Ernani, Luisa Miller*, and *Don Carlo*. (I myself have been able to hear ten Verdi operas in more than two decades of opera-going.) But he who can come away from Mr. Toye's book with no desire to hear all he does not know of the above, plus *Nabucco, La Battaglia di Legnano*, and *I Vespri Siciliani*, is impervious to literary persuasiveness or congenitally unfriendly to opera. Mr. Toye has left me with an undying wish to attend an up-to-the-hilt mounting of *Alzira*, which he describes as "undoubtedly the worst of Verdi's operas," and which deals with blood and passion among the Incas!

My final plea in this defense of musical biography is simple. Having read Mr. Toye's masterly book, watch your own reactions the next time you are present at *Rigoletto* or *La Traviata* or *Aïda*. Watch them closely (it will be fun in itself), and decide for yourself whether or not it is true that you cannot approach closer to an understanding of the art of music through a first-rate biography. I think that you will discover that *"Caro nome"* or the Prelude to Act III of *La Traviata* or the tomb scene of *Aïda*, will have new meanings for you. They will have those new meanings not because Mr. Toye has obtruded himself between you and the operas or taught you to read a score, but because an intimacy with Verdi, his methods, and his times has helped you place his work in a new, more just, and more searching light. A book capable of doing that for its readers, especially a book that deals in part with such masterpieces as *La Traviata, Aïda, Otello, Falstaff*, and the "Manzoni" Requiem, is more than a parasite on the body musical. It is, or should be, an essential organ of that body's functioning.

I do not count as the least of this book's virtues that it introduces its readers to two fascinating men. One of them is Giuseppe Verdi. The other is Francis Toye.

Mr. Toye has asked me to say that his inability to consult papers left in Florence during the recent war has prevented him from correcting one or two small errors in his text. One of these concerns the deaths of Verdi's first wife and two children. Later research has proved that the three deaths did not occur, as stated herein, within a space of three months, but during a period of approximately two and one half years. As at least one of them occurred while the composer was at work on *Il Finto Stanislao*, however, the point made concerning that opera remains valid.

HERBERT WEINSTOCK

PREFACE

THE ORIGIN and above all the length of this book demand a few words of explanation. The origin is simple enough. Some five years ago I was lucky enough to hear several performances of Verdi operas at La Scala under Toscanini, and these performances brought with them a conviction that the importance attached to Verdi by conventional musical opinion in England was miserably inadequate. I was not unprepared for this. Nobody who had the good fortune at Cambridge to come under the influence of Professor Dent, most large-minded and stimulating of teachers, was likely to consider the composer of *Il Trovatore* a mere purveyor of tunes. Performances, usually indifferent, of the operas in England and Germany had already given me great pleasure; a few, in Italy, greater pleasure still. But in Milan I was carried away by a new enthusiasm, a sudden realization that this music contained vital and poetical elements distinct from those of any other music even when presented by the same conductor in the same conditions. Elements, it should be explained, not necessarily better but different, and capable, moreover, of awakening a particularly responsive echo in me.

Needless to say, with the exception of one or two individuals who had already arrived at much the same conclusions, nobody believed that my enthusiasm was justified in regard to the superlative excellence either of the operas themselves or of their interpretation. Lip service might be paid to the merits of *Otello* and *Falstaff;* otherwise there was the same dreary repetition of the nonsense — for it is nonsense — about the "guitar-like orchestra" in *La Traviata* or *Rigoletto;* *Aïda* was "flashy" or "empty"; *Il Trovatore* just "absurd." Operas like *La Forza del Destino* or *Don Carlo* remained mere names, remembered, if at all, by some isolated numbers associated with famous singers. The essential unity of Verdi's output, its unfailing dramatic significance even when expressed in simple melodies — above all, the unswerving artistic integrity of it all — were not so much denied as ignored.

Nor was the case helped by the fact that a musician of Toscanini's genius lavished so much care and enthusiasm on the performance of Verdi's music. In those days, it must be remembered, the name of Toscanini meant little or nothing to the English musical world. The average musician, professional or amateur, if he had heard of him at all, thought that here was a question merely of some exceptional virtuoso with a gift for making the worse appear the better music. There was no world-wide realization then, as there is now, that the greatness of Toscanini lay precisely in his presentation of music in exact accordance with the intentions of the composer, not in the manufacture of brilliant glosses of his own. I do not think that the great maestro will regard it as any belittlement of his genius if I suggest that this incomparable quality may be traced in some measure to the influence of that Verdian probity which excited his admiration and held his allegiance in early days.

Such, then, were the reasons that first prompted me to embark on a book that might assist some of my fellow countrymen to capture a portion of my own delight in the music of a man about whom they knew less, perhaps, than about any other composer of equal standing; for at that time, to the best of my belief, there was not a single adequate biography of Verdi in the English language. Then (as now) it was not so much the professional musicians, especially the composers, or the leading critics who stood in need of conversion. They might, with perfect justice, appreciate Verdi less or more, but they rarely dismissed him as negligible. The mass of the public, too, was faithful to the more popular operas after its fashion. Only the amateurs of superior musical culture appeared to think a liking for Verdi slightly incompatible with their reputation for good taste. There was no merit to be gained by professing admiration for a composer whose music could be enjoyed by anybody gifted with any musical receptivity whatever. Moreover, quite apart from snobbishness, conscious or unconscious, Verdi's shortcomings as a musician were calculated to antagonize such people, just as his virtues were not of a kind to attract them. About Verdi as a man they knew nothing and cared less. The last two years have witnessed a considerable change in this respect among certain circles of the intelligentsia; but the attitude is still common, and one of the objects of this book is to persuade those who adopt it to examine their position again in the light of facts that may be new to them.

I have given this perhaps excessively personal explanation because I am most anxious that it should not be thought that this book was prompted by a mere desire to take advantage of the Verdi renaissance in Germany which has been so remarkable a feature of musical history during the last few years. I did not even know of this renaissance at the time I first determined to write a book. What it did eventually cause me to do was to write a long book instead of a comparatively short one.

The extent of the revival of interest in Verdi in Germany is still imperfectly realized in this country. Figures published in the organ of the Imperial League of Opera provide the best illustration of it. They were based on operatic performances in 135 opera houses during the 1927-8 season. Two composers easily headed the list,

Preface

Wagner and Verdi; and the actual number of performances of works by these two masters was as follows: Wagner 1,576, Verdi 1,513, both figures being nearly 600 more than that achieved by any other composer. An analysis of performances at the Vienna Opera proves that there has been no alteration in this state of things. There were 339 performances at that Opera during the year 1930, of which Wagner was responsible for 49, Verdi for 46, while no other composer reached the figure of 30. Ten years earlier, any such correlation between Wagner and Verdi in Germany would have seemed frankly incredible. Nor must it be imagined that the figure of Verdi performances was swollen only by more numerous presentations of popular operas already in the repertory, such as *Rigoletto, Il Trovatore, La Traviata, Un Ballo in Maschera*, though these have acquired, of course, enhanced reputations. It was not merely a question of operas such as *Otello* and *Falstaff*, formerly regarded, more or less, as preserves of the *cognoscenti*, becoming popular successes. Operas wholly or practically unknown were introduced into the repertory, sometimes, as in the case of *La Forza del Destino* and *Don Carlo*, with triumphant success; sometimes, as in the case of *Simon Boccanegra*, with genuine if less pronounced success. Not only *Nabucco* and *Macbeth* and *Luisa Miller*, all exceedingly interesting works, have been revived, but works admittedly of the second order, such as *I Masnadieri* and *I Due Foscari*, have received attention. Nor, in fact, has this revival of interest in Verdi's work been confined to Germany, though found there in its most striking form.

In such circumstances an exhaustive study of the man and his work seemed imperative. How far the Verdi renaissance may be proved to be transitory no one can tell. It is of course based on reaction — reaction against Wagner, reaction against mere complexity. As the convention of Wagnerian music drama becomes in its turn old-fashioned, music expressed in other conventions is enabled once more to compete on equal terms. This has worked in favor of Verdi's early and middle operas — that is to say, the majority of his output. One thing, however, is certain: if an operatic composer of genius equal to that of Verdi or Wagner makes his appearance among us, both masters will retire to Valhalla, there to await comparative destruction, a fate of which Verdi himself would have been the first to proclaim the justice. Only no such genius has appeared, and the interest in Verdi's work of every period and style seems to be on the increase rather than the decrease. Wherefore any excuse that may have existed for skimping the treatment of any portion of the subject is gone; the time has clearly come for all the material to be reviewed afresh, and I have tried to do this as regards Verdi's life and music alike.

This book makes no pretense to contain any great quantity of new, unchronicled facts; it is rather an attempt at correlation of the enormous mass of facts and opinions already in existence. This has been a considerable task. Several biographies are not wholly accurate, especially in the matter of dates, and it has not always been possible to check them by the *Copialettere,* wherein, incidentally, the dates are too often misprinted. Then, in addition to a study of the music itself, there was the reading, where possible, of the plays from which the librettos had been taken. There were also the stories of these librettos to be related in a manner that should render the psychology as well as the action of the plots intelligible. This, as a matter of fact, was one of the most arduous tasks of all, as anyone who attempts it will soon find out for himself; I can only hope that the expenditure of labor and space will be justified by the enhanced interest of the opera-goer or the student. Lastly, there was the collection of contemporary press criticisms. On these I have laid unusual stress because they help to illustrate the point of view of the time, without which it is impossible to envisage justly a work of art. Thus, in the total result, despite every effort to the contrary, this volume has swollen to proportions such as Verdi, who once twitted the Germans with their passion for writing a hundred pages about the leg of a flea, would have approached with a bias at least as unfavorable as that of his biographer.

The structure of the book explains itself. The first part, intended for the general reader, describes Verdi's life and activities, gives a summary of some of the most important criticisms of his operas, and deals only with the most general characteristics of the music. This is treated in detail in the second part under the headings of the various works. Every effort has been made to avoid unnecessary overlapping, but a certain amount was inevitable. Here, too, will be found an account of the librettos and their origin. In short, the second part is designed to meet the requirements of specialists and students and, above all, of those persons who wish to learn something about the libretto or the music of an opera before going to hear it. Should they desire to link up the historical facts about any particular work with the details of the libretto and the music, reference to the first part of the book by means of the index will, I hope, enable them to do so quite easily.

One or two explanations seem called for. For instance, I have used the word "scene," not in its technical operatic meaning but as denoting a change of set. After some deliberation I decided, in telling the stories of the librettos, to preserve the Italian names throughout. Having once adopted the principle, I had to be logical about it, but I must confess that Bardolfo and Pistola still cause me pain. Fortunately Piave saved me from the ignominy of calling Macduff or Macbeth by anything but their proper names. In the librettos based on Shaksperian subjects the use of Shakspere's own language is intended to indicate roughly where the libretto and the play correspond. I realize only too well that I have failed to solve the thorny problem of musical illustrations, of which there are always too few for the specialist and too many for the ordinary reader. I have endeavored to effect a compromise by selecting musical illustrations that, in the main, bear only on one or two points, such as Verdi's development and typical procedure. I have given no musical illustrations at all in the case of the last three operas or of the Requiem Mass, preferring to assume that the scores are in the possession of everyone sufficiently musical to be interested. If they are not, they ought to be.

It is never easy to determine the exact extent to which acknowledgment should be made to other authors. I have gone on the principle of indicating the reference in a footnote only when the fact in question seemed exceptionally remarkable or disputable. I have tried to be wholly honest in the matter, but I cannot delude myself with the belief that there will not be certain passages for which some readers may think that a reference should have been given and others where they may think that it might have been dispensed with. Generally speaking, the book is based on letters, mainly, of course, the *Copialettere*, before the publication of which, in 1913, no adequate biography of Verdi was in fact possible, supplemented by other biographies in the case of lacunæ or special information. Thus, the anecdotes are mainly derived from Pougin; the facts about the last days of Giuseppina from Martinelli; the information in regard to Verdi's librettists (with the exception of Boïto) from Mantovani in *Musica d'Oggi*, and so on.

My thanks are due to many persons who have helped me in the preparation of this book. First and foremost comes Professor Dent, to whom I owe a special debt of gratitude, for not only was he responsible for putting some valuable material in my way, but he was the first person to awaken in me an interest in Verdi. Indeed, in a sense I regard him as the godfather of this book; which by no means implies any expectation that he will necessarily approve of his godchild. I am also deeply grateful to my wife and to Dr. Malcolm Sargent, who respectively revised the first and second portions of the book. Dr. Sargent, moreover, extended his kindness by making many valuable suggestions and criticisms, in addition to copying out some musical illustrations. I must thank, too, Sir Thomas Beecham who was responsible for several illuminating ideas about *Don Carlo*, and Miss Mary Newcomb, whose theatrical insight has suggested many interesting lines of thought, especially in the case of *La Dame aux camélias*.

I am indebted to Mr. Prime-Stevenson for sending me a copy of his excellent book, *Long-Haired Iopas;* to Mr. Ernest Newman for giving me his edition of Chorley's *Musical Recollections* and the benefit of invaluable advice on one or two points; to Miss Eva Greves for furnishing me with a detailed synopsis of those scenes of popular life in *Don Alvaro* which made excessive demands on my faltering Spanish, as well as with information about the noble author of the play. Signora Toscanini most kindly allowed me to copy the *envoi* found at the end of the score of *Falstaff*, and Major Longden considerately arranged for the photographing of Gemito's magnificent bust of Verdi while on loan at the Italian Exhibition at Burlington House. Signor Bellezza performed the invaluable service of introducing me to Busseto and Sant' Agata, a service for which, like the experience itself, I can never sufficiently thank him.

Nor can the helpfulness of everybody connected with Messrs. Ricordi be exaggerated. Commendatore Valcarenghi, now the head of the firm, in addition to providing me with every facility to work in his jealously guarded library, gave me many photographs and letters for the purpose of reproduction; Dr. Tasselli, their London representative, both gave and lent me music; while to Maestro Zanon, head of their musical department in Milan, go my special thanks not only for the ungrudging bestowal of much of his valuable time, but for first pointing out to me the alterations in the score of *Falstaff*. Needless to say, I further owe to the courtesy of Messrs. Ricordi authorization to reproduce the various musical illustrations, for which I have also to thank the four French publishers who own certain copyrights in France and Belgium.

Last and, in one sense, greatest of all my debts is that owed to the devotion and enthusiasm of my secretary, Miss Pamela Buchanan, who has shown a supreme contempt for trade-union principles in her invariable readiness to work at any hour and for any length of time, could she thereby contribute to the better making of our book.

F. T.

London, December 1930

The following are the principal works and periodicals that have been consulted in the preparation of this book:

ITALIAN:

I Copialettere di Giuseppe Verdi. Gaetano Cesari e Alessandro Luzio.
Verdi, Lettere Inedite. G. Morazzoni.
Rivista Musicale Italiana: Lettere Inedite di Verdi a Escudier.
Giuseppe Verdi: Vita e Opere. Anton Giulio Barrili.
Studio sulle Opere di Giuseppe Verdi. A. Basevi.

La Vita di Giuseppe Verdi. G. Bragagnolo — E. Bettazzi.
Verdi. Eugenio Checchi.
Giuseppe Verdi. Elviro Ciccarese.
Giuseppe Verdi. Franco Temistocle Garibaldi.
Raggi e Penombre. Aldo Martinelli.
Giuseppe Verdi: 1839 — 1898. Gino Monaldi.
Le Opere di Giuseppe Verdi al Teatro alla Scala. Gino Monaldi.
Re Lear e Ballo in Maschera. Alessandro Pascolato.
Cenni Biografici su Giuseppe Verdi. G. Perosio.
Ricordi Verdiani Inediti. Italo Pizzi.
Giuseppe Verdi. Gino Roncaglia.
Le Opere di Verdi. A. Soffredini.
Viaggio Musicale in Italia. Adriano Lualdi.
Musica d'Oggi: Librettisti Verdiani. T. Mantovani.
Arrigo Böito. Corrado Ricci.
Gioacchino Rossini. Giuseppe Radiciotti.
L'Italia Moderna. Pietro Orsi.
Memorie di un Ottuagenario (a historical novel). I. Nievo.

FRENCH:
Verdi. Camille Bellaigue.
Verdi. A. Bonaventura.
Verdi. Arthur Pougin.
Verdi et son œuvre. Le Prince de Valori.
Vie de Rossini. Stendhal.
Cavour: un grand réaliste. Maurice Paléologue.

GERMAN:
Verdi — Briefe. Franz Werfel.
Giuseppe Verdi. Max Chop.
Giuseppe Verdi. Arthur Neisser.
Giuseppe Verdi. C. Perinello.
Verdi. Adolf Weissmann.
Verdi: Roman der Oper. Franz Werfel.
Gesammelte Schriften. Richard Wagner.

ENGLISH:
Verdi. F. Bonavia.
Verdi: Man and Musician. F. J. Crowest.
Thirty Years Musical Recollections. Henry F. Chorley.
Long-Haired Iopas. Edward Prime-Stevenson.

CONTENTS

PART I   PAGE 3

PART II
OPERAS

Oberto, Conte di Bonifacio	199
Il Finto Stanislao	201
Nabucodonosor	203
I Lombardi alla Prima Crociata	207
Ernani	212
I Due Foscari	220
Giovanna d'Arco	223
Alzira	227
Attila	229
Macbeth	233
I Masnadieri	244
Il Corsaro	248
La Battaglia di Legnano	251
Luisa Miller	255
Rigoletto	263
Il Trovatore	273
La Traviata	281
I Vespri Siciliani	290
Simon Boccanegra	295
Aroldo	307
Un Ballo in Maschera	311
La Forza del Destino	321

Don Carlo	PAGE 332
Aïda	345
Otello	359
Falstaff	374

ECCLESIASTICAL WORKS

A Requiem Mass	388
Ave Maria; Pater Noster	392
Quattro Pezzi Sacri	393

MISCELLANEOUS WORKS

Songs	397
Inno delle Nazioni	398
String Quartet in E Minor	399

VERDI THE MUSICIAN 401

INDEX   FOLLOWS PAGE 414

ILLUSTRATIONS

Portrait of Verdi by Boldini	*frontispiece*
Verdi's birthplace	34
Verdi in early life	35
Verdi and Giuseppina Strepponi	88
Rehearsals of Simon Boccanegra	89
Nabucco, *Act I, Introduction*	120
Letter to Piave	121
Verdi and Boïto	136
Verdi at Sant' Agata	137
Un Ballo in Maschera, *Act II*	168
Falstaff	169
Verdi and his dogs at Sant' Agata	184
Verdi at Sant' Agata	185
Bust of Verdi by Gemito	196
Verdi's death-mask	197

GIUSEPPE VERDI

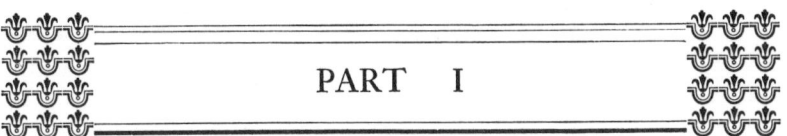

PART I

CHAPTER I

In common with most of the inhabitants of the Italian peninsula the villagers of Le Roncole, a hamlet near Busseto in the old Duchy of Parma, enjoyed during the opening decades of the nineteenth century ample opportunities to reflect on the three major fallacies of abstract democracy. In the cause of liberty they had for many years alternately been cajoled and bullied by an irascible Corsican general with a name, Napoleone Buonaparte, so ludicrous that it was widely considered a vote-catching invention of the French Directory.[1]

As to the nature of equality they had even more intimate knowledge; for were they not equal in subordination to any foreign power strong enough to make use of them? Sometimes that power was Austria, sometimes France. Only the subordination remained constant.

They had to wait a little longer to appreciate the full implication of the principle of fraternity. In due course, however, the general with the odd name became the Emperor Napoleon; Beethoven destroyed the original inscription of his *"Eroica"* Symphony, and the shades of that rather musty Roman trio, Curtius, Cato, and Scevola, so pompously invoked at the foundation of the Cisalpine Republic by Serbelloni a few years before, returned (presumably forever) to the limbo of the unwanted and the forgotten. Wherefore in 1812, as a belated tribute to the fraternal ideal, the inhabitants of Busseto, if not of Le Roncole itself, doubtless had the opportunity to contribute their quota to the forty thousand Italian corpses that lined the roads from Moscow to the German frontier.

On the 12th of October 1813, however, France still remained the dominant power, so that when a certain Carlo Verdi, the keeper of the local *osteria*, went into Busseto to take out a birth certificate for his son, "Joseph Fortunin François," born two days previously, the document was, inappropriately enough, drawn up in French. Had the event been postponed a few months, it might never have been

[1] Nievo.

drawn up at all, for in 1814 the Département Au Delà des Alpes ceased to be a French department and became an Austrian province, the process of transfer being marked by the kind of violent incidents to which the people of Le Roncole, experienced in a succession of warlike operations intended to make the world alternately safe for or against democracy, must have been well accustomed. One general, Prince Eugene, had retired, pursued by the advancing soldiers of another general. Among these soldiers there was a particularly bloodthirsty troop of cavalry who penetrated as far as Le Roncole, pillaged the houses, and killed a number of the inhabitants. Some of the women, panic-stricken, took refuge in the little church, but even here could find no certain sanctuary. One of them with uncommon presence of mind ran a few yards across the road and hid herself and her baby in the obscurity of the belfry. She was Luigia Uttini, wife of Carlo Verdi, the innkeeper, and the baby was Giuseppe (no longer Joseph) Verdi. A tablet on the church commemorates the story — a prelude to the life of the greatest dramatic composer of nineteenth-century Italy which might otherwise seem too appropriate to be credible.

Le Roncole is nothing but a hamlet, and the tiny inn wherein Verdi was born and passed his infancy is little more than a hovel on the side of the road. A modern millionaire might think it not quite good enough for his prize cows. We know that, to make both ends meet, Carlo Verdi sold coffee and sugar and tobacco as well as wine, the circumstances of the family differing in no wise from those of the peasants by whom they were surrounded. In fact they were peasants, and to the day of his death Verdi retained some characteristics, bad as well as good, of his class and upbringing.

The little Giuseppe was a serious child, the idol of his mother, whom he adored. He seems to have been a queer mixture of shyness and fierceness, and we are told that nothing brought him out of himself except music. Thus, when quite a little boy, he used to stand in ecstasy at the exploits of an old wandering violinist who came from time to time to play for the delectation of Carlo Verdi's patrons. Indeed, it is said that it was this strolling minstrel, struck by the boy's musical sensitiveness, who first advised the father to give his son a musical education.

When he was only seven years old, little Giuseppe Verdi gave a further striking proof of his musical sensibility. Like many Italian peasant boys to this day, he was employed on Sundays and feast-days to sing in the choir of the church and to serve the priest as acolyte during Mass. On one of these occasions he heard the organ played for the first time and the novel sound seems almost to have paralyzed him. So absorbed was he in the delicious sensation that when the priest asked him three times running for water, he paid no attention. Whereupon the exasperated ecclesiastic, to rouse the boy from his trance, gave him such a push that he fell down the three steps leading to the altar and fainted away. It is characteristic of his determination even in these early years that, on his recovery, he did not cry or rage as most children would have done, but merely asked his father once again if he could study music.

The story of the music-enchanted acolyte must have made some stir in the community, for a short time afterwards, when his father, yielding at last to the boy's desire for instruction in music, bought for him an old spinet, a neighboring workman volunteered to repair it for nothing; the pedals had gone (if they ever existed) and the hammers were without leather. Its condition, probably dilapidated enough anyhow, was further aggravated by an assault with a hammer made by the hot-tempered little boy, who had by chance lighted on the wholly satisfying chord of C major and vented on the instrument his fury at not being able to find it again.

With a true Latin sense of craftsmanship the repairer left a record inside the instrument of the extent of his labors. As an example of simple pride and as a record of a generous action the inscription is worth recording in all its original inexactitude:

Da me Stefano Cavaletti fu fato di nuovo questi saltarelli, e impenati a corame, e vi adatai la pedagliera che io ci ho regalato; come anche gratuitamente ci ho fato di nuovo li detti saltarelli, vedendo la buona disposizione che ha il giovinetto Giuseppe Verdi d'imparare a suonare questo instrumento, che questo mi basta par esserne del tutto sodisfatto. — Anno domini 1821.[2]

It is possible to attach too much importance to the stories of Giuseppe's musical precocity; the history of music is littered with such anecdotes among both professionals and amateurs who have, nevertheless, failed to achieve fame. It is easy, when a man has become great, to be wise after the event. As a matter of fact, Verdi's early compositions prove conclusively that he possessed none of the miraculous facility of a Mozart or a Mendelssohn. Like Wagner he attained to musical power by the sweat of his brow. There can be no doubt, however, that this spinet played the leading part in the first scenes of his life's drama. It was the great friend of his childhood. Seated at the miserable instrument when tired of working in the fields

---

[2] "By me, Stefano Cavaletti, these key-hammers were renewed and lined with leather, and I fitted pedals, which I gave as a present; as I also repaired gratuitously the said key-hammers, seeing the excellent disposition the young Giuseppe Verdi shows to learn how to play this instrument — which suffices to give me complete satisfaction."

or the inn, when bored with playing the inevitable game of bowls with the village children, he dreamed those dreams which, one biographer tells us, seemed inexplicable even to himself.

There is nothing Arcadian about the plain of Parma, in the winter cold, foggy, or wind-swept, in the summer sunbaked and unshaded. The roads during the hot weather are so dusty that today, when a motor-car passes over them, there is a dense cloud as of steam escaping from the pistons of a locomotive. The trees (such as they are), the vines, the fields of corn within fifty yards of the road, are gray with a layer of dust. Emphatically Verdi's boyhood was no Theocritean idyll; it was essentially practical and poverty-stricken. Many years afterwards the composer summed it up, with typical conciseness, to a friend: "My youth was hard." From Verdi, who hated talking about himself, the avowal indicates much. The best proof of what the spinet meant to him is that he kept it all his life. Can it not still be seen in the museum at Milan?

When Verdi's father bought the spinet, he arranged at the same time with the local organist, an old man called Baistrocchi, to give the boy some musical instruction, perhaps in the elements of music, certainly in organ- and spinet-playing. Here, for the first time, we catch a glimpse of superior musical gifts, for after three years' study little Giuseppe replaced his old master as organist of Le Roncole. The instrument [3] at his disposal was primitive and the duties cannot have been exacting, but few boys of twelve would have been able to undertake them at all. The salary was proportionately modest — rather less than two pounds a year, increased by special fees for funerals, weddings, and the like to about four pounds. Apparently, also, the youthful organist was allowed to make a collection for himself once a year at the harvest festival. This represented little enough, but the inhabitants of Le Roncole probably did their best for the lad. We know that they were both proud and fond of him, for when, a little later, there was talk of his being replaced by a protégé of the Bishop, there was almost an insurrection among the villagers, who clamored loudly and successfully for the retention of their *"maestrino."*

To his credit, Verdi's father, almost immediately after the appointment of the boy as organist at Le Roncole, saw that an education beyond that available in the tiny village was indispensable to his son. So at some sacrifice to himself he arranged for Giuseppe to go to Busseto to live with a shoemaker, a friend of the family. The humbleness of their circumstances, to say nothing of the standard of living in the Italy of that time, is shown by the fact that this board and

---

[3] Devoid of diapasons and terribly out of tune, it is still in use, though unfortunately the pedal that calls into action a "Chinese bell and a drum" no longer functions.

lodging cost fourpence a day. At Busseto the boy attended the local school (where he seems to have worked hard) and very soon mastered the mysteries of reading, writing, and arithmetic. On Sundays and feast-days he trudged the three miles into Le Roncole to play the organ, and on one of these occasions, when he had to start before dawn to play at early Mass on Christmas Day, he fell into a ditch full of water. To understand the accident the reader must imagine a flat winding road with at least one hairpin bend and lined on the side by a ditch as formidable as those in the fen country. Unable to extricate himself, the boy would almost certainly have been drowned but for the help of a passing peasant woman who went to the rescue of the innkeeper's son and, incidentally, of the future composer of *Falstaff*. Still, ditch or no ditch, a hundred francs a year was well worth a six-mile walk once or twice a week, and young Verdi did not abandon his functions of organist of Le Roncole till he went to Milan six years later.

It was Verdi's transplantation to Busseto that determined his career. The ambition of his parents, if not his own, would have been fully satisfied with a post as village organist. Perhaps, as a scarcely credible achievement, he might eventually have written a march for the military band of Busseto and some music for his own or even his colleagues' church services. That was all. The boy's entrance into the larger environment of Busseto, thanks partly to sheer good fortune, partly to his own talent and determination, opened up possibilities undreamed of at the time.

The part of good fortune was played by Antonio Barezzi, who may be described as the fairy-godfather of Verdi's adolescence. Barezzi was a prosperous grocer at Busseto, who must have known young Verdi from infancy, for Verdi's father used to buy from his establishment sugar, coffee, wine, and liqueurs, of which Barezzi seems to have made something of a specialty. The boy certainly accompanied his father on these expeditions to Busseto and most probably often undertook them on his own account, because little boys in Italy are accustomed to shoulder responsibility at a very early age. Now, Barezzi, apart from his commercial pursuits, was passionately fond of music; he not only played the flute well but had a working acquaintance with the clarinet, the horn, and the ophicleide. What is more, he was president of the local Philharmonic Society, of which both rehearsals and performances were given in a large room in his house.

Barezzi belonged to a class of society very different from that of the Verdis, and it was not till young Giuseppe had been living with the cobbler at Busseto for two years that his attention was seriously drawn to the industrious and talented lad. He offered him employment in his business, wherein music during the evening played at least as important a part as groceries during the day. From that moment the foundations of Verdi's musical career were irrevocably laid.

Thanks to a well-timed murder in the neighborhood, which seems to have scared Signora Barezzi, the boy was presently removed from the cobbler and lodged in the Barezzi house for his or her greater protection. With increased intimacy the liking of Barezzi and his family for their gifted employee developed into warm affection. Young Verdi continued to handle groceries, but he was set to learn Latin with a priest by the name of Pietro Seletti and to continue his musical studies with Ferdinando Provesi, the organist of Busseto Cathedral and director of the Philharmonic Society. Young Verdi must have found some difficulty in fitting his various activities into the twenty-four hours of each day. He worked so hard and so successfully at Latin that Seletti complained of the time he was wasting on music. He worked so hard and so successfully at music that Provesi complained of the time he was wasting on Latin. He attended all the rehearsals of the Philharmonic and helped to copy out the parts. He frequented the public library, reading with avidity everything that came to his hand, especially the Bible. He played on the Viennese piano that Barezzi, doubtless considering the overworked spinet inadequate, had placed at his disposal. Sometimes he played alone, sometimes (and with increasing frequency) he played duets with his employer's attractive daughter, Margherita. One rather wonders where the groceries came in.

Verdi was fortunate in his music teacher, for old Provesi seems to have been not only a skilled contrapuntist and an agreeable composer but a man of parts. He had written both the words and the music of several comic operas which had been produced at the local theater. He recognized with admiration the aptitude of his industrious pupil and gradually began to delegate to him some of his own duties. In this manner young Verdi deputized not only at the cathedral organ but at the conductor's desk at the Philharmonic and, like many other great composers, acquired much of his knowledge of music by the satisfactory method of practical experience. He began to compose in earnest, writing music in the various forms practical at Busseto. Thus in 1828 he wrote an overture and marches for the military band, which then, as now, played so important a part in local Italian life; he wrote a motet and a Te Deum for the cathedral and an odd piano piece or two for himself or Margherita. More ambitious still, he composed various orchestral pieces for the Philharmonic Society, himself rehearsing them and copying out the parts. Some may be seen to this day in the archives of Busseto.

Doubtless none of this music possessed any value. Doubtless, despite the high-sounding title, the performances of the enthusiastic amateurs of the Philharmonic left much to be desired. But as an initiation to a musical career the conditions might have been worse. The Philharmonic probably played a good deal of Porpora and Haydn, whose music was popular in Italy at the time. They certainly played the brilliant new overtures to *The Barber of Seville* and *Cinderella*, with which Rossini had first delighted the world some ten years previously. Verdi thus acquired a familiarity with the works of the great masters and, most important of all, developed that instinct for conscientious and practical craftsmanship so characteristic of his whole career as a composer. Like all Italian composers, like all composers in every country indeed, up to the dawn of the romantic movement, Verdi was a practical musician, a craftsman writing music to meet the current requirements of the day. In his youth those current requirements were represented by the cathedral, the military band, and the Philharmonic Society of Busseto; in later days by the opera houses of Milan, Paris, Cairo, London, and St. Petersburg. The principle, however, remained the same.

Young Verdi had by now acquired a certain local fame. We are told that people used to come in from the country round about to hear his music. Provesi declared he could teach him nothing further. Even Seletti, hearing him one day improvise on the organ, admitted that the claims of music must be preferred to those of Latin. In October 1829, backed by a warm recommendation from Provesi, he applied for the post of organist to the parish church of Soragna, but failed to obtain it; perhaps because he was too young, more probably because another candidate, eventually successful, had the advantage of powerful local backing. Verdi continued studying and writing music for a while, but both Barezzi and Provesi felt that Busseto did not offer sufficient scope for the young man's talents. So after a couple of years it was decided to send him to Milan.

Fortunately for him, Busseto possessed a tradition of culture that it would be difficult to match in an English provincial town of the same kind. More fortunately still, it possessed an institution called the Monte di Pietà e d'Abbondanza, founded in the seventeenth century during an epidemic of cholera. At that dreadful time some of the inhabitants of Busseto, who had lost their children, decided to bequeath their property to the foundation of an institution destined to relieve poverty in general and to provide four grants for poor children desirous of adopting a liberal career. One of these grants was made to young Verdi.

Normally they were worth three hundred francs a year and were tenable for four years, but the administrators of the trust, with rare intelligence, managed to meet young Verdi's requirements by allotting him six hundred francs for two years. Even this was not sufficient great importance to personal impressions, was not encouraged by the student's appearance. The long and the short of the matter is that these worthy gentlemen made a mistake — a bad mistake, but not inexcusable. Verdi's Busseto compositions were probably more remarkable for their mere existence than their actual merits, and a friend of Verdi told a friend of mine that Verdi himself once admitted that the exercise that he submitted was very poor. Moreover, Basily, if Fétis is correct, was not perhaps such a fool as might appear at first sight; one of the most successful branches of our public services was for a time recruited on very much the same principle. The appearance and manners of young Verdi at that time, his almost pathological reserve, his awkwardness, his thin, compressed lips, must have suggested anything rather than the promise of a great composer. He probably looked the peasant that he was and, in a sense, always remained. The British navy of today and the Egyptian civil service of yesterday may have lost one or two promising candidates by following a method not unlike that of Basily; they certainly gained a number of highly efficient officers. One cannot legislate for exceptions. Unfortunately the history of great music consists in little else.

Verdi, though profoundly discouraged by such a rebuff, was not of a nature to be overwhelmed by it. Of the two teachers indicated by Rolla, Seletti advised Lavigna, and to Lavigna he went. It was a fortunate choice, for Lavigna must be reckoned a first-class musician, one of those highly skilled craftsmen who seem to have been remarkably plentiful in Italy. A master of theory, he had also proved himself a successful composer in practice, several of his operas having won considerable success. He had received his musical training at Naples, but was now employed as *maestro al cembalo* [2] at the opera. In addition to harmony, counterpoint, and fugue, Lavigna set his pupil to study the works of the masters, and it may have been at this time that Verdi conceived that admiration for Palestrina and Marcello which later became the dominant musical passion of his life. There was also a dose, perhaps an overdose, of Mozart, for Verdi tells us somewhere that he could hardly bear to hear his music again in later years. The thoroughness and austerity of the instruction will come as a surprise to many people who always seem to imagine the technical knowledge of Italian composers to be inferior to that of the Germans.

[2] The Italian term must stand. Apart from rehearsals nobody seems certain as to what were the exact duties of a *"maestro al cembalo"* in those days. He was not what we should call a conductor, for the leading violinist conducted. It is possible that he sat at his instrument in readiness to come to the rescue in case the orchestra broke down — which in view of the low standard of Italian orchestras at the beginning of the nineteenth century must have happened fairly often. It is probable that, like the pianist in the small orchestras familiar to the patrons of most English seaside resorts, he "filled in" generally.

Yet Verdi's musical studies were typical, not exceptional, though Monaldi would seem to exaggerate when he writes that men like Rossini, Donizetti, and Bellini were almost as well equipped and, if they avoided as a rule a display of learning in their operas, did so from choice rather than necessity.

Lavigna appears to have been kind to his rather strange pupil, and to have divined that under the mask of boorishness lay something remarkable. When not engaged at the theater he had him very frequently at his house in the evening, a piece of thoughtfulness or good fortune that must have meant much to young Verdi, who seems to have had scarcely any friends but this old man of fifty-five and, of course, no money wherewith to amuse himself. The world owes a considerable debt of gratitude to Maestro Lavigna.

Verdi certainly repaid his teacher with the most unflagging industry and, incidentally, after some two years, was enabled thereby to pour coals of fire on the head of the most important of the professors who had refused him admission to the Conservatoire. Basily was a friend of Lavigna and often came to see him. One evening the two old *maestri* were shaking their heads over the deplorable result of an examination recently held to fill the post of organist at the Church of San Giovanni di Monza. There had been twenty-eight competitors, of whom not one had been able to construct a correct fugue on the subject set by Basily. Lavigna, perhaps a little maliciously, suggested that his doubtless silent pupil should attempt the task. Basily wrote out the subject which was handed to young Verdi, and the two friends went on with their conversation. A little later, to Basily's unconcealed astonishment, Verdi handed back the subject, not only correctly developed, but enriched with a double canon, because, as he said slyly, "the subject was rather thin."

A fortunate accident about this time was the means of Verdi's attracting some attention to himself. There existed in Milan a body of rich amateurs and social notabilities who met every Friday during the winter in the Filodrammatici Theater under the nominal direction of one Masini, a musician less remarkable for learning than for patience and tenacity — "the qualities especially necessary for dealing with amateurs," as Verdi himself succinctly observed later. In 1833 or 1834 these distinguished ladies and gentlemen were rehearsing Haydn's *Creation*, and Lavigna thought it might be profitable for his pupil to attend. Masini was either too grand or too incompetent to take the rehearsals himself, this duty being shared between three *maestri* in turn. One evening none of them put in an appearance, so Masini, diffident of his own powers of accompanying on the piano from score, turned to the retiring young man seated at the back of the hall and asked him whether he would act as accompanist, adding with revelatory candor: "So long as you play the bass, that will do."

An orchestral score had no terrors for young Verdi, who immediately seated himself at the piano. The accompanist's youth, his homely appearance and dress, did not inspire much confidence in the ladies and gentlemen of the chorus, but as the rehearsal proceeded and Verdi warmed to his work, their skepticism turned to delight and surprise, for in addition to accompanying with his left hand, he conducted with his right. At the end everybody congratulated him. The trinity or maestri found it inconvenient or unwise to make a further appearance; Verdi was entrusted with the direction of the concert. It was a brilliant success, so brilliant that it had to be repeated, not only a second time in the Casino de' Nobili in the presence of all the aristocracy of Milan, but a third time, at his own express wish, in the house of the Austrian Viceroy.

The results for Verdi were of the highest importance. It was doubtless gratifying to be asked, as he was, by the president of the society, Count Renato Borromeo, to write a wedding cantata on the occasion of the marriage of a member of his family, but that did not matter much, especially as he was not paid for it. What did matter was that Masini suggested his writing an opera for the Filodrammatici Theater, at that time under his direction, actually handing him a libretto by one Piazza,[3] which, after considerable retouching by Solera, was destined to become, three years later, the libretto of Verdi's first opera, *Oberto, Conte di Bonifacio*. Solera, the Filodrammatici, all seem very small beer to us, but they must have represented unheard-of glory to the still very callow youth from Busseto. One can imagine the young man's delight. He had already, in addition to a couple of orchestral pieces, written some *buffo* numbers for Lavigna, and, in view of his master's theatrical connections and his own natural inclinations, it is safe to postulate in him that enthusiasm for the theater which comes, in any case, so readily to the young. Then the death of his old master Provesi called him suddenly back to Busseto.

Apparently the intention of the administrators of the Monte di Pietà had all along been that Verdi should succeed Provesi in his functions. Hence the recall from Milan. The ecclesiastical authorities, however, had other views. They did not much like Verdi, whom they called the *maestrino* in vogue, and they detested Barezzi and his friends of the Philharmonic Society. It was, in short, a case of one of those tugs-of-war between the clerical and anticlerical elements familiar to every dweller in Latin countries. So the ecclesiastics chose as organist a certain Giovanni Ferrari; his musical talents might be suspect, but he enjoyed the advantage of the support of no less than

[3] Neisser.

His Life and Works

two bishops. Thus Verdi, for the second time in his life, saw his ambitions frustrated by clerical influence; and it seems extremely likely that his lifelong dislike for priests and priestcraft originated in these early impressions. The Philharmonic Society, however, did not take the rebuff lying down. Verdi, not Ferrari, was appointed their director; the municipality of Busseto was persuaded to pay him for three years the yearly salary of three hundred lire, usually regarded as the perquisite of the cathedral organist. This, augmented by the Monte di Pietà allowance and a few private subscriptions, brought his income up to the same level as that of the unfortunate Ferrari.

Feeling naturally became bitter on both sides. The clergy tried to get the Philharmonic Society declared illegal; the Philharmonic Society retaliated by invading the cathedral and taking away their music. There were insults, satires, even brawls and imprisonments. The famous quarrels between Gluck and Piccini, Handel and Bononcini, pale in comparison with the excess of the Verdians and the Ferrarians. Apart from this new excitement Verdi found the country little changed except for the death of his old master and of his only sister. He wrote more and doubtless rather better music for the *"signori dilettanti"* of the Philharmonic Society — in 1838, for instance, a *Capriccio* for horn, a *Duetto Buffo*, a Set of Variations with Introduction and Coda for bassoon figured in the programs — and himself played the piano at their concerts. Pougin tells us that he especially favored the works of Hummel and Kalkbrenner, but that his greatest success was an arrangement by himself of the overture to *William Tell*. He wrote more and certainly better marches for the municipal band, of which one, a funeral march, was used subsequently in the opera *Nabucco*.[4] He wrote a *Stabat Mater*[5] and other church music for the edification of the Monte di Pietà. Here arose a complication, for the cathedral was naturally barred to the performance of these works, which had to be given in the chapel or the church of the Franciscans, which lay outside the jurisdiction of the ecclesiastical authorities. Enthusiastic biographers paint a lively picture of the popularity of the young man at the time. When his music was being played at the Franciscan church, the cathedral was deserted. After service was over, the municipal band performed in the crowded piazza, and sometimes there were fireworks in the evening. As if that were not enough, the little towns round about used occasionally to send omnibuses to fetch Verdi and his musicians on Sundays so that they might have the advantage of hearing him play on the organ in their own churches, while the band accompanied the procession.

Then there were the piano duets with Margherita, doubtless more

[4] Barrili.   [5] Perosio.

frequent than ever, because in 1835 young Verdi ventured to ask Barezzi's permission for their marriage, a permission which that sensible man readily granted. On the 4th of May 1836 they were married, so that, with the possible exception of Franz Schubert, piano duets played a greater part of the life of Giuseppe Verdi than of almost any other great composer, for they brought him a wife. And all the while he was working at *Oberto, Conte di Bonifacio*, perhaps dreaming of glories to come.

Some biographers have expressed surprise at the length of time Verdi took to write this, his first opera,[6] because later in life he composed operas, as we know, with great rapidity; but there is no evidence, apart from scholastic exercises, that he had yet acquired the fluency characteristic of his later years. Moreover, his duties with the Philharmonic Society, his many compositions, the alarums of the miniature civil war, and the excursions with the band on Sundays must have made very considerable demands on his time and attention. At last, however, when the opera was finished and his three years' contract with the municipality at an end, Verdi with his eighteen-year-old wife and their two little children, Icilio and Virginia, said good-by to their home in the Palazzo Rusca and moved to Milan.

They lived near the Porta Ticinese in very humble circumstances. The outlook did not seem promising. Never had the political situation been so black. The grip of Austria on her Italian provinces was tighter than ever. Cavour, the future architect of Italian unity, then a young man of twenty-nine, known only as an indefatigable gallant and an officer of liberal opinions, was living as a gentleman-farmer on his estates at Leri. Music hardly seemed in a better way than politics. Rossini, despite or because of *William Tell*, had given up composition; Bellini was dead. Worst of all, from Verdi's personal standpoint, Masini, for whom *Oberto* had been written, had resigned the direction of the Filodrammatici Theater; Lavigna had died while he was at Busseto.

Masini, however, had not forgotten the young musician who had been so useful to him in the matter of *The Creation*. He exerted himself to bring *Oberto* to the notice of the authorities of La Scala, with such success that arrangements were made to produce the opera in the spring of 1839. But almost immediately after rehearsals had begun, the production had to be postponed owing to a serious illness of the tenor. Verdi, in despair and not improbably at the end of his financial tether, was, it is said, preparing to return to Busseto when

---

[6] As a matter of fact, it seems that *Oberto* was anticipated by another opera, called *Rocester*, which, as a letter written in 1837 and quoted by Perinello shows, he hoped to get produced in Parma. But nobody appears to know anything about it except that the libretto was by Piazza. Neisser says that Boïto had never even heard its name.

one morning there arrived at his door a messenger from La Scala asking him to come at once and see the impresario, Merelli. Apparently Merelli had heard two of the artists who had taken part in the rehearsals of *Oberto* commenting on the opera in very favorable terms. One of them, in fact, was no less a person than Giuseppina Strepponi, whose influence on the composer's life began thus early in his career. To cut the story short, Merelli decided to produce *Oberto*, and, like the honorable man that he was, did not take advantage of the youth and obscurity of the composer to saddle him with an unfair contract. He undertook to defray all expenses and to share the profits — an arrangement that, as Verdi himself said in later years, was a very generous one, it being then the practice of impresarios to receive rather than give payment for the production of operas by unknown composers.

There was at that time in Milan an enterprising individual called Giovanni Ricordi, who had started life as a copyist of music at La Scala, where, according to Stendhal, he had already made very considerable profits by acquiring the publishing rights of Rossini's operas. Ricordi bought the rights of *Oberto* for 1,750 francs and thus laid the foundations of a connection between his publishing house and the composer that was never seriously broken. What his enterprise and foresight have meant to him and his descendants in terms of mere money it would be difficult to estimate.

Thus on the 17th of November 1839 the first of Verdi's operas was presented to the world. It was not a failure; it was certainly not a triumph. We should call it nowadays a *succès d'estime*. Apparently the performance was little more than adequate and the libretto was blamed for its absurdity. "The music of this opera," wrote the paper *La Fama*, "has much in common with the style of Bellini. There is an abundant, perhaps a too abundant, wealth of melody. In some passages where the words demand energy and passion, the vocal line is languid and monotonous." The paper then goes on to praise two arias and a quartet in the second act, a judgment shared by the periodical *Figaro*, which, incidentally, advised the composer to make a further study of the classics. As a matter of fact, the quartet in question may be described as an afterthought, Merelli himself having suggested it when Verdi was making certain alterations in the opera to meet the requirements of the new cast. Verdi himself had no doubt that it was the best number.

Oberto meant more to Verdi than a comparatively modest public success. To begin with, Merelli was sufficiently struck by its merits to offer the composer a contract to write three more operas, one every eight months, for production either at La Scala or at the Imperial Theater at Vienna, of which he was also director. More important still (though she did not sing in the actual performance), it brought him into contact, as we have already seen, with Giuseppina Strepponi, without whom Verdi would scarcely have been Verdi. Moreover, by a fortunate accident, of which very probably Verdi himself was unaware, there figured in the cast a young Englishwoman called Shaw who developed a great enthusiasm for his music and wrote letters home which, according to Chorley, were first responsible for bringing the name of Verdi to the notice of English musicians. Perhaps, also, there should be added his association with Solera.

Themistocles Solera is not usually considered a very important person. He enjoyed in his day, however, some reputation not only as a poet but as a musician. In fact, eight days after the performance of *Oberto* he wrote both the words and the music of a cantata called *Melody*, which was performed at La Scala, not to mention an opera, produced a year later, of which he also wrote both words and music. A wild bohemian, he had started life by running away from school in Vienna to join a circus, and at least one biographer thinks that he must be credited with having done much to lift Verdi out of the stilted and narrow atmosphere of Busseto. It seems extremely likely, moreover, that as the son of a father imprisoned by the Austrians for revolutionary activities, he was largely responsible for stimulating the passionate devotion to the cause of Italian freedom that played so important a part in Verdi's career.

The first libretto suggested by Merelli to Verdi in accordance with the terms of their contract was *Il Proscritto* by a certain Rossi. Verdi read it, found it unsatisfactory, and dallied with the composition of the music to such an extent that, when the impresario returned from Vienna early in 1840, he had not written a note of the music. It was just as well. Merelli had decided in the meantime that he must have an *opera buffa* for his autumn season, and asked Verdi to write one immediately, sending several librettos by Romani to choose from. None of them was attractive to the composer, but he chose that one which seemed to him the least unsatisfactory. Based on a French farce, it was called *Il Finto Stanislao*[7] and had in fact already been set to music by one Gyrowetz — in those days a circumstance of no importance whatever.

It may be doubted whether the opera would have been a success in any event. Clearly Verdi was not attracted by the form in general or the libretto in particular. Circumstances, however, combined to turn a tiresome duty into nothing less than torture. Almost immediately after starting work on the score he was taken seriously ill with angina and had to retire to bed; the drain upon his resources was

[7] *The Sham Stanislaus.*

such that Margherita's trinkets had to be pawned and money borrowed to pay the rent. Then, at the beginning of April 1840, his little boy fell ill and died, followed by his little girl two days afterwards. As if that were not enough, poor Margherita had an attack of acute encephalitis in June and herself died after a short illness. So in the space of three months, while working on a comic opera, Verdi lost everything in the world that he held most dear. It was a tragic situation, quite operatic in its exaggeration, that left Verdi, who adored his young wife, stunned and resentful, and certainly affected his outlook on life and art during the rest of his days.

Nevertheless, the opera was finished, rechristened *Un Giorno di Regno*,[8] and produced at La Scala on the 5th of September. It was a complete failure. The public was indifferent or hostile. Those curious people who always take pleasure in other people's misfortunes made bad jokes about "the verdant promise" of the composer having withered before it had time to bud. Only the musical critics were scrupulously fair. With justice they blamed the libretto, found little or no originality in the music. But they agreed unanimously in assigning a large part of the responsibility of the failure to the very indifferent performance, while one of them, in the *Figaro*, had the grace to remind his readers of the circumstances in which the opera had been written.

[8] *King for a Day.*

CHAPTER III

V ERDI, in his hypersensitive state, never forgave the Milanese public. The reception left an ineffaceable trace on his memory, for twenty years later, writing to Tito Ricordi, all the bitterness wells up again. "How they make me laugh," he writes, "those who tell me that I owe much to this or that public. It is quite true that *Nabucco* and *I Lombardi* were greeted with enthusiasm at La Scala . . . but less than a year before, the same public had dealt hardly with the opera of a poor young man, himself ill, working against time and with a heart ravaged by horrible misfortune. All this, though known to all, did not serve to moderate their discourtesy. From that day I have never set eyes on *Un Giorni di Regno;* it is certainly a bad opera, although many other operas no better have been tolerated; perhaps even received with applause. If only the public had, I do not say applauded, but received the opera in silence, I could not have found words to thank them. . . . I am not condemning them, I bow to their severity, I accept their hisses; but only on condition that I am not asked to be grateful for their applause. We poor gypsies, mountebanks, call us anything you like, are forced to sell our labor, our thoughts, our dreams, for gold — for three lire the public buy the right to hiss or applaud us. Our destiny is to put up with it." The theme of *Pagliacci,* in short.

Verdi was not quite fair. The public cannot be expected to concern itself with the circumstances in which a work of art is produced. But his feelings were excusable if not justifiable. He was not in a normal state of mind. Indeed, he can only be described as being morally knocked out. He went back to Antonio Barezzi at Busseto, hoping to find there comfort and peace, but, failing to find them, he returned to Milan with the intention of supporting himself by teaching. He vowed to write no more music and actually prevailed on Merelli to tear up his contract.

Merelli behaved very well. Appreciating the crisis through which his young protégé was passing, he saw that the only thing to do was to leave him to himself, not to attempt to disturb the kind of intellectual and spiritual coma that afflicted him. Though acceding to Verdi's wishes in the matter of the contract, he left the door open for future possibilities by a promise that, if he happened to change his mind and write another opera, it should be produced. Then he left the poor young man to himself and the trashy novels that had momentarily supplanted his hitherto respectable if limited literary fare.

Three months passed in this way till, one snowy evening, Verdi ran across Merelli in the Galleria de Cristoforis, the precursor of those huge glass arcades now so prominent a feature of Milanese life. Merelli took him by the arm and, as they walked together towards La Scala, confided to him his difficulties. Nicolai had refused to set a libretto by Solera on the subject of Nebuchadnezzar; he could not provide him with another; he did not know what to do. Verdi suggested handing over *Il Proscritto*, which Merelli thought an excellent idea. They entered the theater together and instituted a search for the manuscript. While waiting, Merelli suggested that Verdi should have a look at Solera's libretto. "What's the use of it to me?" said Verdi; "I don't want to read any libretto."

"Read it; it can't do you any harm," answered the impresario. "Read it anyhow, and then you can bring it back."

Verdi took the book and went home. He has told us himself how, as he walked, he felt overcome by an undefinable perturbation, a sadness that he could not explain. When he got home, he threw the manuscript on the table. It opened at the verses "*Va, pensiero, sull'ali dorate.*"[1] He read them and was much struck by them; they seemed to bring back all the memories of the Bible, which he had read with such enthusiasm in his boyhood. Then he remembered his resolution to write no more music. Closing the manuscript, he went to bed; but the idea of the libretto would not be banished from his mind. He could not sleep. He got up and read the whole manuscript three times. By the morning, he tells us, he knew Solera's poem almost by heart. Later on in the day, again repenting, he took the manuscript back to Merelli. "It is very fine," he said.

"Then set it to music."

"Not a bit of it."

"Set it to music, I tell you; set it to music." And Merelli, shoving the manuscript into the composer's overcoat pocket, literally ran him out of the room and locked the door.

The evil spell was broken. At first the music would not come. Then slowly, but with ever increasing speed, Verdi began to write the opera called *Nabucodonosor*,[2] destined to be the foundation of his fame and fortune. Even in those early days we catch a glimpse of the Verdi who was to play such an intimate part in the composition of the libretto of *Aïda*, for he tells us that he prevailed on Solera to take out of the third act a love duet that seemed to him to hold up the action, and to substitute an air for Zaccharias, eventually one of the most successful numbers. So keen was Verdi on the change and so well did he know the unstable Solera that he ran to the door and

[1] "Go, my thought, on golden wings."
[2] *Nebuchadnezzar*. The opera is always called *Nabucco* for short.

turned the key *à la* Merelli, refusing to let the poet go until he had written the required verses — a risky enterprise because Solera was renowned for his strength and size as much as for his quick temper.

In the autumn of 1841 *Nabucco* was finished; once the period of incubation over, Verdi took but three months to write it. Merelli, at any rate, never expected the score to be delivered so soon, and when Verdi brought it to him with a reminder of his promise, protested that he could not possibly produce it until the spring. Three new operas had been commissioned from well-known composers for the Carnival season — that is to say, the season that began immediately after Christmas. How could he add a fourth? But Verdi had set his heart on having the opera produced at that particular season, mainly, it appears, because the artists engaged included Giuseppina Strepponi and the famous baritone Ronconi, one of the finest singers of the day, who a year later was to move Donizetti to tears by his singing of *Maria di Rohan*; partly because the Carnival season was the most important of all.

Then the Cartellone — what we should call the prospectus — of the season at La Scala was published — and there was no mention of *Nabucco*. Verdi, nervous and hot-tempered, wrote an insulting letter to Merelli. Directly he had written it he was ashamed of himself, expecting, as he confessed in later life, that it would mean the ruin of all his prospects. And so it might have done had not Merelli been a remarkable man. Doubtless he was not actuated entirely by philanthropy; doubtless he had felt, as we can still feel today to some extent, that there was something in the score of *Oberto* quite new in Italian music and that it was worth his while to be patient with this young and troublesome composer. Nevertheless, leaving his patience and his reasonableness out of the question altogether, except to note that they can with difficulty be paralleled in the history of operatic enterprise, we must give full credit to Merelli for uncommon perspicacity. He sent for Verdi and after a gentle lecture on bad manners said that he would give *Nabucco* during the Carnival season provided the composer would be content with costumes and scenery out of stock.

Verdi thankfully agreed. *Nabucco*, announced as the last of the four novelties, was given for the first time at La Scala on the 9th of March 1842, after only twelve days' rehearsal. To describe it as a brilliant success would be an understatement. The public went mad. Merelli's scenery and costumes may have come out of stock, but they were effective enough to arouse enthusiasm on their own account. Strepponi as Abigail; the bass Derivis as the prophet, Zaccharias; Ronconi, especially, as Nebuchadnezzar, were more warmly welcomed still. But in justice to the public it is only fair to say that what aroused the greatest enthusiasm of all was the opera itself. There was such an uproar at the end of the first act that Verdi, who, according to the custom of the time, was seated in the orchestra between the first double bass and the first cello, thought for a few moments that the audience were after his blood. The beautiful chorus of the Hebrews in captivity, "*Va, pensiero, sull'ali dorate*," aroused such enthusiasm that it had to be repeated. At the end the orchestra joined with the public and the singers in giving the young maestro an immense ovation. When, after the performance, Verdi went home with a friend to his humble room on the fourth floor of a house in the Strada degli Andeghari, he was a made man.

The press criticisms, though more reserved, were hardly less favorable. Lambertini in the *Gazzetta di Milano*, after a few rather condescending words of encouragement to the young composer and an exhortation to continue to do even better, singled out the Hebrew chorus for special praise. He then congratulated Verdi on having, unlike so many of his colleagues, written a proper and effective overture — which must have given Verdi considerable satisfaction, for while rehearsals were actually in progress he had composed it in a café as an afterthought at the suggestion of his brother-in-law.[3] With considerable discrimination, the *Gazzetta Musicale* praised the young composer for not sacrificing the truth of the dramatic situations of his fine theme to essays in mere conventional effectiveness.

Felice Romani in the *Figaro*, after commending Solera's libretto as worthy of the subject, wrote: "Verdi has imbued his opera with an austere, grandiose atmosphere which is lost so seldom that he could easily make it absolutely perfect if he would only revise one or two places in a little calmer state of mind." Then, having discussed the sources to which Verdi was indebted for some of his musical ideas, he added: "This new music by Verdi has an emotional quality all its own that profoundly affects the spectators and on occasion arouses them to enthusiastic applause." Though agreeing with his colleague of the *Gazzetta di Milano* in admiring the Hebrew chorus, he found it somewhat long and reserved his main enthusiasm for Zaccharias's prophecy and the *stretto* in the finale of the first act.

Nabucco made Verdi the fashion. As with *Trilby* in our own time, ties, hats, and even sauces were named after him. It brought him many acquaintances, among them Rossini, whom, according to Radiciotti, he first met in this year at Bologna, and at least one devoted and lifelong friend, the Countess Clara Maffei, to whom many of his most intimate letters were written.[4] Most important of all, it was the

[3] Pizzi.
[4] She held in Milan a regular salon which afterwards became famous, Liszt and Balzac being among its frequenters. Four years later she and Verdi were sufficiently intimate for him to be asked to be one of the witnesses to the deed registering her legal separation from her husband, Andrea Maffei.

means of consolidating the friendship with Giuseppina Strepponi inaugurated in the early days of *Oberto*.

This remarkable woman, born at Lodi, near Milan, on the 8th of September 1815, was the daughter of Felice Strepponi, a composer of operas and musical director at Monza. After having studied and taught at the Milan Conservatoire she made a successful first appearance at Trieste, where her father had died three years previously. A dutiful daughter and a conscientious sister — she paid for the education of her two brothers — her talents as an artist were held in the highest esteem. A criticism of the time thus describes her: "Her voice is clear, sweet, and penetrating. Her acting is adequate, her figure graceful; and to the other many gifts with which nature has endowed her must be added a mastery of vocal technique that will in a short time make her shine among the most brilliant stars in the Italian theater." Even in those early days Verdi seems to have been intimate enough with her to rely on her advice. After the third performance of *Nabucco* Merelli told the composer that the directors of the theater considered his reputation now sufficiently established for him to be asked to write the *opera d'obbligo* for the next season. It should be explained that the *opera d'obbligo* was an opera, either completely new or never before heard in the town, that every impresario undertook in his contract to produce during the season. The commission to compose such an opera was therefore a hall-mark of operatic success. Merelli, with a characteristic gesture, produced a contract in which the sum to be paid to the composer was left a blank, telling him to fill it in as he thought fit. The inexperienced Verdi, quite at a loss, turned to Giuseppina, who, with the good sense typical of all the advice she was to give Verdi during nearly fifty years, told him that, while he must of course take advantage of his good fortune, he must on no account ask more than Bellini had received for *Norma*. So the *Norma* tariff was adopted, and Verdi asked and received the sum of 6,800 francs for the opera he was next to write. It was very good pay. Rossini thought himself lucky to get 4,200 francs for *Mosé*, while *Tancrede* had been valued at only 600.[5]

Even today *Nabucco* stands out among the early operas of Verdi. Whether owing to the emotional circumstances in which it was conceived and brought to birth, whether to the appeal made by the Biblical subject matter to the composer, the score has a quality that can still make itself felt despite the passing of the convention in which the music is presented. I am informed that when *Nabucco* was given at La Scala under the direction of the veteran conductor Mugnone on the occasion of the Verdi centenary in 1913, its effect on the public rivaled that of *Falstaff* itself, even though the latter was entrusted

[5] Stendhal.

to Toscanini, the greatest operatic conductor alive. No doubt the elusive thing called quality made itself felt at least as strongly in 1842; but what seems to have struck its contemporaries was mainly the new flavor of the music. Even during rehearsals, we are told, the stage hands stopped their work to applaud and comment on the fact; it was what mainly impressed the public if not the press. Yet this is precisely what we can by no means appreciate without the historical knowledge and perspective peculiar to the specialist. As a matter of fact, Soffredini, who has written minute analyses of all the Verdi operas, is quite right, in a sense, in claiming the best parts of *Oberto* as more truly Verdian than *Nabucco*. For instance, the chorus, "*Va, pensiero, sull'ali dorate,*" lovely as it is, might have been written by Rossini or Bellini. Perhaps the truth of the matter is that *Nabucco* had sufficient in common with its predecessors like *Semiramide, Norma,* and *Lucia di Lammermoor* to make the idiom as a whole immediately intelligible to the public without prejudice to the new element in the music. The libretto, too, not to mention the performance, was rightly considered far more satisfactory than that of *Oberto*. In short, the success of *Nabucco* as a whole, reacting, so to say, on every characteristic of the score, focused attention on all the salient points, including the novelty.

To appreciate this novelty we must understand something of the general operatic taste of the time not only in Italy but elsewhere; and the first point to be emphasized in this connection is the undisputed hegemony of Rossini.

In the fourth decade of the nineteenth century Mozart may have been God, but Rossini was his prophet. A typical cultured amateur of the day, Prince de Valori, writing many years later, calls him "the living encyclopedia of every kind of genius in music," and claims that even in ecclesiastical compositions he is only rivaled by Palestrina. Stendhal, in a delicious if not always strictly accurate biography that is almost unique as a book by one man of genius about another, is a little more critical in general but scarcely less enthusiastic in particular. A perhaps typical instance of his judgment is the statement that, whereas the star of Rossini would probably pale more rapidly than that of Mozart, there were some things in music that Rossini had accomplished better than anybody else who ever lived. "The glory of this man," he writes in 1823, "is limited only by the limits of civilization itself, and he is not yet thirty-two!" The chorus of praise sung by Boïeldieu, Stendhal, Cherubini, de Musset, and Lamartine over an opera like *Otello* can scarcely be surpassed in the annals of music. These, be it remembered, were not the views of men ignorant in matters of music or general æsthetics. They recognized the supremacy of Bach, Beethoven, Mozart, and Haydn; they appreciated the best contemporary literature. A few of the more straitlaced musicians held aloof, but such views were typical of the most enlightened Latin opinion. Nor must we imagine that the German musicians regarded Rossini as anything like the wanton trifler depicted in our superficial or pedantic textbooks. Schubert differentiated sharply his operas from "the rest of the rubbish" heard in Vienna, and Mendelssohn, it is well known, defended him. Wagner is often depicted as a wholehearted opponent of Rossini, but there is, to say the least, another side. In so far as Wagner disliked Rossini at all, he disliked him as the embodiment of the hated Italian opera; but he had no doubt whatever of the true genius of that embodiment. Indeed, he seems to have agreed with Rossini himself that his eclipse (after *William Tell*) meant the end of opera as distinct from music drama. In the very fair and kindly article on the composer written in 1868, he describes him as "the expression of his public and environment as Bach, Palestrina, and Mozart were expressions of their environment." And, more significant still, he calls him "the first truly great and reverable man I had as yet encountered in the art world."

In a book written primarily for English readers these tributes have to be stressed, because there is something more than a tendency among the English musical pundits to belittle the undoubted genius of Rossini or even to deny it altogether. Doubtless his genius was exaggerated by his contemporaries; doubtless he was not so great an innovator as they imagined. But the undimmed sparkle of *The Barber of Seville* and the true inspiration of the overtures to *Semiramide*, *L'Italiana in Algeri* and *William Tell* (to mention only works familiar to everybody) sufficiently attest the first attribute; while those who are inclined to deny the second should remember that Rossini has been singled out as the man first responsible for grafting the fruitfully dynamic principles of *opera buffa* on the more static traditions of *opera seria*;[6] and they will be positively surprised to read the reproaches leveled at him by his own admirers for attaching in his later works, such as *Mosé*, an undue importance to the orchestra. Only in the matter of vocal reforms has comparative justice been done to him in England. The long and short of the matter is that the legends (often apocryphal) of Rossini as a wit and a gourmet have obscured the true greatness of the man. In time Radiciotti's monumental biography will probably do much to correct the false perspective in which he is usually seen.

Rossini, then, may be described as the composer who set the standard of taste, while following close behind him came Bellini and Donizetti. They were more freely criticized, it is true. Even Italian critics

[6] Stendhal.

had been found to complain that their attention was concentrated too exclusively on the melodic line. Nevertheless, no one thought of contesting the supreme beauty of their melodies or the claims of these to be regarded as the ideal vehicle for vocal expression. Bellini was, of course, a man of undoubted genius who, but for his premature death at thirty-three, might have carried his gift for lyrical expression to unsuspected heights. Wagner, in early days at Riga, waxed enthusiastic over the "solemn, grandiose character" of *Norma*, wherein "all the passions which his song so majestically transfigures thereby obtain a majestic background"; while, after hearing Schröder-Devrient's performance in *I Montecchi ed i Capuletti* he wrote: "After I had grown heartily sick of the eternally allegorizing orchestral bustle, at last a simple, noble song showed forth again." Wagner, needless to say, later changed his mind to a great extent. Chopin, on the other hand, never lost his enthusiasm for Bellini, whose arias left a permanent imprint on his music. Indeed, it is impossible to explain the new contours of certain *cantabile* phrases in Chopin's piano works without reference to the operas of Bellini.

Donizetti's talent was of an indubitably lighter caliber, but his comic operas, such as *Don Pasquale* and *Elisir d'Amore* are veritable masterpieces, while even a work so preposterous in some ways as *Lucia di Lammermoor* shows an unexpected reluctance to die.

In 1840, then, Italian, not to say European, operatic taste proudly based itself on the various styles of these three men with far more justification than is usually supposed; and in the case of Italy, at any rate, their purely musical appeal was reinforced by their international prestige. Politically and intellectually the Italian provinces then counted for nothing in Europe; the country, to recall a famous saying, was merely "a geographical expression." The sole Italian ambassadors to the Court of European Esteem were her musicians, of whom these three were the chief. Only through them could Italy speak to the world at all, and the fact naturally enhanced their importance in Italian eyes.

At this time, however, a new feeling was discernible in the peninsula. Political acquiescence was beginning to give way to a more virile spirit of revolt and independence. This new spirit, manifested from force of circumstances especially in the theater, felt the lack of something in the wit of Rossini, the melancholy of Bellini, the fluency of Donizetti, which it found in the operas of Verdi. Connoisseurs might sneer at the crude vehemence of the peasant lad from Busseto, but the public sensed in his music the presence of an unfamiliar element that satisfied their secret longings, that translated into a new language their hopes and fears. As Lualdi has well said,

Verdi's music at this time was "agitator's music." A fresh wind was blowing; his characteristic genius provided just the new set of sails fitted to take full advantage of it.

Neither at first nor subsequently did this new forcefulness, this striving after new expressiveness, please everybody. In its own way, as we can see from the writings of Chorley, an excellent English critic, it provoked almost as great a disgust as did the music of Wagner. Accusing Verdi, among other things, of placing an impossible strain on the human voice, those men of taste who are always the most bitter opponents of genius sighed audibly for the greater skill, the more cultivated restraint, of the old masters. And let there be no doubt about it, they were more skilled, more cultivated; but they had not in them the quality that could identify their music with national aspirations. "*Va, pensiero, sull'ali dorate*" might remind the connoisseurs of Bellini in a purely musical sense; but it was the particular poignancy of Verdi's emotional inspiration that led the audiences of La Scala and subsequently at other Italian theaters to identify the longing for home of the Jewish exiles in the opera with their own longing for a country that should really be their own. As will be seen in the course of Verdi's life, this process of subjective identification, established for the first time in *Nabucco*, later became something very like a habit. It is a significant and amusing coincidence that while Wagner was turning out reams of prose to show that Italian composers of opera had sinned in neglecting the national songs of their country, Verdi was, in fact, writing them.

CHAPTER IV

Eleven months after the production of *Nabucco* Verdi's second opera was finished; it was called *I Lombardi alla Prima Crociata*.[1] Solera, drawing his ideas from a poem of Grossi, had written the libretto, an extravagant medley of time and place, love and religion, Crusaders and Moslems, Jerusalem and Milan. Verdi, it appears, had composed the music in six or at the most seven months. Everything was ready for production when the censorship interposed its veto. Cardinal Gaisruk, the amiable Archbishop of Milan, had received information that in the new opera were represented not only ecclesiastical processions, a conversion, and a baptism, but the actual Valley of Jehoshaphat. Such things, in his opinion, could not be shown on the stage without sacrilege, so he wrote to the Chief of Police demanding the suppression or drastic modification of the opera. The police themselves were not very easy in their minds about Solera's libretto. Gioberti's famous book *The Moral and Civil Primacy of the Italians*, a plea for the unification of Italy under the presidency of the Pope, had just appeared and was being read by everybody with all the avidity attaching to a work officially suppressed for political reasons. Several of Solera's lines might, they thought, be taken as a reference to the ideas of the book in general if not as an appeal to the Papacy in particular. Merelli, Solera, and Verdi were commanded to wait upon the Chief of Police.

Verdi refused to go. Either, he said, the opera should be performed as he had written it, or it should not be performed at all. Merelli and Solera were more diplomatic. They went to see the Chief of Police, an Italian called Torresani. Merelli pleaded eloquently for the opera. All the scenery and costumes were ready; principals, orchestra, and chorus were alike enthusiastic about the music; the composer would tolerate no cuts, no changes. Were the police prepared to take the responsibility of suppressing an undoubted masterpiece? No Italian could listen unmoved to such a plea. Torresani, declaring that he was the last person in the world to wish to spoil the future of a young man of genius, promised, if only the words "Ave Maria" were changed to "Salve Maria," that he would license the production on his own responsibility. Even Verdi's pride could find no fundamental objection to such a trivial alteration, and on the 11th of February 1843 *I Lombardi* made its appearance at La Scala.

It was as successful as *Nabucco;* from the popular point of view

[1] *The Lombards at the First Crusade.*

perhaps even more successful. The story of the dispute with the Censorship had been noised abroad, and from three o'clock in the afternoon the approaches of the theater were packed with people carrying their own provisions, waiting to gain admission. Verdi, never an optimist, was apprehensive. The rehearsal had gone none too well and he confided his fears to the prima donna, Frezzolini, just before the performance. The lady, one of the best singers of her time, reassured him. "Either your opera will be a great success," she said, "or I will die on the stage." But there was no necessity for any such immolation; the triumph of the opera was assured from the outset. The police prohibited one encore, but had to allow others, while the famous chorus: "*O Signore, dal tetto nation,*" [2] roused the audience to an enthusiasm that surpassed even that which had greeted the popular chorus in *Nabucco*. Once again they identified themselves with the sentiments of the characters on the stage, and on this occasion it was even easier than before to adapt the longing of the Lombard Crusaders for their native land to the actualities of present aspirations. Ten years later the poet Giusti was to recall in a well-known poem the unparalleled effect made by this chorus on the Italians of the forties.

The enthusiasm of the critics was hardly equal to that of the public. The *Gazzetta di Milano*, after much vague praise, cautiously said that *I Lombardi* would confirm the reputation brought to Verdi by *Nabucco*. The *Figaro* thought both the structure and versification of the libretto good, but decided that it was far from being a masterpiece, which strikes us today as over- rather than under-praise. While recognizing that the noble and imposing characteristics of the music as a whole justified the tribute paid to the composer, the critic found fault with him for sacrificing everything to grandiose effects and for never allowing his artists to sing together in the concerted numbers. Vitali, in the *Gazzetta Musicale*, though lavish of his praise of the score as a whole, suggested that the scoring was too noisy and that greater moderation in the use of the big drum would be an advantage. A correspondent of the *France musicale* was much more severe. "Nothing could be poorer than this work from the technical point of view," he wrote. "Counterpoint is inexcusably neglected and the deafening noise of the brass instruments and the big drum does not suffice to hide the emptiness of the orchestration. Mme Frezzolini, having nothing to sing, shouts at the top of her voice from beginning to end."

These criticisms, taken as a whole, give a by no means unjust impression of *I Lombardi*, particularly when one remembers that the public had already expressed perhaps exaggerated admiration for all

[2] "Lord, from our homes."

that was worth admiring in the music. The influence of the Busseto band is prominent in the composer of *I Lombardi*, a very unequal opera with some magnificent choruses and a fine trio, but as regards both text and music decidedly inferior to *Nabucco* as a work of art. Still, the public did not think so, and, finding in it exactly what they wished to find, exalted it to the skies. Incidentally, there is no evidence that Verdi, when composing it, had consciously intended to take advantage of its patriotic attributes. Indeed, the critic Vitali, writing a week later, paints a most attractive portrait of the young composer at the time as totally absorbed in the cultivation of his art, conspicuously free from any taint of charlatanry or intrigue, and distinguished among his fellow musicians as much for his modesty as for his moral qualities. If extra-musical considerations contributed to the success of *I Lombardi* they were fortuitous, though Verdi may, as Bonavia says, have at times identified himself with the "ideal and unknown youth" prophetically apostrophized by Mazzini in 1836 as destined to consecrate music to the cause of Italian independence.

Soon after the success of *I Lombardi*, Verdi went to Venice to supervise the production there. It was not a success, and Verdi's letter to a friend describing the first night provides the first instance of that laconic restraint with which he always faced failure, comparative or total. "*I Lombardi*," he writes, "was a complete fiasco — what may be called a really classical fiasco. Except for the cabaletta of the Vision it was all received with disapproval or, at the best, tolerance. This is the plain and simple truth, which I retail with neither pleasure nor grief."

I Lombardi may not have been a success at Venice, but the prestige of the composer had grown greatly in the Italian peninsula. With two leaps, so to say, he seems to have sprung into a position at least equal to that of his contemporaries such as Mercadante or Pacini — indeed, probably superior to that of any other Italian composer except Rossini and Donizetti. His reputation was great enough at any rate for the director of La Fenice at Venice to commission a new opera from him. Despite the most flattering offers from Merelli, he accepted it, for he seems to have felt that after two such outstanding successes as *Nabucco* and *I Lombardi* it would be unwise to tempt fortune again in Milan. The choice of a libretto presented much difficulty. Had a sufficiently good baritone been available, Verdi would have liked to tackle *King Lear* or *Il Corsaro*, two subjects of which more will be heard subsequently. His suggestion of *I Due Foscari* was rejected by the management; he dallied with the idea of an opera on Cromwell. Finally Count Mocenigo, the director of the theater, suggested Victor Hugo's *Hernani*, recommending a certain Francesco Piave as a suitable person to turn it into a libretto. Verdi, though nervous of the police, was enthusiastic about the play and satisfied with the competence of the experienced and exceptionally docile adapter, who, whatever his other shortcomings, had an undoubted sense of the stage.

Piave, a Venetian, was then thirty-three years old. Originally destined for the law, a passion for everything theatrical, from plays to actresses, had at this time led him to the Fenice, where he combined the offices of resident poet and stage manager. Thus began the association between the two men destined to last for so many years. Even at this date Verdi found much to criticize in the work of his collaborator, whose theatrical knowledge he compared unfavorably with Solera's, and was by no means sparing of his own suggestions. Finally, however, everything was arranged and Verdi went to Venice, strictly temporarily; for it is characteristic of the man that, while recognizing "the divine, beautiful, and poetic" quality of the city, he had no wish to stay there.

Then the usual troubles began. First, the inevitable trouble with the censorship, doubtless suspicious in general of a play which had been hailed throughout Europe, not to say proclaimed by its distinguished author, as the embodiment of romantic liberalism, and hostile in particular to any representation on the stage of a conspiracy against an emperor. The change of a few verses, however, provided an unexpectedly simple solution of this difficulty. The next was no less serious if more absurd. A horn-call, representing Ernani's promise to commit suicide when and where required, plays a prominent part in the opera. Count Mocenigo, the director of the theater, thought that the presence of a horn on the stage at La Fenice was out of keeping with the dignity of his establishment, and all the power of Verdi's inflexible will had to be used in order to make him change his mind. Finally, the prima donna, a German singer called Loewe, was dissatisfied with the trio that ends the opera. She wanted a brilliant solo for herself, whereof the docile Piave, always ready to invent, change, or delete anything for anybody, had already written the words when Verdi rose in his wrath and forbade the alteration. It was the first engagement in that battle for supremacy between Verdi and his singers so resolutely waged throughout his entire career. He emerged victorious, but at the risk of ruining the chances of his opera; for Loewe was furious. Relations between the composer and his principal interpreter were, indeed, so strained that when later he left Venice, he satisfied the demands of politeness by merely sending her a visiting-card, even though the success of the opera in the meantime had induced her to confess the error of her ways. She did not, in fact, receive absolution till the autumn at Bologna, when, during the performance of the same opera, the quarrel was finally composed.

On the 9th of March 1844 *Ernani* made its first appearance. Its success was definite, but in no way comparable with that of *Nabucco* and *I Lombardi* in Milan. Verdi himself held the singers responsible. "Nobody," he writes, "could have sung more out of tune than Loewe, and Guasco [the tenor] was in bad voice and frightfully hoarse." It is clear, however, that these shortcomings must have been largely due to the nervousness so often associated with first nights. The *Gazzetta di Venezia* does not mention them, but contents itself with saying that Loewe was "even more successful" at the second than at the first performance. It is not an uninteresting notice. The writer, after criticizing certain numbers, praises equally the slow movement of the finale of the first act and the chorus of conspirators in the third. He especially congratulates the composer on having succeeded, despite all the fine music that had gone before, in preserving the climax of interest and inspiration for the final trio; while in two sentences that throw much light on the tastes and standards of the time, he concludes as follows: "The music made such an impression that even on Sunday people came out of the theater already humming the tunes. To impress itself on the mind at a first hearing and become popular is the privilege of good music. Maestro Verdi has an abundant and felicitous imagination, only equaled by his good taste."

Good taste is about the last attribute in the world that we should discover in the score of *Ernani*. There are some magnificent pages in it, particularly in the last two acts, but its outstanding characteristic is a rough sincerity of emotion that, if not inappropriate to a subject dealing with the passion of three men for one woman, is crude, almost brutal. *Ernani* remains of interest primarily as Verdi's first important analysis of romantic passion. There is more humanity about it than any of its predecessors.

Victor Hugo considered with some reason that Piave's libretto had not done justice to his play; indeed, when the opera was produced in Paris in 1846, he insisted not only on the title but the very names of the characters being changed. Verdi's carelessness of literary detail, perhaps his greatest weakness, led him to tolerate downright absurdities. Exceptionally, as, for instance, when Piave wrote the final trio in Metastasian strophe, he insisted on that excessively pliable librettist recasting the verses in accordance with a prose formula written by himself. But his interest first and foremost lay in the musical possibilities of a situation in general, not in its detailed exposition. These situations in *Ernani* were just what he wanted, new, violent, and highly effective. They were also, apparently, what his listeners wanted; for despite the singularly ill-inspired criticism of a Florentine journalist a few months later to the effect that the opera was lacking in popular appeal, it surely, and not very slowly, became one of the popular successes of the day.

So far as Italy was concerned, this may be ascribed in part to the inevitable patriotic catchwords that could be discovered in or manufactured out of the libretto. Conspirators and plots! What more appropriate to the continually increasing ferment of revolt? If ever there was an opera charged with the heady wine of liberty, *Ernani* was such an one. The hero became the embodiment of the proscribed patriot. The chorus "*Si ridesti il Leon di Castiglia*" [3] could easily be changed into an invocation to the Lion of Venice or even of Italy; just as in 1847, when the accession of the liberal Pius IX to the Papacy led the credulous Italians to believe for a short time that Gioberti's dreams might actually be realized, the other famous chorus, "*A Carlo Quinto sia gloria e onor!*" [4] could be changed, mid the waving of flags and manifestations of the wildest enthusiasm, to "*A Pio Nono sia gloria e onor.*" The Venetian censors must often have repented of their leniency.

Nevertheless, the success of *Ernani* outside Italy proves that the opera could stand on its own feet without any considerations of local patriotism. A few months after its original appearance it was produced at Vienna, where Donizetti, at that time director of the Italian Opera, earned Verdi's gratitude and esteem by offering to supervise the rehearsals himself. Von Bülow found merit in the music,[5] and from Vienna the opera made its way sooner or later to the principal opera houses of other countries. What *Nabucco* and *I Lombardi* had done for Verdi in Italy, *Ernani* did in Europe. Henceforward he was an international figure.

Less than a fortnight after the production of *Ernani* Verdi was back in Milan considering, almost simultaneously it appears, no less than three librettos. The management of the Teatro San Carlo at Naples had written to suggest that he should compose an opera in collaboration with Cammarano based on Voltaire's *Alzira;* he himself, having found some "most effective and magnificent" things in a tragedy by Verner on the subject of Attila, was in correspondence with Piave on the subject. But the opera destined first to come to birth was *I Due Foscari*, founded on Byron's historical tragedy of the same name and definitely commissioned by the impresario of the Argentina Theater in Rome.

From this time onwards we have at our disposal Verdi's own files

---

[3] "Let the Lion of Castile arise."
[4] "Glory and honor to Charles V."
[5] Weissmann.

VERDI'S BIRTHPLACE AT LE RONCOLE

Courtesy of Messrs. Ricordi

Courtesy of Messrs. Ricordi

VERDI IN EARLY LIFE

of correspondence, collected, edited, and supplemented in the year of his centenary by Cesari and Luzio, one of the most typical collections of papers and letters ever left to posterity by a composer. From this *Copialettere* it is often possible to follow Verdi's movements and states of mind and body in minute detail. For instance, it is clear that during the spring and summer of this year he was suffering from digestive trouble. Owing partly to this, partly to the amount of work on hand, he had to refuse to write a cantata to Romani's words intended for an evening party at the Casino de' Nobili on the occasion of some learned congress or other.

In the summer he went to Busseto to stay with Barezzi, hoping to benefit his health and perhaps to obtain greater leisure for the composition of his opera, which had not progressed as rapidly as he had hoped. Busseto does not seem to have answered his expectations in either respect. He complained of dullness, of a feeling of isolation from everything and everybody, and, despite the solitude, of an inability to work. At the end of August or in the first days of September he returned thankfully to Milan, where the change seems to have had a beneficial effect, for by the end of the month he was ready to go to Rome to supervise the production of *I Due Foscari*, which was performed for the first time at the Argentina Theater on the 3rd of November 1844.

It is scarcely accurate to say, as has been said, that the opera and its composer met with a cool reception. The public were annoyed at the high prices of admission, especially in view of the fact that the performance was none too good and that there was no ballet, but a contemporary press notice tells us that the composer was called before the curtain again and again amid scenes of great enthusiasm. A few days later the noble concessionaire, Don Alessandro Torlonia, entertained him at a banquet, where he was presented with a poem written in his honor. In short, if the public showed dissatisfaction, it was rather with the management than with Verdi and his opera.

He had certainly done his best to satisfy their tastes, for in a characteristic letter written to Piave in the summer he had instructed that docile poetaster to make a certain cabaletta energetic, "because we are writing for Rome," suggesting, moreover, that in the third act a gondolier's song should be mingled with the chorus and that the action should take place, if possible, towards evening so that there might be a sunset effect, "which is always so fine." As a matter of fact, the whole of the letter to Piave is interesting apart from these rather naïve bids for popularity, because it shows the meticulous care that Verdi bestowed on certain aspects of his librettos even at this date. For instance, he points out that nobody knows the crime for which the younger Foscari was condemned; that at the end of the tenor's cavatina the singer remains on the stage, "which is always ineffective"; that the mood and idea in a certain place are insufficiently differentiated as between one number and its predecessor. We see, too, for the first time his characteristic feeling for conciseness in the instructions to make the duet that concludes the first act short, "because it comes at the end." If only Verdi had shown the same care for the literary as for the theatrical details of his librettos! If only Piave's virtues of docility and pliability had been matched by other, more stalwart gifts! Lord Byron is said himself to have thought little of his tragedy, and where Piave was concerned the question was generally how much he would spoil a subject rather than how much he could improve it. *I Due Foscari* is decidedly a monotonous and gloomy opera, relieved by one or two flashes of inspiration on the part of the composer, from the æsthetic point of view inferior rather than superior to any of its three predecessors. At least one of the contemporary critics, however, thought otherwise. "It seems to me," he wrote in the *Rivista di Roma*, "that Verdi, even more than in *Ernani*, has endeavored to shake off his former manner, to return to the springs of affection and passion. In this opera he wished to hark back to the pure and simple style of the old masters." Then, after rather florid praise of the "passionate and sweet melodies accompanied by exquisite harmonies, quite Oriental in their opulence," of the "unsurpassable richness and variety of the tunes," of the absence of "odious dissonances" and of "crude noise," the critic is perspicacious enough to lay his finger on what was, perhaps, Verdi's chief merit as a composer of opera. "Every personage," he says, "speaks his own language; every character expresses his own passions in a manner eminently dramatic."

For which piece of prophetic analysis may his previous sins of bombast receive plenary absolution! Besides, it is only fair to remember that it was *I Due Foscari*, not any of its predecessors, that drew from Donizetti the perhaps unwilling admission: "Frankly, this man is a genius." [6]

[6] Monaldi.

CHAPTER V

Within three months Verdi's next opera, *Giovanna d'Arco*, was ready. Its admittedly unsatisfactory nature is usually ascribed to the fact that it was written in so short a time, but the point has been overemphasized. We know that as early as December 1843 Verdi had definitely arranged to write a new opera for La Scala, which could scarcely have been either *Attila* or *Alzira*. So the subject must have been in his mind for a considerable time, and it is at least possible that he had jotted down some ideas. Moreover, three months was not an especially short period for the composition of an opera in those days; nor, in any case, does *Giovanna d'Arco* seem to me notably inferior to its predecessor, while it is certainly superior to its immediate successor.

His old associate Solera was responsible for the libretto, based on Schiller's well-known *Maid of Orleans*. The comparative failure of the opera has been ascribed to its absurdity; but it may be doubted whether the Schiller play, despite Wagner's admiration and German patriotic prejudice, appears any less absurd to the modern mind. The figure of Joan of Arc is to us nowadays equally incredible in both, and Solera's version has at least the advantage of being the shorter. We know nothing of Verdi's approach to the subject, because unfortunately there is a nine months' lacuna in the *Copialettere* just at the time when he was engaged in the composition of the opera. He was probably attracted in theory by the theme of an oppressed country battling for liberty, but he may have been equally attracted in practice by the idea of writing an opera for his personal friends, the well-known singer Frezzolini and her husband. Contemporary criticism, at any rate, seems to have been mainly concerned with her performance, for when the opera was first produced at La Scala on the 15th of February 1845, only the most general mention is made of the music (except in the case of Lambertini, who, incidentally, bestowed warm praise on the overture), all attention being concentrated on the beauty of Frezzolini's singing and the loveliness of her appearance in her white warrior's dress with the fleur-de-lis clasped to her bosom. Nevertheless, the music of *Giovanna* is not without interest. The overture gives an appropriate atmosphere at once; there is at least one lovely aria; a great deal of the chorus-writing is admirable, while in Joan's "voices" (represented in this case by two choruses of angels and demons) we find Verdi for the first time experimenting, though not altogether successfully, in the fantastic. He himself, at any rate, thought well enough of the opera to permit Teresa Stolz, a singer especially dear to him, to appear in it twenty years later. Incidentally, *Giovanna* was revived in 1847 at Palermo with an entirely new libretto manufactured to meet police objections, Joan being changed to a compatriot of Sappho and the title to *Orietta of Lesbos*.

Almost immediately after the production of *Giovanna* Verdi turned his attention once more to *Alzira*. A year previously, in correspondence with Flauto, the Naples impresario, he had expressed his delight at the idea of being associated with the Neapolitan poet Cammarano,[1] famous throughout Italy as the librettist of Donizetti's *Lucia di Lammermoor*. Indeed, he had written to that gentleman a very flattering letter in which he expresses the assurance that in his expert hands "Voltaire's tragedy will become an excellent melodrama." Incidentally, the letter is interesting as showing the equanimity with which Verdi met the charges leveled at him by his detractors. "I am accused," he writes, "of loving noise and maltreating the voice. Pay no attention; only put some passion into your libretto, and you will see that I shall write all right." No progress, however, seems to have been made with the opera in 1844 except as regards some correspondence about the exact terms of the contract. In this connection we have the first of those typical letters written by Verdi to Ricordi, who acted as a kind of agent as well as publisher, in which the composer puts forward his conditions and terms with meticulous care. From the details of the contract sketched in this letter we learn the casual fact that Verdi was to receive for his opera about one third as much again as the sum he had himself suggested for *I Lombardi;* while the condition that Cammarano should deliver the completed libretto to the composer at least four months before production throws a significant light on the musical habits of the time.

So it was not till the spring of 1845 that Verdi turned his serious attention to *Alzira*, and even then he was much handicapped by his digestive troubles. To such an extent that at the end of April he wrote to Flauto that the doctors had ordered him at least a month's rest and that the production of *Alzira* would have to be postponed till the end of July or the beginning of August. He even enclosed a medical certificate. Flauto answered in a very odd letter in which he assured Verdi that his trouble was in no way serious and could be cured by taking tincture of wormwood; that the doctors would do him more

---

[1] He was twelve years older than Verdi and seems to have been something of a character, his love of solitude being a byword in Naples. He had a special affection for the porch of the Church of San Francesco di Paolo, where he could often be seen, a slim, tall figure with spectacles that never left his nose, leaning against a pillar and writing verses. When he was tired he just sat down and went to sleep.

harm than good; that if he would only come at once to Naples, the good air and the "excitability of our Vesuvius" would repair all his disorders, notably his lack of appetite. Verdi, whose sense of humor was not his strongest point, resented the tone of this letter, especially the advice about the wormwood, and tartly insisted on the delay, writing at the same time to Cammarano that, but for the pleasure of setting his libretto to music for such a theater as the San Carlo, he would have followed the advice of the doctors and done nothing the entire summer. There is little doubt that he regarded Flauto's belittlement of his ailment as a kind of slur on what may be called his craftsman's conscience. He prided himself on his reliability, on the business-like execution of his engagements; and particularly disliked being treated as a temperamental malingerer.

Towards the end of June, however, Verdi was well enough to go to Naples, where he spent the month of July finishing and scoring the opera. He did not enjoy himself. Harassed by journalistic and public curiosity as to his habits and movements, he was deprived of the solitude especially dear to him. However, the opera was produced on the 12th of August and appears to have had a fair reception, described by Verdi himself as akin to that of the first performance of *Ernani* in Venice. The correspondent of the *Gazzetta Musicale*, in his account of the evening, hedges carefully, suggesting that the beauties of the opera are such that they might well become more manifest as time went on and that *Alzira*, like *I Due Foscari*, would gradually grow in popular favor. He was wrong. *Alzira* neither achieved nor deserved popularity. Verdi himself admitted as much, for when the opera failed utterly in Rome four months later, he wrote to a friend that only the introduction and the last finale might possibly have compensated for the defects of the rest of the work. Later in life he was even more explicit. "*Alzira* is thoroughly bad," he said to the Countess Negroni Prati. He was right. *Alzira* is the worst opera he ever wrote and the fault was his. True, the libretto is as monotonous as Voltaire's original play, but Verdi had welcomed it and, indeed, waxed enthusiastic over the verses of Cammarano, whom, incidentally, he treated with far more deference than the too obliging Piave. The secret of his failure is probably to be found first and foremost in the prosaic fact of his indigestion, while in a letter written to his friend Maffei at the end of July he makes the significant admission that, even if *Alzira* proved a failure, he would not grieve overmuch, because he composed it "almost unconsciously" and "without effort."

The truth is that during the whole of the year 1845 Verdi was not at all himself, as is shown by the fact that his digestive troubles grew steadily worse till, at the end of the year, he was definitely on the sick-list in Venice. On Christmas Eve he was too ill to attend the production of *Giovanna d'Arco* at the Fenice Theater, where, despite the presence of the Emperor of Russia and a new number specially written for his erstwhile antagonist Loewe, it was very coldly received. On the 2nd of January he was confined to bed for three weeks with gastric fever so that there can be no doubt of the genuine nature of his illness. The assurance is welcome, because a certain tendency to hypochondria in Verdi must be admitted. Even in later years, when the excellence of his health verged on the miraculous, his devoted admirer Pizzi noticed that he attached exaggerated importance to the slightest indisposition. It is not an uncommon phenomenon among those fortunate enough to be able to take perfect health for granted. At this period of his life, however, there was no question of perfect health, and that his disorder provides an obvious explanation of the poor quality of his work can scarcely be doubted, though the fact seems to have been overlooked by too ingenious commentators.

Verdi, after his return to Milan from Naples, had gone to Venice to finish his next opera, *Attila*, and to supervise the production. The libretto, at any rate, had been under consideration since the period immediately following the production of *Ernani*. It had been originally entrusted to Piave, who had received the strictest possible marching orders. He was to have Verner's original play translated; he was to make a point of reading Mme de Staël's book on Germany; he was to invent a new character; he was to change this and to change that. Meanwhile, however, Solera and Piave had effected what may be called a deal in librettos, and *Attila* was handed over to the former, not with altogether happy results. Solera, though more gifted than Piave, was less reliable. When Verdi returned from Milan after the production of *Alzira*, he found that the volatile Solera had gone to Barcelona, and experienced the greatest difficulty in getting from him complete details of the libretto. Even in December, when he had actually finished most of the music, various changes in the last act had not reached him, so that he had to have recourse to the faithful Piave. Then, as we have seen, Verdi had to keep his bed, and the whole production of *Attila* was postponed. It eventually took place on the 17th of March 1846. Verdi wrote to the Countess Maffei that, on the whole, it was very successful. The correspondent of the *Gazzetta Musicale* was less certain. He writes that the expectations he had entertained from a preliminary glance at the libretto had not been fulfilled. Though he praises certain numbers, notably the famous duet between Attila and Ezio and the music that accompanies the passing of the storm at the end of the prologue, he comes to the general conclusion that the friends of the composer rather than the general public were responsible for any enthusiasm there may have been. That Verdi's friends were particularly enthusiastic about *Attila* cannot be doubted, because Verdi himself tells us that they insisted that it was the best of his operas. He probably thought the same. He had been exceptionally attracted by the musical possibilities of the libretto and he had taken infinite trouble, using the respite due to his illness to beg his friend in Rome, the sculptor Luccardi, for details of the figure of Attila shown in the Vatican tapestries or frescoes. With typical, laconic caution he writes that the public seem less certain than his friends of the opera's merits, that all he himself will say is that it is not inferior; time will decide.

Time has decided — on the whole in favor of the critic. Yet there are one or two points that do not seem quite clear — points not of opinion but of fact. Thus the critic speaks of a cool reception while Verdi complains that the applause and the calls were excessive for his weak state of health. More odd still, the critic, though admitting that the duet between the bass and the baritone "pleased much," gives us no indication that it actually contained the famous line "*Avria tu l'universo, resti l'Italia a me!*" [2] which, as we know from other, independent sources, roused the house to a frenzy of patriotic excitement and became, in fact, one of the catchwords of the time. Monaldi, who has specialized in these matters, describes the reception of *Attila* by the Venetians as one of "frantic enthusiasm, surpassing that of *Ernani*." A partial explanation of the discrepancy may be hazarded in the suggestion that the success of *Attila* increased with great rapidity at each performance. It could hardly have been otherwise. Nobody knew better than the fiery Solera how to make the most of the patriotic possibilities of the libretto. The public was shown the founding of Venice; the heroine (inappropriately enough represented by Loewe, a German) was intended to be the embodiment of Italian womanhood; there was an apostrophe to Italy "as formerly queen-mother of powerful and valorous sons." All this could scarcely leave unmoved Venetians in particular and Italians in general. *Attila* triumphed for a time throughout the entire peninsula. We must remember that there were but two years to run before the explosion of 1848.

As regards the music pure and simple, the overwhelming sincerity, if not the skill, of the score raises *Attila* to a level superior, at any rate, to that of its immediate predecessors. Outside Italy, however, the opera never achieved much success. When, two years later almost to a day, it was produced in London, the receipts only amounted to eight pounds, and a contemporary critic remarked with some acidity that the sole merit of the opera seemed to be that it was short, unlike other works by the same composer.

It was during the preparations for this very *Attila* that Verdi seems first to have established personal contact with England. Things

[2] "You may have the universe, but let me keep Italy."

were going very well with him. In Italy his operas were all the rage; even the unfortunate *Un Giorno di Regno*, become once again *Il Finto Stanislao*, was keeping its place in the repertory. Not only had *Nabucco* been successful at the Théâtre Italien in Paris but, with the names of the characters changed in order to maintain the prestige of the Old Testament and the title changed to *Nino*, it was due for production in London, where it had been preceded a year before by *Ernani*. Lumley, at that time director of Her Majesty's Theatre, had contracted with Verdi to come to London to produce an opera especially written for his theater. He seems to have arranged this in conjunction with a certain Lucca, a publisher at Milan, who, jealous of Ricordi's success, had been maneuvering for some time to secure the property in an opera on his own account. His jealousy was certainly intelligible. Emanuele Muzio, already the master's pupil and later his intimate amanuensis, told Antonio Barezzi that Ricordi had at that time made 30,000 Austrian lire (rather more than 3,500 dollars) out of the sale of *Ernani* alone. The contract, however, was not destined to be fulfilled. Immediately after the production of *Attila* Verdi wrote to Lumley that he was not well enough to go to London, much less to write an opera, forwarding via Lucca medical certificates from doctors at Venice and Milan. Then the Flauto comedy began anew. Lumley had no Vesuvius to offer, but he wrote in April expressing the hope that in a few days the composer would be well enough to visit England at a time when "our weather is at its best, with a climate less fine but also less exciting than that of Italy." The change of environment, he added, and the visit to London during such a brilliant season would do the composer more good than all the remedies in the world. The letter remained unanswered; so a month later the enterprising impresario tried again. This time he was able to announce the successful production of *I Lombardi* in the presence of "all the most important personages in England, not excepting the Queen-Dowager and the Princes and Princesses of the Blood-Royal." He hoped that this pleasant news would serve as an antidote to the composer's indisposition and that he might come in person to take an even stronger dose in the form of the applause that would inevitably greet his appearance. Verdi, however, despite such inducements, remained unmoved. He wrote a friendly but firm letter to Lumley in which he said he considered the matter closed, and a couple of months later went to take the waters at Recoaro where his extreme boredom was only mitigated by the pleasure of neither making nor hearing any music.

Recoaro, however, did its work. Early in August Verdi was back again in Milan with his health completely restored, and very busy. He was under contract to Lanari to produce an opera at the Pergola

Theater in Florence; the choice had to be made between three librettos. He had to carry through with Flauto delicate negotiations as to the postponement of a new opera promised for Naples, on the result of which depended the possibility of reopening with Lucca and Lumley the question of a visit to London. Apparently Lumley was keen enough on the project to come to Milan to discuss it, and eventually Verdi, who had managed to get his own way in the matter of Naples, was able definitely to accept his offer for the following summer.

CHAPTER VI

Of the three librettos under consideration for Florence, *Macbeth* was the one eventually chosen, mainly, it appears, because a first-class tenor was not indispensable. Verdi's love for Shakspere dated from very early years and it is well to remember in this connection that the attitude towards Shakspere at this time was very different from ours. He represented to the romantic movement the negation of that classical tradition which they so much disliked; he was the very embodiment of passion and horror, as will be evident to anybody familiar, for instance, with the career of Berlioz; he was not quite respectable. Verdi felt irresistibly attracted by *Macbeth* or, to be more accurate, by the dramatic situations in *Macbeth;* for the beauty of the details, especially as regards the language, seems to have appeared to him as secondary in importance. He himself completed the libretto in prose, merely handing it to the dutiful Piave to turn into verse. Piave, always enthusiastic, wrote to the impresario Lanari that *Macbeth* would be the most remarkable production yet seen on the Italian operatic stage, which, if it were a success, would open out undreamed-of possibilities to composers both present and future. Lanari, essentially practical, neither affirmed nor denied, but contented himself with pointing out to Piave that his scenic indications were not sufficiently detailed, that a ballet for aerial spirits would have to be cut because the opera was due for production in Lent. Meanwhile Verdi was working at the music, on which he had been engaged during the autumn, but eventually he, too, was drawn into the correspondence. He wrote towards the end of December to Lanari giving precise instructions as to how the ghost of Banquo was to be treated. It was to be impersonated by the same actor who played Banquo in the first act; it was to emerge from underground, very lightly draped in an ashen-colored veil, with disheveled hair and wounds visible on the neck. "All these ideas," he writes, "I have got from London, where this tragedy has been continually played for two hundred years." On the 21st of January he wrote again. He had been talking with the scenic artist at La Scala, who suggested that the scene of the apparitions in the third act could be admirably executed by that wonderful new invention the magic lantern. He thought this an excellent idea, suggesting that the novelty of the effect would draw crowds of people to the theater and more than cover the expense of buying the apparatus. The witches were to be divided into three sections of six each. The choruses and the concerted pieces were of special importance. He had procured from London various sketches for costumes. These precise instructions show the anticipatory care that Verdi bestowed on the production. How necessary they were is proved by the fact that the stage manager at La Pergola apparently thought that the period of *Macbeth* was that of Ossian and the late Roman Empire! Verdi read him a little lecture on dates, precising 1040 as the year in which Duncan was assassinated, and adding a list (inaccurate) of contemporary English kings. At the very end of January or in the first week of February 1847 the score was finished, and during the first few days of March Verdi, accompanied by his faithful Muzio, left Milan for Florence.

He found there a very agreeable and cultivated circle of people. There had been procured for him a letter of introduction from Alessandro Manzoni to the famous poet Giuseppe Giusti, with whom he became intimate. The sculptor Dupré, a warm admirer, called on him and laid the foundation of a friendship that was destined to be lifelong. His friend Andrea Maffei, who had been engaged since the previous summer in adapting a libretto for the composer from Schiller's play *Die Räuber*,[1] was also there. The four men saw each other nearly every day. Maffei obliged Verdi by touching up the weakest points of Piave's versification and adding one or two lines of his own. Dupré modeled the composer's hand and introduced him to the art treasures of the city. The sculptor has left us an interesting account of Verdi's great delight in painting and sculpture, on which he discoursed, it appears, with real intelligence, his favorite artist being Michelangelo. At night Verdi took them to the rehearsals of *Macbeth*. It must have been a very agreeable and stimulating life, wherein the intimate contact with men of such culture doubtless proved of incalculable value to the composer.

If Verdi enjoyed exceptional popularity among his friends, new and old, he made up for it in the theater. Never had he been so exacting; never so taciturn and resolute. There he was definitely unpopular. Trouble had been brewing among the singers even before his arrival. The gentleman cast as Banquo had protested against doubling the part as ghost. Verdi followed his usual method of redoubled severity. Rehearsal succeeded rehearsal. The leading lady, Barbieri-Nini, herself a most competent and conscientious artist — she had studied the sleepwalking scene for three months in order to give an accurate impression of a woman talking in her sleep — has left us a most amusing account of them. The climax came on the very evening of the *répétition générale*. Incredible as it may appear, Italian theaters at that time do not seem to have indulged in the luxury

---

[1] *The Brigands*. The commission was not given after *Macbeth*, as is usually implied.

of a proper dress rehearsal. Verdi, however, had insisted on it, and as the invited public was pouring into the theater, went in search of Barbieri-Nini and the baritone, Varesi, who was Macbeth, asking them to come into the foyer to rehearse the duet, "*Fatal, mia donna,*" once more. The baritone objected that they were in costume and had already rehearsed the duet a hundred and fifty times. "Then you will put on a coat and rehearse it the hundred and fifty-first," replied the composer, getting his way as usual. All through his career Verdi subjected his singers to similar inflexible discipline. As he himself admitted, he was unwilling or unable to pay them even the conventional compliments expected in the operatic world. Yet many of them — and those as a rule the best — adored him.

There can be no doubt that he was absolutely right, in this instance at any rate. He felt that in *Macbeth* in general he was, as Piave had written to Lanari, trying something new, an opera without love interest, and in this duet in particular he was aiming at a dramatic declamation that must have seemed strange to singers brought up in the school of Bellini, Rossini, and Donizetti.

In the result the duet, together with the sleepwalking scene, carried off the honors of the evening when *Macbeth* was produced on the 14th of March 1847. Otherwise, with the exception of a few numbers, the opera failed to arouse remarkable enthusiasm. The Florentine correspondent of the *Gazzetta Musicale* (who gives an account rather than a criticism), while noting that the house was packed, that the composer received twenty calls, and that there was much applause here and there, declared that the atmosphere as a whole was too "Satanic" and that the *mise en scène* left a great deal to be desired. At the second performance, however, everything went differently. "From the reserve of the first evening," the critic writes, "the public passed suddenly to wild applause. So much so, that all the numbers, even those that had been received with indifference on the first night, were greeted with enthusiasm. . . . The composer was called over and over again and a cheering crowd of his warmest admirers and friends followed his carriage from the theater to his apartment, where he had to come out several times on the balcony to acknowledge the applause." The notice then concludes with a few lines of praise for the composer's happy new orchestral effects and the power of his declamatory writing.

There can be no doubt of the real merits of *Macbeth*, which represents the high-water mark of Verdi's achievement up to this time. Even today, despite the absurdity of some — not all — of the witches' music and of one or two other numbers, we can hardly fail to be impressed by the power and sincerity of this very somber score. *Macbeth* is a true music drama. It may be doubted whether the public at large fully appreciated the æsthetic merits of the work, though Giusti wrote to the composer affirming that the more often his opera was heard, the more clearly would its excellence be evident. But he rather spoiled the effect of this tribute by belittling the importance of the fantastic and urging the composer never to neglect an opportunity to reproduce in his music that "chord of grief which wakes the readiest echo in our hearts."

The public, however, rose to no such heights of analysis. It wanted music of action, and thought to have found it once more in *Macbeth*. We can scarcely credit the fact that this eminently Scottish melodrama should have provided occasion for manifestations of Italian patriotism, but it did. Italy was like a tinder-box at this time. Cavour had been frightening Carlo Alberto by openly advocating railway-construction as a means of unifying the country. The accession of the liberal Pope Pius IX to the throne of St. Peter had aroused the most extravagant expectations. A learned congress at Genoa had just interrupted its deliberations to celebrate the anniversary of the day when the Austrians were expelled from that city. Patriotic fervor sought an outlet everywhere. So when, a year later, *Macbeth* was produced in Venice and a Spanish tenor, as Macduff, sang Maffei's stirring lines so fortunately grafted on Piave's pedestrian verses:

> *La patria tradita*
> *Piangendo c'invita:*
> *Fratelli, gli oppressi*
> *Corriamo a salvar,*[2]

the whole audience was moved to frenzy and the police had to be called in to restore order.

One person, at any rate, had no doubt of the purely musical worth of *Macbeth* — Verdi himself. He dedicated it to his father-in-law and benefactor, Antonio Barezzi and in the charming letter sent with the score wrote as follows: "Here is this *Macbeth*, which I love above all my other operas and therefore think the most worthy to be dedicated to you." Twenty years later, as we shall see, he still cared enough about it to submit it to drastic revision.

After the production of *Macbeth* Verdi returned to Milan, where one of his first cares was to occupy himself with matters concerning Lumley's production of his new opera in London. Originally Verdi had intended this to be *Il Corsaro*, but, despite a strange enthusiasm for the subject in the first instance, dissatisfaction with the libretto as well as the various complications of the previous year had led to his substituting for this *I Masnadieri*, an adaptation by his friend

[2] Our country, betrayed, invites us with tears:
Brothers, let us speed to succor the oppressed.

Maffei of Schiller's play *The Brigands*. He had by the end of 1846 already written half the music and, before finishing it, only waited to obtain assurances, first, that the interests of his opera would not be sacrificed to the production of Meyerbeer's German opera, *Feldlager in Schlesien*, announced (as it turned out, vainly) for the same season at Her Majesty's; second, that Jenny Lind, who had just made a brilliant success in Vienna in this very opera of Meyerbeer's, would be available for his opera also. These questions settled, he set out at the beginning of June for London, taking on his way the Rhine, Brussels, and Paris, where he stayed two days. A first visit to the Opéra did not impress him; he found the singers execrable and the orchestra mediocre. Finally he arrived in London, very curious, very nervous, and prepared on the slightest pretext to tear up his contract and return to Paris.

Some of Verdi's biographers give the impression that Verdi disliked London very much. This is inaccurate. He disliked the climate, which he held responsible for destroying all his desire to work and even for his inability to pass judgment on his own opera after two orchestral rehearsals. "I hate this smoke," he writes to the Countess Maffei, "and this smell of coal; it is like being on a steamboat." He failed to understand why he was not in the least ill. Nevertheless, he conceived an extraordinary admiration for the town. He liked the clean houses, the immensity and opulence of the city, the beauty of the streets, the Bank, the Docks. "If only," he writes, "London had the climate of Naples, there would be no need to sigh for paradise."

Despite climatic handicaps Verdi managed to finish *I Masnadieri* in time for production on the 22nd of July. If he bothered his head about the critics — which is, to say the least, doubtful — he must have been rather nervous as to its reception. Davison, the critic of *The Times*, and Chorley, of the *Athenæum*, were almost as hostile to him as later they were to be to Richard Wagner. Both denied him any gift for melody, Chorley being particularly emphatic. "Neither in 'Ernani' nor in 'I Lombardi,'" the critic had written in 1846 on the occasion of the production of *Nabucco* under its Assyrian title, *Nino*, "nor in the work introduced on Tuesday is there a single air of which the ear will not lose hold. . . . How long Signor Verdi's reputation will last seems to us very questionable." Perhaps the composer's most intelligent as well as consistent supporter in the press was the critic of the *Illustrated London News*, who had described *Ernani* as a "real type of lyrical tragedy where feeling finds its appropriate expression in music," and had praised *Nabucco* as "bearing the stamp of genius and deep thought." Apart from the press, moreover, Verdi could hardly have felt certain of the public. *I Due Foscari*, produced earlier in the year, had been a failure, and *I Lombardi*, though Lumley had written to the composer of its triumph, had in fact, according to the later and more candid reminiscences of that enterprising manager, split the town into the usual two factions of partisans of old and new.

Nevertheless, *I Masnadieri* was a decided success, though, again according to Lumley himself, not so successful as it appeared to be. "The interest that ought to have been centred in Lind was thrown on Gardoni; while Lablache (a portly giant) as the imprisoned father had to do the only thing he could not do to perfection — having to represent a man nearly starved to death." Contemporary press notices hardly seem to bear out Lumley's complaint of insufficient interest being centered in Jenny Lind, because the main concern of all of them was the excellence of her performance and the beauty of her singing. In any case it was an exceptionally brilliant first night, with the Queen, the Prince Consort, Prince Louis Napoleon, and the Duke of Wellington among the audience. There were calls for the artists. Verdi, who himself conducted the orchestra and secured, according to the *Morning Post*, "a faultless performance," was repeatedly acclaimed. Despite the fact that the season had only three weeks more to run and that a general election was imminent, the opera was given four times.

With the exception of Chorley, the critics were reasonable enough. *The Times*, after warmly praising the libretto, singled out several numbers for commendation, incidentally remarking with some discernment that "it must always be remembered that Verdi writes more for the ensemble than for bringing forward any single personage and hence there are not those opportunities for individual display which are to be found in the works of earlier composers. Even Amalia, with an ordinary vocalist, would not have risen into remarkable prominence but the beautiful singing of Jenny Lind rendered every air she executed a boon to the hearers." The *Morning Post*, it is particularly interesting to note, was almost as much struck by the novelty of certain instrumental effects, especially by the substitution of an introduction for the conventional overture, as it was by the vocal numbers. One scene (that where Carlo summons the robbers to avenge Massimiliano) is described by the enthusiastic critic as "the most dramatic scene extant." The *Illustrated London News*, after decrying the story as excessively horrible, wrote that "the music is dramatic in the extreme and somewhat excels the masterpieces of Meyerbeer and other composers of the German Romantic School." Chorley in the *Athenæum*, however, was implacable. "We take this," he says, "to be the worst opera which has been given in our time at Her Majesty's Theatre. Verdi is finally rejected. The field is left open for an Italian composer."

He had not changed his mind many years later, for in his reminiscences he describes *I Masnadieri* as "Verdi's most paltry work," only remembered by the stage appearance of Jenny Lind, "whose Amalia could not have pleased had it been given by Cecilia and Melpomene in one, so worthless was the music."

Generally speaking, the critics' judgment of *I Masnadieri* was fair. Nearly all of them praised the final trio, which is certainly the best number in the opera, and most of them recognized the excellence of Amalia's cabaletta, "*Carlo vive*," quite apart from Jenny Lind's superlative interpretation of it. On the whole, however, *I Masnadieri*, being decidedly conventional in every particular, is an unsatisfactory opera, which never, anywhere, achieved notable success.

After two performances Verdi relinquished the direction of the orchestra at Her Majesty's Theatre in favor of Balfe, already famous as the composer of *The Bohemian Girl*, and went to Paris. Before his departure Lumley had sounded him as to his willingness to undertake the musical direction of the theater and compose one new opera each year for three years. Balfe could not be compared as a conductor with Costa, who had just transferred his allegiance to Covent Garden, so that this offer from such an astute person as Lumley proves beyond a doubt Verdi's excellence as a conductor as well as his popularity with the public at large.

Verdi considered the idea seriously, though he was not enthusiastic about it. He did not like the idea of conducting during a whole season; he liked even less the idea of writing only one opera a year — an interesting, revelatory objection. Shortly after his arrival in Paris, however, he wrote a letter to Lumley stating his exact terms. He must have 60,000 francs each year for the new opera, 30,000 for his duties as a conductor; a house in the country and a carriage. The terms were high for those days, but London then was to Europe what New York is now. It is clear from his letters that Verdi, accustomed to the modest standard of life in Italy, was overwhelmed by the riches and expenditure of the English. He wished to make hay while the sun shone. But a week later Lumley wrote that circumstances had arisen that made it advisable to postpone the discussion of the contract for a little time. Verdi was not even able, as he had intended, to return to England with a new opera in the following year. He had signed an agreement with Lucca for a second opera, and that unwise publisher refused, for any compensation whatever, to release him from the contract. Verdi, by no means indifferent to money, was highly displeased. He kept his bargain; but, as we shall see, he produced a thoroughly bad opera and never again had anything to do with Lucca. Lumley's scheme, it should be observed, never materialized, for which we may perhaps be thankful. The routine of a conductor's life is not as a rule conducive to successful composition, and Verdi, an Italian of the Italians, was rarely at his best when exposed to cosmopolitan influences.

Verdi settled down to enjoy in Paris the solitude that can always be found in the midst of a crowd, the distress caused him by the presence of the dying Donizetti being doubtless relieved by frequent visits to Giuseppina Strepponi, who had settled there as a singing teacher when her voice showed signs of wear. Except in the matter of climate, however, he preferred London to Paris, as he himself states in so many words, disliking especially the noise and animation of the boulevards. The only advantage was that at first nobody paid attention to him or his affairs. But this advantage did not last long. By the middle of August the directors of the Opéra had got in touch with him. "All day," he humorously complained, "I am confronted with two impresarios, two poets, and two publishers, for in Paris everybody seems to hunt in couples."

The matter under discussion was the production at the Opéra of a French version of *I Lombardi*, which eventually, after two months' rehearsal, materialized on the 26th of November under the title of *Jérusalem*. It was perhaps Verdi's least successful effort at reconstruction. The librettists, the two poets Royer and Vaez, by abolishing the Crusades, by turning Milan into Toulouse, by dressing up Italians as Frenchmen, had managed to contrive a remarkably complete disguise for the original. Verdi did his best to second their efforts, inserting a new ballet, indispensable, of course, at the Paris Opéra, making many changes, and substituting some new numbers for old. Unfortunately the alterations as a whole were by no means for the better; much of whatever primitive charm *I Lombardi* possessed evaporated in its metamorphosis. From what Verdi does not say it is clear that his main impression of the production was gorgeousness rather than any particular musical merit. Nevertheless, *Jérusalem* had a fair success, and three years later it made its appearance in Italian at La Scala, without, however, equaling, much less surpassing, the reputation of *I Lombardi* in the peninsula — or anywhere else.

After the production of *Jérusalem* Verdi spent the next month or two, apparently, writing *Il Corsaro*, the opera promised under contract to Lucca. He seems to have finished it by the beginning of February, for at that time he handed over all the rights in it to Lucca for the sum of 1,200 napoleons, or about 20,000 francs. Since, with the exception of *Alzira*, this is the worst opera ever written by the composer, little more need be said about it. *Il Corsaro* contains one excellent scene, that depicting the hero in prison; otherwise the only point of interest about the opera is that it provides almost the only instance of a lapse on Verdi's part from the standards of conscientious craftsmanship. He took the execrable libretto exactly as it came from Piave; he displayed no interest in the production. We may dispose of it as summarily as he did. *Il Corsaro* was produced on the 25th of October 1848 at Trieste, failed completely and deservedly, was buried without hope of resurrection. Lucca must often have repented of an unwise, though perhaps inevitable, insistence on the terms of his bond. By a curious coincidence his publishing house subsequently became identified with the introduction of Wagner's works into Italy and, in consequence, with the opposition to Verdi that was for some time associated with that movement.

CHAPTER VII

Except for the Napoleonic upheaval the year 1848 was perhaps the most disturbed known by Europe during the entire nineteenth century. It opened with a revolt against the Bourbons, leading to the independence of Sicily and a temporary constitutional monarchy at Naples. In February Louis Philippe lost the throne of France. There were revolutionary movements in Vienna and Germany, in which Richard Wagner played a part sufficiently conspicuous to cause his exile. Most important of all, from Verdi's point of view, the whole of Italy, united for the first time (though united, as a matter of fact, more in appearance than in reality), made a determined effort to sever the Austrian connection. The pot which had been simmering so long had at last boiled over.

These events affected the composer in various ways. The disturbances at Naples entailed the necessity or the excuse for the cancellation of his contract to write an opera for the San Carlo. The revolution in Paris, which seems to have been a kind of tragicomedy, provided him with considerable amusement. It appears to have affected him personally only to the extent that he felt constrained to buy twenty newspapers a day, not, as he tells us, in order to read them, but to avoid the persecution of the newsboys. He was exceedingly gay.

The uprising in Italy, however, was a very different matter, shaking every fiber of his emotion both as man and as musician. As man he felt himself irresistibly drawn to his countrymen in such a crisis, and by the beginning of April he was in Milan just after the glorious "Five Days" in which that city had managed to assert her independence. But it was soon only too clear that the cause of Italian liberty was doomed, so on the last day of May Verdi once more set out for Paris. Things went rapidly from bad to worse. The leadership of the Italians was as incompetent as their bravery was commendable. By August Verdi, in common with other prominent Italians residing in Paris, signed a despairing appeal to the French government to intervene in Italy, in the vain hope of averting the disastrous armistice of Salasca. Needless to say, nothing happened. The contrast between Verdi's high spirits in the spring and his depression in the autumn of the year is very striking. He was equally disgusted with the various rulers of the Italian states, who by their vacillation and jealousy had in reality compromised the Italian cause from the outset, as with the politicians of the French Republic, who, like all politicians, had so signally failed to translate theory into practice. As a matter of fact, he did not believe in the vitality of the French republican movement at all, prophesying with remarkable political prescience its collapse within a short time.

The most important musical outcome of the revolution was the composition for the Argentina Theater in Rome of an opera on a patriotic subject, *La Battaglia di Legnano*. It appears that the poet Cammarano had suggested this to Verdi while he was in Italy, and the composer, only too anxious to find an outlet for his patriotic feelings, jumped at the idea. The failure of the Neapolitan management to deliver a libretto by the date stipulated had invalidated their contract, so that, immediately on his return to Paris, Verdi was able to devote himself wholeheartedly to the composition of Cammarano's opera. It has been suggested that Verdi wrote *La Battaglia di Legnano* in extreme haste — Monaldi even speaks of a few days — but this is inaccurate. He was working on it all the summer, and a letter to Cammarano on the 23rd of November shows that he had given much thought to the libretto, while even at that date the score was not finally finished. There is no doubt that the subject, which deals with the victory of the Lombard League over Frederick Barbarossa, appealed strongly to Verdi. For one thing, it was so topical. Was not Legnano one of the strong points of the quadrilateral still held by the Austrians? By the end of the year the opera was finished and as a manifestation of patriotism Verdi consented himself to go to Rome to supervise the production. This took place on the 27th of January 1849, when the opera was received with delirious enthusiasm. In view of its character and the circumstances in which it was given, how could anything else have been expected? Pope Pius IX had fled to Naples; the shortlived Roman Republic was to be proclaimed within a fortnight. The theater and the audience were decorated with the national colors; the composer and the artists were called over and over again; the whole of the fourth act was encored. Never can an opera have been produced in circumstances quite so appropriate. Yet this very fact has tended to detract from rather than emphasize the merits of an opera that has been dismissed far too summarily as a mere *pièce d'occasion*. Such, of course, *La Battaglia di Legnano* is; but the fact does not necessarily condemn it. Cammarano's libretto, in some respects highly ingenious, is admirably suited to its purpose. Verdi's music, conceived on the broadest possible lines, burns with a patriotic fire that can warm our hearts even today, after a lapse of the best part of a hundred years. In those troubled times musical criticism was at a discount, but an account of the production in a local evening paper, the *Pallade*, has been preserved. To be frank, the critic has little of interest to say, mainly confining himself to outbursts of patriotic enthusiasm; but he emphasizes the fact that in this opera Verdi's "melodies are not mere mechanical combinations of notes but a happy instance of how the musical phrase should be grafted on to the poetical expression and interest of the drama. . . . Far from following the old conventions, Verdi has felt that his spirit needs freedom as Italy needs independence."

The other musical child of 1848 was of far less importance. A year before, in London, Verdi had made the acquaintance of Mazzini, at whose request he now set to music some verses by the young Genoese poet Mameli to serve as a popular song. He set them, but too late; not in fact till October, when all the fighting, at any rate, was over. For this reason, perhaps, Verdi's *Inno di Mameli* never succeeded in achieving the popularity of Novaro's, which had the advantage of being written before, not after, the event, and remains, worthily, one of the national songs of Italy to this day. There seems to be an impression in some quarters that both composers set the same words. This is not so, Novaro's setting being of *Fratelli d'Italia*, Verdi's of *Suona la Tromba*. Nor is there any musical reason to regret the survival of Novaro's rather than Verdi's tune, for, the last phrase excepted, there is nothing individual about the latter in any way.

Apart from the brief excursion to Rome to produce *La Battaglia di Legnano*, Verdi remained continuously in Paris for nearly a year. During this time Giuseppina Strepponi and he decided definitely to set up house together. Riemann gives the date as 1849, but the decision may well have been made earlier. At any rate, in January 1849 he gave Giuseppina's address, 13 bis, rue de la Victoire, as the place where the directors of the Opéra were to deliver to her in person a contract canceled by mutual agreement. Thus began an association that proved of incalculable moral, physical, and artistic benefit to the composer. Peppina, as her intimates called her, was not an intellectual woman, though Berlioz had a warm admiration for her personality; but she was clever and charming and extremely sensible. Her letters to the Escudier brothers, to the Countess Maffei, to all her friends, are a delight. No composer was ever more fortunate in his life companion.

There was a great deal of correspondence with Ricordi, very precise, very business-like. Havana and a mysterious place mentioned for the first time by the composer under the name of "Nuova Jork" were negotiating for performances of some of his operas. He was urgently in need of money, 12,000 francs, in particular, being required to pay a Jew called Levi, of Soragna, who had advanced that sum on mortgage to a certain Merli, the owner of property just outside Busseto. By making himself responsible for this and other mortgages Verdi had acquired the property in May 1848, having ceded in part exchange a little farm he had bought four years previously at Le Roncole and having put in his father as a kind of caretaker until he himself should take possession. Thus, for the first time, we are introduced to the Villa Sant' Agata, destined henceforward to be indissolubly connected with Verdi's life and works. As Verdi took it over, it was a farm of moderate dimensions with vines and arable land and, best of all, a depressing but invaluable river just outside the front gate, whence the kitchen-garden could be irrigated. Some slight repairs and alterations were at once made to the house, and in August and September Verdi went to live in Busseto to look after things, fortunate to find this escape from the epidemic of cholera that was raging in Paris.

Verdi's main musical preoccupation throughout this period was the composition of *Luisa Miller*, or, as it was first called, *Eloisa Miller*. This was written in fulfillment of the Neapolitan contract canceled owing to the political troubles of '48. Verdi undertook to write it mainly to oblige Cammarano, for whom he seems to have entertained great liking and respect, and they were in correspondence about it during the composition of *La Battaglia di Legnano*. Verdi, who was extremely busy, had left the choice of a subject to his librettist, only begging him to provide "a short absorbing drama with plenty of action, plenty of passion, so that I shall be able to set it easily to music." Cammarano's first idea had been a play called *Maria De' Ricci*, which dealt with a certain siege of Florence, but the authorities, thinking it far too topical and dangerous, vetoed the subject altogether. Cammarano then suggested *Luisa Miller*, a libretto based on Schiller's play *Kabale und Liebe* [1] which had previously attracted the attention of Verdi himself. On the 3rd of May 1849 the completed scenario was dispatched to Verdi in Paris, when an interesting correspondence began between the two collaborators with regard to the details of the libretto, Verdi making several suggestions and Cammarano accepting them or making counter-suggestions in a manner that does great credit to his intelligence. For Cammarano, despite the handicap of what we now consider the bad taste of his time, was extremely intelligent. Essentially a dreamer, as little like the typical lively Neapolitan as can well be imagined, he had thought much about the problems of operatic production and had come, apparently, to very much the same conclusions as Richard Wagner. "Did I not fear," he wrote to Verdi in connection with this very *Luisa Miller*, "to be branded as an Utopian, I should be tempted to say that for an opera to obtain the maximum of perfection one mind should be responsible for both text and music. From this it will be clear to

[1] *Intrigue and Love.*

you that when two authors are in question, I think that the least they can do is to collaborate with the greatest possible intimacy. Poetry should be neither the slave nor the tyrant of music."

Though the concluding portion of the libretto was not in fact ready till the middle of August, Verdi had begun writing the music about the beginning of July, and in the first week in September he was able to promise completion, except for the scoring, by the time he was due to arrive in Naples in the second week in October. "Arrange that rehearsals begin the day after my arrival," he writes, "and the opera can be produced at the end of the month" — a significant commentary on the rapidity of orchestration in those days.

As a matter of fact, owing to the quarantine that had been imposed in consequence of the cholera epidemic now spreading into Italy, Verdi did not arrive in Naples until much later. He had never wished to go at all, only having yielded to the urgent entreaties of Cammarano and the impresario, Flauto. He had an unpleasant recollection of his first visit when gossip dogged his footsteps at every turn. Indeed, a year before he had categorically refused the request for his presence in a letter that throws an interesting light on his mentality at the time. "If you think that my presence will contribute to the success of the opera, you are wrong. I repeat what I told you at the beginning: I am a bit of a savage, and if the Neapolitans found so many defects in me the first time, they will not change their opinion now. True, I have been living for a year and a half in Paris (that city in which everything is said to acquire a certain polish), but, to be frank, I have become more of a bear (*orso*) than ever. I have now been writing operas and wandering from place to place for six years and I have never in the pursuit of success addressed a word to a journalist or asked a favor from a friend or paid court to a rich man. Never, never! I shall always despise this kind of thing. I write my operas as well as I can; then I let matters take their course without any effort to influence public opinion."

However, he did go — and must often have repented. The quarantine in Rome (which to Verdi's inexpressible chagrin had reverted to its Papal master a few months previously) was bad enough, but things in Naples were worse. To begin with, the financial condition of the management was so precarious that Verdi, acting on a friendly hint from Cammarano, wrote a formal request to Flauto for the three thousand ducats due to him in advance, with a threat to leave immediately unless he received satisfaction. Whereupon a certain Duke of Ventignano, superintendent of the royal theaters, thought to checkmate him by invoking a curious law by which no artist could leave Naples without a passport bearing the visa of his own bureau. Verdi, countering with a proposition immediately to take himself and his opera on board a French frigate that lay in the bay, won the game as usual, and rehearsals duly began.

During this another exasperating comedy was staged. A certain amateur composer called Capecelatro was credited in Naples with the possession of the Evil Eye. According to Verdi's friends, this had been directly responsible for the failure of *Alzira* four years previously. So, in order that the redoubtable Capecelatro should not approach him, they arranged to watch over the composer from morning till night. They mounted guard in his hotel; they carefully surrounded him in the street, the theater, the restaurant. Anything less congenial to Verdi, that passionate lover of solitude, could scarcely be imagined.

Finally, there was an annoying encounter with a journalist, a particularly contemptible member of a species obnoxious to Verdi at its best. This gentleman had prepared beforehand two notices of *Luisa Miller*, one favorable, the other the reverse. He showed them both to the composer, insinuating that a little present would suffice to ensure the publication of one rather than the other. "Print whichever you like," dryly said Verdi, turning to Giovanni Barezzi, his frequent companion at first nights.[2] Wherefore, despite delightful excursions to Vesuvius, Capri, and Sorrento, not to mention the consumption of a considerable quantity of Lacryma Cristi wine, Verdi can have found little pleasure in his life at Naples. But there was at least one compensation. Whether owing to the successful precautions taken against the Evil Eye, whether owing to the intrinsic merits of the opera itself, *Luisa Miller* won a great success. Details of the first performance are lacking, the troubled state of the times being responsible for a lacuna here in the files of the *Gazzetta Musicale*, that precious mine of press notices. Nevertheless, the success remains beyond dispute and was, moreover, repeated in Rome a few months later, though, curiously enough, the last act, indisputably the best of the whole opera, seems at the first performance to have been the least successful of all. Can it be mere coincidence that in the interval immediately preceding it the terrible Capecelatro contrived for the first time to approach the composer and embrace him warmly?

Outside Italy, however, *Luisa Miller* was never received with conspicuous favor, though many years later no less a person than Boïto, writing to Camille Bellaigue, confessed that he could never hear the lovely tenor song *"Quando le sere"* [3] unmoved: "Ah, if you knew the kind of echo and ecstasy that this divine cantilena awakes in the soul of an Italian, especially in the soul of one who has sung it from his earliest youth! If you only knew!"

[2] Pizzi.   [3] "At Eventide."

Luisa Miller is of particular interest in that it has been singled out by Basevi and others as the inauguration of Verdi's "second manner," a subject discussed elsewhere. Some have found in it a musical expression of the war-weariness subsequent to the excitements of 1848; others, the first evidence of Parisian polish on Verdi's exuberant vitality. The only point on which everybody seems agreed is that *Luisa Miller* is an opera different in kind from anything that Verdi had written before. It is equally passionate, but more intimate; there is nothing grandiose about it as regards either subject or treatment. We are asked to weep over the woes of the virtuous Luisa in very much the same way as we are asked later to sympathize with the agony of the profligate Violetta; both the demi-mondaine and the little bourgeoise are sacrificed to the conventions of their times. It seems impossible to accept unreservedly the theses of war-weariness or Parisian polish, for the reason that Verdi was first attracted to the subject in 1848 — that is to say, before either factor could be considered paramount. It would be equally justifiable to claim that Verdi, thinking of himself and Peppina, wrote the opera as a protest against the conventional attitude towards the relations of men and women. The least self-conscious of men, he was almost certainly unaware of any definite stimulus at all. Indeed, so much is fairly clear from the letter to Cammarano already quoted. In the theme of *Kabale und Liebe* he saw a new kind of subject fraught with dramatic possibilities and, following his instinctive genius for the dramatically appropriate, he produced a new kind of music — that is all. We are too inclined in these matters to be wise after the event.

CHAPTER VIII

Verdi passed practically the whole year 1850 at Busseto, though not, as has been sometimes taken for granted, at his new villa, but in the Palazzo Orlandi,[1] in the town itself. Very probably the extensive alterations to Sant' Agata, which Verdi himself always described as contemporaneous with *Rigoletto*, were first started about this time. It was an extremely busy year for the composer, starting off with a typical interchange of letters with Ricordi. Things were not going too well, his publisher wrote. *La Battaglia di Legnano* had been a comparative failure. The prevalence of pirates throughout Europe, particularly in Seville, where a certain maestro drove a regular trade in making orchestral versions from piano scores,[2] entailed enormous expenses for the maintenance of agents in every city of importance. Verdi must reduce his royalties on performances and sales; otherwise there would be a danger of outcry against musical and literary property, a principle by no means universally recognized. Such letters from publishers are not unfamiliar to authors and composers, but Ricordi was in this instance not wholly unjustified. Verdi, a match in matters of negotiation for any publisher who ever lived, agreed to Ricordi's proposals after a certain amount of satirical commiseration with the woes of his rich friend, protesting only against what he considered the excessive reduction of his percentages in certain details.

He had promised a new opera to Ricordi on the interesting condition that it should be produced at any Italian theater of the first class except La Scala, to which Verdi had taken a dislike destined to last for a long time. The opera in question was *Stiffelio*, originally intended for Naples, but withdrawn thence by Verdi owing to his dissatisfaction with the management of the San Carlo. This withdrawal entailed, apparently, a change of librettist, Piave being substituted for Cammarano. Whether any librettist in the world could have produced anything satisfactory with such a theme may be doubted. The forgotten French play by Souvestre and Bourgeois on which the opera is based deals with the attitude of a mystic, evangelical German clergyman to his faithless wife. To begin with, a Catholic audience could not understand a clergyman having a wife

---

[1] Bonaventura.
[2] Compare the experience of Sullivan later in the United States, where the principle of international copyright was not established till much later and cannot be described as satisfactory even today.

at all. Second, as Latins, they found great difficulty in distinguishing between the attributes of the leading character as an outraged husband and as a mouthpiece for the expression of Christian forgiveness. Worst of all, the clergyman was a tenor, which struck everyone as ludicrous. The opera, therefore, seemed doomed from the outset, especially as the censorship practically suppressed the last act, considering the scene in the church and the clergyman's address, based on the actual words of the New Testament, flagrantly profane.

Nevertheless, when *Stiffelio* was first produced at Trieste on the 16th of November 1850, under Verdi's own supervision, it was by no means a failure. The local correspondent of the *Gazzetta Musicale* tells us that not only at the first performance but at several subsequent performances the theater was sold out, while a greater or less measure of applause greeted every number. The critic makes an interesting, though not perhaps wholly justifiable, comparison between *Stiffelio* and *Luisa Miller* in view of the "passionate quality of the vocal expression and the careful and effective orchestration." Writing a second notice ten days later, he gives his considered opinion as follows: "This is a work, at the same time religious and philosophical, in which sweet and tender melodies alternate in the most attractive manner; it achieves the most moving dramatic effects without having recourse to bands on the stage, choruses, or superhuman demands on vocal chords or lungs." The critic's perhaps partial enthusiasm was not justified by the opera's subsequent career, though it does contain, in fact, one or two excellent numbers. Had the music of *Stiffelio* been twice as good as it actually was, however, the opera could scarcely have overcome the obstacles of its own libretto and of the mutilation of the last act perpetrated by the censorship. As we shall see, Verdi eventually abandoned the unequal contest in despair, using most of the music for an entirely new libretto supplied by the always obliging Piave. Thus seven years later *Stiffelio* became *Aroldo*.

Many other matters actually or potentially more important than *Stiffelio* occupied Verdi during this year. For instance, in February he sent Cammarano a detailed scenario of his own based on Shakspere's *King Lear*. The letter that accompanied it shows that the two men must already have discussed the matter, and, as a matter of fact, Verdi had been considering the subject in a general way for some time; but this is the first appearance in definite form of an idea that frequently recurred in subsequent years. By the summer, however, Verdi realized that he was too busy even to think of tackling such a subject and for the moment dismissed the idea of *King Lear* from his mind. He also had to refuse, perhaps unwillingly, to consider a libretto based by his friend Carcano on *Hamlet*; while, altogether willingly, he declined an offer from the Paris Grand Opéra to set Schiller's *Don Carlos*, being typically piqued that the director, Roqueplan, instead of writing himself, had asked the librettists, Royer and Vaez, to arrange the matter on his behalf. Whatever Verdi's wishes, he could not very well have done otherwise; he was busy not only with *Stiffelio* but with another opera for the Fenice Theater at Venice, which on the 9th of March had commissioned a new work destined to be the first of those by which the name of Verdi still lives today for the public at large — *Rigoletto*.

This was not the subject Verdi had in mind when he originally accepted the Fenice's offer. Piave had been ordered to look for a certain Spanish play (it was, in fact, *El Trovador* [3]) that he had apparently failed to trace. Failing that, Verdi first thought of a play by the elder Dumas called *Kean*, but eventually chose Victor Hugo's *Le Roi s'amuse*, produced in Paris some twenty years previously. Verdi's contract with the Fenice was only to write an unspecified *opera seria* to be produced during Lent 1851. The details of this contract are interesting in many respects. For instance, it is significant that Verdi thought it necessary to insert a clause guaranteeing a full-dress and lighting rehearsal which should rank almost as a *répétition générale*. He was to choose the singers and, as was the invariable rule at that time, himself to pay for the libretto. For the performing rights at the Fenice he was to receive 6,000 Austrian lire (about 700 dollars), for which the management had the right to make, only for their own use, a copy of the original score to be "jealously preserved in the archives of the theater." To avoid misunderstanding it should be pointed out that the sum above mentioned by no means represented Verdi's sole profit in the transaction. He sold the opera to Ricordi for 700 napoleons, besides receiving royalties on performances at other theaters.

The management of the Fenice accepted the subject, though with some misgivings. Victor Hugo's *Le Roi s'amuse* had created a scandal in Paris on its first production. Indeed, it had been withdrawn from the stage after one performance, ostensibly owing to the immorality of the theme, in reality, the author maintained, because it was politically distasteful to the government. Hugo, consciously or not, probably deceived himself. *Le Roi s'amuse* did strike its contemporaries as shocking. Even Basevi, writing many years later, maintains that vice is therein glorified at the expense of virtue. He stigmatizes Gilda's final sacrifice as nothing better than suicide, while Rigoletto's passion to preserve his daughter's innocence amid the welter of his other corruption he not unreasonably characterizes as selfish and illogical. Piave, however, assured both Verdi and the management

[3] *The Troubadour.*

that everything would be all right. Owing, doubtless, to one of those subterranean channels of information so precious to an Italian, he knew for a fact that no objection would be raised by the censorship. The management, however, was not completely satisfied; a letter was written to Verdi, still living in the Palazzo Orlandi at Busseto, that caused him considerable perturbation, and Piave, who seems to have been with him at the time, was sent post-haste back to Venice personally to deliver his answer. "The doubt about *Le Roi s'amuse* being allowed," wrote the composer, "causes me grave embarrassment. I was assured by Piave that there would be no objection to the subject and I, relying on his assurance, began to study and think about it very deeply. I have made up my mind as to the general musical idea and coloring. Indeed, I can say that, so far as I am concerned, the main part of the work is already done. If I am now compelled to tackle another subject, I shall not have time to devote the necessary study to it and shall be unable to write an opera satisfactory to my conscience." The letter is important as showing the manner in which Verdi approached composition. Much has been made of the fact that the actual writing and scoring of *Rigoletto* were completed in forty days; the more important gestatory period is altogether forgotten. The reader would be well advised, when listening to tales of compositions so spectacularly rapid as, for instance, those of *The Messiah* or *The Barber of Seville*, to remember the facts about *Rigoletto*. The explanation, as Verdi himself once insisted in connection with Rossini's opera, is generally the same.

Piave, still relying on his mysterious source of information, continued to insist that all was well, and under the title of *La Maledizione* [4] completed his libretto. Then, on the 10th of November, the censorship suddenly demanded a copy, which Verdi, who was at Trieste supervising the production of *Stiffelio*, was asked to dispatch immediately. On the 1st of December the bomb exploded. In the name of the Military Governor of Venice, *La Maledizione* was prohibited altogether, the prohibition being accompanied by a stinging rebuke to "the poet, Piave, and the famous maestro, Verdi, for not having chosen a more worthy field in which to display their talents than that of a plot so revoltingly immoral and so obscenely trivial." In vain the distraught Piave, by substituting a contemporary feudatory prince for the King of France, by toning down the more daring portions of the text, hoped to pacify the outraged Governor. The management decided that Verdi must be told the worst at once.

He took it badly. Some of the music was written; there was no time to choose another subject. In despair he suggested *Stiffelio*, with a new last act, if necessary. In view of the proximity of Venice to

[4] *The Curse.*

Trieste, the management of the Fenice naturally thought little of this proposal, and Piave feverishly recast the offending libretto with a hope of meeting the censor's objections. This time, however, he reckoned without Verdi, who would have none of it. He objected to the tepidity of some of the new action; he objected to Francis I becoming the Duke of Vendôme and especially to the toning down of his profligacy, without which, indeed, the play is meaningless. He very reasonably failed to see how or why the Duke should go to a lonely, disreputable inn unless something definite took him there. Most stubbornly of all, he refused to let Triboletto (Triboulet in Victor Hugo's original) be turned from a hideous hunchback into a fine, upstanding figure of a man, as the excessively pliable Piave was quite ready to do. His letter to the management ends as follows: "A hunchback who sings? Why not! Will it be effective? I do not know. But if I do not know, neither does the person who suggested these changes. In my opinion the presentation of this character, so deformed and ridiculous outside, so full of love and passion within, is a fine idea. Indeed, it was precisely on this account that I chose the subject. If these original characteristics are removed, I can no longer write the music. Should you tell me that my music can stand with the drama as it is, I make answer that such reasoning is incomprehensible to me. I tell you frankly that my music may be good or bad, but it is never fortuitous; I always try to give it a definite character."

The deadlock seemed complete, Piave's peace-offering of some Venetian sweets and fish being very coolly received at Busseto. Then the unexpected happened. A certain official of the censorship, one Martello — by a curious coincidence the actual signatory of the letter prohibiting the libretto altogether — who had in the first instance indicated to Piave the kind of modifications likely to make the subject acceptable, came once more to the rescue. The original situations of Victor Hugo's play could be left essentially unaltered; only the names of the characters were to be changed and the action transferred from France to Italy. In this way Francis I became the Duke of Mantua; Triboulet, Rigoletto; Blanche, Gilda; and so on. The storm in what appears to us an extremely diminutive teacup had subsided.

One of the main and least comprehensible causes of offense had apparently been the sack in which Gilda's body is placed at the end of the opera. This, Verdi, subject to certain strict conditions, was now allowed to keep, giving up in exchange the latchkey by which the Duke boasts his ability to enter at his own pleasure the room where Gilda has taken refuge, an incident so revolting, apparently, that it could not be tolerated. Verdi, Piave, and the secretary of the Fenice, assembled in conclave at Busseto on the 30th of December

1850, drew up and signed a solemn agreement embodying these absurdities, surely one of the most remarkable documents in the history of opera. On the 26th of January 1851 the irrepressible Piave, now, apparently, restored to favor, was able to open a letter to the composer with a Te Deum, a Gloria, and a couple of Alleluias; *Rigoletto* had finally been passed.

About three weeks later Verdi went to Venice to start rehearsals and on the 11th of March *Rigoletto* was finally produced. It was a very great success. How great may be measured by the fact that Verdi, the most restrained of men, himself used the extreme superlative in describing the reception to a friend a week later. The public as usual went mad; the press was enthusiastic. "An opera like this," wrote the *Gazzetta di Venezia*, "cannot be judged after one evening. Yesterday we were, so to say, overwhelmed by the novelty of it all — the novelty, or rather the strangeness, of the subject; the novelty in the music, in the style, in the very form of the numbers. We could not take it all in at one hearing. . . . The composer and the poet have developed a posthumous affection for the Satanic school now so discredited and outmoded. They have searched for their ideal of beauty in the horrible, the deformed. To achieve their effects they have had recourse not to the usual emotions of passion and terror, but to those of anguish and horror. Frankly we cannot praise their taste in these matters.

"Despite all this, however, the opera had the most complete success and the composer was acclaimed, applauded, and called after almost every number, two of which had to be repeated. And, truth to tell, the orchestration is admirable, marvelous; this orchestra speaks and weeps with you and arouses your every passion. . . . Never was sound more eloquent. Less admirable, however, so it seemed to us on a first hearing, is the writing for the voice. Notably as regards the lack of important concerted numbers; this departs from the style hitherto in use; one quartet and a trio towards the end, in which it is difficult completely to grasp the musical thought; that is all. On the other hand, there is an abundance of airs and duets, some of which, owing to their admirable execution, their novelty of phrase or cadence, the originality of their general contours, are truly delightful. . . ." In a second notice, written a week later, the critic of the same paper was still more enthusiastic, for by this time he had managed, apparently, to digest the unfamiliar beauties of the last act.

As might have been expected, the enthusiasm of the general public was focused on *"La donna è mobile."* [5] In writing it Verdi had been fully aware that this would happen. He had not given the music to the tenor until the last moment, and then only under the strictest in-

[5] "Woman's a fickle jade."

junctions to neither sing nor whistle it outside the theater, whereof the whole staff had also been sworn to secrecy. Everything went according to plan. People came out of the theater singing both words and music, and within a few days every Venetian gallant was teasingly humming them into the ear of his lady-love. Piave himself tried the joke on his own mistress, receiving a well-merited snub for his pains.[6]

Nevertheless, "*La donna è mobile*," despite its great merits as a dramatic aria, discussed elsewhere, was in reality by no means the outstanding feature of *Rigoletto*, which is, in my opinion, one of the most satisfactory operas ever produced. To begin with, Victor Hugo's original play is an extremely good one, and the libretto founded on it by Verdi and Piave as the result of their confabulations at Busseto (of which unfortunately we have no record) is scarcely, if at all, inferior. Indeed, Victor Hugo himself, who started off with a violent prejudice against *Rigoletto*, ended as one of its most fervent admirers. Doubtless one misses the real historical background. Doubtless it is a pity that audiences fail to realize that the lady whose betrayal caused Monterone's portentous curse was none other than Diane de Poitiers. These, however, are small matters; the main situations and motives of the original are faithfully reproduced, in some cases with heightened effect. This is especially true, of course, of the last act, where, thanks to music, Verdi was able to paint the simultaneous emotions of the characters with a vividness impossible to any writer. The quartet in *Rigoletto* is admittedly one of the masterpieces of opera, worthy to rank in musical beauty with the quintet in Wagner's *Meistersinger* and, psychologically, more dynamic. Contemporary critics were right in their praise of the orchestration, which, if apparently simple to us nowadays, remains in many instances extraordinarily original and effective.[7]

There is no doubt that Verdi himself was completely satisfied with his work. Immediately after the performance he told the baritone,

[6] She improvised in the same metre: E Piave è un asino
Che val per cento.

Which may be sung as: (Piave's a perfect ass,
One in a thousand.)

[7] A contributor to the discussion, in a paper read by the writer to the Musical Association, gave an interesting illustration of the point. While conducting a touring company in South Africa, he, never having heard the opera, had to orchestrate it from the piano score. On his return to Europe he made a point of hearing the original and found to his chagrin that, despite what he modestly described as his own reasonable professional competence, not to mention the benefit of knowledge of the progress made in orchestration since the days of *Rigoletto*, Verdi's score was entirely different and, as he candidly admitted, infinitely better. The testimony of such an honest and practical "pirate" **is of exceptional value.**

Varesi, that he did not think that he would ever do anything better; and in a sense he was right. *Rigoletto*, though it contains several weak passages, attains to a force of dramatic sincerity and expression that could scarcely be improved upon. I always feel in it something of the inevitability of Greek drama. Verdi himself liked it mainly on account of its strong contrasts. Indeed, writing two years later, he singled it out once again as the best of his operas for that very reason. Just before *Otello*, when it was to be given at the Paris Opéra, he was still sufficiently interested to be sorry that he was too old to come and revise it. Nor must it be forgotten that *Rigoletto* was the opera that caused Rossini to exclaim: "In this music I at last recognize Verdi's genius." [8]

[8] Monaldi.

CHAPTER IX

Immediately after the production of *Rigoletto* Verdi returned to Busseto, where he remained until the end of the year, in company with Peppina, mainly occupied in enlarging the garden at Sant' Agata and probably the house as well. There were negotiations to write an opera for Madrid on a libretto by Solera. That versatile gentleman had now settled in Spain, where, after being conductor-in-chief of the theaters of Malaga, Granada, Córdoba, and Gibraltar, he had become the conductor at the principal theater in Madrid. He was very anxious, apparently, again to be associated with his old collaborator; but the negotiations came to nothing, for Verdi's terms, which included traveling expenses for two, a convenient residence in Madrid, a piano, and the exclusive rights in the opera for all countries except Spain, were thought too high.[1]

In the main, however, his interests were concentrated on affairs at home. There was certainly little calculated to please him outside. Executions and imprisonments marked the definite collapse of the movement for independence throughout the peninsula; his two latest operas were in trouble with various censorships. In Rome, especially, *Rigoletto* was presented in so mutilated a form that Verdi seriously considered writing to disown it. "What would you say," he wrote on the 1st of December to his friend the sculptor Luccardi, "if a

[1] Incidentally this was the last definite contact between Verdi and his first librettist, whose career continued as incredibly as it had begun. Abandoning art for politics, Solera entered the secret service of Napoleon III in 1859, and in 1860 transferred his allegiance to the newly formed Italian government, which detailed him to deal with the brigandage then rife in the Basilicata. He seems to have tackled this with such success that he was later made head of the police in Florence, where, in the absence of anything exciting to report, he distinguished himself by his wild inventions. Hoping, perhaps, to find a more suitable outlet for the imagination of their strange functionary, the Ministry of the Interior transferred him in rapid succession to Palermo, Bologna, and Venice, and finally, when the Khedive asked for the loan of an official to reorganize the Egyptian police, thankfully recommended him for the post. For a while things went well with him in Egypt, and he even made a casual return to literary composition; but eventually he left the country to establish himself in Paris as a dealer in antiques, his hopes of success being centered, apparently, on a bust of Christ, which he fondly believed to be the work of Benvenuto Cellini. His last days were spent in Milan, where, penniless and unknown, he died on Easter Sunday, 1878, after what must surely have been the most extraordinary career that ever fell to the lot of an opera librettist.

During the sixties the Countess Maffei raised a fund on his behalf, to which Verdi contributed anonymously and, one is sorry to add, rather unwillingly. Somehow, some time during Solera's activities at Bologna, he had done something that seriously offended the composer. In circumstances and matters like these Verdi showed the defects of his qualities.

black mask were stuck on to the nose of one of your fine statues? . . . These impresarios have not yet realized that operas, when they cannot be presented whole as conceived by their authors, had better not be given at all. They do not know that the transposition of a number or of a scene invariably leads to failure. Imagine, then, what happens when the plot itself is altered."

As a climax to his troubles during 1851 his mother, to whom he was deeply attached, died on the 13th of June, and he buried her at Vidalenzo, near by. His grief for her loss was not without compensations from the æsthetic point of view, however, for the fruits of it may be traced in some of the most inspired pages of *Il Trovatore*,[2] those that depict the maternal and perhaps the filial devotion of Azucena. It must not be thought, however, that Verdi's loss had anything to do with his choice of subject. Not only, as we have seen, had Verdi indicated Gutierrez's drama *El Trovador* to Piave before the composition of *Rigoletto*, but already in April 1851 [3] he was in intimate correspondence about it with Cammarano, to whom the task of making the libretto had been transferred. Moreover, from the very outset Verdi had been principally attracted by the character of Azucena and had, apparently, at one time even thought of calling the opera by her name.[4] As a matter of fact, Luigia's death definitely interrupted, for a time, his preoccupation with *Il Trovatore*, and in January 1852 he was again in Paris. His old friend Lumley, who had, two years previously, assumed the direction of the Théâtre Italien in Paris, wished him to write a new opera, a project, however, that came to nothing. Instead, on the 28th of February he signed a contract with Roqueplan to compose, for production in 1854, "the music of a poem in five acts or in four acts, to be written by Mr. Scribe alone or in collaboration," which was destined to be the opera known later as *I Vespri Siciliani*.[5] There was trouble about an unauthorized translation for the Paris Opéra of *Luisa Miller*, entailing much tiresome correspondence with Ricordi, which, to the credit of both men, did not affect their personal regard for each other, though their disagreement was complete. Incidentally, this question of *Luisa Miller* illustrates once again the small regard entertained for musical or lit-

---

[2] *The Troubadour*.
[3] Indeed, if the date of the letter, January 2, 1850, quoted by Monaldi, be not a misprint, this correspondence with Cammarano began even earlier. But 1850 must almost certainly be a misprint for 1851.
[4] Prime-Stevenson says that it was actually called *The Gypsy's Vengeance* in one of the earliest English versions.
[5] *The Sicilian Vespers*. Collaboration with the famous Scribe was then the blue ribbon of operatic success, and the news of it sufficed to elicit a request for a performance at the Italian Opera in Vienna, accompanied by something more than a hint that the composer could, if he wished, succeed to the post of Hofkapellmeister, once occupied by Donizetti.

erary property at that time, for neither Verdi nor his publisher was able to prevent a performance in a pirated version at the Théâtre Italien.

By the 23rd of March he was back again in Busseto intending to work on *Il Trovatore*, a plan frustrated after a few weeks by the nearly fatal illness of his father. In the midst of this anxiety he signed on the 4th of May a contract for a new opera with the Fenice Theater in Venice, and then, in July, the unexpected death of Cammarano at Naples once more broke in on the peace of mind that he had vainly hoped to find in his native country. Poor Cammarano had finished in the main the libretto of *Il Trovatore*, though, as a matter of fact, for the final touches Verdi had eventually to have recourse to a certain Bardare. With characteristic generosity, however, he immediately paid Cammarano's widow not only the five hundred ducats agreed upon as the price of the libretto, but one hundred ducats in addition.

As already indicated, the subject of *Il Trovatore* had at intervals occupied Verdi's attention for a long time. In March of the previous year he had written a long letter to Cammarano, freely criticizing the original scenario submitted to him and outlining a new one of his own that embodied several suggestions afterwards adopted. By September 1851 the libretto, though not finished, was well advanced, and in the same month Verdi was debating to which theater the opera, when completed, should be given. Both Venice and Rome had asked for a new work, and to Rome *Il Trovatore* eventually went, because the composer thought the company better suited to his requirements. There was only one drawback: no singer in the Roman cast seemed to him suitable for the part of Azucena, "that Azucena to whom I attach so much importance!" So much importance, indeed, that it seems as if any theater that, in addition to a first-class tenor, could have offered him in this respect exactly what he wanted would have secured the first production of the opera.

The actual writing down of the music is said to have taken place between the 1st and 29th of November 1852.[6] It is certain that the score was finished by the 14th of December, though once again, even more strongly than in the case of *Rigoletto*, the reader must be warned against attaching undue importance to the speed of the actual writing. For all we know, Verdi may have noted down the principal ideas for his opera any time during the preceding year and a half. At any rate, he was able in December to write to his friend Luccardi, in Rome, asking for an apartment to be taken as from Christmas Day (though in fact he seems to have arrived a little later), and on the 19th of January 1853 *Il Trovatore* was duly produced at the Apollo Theater.

[6] Weissmann.

Despite an overflow of the Tiber flooding that portion of the city near the theater, despite increased prices of admission, despite the nervousness of the baritone, *Il Trovatore* was received with the greatest possible enthusiasm. Queues had been formed from eight o'clock in the morning; by midday the house was sold out. The Roman correspondent of the *Gazzetta Musicale* gives an account of the evening:

"Last night *Il Trovatore* was produced in a theater overflowing with people . . . the music transported us to heaven; and, of a truth, it could not be otherwise, because this is, without exaggeration, heavenly music. The composer deserved this splendid triumph, in that he has here written music in a new style, imbued with Castilian characteristics. The public listened to every number in religious silence and broke out into applause at every interval, the end of the third act and the whole of the fourth arousing such enthusiasm that their repetition was demanded. My own opinion is that in this score Verdi has effected a combination of musical learning with true Italian fire, and that the fourth act in particular is unmatchable." The detailed criticism of the music, though sound enough, is not particularly noteworthy. The paucity of concerted numbers is commented upon; the slow portion of Leonora's first aria is considered a failure; after the "*Miserere*," Azucena's narration is singled out for especial praise on account of its "originality and exquisite artistry." It is interesting, however, to note that the final trio of the opera, "with its horrible situation," was too much for the sensibility of some of the audience and that the orchestration was described as "deliciously new."

These final remarks well illustrate the difference between our attitude and that of a contemporary audience. No one today would think of describing the orchestration of *Il Trovatore* as either new or delicious. It may be — in fact, is — adequate; but the outstanding characteristic of the opera that obliterates all else to us is the expressive passion of the melodies, the reason being, of course, that, whereas composers have brought the art of orchestration to a pitch then undreamed of, nobody has ever surpassed the magnificent collection of tunes assembled by Verdi in *Il Trovatore* — tunes throbbing with sincerity and emotion. True, even at the time, it was the quality of these tunes that principally impressed itself on the imagination of the public all over the world, but it is interesting to know that the orchestral factor was considered by no means negligible.

Nor can we appreciate, or even understand, any detail of the libretto of *Il Trovatore* causing genuine horror, so far are we removed from the conventions of the period. Yet it is certain that Gutierrez's original play, *El Trovador*, impressed its contemporaries as being a singularly potent and original drama, for it raised the author in one night, at the age of twenty-three, from obscurity to an important position among nineteenth-century Spanish dramatists. Young Gutierrez was a typical disciple not only of Victor Hugo but, by a curious coincidence, of that Duke of Rivas whose *Don Alvaro* (the original of the libretto later to be known as *La Forza del Destino*) is said to have directly influenced the composition of *El Trovador* in particular. In short, this work was considered at the time to possess definite literary significance; and Cammarano, thanks largely to Verdi's own insistence in the matter, adheres far more closely to the spirit and characteristics of the original than is often supposed.

Far too much has been written of the unintelligibility of the libretto of *Il Trovatore*. It is complicated, but not unintelligible, provided it is read carefully and the reader remembers that the central figure is neither Manrico nor Leonora but the gypsy woman, Azucena. There is no doubt that Cammarano, encouraged by Verdi's passion for brevity, did excessively condense certain matters important in the unfolding of the dramatic action. There is no doubt that Verdi concentrated too exclusively his attention on the individual reactions of the characters to the detriment of their general correlation. But anyone who is prepared to devote an hour's study to the Italian libretto of *Il Trovatore* can follow its thread perfectly well. This is not done, partly because Verdi's music is so easy to follow, so immediately expressive of the individual emotions and situations therein portrayed, partly because study of Italian opera librettos is not considered a proper pastime for the intelligent. Incidentally, Gutierrez's fondness for babies changed in their cradles is of especial interest to English people, since it probably suggested to W. S. Gilbert that particular imbroglio parodied in two of his comic operas.

Verdi's score, whether its "Castilian characteristics" are admitted or not, remains a remarkable expression in music of the romantic, hot-blooded drama of chivalry. There is no need to praise the tunes, which have survived imitation, parody, inadequate singing, and barrel organs for three quarters of a century. All over the world, almost immediately, *Il Trovatore* captured the heart of the public, if not the admiration of the learned. It has by no means lost the first even today, while its claim to the second seems greater, not less, than formerly. *Il Trovatore*, which, all things said and done, is only *Ernani in excelsis*, may be regarded as the apotheosis of both the good and the bad qualities of early Verdian opera.

The opera for which Verdi had signed a contract with the Fenice Theater on the 4th of May was destined to be *La Traviata*.[7] We know practically nothing as to the details of the turning of Dumas fils's *La Dame aux camélias* into *La Traviata* or as to when Verdi defi-

---

[7] *The Erring One.*

nitely decided on an operatic treatment of the theme. It is clear that the decision was not taken before the signature of the contract with Venice, because as late as August 1852, other subjects were under consideration; but there is little extant correspondence with Piave or anybody else on the subject. Dumas's play had been produced on the 2nd of February of the same year. Pougin says that Verdi saw it and was wildly enthusiastic about it, which is at least possible, because he was in Paris at the time. On the other hand, he does not seem to have been actually in possession of a copy of the text until the last day of October, when one of the Escudier brothers sent it to him at Busseto. A little-known letter to Piave in which Verdi complains that the excessively slow movement of the action, in the last act especially, is "calculated to send the public to sleep" proves that the libretto was not finally completed in January 1853. We are better informed about the composition of the music. Verdi is said to have begun writing it on the ship between Genoa and Civitavecchia;[8] he was certainly at work on it during the rehearsals of *Il Trovatore*, for in the letter to Luccardi already quoted he asked to be provided with a pianoforte, "either a good one or none at all," for that specific purpose; and immediately after the production of *Il Trovatore* he was back at Busseto working hard and apparently with difficulty on the score. "My notes are a real penance," he wrote to his friend the Countess Maffei.

On the 6th of March 1853 *La Traviata* was duly produced at the Fenice Theater and failed completely, even the second performance being no more successful than the first. Verdi's typically laconic letter to his amanuensis, Muzio, is well known: "*La Traviata* last night a fiasco. Is the fault mine or the singers'? Time will show." If only other composers had learned to accept reverses with such dignity and restraint!

In his heart Verdi undoubtedly thought that the singers were to blame, and he was, in the main, right. Unfamiliar with *Luisa Miller*, which might have helped them, they found the new, intimate style of the opera alien to their methods, perhaps uncongenial. The tenor was hoarse; the baritone in particular, considering his part of insufficient importance, took little trouble; the prima donna, though a good singer, was a very plump, robust lady, whose death of consumption in the last act provoked a regular epidemic of laughter among an audience as yet operatically unvaccinated by a succession of flabby Brünnhildes, pot-bellied Siegfrieds, and bediamonded Mimis. There were, however, contributory causes, notably the contemporary action and the contemporary dresses, an unheard-of innovation in seri-

[8] Weissmann.

ous opera: while the staging of the ball scene, which left, apparently, a good deal to be desired, also provoked considerable hilarity among the experienced Venetians.

The criticisms entirely bear out Verdi's dissatisfaction with his singers. Indeed, the critic of the *Gazzetta di Venezia*, after praising the orchestral performance, especially in the prelude to the third act (which, he tells us, was played by the violins like one man and aroused great enthusiasm), and after noting that the first act, "full of beauties worthy of the palmy days of Rossini," pleased greatly, in particular the prelude, the toast to pleasure, and the duet between Violetta and Alfredo, wisely refused to criticize the rest of the opera until it was better sung.

The Venetian correspondent of the *Gazzetta Musicale* was equally severe on the singers, whom he held directly responsible for the cool reception of the opera. "Let us summon up courage to say," he continues, "that *La Traviata*, too, is a worthy product of that inexhaustible genius which has given to Europe *Nabucco, Ernani, Rigoletto,* and so on. Let us say that the music is marvelously effective and throws the dramatic evolution of the passions into terrible relief." This critic also was much impressed by the first act, especially with the faithful interpretation of the dramatic situations in the music, Violetta's "*Ah, fors'è lui*" [9] being singled out in particular as an ideal expression of the psychological state of mind of a woman who, after hesitating between remorse and tender love, abandons herself in despair to unbridled pleasure. The second act is praised for its sensitive musical interpretation of the text; while the orchestral accompaniment of the gambling scene is noted for its novelty and apt interpretation of the moods of the characters.

But the third act seems to have been the critic's favorite. He describes it as "a perfect jewel from the very beginning of that tender prelude on the violin which so piteously prepares us for the tragic catastrophe." In the soprano's aria, in the following duet, in the pathetic melody of the quintet, "accompanied by those pulsations of drum and trumpet which, like the sound of a funeral bell, tighten the heart-strings — in all these places the conception is so philosophical, the music so dramatic, that they are worthy to be ranked with Auber and Meyerbeer." A tribute none the less striking because to us more than a little ludicrous.

Better than Verdi's own judgment, however, better than the opinions of musical critics, facts soon established once and for all the responsibility for the original failure of *La Traviata*. Just a year later a devoted admirer of Verdi, Antonio Gallo, decided to revive *La Traviata* at his own theater at San Benedetto, also in Venice. Verdi

[9] "Ah, perchance 'tis he."

made a few changes in five of the numbers; the opera was re-dressed in costumes of the Louis XIII period — an unfortunate precedent that has only been discarded of recent years — and a really adequate cast of singers was secured. On the 6th of May 1854 *La Traviata*, thus equipped, was launched once more, this time with complete success. With such success, indeed, that it very speedily became, not only in Italy but throughout Europe, the most discussed opera of the day and one of the most popular, though, frankly, the triumph must be admitted to have been something of a *succès de scandale*.

It is difficult for us nowadays to realize the sensation that the very young Dumas caused with *La Dame aux camélias*, his first play. Here for the first time the emotions and the surroundings of a Parisian courtesan were presented on the stage without picturesque trappings or any pretense at historical disguise whatever. The author himself had emphasized the fact in his preface to the play, the character of Marguérite Gautier being admittedly based on Marie Duplessis, a demi-mondaine well known in Paris. His play was regarded by the old-fashioned as a deliberate attack on the institution of marriage, a defense of free love, a plea for easier divorce. The conventional Basevi even devotes several pages of his analysis of the opera to a recital of his horror at the poison being thus administered to Europe by the author and other French literary persons of like tendencies. The opera was considered even more objectionable, because more insidious, than the play. Piave, able to follow the original very closely, had produced an excellent libretto. Except for the elimination of certain subsidiary characters, the compression of certain scenes, and the reduction of the whole from four acts to three, *La Traviata* is almost identical with *La Dame aux camélias*, with the appeal of the latter heightened by the genius of Verdi's expressive music. It was considered an extremely erotic opera. One aristocratic French lady, well known in cosmopolitan society, was famed for her attendance at performance after performance in various capitals, though the poignancy of her emotion not infrequently caused her to leave the theater in the course of the evening.[10] Lovers, especially lovers whose love was illicit, attended it in very much the same spirit as they afterwards attended performances of *Tristan and Isolde*. In short, *La Traviata* became the symbol of revolt against current sexual conventions.

No one acquainted with Verdi's character can imagine for one moment that he was attracted by the erotic ingredients of Dumas's play, even if they exist, which is by no means certain. What appealed to him, as always, was the dramatic clash between Marguérite Gautier's profession and her wholly unselfish love for Armand, the emotional poignancy of her scenes with Armand's father, the contrast

[10] Ciccarese.

between the glitter of her wanton life and the pathos of her miserable death. When Marguérite became Violetta, Armand Alfredo, and Duval Germont, these features were more rather than less marked. Never had Verdi's music been imbued with deeper emotion, with a greater sense of dramatic fitness. But the emotion, like the drama, remained intimate; there was nothing heroic about it, little even rhetorical; even the undoubted romanticism appeared in realistic guise. The Italian critic who described *La Traviata* as "chamber music" was, speaking comparatively, right.

Moreover, the orchestra as never before served to illustrate the moods and motives of the characters. Those people, comparatively rare, who can distinguish between what is simple and what is commonplace will find in the score of *La Traviata* a certainty of effect, a power of expression, that show infallibly the touch of a great master. In short, alike from the orchestral and the vocal point of view, *La Traviata* is a genuine music drama, in that the music, even in a few inferior passages such as Germont's popular *"Di Provenza il mar,"* [11] is indissolubly linked with and conditioned by the dramatic action. Verdi himself was satisfied with the result, for a few years later, when asked which of his operas he liked the best, he said that were he a professional, he would prefer *Rigoletto*, but as an amateur he would certainly vote for *La Traviata*.

[11] "The sea of Provence."

CHAPTER X

Verdi passed the spring and summer of 1853 at Sant' Agata, where his sole artistic preoccupation seems to have been the preparation of a libretto founded on Shakspere's *King Lear*. The subject had been in his mind for some time — it will be remembered that he had prepared a detailed scenario for Cammarano three years previously — but on this occasion the design was carried many steps further. A certain Antonio Somma, a lawyer from Udine, well known throughout Italy as a patriot and the author of successful tragedies, wrote to the composer suggesting several subjects with a view to collaboration. Verdi answered on the 22nd of April in an exceptionally interesting letter. "I can imagine nothing more agreeable to me," he wrote, "than to see your great name united with mine. But to provide worthy music, or, at any rate, the best music that I can produce, for the excellent poetry that you could hardly fail to write, you must allow me to indicate a few of my opinions for what they are worth. Long experience has only confirmed the ideas I always had with regard to theatrical effectiveness, although in my early years I had the courage only partly to put them into practice. (For instance, ten years ago I should never have dared to write *Rigoletto*.) In my opinion, monotony is the besetting sin of our opera. So much am I convinced of this that I should refuse today to treat subjects like *Nabucco, I Due Foscari*, et cetera. These operas have interesting isolated themes, but they lack variety. They are played, so to say, on one string, of a fine quality if you will, but always the same. To explain myself more clearly, Tasso's poetry may be superior, but I prefer Ariosto a thousand times. For the same reason I prefer Shakspere to every other dramatist, the Greeks not excepted. In my opinion the best subject that I have yet set to music as regards effect pure and simple (I am not talking of its poetical or literary merits) is *Rigoletto*. . . ." Then, after giving his reasons for this preference, Verdi politely dismisses various subjects proposed by Somma in favor of *King Lear*, which he asks him to read, promising at the same time to refresh his own memory at the original source.

A second reading only confirmed Verdi in his enthusiasm for what is, perhaps, Shakspere's greatest play. A month later he wrote again to Somma indicating his appreciation of the difficulties of reducing such a vast canvas to manageable proportions. He suggested three acts or at the most four — in this point as in most others following closely the scenario originally sent to Cammarano — and recommended especially to the librettist's attention the part of the Fool, "so original, so deep," warning him at the same time not to make the part of Lear too exacting.

The correspondence continued throughout the summer. Verdi was at first not altogether pleased with Somma's work. The verses did not appear to him well adapted for music; there were too many changes of scene. Incidentally, we learn from Verdi's objections that he considered the French convention of unity of time and place superior to the Elizabethan convention in the matter of scene-changing: "the only thing that has always made me hesitate to treat Shaksperian subjects more frequently." His last act before leaving Busseto for Paris on the 15th of October was to pay Somma two thousand Austrian lire for the libretto, of which two acts at least were already completed. In Paris the correspondence became slightly less intense, though it continued intermittently during the next two years, Verdi criticizing every scene, almost every verse, with the most meticulous care. He wanted Edmund to be a complete but cheerful villain; he did not wish Cordelia to put on warrior's clothes; he did not like her Prayer, "cold, as are all operatic prayers"; he planned to open the opera with a fanfare of old-style trumpets. But mainly he wrote the long-suffering poet detailed lectures on the different nature of words for arias and ensembles, and above all he was continually expressing his fear of excessive length, here as always his especial bugbear. "In the theater," he insists, "excessive length is synonymous with boredom, and of all styles the boring is the worst." Verdi was extremely exacting in the matter of this libretto, for which he obviously entertained the greatest possible affection, but he was not unreasonable. For instance, he allowed his original objection to the inadequacy of Lear's motives in disinheriting Cordelia to be summarily disposed of by Somma with the frank admission that he had been mistaken. It certainly was the closest collaboration on which he had as yet been engaged.

His first idea had been to write the music for some Italian theater before setting Scribe's opera, but this proved impossible. Not entirely to Verdi's dissatisfaction. "Perhaps better so," he confessed when, in January 1855, he wrote to Somma that there was no hurry for the libretto in its final form, but that he would like to have it completed by the time he returned to Busseto; "for thus I shall be able to occupy myself with this opera at my leisure and produce, I dare not say something new, but at any rate something different."

The libretto was duly completed, except for a few minor alterations, at the time indicated. But it was never destined to become an opera; something always got in the way. Yet as late as 1868, four years after Somma's death, Verdi appears not to have abandoned the idea, for he refused to allow the play to be included in a collection of the poet's works. Even after the composition of *Falstaff* there were rumors of an opera on the subject of Lear, which, incidentally, figures largely in Werfel's imaginative novel about Verdi's visits to Venice in the eighties. It is more than probable that sketches for the music were made; it is possible that the composition proceeded considerably beyond the stage of mere sketches. We shall never know, for, whether in the form of sketches or partially finished product, the music (if it existed) perished in the funeral pyre expressly provided for uncompleted or immature compositions by a clause in Verdi's will.

When Verdi arrived again in Paris in October 1853, the Republic had become an Empire and the Opéra the Académie Impériale de Musique. He gave as his address for letters No. 4, rue Richer, where he possibly resided; but in the spring he certainly went to live in the suburbs, at Asnières or Saint-Germain-en-Laye.[1] In the main he was occupied with the composition of *I Vespri Siciliani*, the libretto of which had been delivered by Scribe and his collaborator Duveyrier on the last day of 1853. Early in the new year he attended the first night of Meyerbeer's *Étoile du Nord*. "Though I can make little or nothing out of it," he writes to the Countess Maffei, "the public understood it all and found everything lovely, sublime, divine! And this is the same public that, after twenty-five or thirty years, has not yet succeeded in grasping *William Tell*, given on this account in a mutilated form, in three acts instead of five, and miserably mounted. And this is the first theater of the world!"

All Verdi's dislike, not to say contempt, for Paris is evident in the sarcasm of this letter. His body may have been in France, but his heart remained in Italy. One can almost feel his homesickness, even in the precise instructions to his lawyer to use the proceeds of the sale of the vintage for the purchase of a small property adjacent to Sant' Agata, even in the letters to Somma about the possible production of *King Lear* before an Italian audience. To the Countess Maffei he is quite explicit: "I have a fierce desire to go home. I whisper you this because I know you will believe me. Others would merely think it an affectation on my part." Probably Rossini's famous Saturday evening parties were what he enjoyed most. Not only at this time but on subsequent visits to Paris he frequented them with some regularity, and on one such occasion Rossini made a performance of the quartet in *Rigoletto*, sung by Patti, Alboni, Gardoni, Delle Sedie and accompanied by himself, the feature of the evening.[2]

Perhaps these remarks require some explanation. If Verdi disliked Paris, why did he spend so much time there? Why did he accept a

[1] Barrili.   [2] Radiciotti.

commission to write a French opera? It was not mere desire for fame, as he himself expressly states, or a desire to make more money. Thanks to improved conditions in Italy, he could now make as much money in his own country. The reason probably was that success in Paris then meant something to a composer that could be matched in no other capital. Paris was the artistic center of the world — the New York, London, Paris, and Berlin of our own day all rolled into one. Apart from its unquestioned supremacy in literature and painting, everybody who was anybody in the world of music or the theater was to be found there. Wagner, whose reactions to Paris were curiously like Verdi's, tacitly admits in his writings the artistic lure and hegemony of the French capital. In his very amusing article, "Parisian Fatalities," he makes great fun of the "Scribe Factory"; of the countless appearances of Rubini and Lablache in Rossini's *Cinderella* at the Théâtre Italien; of the ingrained habit of putting on *Robert le diable* when any other opera was a failure, and so on. But his praise of Auber, his instance of the "grander faculties that distinguish the French school," his enthusiastic account of the performances of Beethoven's symphonies given by Habeneck and the Conservatoire Orchestra, prove that a great deal of respect was mingled with his sarcasm. More respect, indeed, as regards the Opéra than Verdi ever showed, for, writing in 1851, he expresses admiration of it as possessing "the most expensive singers, the most ample ballet-corps in the world, an orchestra of unrivaled strength and eminence accompanying never ending masses of chorus singers"; while again, in 1863, he repeats his praise of the constitution and efficiency of the Opéra as contrasted with that of Vienna.

In short, the Paris Opéra was the Mecca of all opera composers in a sense that can with difficulty be appreciated today. Verdi may not have wished for fame or money; he must have desired the *cachet* that a successful production at the Paris Opéra could alone bestow. True, *Jérusalem* had been written for it; but *Jérusalem* was only, after all, an adaptation. To have been asked to set a libretto by no less a person than Scribe for an occasion like the Great Exposition of 1855 was a very different matter. In fact, it made him many enemies, because it was naturally felt in certain quarters that the honor should have been given to Auber, Berlioz, Halévy, or some other French composer. The opposition had been embittered, further, by the too ardent championship of his Parisian agent-publishers, the brothers Escudier, whose idea of publicity on Verdi's behalf, apparently, was to decry all other operas and to insult the critics who did not agree with their incessant praise of the Italian composer's each and every composition. All this had produced a considerable anti-Verdi faction in Paris, headed curiously enough by an Italian musical critic called

Scudo. It cannot be said, moreover, that any of Verdi's operas produced in France up to that time, even *Ernani*, the most popular of them, had achieved any success comparable with their Italian triumphs. Wherefore the importance for Verdi of establishing his reputation once and for all at the Opéra must have seemed paramount. Supreme professional reputation is by no means the same thing as mere fame.

Work on *I Vespri Siciliani* proceeded slowly, but on the 1st of October 1854 the opera was either finished or sufficiently advanced to be put into rehearsal. Nine days later, however, the lady who was to sing the principal part chose to disappear. She was a certain Mlle Cruvelli, the idol of Paris for her beauty and her talent, who had made her greatest success in the part of Valentine in *Les Huguenots*. With the unerring publicity-sense of the born prima donna, she chose the performance of that opera for the night of her disappearance. Nobody knew where or why she had gone. Not only Paris but Europe rang with the scandal; even the Strand Theatre in London produced a farce called *Where's Cruvelli?* An order of distraint was made upon the furniture of her flat to meet the penalty of a hundred thousand francs to which her flight had rendered her liable. Still there was no news of the fugitive, variously reported to be in America, St. Petersburg, and Frankfurt. Rehearsals of Verdi's opera were perforce suspended, and the composer's feelings may be gauged by the fact that he jumped at the opportunity to propose that his contract should be canceled. In addition to his longing for home he may also have desired to avail himself of the opportunity to write the music for *King Lear*. A new theater was being built in Genoa, and the authorities had approached him with a request to be allowed to call it by his name and to be honored with the production of a new opera. Verdi unhesitatingly refused the first request (the theater was eventually christened Paganini in honor of the celebrated violinist, a native of Genoa), but the idea of a new opera pleased him. There was a good cast available, not to mention a particularly talented young conductor called Mariani. Ricordi, who knew all about *King Lear*, suggested that opera for the purpose. It is more than possible that the plan would have materialized if, on the 7th of November, almost as suddenly as she had vanished, Mlle Cruvelli had not reappeared in Paris. She seems to have gone on a kind of anticipatory honeymoon with one Baron Vigier, whom she married shortly afterwards, excusing herself on the grounds that the person charged to inform the authorities of the Opéra of her proposed departure had forgotten to do so. The Parisian public, always indulgent to a theatrical favorite, readily forgave her, all the more readily because they were able to indulge in a good laugh at her expense. When Cruvelli made her first reappearance as Valentine in *Les Huguenots*, almost the first words addressed to her by Marguerite of Navarre were: "Tell me the result of your adventurous journey?" Inevitably, the theater was convulsed by the apt illusion.

Rehearsals were resumed at once, but disagreement with the author succeeded to trouble with the prima donna. Verdi complained that Scribe refused to make the changes promised in the fifth act, "which everybody agrees lacks interest"; some of the words were awkward to sing; above all, the subject was dangerous, hurting French susceptibilities because the French are massacred, and insulting to the Italians because Procida (the leader of the Sicilian revolt with which the play deals) is turned in Scribe's favorite manner "into a common conspirator complete with the inevitable dagger." "Whatever the consequences," wrote Verdi to Crosnier, who, subsequent to the Cruvelli scandal, had succeeded Roqueplan as director of the Opéra, "I am an Italian first and foremost and I will have no part in anything that is insulting to my country." The letter concluded with a second demand for the cancellation of his contract.

Verdi's claims were just, but the tone of the letter is indubitably harsh. There can be no doubt that Verdi entertained a deep mistrust for the Paris Opéra, which had given *Luisa Miller* in an unauthorized translation and compressed *Jérusalem* into three acts. If Berlioz's account of Roqueplan and the Opéra generally is accurate, his mistrust was amply justified.

He was on even worse terms with the Théâtre Italien, which seems to have given a performance of *La Traviata* based on a score from the well-known Spanish pirate factory. A friend, obviously put forward to try to mend matters, only received an adamantine letter and a snub for his pains, Verdi refusing his consent to performances of any of his recent operas. Such incidents show better than any comment the suspicious, not to say hostile, state of mind induced in the composer by his Parisian experiences.

His letter to Crosnier, however, produced the desired effect, probably because a week later he refused to attend rehearsals owing to its having remained unanswered. The haughty and indifferent Scribe consented to make some changes; but later there was further trouble between author and composer, reports of which appeared in the press. The dress rehearsal, according to Berlioz, was the scene of a final explosion. On the 13th of June 1855, however, *I Vespri Siciliani* was at last given to the world.

It was a definite success. Even Verdi's opponent, the Italian critic Scudo, had to admit as much, though he sought to belittle it by a political explanation. "It is hardly an exaggeration to say," he wrote, "that almost all the wealthy amateurs of Milan, Turin, and other cities of Lombardy were present on an occasion that had for them all the importance of a political event. In fact, the Italians of today do not regard artistic questions as simple problems to be solved and discussed in the serene regions of the mind. . . . In the success of a singer or of a work of any kind they see a national success, one more title to the esteem of civilized Europe." For which piece of accurate observation the unfortunate music-critic has never been forgiven by some of his compatriots.

Nevertheless, the success of *I Vestri Siciliani* was genuine enough. It achieved fifty consecutive performances and, with the exception of Scudo and two Italian colleagues, was remarkably well received by the press. According to *Le Siècle* the opera showed a marked improvement in the composer's style; *La Presse* defined its primary beauty as one of perfect clarity in both the vocal and the orchestral writing, praising further "the powerful unity of conception, the sense of the stage never before so clearly manifested, the unfailing orchestral restraint and economy of detail. . . . Entering the Opéra, Verdi's music has conformed to the procedure invented by French genius without losing anything of its Italian ardor." Adolphe Adam in the *Assemblée Nationale*, after an interesting account of Verdi's previous success in substituting his own qualities of dramatic energy and passion for the sweetness, the fluency, the melodic richness of his Italian predecessors, congratulates the composer on having triumphed in Paris by means of the wealth of fresh, attractive melodies, which he considered to be the outstanding characteristic of the opera. So impressed, indeed, was Adam, a devotee of the old school, by the qualities of these melodies that he confesses *I Vespri Siciliani* had now definitely forced him to take a more favorable view of Verdi's genius.

"Verdi," wrote the *Débats*, "does not play on the intimate, exquisitely melancholy string of Bellini, the only one, perhaps, on that lyre so prematurely broken; he does not possess, perhaps, the transparency or the abundant, if superficial, fluency of Donizetti. Verdi, however, has one great advantage over his predecessors: he has rid the school to which he belongs of conventionality of form. He has carried further the respect for dramatic proprieties and dramatic truth; his writing for the orchestra shows colors and accents previously unknown in Italian music. A great and fine work! A great and fine success!"

A tribute all the more interesting because the musical criticism of the *Débats* was under the direct inspiration of Hector Berlioz, though a remark in his *Mémoires* seems to suggest that he may not have been personally responsible for this notice.

Despite such a flattering reception, *I Vespri Siciliani* did not, after the close of the Great Exposition, maintain its initial popularity. Possibly the libretto was in great part to blame, for the subject, as Verdi had foreseen, provoked resentment in many quarters.[3] Scribe found it necessary to defend himself on the plea that there was little or no history in question at all, a lame excuse, though perfectly accurate, as is indeed proved by the fact that, when the opera acquired an Italian domicile at Parma on the 26th of December of the same year under the title of *Giovanna di Guzman*, the new Portuguese environment and a skip of some five centuries made apparently little difference to the success of the opera as a whole.

Most people today will agree that the music of *I Vespri Siciliani* was over- rather than under-praised. It is particularly difficult to understand the enthusiasm lavished on the melodies, which, with one or two exceptions such as the duet between Monforte and Arrigo, are obviously inferior to those of many preceding operas. From the orchestral point of view the opera does, perhaps, show some technical progress; and it is significant that the overture, a fine piece of work, is undoubtedly the most satisfactory feature of the whole score. The long and short of the matter is that Verdi in *I Vespri Siciliani* was trying to write a second *Les Huguenots*. The two operas have a good deal in common. Luckily for him, Verdi had little in common with Meyerbeer, and his efforts to cut his coat according to Meyerbeerian cloth, though they may have taught him something, strike us nowadays as decidedly rigid and self-conscious.

[3] Later Saint-Saëns asked sarcastically why Verdi did not set the Battle of Pavia or the Battle of Waterloo to music. Even Wagner referred contemptuously to "*I Vespri Siciliani* and other nights of carnage."

CHAPTER XI

Verdi had intended to leave Paris a week or two after the production of *I Vespri Siciliani*, but affairs at the Théâtre Italien prevented him. The management planned to produce *Il Trovatore*, which Verdi determined should not be given in the manner proposed. His disappointment and irritation were shown in or even aggravated by a highly acrimonious correspondence with Ricordi about translation rights, performing rights, piracy, royalties, and so on. When Verdi wished to be disagreeable he could be very disagreeable indeed, and such he certainly was on this occasion, telling Ricordi, among other home truths, that he thought it a scandal that the publisher of *Il Trovatore* should have made four times as much as the composer. To make matters worse, the question of his English rights became acute. For ten years or more there had been a legal squabble as to the rights in Bellini's *La Sonnambula*. On the 1st of August the House of Lords gave their final decision. By this decision all nationals of states united to Great Britain by reciprocal copyright treaties seem to have been deprived of their rights in foreign operas unless the author were present in England for the first performance and the sale made in the presence of two witnesses. This exposed to piracy nearly all the compositions of Verdi, a subject of the Duchy of Parma, which had never negotiated such a treaty. To escape from the difficulty, it was suggested to him that he might become a Piedmontese or even a French or English citizen; but it is characteristic of Verdi's staunch patriotism that he preferred to launch an agitation for the making of the necessary treaty by his own government.

The only consolation was that, thanks to what might not inaptly be called his "mailed-fist" policy, relations with the Théâtre Italien rapidly improved. Actually in September he again postponed his departure for Italy in order to give personal aid to the production of the much buffeted *Il Trovatore*. Just before leaving Paris in the middle of December he wrote quite an amicable letter to the director, Calzado, congratulating him on his decision not to give *La Traviata* or *Rigoletto*, and protesting only with comparative mildness against a projected performance of *Ernani*. "I am only too delighted to give you my assistance (as you put it), provided that my interests permit me to do so and provided *especially* that you are able to engage the right singers for these works. A clever director must either choose operas for the artists he has engaged or engage artists for the operas he has chosen, a matter that is far more difficult than is usually supposed. Believe my long experience."

With which parting words of wisdom he quitted Paris for the "sky and desert" of his beloved Sant' Agata.

He was not destined, however, to stay there as long as he would have liked, nor can he have written much, if any, music. One of his first cares was the revision of the unfortunate *Stiffelio*. The never ending difficulties with the censorship had led him to this decision some time previously; so on the 10th of March 1856 Piave was commanded to Busseto, with instructions to bring with him all the literary materials necessary for the change. A large new theater had been built at Rimini, for which Verdi had been commissioned to write the first opera. The management would have liked one on the subject of their famous compatriot Francesca, but Verdi insisted on a new version of his old opera, furnished with a new last act and a new title, *Aroldo*, the period of the action being transferred from early nineteenth-century Germany to the Crusades. Incidentally, the change of the principal character into a Crusader provides almost the only instance of a suggestion by Piave surviving Verdi's objections. The composer, as well he might, found this violent transmutation incongruous, but a Crusader the protagonist became, and remained.

Not improbably Verdi's exceptional compliance in the matter may be ascribed to the fact that he was once again preoccupied with the more important possibility of the composition of *King Lear*. In April definite negotiations for the production of that opera began with the management of the Neapolitan San Carlo, which continued sporadically during that year and the first six months of the next. The Fool was to be a contralto. There was not much for a tenor to do, but Verdi considered a baritone of the first class indispensable for the part of King Lear and he wanted Mlle Piccolomini,[1] a singer famous for expression rather than voice, to sing the part of Cordelia, even taking the unusual step of himself approaching her in the matter. Nevertheless, the rock on which the project eventually foundered was the question of the cast, though at one time all the difficulties, including that of the baritone, seemed in a fair way of settlement. Had Verdi been willing to accept the San Carlo soprano as Cordelia,

[1] The aristocratic and fascinating Piccolomini became the outstanding Violetta in *La Traviata*. It is hardly an exaggeration to say that she was at one time to that opera what Chaliapin has been in our day to *Boris Godunov*. Perhaps the best tribute to her merit comes from Chorley, who was so scandalized that he wrote as follows: "Never did any young lady, whose private claims to modest respect were so great as hers are known to be, with such self-denial fling off their protection in her resolution to lay hold of her public at all costs. Her performances at times approached offence against maidenly reticence and delicacy."

we should almost certainly have had the opera; but he was not. "It is one of my customs," he wrote from Paris, "to which I should adhere even if Malibran herself returned to the world, not to have my singers imposed on me."

At the beginning of August, Verdi was forced to return to Paris. Calzado was threatening litigation, the Opéra a French version of *Il Trovatore*. Verdi, who had written to Léon Escudier in July that he was coming to Paris on purely private affairs — "Verdi is coming to Paris, but the maestro remains in Italy" — found himself detained there until the end of the year, consoled only by a most successful performance of *La Traviata* which his presence and his resolution had wrested from the recalcitrant Théâtre Italien.

Though, as we have seen, Verdi had already begun to occupy himself with the metamorphosis of *Stiffelio* into *Aroldo*, this opera was not the one destined first to see the light in 1857. On the 15th of May of the previous year Verdi had signed a contract with the Fenice Theater at Venice for a new opera, and this was in fact produced before *Aroldo*. It was *Simon Boccanegra*, founded on a play written fourteen years previously by the same Gutierrez who had supplied the original material for *Il Trovatore*. Gutierrez was at one time Spanish consul at Genoa,[2] and seems to have been attracted by the romantic figure of Boccanegra, the ex-pirate who became Doge of the Republic in succession to the patrician Fiesco.[3] We know little of the details of the composition of the opera and nothing as to Verdi's share in the fashioning of the libretto, for which Piave was again responsible. He was certainly writing the music in February 1857, for Peppina describes him in one of her letters to Escudier as "working like a slave." In other respects, too, it is an interesting letter, because it reveals the fact that Lumley was again trying to angle for Verdi's return to London, with productions of *Luisa Miller* and *Il Trovatore* and a fee of five hundred pounds as a bait. The bait, however, was insufficiently tempting, much to the disappointment of Peppina, who would have liked to spend two or three months in London. Even more remarkable was her curious, rather naïve premonition that things were going too well. The press was too unanimous in Verdi's praise; *"midi est sonné."*

She disturbed herself unnecessarily, for when, on the 12th of March, *Simon Boccanegra* was produced in Venice, it was a failure. The press, however, was favorable enough. The *Gazzetta di Venezia* described the music as "decidedly elaborate. worked with the most

---

[2] Weissmann.
[3] It was long thought that *Boccanegra* was inspired by Schiller's play about the Fieschi and that its subsequent revision was due to Verdi's seeing the play in Germany. This is an error.

exquisite ingenuity and worth studying in every detail." The Venetian correspondent of the *Gazzetta Musicale*, after praising the music for its fidelity to the spirit of the text, for its beautiful melodies and profound philosophy, roundly declared *Simon Boccanegra* to be one of the most inspired of Verdi's works. "We assert," the critic continues, "that in none of his previous operas has the composer carried dramatic interpretation to such a high pitch of expression, that his scoring has never been so elegant, at the same time so simple, so ingenious, so rich in absolutely new effects, being quite unlike any heard here or abroad. We assert that there is here an abundance of melody, charming, new, inspired. . . . There is something for every taste, but the various tints, as is always the case in Verdi's operas, are invariably subordinated to the general atmosphere and to the logic of the whole."

The public, however, was almost bitter in its indifference; so much so that the press was moved to protest. There even seems to have been some kind of organized opposition, to judge by certain allusions in the *Gazzetta di Venezia* to disturbances "such as could not possibly have been engineered by a public so notoriously courteous as that of Venice." The fact of the matter was that the audience were thoroughly bored. They found Piave's libretto unintelligible, the proportion of recitative excessive, the opera as a whole monotonous, cold, and gloomy. Verdi himself was under no illusions as to his failure, a failure, moreover, accentuated later at Milan, though partially retrieved at Naples, where the opera was received with favor. As usual Verdi did not bother to defend his own share in the opera; but he thought that Piave, "a libretto by whom is always condemned in advance," had been unfairly treated, and he said so. As a matter of fact, Verdi must in his heart have resented the reception of *Simon Boccanegra*, for we know that he entertained for it much the same kind of liking as for *Macbeth*. "Whatever friends or enemies may say," he wrote to Tito Ricordi after the hostile reception given to the opera when it was produced at La Scala in 1859, "*Boccanegra* is not inferior to many of my other operas that have been more lucky, but perhaps it needs a higher standard of performance and a public really willing to listen." An even more convincing proof of his attitude towards it is the fact that more than twenty years later he persuaded Boïto to revise the libretto and himself revised the score. Since this is the only version of the opera now extant, any consideration of *Boccanegra* as a whole may advantageously be postponed till that time.

The reception of *Aroldo* at Rimini, where it was produced on the 16th of August 1857, must also have contributed to temper Peppina's apprehension of excessive success. Though it did not encounter the

Courtesy of Messrs. Ricordi

VERDI AND GIUSEPPINA STREPPONI IN
MIDDLE AND LATE LIFE

Courtesy of Messrs. Ricordi

INCIDENTS DURING THE REHEARSALS OF *Simon Boccanegra* AT NAPLES. CARICATURES BY DELFICO definite hostility aroused by *Boccanegra*, *Aroldo* fell comparatively flat. The press notices were mainly concerned with the beauties of the new last act, especially the storm and the finale. The judgment of the critic of the *Gazzetta Musicale*, who concluded his notice by christening *Aroldo* a "magnificent work that cannot fail to elicit universal approval," was soon proved wrong by events; for, with the exception of a performance at Treviso in October, the opera can scarcely be said to have survived Rimini. Probably Piave's libretto did not convey to its contemporaries quite the impression of absurdity it conveys to us. This medieval Crusader, living in a castle "near Kenth," and retreating finally to the bonny banks of Loch Lomond, inevitably strikes an Englishman as ridiculous; while the lifeless characters, especially the incredible heroine, are of a stuff particularly unsympathetic to the twentieth century. Even a contemporary audience, however, must have felt the libretto of *Aroldo* to be inferior to that of *Stiffelio*, for the good reason that the psychology of the original is more consistent and intelligible. The music of the second version, on the other hand, is superior, though objectors were not wanting even at the time to point out that the fusion of the two styles was by no means wholly satisfactory. Still, nearly, though not quite, all the best music of *Aroldo* dates from Rimini rather than Trieste, and the level of orchestral writing remains consistently on a higher level.

Perhaps the most important thing about *Aroldo* was that it seems to have been the first occasion on which Verdi was brought into contact with Angelo Mariani, a conductor destined to play an important part in the life of the composer as well as in the general history of opera. Mariani, who was about thirty-five years old at this time, was already known as one of the best conductors in Italy. At one time a pupil of Rossini himself, he had been conductor of the Court Theater at Copenhagen, but, returning to Italy to serve as a volunteer in the fighting of 1848, he had since 1854 made his headquarters at the Carlo Felice Theater in Genoa. Here, by a curious coincidence, Chorley heard him in this very same year, being moved to great enthusiasm by his conducting, to which he ascribes the "only good orchestral performance execution I have ever encountered in that country. . . . The exquisite sentiment of this gentleman [Mariani] as a conductor of Southern Music left nothing to be desired." At one time Mariani had had lessons in composition from a celebrated contrapuntist of Rimini, a monk called Levrini, and this may have been the reason for his being invited during the summer season, when the opera at Genoa would be closed, to direct the opening performance of the new theater at that seaside resort. Verdi, who had conceived the greatest admiration for Mariani's talents, attended his orchestral rehearsals and, it is said, was so struck by the comparatively poor effect made by the storm music in the opera despite such able direction that he took it away and rescored it [4] — an example of intellectual honesty typical of him. From this time seems to date that close friendship between the two men which, in its final rupture, had such far-reaching effects on the history of music.

Except for the journeys to Venice and Rimini and a brief excursion at the beginning of June to Reggio to tempt fortune again with *Boccanegra*, Verdi spent practically the whole of the year 1857 at Sant' Agata with Peppina and his father-in-law, Antonio Barezzi. Five years before, relations between Verdi and Barezzi had been momentarily clouded by his association with Peppina, whose presence at Busseto had occasioned a great deal of local gossip, some of it definitely malevolent. Antonio Barezzi had apparently taken it upon himself to write some kind of protest, for Verdi's answer, sent from Paris in January 1852, though affectionate in terms, is very uncompromising. Busseto, including Barezzi, was told to mind its own business and not to interfere in the relationship of two people so absolutely independent as Peppina and himself. However, Barezzi seems soon to have accepted the situation, for Escudier gives us an illuminating account of *"Le père Antoine"* in Paris, where he went, as was his wont, to attend his son-in-law's productions and spent the day wandering about the city.

In any case, in August 1857, all three were living together in complete harmony. It was a wholly simple, practical life. Verdi's love for the country had become almost a mania, as Peppina tells us in one of her charming letters. He was up at daybreak to examine the wheat, the corn, and the grapes, returning so tired that it was impossible to get him to write letters. She adds with characteristic humor: "Luckily our tastes coincide except in the matter of sunrise, which I prefer to see from my bed, but Verdi up and dressed."

As a matter of fact, it was Peppina herself who was responsible for guiding Verdi's tastes towards country life. Biographers have written as if Verdi during his whole career always longed to get back to the country. This is inaccurate. Perhaps from a surfeit of it in early days, Verdi in his thirties detested the country. It was Peppina who persuaded him — with difficulty — to take the house outside Paris where was laid the foundation of those tastes which subsequently developed into a passion for the solitude of Sant' Agata. Indeed, his passion soon surpassed that of Peppina, for Verdi was content to be at Sant' Agata in any season of the year, while Peppina, as well she might, found the plain of Parma excessively dreary in the winter time.

[4] Checchi.

CHAPTER XII

Despite his preoccupation with his crops and his animals, despite his refusal to write letters, Verdi was at work again in September. He had found another play by Gutierrez called *El Tesorero del Rey Don Pedro*,[1] of which he thought so highly that he himself began to construct the scenario; he threw a passing glance at *Ruy Blas*; he proposed to recast *La Battaglia di Legnano* à la *Stiffelio*, suggesting to the management of the San Carlo Theater that they might do worse than produce it together with *Aroldo* and *Boccanegra*. But nothing came of any of these projects. The Spanish play proved unsuitable for musical treatment; the principal baritone at the San Carlo was unsuited to *Ruy Blas*; the management, though they had nibbled at *Boccanegra*, wanted a new opera. Finally Verdi's choice fell on the opera we know as *Un Ballo in Maschera*.[2]

The libretto, written by Scribe on the subject of Gustavus III of Sweden, had already been set by Mercadante as well as made the subject of an opera by Auber, produced in Paris in 1833. Verdi found it excellent, though he complained of "the typical operatic conventionalism which I have always disliked and now find unbearable." In October, as some consolation, perhaps, for the disappointment of *King Lear*, Scribe's libretto was sent to Somma for translation — in the first instance it was little more — and a prose version of the plot was submitted to the management for purposes of censorship. By the 6th of November Somma had finished the first act more or less to the satisfacton of Verdi, who contended himself by suggesting some verbal alterations and the addition of a few verses here and there to justify the presence of certain characters on the stage. The second act, which was ready a fortnight later, likewise pleased him well with the exception of the trio, in respect of which he wrote Somma a most illuminating lecture on rhythms and meters. The whole libretto was completed, except for some afterthoughts, by December, and Verdi, who had been working all the while, had finished his music by the end of the year.

Then his troubles began. The management of the San Carlo, frightened by the subject, at once suggested a change of time, place, and nomenclature. Scribe's Gustavus of Sweden is first cousin to Victor Hugo's Francis I, and the censorship in those days was very jealous of the virtue of reigning princes. Moreover, a conspiracy against

[1] *The Treasurer of King Pedro.*
[2] *A Masked Ball.*

him is the mainspring of the play, and in the view of the censorship, conspiracies against the lives of kings were, if anything, more objectionable than an exposition of their amours. Verdi accepted the idea of change in principle, proposing only that Somma should finish his versification first and make the necessary alterations afterwards. Somma, when consulted, suggested transporting the action to the thirteenth century, an idea that did not in the least appeal to Verdi, who rightly felt that the characters of Scribe's play, conceived on essentially French and modern lines, would be incongruous in such a remote and barbarous period. "We must find a princeling, a duke, a devil; from the north, if you will, but one who has seen something of the world and breathed the atmosphere of the court of Louis XIV," he wrote to Somma at the end of November.

Except for the title, however, which had been altered at the outset to *Una Vendetta in Domino*, and the substitution of the Duke of Pomerania for the King of Sweden, the main features of the libretto remained unaltered when Verdi, with his completed score, set sail in the second week of January 1858 from Genoa to Naples. Here another unpleasant surprise awaited him. The Neapolitan censorship made it a rule that only completed librettos could be read; prose summaries, such as that submitted by Verdi in the previous October, were inadmissible. Torelli, the director of the opera, had, it appears, deliberately refrained from informing Verdi of this fact in order that he should write the music and come to Naples. His fury at such deception may be imagined. There was nothing for it, however, but to submit the libretto in its present form and wait. To Verdi, who felt himself a foreigner, whose associations with Naples had in any case never been pleasant, the delay must have been exasperating, all the more so because there were continual negotiations with officials as to changes and cuts that seemed to presage the ruin of his opera. On the 14th of February he wrote to the manager, Torelli, demanding a decision one way or the other and suggesting that a cancellation of his contract would be more than agreeable to him. Apparently Torelli had been trying to persuade him that an opera in any form was better than no opera at all, because after a recapitulation of the various mutilations proposed by the censorship there occurs in the letter the following remarkable passage: "I have told you already that I cannot commit the outrages that have been perpetrated here in the case of *Rigoletto*, outrages that I would prevent if I could. And do not talk to me about success because one or two isolated numbers have been received with applause. That is not enough to constitute a musical drama. In artistic matters my ideas and my convictions are quite clear and well defined, and I can and will not abandon them."

Three days later the censorship officially released the libretto in a form acceptable to them, but totally unacceptable to Verdi. The title had been changed to *Adelia degli Adimari*, which seemed to him meaningless; the action had been transferred to Florence; the date altered from the eighteenth to the fourteenth century. Further, the most salient characteristics of the principal characters had been tampered with and one of them had been changed from a frivolous, rather effeminate page to a young warrior. Worst of all, a scene, the climax of the whole opera, where lots are drawn for the privilege of killing the King, had been suppressed altogether, and the masked ball at which the assassination was to take place was converted into an ordinary evening party.

The scarcely explicable obstinacy and stupidity of the censorship in this matter seem to have been due to the attempted assassination of Napoleon III by Orsini, news of which arrived in Naples on the 15th of January. It is scarcely correct to say, as has been said, that permission was revoked, for no permission was ever given. But demands became more, not less, exacting as negotiations proceeded.

Verdi, not at all the kind of man to suffer such a mutilation of his opera, refused to allow its production. The theatrical authorities, represented by his old enemy the Duke of Ventignano, threatened him with arrest and an enormous fine; he counterclaimed for damages, exposing at length before the tribunal the æsthetic reasons that had prompted him to refuse consent to the production. The quarrel aroused the passionate interest of the Neapolitans of all classes. Every influence was brought to bear to induce the composer to alter his decision, the Count of Syracuse even proposing to arrange an audience for him with King Ferdinand in order that royal pressure might be brought to bear upon the censorship. Verdi remained adamant to supporters and opponents alike. The populace, especially, were with him heart and soul; not so much, it may be suspected, on æsthetic grounds as because they associated the composer with the cause of Italian independence, to which Napoleon III was regarded as a traitor and the rulers of Naples were, in fact, bitterly hostile. There were demonstrations in front of Verdi's hotel, and here for the first time were heard those cries and seen those inscriptions of *"Viva Verdi"* intended as a tribute not only to the composer but to the cause of United Italy.[3] Eventually the authorities, frightened perhaps by this popular clamor, decided to compromise. Towards the end of April Verdi was allowed to depart with a promise to return in the autumn to produce *Boccanegra* in the place of the opera that had been the cause of so much trouble.

[3] *"Viva Verdi"* was a simple acrostic on *"Viva Vittorio Emmanuele, Re d'Italia,"* the first letters of the last five words forming by a fortunate coincidence the name of the composer.

In the meantime Verdi had not been idle. As early as the 27th of February, while the trouble was at its height, he had written to his friend Luccardi, in Rome, suggesting that the impresario of the Apollo Theater, Jacovacci, might be interested in his opera. Rumors of the dispute at Naples had reached Milan, and the directors of La Scala had approached him through Ricordi with a view to producing the opera there. Verdi, however, preferred Rome, partly because Rome was near Naples and he wished to give that disagreeable city a lesson; partly because Scribe's original libretto, in play form apparently, had been performed in Rome, which seemed encouraging. This roundabout approach to Jacovacci was dictated not only by the imperative necessity for secrecy, but by Verdi's knowledge of that impresario's meanness. "If Jacovacci plays the Jew," he wrote to Luccardi, "tell him to go ot the devil." Jacovacci swallowed the bait and went to Naples to see the composer, then in the midst of his case. The impresario's enterprise in this matter has been much praised by nearly all the biographers, but it is now clear that the initiative came from the composer himself. It was arranged between them that Verdi's opera should be given at the Apollo Theater early in the following spring, Jacovacci undertaking to arrange everything with the Roman censorship, thanks to his influence in ecclesiastical circles. He had, however, overrated his powers, for he was obliged, a month later, to write to Verdi to the effect that the censorship would not pass the libretto as it stood. Verdi, on the point of quitting Naples for Busseto, contented himself merely with observing in the manner of Beaumarchais that it seemed odd that what could be spoken in Rome could not be sung, and asked for the return of the libretto. At the beginning of May he was back at Sant' Agata, delighted to be quiet. "It would be impossible," he wrote to the Countess Maffei, "to find an uglier place than this, but on the other hand it would be impossible to find a place where I could live with greater freedom. And this silence that leaves you time to think and this absence of uniforms of every color! How good both are! . . . Perhaps I shall go back to Naples in the autumn and to Rome for Carnival if the censorship there will pass the opera that was written for Naples. If not, all the better! For thus I shall not write anything, even during the next Carnival season. Since *Nabucco* I have not had, I may say, one hour of repose. Sixteen years' hard labor!" The letter of a tired man and substantially, if not literally, accurate; for in those sixteen years he had written nineteen operas, two of them twice over!

Jacovacci, however, had not retired from the contest. Pulling every string at his disposal, he finally induced the Roman censorship to pass Somma's libretto very much as it stood, subject to the change of a few verses and the transplantation of the action to some place outside Europe. Verdi communicated the glad tidings to Somma on the 8th of July, suggesting "North America at the time of the English domination, or, if not America, the Caucasus!" Somma was, apparently, not too pleased at having to do so much of his work over again, for when Verdi wrote to him in August, enclosing a list of all the verses and expressions objected to by the censorship, he found it tactful to urge the poet to be courageous and patient, "especially patient." By September the reconditioned libretto was finished except for a few minor changes; Scribe's original subtitle was selected and literally translated as *Un Ballo in Maschera*, and Verdi was able to enjoy two months' quiet before returning to Naples in November for the promised production of *Boccanegra*. Even then his plans were nearly upset owing to the difficulty experienced by Jacovacci in casting the part of the page, to which Verdi attached great importance. "I would rather that the opera were not given at all than that such an important part should be ruined," he wrote to Luccardi on the 27th of November. Finally, at the end of the first week of January 1859, he arrived in Rome, proceeding immediately to the flat that, together with a cook and a piano, Luccardi had been commissioned to procure for him.

On the 17th of February, despite the shortcomings of the female members of the cast, *Un Ballo in Maschera* was produced with success. At first the public seem to have been somewhat disconcerted by the novelty of its idiom, but at the second performance the opera was greeted with genuine enthusiasm by the public and the majority of the press, the critic of the *Gazzetta Musicale* being especially struck by the success with which Verdi had contrived new orchestral effects and achieved expressiveness without any sacrifice of melodic beauty. Later on he wrote a detailed study of the opera, interesting but too long for complete quotation, in which he describes the opera as "a huge step forward in a new manner, but no more so than his other operas, either singly or in groups." After praising the development of the action, the delineation of the characters, and the contrast of the situations, the critic concludes, rather curiously, as follows: "In *Un Ballo in Maschera* the music is everything — words, action, sentiment, passion, and character. Taking its inspiration from the moods of the characters and the movement of the action, the music in this case exercises such complete domination that in comparison and in relation with it the poetry becomes less than an accessory. Here we can say in truth that the notes begin their discourse where the poetry stops; anger, entreaty, jealousy, love are felt and heard above, if not quite apart from, the words in which they are expressed. . . . Verdi in *Un Ballo in Maschera* has achieved the great ideal of harnessing dramatic truth in its most minute particulars to the fluency, the clarity, and the popular appeal of his melodies." On the whole the criticism is an intelligent one, though it lays no emphasis on what are usually considered the two outstanding characteristics of *Ballo:* to wit, the new polyphony in the orchestral writing and the definitely humorous aspect of certain passages of the score, a novel feature in the composer's style. The *fugato* passage that serves as a kind of motif for the conspirators attests the first, as the whole of Oscar's music, not to say the laughter of the conspirators when they discover Renato's apparent assignation with his own wife, is evidence of the second, attribute. However, in regard to the beauty and preponderance of the melodies, the happy orchestral touches, and, above all, the delineation of character, the critic's judgment was remarkably acute. Riccardo and Amelia, it is true, live only in the lyricism of their music, and the soothsayer, Ulrica, is perhaps too legitimate a descendant of Azucena; but Renato, the loyal friend who becomes an implacable enemy, is beautifully drawn, while the frivolous page, Oscar, is a real creation, for which Verdi, as has already been noted, entertained a very special affection.

The present libretto makes a realization of the great musical qualities of *Ballo* particularly difficult. In fact, Somma had produced a workmanlike version of Scribe's *Gustave III*, marred, it is true, by uncouth verbal extravagances. But the fantastic nature of the locale into which the action had been transplanted owing to the vagaries of the censorship makes it hard for us to appreciate what is in reality a very human and moving drama. It is perhaps not mere coincidence that the three most satisfactory characters in the opera as we know it are, with the exception of Amelia, the characters that suffered least from the change. Oscar is the same in both; Renato is quite a tolerable version of Ankarstroem; Ulrica loses only some of the historical authenticity of Scribe's fortune-teller. But the metamorphosis of Gustavus of Sweden into the Earl of Warwick, Governor of Boston, makes him a wholly incredible character, for the actions and psychology conceivable in an absolute monarch are inconceivable in an English colonial governor; and as for Samuel and Tom (the Counts Horn and Warting in Scribe's play), their very names make them grotesque figures to an Anglo-Saxon. It is unthinkable that Verdi, who, as we have seen, was specially concerned with the psychological plausibility of his characters, should not have felt the incongruity of these metamorphoses. He probably consented to them in part from sheer weariness, in part because the acceptance of them enabled the original action to take place without change. If the listener can bring himself to realize who these characters really are, the drama of *Ballo* remains credible and poignant enough to carry conviction. It seems odd that nobody has ever attempted to restore them to their proper condition, for it is impossible to take seriously the compromise reached two years later in Paris, when, to satisfy the vanity of the tenor Mario, who refused to wear the kind of Puritan clothing associated with Boston in the eighteenth century,[4] the action was transplanted to the Kingdom of Naples.

Despite the opposition of a certain portion of the Roman press, which the grasping Jacovacci seized upon as an excuse to ask Verdi for a reduction of fees — a request that earned him one of the most tart snubs ever administered by a composer to a manager — despite Chorley's sneer that it was Verdi's setting of Scribe's libretto that had first made him appreciate Auber's genius at its proper worth, *Un Ballo in Maschera* gradually won, not only in Italy but in France, Germany, and England, a popularity that it has kept, deservedly, to this day.

[4] This is the reason given. But Mario or the producer must have been singularly ill-informed, because there was no reason why the Governor of an English crown colony at that time should not have worn ordinary Georgian costume.

CHAPTER XIII

Verdi's desire to take a rest from composition was certainly fulfilled, for during the next two years music seems to have played a very small part in his life. In view of the times, his temperament, and political ideals, little else could be expected, quite apart from any actual desire for repose. For when Verdi returned to Sant' Agata after the production of *Un Ballo in Maschera*, Cavour had already started the diplomacy of Piedmont on the road deliberately planned to lead to war with Austria. Four years previously he had, with unerring foresight, secured alliances with England and France by participation in a war that his compatriots neither understood nor desired and he was now using the new prestige won by Piedmont in the Crimea to entangle the more pliable of his former allies in a war against the hereditary enemies of his country. To attain this object he shrank from nothing, not even the marriage of the daughter of Victor Emmanuel with a prince she both detested and despised. He played with consummate skill on the vacillating temperament of Napoleon III, especially on the fears of assassination, which, as Orsini's attempt on his life had already proved to the Emperor, could only be removed by some practical manifestation of his early enthusiasm for Italian independence. Most important of all, he had to arrange matters so that the Austrians appeared to be the aggressors, for France and Piedmont were bound only by a defensive alliance. The Austrians, too confident or too headstrong, fell into the trap, crossing the Piedmontese frontier on the 29th of April.

These must have been exciting days at Busseto, still under Austrian domination, and it was not improbably about this time that Verdi received from a passing stranger the anonymous warning that led him and Giuseppina to sit up all night burning in their bedroom all the documents in their possession that might be considered compromising. The threatened search of his house never materialized, but in view of the prominent association of Verdi with the cause of Italian independence the danger must have seemed real enough. By the 8th of June, however, all such fears were at an end, for the preliminary successes of the Franco-Piedmontese allies had rid Parma of the Austrians. Verdi was in an ecstasy of delight. Together with Giuseppina, his father, and his father-in-law, he headed with twenty-five pounds a local subscription list for the wounded and orphans; he wrote to the Countess Maffei a pæan of surprised gratitude on the apparent disinterestedness of the French and their Emperor, whom, "if he keeps his promise, I shall adore as I have adored Washington and even more." The crowning victory of Solferino brought his enthusiasm to such a pitch that, but for lack of time, he would have broken his own strict rule by acceding to the desire of the city of Milan to write a cantata in honor of the Emperor's name-day.

It was as well that he did not do so, for in less than a week the Treaty of Villafranca, which left Venice to the Austrians and envisaged an Italy united only under the nominal suzerainty of the Pope, destroyed forever the chances of Napoleon III ranking equally with Washington in Verdi's esteem. Every historian knows that Napoleon could not well have acted otherwise than he did. The war was unpopular in France, where people were asking with some show of reason why French blood should be shed to set up a potential rival on a new frontier; the Emperor, his pacific nature sickened already by the sights of the carnage around him, had reason to believe that Germany was preparing to intervene; his cousin, originally one of the most ardent supporters of the war, was now equally ardent for peace, perhaps owing to the discovery that his fine promised Kingdom of Tuscany was nothing but a dream, a French monarch being only less obnoxious to the Tuscans than an Austrian duke. But the Italian patriots could not forgive Napoleon. Cavour, who must have known the facts, resigned in bitter anger. Orsini's photograph reappeared as if by magic in the shop windows. The intensity of feeling is perhaps best shown by the fact that it was not till 1927 that the statue of Napoleon III, thanks to the intervention of Mussolini, was re-erected in the streets of Milan, a city that, all things said and done, owed primarily to him its liberation from a foreign yoke.

One of the stipulations of the Treaty of Villafranca was that various regions of Italy, the Duchy of Parma included, should hold a free plebiscite as to whether they desired or not to be united with Piedmont. As often in times of Italian crises, a dictator was appointed, an ardent republican, by name Farini. The plebiscite resulted, needless to say, in an overwhelming vote in favor of Piedmont, and Verdi, originally, at any rate, another republican, was chosen with four colleagues to carry to Victor Emmanuel the official notification of the latest addition to his kingdom. The fact that all but the most extreme republicans seem to have been willing to place themselves beneath the scepter of the house of Savoy not only possesses general historical significance but throws an interesting light on Verdi's political psychology in particular. He was always ready to abandon theory for practice, to be influenced by the personality of a man rather than by the abstract principles for which the man stood. He thought Victor Emmanuel the right man in the right place. The King might be a rough, not to say, a boorish, soldier, but, alone of all the reigning princes in Italy, he had never broken his word to his subjects. That was enough for Verdi, for whom a high standard of honor remained always of paramount importance. He might believe in the theoretical tenets of Mazzini, but he worshipped the practical accomplishments of Victor Emmanuel. Besides, was not Cavour the King's Minister? And Cavour could do no wrong.

When Verdi, together with his fellow delegates, arrived at Turin on the 15th of September, he sought to make the personal acquaintance of his idol. The meeting was arranged by Sir James Hudson, since 1851 the British Minister to the court of Piedmont, who on behalf of the composer requested an interview from Cavour, buried, since his resignation, on his estate at Leri. Cavour was delighted. Verdi, after all, was a European celebrity besides being the composer of *"Di quella pira,"* [1] that tune which Cavour had sung five months before to express his joy and excitement at the news that the Austrians had actually crossed the river Tessino. The interview seems to have been a great success, for when Verdi returned to Busseto a week later, he wrote to Cavour a moving letter in which he thanked the former Prime Minister for the opportunity of "shaking hands with him whom every Italian should call the father of his country," begging him to believe in the "sincerity of a poor artist who possesses no other merits except that of loving, as he has always loved, his own country." Cavour answered in equally warm terms, and the mutual regard of the two men lasted till Cavour's death, in 1861.

It may seem odd that an interview between two such important Italians should have been arranged by an English diplomat; but Sir James Hudson, a Yorkshireman, once described by Disraeli as "Hurry Hudson," must have been an odd diplomat. Even in those days, when the diplomatic service enjoyed a considerably greater freedom of action than it does now, his independence provoked much criticism. As *The Times* said of him in an obituary notice: "He disobeyed the instructions of two successive governments and acted according to the wishes of the people of England." Lord Malmesbury wrote in this very year, 1859, that Hudson "is more Italian than the Italians themselves and he lives almost entirely with the ultras of that cause. I had reason to complain of his silence and quite understood how disagreeable to him it must have been to aid, however indirectly, in preventing a war which he thought would bring about his favourite object, namely the unification of Italy."

Certainly Sir James Hudson's enthusiasm in the cause of Italian independence carried him to extreme lengths, for he gave Verdi at Turin a letter to one of Garibaldi's officers so that the composer might know where, if necessary, rifles could be bought. Verdi took

[1] "Of that pyre." A well-known tune from *Il Trovatore*.

advantage of the information, and that very soon. In Parma there was talk of the return of the Austrian Duchess Maria Louisa, and, to maintain order or to defend their liberty, the inhabitants of the Duchy decided to call out the National Guard. But the National Guard at Busseto had no rifles, and the Commune no money to pay for them. So Verdi, at his own expense, using the information put at his disposal by Hudson, ordered in Genoa a hundred and seventy-two rifles of English manufacture, charging Mariani, now his intimate friend, to expedite the deal — surely one of the most incongruous transactions ever arranged by a composer and a conductor!

The emphatic result of a second plebiscite, held on the 12th of March 1860, fortunately rendered the rifles superfluous, and in April the Emilian province was quiet enough for the King to visit his new subjects. The municipality at Busseto presented His Majesty with a fully equipped piece of artillery, to the delight of Verdi, who wrote to congratulate his fellow citizens on having been sensible enough to choose a gift of practical value instead of wasting their money on festivities and illuminations like some other Italian towns. He did not see his way, however, to accede to their desire to write a hymn in honor of the event, repeating once again his disapproval of such compositions and pointing out that he could not very well give to Busseto what he had already refused to Turin and Milan on several occasions.

At the end of 1860 Cavour decided to summon the first national Parliament, for which Verdi was invited to stand as the local candidate. He refused the honor with the greatest vigor, a certain Minghelli Vaini being nominated in his stead. Then a very pretty little comedy began. Minghelli, who was friendly with Verdi, wishing to know if he had in fact decided not to stand, wrote for what may be called official confirmation. When the letter reached Sant' Agata, Verdi was absent. Peppina opened it and, knowing Verdi's determination, wrote to inform Minghelli that his information as to Verdi's attitude was correct. But Verdi, while at Parma, had received a personal letter from Cavour asking him to enter Parliament, as the prestige of his name would be useful to the Italian cause. Verdi set off immediately for Turin in the hope of being relieved of the responsibility. In vain, however. Not only Cavour but, even more, "Sir Hudson," the extent of whose participation in the internal affairs of the country to which he was accredited seems scarcely credible, insisted so strongly that it was his duty to stand as a candidate that Verdi finally consented, reserving only his right to be allowed to resign at the first possible opportunity.

Not unnaturally Minghelli was displeased to learn the new state of affairs on the return of the composer to Sant' Agata. He had had considerable experience in politics and did not at all relish the prospect of losing what otherwise would have been a certain seat. He wrote to Verdi protesting that the administration could easily procure the election of so distinguished a person somewhere else. Verdi, however, was inflexible. He did not, he repeated, want to be elected; he would not move one finger to secure election, but if he were nominated, he would stand in accordance with his promise. So the two friends were rival candidates in the election which took place on the 27th of January 1861. Verdi received the majority of votes, but, the majority not being sufficient, a second ballot was necessary, in which Verdi was definitely successful. On the 18th of February he went to Turin to take his seat in the first Italian Parliament.

It cannot be said that Verdi played a very glorious part in the Italian legislative deliberations. So long as Cavour lived, he followed his lead blindly, and the death of that statesman on the 6th of June 1861 affected him so profoundly that he could not bring himself to go to the funeral in Turin; even the memorial service at Busseto was almost too much for him. It seems not improbable that his comparatively long membership of the Italian Parliament — he remained a deputy until 1865, when he refused to be re-elected on any terms whatsoever — may be ascribed to his veneration for the memory of that great man and his respect for the promise he had given him. We know, too, that in 1861, not long before Cavour's death, he had a detailed discussion with the Prime Minister with regard to musical education in Italy, proposing that it should be linked up with free evening instruction classes in singing and subsidies for the three principal opera houses. Otherwise we know little of his parliamentary activities, except that he was as adverse to the extreme Left as he was to the extreme Right, and that he once amused himself by setting a "scene" to music in the manner of the choral writing in the last act of *Rigoletto*. He used, in the Chamber, to sit next to Quintino Sella, who has given an account of at least one interesting conversation. During a dull debate on a land-tax bill Sella thought fit to question Verdi as to his methods of composition, eliciting the very significant reply that his musical ideas always came to him as destined for the voice or for some particular instrument or other, and that the only difficulty was to write them down quickly enough.

Detailed information about this period of Verdi's life is comparatively scarce, because, after the production of *Ballo*, not only did he, for a considerable time, cease to compose, but he failed, apparently, to maintain that habit of preserving his correspondence which gives us such a valuable guide to his actions and thoughts. At any rate, after the end of 1858 there is a lacuna of nine years in the *Copialettere*, a period that, if not of the first importance from the musical point of view, comprises all his political life. From extraneous sources, however, a certain amount of information is fortunately available. A general outline of Verdi's political career has already been given, but other events of interest took place during this period.

First and most important of all was his formal marriage with Giuseppina. This took place in 1859 on the 29th of April, the very day when the crossing of the Tessino by the Austrians made war inevitable. They were married at Collange, a little village in Savoy, quite close to Geneva. Savoy at that time formed part of Piedmont, and it looks as if Verdi and Peppina had slipped away from Turin during the excitement of those fateful days to legitimize their union with the least possible fuss. They certainly returned almost immediately to Sant' Agata, where, apart from parliamentary duties and occasional excursions to neighboring cities, Verdi passed the main portion of the next two years and a half.

The city most favored by Verdi in their excursions was Genoa, where Garibaldi was in 1860 preparing the famous expedition of the Thousand. It would be interesting to know how far, if at all, Verdi, during his frequent visits to that city, came in contact with him. He was certainly in sympathy with his aims, for in the subsequent year he was only too delighted to allow one of his servants to go and join the condottiere's army in Sicily. But Verdi was essentially Cavour's man; and Garibaldi could never forgive Cavour for having allowed his native town of Nice to be ceded to the French. Indeed, it is one of the curious paradoxes of history that there was more real sympathy between the irreconcilable republican Garibaldi and King Victor Emmanuel than between Garibaldi and Cavour.

One wonders, too, if Verdi was at Genoa when Alexandre Dumas made a typical entrance into the port in his yacht, *Emma*, with a party of friends including a young woman dressed as a midshipman, and a store of champagne and fireworks among the cargo. Dumas — so like him! — had set out to visit the "world of Napoleon, Augustus, Constantine, Christ, Sesostris, Mahomet, Hannibal, and the Cid," but succumbed at Genoa to the lure of Garibaldi, whom he subsequently followed to Sicily and Naples. What brave, incredible times! Mariani and Verdi gun-running! Dumas living a page out of one of his own novels! Garibaldi reviving the exploits of a medieval condottiere! Without catching a glimpse at least of that spirit it is impossible to appreciate the literature or, what is more germane to our purpose, the music of the period.

As regards Verdi and Mariani, however, their interest in firearms was now limited to those of a peaceable variety. During the last months, if not before, the two men had drawn very close together. Whenever Verdi and Peppina were in Genoa, it was always Mariani who accompanied them on their frequent expeditions to the villages round about, when they feasted on *paste* or fish. But their principal bond was a passion for shooting. Verdi gave Mariani a gun, accompanying the gift with a letter in which he signed himself "a deputy of central Italy who has been idiotic enough to write music for many years." Moreover, he was always writing to the conductor from Sant' Agata with the most varied requests. Would Mariani buy ten magnolia grandiflora, not less than a yard high, and dispatch them by train? Would he go to a certain manufacturer and change one gun for another, taking care that it was accurately sighted and did not kick? Would he buy some iron shutters to be put on the french windows of the ground floor? And in almost every letter there is a reference to the shooting conditions round about. In March the woods on the banks of the Po were said to be full of wild duck, but the ground was too sodden from the melting snow to get anywhere near them. In August there were dozens of quail to be shot or caught in a net; even a partridge or two. Mariani was to come quickly from Genoa to take his share of the sport. In the first week of September he arrived, and the two musicians used to get up at five o'clock in the morning to go and shoot their quail.

Shooting or no shooting, Verdi always seems to have been up and about very early in the morning. It was his habit, even before his morning coffee, to inspect his crops and visit his horses, in the breeding of which he made something of a specialty. Luncheon was at half past ten; dinner at five in the winter, six in the summer months. After an occasional game of cards or billiards everybody went to bed at ten o'clock.

The principal event of the day seems to have been the arrival of the afternoon post, which Ghislanzoni, who paid a visit to Verdi in the country a few years later, describes as the only thing that brought the isolation of Sant' Agata into momentary contact with the outside world. Certainly the sense of isolation produced by Verdi's house can scarcely be exaggerated. The Plain of Parma in general is a region inhospitable enough, and, as if to shut out even that, Verdi planted round his house a thick belt of trees, which, now that they have grown to maturity, give almost the effect of an oasis amid these desolate miles of practical cultivation. Shooting, rowing on the little artificial lake, supervising continual additions to the house and grounds — above all, the companionship of his dogs — were Verdi's principal pleasures. Farming ranked with music as business. It might, however, be mentioned, while any discussion of music was for the casual visitor, at any rate, taboo.

Outside Sant' Agata, Verdi occasionally went for a walk, more often for a drive, on which he was sometimes accompanied by a favorite cock, whose devotion was the talk of the countryside. Of social life in the ordinary sense of the term there was none. The great house of the neighborhood, on the other side of Busseto, was that of the Marchese Pallavicino, to whom, incidentally, belonged the house in which Verdi was born. The composer does not seem to have been on very good terms with Pallavicino. Above all things he liked getting his own way, and the Marchese had refused to sell him his birthplace. Before the Duchess Maria Louisa lost the throne of Parma, she came to visit the Pallavicino, and Verdi was asked to come and play the piano for her entertainment. This he refused to do, to the unconcealed admiration of the neighborhood. The Duchess, who must have been aware of the composer's political views, does not seem to have minded, but the refusal can hardly have promoted more harmonious relations between Sant' Agata and the Villa Pallavicino.

Nor was there that contract between Verdi and the town of Busseto which might have been expected. Indeed, the relations between the composer and the community to which he owed so much are one of the most curious features of his career. All the more so because his natural bias in favor of local patriotism was very strong.[2] Not that he denied or forgot the extent of his obligations. On the contrary, he repaid all the money advanced to him in his early years by the Monte di Pietà, was always ready to assist local charities, both public and private, and went out of his way to contrive work on his estate to provide employment in times of distress. But the fact remains that his relations with the little town were at this time fundamentally unfriendly. He would never enter it unless he had to, preferring to drive round whenever possible. His typical attitude towards the local theater is worthy of a brief description.

In quite early days, in 1845, there was friction between the composer and his friends at Busseto because they thought that he had promised to use his influence to secure the appearance at their theater of two famous singers during the summer, a promise that he strenuously denied. This misunderstanding may be regarded as a prelude. Many years later, in 1857, the municipality decided to build an entirely new theater, which was, in fact, begun in August 1859.

---

[2] For instance, he was extremely proud of the artistic accomplishments of Parma. The point is well illustrated in an anecdote related by Pizzi. On one occasion a double-bass player in the orchestra of La Scala declared at rehearsal that a certain passage was unplayable. Verdi said nothing, but wired to Parma for a player called Pinetti, a native of that very Le Roncole where Verdi was born. When the fat, countrified musician arrived, the whole orchestra laughed. Their laughter, however, turned to admiration when he played the passage through with perfect ease. "That, gentlemen, is how we play at Parma," was Verdi's triumphant comment.

Incidentally, Parma enjoys to this day a reputation for exceptionally high standards, and many singers, it is said, refuse to appear there on this account.

Verdi disapproved of the expenditure of money on such a scheme at such a time, writing to urge the restoration of public finances as the first duty of every Italian community. Nevertheless, not only was the scheme not suspended, but it was decided to call the theater by Verdi's name and to present him with a box in perpetuity. In 1868 the theater was ready and the inhabitants of Busseto undoubtedly would have liked their illustrious fellow citizen to write the first opera. Not only that. In 1865 the Mayor, taking advantage of some casual words spoken by Verdi many years before, most unjustifiably alleged that the new theater was being built entirely for Verdi's benefit and that he had promised to secure the three most important singers in Europe for the opening — a promise again denied most strenuously by the composer. Feeling ran high on both sides. Thanks to the intervention of Dr. Carrara, Verdi was induced to allow the theater to bear his name and actually subscribed ten thousand lire towards the expense of construction. But, considering that he had been maneuvered into a false position, he never, in fact, entered it [3] and aroused considerable local resentment by giving his box away to a friend, though Pizzi says that he sometimes listened to performances outside, in the adjoining meadow.[4]

The fact of the matter was that Verdi strongly resented the attempt on the part of the inhabitants of Busseto to establish a claim on him. Rightly or wrongly he felt that the claim, whatever it was, had been paid with interest in the form of world-wide celebrity for the town primarily associated with his name. But this was not all. Somewhere it has been suggested that the memory of the old quarrel with the clerical party in his youth never ceased to rankle. In my view this was a contributory cause at the most. The real reason was almost certainly the attitude taken up by some people in Busseto towards Giuseppina. There had always been and still was an anti-Verdi party in Busseto, which, as we have already seen, had previously given expression to their views in a manner that was very distasteful to the composer. His international fame, even his marriage, do not seem entirely to have put an end to their malevolence, for at the very time under review Verdi received anonymous letters that were a source of great mortification to him. Indeed, Pizzi says that it was after the receipt of one of these that he gave away the box presented to him by the municipality. One hopes this is true, for it was an ungenerous and ill-advised action that needs definite excuse.

Had, however, his relations with Busseto and neighboring society

---

[3] Neisser, however, says that later he once attended a performance of *Luisa Miller*.

[4] It is a most attractive theater, small but spacious for its size, which forms part of the block of municipal buildings. Extending, as it does, to the old city wall, a listener in the meadow could quite well hear what was going on inside.

been more harmonious than they in fact were, it may be doubted whether his mode of life would have been notably affected. Verdi did not excel in social qualities. He was exceedingly shy and taciturn to the point of boorishness, particularly in his early and middle life. Once at a friend's house an unfortunate young lady thought to please him by playing some of his own compositions, only to be told curtly to "stop playing that music at once and shut the piano." Even in later years his shyness became at times almost pathological. A story is told of how on one occasion he improvised a sling for his arm in order to have an excuse for refusing an autograph. His hatred of publicity, his pessimism, will be evident to any reader of this book.

With his intimate friends he was quite a different person. Though always basically inclined to melancholy, he could be very cheerful and gay, and Peppina in one of her letters to Léon Escudier says that "Verdi's laugh, when he laughs at all, is a great laugh." Life at Sant' Agata, then, though by no means suited to the tastes of everyone, was exactly suited to Verdi's peculiar temperament and must, moreover, be credited with having turned the pale, rather delicate young composer of *Ernani* and *I Due Foscari* into the virile old man whose vitality in writing *Otello* and *Falstaff* after the age of seventy remains one of the wonders of the world.

CHAPTER XIV

IN APRIL 1861 music came creeping back into this world of farming and politics. The Imperial Theater of St. Petersburg wanted an opera, and on June 3 of that year the contract was signed. Somehow, somewhere, Verdi had come across a famous Spanish play called *Don Alvaro, o La Fuerza del Sino*,[1] by Don Ángel de Saavedra, Duke of Rivas. It seems to have appealed to his imagination, for he describes it in a letter to Escudier in August 1861 as a "powerful, singular, and vast drama," though he is careful to add that he is not sure whether the public will share his admiration. The Duke of Rivas's play undoubtedly deserved the last two epithets, at any rate; it is very singular and very vast, almost as remarkable in its way as its noble author. Verdi's biographers have habitually dismissed both in a couple of lines, but they are of interest and importance.

Rivas, who started his career as a cavalry officer and ended it as Ambassador Extraordinary to the court of Naples, was a typical figure of the romantic period. He fought gallantly against Napoleon in the Peninsular War, in which he nearly lost his life. After the return to the Spanish throne of Ferdinand VII he had to fly from Spain, owing to his liberal opinions, and lived an exile for many years, mainly in Malta and in France (where, at Tours, he incidentally wrote *Don Alvaro*), but also in England, where he came under the influence of Walter Scott. After the death of Ferdinand, Rivas was able to take advantage of the general amnesty to return to Spain, and two years later, in 1836, he became a member of the Spanish government. Almost immediately, however, owing to fresh political disturbances, he had to fly to Portugal, returning after the proclamation of the Constitution in 1837 once more to his own country, where he eventually was made the Vice-President of the Senate and might, had he so wished, have become prime minister. He died in 1865, in Madrid, at the age of seventy-six, having survived his political activities by fifteen and his radical opinions by some thirty years. His most striking action at Naples was the exercising of pressure on the government to send an expeditionary force to assist Pius IX in recovering the pontifical throne. One wonders if Verdi knew this.

Despite all his political activities, Rivas always remained first and foremost a man of letters. He was, according to an enthusiastic biographer, the last of the great poets who might be called genuinely Spanish, a man who deserved to rank as one of the greatest exponents

[1] *Don Alvaro, or the Force of Destiny.*

of Spanish literary art in his day. Moreover, he was not only a poet but a historian of merit, and, in view of the æsthetic tendencies of the present time, it is interesting to know that he delighted particularly in describing the most minute details of his settings, such as the aspects of the country, the furnishing of a room, and so on. Needless to say, he was a romantic of the romantics; indeed, this very *Don Alvaro* is said to have been the means of finally banishing the French classicism that had dominated the Spanish stage for many years.

To dismiss such a play by such a man merely as a "popular Spanish drama produced in Madrid in 1835" betrays a lack of historical and literary perspective. The Duke of Rivas was a very important person, though his style and his subject-matter are uncongenial to us; and *Don Alvaro*, though suggesting to the modern reader a cinema drama rather than a tragedy, was an important play. The point is worth making, because it has been suggested that the choice of such a subject indicates a certain carelessness or even a definite step backwards on the part of Verdi. Nothing of the kind! He thought, doubtless wrongly, that he had found a masterpiece full of just those dramatic contrasts which particularly appealed to him. At the worst he can only be accused of lack of judgment in choosing a highly romantic subject at a time when romanticism was on the wane.

We know little of the details of the construction of the opera subsequently known as *La Forza del Destino*, which Verdi and Piave together fashioned on the basis of Rivas's play. As far back as 1859 Verdi seems to have been attracted by the psychological situation of Don Alvaro, who with the best intentions is forced into the very actions he would willingly have avoided. In 1860 he referred to the composition of the opera in conversation with friends. He was certainly working on the music during the summer and autumn of 1861, and the whole was completed, except for the scoring, by January 1862, when he went to St. Petersburg to supervise the production. Owing to the illness of a singer, however, the production had to be postponed; so, after brief interludes in France and Italy, Verdi exchanged the rigors of a Russian winter for the treachery of an English spring.

It was the Exhibition of 1862 that brought Verdi to London. The opening of that unsuccessful attempt to repeat the glories of 1851 was to be celebrated by the performance of compositions by four of the most representative composers of the day, one from each of the countries principally concerned. Sterndale Bennett contributed a setting of one of Tennyson's worst official poems, Meyerbeer an overture, Auber a march. The honor of representing Italy, offered in the first instance to Rossini, who declined it on the plea of age and infirmity, fell to Verdi. That he willingly accepted it is extremely unlikely. His distaste for compositions of this nature was fundamental and we can only conjecture that political and patriotic considerations induced him not to let the representation of Italy lapse, so to say, by default in comparison with that of France and Germany.

The choice of Verdi as Italy's representative was probably more agreeable to popular than to critical opinion. Since the production of *I Masnadieri* fifteen years previously, most of Verdi's subsequent operas had been introduced into England and nearly all had been condemned by the two leading critics of the day, Davison of *The Times* and Chorley of the *Athenæum*. When *Rigoletto*, for instance, was produced at Drury Lane in 1853 under Gye, Chorley wrote that there was hardly one phrase in the part of the buffoon that might not have been taken from some other baritone part by the composer. Not only the scene between Rigoletto and the courtiers in the second act but the magnificent music of the last act were singled out as "miserable in their patchiness and want of meaning." Davison was even more severe. Describing the opera as a strain after novelty, he summed it up as follows: "In short, with one exception ('Luisa Miller'), 'Rigoletto' is the most feeble opera of Signor Verdi's with which we have had the advantage to be acquainted."

Il Trovatore, produced in 1855, had fared somewhat better. Chorley, finding it all commonplace, remarked at the end of his notice that Verdi is said "to be a thoughtful, cultivated gentleman, as anxious according to his measure of light for dramatic reality in opera as Herr Wagner himself." Davison condescendingly wrote that *Il Trovatore*, "though it exhibits Signor Verdi in his best holiday attire, is hardly destined to raise him in the estimation of real judges. . . . He is neither a Rossini, nor an Auber, nor a Meyerbeer; far from it; but he is not, as some would insist, a nonentity."

The most terrific thunders of all were, of course, reserved for *La Traviata*. When the opera was introduced to London in 1856, Davison spoke of its "foul and hideous horrors" and dismissed the music as being of no value whatever; Chorley spoke of "poor, pale, consumptive music." Even the *Illustrated London News*, usually a faithful admirer, described it as the weakest of all the composer's operas. The great popular success of *La Traviata* only made the moralists and critics more furious. It is quite clear that both Chorley and Davison were convinced that here was a case of nothing but a *succès de scandale*, a flash in the pan. Even the principal interpreter, Mlle Piccolomini, came in for her share of abuse. "Her performance," we are told, "at times approximated to an offence against maidenly reticence and delicacy." It was "an exhibition of simple and compound female frailty in modern guise."

His Life and Works

How or why Davison managed to class the very inferior *I Vespri Siciliani* (1859) among the best operas of the composer, it is difficult to understand. But he made up for it in 1861, when his condescending praise of *Un Ballo in Maschera* was tempered by reference to *Rigoletto* as "beyond comparison a better work," and to *Il Trovatore* as "containing isolated passages of marked superiority." Eight years seem to have been responsible for either a very marked change in taste or a very decided lapse of memory on his part. Both he and Chorley agreed in considering superior in every way Auber's *Gustave III*, a setting of the same plot now remembered only because of its affinity with Verdi's opera. Chorley was particularly emphatic. "I was never fully aware of the value of Auber's music," he wrote in his *Reminiscences*, "till I heard the assault made by Signor Verdi on the same subject."

These quotations are of interest as showing the trend of contemporary English critical opinion on Verdi; they are not intended as a pillory for Davison and Chorley, who were honest, competent critics, not afraid to oppose public opinion when they thought it wrong. Nor were their standards contemptible, for they judged music in accordance with the ideals of men like Mozart, Rossini, and Bellini. They were just shocked, almost physically, by the new striving after expressiveness in Wagner's and Verdi's music, which to them seemed merely vulgar. Above all, they felt, not altogether without reason, that this new kind of music tended to prejudice the art of singing, which they understood and loved so well. Chorley is quite definite on this point, for at the end of his *Reminiscences* he speaks of "the years during which singers' music has been stamped into such trash by the Wagners of New Germany, and bawled into premature destruction by the Verdis of infuriate Italy." Doubtless they were wrong, hopelessly wrong; but as regards Verdi, at any rate, they never sank to the imbecility of certain modern amateurs who regard him merely as the writer of pretty tunes.

Although Verdi liked his London quarters, which were at 43 Alpha Road, a house with a little garden near what he calls "Regent Saint Park," he must have been disappointed, for when the day of the opening of the Exhibition came, his composition was not performed. Apparently the whole opening function was something of a fiasco. Owing to the death of the Prince Consort the year before, the Queen did not attend in person, but was represented by her Commissioners, in whom the public took not the slightest interest. The Exhibition itself, like all exhibitions, was not nearly ready, and Verdi, who was present, thought little of the contributions of his musical colleagues, describing Bennett's work as quite ineffective and

Meyerbeer's as very little better: only Auber's march seemed to him meritorious.

Exactly why Verdi's composition was not performed is uncertain. The Commissioners gave out that it had not been received in time for rehearsal. This, however, was untrue, as Verdi felt obliged to point out in a letter to *The Times*. It had actually been delivered on the 5th of April, while the Exhibition did not open until the 1st of May. Probably the reason was political. Verdi had originally intended to write a march, but, on finding that Auber had already done so, decided on a short cantata with words by a young Italian called Arrigo Boïto, who had just arrived in Paris and was much in evidence at Rossini's house. The cantata was called *Inno delle Nazioni*,[2] but in fact only three nations, England, France, and Italy, figured in it; which was not perhaps in accordance with the cosmopolitan views of Her Majesty's Commissioners, especially as France was represented by the revolutionary strains of *La Marseillaise* and Boïto's poem ended with an aspiration for a completely free and united Italy.[3] At any rate the cantata was not performed, to the considerable indignation of the public. A few days later the *Morning Post* devoted a leading article to the discourteous treatment of Verdi by the Commissioners, who indeed seem to have been thoroughly unpopular, because the newspapers of the time abound with complaints of the management of the Exhibition, for which the public showed little or no enthusiasm.

Either as a shrewd stroke of business or as a graceful gesture, Mapleson decided to give the cantata at Her Majesty's Theatre. The solo part, originally intended for the tenor Tamberlik, was altered to suit the requirements of Mme Titiens, and as a compliment to the composer the whole company sang in the chorus. The production, which followed a performance of *The Barber of Seville*, took place successfully on the 24th of May. The cantata was encored, the reluctant Verdi being called six times before the curtain. Some of the enthusiasm may be ascribed to the circumstances already mentioned as well as to the large Italian element in the audience; but it is clear from contemporary accounts that the *Inno delle Nazioni* was a genuine success even with the critics. The *Morning Post* speaks of "the broad vigorous subject of the first chorus supported by pompous and brilliant instrumentation." The chain of melodies for solo voice is commended, especially the "solo with choral responses in which harps are employed with brilliant effect," while the final apostrophe

[2] *Hymn of the Nations.*
[3] Personal dislike or jealousy on the part of Costa, who conducted, has also been alleged, and it is perhaps significant that no effort was ever made to present the cantata at Covent Garden, where not only was he in musical command, but Tamberlik, for whom the solo part had been written, was the principal tenor.

to England, France, and Italy, in which Verdi had the strange idea of combining *God Save the Queen,* an Italian national tune,[4] and *La Marseillaise,* is greeted as an example of "polyphonic ingenuity rarely heard in his operas." *The Times,* though slightly shocked by the inclusion of the revolutionary *Marseillaise,* was no less impressed than its contemporary by the skill of the finale, describing the whole cantata as "not merely effective but in every sense good." The only reservation made by *The Times* was in regard to Boïto's verses, which it dismissed as "the somewhat bombastic stanzas of the poetaster whom it has been the fortune of the popular Italian composer to immortalise."

Neither the music nor the verses of the *Inno delle Nazioni* can be said to have achieved immortality, and Verdi himself did not regard either as deserving of it. Indeed, in later years he regretted having written a work the sole interest of which lies in the fact that it first brought together Verdi and Boïto, "the poetaster" destined later to become the incomparable librettist of *Otello* and *Falstaff.*

Verdi passed the summer months in Italy scoring *La Forza del Destino* — the first occasion, so far as can be gathered, on which he did not orchestrate an opera during rehearsals — but by the 25th of August he was off again, accompanied as always by Giuseppina, making for St. Petersburg. He arrived by way of Paris in the middle of September, in ample time to supervise the production of his opera as well as to make a four days' visit to Moscow, where he attended a performance of *Il Trovatore.* He seems much to have enjoyed his stay, going out into society far more than was his wont. He was especially struck by the exquisite politeness of the Russians of every class, which he compared favorably with the "impertinent politeness" of the Parisians. On the 10th of November *La Forza del Destino* was produced at the Imperial Italian Theater. It was not a failure; it was not a success, though there were the usual scenes of enthusiasm at the end and the Czar, Alexander II, bestowed on the composer the Order of Saint Stanislas, not usually given to an artist. Apparently the opera had encountered the inevitable opposition of the Nationalist party, who were just beginning to make their influence felt. They actually staged a hostile demonstration at the second or third performance, and one of them tells us in his reminiscences that he was principally struck by the fact that Verdi had been paid 22,000 roubles instead of the 500 usually given to a Russian operatic composer.

"There was nothing of technical or artistic merit in the opera," he writes; "its purely mechanical nature is demonstrated by the fact

[4] Not the present Italian National Anthem, as is usually implied, but Novaro's *Inno di Mameli.*

that it has never been played since" — perhaps one of the most unfortunate attempts at æsthetic deduction ever made.

The correspondent of the *Gazzetta Musicale*, after having stated that Verdi, on the one hand, had produced many numbers destined to become popular and, on the other, had never shown so much care and discernment in his orchestration and general musical construction, claims that the score is quite unlike any of its predecessors and will doubtless be even better appreciated when the great beauties that it contains become more familiar. In view of the close connection of the *Gazzetta Musicale* with the house of Ricordi, it cannot be said that this notice suggests a striking success of any kind. More interesting are the remarks of the Russian correspondent of the French musical paper *Nord*. After dismissing the Nationalist opposition as prejudiced and unjust, he continues as follows: "The real music-lovers are agreed that Verdi has never produced so conscientious a score or paid so much attention to the form in which his ideas are molded. The originality and beauty of the choruses are undeniable, that of the monks at the end of the second act and that of the 'Rataplan' in the third being quite irresistible. How many fresh and new ideas are scattered in this so scholarly work! How many numbers so elevated in their style, so dramatic and sincere in their expression! The orchestration shows very striking progress; and if a certain portion of the public felt rather disappointed, it was because they expected something different. In place of a light opera in the ordinary Italian manner the composer of *Rigoletto* has given us on this occasion a work more akin to the productions of Meyerbeer and Halévy."

Certainly anybody who went to *La Forza del Destino* expecting any form of light entertainment must have been disappointed, for a more lugubrious opera has rarely been seen on the stage. Rivas had lightened his huge and somber canvas by a number of vivid scenes illustrating popular life, which are, in fact, the best feature of the play. In Piave's libretto these were necessarily relegated to a subordinate position, attention being almost exclusively concentrated on the somber drama of the evil fate that pursues the heroine, her father, her brother, and her lover. From the opening act, when the father is killed by the accidental discharge of a pistol, to the final scene, which concludes with a Shaksperian massacre of all the principal characters, the atmosphere is one of intense gloom, relieved only by occasional passages of a lighter character, some borrowed from Rivas, others invented by Piave or Verdi. The result is a curious jumble, regrettably — for Verdi, exceptionally — diffuse, though not devoid of character. Indeed, in some respects *La Forza del Destino* shows, by a curious coincidence, a certain affinity with that Russian shapelessness and incoherence which we are now often asked to admire on the score of sincerity and intensity, qualities that the opera, too, possesses in a marked degree. Rivas's play possessed them in the first instance; Verdi's music possesses them even more; Piave's contribution hardly counts one way or the other.

It is clear that Verdi himself was conscious almost at once of the necessity of making some changes in the opera, for which, as we shall see, the opportunity presented itself later. In the meantime he was sufficiently satisfied to allow it to be performed in its original form in Madrid, whither, much bothered by a carbuncle, he went direct from St. Petersburg to supervise the production. He certainly had no reason to be ashamed of his part of the work. There are some conventional and even some trivial pages in *La Forza del Destino*, but there is also some of the most lovely music that he ever penned, and the score as a whole is characterized by a profusion and quality of melodic invention that can scarcely be overpraised. The critics were right in especially commending the choral writing and the always apposite orchestration; but the public has also been right in its uninstructed love for the tunes of an opera that, from the purely musical point of view, remains one of the most typical and spontaneous of all Verdi's compositions. Until quite recent times, when, mainly owing to Franz Werfel, *La Forza del Destino* took musical Germany by storm, the opera never enjoyed the favor of the critics. But the Italian public, at any rate, never lost faith in it; and in view of the poignancy of Leonora's music, the irresistible vigor of the duet between Don Carlo and Don Alvaro, immortalized by Scotti and Caruso, the dignity of the utterances of the Father Superior, the humorous characterization in music of Brother Melitone, first direct ancestor of Falstaff, who shall say that they were wrong? They have, in fact, been proved right.

CHAPTER XV

By the 11th of January 1863 Verdi was in Madrid, where *La Forza del Destino* was produced a fortnight later. Though only two of the singers and (especially) the chorus and orchestra seem to have satisfied him, the opera was a success. It had also been produced successfully a few days before in Rome, whence his friend Luccardi had been charged to write an absolutely truthful account of the event. Apparently here also the performance had been none too good, for in his answer to Luccardi's letter Verdi complained that its effect would have been much greater if Jacobacci, like every other impresario, would only realize that it is of the first importance to have either an opera suited to the cast or a cast suited to the opera. "True, to sing *La Forza del Destino* a singer need not be an expert in *solfeggi*, but a soul and a capacity for understanding and expressing the words are indispensable."

After a brief holiday in Andalusia and a stay of some months in Paris on professional business, Verdi returned to Sant' Agata, where, except for a visit to Tremezzo, he remained most of the summer and autumn. His bailiff had left and for some of the time, at any rate, he was personally supervising all the farm work. He found leisure, however, to reflect on the unsatisfactory nature of the end of *La Forza del Destino*, which, in a letter written to Escudier at the beginning of October 1863, he describes as "so terrible that I shall think how it can be altered when the opportunity occurs." One of the letters here reproduced proves that he wrote to Piave in the same sense.

In February and March 1864 he was in Turin, attending, for a change, to his parliamentary duties. But even here music was not neglected, for Escudier received letters on official notepaper about *Rigoletto, Il Trovatore*, and *La Traviata*. Apparently there was a question of doing not only *La Forza del Destino* but *Simon Boccanegra* at the Théâtre Italien in Paris. Verdi, however, was opposed to the project. He wished, as we have seen, to make some alterations in the former; he considered the latter in its original version too monotonous. Moreover, as regards *La Forza del Destino*, he was always doubtful whether the singers at any theater in Paris were of a caliber to do the opera justice.

In June 1864 Escudier came to pay him a visit. The intention had been that he should stay at Sant' Agata, but owing to Peppina's illness the visit had to be transferred to Genoa, where she lay in bed with gastric fever. Escudier must have made some suggestions about the refashioning of *La Forza del Destino*, for we find Verdi writing to him in Paris in August that "Fate cannot allow a reconciliation between the two families, and the brother (who, remember, is a Spaniard) must necessarily revenge his father's death." Nor did he like the suggestion made by de Lauzières, who was preparing a French version, to insert a trio at the end in the manner of *Ernani*. Something, however, had to be done about Paris, the more imperatively, perhaps, because Verdi had just been elected a foreign member of the French Academy. So eventually it was decided that a new version of *Macbeth* should be prepared to follow the successful revival of *La Traviata* at the Théâtre Lyrique.

We are exceptionally well informed as to Verdi's attitude towards this revision, details of which are given elsewhere, for he wrote several interesting letters to Escudier on the subject. Since 1860 the Escudier brothers had been on bad terms, but Verdi's relations with Léon seem to have remained as much those of a friend as of a business associate; otherwise he would scarcely have invited him to stay at Sant' Agata. It was Léon who was charged to give Verdi's love to "that little devil Patti," and who presented the establishment with a golden pheasant, receiving in return a typical missive from Peppina with inquiries after the health of his parrot. It was Léon, too, to whom Peppina wrote in 1865 that charming and revelatory New Year's letter "wishing, for you and dear Laure and for Marie and Gaston, all that you may desire and all that I wish for myself, that is:

"1. To be twenty years younger.

"2. A Greek nose.

"3. Legs ten centimeters longer, except for Laure.

"4. An iron constitution.

"5. An income of £365,000.

"6. . . . I will tell you another time."

Not even with Ricordi do the Verdis seem to have been on more intimate terms.

During December 1864 Verdi was at work on the revision of *Macbeth*, of which he had promised delivery early in the next year. His particular affection for this opera has already been mentioned, but, on taking up the score again, Verdi seems to have been surprised, perhaps a little distressed, to find how much alteration was required to make the work conform to his present standards. Apparently Escudier's original idea had merely been the addition of a ballet, but as early as October Verdi had decided that far more drastic treatment was necessary. The changes that he made are described in detail elsewhere; it will suffice to state here that most of the third act was rewritten, as were two important arias; while the end of the opera was completely changed, a very vigorous fugue being added to describe the final battle. Nuittier and Beaumont, the translators of *Tannhäuser*, were entrusted with the French version; Verdi, as his revision proceeded, wrote the most precise instructions to Escudier with regard to production and interpretation; on the 3rd of February 1865 the work was completed.

It was produced on the 21st of April at the Théâtre Lyrique, where it received only fourteen performances. There is no doubt that Verdi was disappointed. "Everything taken into consideration, *Macbeth* is a fiasco. Amen. But I confess I did not expect it. I thought I had done pretty well; it seems that I was wrong." Only one detail of the failure of *Macbeth* seems really to have annoyed him — the remark of a critic to the effect he did not know his Shakspere. "I may not have been successful in *Macbeth*," he writes indignantly, "but to say that I do not know, do not understand and feel Shaspeare [*sic*], no, by heavens, no! He is one of my very special poets; I have had him in my hands from my earliest youth and I read and re-read him continually." Despite the faulty spelling, typical of his literary carelessness, Verdi's insistence on his appreciation and understanding of Shakspere was justified. An incongruous drinking song allotted to Lady Macbeth, some of the witches' music, and a few other passages should not blind us to the fact that much of the score of *Macbeth*, especially the new portion written for Paris, is worthy of and apposite to the subject. Doubtless the opera is not wholly successful, in the main because the new wine was too strong for the old bottle; but *Macbeth* shares with *Simon Boccanegra* the honor of being the most interesting of all Verdi's more or less experimental operas.

Much to the disappointment of Peppina, who was feeling depressed at the wintry desolation of Sant' Agata, Verdi did not go to Paris for the production of *Macbeth*. Indeed, he stayed at Sant' Agata almost continuously during the year 1865 until the month of November. It was during this time that he finally resigned his seat in the Italian Parliament. In view of his peregrinations already described, he must have been a frequent absentee from the debates, though it is said that he did useful work in committee on occasions. He himself, however, was under no illusion as to the importance of his parliamentary career. When the admiring Piave wished to compose an account of his activities as a member of Parliament, Verdi advised him merely to take a piece of paper and write in the middle: "The four hundred and fifty deputies are in reality only four hundred and forty-nine, because, as a deputy, Verdi does not exist." It appears that he was, in fact, not favorably impressed by his colleagues, who seemed to him to waste their time and his in petty quarrels. His last direct political act, however, was to do his utmost to ensure the worthiness of his successor.

In November the Verdis went to Paris, where they remained until the following March (1866). It is clear that Verdi was at this time generally dissatisfied with the theaters in his orbit. He described La Scala as "the opera house where they no longer know how to do operas." He was annoyed with the incompetent management of the Théâtre Italien, writing some decidedly stiff letters in which he suggested that the only way to retrieve the musical situation would be the appointment of Mariani as conductor. He was equally critical of the Paris Opéra — "La Grande Boutique" as he called it — which he accused of sacrificing everything to stage effects. When there was a question of *King Lear* being done there — a project dismissed almost immediately owing to the subject being insufficiently spectacular — he showed his distrust by making it a condition that "Shaspeare" should be treated with the respect due to so great a poet. He disliked especially the precedents set by Mme Meyerbeer, who had been in the habit of giving expensive presents to everybody concerned in the production of her husband's operas. "What a business!" he had written to Escudier in June 1865; "even art becomes a matter of banking, and to succeed one needs to be a millionaire."

Nevertheless, Escudier had managed to persuade him that a performance of one of his works at the Opéra was desirable, and it was doubtless with this in view as well as with the idea of clearing up various misunderstandings with Bagier, the director of the Théâtre Italien, that he went to Paris. He liked and trusted personally Perrin, the new director of the Opéra, and was prepared to let him give the first French performance of *La Forza del Destino*. Indeed, negotiations to this end were far advanced, but were abandoned soon after Verdi's arrival in Paris, for on the 31st of December he signed a contract with the Opéra to write a new work to be put into rehearsal in July and produced in November, the libretto being an adaptation by du Locle and Méry of Schiller's tragedy *Don Carlos*.

Verdi went home to write the music. He was having trouble with his throat and perhaps on that account took ship from Nice to Genoa, where for three days he reveled in the mild sunny climate that "restores the blood and opens out the lungs." By the 25th of March he was back at Sant' Agata, but the throat trouble interfered considerably with his work. Indeed, sometimes, when it was acute, he could not work at all. His customary country pursuits failed to provide the usual solace; not even the breaking in and schooling of his fine new horse, Gisella, succeeded in distracting him. He did little but stroll about the garden, working when he felt able.

A new and even more serious affliction soon came further to interrupt his labors. As a result of the secret treaty signed in April 1866 between the King of Prussia and Victor Emmanuel, Italy again became involved in hostilities with Austria. In May Verdi, seeing war to be imminent, feared (unnecessarily as it proved) that he would be unable to stay at Busseto owing to its exposed position. He did not want to go away at all. Work had been more satisfactory of late; the first three acts of *Don Carlo* were finished. There was a suggestion of his seeking repose in France, but his patriotism forbade him to leave Italy at such a moment. Worse, however, was to come. On the 24th of June the Italian army was severely defeated at Custoza, and though the crushing victory of the Prussians at Sadowa nine days later decided the general issue of the campaign in favor of the Allies, Italy was practically in the position of a defeated nation. At the end of the war the Austrians did not even hand over to her the province of Venetia, but enacted the comedy of ceding it to Napoleon III, who eventually passed it on, so to say, to King Victor Emmanuel after the formality of a plebiscite. The Trentino, where the Italian troops under Garibaldi had greatly distinguished themselves and won notable successes, was to be evacuated as a preliminary to peace negotiations.

Nothing could have been more galling to the pride of an Italian patriot such as Verdi. Conscious of the fact that the disaster of Custoza had been due to bad leadership and faulty equipment, not to any lack of bravery on the part of the Italian troops, he would have preferred the war to go on rather than to see Italy acquire Venice in such an ignominious fashion. He felt the greatest disinclination to visit Paris under the circumstances and made a vain attempt to obtain the cancellation of his contract. His throat was still troubling him; he could not make up his mind as to the value of *Don Carlo*. "Written in the midst of flame and fire, either this opera will be better than the others or it will be a horrible thing," he had written to Escudier in June.

By the end of July, however, Verdi, resigning himself to the inevitable, left Italy for France. He first went to Cauterets in the Pyrenees to do a cure for his throat; then, at the beginning of September, he returned to Paris, to 67 avenue des Champs-Élysées, for the rehearsals of the much buffeted *Don Carlo*. Partly owing to the troubles in Italy, partly owing to a lawsuit between a singer and the Opéra management, the production of *Don Carlo* was considerably retarded. The news of his father's death, received on the 15th of January 1867, further delayed matters, for Verdi, who was persorally coaching individual singers, was so upset that he could not proceed with his labors for some time.

On the 11th of March 1867 *Don Carlo* was finally produced. Verdi himself wrote to his friend Piroli the next day that it had not achieved the success that he had hoped for. Nevertheless, on the whole, the

MANUSCRIPT SCORE, *Nabucco*, ACT I, INTRODUCTION

A LETTER TO PIAVE, WRITTEN IN 1863

about the necessity of changing the end of La Forza del Destino press notices were favorable enough, though not particularly interesting. Théophile Gautier wrote an enthusiastic article in the *Moniteur*, in which he waxed especially eloquent about the beauties of the great *auto-da-fé* scene. The professional music-critics were by no means unanimous, but the *Temps* considered that Verdi, "realizing the poverty of the melodic forms of the school of Rossini and their inadequacy for theatrical expression, had enriched his style by resources borrowed from the German and French schools. In search of the true dramatic style he has consciously or unconsciously been forced to draw near to the school of Gluck. If he had only aimed at success, he would have made no advance after *Il Trovatore* and would not have gone so far as he has done, now surpassing even Meyerbeer." The musical critic of *La France*, after praising the libretto and defending the composer from the charge of having become a mere follower of Wagner or even of "that greatest contemporary dramatic genius, Meyerbeer," notes that Verdi had been exceptionally successful in differentiating the moods and the characters in his vocal and orchestral writing. Where Verdi might have been expected to produce only a brilliant essay in a strictly contemporary idiom, he had in fact produced a masterpiece which showed notable attempts to explore the future. But what seems to have pleased this critic most of all was that Verdi had produced an "exclusively French work, which, more certainly than his best Italian operas, will carry his name down to posterity."

It is clear from these typical extracts that the usual statement to the effect that *Don Carlo* met with a merely respectful reception from the press is scarcely accurate. It is also clear to any person accustomed to reading between journalistic lines that the opera had been widely accused not only of Meyerbeerism but of Wagnerism. Indeed, this was the first occasion on which Verdi was charged with having succumbed to the influence of Wagner. The charge was untrue and Verdi resented it, telling Escudier that the germs of all the so-called Wagnerism in *Don Carlo* could be found in the trio of *Ernani*, the sleepwalking scene in *Macbeth*, and many other places. Verdi, like all Italian composers, regarded himself primarily as a craftsman whose duty it was to keep abreast of the times,[1] to write the best possible music of which he was capable consonant and compatible with particular circumstances. Disliking conscious æsthetic theories, he much resented being accused of having written an opera in accordance with one. His attitude is well defined in the same letter to Escudier, wherein he says that the point is not to what system *Don Carlo* belongs, but whether the music is good or bad.

[1] The first act of Puccini's *Turandot*, with its choruses *à la* Mussorgsky, is a good parallel instance.

The influence of Meyerbeer cannot, need not be denied, but that influence was accepted, so to say, as part and parcel of the condition of writing an opera for a theater where the ideals of Meyerbeer still reigned supreme. The dominating role played by Verdi in the fashioning of his Italian librettos has been repeatedly emphasized. He seems, however, to have accepted Méry and du Locle's libretto without question, practically as it stood. We know very little about his attitude to it. He certainly wrote to du Locle some letters on the subject, which were lost in the post; in later years he told Pizzi that the character of De Posa both in the opera and in Schiller's play was an anachronism that he would gladly have suppressed if he could. In the main, however, he seems to have felt that his librettists understood better than he did the requirements of the Paris Opéra, accepting without demur the spectacular element, the ballets, even the conventional but excessive length of five acts. The libretto of *Don Carlo* is not exactly bad, but few would rank it as in any way equal to Schiller's play. Apart from the activities of the Inquisition, most of the interesting political side is necessarily omitted. Rodrigo, in the opera merely a kind of Wolfram, is a real person in the play, where the bond between him and Don Carlos is made very much more clear; while the final arrest of Don Carlos in Schiller is far more satisfactory than the wholly absurd ending provided by Méry and du Locle.

It is clear that Verdi realized that he had made a mistake in tolerating the excessive length of the *Don Carlo* libretto. It was too long anyhow, anywhere; it was criminally long for a composer who made almost a fetish of brevity and swift-moving action. "To write well," he once said, "one must be able to write quickly, in one breath, as it were, leaving till later the work of correction and revision. Otherwise there is a risk of writing music like a mosaic, devoid of style or character" — a principle that, as Bonavia truly observes, does not apply to all composers, but is certainly true of Verdi and moreover helps to account for the strong individuality of his music.

Verdi felt with justice that he had on this occasion lost his way in a maze of words. Contrary to his usual custom, he authorized several important cuts before the second performance, and sixteen years later he commissioned Ghislanzoni to prepare an abbreviated version in four acts, which, if not an improvement in every respect, minimized some drawbacks of the original libretto.

Nevertheless, Méry and du Locle had provided the composer with a frame in which his talents were often displayed to advantage. The great scene at the end of the third act contains some of the finest ensemble-writing that Verdi ever penned, the effectiveness of which can scarcely be appreciated by anyone who has not heard the opera in performance. The musical delineation of the characters is, on the whole, excellent; the harmony and orchestration register a decided advance. There are many beautiful and typical melodies, by no means confined to the familiar "*Ella giammai m'amò*" and "*O don fatale*." [2] Rossini, notoriously difficult to please, was sufficiently impressed to say that *Don Carlo* proved Verdi to be the only man alive capable of writing grand opera.

The general feeling in Paris seems to have been that the opera fell between two stools: it was not sufficiently traditional to belong to the old school, not sufficiently venturesome to be reckoned as typical of the new. Such criticism was not altogether unjustified. *Don Carlo* does show traces of incompatible styles. There is also, at times, a sense of strain, and in this respect, as in several others, *Don Carlo* has a decided affinity with *I Vespri Siciliani*. Both operas were modeled on Meyerbeerian lines; both were written for the Paris Opéra to typical French librettos; both were associated with international expositions; both aroused nationalist opposition. As regards intrinsic merit, however, no comparison is possible, for *Don Carlo*, despite defects of detail, despite a certain lack of the charm and unity perceptible in such previous works as *Ballo*, *Traviata*, and *Rigoletto*, remains on the whole the most interesting product of Verdi's middle age. Had he not written it, we may doubt if he could ever have written *Aïda*.

Extraneous causes contributed to the failure of *Don Carlo*, for an opera launched so splendidly, which achieved only a dozen performances in one season, cannot be described in any other way. Certain Italian writers maintain that the subject offended the clerical prejudices of the Empress Eugénie. This may or may not be true, because there has always been a tendency in Italy to make the Empress a scapegoat on every possible opportunity. What is certain is that the actual performance left a great deal to be desired. True, *Don Carlo* calls for a perfection of cast not easily attainable; no less than five singers of the first class are indispensable. But Verdi himself was dissatisfied not so much with the singers as with the general ensemble, and in connection with it he designated lack of rhythm and enthusiasm as the capital defects of the Paris Opéra, where far too much importance was attached to good taste at the expense of inspiration. He told Escudier that he was not at all surprised that *Don Carlo* had won greater success in London, where it was produced a few months later, because Costa was a really good conductor, almost if not quite the equal of Mariani, whose orchestra, moreover, was not handicapped by using Sax's [3] brass instruments. "Any instruments

---

[2] "She Never Loved Me" and "Oh, Fatal Gift."
[3] Immortalized in the invention of the saxophone. Meyerbeer and Berlioz both supported him.

are better than Sax's." Mariani, who was present at the first performance, was so dissatisfied that he told his friends that he would not be happy until he had himself produced the opera at Bologna.[4] This he did in the autumn of the same year with the happiest possible results; a significant fact that Verdi, not unnaturally, pointed out to Escudier, to be passed on by him to the authorities of the Paris Opéra.

[4] Monaldi.

CHAPTER XVI

Delighted to escape from France, "the greatest country in the world, it is true, but one I can't stand for long," Verdi left Paris the day after the production of *Don Carlo*, going straight to Genoa, where in the previous December he had taken a permanent flat in the Palazzo Sauli on the eminence of Carignano. The position, with its view over the port and the open sea, is a delightful one, and the residence in the same building of Mariani, who was at that time living with Teresa Stolz, must have been an added attraction. Though the flat was still in the hands of upholsterers, carpenters, and builders and Verdi had to spend much time in the train between Genoa and Busseto, his delight at being home again was unlimited. "This seems truly a paradise after having to do with the Opéra for eight months," he wrote to Escudier at the end of March. He made Genoa his headquarters, but went very frequently to Sant' Agata, where his father-in-law and benefactor, Antonio Barezzi, lay dying. Ever since January, when he had rushed from Paris to Sant' Agata for a few days, Verdi had known that Barezzi's days were numbered, but the knowledge availed little to lessen his grief. To Barezzi and to Barezzi alone he owed everything. It was Barezzi who had saved him from a return to Le Roncole when his own father had no money to send him to the University at Parma. It was Barezzi who had enabled him to pursue his musical studies at Milan; it was Barezzi who had given him his daughter as a first wife. "I have known many men," Verdi wrote to the Countess Maffei, "but never a better one. He loved me as his own children and I loved him as a father." The end came on the 20th of July. Barezzi's favorite among all Verdi's compositions had always been the chorus of Hebrews from the early opera *Nabucco*, and just after Verdi had played the beautiful tune to him for the last time, he died, an exclamation of affection and admiration on his lips.

There is no doubt that Verdi felt the shock very keenly. Indeed, he himself says that the year 1867 was as bad for him as that year, 1840, when his wife and two children died in rapid succession in Milan. Nor were his troubles yet at an end, for on the 5th of December the faithful Piave, to whom he was sincerely attached, had a stroke on his way to a rehearsal at La Scala. Poor Piave lingered on for eight years, till the 5th of March 1876, unable to move, unable to read, write, or speak, but perfectly conscious. His thoughts, we are told, centered on two things only: Verdi and the future of his illegitimate daughter. Verdi, at any rate, repaid his constant devotion in the most generous manner, defraying all expenses, settling ten thousand lire on the daughter, and putting himself to infinite trouble to get six of the most famous composers of the day, including Auber and Thomas, to contribute to an album of six songs the royalties on which should provide her with a little income.

Almost immediately after Barezzi's death Verdi paid another short visit to Paris, stopping a few days at Turin on the way. As usual, however, his heart remained at Sant' Agata. Wherever he found himself, he was always writing instructions to his bailiff about the care of his horses, about the precise manner in which irrigation pipes were to be painted, and so on. But on this occasion the letters were more frequent, more detailed, far more severe than usual. It is clear that Carlo Verdi's death and Barezzi's long illness had caused a certain disorganization on the estate, and lack of order and discipline was highly obnoxious to Verdi, particularly in his present mood. The bailiff is severely reprimanded for using a certain machine that should have remained unused until Verdi's return; he is to see that the groom exercises the horses every other day without taking them into Busseto; he is to tell the gardener that nobody is to be allowed to go into the garden; he is curtly informed that he himself knows neither how to command nor how to obey; his accounts are as unsatisfactory as the information in his letters is insufficient. Verdi could be a very exacting master when he thought fit.

By October he was back again in Genoa, where he remained during the winter, as henceforward was to be his custom. He wrote many sarcastic letters to Escudier about the shortcomings of "La Grande Boutique," rubbing in the fact that even at Parma, where the orchestra was weak, effects had been produced unknown in Paris. He read the libretto of Thomas's *Hamlet*, which he considered as bad as it could be and a positive insult to Shakspere. He sat in the sun and gradually recovered his equanimity. In May 1868, if not before, he was back again at Sant' Agata, paying a short visit to Milan at the end of June to see the new Galleria, which he much admired, and to offer his respects to Manzoni, whom he idolized. He had not entered the city, the scene of his early triumphs and failure, for twenty years. In August he left Sant' Agata again for a village called Tabiano, at the foot of the Apennines, partly to do a cure, mainly to avoid the opening of the Busseto theater, which took place on the 15th of August. The not very edifying story of Verdi's relations with his local theater has already been told. The season lasted a month; he stayed away a month. Further comment is unnecessary.

On the 13th of November 1868 Rossini died at Passy. The news deeply moved Verdi. The two men had never been on intimate terms, though their personal relations were friendly enough. An amusing and typical letter, written in 1865, by "Rossini, ex-composer and pianist of the fourth class, to the illustrious composer Verdi, pianist of the fifth class," sufficiently attests the fact; otherwise Verdi would not have preserved it so carefully at Sant' Agata. But it was the public rather than the private loss that remained uppermost in his mind. "Rossini's reputation," he wrote to the Countess Maffei, "was the most widespread and the most popular of our time; it was one of the glories of Italy. When the other like unto it (Manzoni's) exists no longer, what will remain to us? Our ministers and the exploits of Lissa and Custoza!" The well of bitterness in these words reveals not only the writer's admiration for a fellow musician but the depth of the wound inflicted on his patriotic pride by the disasters of 1866. Verdi felt, then, that something should be done to dramatize, so to say, this sense of loss. He highly approved the proposal of the Italian government to bring Rossini's body to Italy and bury it with the highest honors, though confident that nothing would come of the project were the decision left to Mme Rossini,[1] because "no Frenchman loves the Italians, but Mme Rossini detests us as much as all the rest of the French nation put together."

Feeling, however, that Italian musicians should do something on their own initiative worthy of the occasion, he wrote to Ricordi, four days after Rossini's death, proposing that the principal Italian composers of the day should be asked each to write a movement of a Mass to be performed on the 13th of November 1869 in the Church of San Petronio, in the city of Bologna, "Rossini's real musical fatherland." Nobody, none of the composers, none of the musicians taking part, was to receive any kind of payment; the score was to be deposited immediately after the performance in the archives of the local Liceo Musicale and never to be used again except for future anniversaries, "if posterity thinks fit to celebrate them," as he adds with typical skepticism. It was a noble if somewhat naïve idea. Nobody knew better than Verdi that from the purely musical point of view the resulting composition must necessarily partake of the nature of a patchwork quilt, but he was not — he says so himself — primarily concerned with the purely musical point of view on this occasion, the Mass being intended as a demonstration of civic rather than æsthetic virtue.

Though an influential committee was formed, though the composers had their respective parts [2] allotted to them, the project came

[1] Originally Mlle Olympe Pélissier, Rossini's second wife.
[2] The portions of the Mass were allotted as follows: Buzzolla, *Requiem;* Bazzini, *Dies iræ;* Pedrotti, *Tuba mirum;* Cagnoni, *Quid sum miser;* Ricci, *Recordare;* Nini, *Ingemisco;* Boucheron, *Confutatis;* Coccia, *Lacrymosa;* Gaspari, *Domine Jesu;* Plantania, *Sanctus;* Petrella, *Agnus Dei;* Mabellini, *Lux æterna;* Verdi, *Libera me.*

to nothing. The municipality of Bologna was lukewarm or merely lazy; the impresario, Scalaberni, who directed the Opera, refused to lend his soloists or orchestra without payment, excusing himself on the grounds that he was a "poor man with six children and a living to make." The fiasco touched Verdi to the quick. To begin with, he liked and was accustomed to have his own way; further, he felt that many of the people concerned had failed to do their duty as good Italians. Worst of all, among these people was Mariani, his most intimate friend. There seems to be no doubt that Mariani's tepidity was due to the fact that he thought that he should have been included among the composers chosen to write the Mass. Whether his talent for composition would have justified such an inclusion it is difficult to say, though it is only fair to recall the fact that Chorley much admired his songs. But Verdi was not the kind of man to forgive any lukewarmness in a matter in which he was vitally interested. He felt that Mariani, as the conductor at Bologna, should have subordinated any sense of personal grievance, justified or not, to the interest of the common cause, and his disappointment and disapproval opened a rift between the two friends that was soon to grow very wide. Doubtless, extraneous causes contributed to his bitterness. Verdi had judged correctly in thinking that Mme Rossini would choose to have her husband buried in Paris though her letters and subsequent conduct in consenting to the removal of the body after her own death to the Church of Santa Croce in Florence hardly bear out the rest of his accusations. The world-famous funeral in Paris, not to mention the success of the commemorative festival at Pesaro, must have been very galling to him in the circumstances. Many years later, when he was to be nominated honorary president of a committee formed for the purpose of bringing back Rossini's body to Italy, he declined on the plea that his memory of the whole episode remained so unpleasant.

In the meantime negotiations were in progress for producing a revised version of *La Forza del Destino* at La Scala, for Verdi's visit to Milan had apparently put an end to the long-standing feud with that theater. As early as December 1864 — that is to say, two years after the original production at St. Petersburg — Piave had been ordered to make some changes, which he carried out so ineptly as to earn a sharp reprimand from his master. Then for four years, owing to *Don Carlo*, the war, and other distractions, the project seems to have lain fallow. When it again materialized, Piave was nothing but a living corpse at Milan; so the task was entrusted to Antonio Ghislanzoni.

Ghislanzoni, one of those wild, bohemian figures who abound in the chronicles of the time, had started life as a student of medicine at Pavia with a passion for playing the double bass. Then he became successively an operatic baritone, a journalist, a poet, and a writer of plays and novels, the titles of some of which, such as *The Art of Making Debts* and *Ugly Women*, seem to invite closer acquaintance. He was famous throughout the north of Italy for his freakish exploits. One, particularly notorious, dated from his baritone days, when he was playing the part of Ezio in *Attila* at some small provincial theater. Suddenly deciding to go to Milan, he left the theater just as he was, in his tunic, plumed helmet, and sword, and, thus arrayed in the full uniform of a Roman general, alighted at his hotel in the Piazza del Duomo.

Verdi and he had been acquainted for many years, but were on nothing like intimate terms till the summer of 1868, when Ghislanzoni seems to have gone to Sant' Agata, presumably to discuss the changes in *La Forza del Destino*. These were not considerable, consisting mainly of an extended overture, some rearrangement, and a new ending. In the original version Piave, following Rivas, made Don Alvaro jump over a precipice after the deaths of Leonora and her brother. Verdi and Ghislanzoni now permitted him to survive, and, despite the objection originally raised when de Lauzières made the same suggestion, a final trio was inserted at the end of the opera.

In its new garb *La Forza del Destino* was produced at La Scala on the 20th of February 1869. Verdi was delighted with the production, which he found excellent in every detail, and the opera certainly achieved a measure of success hitherto denied it. The municipal band serenaded the composer in his hotel after the performance; the public flocked to the theater; the press was unanimous in its praise, though the excellent critic Filippi thought Leonora's "*Madre, pietosa Vergine*," excessively reminiscent of Schubert's "*Ave Maria*."

This criticism seems to have annoyed Giulio Ricordi, who had a special affection for that lovely aria; whereupon Verdi wrote to the critic a letter so interesting that it must be quoted. After thanking Filippi for the generally favorable tone of his notice and conceding his perfect right to criticize anything that seemed good to him, Verdi continued as follows: "In my consummate musical ignorance I really could not say how many years have passed since I heard Schubert's '*Ave*'; so to imitate it would have been difficult for me. Do not imagine when I talk of 'consummate musical ignorance' that I am joking; it is absolutely true. In my house there is hardly any music; I have never been to a musical library or to a publisher's to examine a composition. I am familiar with some of the best contemporary operas, not from having studied them, but from having heard them in the theater. In all this there is a definite policy, as you will doubtless realize. I repeat that of all composers past and present I am the least erudite. Let us be quite clear, eschewing all nonsense: I refer to erudition, not musical knowledge. In this respect I should lie if I said that I had not studied hard and thoroughly in my youth. Indeed, it is for this reason that I have a hand strong enough to bend the notes to my will and sure enough to obtain as a rule the effects that I have in mind. So when I write something irregular, the reason is because the strict rule does not give me what I want, also because I do not think all the rules at present established are good. The treatises on counterpoint need to be revised."

Words very revelatory in their simplicity and very admirable in their lack of affectation.

The summer and autumn of 1869 were mainly devoted to efforts on behalf of the Rossini Mass, efforts that resulted in the fiasco already mentioned. When it became clear that the Mass could not be given at Bologna on the anniversary of Rossini's death, Verdi, taking the line that he was only one of the composers selected to write the music and that all responsibility now rested with the committee, abandoned the project for good, with the expression of his personal view that to resuscitate it in Milan under different conditions would be a mistake. Du Locle wanted him to set Meilhac and Halévy's *Frou-Frou*, but he refused, saying that he had definitely come to the conclusion that his characteristics as a composer were not suited to Paris. As was not infrequently the case, he spent August at Genoa, returning to Sant' Agata in the autumn. During the summer he had been made Knight of the Order of Civil Merit of Savoy, an honor that carried with it an annual pension of six hundred lire, and this he now allotted in equal parts to the most promising and industrious boy and girl in the national schools of Busseto. But undoubtedly the most important feature of this period was the ever increasing coldness between himself and Mariani, a coldness that brought about musical results of the greatest importance.

Memories of a splendid performance of *La Forza del Destino* under Mariani's direction in the summer and of the Bologna interpretation of *Don Carlo* two years previously — an interpretation so remarkable that from it has been dated the modern efficiency of Italian orchestras — served in no wise to temper it. To a certain extent, indeed, Mariani's triumphs may have been something of an aggravation. Mariani was a conductor of genius — there is no doubt of that — but he was essentially a virtuoso conductor who did not scruple to alter marks of expression, even rhythms and notes, if he thought the change would contribute to greater orchestral effectiveness. In *La Forza del Destino* and more especially in *Don Carlo* he had ventured to take liberties that Verdi resented; all the more, perhaps, because the public liked them. Verdi always insisted that the composer was a dictator whom both conductors and singers only existed to serve; he conceded to them no creative importance of any kind. Doubtless the divergence between his and Mariani's point of view in this respect mattered little while their personal ties of friendship were strong; but after the shock and disappointment at Mariani's action (or, to be accurate, lack of action) in the matter of the Rossini Mass, it may well have begun to assume greater importance. One thing is certain: by the beginning of the year 1870 relations between the two men were so strained that Verdi refused, except in the presence of a common friend, to grant Mariani's desire for an interview.

Either at or before that time another factor, in the shape of Teresa Stolz, a singer from Bohemia, came to aggravate the situation still further. Stolz was not only a first-class dramatic soprano, who had created the part of Leonora in *La Forza del Destino* at La Scala, but, as her picture in the theatrical museum there shows, a handsome if rather hard-faced woman. She lived with Mariani as his wife, though she was not in fact married to him. As already mentioned, Verdi and Peppina, Mariani and Stolz resided in the same block of flats at Genoa, where all four were on terms of the greatest intimacy; but during the time under review Stolz left Mariani and went to live in Milan. It is frequently asserted in Italy, and by at least one German biographer, that the reason of this separation was due to an intrigue between Verdi and Teresa. It has even been said that there exist letters at Sant' Agata, unavailable to the public, that contain Giuseppina's comments to the Countess Maffei on the episode. Despite questioning, no proof of the assertion has yet materialized sufficient to carry conviction to me. *Prima facie*, the story seems possible but hardly probable. To begin with, Verdi was nearly sixty years old at the time. Further and more important, not only he but Giuseppina remained on the most intimate terms with Stolz for the rest of her life. The Requiem Mass is dedicated to her; she was a constant visitor at Sant' Agata in the eighties and the nineties; she frequently accompanied the Verdis to Montecatini and elsewhere. To brush aside the whole story on these grounds, as some have done, is perhaps unjustified. Verdi would not have been the first man of fifty-seven to have an intrigue with a young and attractive woman. Peppina, a very remarkable and broad-minded person, would not have been the first wife to make friends with her husband's mistress. Moreover, in the operatic world, where she had acquired her standards of conduct, the matrimonial tie cannot be said to be regarded in quite the same way as in ordinary society. Giuseppina was a very ardent Catholic, but the story of her own relations with Verdi, not to mention the intimacy of both with the irregular ménage in the flat below, proves this much. Inherently, then, an affair, serious or light, transitory or of some duration, between Verdi and Stolz does not seem impossible and might be accepted if no other reason could be found for the separation of Stolz and Mariani.

In fact, however, a very different explanation has recently been made public.[3] The widow of the well-known conductor Mancinelli told a Genoese journalist who writes under the name of Belviglieri the following story: Stolz had become at this time increasingly irritated by Mariani's failure to fulfill his repeated promises to regularize their union. Finally deciding to bring matters to a head, she asked him to return to her a considerable sum of money that she had entrusted to his care during the period of their intimacy. This Mariani failed to do; whereupon Stolz left him and, instead of going to law, asked Verdi to act on her behalf in the matter. Intervention, however, was fruitless. Apparently Mariani had speculated with and lost the money, a breach of trust that particularly scandalized Verdi, whose sense of honor and punctiliousness in business matters was very strong. From that date he would have nothing more to do with Mariani in the way of personal friendship. This explanation of the final break between Stolz and Mariani, Mariani and Verdi, seems to me more probable than the romantic version often accepted, not to say welcomed. Signora Mancinelli, who as a girl lived in the same building as the Verdis and later saw them frequently at both Genoa and Busseto, was in a position to know the facts. It seems also more consonant with subsequent events as well as with the psychology of everybody concerned.

The rest of the tragic tale is soon told. Verdi, though no longer believing in Mariani as a friend, still considered him the greatest orchestral director in Italy; he would gladly have had him go to Cairo to conduct the first performance of *Aïda* in 1871. Mariani refused. Either from conviction, from restlessness, or from a desire to hurt his former friend, he had in the meantime deserted, bag and baggage, to the camp of the Wagnerians, and it was he who in the same year (1871) conducted at Bologna those performances of *Lohengrin* which so delighted Wagner. Thus, thanks to vanity, a woman and/or shady finance, Wagner made his first entrance into Italy. Dare one say in view of Wagner's own record that two of the motifs were not wholly inappropriate? Poor Mariani, however, gained little from his new orientation. He had lived — and loved — too well and he died miserably at Genoa on the 13th of June 1873. Verdi, who forgave with difficulty, does not in the letters preserved in the *Copialettere* even men-

[3] It appeared in the paper *Il Lavoro* on the 4th of September 1929.

tion his death, and though he was almost certainly at Sant' Agata, did not attend the funeral, merely sending a formal telegram of condolence. We may be less hardhearted. Mariani's disease was of a nature that notoriously undermines moral responsibility; Italian, not to say European, music owes a real debt of gratitude to his genius.

CHAPTER XVII

In 1869, before the final liquidation of the Rossini Mass, before the definite break with Mariani, Verdi was asked to "write an opera for a very distant country." He did not even tell Ricordi what the country was or who had given him the invitation, though we now know that the invitation was on behalf of the Khedive to write an opera for the new Cairo theater on the occasion of the opening of the Suez Canal. Verdi refused it. In the spring of 1870, while on a short visit to Paris, he was again approached through his friend and collaborator du Locle and offered a large sum of money to change his mind. He again refused. He then went home, thoroughly disinclined, as he says, to write any music at all. A week or two later, however, du Locle had the happy idea of sending him a précis of the proposed opera with the request that he would at any rate read it. There were only four small pages, but they sufficed to awaken Verdi to its great possibilities. He did not know who had written the scenario though he had been led apparently to believe that the author was none other than the Khedive himself, on which point he rightly remained skeptical. This, however, was of no importance. His unerring theatrical instinct told him at once that here was a subject that lent itself admirably to musical expression and he consented to accept the commission. His artistic conscience once satisfied, Verdi's business instincts were not long in asserting themselves. On the advice, it is said, of his old pupil Muzio, who was at that time Bagier's right-hand man at the Italian Theater in Paris, he asked a fee of 150,000 francs, reserving his rights for all other countries except Egypt, but undertaking, as was his custom, to pay the expenses of the completed libretto as well as of a representative to be sent to Cairo to rehearse and produce the opera on his behalf. Even so, these details were not agreed upon till much later, only the general principles being stated at the time.

This precise sequence of events is of importance, because it is frequently suggested that pecuniary considerations primarily induced Verdi to write the opera we now know as *Aïda*. This is not so. Nobody was more careful about money than Verdi, but in this case practical considerations came second, not first.

His terms were immediately accepted in principle and du Locle set out for Sant' Agata to prepare with Verdi a detailed scenario based on the original précis. Verdi still seems to have remained in ignorance of the name of the author, one Mariette, a famous French Egyptologist who had received the title of Bey in recognition of his learning and excavations. Nor was the contract definitely signed. Nevertheless, Verdi and du Locle, probably in the month of May, were working together on a detailed scenario in French prose, of which several details, notably the final scene, were suggested by Verdi himself. Next an Italian poet had to be found to versify the scenario. Verdi wrote confidentially to Giulio Ricordi, asking him to find out whether the proposition would be agreeable to Ghislanzoni, who, in fact, accepted the task with enthusiasm, leaving the amount of his remuneration to the composer. In the first week of July, accompanied by Ricordi, he came to Sant' Agata to talk over the project. Verdi wanted information about several historical details: the possible identity of Ethiopia and Abyssinia in remote times; facts about the mysteries of Isis, and so on. Ghislanzoni did not remain at Sant' Agata, though he returned there for a few days later in the summer, but at frequent intervals, sometimes twice in one week, letters were exchanged between the two men. In the meantime Verdi learned the identity of Mariette, with whom he was soon in communication, and definitely signed his contract.

It was fortunate for posterity that so many of the details of the libretto of *Aïda* had to be settled by correspondence, for the letters, which extended all through the year 1870 and even overlapped into 1871, give us an exceptional insight into the construction of the libretto of *Aïda* as we know it. Verdi took command from the outset; Ghislanzoni was only his lieutenant, though, unlike Piave, a lieutenant with many ingenious and valuable ideas. The preponderant part taken by Verdi in the construction of the libretto of *Aïda*, which is treated in some detail in the section devoted to that opera, is not generally realized. All the reader need be told here is that several of the most effective scenes, many of the most striking passages of the dialogue, much of the ingenuity of the metrical scheme, are directly due to his commands or suggestions.

So far from waiting for the completion of the libretto in every detail, Verdi was working at the music while in active correspondence with Ghislanzoni. Indeed, it is fair to say that words and music grew up side by side. By November the task was accomplished except for the fourth act and the scoring of the entire opera, "at least a month's work," before the completion of which Verdi would not move from Sant' Agata. During his collaboration with Ghislanzoni he continually insisted that time was short, as in fact it would have been had *Aïda* been produced on the date stipulated in the original contract: January 1871.

But the outbreak of the Franco-Prussian War on July 14, 1870 upset all calculations. We are not concerned here with Verdi's personal reactions to the war, though it may be stated that the French disasters obliterated any rancor he may ever have felt against France. All his sympathy went out to her in her time of trouble and he instructed du Locle to devote to the benefit of the French wounded two thousand francs of the advance received on account of *Aïda*. The serious thing from the practical point of view was that Mariette Bey, who had been conducting all the negotiations, was shut up in Paris, where, besides, all the scenery and costumes were being manufactured. The facilities of the balloon post were hazardous, limited, and one-sided. In the circumstances Draneht Bey, the director of the Cairo Opera, decided to get into communication with the composer himself.

One of Verdi's stipulations in the original contract had been that *Aïda* should be produced at La Scala immediately after the date fixed for its performance at Cairo. Draneht Bey feared that the La Scala production might take place, as arranged, in February. He naturally wanted the first production for his own theater and laid the whole matter before the Khedive. But in this matter, at any rate, Draneht disquieted himself unnecessarily. Verdi, like the honorable man that he was, had, even before the reception of Draneht's letter, suspended negotiations with La Scala and canceled the arrangements for sending to Egypt his old and trusted pupil Muzio, who had been chosen to represent him during rehearsals. He recognized at once that the war and the siege of Paris constituted an undeniable case of *force majeure* of which it would be unfair to take advantage. In view of Verdi's sometimes excessively rigid insistence on the terms of his bond, the reasonableness that he showed on this occasion is worth recording.

Paris finally surrendered in January 1871, too late, however, to permit the production of *Aïda* during the current season at Cairo. In the course of the year there were the usual discussions about the suitability of this or that singer. Draneht himself came to Italy, when he paid a visit to Sant' Agata, hoping, apparently, that Stolz and "her future husband Mariani" — the expression is his — might be induced to go to Cairo; which owing to circumstances already known to the reader did not, of course, take place. Verdi made no secret to Draneht of his opinion that Mariani would be the ideal conductor — "if we cannot get him all the others are very much of a muchness" — and at one time seems not to have despaired of securing his services. Muzio's presence having been made impossible owing to the postponement, the responsibility for everything was finally left to Giovanni Bottesini, who seems to have fulfilled his task with exceptional competence, for on the 24th of December 1871 *Aïda* was produced with triumphant success.

Though Verdi did not attend the production, and never intended

Courtesy of Messrs. Ricordi

VERDI AND BOÏTO

during the preparation of Falstaff

Courtesy of Messrs. Ricordi

VERDI IN THE GARDEN OF SANT' AGATA

to, he followed it with the greatest interest. Only ten days before the first performance he sent to Bottesini an amended version of the *stretto* at the end of the duet between Amneris and Aïda in the second act. He was especially anxious, moreover, to know how the final duet of the opera came off in performance. He had, he wrote to Bottesini, taken great pains with this duet, but "in view of the fact that it belongs to what I may call the vaporous style, maybe the effect will not correspond to my intentions." Bottesini was urged to be wholly frank and to tell him the whole truth about the passage in D flat where Aïda sees the approach of the Angel of Death and the duet in G flat where the lovers sing together in unison.

Verdi was only concerned with the musical aspect of the performance; what may be called the publicity side left him completely indifferent. The Egyptian authorities had invited to the performance two well-known musical critics, Reyer from Paris and Filippi from Milan. Verdi would have preferred them not to go. When Filippi wrote offering his services in case they could be of use in any way, Verdi expressed his views in a letter that is worth quoting:

My dear Filippi, —

What I am going to say to you will seem strange, very strange; but you must forgive me if I feel I must unburden myself of what is on my mind.

You at Cairo? Why, nothing could be more important for *Aïda* in the way of publicity. To me it seems that art practiced in this manner is no longer art, but a trade, a diversion, a sport, something to be run after, to be made, if not successful, at least notorious at any cost! The feelings roused in me are those of disgust and humiliation. I always remember with joy the early days in which, almost without friends, without any personal mention, without preparations, without any kind of influence, I came before the public with my operas ready to be shot at, only too glad if I were able to make some kind of favorable impression. And now what a pother about an opera! Journalists, singers, players, choristers, and directors, etc., etc., all have to contribute their stone to the edifice of publicity, to make in this way a cornice of nonsensical trifles that add nothing to the merit of an opera and may quite possibly detract from its real value. It is deplorable, absolutely deplorable. . . . All I desire for this opera is a good and, especially, an intelligent production from the vocal, instrumental, and scenic point of view. As for the rest — *à la grâce de Dieu*. So I began and so I wish to finish my career.

Verdi's diatribe seems to have had little effect on the worthy Filippi, who sent back to Italy highly colored accounts of the enthusiasm that accompanied not only the first performance but the *répétition générale* of *Aida*. The latter lasted from seven o'clock till half past three in the morning, but the Khedive himself, with his suite in attendance, sat it out and was so delighted that he wished to send a telegram of congratulation to the composer. His enthusiasm seems to have been shared by the rest of the audience, who applauded in and out of season, to the mingled disgust and delight of Bottesini. The reception of the actual performance was equally favorable, Filippi being so impressed by the glories of the theater, the unfamiliar public, the bright discordant colors favored by the Copts and Jews, the veiled ladies of the harem in three boxes on the first tier, that he forgot, or at any rate is not allowed by Pougin, to chronicle anything but the most general impression of the music.

Reyer's account of the evening is more interesting, as might be expected from the future composer of *Sigurd*. By no means an admirer of Verdi, his tribute to the success of the opera is on that account the more striking. He did not like it all; he found some of the style exaggerated, some of the contrasts too violent; but he praised wholeheartedly the new harmonic sense, the unexpected modulations, the original melodic line, the unaccustomed orchestral richness of a score that showed, in his opinion, the composer's familiarity with all the latest music from Wagner and Meyerbeer to Gounod and Berlioz. "If," he concludes prophetically, "Verdi persists in his new orientation, he may lose some enthusiasts, but he will make many converts and will find followers in circles in which he has never hitherto been received."

The Milan production took place six weeks later, on the 8th of February 1872, with that bone of contention, Stolz, in the title role and with a singer equally favored by Verdi, Maria Waldmann, as Amneris. Franco Faccio, the successor of Mariani in the composer's esteem, conducted. Verdi experimented with a new overture for this production, with which, however, he seems to have been dissatisfied at rehearsal, for to this day it exists only in manuscript at Sant' Agata. Otherwise, except perhaps for a few trifling alterations, the opera remained precisely the same as at Cairo. Verdi was at great pains to ensure its success. Before finally consenting to the presentation of the opera, he had made the most minute inquiries from Ricordi about the constituent elements of the theater, even going so far as to inquire whether the big drum and the timpani had been changed for those of a larger size. He was particularly insistent about the arrangement of the orchestra in accordance with his own views, making no secret of the fact that Wagner's idea of placing it out of sight had his complete sympathy. When all these matters had been settled to his satisfaction and the singers he wanted had been engaged, he attended nearly all the rehearsals, which, incidentally, caused him considerable trouble owing to the stupidity of the tenor, Fancelli, who could not understand how a singer should at one and the same time be expected to sing accurately and with a proper appreciation of the words! There was an orchestra of ninety and a chorus of a hundred and twenty, and the scenic *mise en scène*, without rivaling that of Cairo, where there had been Arab trumpeters, a native military band, and three hundred people on the stage at the end of the second act, completely satisfied the composer.

Needless to say, the performance was a brilliant success, Verdi being called before the curtain over and over again. Contemporary accounts are little but chronicles of an evening of enthusiasm and triumph. But Fortis, the most important journalist of the time, makes the interesting reservation that, while everybody recognized the greatness of the conception in every particular, a minority resented what they agreed with Reyer in considering a new orientation on the part of the composer and would have preferred an opera written more in accordance with his earlier principles. The critic of *La Fama* was quite precise. He roundly accused Verdi of following the "strange erratic paths of Wagner," commending to the composer the example of Julius Cæsar, who "preferred to reign in a village rather than to be second at Rome."

Though the Cairo-Milan success of *Aïda* was repeated not only throughout Italy but, before five years had elapsed, in Paris and other European capitals, the accusation of Wagnerism quite spoilt it for Verdi. In letters written to Ricordi he revealed the bitterness of his soul on many occasions. He congratulated himself on *Aïda* being performed for the last time at Milan. "They won't talk about it any more or, at any rate, there will be only a few final words; perhaps some new insult accusing me of Wagnerism and then . . . *requiescat in pacem* [sic]." He considered the attitude of the press beneath contempt, its praise appearing to him even more stupid than its blame. He resented the fact that in Milan there had been no official recognition of his efforts to produce an opera in the best possible manner. "Let us speak no more of this *Aïda*," he wrote later; "if it brought me a good deal of money it also brought me a multitude of worries and the greatest possible artistic disappointment."

Beyond question most of the "artistic disappointment" lay in the accusation of Wagnerism. It is difficult for us nowadays to understand, much less accept, the accusation — almost as difficult, in fact, as to understand how the opera could have been accused of being too "metaphysical." Nevertheless, these things happened and caused Verdi great pain. Only he and Ghislanzoni knew what trouble had been taken with *Aïda*, what an effort had been made to effect a fusion between words and music more complete than any known hitherto in Italy. Whereas Verdi realized, none the less fully because secretly, that *Aïda* was but the logical outcome of all that he had been striving for throughout his career, he was now told that it was a mere imitation of Wagner! He knew that Wagner could no more have written the melodies, even the declamatory vocal passages, of *Aïda*, than he himself could have written the overture to *Tannhäuser*. Not only that, the new·richness of the scoring was his own, the greater freedom of the harmonic scheme his own, and, above all, the basic flavor of the whole of the opera was as quintessentially Italian as it could possibly be. Even nowadays some people, misled by the setting and the undoubted Oriental atmosphere of certain isolated scenes, have insufficiently appreciated this point. Verdi definitely rejected the idea of writing "Egyptian music." He did, we are told, go so far as to examine an Egyptian flute in the Florence museum, but showed his opinion of it by a contemptuous comparison with the primitive pipe in use among the urchins of his own village.[1] The famous long trumpets were employed, not because of their association, if any, with Egypt, but because of their exceptional capacity to suggest festal pomp. The characters of the opera, despite their swarthy skins, were essentially the characters of Verdi's own land and epoch. The fervent Radames, torn between love and patriotism; the jealous Aïda, struggling to reconcile her duty to her father with her passion for his conqueror; the very human Amneris, fundamentally decent despite all her vengeance and hate — they might equally well have figured in any Italian libretto. As for the priests, one has a shrewd suspicion that they were nothing but his old enemies the clerics of Busseto in fancy dress. By means of his skill and new-found mastery of expression alike in the vocal and orchestral writing, Verdi was able to depict them all in a manner appropriate to their surroundings; but normal, intelligible products of his own culture and civilization they, nevertheless, fundamentally remained. *Aïda*, then, despite its superficial exoticism, is in reality the most Italian of grand operas. Its dramatic sincerity, its effective pageantry, its glowing passion — above all, its exuberant, irresistible vitality — justify, perhaps, its classification as the best grand opera not only of Italy but of Europe.

Even before the composition of *Aïda* was finally completed, Verdi had to face two important decisions. In December 1870 Mercadante, a well-known composer and director of the Naples Conservatoire, died. The professors, who felt that the institution was in need of radical reform, endeavored, through Verdi's friend Florimo, to persuade him to fill the vacancy. Verdi was undoubtedly pleased and flattered by the invitation, for the Naples Conservatoire was one of

[1] Pizzi.

the most famous in the whole annals of music. But he loved his country life at Sant' Agata, his solitude, his independence, too well to accept it. He was not at all the kind of man to undertake halfheartedly what he felt to be a great responsibility. His letter to Florimo, written in January 1871, in which he finally refused the offer, outlines the severe training in counterpoint and fugue that, following the example of old masters like Alessandro Scarlatti and Durante, he would have thought it his duty to impose upon the pupils. It is this letter that finishes with the often quoted and nearly as often misunderstood aphorism: *"Torniamo all' antico: sarà un progresso."* [2] Verdi did not mean by this that the old should be imitated, but that a reversion to the strict principles practiced by the older masters would be an improvement on present methods.

Subsequent efforts on the part of the Naples municipality and even of the Minister of Education did not suffice to make him change his mind. The terms, however, in which his refusal was expressed seem to have caused some stir, for they led to the appointment of a commission to study the reforms necessary to the improvement of Italian conservatoires in general, of which Verdi was asked to become president. At first he refused this request also. He did not believe in systems; he believed in personalities. He pointed out that in the palmy days of the Naples Conservatoire directors such as Durante and Leo had made their own rules for instruction. He instanced the independence at Bologna of the famous Father Martini, object of the especial reverence of composers so distinguished as Gluck and Mozart. In none of the institutions directed by these men were there any set rules; and in the Paris Conservatoire, where the rules were as excellent as they were rigid, the results had only been satisfactory when they were interpreted by a musician of the highest order like Cherubini. In the end, however, Verdi, yielding to the solicitations of his friend Piroli and the Minister of Education, Correnti, consented to take part in the commission, which sat in Florence during March 1871 and drew up its report on the 20th of that month.

As a kind of sop for his refusal to assume the directorship of the Naples Conservatoire, Verdi consented to become first honorary member of the Naples Philharmonic Society, which was more than he condescended to do in regard to the Philharmonic-Dramatic Society at Busseto. This grandiloquently named body had enlisted the services of Verdi's great friend Dr. Carrara to try and induce him to become their honorary president. Verdi was very fond of Dr. Carrara, but he did not believe in the practicability or the utility of his society any more than he believed in the desirability of the Busseto theater. Partly on this account, partly because the memories of the calumnies

[2] "Let us get back to the old; it will be a step forward."

and malicious gossip still rankled, Verdi refused to have anything whatever to do with the project.

There is no doubt that Verdi was in an exceptionally touchy state at this time, induced in the first instance, perhaps, by the Franco-Prussian War. He had viewed with dismay the triumph of the Germans; his letters to the Countess Maffei, in which he was always exceptionally candid, reveal his disgust at the idea of Latin culture being trampled underfoot by "these damned Goths." He might have had his own quarrels with France in general and Paris in particular, but they represented to him the acme of civilization. Even the fact that the collapse of Napoleon's power had meant the end of the temporal power of the Papacy and the long-desired establishment of Rome as the capital of Italy did not console him. He would have liked Italy to throw in her lot with France. A hundred and fifty thousand Italian troops might have sufficed to turn the scale; better defeat at the side of France than a condition of things which, as he judged with remarkable prescience, must one day lead inevitably to another great war. In short, during this period Verdi was suffering from what nowadays we should call an anti-German complex, and it is not merely fanciful to link up this general state of mind with his personal attitude to Wagner. So far as he was concerned, Wagner represented the new triumphant Germanism in his own sphere of action. He especially resented, therefore, the idea that he had capitulated to the German conqueror at a kind of miniature musical Sedan. Subsequently his attitude to Germany was much modified; nor, despite Werfel's admirable but purely imaginative novel, did his excessively self-conscious attitude towards Wagner persist. But in the early seventies there can be no doubt that the very name was anathema to him as synonymous with the infiltration into Italy of everything he most disliked.

The main preoccupation of the remaining months of the year 1872 was the production of *Aïda* at various Italian theaters. Many managements, both then and later, wished to mount the sensational new opera, but Verdi himself only consented to supervise the productions at Parma and Naples. To an urgent invitation from Trieste to attend the first performance he replied that, as his presence was not essential to the production, he preferred to adhere to his custom of never entering a theater for the mere purpose of exhibiting himself.

An amusing incident characterized the Parma production. A certain Prospero Bertani, living in Reggio, near by, wrote Verdi a letter couched in the most formal terms to complain that, having heard much talk of *Aïda*, he had gone twice to Parma to hear the opera. He was satisfied with the singers, impressed by the mounting, but found the music worthless. Since he was entirely dependent on an allowance from his family, the useless expenditure of so much money haunted him like a nightmare, and he therefore suggested that Verdi should repay him his expenses, of which he enclosed the following account:

2.5.'72.
Return railway ticket	lire	5.90
Theater	"	8
Detestable supper at the station . . .	"	2
		15.90

4.5.'72.
Same as above	lire	15.90
Total	"	31.80

Verdi, with real kindliness and a refreshing sense of humor, gave instructions to Ricordi to satisfy the claim, deducting only the price of the supper, which, as he truly observed, might quite well have been eaten at home. He, further, made it a condition that the complainant should promise never to attend any of his operas in the future, a condition which Bertani, with imperturbable gravity, accepted and acknowledged in a document even more formal than his original complaint.

Verdi had gone to Parma mainly because of his local associations with that city. Quite different considerations drew him to Naples. He entertained a profound mistrust for the manager of the San Carlo, Musella, whom he describes as disliking equally himself and his works. Even more than the management in particular, he distrusted general conditions at Naples, where, "because they have had Palestrina, Scarlatti, Pergolesi, they think they know more than anybody else." He went, then, to Naples towards the end of 1872, determined either to have his way in every respect or to withdraw his opera at the last moment, if necessary even after the dress rehearsal. His iron will triumphed as usual, for an excellent performance seems to have been obtained. On this occasion, too, the bad luck that appeared to dog his visits to Naples was once more in evidence. Teresa Stolz, who was singing Aïda, suddenly fell ill and the production had to be postponed, to the disgust of Verdi, who desired nothing so much as to exchange the intrigues and worries of theatrical life for the peace and solitude of Sant' Agata. His enforced leisure had one good result, for, to while away the time, he composed during the month of March 1873 a String Quartet, which, if in no way a masterpiece, is a most agreeable piece of music. He attached so little importance to it that for some time he would allow neither publication nor public performance. The sole presentation of the quartet at that time was a private one in his own house, immediately after the Neapolitan production of *Aïda*. Subsequently he relented and, according to Weissmann, even became enthusiastic about a proposal, originating in London, to play it on a full string orchestra.

CHAPTER XVIII

B<small>Y THE</small> middle of April Verdi was back at Sant' Agata, but the death of Alessandro Manzoni on the 22nd of May 1873 soon came to disturb his repose. He entertained for the author of *I Promessi Sposi* a veneration similar to that which he had felt for Cavour. As with that statesman, he could not bring himself to go to the funeral, but on the 2nd of June he made a secret journey to Milan to visit the grave. A day or two later he wrote to the Mayor of Milan offering to compose a Requiem Mass for the anniversary of Manzoni's death. "It is," he said, "a heart-felt impulse, or rather necessity, that prompts me to do honor as best I can to that Great One whom I so much admired as a writer and venerated as a man." The offer being gladly accepted, the rest of 1873 was divided between Sant' Agata and Paris, where the sight of the ruins of the Hôtel de Ville and the Tuileries much affected him. He worked at the Mass in both places, using, apparently, as a basis for his labors, an Italian version of the Latin text, a joint product of the independent collaboration of Angelo Fava and Carlo Borri — which seems to suggest that little of his Latin had followed him from Busseto to Milan in the old days.

Possibly a substantial portion of the general scheme was already in his mind. It will be remembered that Verdi's allotted share in the Rossini Mass had been the final number, *Libera Me*, which he had completed and almost forgotten. Somehow or other it came to the notice of Mazzucato, a professor of composition, æsthetics, and history at the Milan Conservatoire, who had sat with him on the Florentine commission for the reform of Italian conservatoires. In his answer to Mazzucato's enthusiastic letter of praise, Verdi, in 1871, confessed that commendation from such a quarter almost made him inclined to finish the Mass himself, especially as he had sketched the main ideas of the *Requiem* and *Dies Iræ*, "but," he added, "reassure yourself; the temptation will pass as many others have done."

This material, therefore, was ready to hand, though the actual process of composition was far from being the only labor in connection with the Mass. Verdi, warned by the previous fiasco of the Rossini Mass, was at great pains to ensure a performance worthy of the occasion. The acoustical properties of the churches of St. Mark and the Madonna de le Grazie were carefully weighed. Maria Waldmann was instructed to see to it that her contract with the Florentine Opera should not prevent participation in the Mass; and when, despite this precaution, difficulties arose with the Florentine management as to letting her and other artists appear at the appointed date, Verdi successfully used all the influence at his disposal to prevent a postponement, which, he felt with reason, would be a stultification of the whole idea. Finally, on the 22nd of May 1874, the first performance took place at the Church of St. Mark in Milan. The soloists were Stolz, Waldmann, Capponi, and Maini; there was a picked orchestra of a hundred and a chorus of one hundred and twenty; Verdi himself conducted.

The Mass was a brilliant success, not only, it seems, because of its intrinsic merit but because of the exceptional excellence of the interpretation. On the latter point all the critics were agreed. The sole flaws found even by the meticulous Filippi were an occasional overemphasis on the part of the soloists and a slightly confused rendering of the fugue, *Pleni Sunt Cœli*. They were practically as unanimous with regard to the musical value. In Filippi's notice, a very fine and learned example of musical criticism, there is the statement that "for *Canto Fermo*, calm, grave, and impassive music without modulations or bar signs, a faith, I would almost venture to say a religious exaltation, quite alien to the spirit of our times, is necessary." On this basis is justified the progressively more human and emotional treatment of the Mass by composers such as Mozart, Cherubini, and Beethoven, culminating in the unabashed drama of the Manzoni Requiem. Filippi then went through the Mass number by number, praising everything, especially the *Dies Iræ*, "a poem full of things terrifying and at the same time moving and pathetic."

The critic of the *Gazzetta Musicale*, though expressly denying Filippi's premises in the matter of religious faith, agreed with him in his conclusions as to the value of the music. Indeed, he took definite pleasure in its dramatic nature, protesting, with Rossini, that music was of two kinds only, the good and the bad, and that any fundamental distinction between theatrical and ecclesiastical music was illusory. *Il Pungolo*, glorying in the fact that an Italian composer should have written a work indisputably worthy to rank with those of any foreign composer "from Wagner to Glinka" (of all odd pairs), asserted that the Mass was not theatrical at all, but purely human. The *Corriere di Milano* delighted in its dramatic nature and asked whether such a virile and theatrical composer as Verdi could be expected to carry the example of the saintly Origen into the domain of music.[1]

The production of the Mass had aroused European interest and people came from France, Germany, and Austria to hear it. The church could not contain anything like all those desirous to gain admission; even such important visitors as journalists from Paris had

[1] The curious reader may be referred to the fifteenth chapter of Gibbon's *Decline and Fall* for an explanation of the allusion.

to be accommodated in the organ gallery. Wherefore three further performances (the first conducted by Verdi himself, the other two by Franco Faccio) were arranged at La Scala. Here the audience, unfettered by ecclesiastical surroundings, were able to give full vent to that enthusiasm which has always been the life-blood of musical performances in Italy. The newspaper *Il Sole* gives a vivid account of the evening. On the left side of the stage was the orchestra; on the right, the chorus. The entrance of the soloists, Stolz in a dress of blue silk trimmed with white velvet, Waldmann in unrelieved pink, was received with acclamations that redoubled when Verdi himself appeared. But Verdi, "severe as ever, taking his place at the desk in the middle of the stage . . . immediately gave the signal to begin and the applause ceased as if by magic." During the performance the enthusiasm grew until the *Offertorium* was actually encored; so was the *Sanctus*. But the climax was reached in the *Agnus Dei*, where "the applause changed to roars, which, though stifled, even broke out during the actual performance, so irresistible was the inspiration of the music." Needless to say, this, too, was encored, and afterwards, amid the wild plaudits of the assembly, "a silver crown on an elegant cushion was presented to Verdi."

This revelatory account of the reception of the Requiem Mass is of importance because it provides the best possible illustration of the difference between the reactions of the public of that time and of our own to a work of this character. True, the performance at the Church of St. Mark had taken place in a very different atmosphere, but that performance was an isolated event. Generally speaking, the Requiem Mass was approached like any other piece of music — like an opera, the reader may well say. Nor was this attitude confined to Italy, though found there in its most extreme form; for at later performances in Vienna and London various numbers were also encored. It is difficult for us, who live in a period when applause is discouraged during performances even of secular music, to understand this point of view. We must, however, try to enter into it to some extent if we wish to understand the nature of what is indubitably a masterpiece. Possibly no work of art could or should be considered apart from the circumstances in which it was produced, and of those circumstances the contemporaneous attitude of the public is an important factor.

If such manifestations tempt us to think that Verdi sacrificed the artistic seriousness and sincerity of his work to considerations of mere effect, we shall be completely wrong. No music has ever been inspired by feelings more sincere than those which prompted Verdi to write this Mass. He had always entertained the warmest admiration for Alessandro Manzoni; since their personal acquaintance in

1868 he had, in his own words, "venerated him like a saint." Verdi was incapable of pose, and his actions, already described, on the occasion of Manzoni's death sufficiently attest the depth of his feeling. Nor must we be led astray by the accident of the music being written in an essentially theatrical idiom. Verdi wrote the music in this way because it was the natural way in which to express himself. With his unrivaled technical skill, his profound knowledge of old Italian music, his almost fanatical devotion to Palestrina, nothing would have been easier for him than to produce an essay in the traditional ecclesiastical manner; but the result would have been less, not more, sincere than the actual idiom of the Requiem Mass; though an Englishman, to whom the terms "theatrical" and "insincere" are practically synonymous and the wholly natural theatricalism of an Italian is very alien, may find difficulty in appreciating the fact. Not all the music of the Requiem Mass is theatrical or even objective — the *Agnus Dei* and the *Lux Æterna* for instance — but the conception as a whole is undoubtedly approached from a dramatic point of view. The *Dies Iræ* is like a canto from Dante's *Inferno*, with the *Tuba Mirum* section as it were an imaginative illustration by Gustave Doré. Even the fugue of the *Libera Me* is expressive of definite emotion, while the beginning and end of the same movement paint the most poignant anxiety and apprehension. The orchestration throughout, extraordinarily colorful and effective, is designed to heighten the emotional and dramatic appeal.

The music of the Requiem Mass is fully dealt with elsewhere, but these few instances should suffice to indicate to the reader the nature of a work worthy to rank among the best compositions of the kind. Doubtless the theatrical idiom prevented its appreciation by a certain school of musicians. Other liturgical works, such as the Requiem Masses of Berlioz and Cherubini, Beethoven's Mass in D, even portions of Bach's B minor Mass had been dramatic, but none, perhaps, with the exception of the Berlioz, is quite so theatrical as Verdi's. It was this aspect of the work that first prejudiced von Bülow against the music, though subsequently he became one of its most enthusiastic champions.

The Mass took Italy by storm. So much so that the law had to be invoked to prevent unauthorized performances in other Italian cities. Bologna had ventured to perform it with four pianofortes instead of an orchestra; Ferrara with a military band. Verdi, who had already had reason to complain of negligence in the matter of faulty performances of *Aïda* at Naples, insisted on Tito Ricordi taking the most drastic steps to prevent such travesties of his intentions. It is clear, however, that his attitude to the Manzoni Requiem was never quite the same as to the Rossini Requiem. Perhaps he felt that what the Romans would have called "piety" had been satisfied by the performance at St. Mark's Church. Perhaps he thought that the publicity of such a tribute to a patriot so well known and esteemed as Manzoni would benefit Italian prestige. Whatever the reason, he treated the Mass like any other of his compositions, arranging for the payment of royalties with all his typical and customary care. So far from standing in the way of further productions, he did his best to promote them and actually himself went to Paris after the first of the Scala performances to launch the Mass there.

Moreover, his letters from Genoa during the winter of 1874-5 attest his personal enthusiasm for a tour of the Mass that was being arranged by Ricordi and Escudier. The cities originally chosen for this tour were Paris, London, Berlin, and Vienna. The Berlin arrangements fell through, and the proposal of Gye to take advantage of the absence of Patti and the presence of Stolz and Verdi to combine the performance of the Mass with a production of Aïda at Covent Garden came near imperiling the London venture. Verdi, by no means the kind of man to allow any work of his to be presented as a substitute for a prima donna, however distinguished, threatened not to go to London at all if the Mass were given at Covent Garden instead of at the Albert Hall. Finally everything was arranged, and on the 19th of April the tour opened in Paris at the Opéra Comique, with Stolz and Waldmann in the parts originally written for them and Masini and Medini as tenor and bass. Its success was even greater than that of the year before; eight performances were given instead of four, and, after the third, Verdi was made a Commander of the Legion of Honor. From Paris Verdi and his colleagues proceeded to London, where the Mass received its first public performance at the Albert Hall on the 15th of May. Barnby, a singularly enterprising musician, had trained the chorus of twelve hundred; Stainer was at the organ. Excluding a semi-public rehearsal two days previously, to which Messrs. Novello invited a number of distinguished or useful persons, there were three performances, and the reception was most enthusiastic, though some people, including the composer's admiring biographer, Crowest, were rather scandalized by the secular flavor of the music.

On the whole, the press shared the enthusiasm of the public. The *Pall Mall Gazette* roundly declared that this was "the most beautiful music for the church that has been produced since the Requiem of Mozart." *The Times*, though its notice was curiously superficial, declared that the composer owed nothing to any of his predecessors. "The intense feeling," it says, "for which certain passages are distinguished cannot but impress all hearers attentively alive to what the composer has to say and willing to accept it in the belief that he is speaking out his mind with earnest sincerity." Perhaps the most interesting notice is that of the *Daily Telegraph*. Except for a surprising lack of appreciation of the fugal writing and the description of the *Tuba Mirum* as "puerile," the critic waxes enthusiastic over the music as a whole. He notes the predominance of the orchestra over the voice in the opening number, which "nobody who is conversant with Verdi's latest manner could be surprised at." He describes the *Mors Stupebit* as a masterpiece in its way; the *Lacrymosa* as "the climax of achievement." He notes in the *Recordare* "a genuine, though distinctive, melody and the masterly use of the orchestra." Most interesting, as showing how little musical conditions in England change fundamentally, is the critic's tilt at "the believers in the exclusive merit of German music"; most sensible is his dismissal of the objection of "Puritans who think all sacred music should conform to English standards."

The one discordant note came from the *Morning Post*, which disliked the Mass from beginning to end. The critic flayed the "shouting" of the chorus in the *Dies Iræ;* "the pale reminiscence" of *La Traviata* in the *Recordare;* the "canine vociferation" of the *Libera Me*. He refused to class the work either with opera or with sacred music; "It is simply a study of orchestral colouring with vocal accompaniment. . . . There is no melody that the mind can receive consonant with the words, and the breaking of those words into short, sharp ejaculations, like a series of barks or yells, is certainly not indicative of reverence. But, if it were possible so far to control the voices as to soften this peculiarity, the droll accompaniment still remains, with its pantomimic melody and ungrammatical, ineffective harmonies." With a tilt at "Beethoven, Haydn and even Weber" for having sinned in the same manner as Verdi, but in a far lesser degree, with regard to sacred music, the scandalized critic then sums up as follows: "Considering the entire want of agreement between the style of the music and the nature of the words, the conclusion that must be made is that the Requiem Mass was never intended to be accepted seriously, but that the whole thing is a *charivari* view of the subject. As such it is clever, and may be quoted as another instance of the power of music to excite humorous feelings."

This diatribe might be received with more respect but for the strong presumption that the writer never attended the performance or, if he did, followed it with little attention. Apart from the fact that no mention is made in the whole article of the quality of the executants or the attitude of the public, the critic, unfortunately for himself, has singled out as the best piece of writing in the work the fugal setting of the words *Liber Scriptus*. Now, these words had originally been set in a fugal style, but just before the Paris performance Verdi had rewritten them as a solo for Maria Waldmann, which was, in fact, given for the first time at the London performances. Clearly what happened was that the critic had made an exhaustive preliminary study of the original piano score, though the fact that he speaks of the primary importance of the orchestra in the eyes of the composer having "the particular advantage of relieving the composition from the general character of humour which the opening presents in the pianoforte score" distinctly suggests a wish to convey the impression that he was present at the concert.

Verdi, who paid scant attention to criticism, was probably little moved by these conflicting judgments one way or the other. He liked London except on a Sunday, when he complained that the city resembled a desert. He found time, too, to go to the Handel Festival at the Crystal Palace, writing to Escudier that "these three or four thousand executants are only a huge *blague*," though he subsequently informed him that the English were certainly more musical than they used to be. But his stay was short, for by the 11th of June he was due in Vienna, where the tour concluded with a performance of the Mass that seems to have been exceptionally satisfactory. Immediately afterwards Verdi returned to Sant' Agata, more than half convinced, apparently, that his career as a composer was now finished.

CHAPTER XIX

In view of what we know did in fact happen, some effort of imagination is necessary to understand Verdi's state of mind at this time, to appreciate his outlook on the probable future. He was, be it remembered, sixty-two years old and, though his health and vitality remained an object of wonder to all who came in contact with him, he may well have thought himself entitled to rest on his laurels. In a letter written to the Countess Maffei in March 1875 he had given his views on the subject: "Are you right when you speak of my conscientious obligation to write? No, no. You are joking, because you know better than I do that the account is balanced (*le partite sono saldate*). That is to say, I have always conscientiously carried out the undertaking I entered into; the public has met me equally conscientiously, with sincere hisses, applause, etc. So nobody has the right to complain, and I repeat once more, 'the account is balanced.'"

After the fatigues of the tour with the Mass we may be sure that Verdi held this opinion more rather than less strongly. Its undoubted success made no difference to his general outlook, which remained, as always, basically pessimistic. He prepared to settle down once more to the life of a practical farmer at Sant' Agata, where, indeed, he passed the greater portion of the next few years. He was often to be seen at Cremona at the weekly market, buying stock. He personally directed the sinking of an artesian well. In the early eighties, when there was much unemployment, he contrived to make work in the house and on the estate for the relief of local distress. Complaining of the stubborn ignorance of the peasants, he endeavored to combat it by technical instruction, especially in the matter of viticulture. Above all, he paid the greatest attention to his beloved horses, about which it may be doubted whether any musician has ever known so much as Verdi. He took charge of their schooling from the very beginning. For instance, in this very year 1875, just before the tour of the Mass, he wrote the most precise instructions to his bailiff on the matter: "The youngest colt should be continually in harness and must never be allowed to break its trot, which should always be slow and gentle. You will see that next year he will go splendidly, perhaps as well as the other. And as regards this other, take great care that he does not develop some vice. He is a horse who is very much above himself and, being at the same time very quick, he might easily come to some harm."

Then there were the dogs which played such an important part in life at Sant' Agata. Verdi had always liked dogs; even in early days the Maltese spaniel Lulu accompanied him and Giuseppina to Naples for the rehearsals of *Simon Boccanegra*, as is proved by Delfico's caricatures. But the big dogs at Sant' Agata were more than pets; they were part of the establishment, guarding the house in the master's absence and on one occasion ungraciously chasing away a band of itinerant musicians who thought to please the composer by playing a selection of his more popular operas outside the gate. Verdi found in them a companionship that he granted to few human beings, and a monument to one: "My true and faithful friend," stands in the garden to this day. The parallel with Wagner's well-known love for animals will strike many, but Verdi's attitude was more that of the true countryman. For this reason, perhaps, he never thought of introducing either dogs or horses into his operas.

In a very charming letter written to Maria Waldmann on her marriage, in 1876, to the Count Galeazzo, thanking her for her collaboration in the past and wishing her every happiness in the future, Verdi thus sums up his life at this period: "About myself in particular I have little to tell you, even less than little. I do nothing and I know nothing about anything. I wander about the fields until I am tired out; then I eat and sleep. That is all. What a fine life! you will say. True, there is little poetry in it, but after all it is a life like any other; and perhaps there are worse."

Nor did his winter sojourns in Genoa materially alter matters, except as regards the mere accident of environment. Genoa has never been and is not now a city characterized by social, artistic, or intellectual activity. Nowhere else in Italy, perhaps, do the inhabitants keep themselves so much to themselves. When one of Verdi's biographers goes so far as to say that he settled there in order to avoid music and musicians, he overstates the case but little. Verdi liked Genoa because of the possibility it offered him for that secluded life he so much valued, the absence of any of those social obligations unavoidable in Milan, Rome, or Turin. Had he had any inclination to live elsewhere, he would undoubtedly have done so at the end of 1874, when he left the Palazzo Sauli (subsequently pulled down to be replaced by the offices of an electricity company) and at the first opportunity moved into new quarters in the Palazzo Doria, just below the railway station, which he occupied for the rest of his life.

Nevertheless, Verdi exaggerated somewhat in saying that he "knew nothing about anything." A very remarkable letter, written in the summer of 1875 to Arrivabene and quoted in full elsewhere, shows that his musical judgment was as acute as ever. At the end of 1876 he was, further, much exercised by the degradation of the Italian Parliament. On his return from the tour of 1875 he had been nominated a senator, partly on account of his artistic eminence, mainly because of the large amount for which he was liable in direct taxation;[1] but he never again took an active part in politics. The vanity and pretensions of all parties were equally distasteful to him. "No [political] color frightens me," he wrote, "but I am afraid of intolerance and violence. What is more, I believe, and always shall believe, that the progress of the world is due to men of talent and good sense." He was of the same opinion in 1881. "What do I care about the constitution or the political color of a government?" he wrote to Arrivabene. "In reading history I observe great exploits, great crimes, and great virtues in the governments of kings, priests, and republicans alike! What do I care, I repeat? All I demand is that those who conduct public affairs shall be citizens of great talent and immaculate honesty." Verdi, though a lifelong liberal, hated demagogues. As previously indicated, he believed in men, not systems. At this time, indeed, when, as he told the Countess Maffei, he was so depressed that he had to take refuge in his usual habit of reading the worst books he could find in order to be able to laugh at them afterwards, he repeatedly sighed for "a man, a man." This attitude in a person of so strong and independent a character as Verdi is of more than individual and contemporary interest in that it explains the welcome extended to Mussolini in our own time by many Italians holding similar views.

Even the death in 1878 of Pius IX awoke in him a sympathetic echo. "Fundamentally he was a good fellow and a good Italian, better than many others who are continually prating of patriotism." Partly, no doubt, this was mere sentiment. All the great figures associated with his active life were passing away: first Cavour, then Rossini, Mazzini, Manzoni, and now the Pope. In any case Verdi was not the man to belittle a worthy and high-minded antagonist.

A curious incident dates from the period under review. Early in 1876 an unsuccessful composer, by name Vincenzo Sassaroli, sent a registered letter to Ricordi in which he demanded rather than asked permission to set the libretto of *Aïda* to music. A prey to one of those musical hatreds not unfamiliar to historians, Sassaroli was under the delusion that the triumph not only of *Aïda* but of the Requiem Mass was entirely due to journalistic propaganda. He was particularly angry at the claim made for *Aïda* as having first achieved the successful fusion of German and Italian styles, stating that the same compliment had been paid to his own early works in 1846, when Verdi was writing cabaletta operas, "as he has always done."

Reading between the lines, it is clear that the unfortunate Sassaroli, who had to earn his living by giving lessons, was suffering from per-

[1] Bragagnolo-Bettazzi.

secution mania. He had had business relations with Ricordi in the past and believed that he had been shelved to make way for an unduly favored rival. Now was the opportunity to prove his worth. He would take the libretto of *Aïda* exactly as it stood and set it to music; judgment on the comparative result would be passed, not by a venal press or an ignorant public, but by a jury consisting of three maestri nominated by himself, three by Verdi, and one other by the six in conjunction, "incapable of being fascinated or dazzled by long trumpets, by double scenes, by niggers, by chariots, by oxen led in triumph, by telegrams, Cairo, or the Khedive." Ricordi published what Sassaroli himself called "this gauntlet of defiance" in the *Gazzetta Musicale* with a few facetious comments, which so infuriated the poor composer that he not only wrote a second letter (also printed) but devoted some of his modest savings to the publication of a forty-page pamphlet entitled: *Considerations on the Actual State of Music in Italy and on the Artistic Importance of Verdi's Opera "Aïda" and Requiem Mass, by Maestro Sassaroli; with Two Letters Containing the Challenge Issued by Him to the Publisher, Tito Ricordi, and the Maestro, Giuseppe Verdi, and Refused by Them.* The grandiloquent title is sufficient evidence of the author's mentality.

Verdi, needless to say, took no notice. To begin with, he was not, as we have seen, in a mood to disturb himself unnecessarily. Moreover, during most of the controversy he was in Paris superintending the production of *Aïda* at the Théâtre Italien. His object in going was twofold: first, doubtless, to secure an adequate production of his most important opera; second, as the leading Italian musician of the day, to set a higher standard of performance at the Italian theater, which, after being closed for two years, had been reopened for his special benefit under the auspices of Léon Escudier. In the latter respect he was not, as he himself admits, permanently successful, but as regards *Aïda* his desires were completely realized, for the performance of the opera on the 22nd of April 1876, the first in France, was a triumphant success. Verdi himself conducted the two opening performances, subsequently handing over the control to his reliable but not remarkably gifted pupil Muzio; Stolz and Waldmann undertook their original roles, and a promising young bass called Édouard de Reszke appeared in the part of the King. So successful indeed was *Aïda* that it sufficed to sustain the tottering fortunes of the Théâtre Italien till 1880, when the theater was pulled down to make way for the present Bank of France and, incidentally, both the brothers Escudier, now fortunately reconciled, died. During the last years of Léon Escudier's life relations between him and Verdi had perceptibly cooled. Apparently he had made unsatisfactory contacts and been unduly negligent with regard to performances. A letter written to

Muzio in October 1879 makes it clear that only their long business relationship prevented Verdi from changing his publisher.

With or without Escudier, however, it became evident that something would have to be done about assuring *Aïda* a permanent place in the Parisian repertory. For many years the Opéra had wanted a French version, for as early as 1873 the director, Halanzier, had approached the composer in this sense; but Verdi, embittered by his past experiences of "La Grande Boutique," frigidly, if politely, refused. In 1879, however, Halanzier had given place to Vaucorbeil, one of whose first acts was to pay a visit to Sant' Agata to beard the lion in his den. Apparently Verdi took a genuine liking to Vaucorbeil, for he granted to him what he had so often refused to others and went himself to Paris in the early spring of 1880 to superintend the production of du Locle's and Nuittier's French version of *Aïda* at the Opéra. When it was produced on the 22nd of March, its success equaled, if it did not surpass, the previous production at the Théâtre Italien. Verdi was acclaimed, fêted, and created a Grand Officer of the Legion of Honor. Reconciliation with the Opéra was complete — and permanent.

During all this period Verdi, so far as he was concerned with music at all, was interested in past more than in future compositions. But a remarkable and very important incident, which took place in 1879, seems to suggest that he was not quite so indifferent as he appeared to be. A certain Dupré had written an article in the *Gazzetta Musicale* in which he quoted Rossini's remarks to him about Verdi's inability to write a comic opera; whereupon Verdi, extremely piqued, to say the least, sent the following letter to Ricordi on the 26th of August:

> DEAR GIULIO:
> I have read in your paper Dupré's description of our first meeting and the judgment of Jupiter Rossini (as Meyerbeer used to call him). But look here! I have been searching for twenty years for a comic-opera libretto and, now that I have practically found one, you with your article instill into the public an unreasonable desire to condemn my opera in advance, thus prejudicing your interests and mine. But have no fear. If by chance, unfortunately, fatally, despite the August Pronouncement, my evil genius should lure me to write a comic opera, have, I repeat, no fear. . . . I will bring ruin on some other publisher!

Ricordi, though admitting that there should have been a footnote in the paper indicating Verdi's success in the delineation of such a comic character as Fra Melitone in *La Forza del Destino*, reasonably disclaimed editorial responsibility for his contributor's opinions. But he could not contain his surprise at learning in so casual a manner that Verdi was seriously considering the composition of a comic opera. Of the seriousness of the consideration, however, there can be no doubt; another letter, written to Filippi a week later, clinches the matter. We do not know what was the libretto that Verdi had in mind. Could it, even in those days, have been *Falstaff*? Hardly.

As a matter of fact, the only new music that did actually materialize was unimportant, consisting of settings of the *Pater Noster* and the *Ave Maria* in the versions of Dante, whom Verdi had grown to admire equally with Shakspere. These were the result, it appears, of a promise made some time previously to the Società Orchestrale of Milan,[2] at whose concert they were produced on the 18th of April 1880, the *Pater Noster*, a fine example of choral writing in five parts, achieving, in particular, a notable success. Incidentally, it is clear from the account of Vaucorbeil's successful visit to Sant' Agata in September 1879 that the *Pater Noster*, at any rate, was then written, for one of the ways to Verdi's heart found by that astute or lucky manager was the playing of the manuscript as it lay on the piano.[3]

The important event at this period, however, was not a production or a composition, but a dinner party.

[2] Neisser, quoting Seletti.   [3] Pougin.

CHAPTER XX

In the summer of 1879 Verdi, Franco Faccio, and Giulio Ricordi were dining together and, in connection with Shakspere's *Othello*, the conversation turned on Boïto. The next day Faccio brought Boïto to see Verdi, and three days later Boïto produced a sketch of a libretto on the subject. Thus was established a contact between the two men destined to give birth to the two greatest masterpieces of Italian opera. It seems to have been the result of a deliberate conspiracy on the part of Ricordi and Faccio, probably aided and abetted by the Countess Maffei. This was not the first time the two men had been brought into contact, for, as we have seen, it was Boïto who wrote the words of the *Inno delle Nazioni*, produced in London in 1862; but between that time and the dinner party in 1879 they had drifted quite apart — indeed, at one time into positions of open antagonism.

Since Boïto was the most interesting as well as the most important of all the people who exercised an influence on Verdi, some exposition of the facts in general and his career in particular seems imperative. When he wrote the words of the cantata he was only twenty years old. Born in 1842, the son of a Polish lady of noble but impoverished family and of an Italian miniature-painter who seems to have been equally indifferent to wife and family alike, he entered the Milan Conservatoire at the end of 1854 and stayed there for seven years, giving, even in those early days, exceptional proofs of his versatility and precocity. Indeed, his verses were considered even more remarkable than his compositions, in which his teachers, it is interesting to note, found so little sense of rhythm that they prescribed a course of dance music. Eventually, however, in 1861, he was sufficiently successful to win a monetary prize that enabled him to proceed to Paris, together with his friend and fellow student Faccio. Here the two young men paid their respects to Rossini, who seems to have been kind to them and often asked them to his house; they further made the acquaintance of Berlioz and Verdi — whence, presumably, the commission to write the words of the cantata.

From Paris Boïto, after paying visits to his relations in Poland, made a journey to Germany, Belgium, and England to improve his mind even more than to extend his musical knowledge. Returning to Milan with his funds exhausted, he then supported himself not only by writing musical and other artistic criticism but by translating stories and poetry from the Polish. He collaborated in an unsuccessful comedy as well as in the editorship of a weekly paper originally founded by Ghislanzoni. He wrote both words and music of an opera called *Hero and Leander*, not to mention a libretto on the subject of Hamlet for his friend Faccio. He produced a quantity of ingenious poetry, some of it of great merit. Then, in 1865, he turned his attention to the composition of *Mefistofele*, interrupted almost immediately by his volunteering to join Garibaldi's expedition to the Tyrol in the Austrian war.

Even before the *Inno delle Nazioni*, however, Boïto had shown scant reverence for Verdi, for as a lad he had amused himself by turning "*La donna è mobile*" into a polka; but the immediate cause of the hostility between the two must be traced to a poem written in 1863 in which Boïto, probably with Faccio in his mind, referred to the advent of a composer who should once again set up the glory of Italian music "on that altar soiled like the wall of a brothel." Verdi, as the most popular composer of the day, naturally took the insult as directed against himself. "If," he wrote to Ricordi, "I am among those who, as Boïto says, have sullied the altar, let him clean it and I shall be the first to come and light a candle in his honor." The rancor, however, persisted, for the name of Boïto did not figure in the list of composers selected to compose the Mass in memory of Rossini, though *Mefistofele* in its original form had been produced at La Scala the year previously. It is impossible, perhaps, to acquit Verdi of all personal feeling in this matter. The case, however, is not quite so black as it seems. Historians, aware of the great importance of *Mefistofele* in the annals of opera, impressed, as they must needs be, by the new ingenuity of the music and, above all, by the masterly synthesis of Goethe's *Faust* in the libretto, too easily forget that these qualities were far from being recognized in 1869. *Mefistofele* had just achieved one of the most sensational failures in the history of La Scala. The critic Filippi, to his great honor, had dared to defend it warmly, roundly asserting that the prologue alone was sufficient proof of Boïto's greatness; but the majority of the press dismissed the music as the ravings of a lunatic, while the public was not so much indifferent as actively hostile. Not till seven years later, at Bologna, did the opera, after undergoing, be it noted, considerable revision, win a success destined to be world-wide. It was reasonable, then, that Verdi, in 1869, should have felt no call to number among the leading composers of the day a young man, however talented, whose sole important work had recently encountered almost unprecedented opposition. It was reasonable, it was even natural — but we could wish that it had been otherwise.

During the seventies Boïto's opinions underwent a complete

change. He, who had been one of the apostles of Wagner in Italy, was so impressed by *Aïda* and the Requiem Mass that his distaste for Verdi's music turned to unbounded enthusiasm. As a matter of fact, it seems to me that Boïto's dislike of Verdi's early operas was more apparent than real. He was only twenty-one when he wrote the offending poem, an excitable, nervous young man, irritated by the excessive admiration poured by an uncritical public on works more distasteful to him, perhaps, for their theoretical æsthetic shortcomings than their practical accomplishments. Certainly in later life he showed no trace of his former opinions (if indeed they ever were his opinions), for it was he who emphasized to Bellaigue the emotions aroused in an Italian by arias such as "*Quando le sere al placido*" from *Luisa Miller.*

Such was the man whom Faccio, playing the part of honest broker between two friends he so greatly admired, brought round to see Verdi in the summer of 1879. Ricordi had long worked for the same end, taking care to keep Verdi informed of Boïto's change of heart and telling him that the composer of the now triumphant *Mefistofele*, though unwilling to write a libretto for anyone else, would esteem it an honor to put aside any composition of his own to write one for Verdi. He emphasized the admiration and friendship felt by himself and Faccio for Boïto and, without excusing past errors, insisted on the fundamental loyalty and honesty of their common friend. The world owes both Franco Faccio and Giulio Ricordi a real debt of gratitude for the tact and enthusiasm that they showed in effecting one of the most important reconciliations in the history of music.

At first things did not go very smoothly. Verdi read and approved Boïto's scenario but, suspicious or merely reluctant, hesitated to commit himself. The idea of *Othello* had originated not with him but with Faccio or Ricordi.[1] The possibilities of *King Lear* still haunted his imagination; there was the comic opera intended to disprove the dictum of Rossini, who, moreover, had himself written an *Otello*. Boïto could send the completed libretto if he so wished, but for fear of disappointments and heart-burnings it would be better if he did not come and discuss the matter in person. "The chocolate venture" (*progretto di cioccolata*), as Verdi and his intimate friends always called the *Othello* project, was being developed at altogether too rapid a pace.

Nevertheless, by the end of the year 1879 at the latest, Verdi had made up his mind, for by the 6th of January 1880 he was already in correspondence with his friend the painter Morelli as to the physical type of Iago. But in marked contrast with his custom hitherto, he approached the matter in the most leisurely fashion, almost immedi-

[1] Ricci.

ately turning his attention to other things — first, the French production of *Aïda* already referred to; second, the revision of *Simon Boccanegra*.

Verdi, who had always entertained a particular affection for this opera despite its decisive failure more than twenty years previously, wished to present it at La Scala. He recognized its defects, for he had told Escudier some years before that it was monotonous and cold, while, writing to Ricordi at this very time, he described the score as "quite impossible in its present state, too sad and dreary altogether." The question was what could be done and who should do it. Boïto was suggested, and he, with considerable reluctance, not improbably to show his good faith, consented to do his best though Piave's libretto seemed to him beyond remedy. Verdi, however, was insistent. In the first letter written to Boïto that is preserved in the *Copialettere*, dated the 11th of December 1880, he confessed that to do nothing would perhaps be the wisest plan of all, but went on to make the curious statement that "what I may call professional reasons prevent my abandoning the idea of putting this *Boccanegra* in order, without an effort at any rate." He admitted that Boïto's general criticisms were just, "but you, absorbed in more elevated labors and with *Otello* in your mind are aiming at a perfection that is here unobtainable. I do not aim so high and, more optimistic than you, refuse to despair. I admit that the table is shaky, but, by putting a leg or two in order, I think it can be made to stand upright. I admit further that none of the characters — a rare phenomenon in any event — is of a kind to make anyone exclaim: 'What a masterpiece of delineation (*è scolpito*)!' Nevertheless, I think something decent might be made of the personalities of Fiesco and Simone."

The crux of the revision lay in what is, in fact, the second act, the first act being called a prologue. Verdi, inspired by some letters of Petrarch, wished to have a scene laid in the Council Chamber at Genoa, wherein the Doge should appeal to the Genoese to remember that both they and the Venetians were Italians. Boïto imagined a scene in the Church of San Siro that aroused Verdi's warmest admiration, but would, he thought, give him too much trouble. Finally Boïto accepted Verdi's idea and made various slight changes throughout the rest of the libretto.

Verdi's revision was far more drastic. Apart from the important new scene, he rescored much of the opera and rewrote many passages throughout. These alterations, which are described in detail elsewhere, sufficed to assure to *Simon Boccanegra* a definite success when it was presented at La Scala on the 24th of March 1881. The performance seems to have been exceptionally good. Verdi, himself the sternest of judges, was satisfied. The cast, which included Maurel as Boccanegra, Édouard de Reszke as Fiesco, Tamagno as Adorno, was exceedingly strong, and the work of the chorus and orchestra under Faccio earned the warmest praise from the critic Filippi, who summed up the evening as one of triumph for everybody concerned; while his colleague Fortis described it as "a most colossal success." Nevertheless, *Simon Boccanegra* cannot be said to have maintained its popularity. The subject, dealing with the election of the ex-pirate Boccanegra as Doge of Genoa and the feuds between the aristocratic and popular parties in that city is a good one. But the details of the plot, wherein everybody is ignorant of the identity of everybody else and the principal female character even of her own, reach a level of obscurity compared with which the tangle of *Il Trovatore* is lucidity itself. From the musical point of view, the score is of great interest, for the recitatives throughout do full justice to the somber dignity of the subject, while nearly all the ensemble-writing is excellent and full of characterization, though only a few of the arias reach the same standard.

But undoubtedly the gem of the entire opera is the important new scene in the Council Chamber. Here Verdi shows a mastery of orchestration and declamatory writing worthy of *Otello* itself, and, did the opera contain nothing else, it would be worth hearing for this scene alone. On the whole, Verdi himself summed up the general characteristics of *Simon Boccanegra* accurately enough when he wrote to Arrivabene that the opera "is gloomy because of its nature it must be gloomy; but it is interesting." Among what may be described as his secondary and less-known works it is the one that usually excites the greatest admiration of connoisseurs. The fact that in 1930 both Vienna and Berlin produced with success Werfel's German version of it sufficiently attests its durable qualities.

Another revision came almost immediately to occupy his attention further. The Opera at Vienna wished to give *Don Carlo*, of which Verdi and Ghislanzoni set out to prepare a new version in four acts, eventually produced in Milan on the 10th of January 1884. The revision seems to have given Verdi more trouble than he anticipated. He was working on it in October 1882, and it was not finished until March 1883, a considerable time for such a quick worker. He was satisfied, however, with the result, which he described to Arrivabene as "more practical and, I think, better from an artistic point of view."

It was almost the only thing with which Verdi was satisfied at this period, during which his pessimism and depression became more marked than ever. In the world of politics the isolation of Italy at the Berlin Congress in 1881 and the occupation of Tunis by the French provoked him to such an extent that he refused even to entertain the idea of producing *Boccanegra* in Paris. The excesses of the Left in Italian politics almost made him despair of his country. In the world of music the outlook seemed just as black. Asked in 1883 to form part of a commission for the reform of musical education, he refused on the ground that all the composers were so tainted with Germanism that nothing worth while could be accomplished. He prophesied the imminent closing of all the Italian theaters. Neither public nor composers knew what they wanted. The government would not grant subsidies; the fees asked by singers were so high that any economic balance was out of the question — an attack of despair that sounds only too familiar to the student of operatic conditions in 1930. Lastly, as was inevitable with so old a man, the hand of death became increasingly active among those intimately connected with him in one way or another. He had never known Wagner personally, but Wagner's death at Venice at the beginning of 1883 strangely affected him. He chronicled the event as follows:

Sad. Sad. Sad!
Wagner is dead!
Reading the news yesterday I was, I say it frankly, bowled over. There can be no question. This is the passing of a great personality! Of a name that leaves a most powerful imprint on the History of Art!

Verdi's feelings were more directly affected in the following year by the death of a friend, Giulio Carcano, the translator of Shakspere, who on his deathbed charged his daughter to send to Busseto the first edition of *I Promessi Sposi*, a gift from Manzoni, bearing the author's signature. The present moved the old man to tears. He was seventy-one; his world was passing away before his eyes. The letters written in answer to the congratulations of friends on his seventieth birthday betray ineffable sadness and discouragement. What was the point of living long? Work? For what object? To please whom? Gratitude is a burden for most men anyhow. To the Countess Maffei, always his most intimate confidante, he was quite explicit: "Gradually I am beginning to find my years excessive and life a sadly foolish, still worse, a useless, affair. What do we do? What should we do? Everything considered, there is only one humiliating, intensely sad answer: Nothing." The kinship of mood between these sentiments and much of Shakspere is evident. Small wonder Verdi considered the author of *Hamlet* "the greatest authority on the heart of man."

CHAPTER XXI

Despite revisions, despite depression, the idea of *Otello* lurked always at the back of Verdi's mind. During the year 1881 and sporadically during the ensuing years he was in correspondence with his friend the painter Morelli about the characters and costumes of the play. Apparently Morelli would have liked Othello himself to be dressed as an ordinary Venetian, but Verdi replied that, as Shakspere had chosen to make a Moor out of Giacomo Moro (a Venetian general in the original Italian story on which the play is based), a Moor he would have to remain. His chief preoccupation was with Iago. Morelli's idea of Iago was a small man of cunning aspect, dressed in black. Verdi approved the black, but confessed that his own idea of Iago was quite different. "If I were an actor," he wrote, "and had to act Iago, I should like to portray rather a spare, tall man with thin lips, small eyes set close together like a monkey's, a high, receding forehead, and head well developed at the back. His manner should be vague, nonchalant, indifferent to everything, skeptical, pungent. He should throw off good and evil sentiments lightly, as if he were thinking of something quite different from his actual utterances. Thus, if somebody reproached him, saying: 'What you propose is infamous,' he would reply: 'Really? . . . I did not think it was . . . don't let us talk about it any more!' A man like this might deceive anybody, even his own wife to a certain extent. A small malevolent-looking man arouses suspicion in everybody and deceives no one." Morelli was told that he ought to paint a picture of Othello prostrate on the ground after the terrible insinuations of Iago, and he in fact made a sketch for such a picture, which Boïto vainly tried to describe to Verdi in March 1884; but the picture itself had not even then materialized. There is no doubt that the figure of Iago, in whom he saw an embodiment of the kind of priest he so much disliked, especially fascinated Verdi. It was no mere coincidence that for a long time he intended to call the opera "Iago."

The whole project nearly came to grief in 1884. After the production of *Mefistofele* at Naples, a banquet was given to Boïto, at which he was reported by a newspaper to have said that he was sorry not to be setting "Iago" himself. Verdi, in his touchy mood, thought that Boïto implied that his music would not be satisfactory and offered to restore the manuscript as a free gift, "without the slightest resentment." Boïto, whose relations with Verdi had been growing steadily more intimate, had no difficulty in proving that he had been misreported. He refused point-blank to accept Verdi's offer, and the storm blew over. Verdi, however, refused to guarantee to complete the opera, writing to Boïto on the 26th of April 1884 that there had been too much talk about it, that he had worked and lived too long, that the years not only of his life but of his labor were excessive: "Heaven forbid that the public should have to say to me too openly: 'Enough.'" Ten days later he wrote to Franco Faccio in much the same strain: "So, in your opinion, I ought really to finish this *Otello*? But why? And for whom? It is a matter of indifference to me and still more to the public."

Verdi speaks of "finishing" the opera, but it is, to say the least, doubtful whether he had as yet composed much of the music. He certainly told both Arrivabene and Giulio Ricordi in March 1883 that he had not written a note at that time. Checchi makes the definite statement that he did not begin writing the score until November 1885 (and, incidentally, that he scored the whole of the first act during the fortnight that he passed at Montecatini during the summer of 1886, working not more than two or three hours a day); but this seems scarcely possible in view of the fact that Verdi wrote to Maurel on the 30th of December 1885 to the effect that *Otello* "is not completely finished, as has been stated, but is well advanced towards completion. I am in no hurry to finish it, because up to now I have not made up my mind to produce it" — his hesitation being due, apparently, to the impossible economic conditions prevailing in the theater.

Besides, he informed the publisher Leduc in January 1886, "my *Otello* (no longer 'Iago') is not finished. True, I did a lot of work on it toward the end of last winter and at the beginning of the autumn, but many things still have to be done to complete the score." Knowing Verdi's habitual procedure, we may surmise that he had most of the music in his mind before he started to write it down. He may even have made definite sketches; in any case it would be perhaps unwise to take his denials to Ricordi and Arrivabene too literally. Where his compositions were concerned, Verdi always showed himself extraordinarily secretive even with his most intimate friends.

Rumor became busy with his intentions. As early as March 1883 Verdi was surprised to read in a paper that "Maurel has again told us that Verdi is preparing a huge surprise for the musical world and in his 'Iago' will give the young 'musicians of the future' a very stiff lesson." He was not at all pleased. "Heaven forbid!" he wrote to Ricordi; "it never has been and never will be my intention to give lessons to anybody. I admire everything I like without prejudice for or against any particular school. I am guided by my own tastes and I let everybody else do as he pleases."

As the facts with regard to the progress of the opera became known, interest not only in Milan but in Paris increased. Maurel wrote, reminding Verdi of a promise to entrust to him the part of Iago. Verdi, though protesting that he never could have made a promise that he was not absolutely sure of being able to fulfill, replied that he could imagine no better interpreter possible, and for the time being closed the subject. A year later, in January 1886, Maurel again returned to the charge, this time trying to persuade Verdi to allow *Otello* to be produced at the Paris Opéra Comique under the direction of Carvalho, who was prepared to do everything conceivable to satisfy the composer's requirements. Verdi, though much pleased, politely refused. "You who know Boïto will not need to be told that in *Otello* he has fashioned a libretto wherein situations and verses alike are extraordinarily powerful. I have tried to give to these verses the most true and significant accents in my power. This quality (it may turn out to be a defect) would be largely lost in translation. It is imperative, then, that *Otello* should be given for the first time in Italian. . . . But, I repeat, any such consideration is premature."

Several celebrated singers wrote in the hope of procuring parts in the new opera, but on some excuse or other all were discouraged except Tamagno, who was told to come quietly to Genoa on his way back from Madrid to talk things over. The journalists began to take a hand in the game, tackling the notoriously reserved Boïto with no success at all and eliciting from Giulio Ricordi, afraid perhaps of his own expansiveness, only the deliberate misstatement that it was a thousand pities that Verdi would or could write no more music.[1] Needless to say, the inscrutable composer himself vouchsafed no information. Outwardly his attention seemed occupied with quite other matters. For instance, he was considering the presentation to the village of Villanova of a tiny hospital with twelve beds, in order to save the poorer inhabitants the tiresome and often fatal journey to Piacenza; while the newspapers credited him with the further intention of restoring the church of the hamlet of Sant' Agata. Since Verdi, who regarded the report as tendentious, never had any such intention, this led to correspondence in which he complained that the newspapers seemed determined to make him out much richer than he was. "You must know better than anybody else," he wrote to Ricordi, "that when I composed a great deal, the price paid for operas was low; now that it is high I hardly compose at all." Even

[1] Checchi.

as late as March 1886 he found time to go to Paris for a week or two, "a little to hear Maurel, a little to see if they are madder than they used to be, a little just to have a change." In July he journeyed post-haste to Milan to be present at the deathbed of the Countess Maffei, his friend for forty-four years and the recipient of his most intimate confidences.

Nevertheless, on the 1st of November 1886 *Otello* was finished, the fact being announced to Boïto in the following laconic note:

DEAR BOÏTO, —
It is finished.
Here's a health to us . . . (and also to Him . . .).
Good-by.
G. VERDI.

On the 18th of December the last pages were sent from Genoa to the copyist. Verdi hated to see them go. He felt as if he had lost a friend. "Poor Otello!" he wrote to Boïto, "he will come back here no more."

The production was announced for the 5th of February 1887 at La Scala, but Verdi had reserved the right, though the public was unaware of the fact, to withdraw the opera at any time during rehearsal or even after the dress rehearsal.[2] Curiosity and excitement were rife in the city. The choice of subject, inseparably associated in the mind of the older generation with Rossini, provoked comment, not all of it favorable. With an insignificant exception, no new work by Verdi had been heard for nearly thirteen years. Some remembered his own declaration that he was too old to write any more, that "music needs youthfulness of the senses, impetuousness of the blood, fullness of life"; that the children of old men "are rickety, anæmic and worse." Others, pointing to Verdi's well-known vitality in comparison with his years, recalled the fact that Professor Fedeli, who looked after him during his annual cure at Montecatini, had declared that he was still perfectly capable of work.[3] Nobody had the slightest idea what the new opera would be like as regards either nature or style, especially as the La Scala rule of exclusion from rehearsals had been enforced even more rigidly than usual.

Though the speculators took advantage of the situation to push up the price of seats to fantastic heights, the theater, with the excep-

[2] This little-known fact is established by a letter to Giulio Ricordi that appeared in the *Berliner Tageblatt* and is included by Werfel in his collection of Verdi's letters. It is of importance as illustrating the sense of experiment felt by Verdi in his new venture.
[3] Bonaventura.

tion of the royal box, was completely filled a quarter of an hour before the performance; the rush for the cheaper seats nearly ended in a free fight, and the approaches to La Scala were thronged throughout the evening by crowds of people unable to gain admission but determined to play some part, however vicarious, in such a historic event.

Monaldi, who was present, gives an extremely vivid account of the scene in the theater, with its atmosphere of tense expectancy. The orchestra, under Faccio, numbered a hundred; so did the chorus. Managers and critics from all Europe were present in force, including Reyer from Paris, Bennett and Hueffer from London. What would their verdict be? As to the reception of the opera by the public there was soon no doubt. Twice in the first act, after the fire chorus and Iago's drinking song, they tried, though vainly, to call Verdi on to the stage. When, at the end of the act, Verdi took his call, "one immense simultaneous shout makes the theater rock. Verdi slightly bends his head and smiles, the frantic enthusiasm of the huge assembly bringing tears to his eyes. He seems to feel the necessity to retire, which the public, with a tardy respect for his age, finally permits him to do."

At the end of the opera renewed and even greater enthusiasm! When the composer left the theater, a crowd of admirers, who throughout the day had lined the streets to applaud his every appearance, unharnessed the horses from his carriage and drew it to the Hotel di Milano, where he always stayed. Bellaigue relates that here, in the midst of those he loved most, Peppina, Teresina Stolz, Faccio, Boïto, and Ricordi, listening to the acclamations of the crowds outside, he was assailed by melancholy. "I feel," he said, "as if I had fired off my last cartridge. Oh, the solitude of Sant' Agata, hitherto peopled by all the creatures of my imagination whom, well or ill, I translated into terms of music! Tonight the public has torn away the veil that concealed my last mysteries. I have nothing left."

And as they spoke of his glory, he continued: "Oh, glory, glory! I so loved my solitude in the company of Otello and Desdemona! Now the crowd, always greedy for something new, has taken them away from me, leaving me nothing but the remembrance of our secret conversation, our dear, past intimacy." But the mood, which will readily be understood by anyone who has experienced the vicissitudes of artistic creation, soon passed, and with a smile on his austere face the old man said: "My friends, if I were thirty years younger I should like to begin a new opera tomorrow, on the condition that Boïto provided the libretto."

When the press notices appeared, the judgment of the critics was as favorable as that of the public. In the *Corriere della Sera*, then

MANUSCRIPT SCORE, *Un Ballo in Maschera*, ACT II

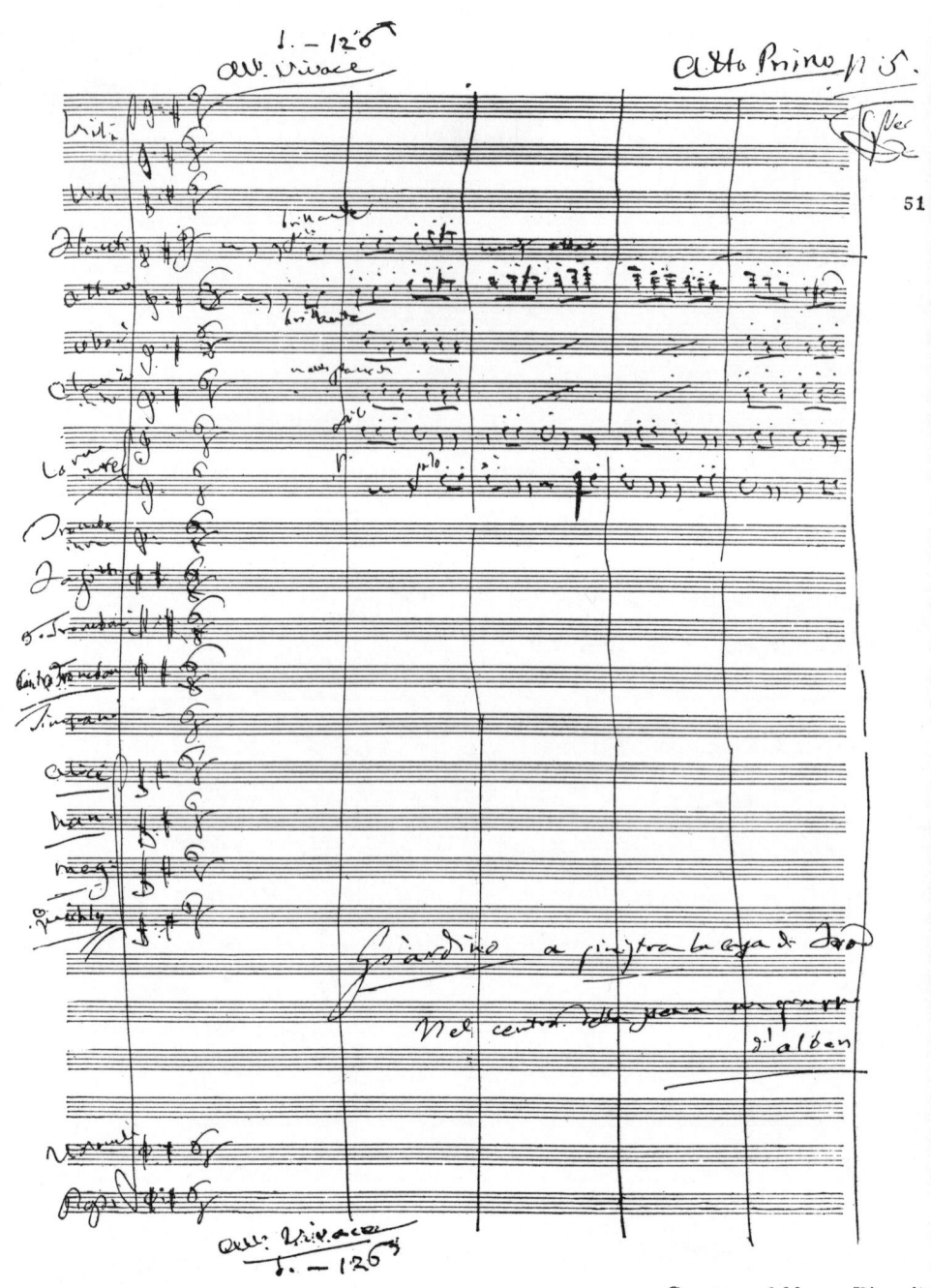

Courtesy of Messrs. Ricordi

MANUSCRIPT SCORE, *Falstaff*: ACT I, SCENE II

beginning to occupy the predominant position in Italian journalism that it still holds, there were criticisms of the first three performances, on the whole exceptionally intelligent. "In no other opera," writes the critic, "has Verdi devoted so much care to detail as in this *Otello*. The recitatives, which are of unique beauty, will, I am sure, after two or three hearings prove to be not one of its least attractions for the public. A most marked feature of this opera is the manner in which Verdi has underlined, as it were, the words that are most important for dramatic expression; while the scoring, even on a first hearing, appeared to be of rare beauty and perfectly balanced." The critic then proceeds to detailed praise, especially of the final duet of the first act, "which alone would suffice to make the fortune of any opera"; of the great ensemble at the end of the third, and of the whole of the last act. He also makes the interesting remark that the measure of the success of the second as compared with the first performance was more like a hundred to one than two to one. Perhaps in part this may have been due to the greater restraint of the audience — an innovation particularly welcome to Verdi. "Do you know the greatest pleasure I had in Milan?" he said to Ricordi; "it was the discovery that the public was intelligent and perceptive enough to guess my wish that the acts should not be interrupted by calls or encores."

The *Nuova Antologia* considered as the greatest merit of Verdi in *Otello* the fact that he had not allowed himself, as regards form, to be bound by any rigid system, especially the Wagnerian system of the leitmotiv. "In his desire for the music to illustrate and comment on the drama he has reserved for himself full liberty of form, abolishing the old divisions and conventions of separate numbers. All the scenes in an act are closely linked together, but it is not true, as has been erroneously asserted, that every act makes an indivisible whole." The critic of the *Secolo* summed up the leading characteristic of the opera with acumen when he wrote: "This is dramatic declamation in strict time substituted for classical recitative on the one hand and Wagnerian polyphony on the other."

The French and the Germans were in agreement with their Italian colleagues. Reyer in the *Journal des Débats* waxed positively lyrical. He particularly emphasized the absence of motifs in *Otello* and the fact that the orchestra, for all the care bestowed upon it, was never allowed preponderance over the singers. "This is sufficient proof, I think, that the score of *Otello*, despite its evident tendencies and the determination to sacrifice every conventional effect to dramatic truth, cannot be compared or likened in any way to works entirely different in type and character. There is no excuse for anybody to believe that the composer in modifying his style has for one moment lost sight of the claims of his own personality." The reference is clearly to Wagner, a similar conclusion being reached by the *Wiener Zeitung*, which affirmed that the obvious change in Verdi's style was due to evolution, not imitation, and that for this reason Verdi's *Otello* was in some respects more remarkable than Wagner's *Parsifal*.

The English critics, Bennett in the *Daily Telegraph* and Hueffer in *The Times*, concurred in the general verdict, the former praising unreservedly Verdi's declamation and power of musical accent, the latter describing his success with the dialogues as astonishing. "The doctrine of Wagner," wrote *The Times*, "is carried out with a rigour that would have astonished Wagner himself . . . but every bar teems with individual and national impulse. In no other opera has Verdi been more himself than in 'Otello.' . . . This is the most remarkable first performance of modern times."

The two English critics agreed, moreover, in rating the last act as the most beautiful of the entire opera and, what is especially interesting, in stating that the performance left something to be desired. This is important, because we are often asked to believe that one of the reasons why *Otello* made its way comparatively slowly in the Italian theaters was the fact that the superlative excellence of the first performance discouraged emulation. As regards detail, the critics differed. Both agreed that the double bass recitative before the entrance of Othello in the last act (strangely enough, encored) was exceedingly badly played. Both agreed that Signora Pantaleoni left a great deal to be desired as Desdemona, that Maurel's performance of Iago was superb. But whereas *The Times* described the famous Tamagno as "almost as good . . . with a voice which though without much charm in the middle register goes up to B flat with perfect ease," the *Daily Telegraph* dismissed him somewhat cavalierly as being "not quite equal to the part." Again, the *Daily Telegraph* characterized the chorus as "moderately good," and wrote that "even Signor Faccio's orchestra, usually so capable, fell short of perfection at important moments." *The Times*, on the other hand, considered the performances of the chorus and orchestra "the most satisfactory features throughout, though the brass was too strong and the wood-wind was not strong enough." Moreover, the critics differed amusingly with regard to certain points about the opera itself, Hueffer singling out the ensemble at the end of the third act for especial praise but thinking that Verdi would have been well advised to make use of motifs in the opera generally, Bennett commending Verdi for the absence of motifs but finding fault with the ensemble in question as "excessively elaborate." Finally, it is interesting to note that nearly all the critics of every nationality concurred in considering the third act as the most difficult of digestion for the public.

On the whole, then, contemporary criticism assigned to *Otello* precisely the merits now universally recognized. It may be doubted whether any other opera has achieved a more satisfactory fusion between music and words, a relationship between voice and orchestra more perfect. We know little or nothing of the details of the collaboration between Boïto and Verdi, what changes, if any, Verdi made in Boïto's original libretto, what share, if any, Boïto had in suggesting a particular line of musical treatment. It is said that Boïto advised against the great ensemble at the end of the third act, but that Verdi insisted, probably because it provided a characteristic example of Italian operatic construction. It is said that Verdi had qualms about Iago's "Credo," which Boïto, drawing on isolated passages in various Shaksperian plays, had inserted in the libretto. Whatever the contributory means, however, the final result was a remarkable, probably unparalleled, example of felicitous collaboration.

A considerable portion of the credit must be assigned to Boïto, for his adaptation of Shakspere's play to operatic purposes is beyond praise. A lesser man could hardly have escaped the lure of the first act. Boïto, to avoid excessive length, discarded it altogether, making use only of some relevant allusions and a few lines of exceptional beauty inserted into the love duet. Certain important points, of course, such as Iago's vague suspicions of Othello and Emilia and the warning by Desdemona's father to Othello that a girl who can deceive her father may also deceive her husband, are inevitably jettisoned; but it is difficult to see how the material as a whole could have been better dealt with. Boïto's treatment of the climax of the tragedy is, if anything, an improvement on Shakspere's, while all through the opera he showed the greatest ingenuity in providing Verdi with every possible opportunity for lyrical expression without sacrificing the truth or the rapidity of the dramatic action. His verses, his general handling, reflect throughout the essential spirit of Shakspere, though it is said that he was only able to read the play in a French translation.

Verdi's music is something of a miracle; in my opinion, more of a miracle than the music of *Falstaff*, usually considered the most extraordinary phenomenon of the century. But is it, in reality, so remarkable that a man of eighty should have written the masterpiece of sparkling wit and mellow wisdom that is *Falstaff* as that a man of seventy-four should have written the masterpiece of intensity and passion that is *Otello*? Doubtless the technical handling of *Falstaff* is, if possible, even more masterly than the technical handling of *Otello;* but the vitality of *Otello* from the first bar to the last, no whit inferior to the vitality of *Aïda* or *Il Trovatore*, would, if it did not exist, be considered incredible in the work of so old a man. The amazing skill with which Verdi follows every shade of meaning, every change of mood throughout the drama; the flexibility of the dialogue, with the points continuously emphasized in an orchestration that is never superfluous, always true to the psychology of the situation; the harmonic invention, as, for instance, in Iago's famous drinking song, where the chromatics suggest in the most subtle manner the Satanic design underlying what appears to be mere boisterous revelry; the ability with which the various personalities are differentiated in the concerted numbers; the lyrical perfection of the opening of the last act, in which, as Mr. Anthony Asquith once beautifully said, "one seems to hear the overtones of Shakespeare" — all these are remarkable enough. But the miracle lies elsewhere. It is to be sought in the intense malignity of Iago, in the passionate, animal jealousy of Othello, in the yearning ache perceptible under the tenderness of that duet between Othello and Desdemona which remains, perhaps, the most satisfactory interpretation of true love, as distinct from passion or lust, in all the annals of opera. How could a man of over seventy feel these things so acutely as to translate them with such poignancy into music? We are fortunately not called upon to solve the riddle, only to be grateful for the fact. There is no question that *Otello* is the greatest tragic opera of Italy; it should rank with *Tristan and Isolde* as one of the two greatest tragic operas of the world.

Despite his triumph, Verdi may well have been glad to leave Milan. To begin with, even his exceptional vitality must have felt the strain of the three months of hard work preparatory to the production of his opera. But this, though exhausting, was not distasteful. What, in view of his temperament, he probably disliked most was the necessity to live so much in public. In addition to the crowds and the journalists, there had been the formal acceptance of tributes from admirers — monstrous things, most of them, such as the cup shaped like a winged dragon carrying a shell with a pearl in the middle, the gift of Signora Pantaleoni — of which the only one that he can have valued at all was a bronze-gilt wreath given him by Faccio on behalf of the orchestra after the dress rehearsal. There had been formal interviews with the authorities of the theater and of the municipality, at which everyone said polite things about everyone else. The sole function of importance that he seems to have avoided was a lunch given by the Mayor of Milan to distinguished foreign visitors, whereat, as a matter of fact, that functionary made an exceptionally illuminating speech descriptive of the bond between Verdi and Shakspere: "In both," he said, "we find the same richness of color, the same capacity to create characters. In the works of the English poet and the Italian composer we feel the same sense of tragedy, making us shudder or weep." Verdi, in spite of his regrets, must have heaved a sigh of relief as his train steamed out of Milan and he became once more "the placid farmer of Sant' Agata."

CHAPTER XXII

With the exception of his usual visits to Montecatini and Genoa, he remained at Sant' Agata most of the year 1887, busy with accounts, farming, and, above all, the building of the miniature hospital at Villanova — a generous action, which, incidentally, caused him considerable trouble, for two years later he was within an ace of demanding its closure owing to complaints about the bad food and general administration. He followed the career of *Otello* with keen interest, being particularly delighted and surprised that the performance given by Faccio at Brescia in the summer of 1887 was a success despite the absence of "stars." Indeed, he waxed quite sarcastic on the subject, writing to Faccio that he had become so accustomed to listening to the praises of the original interpreters of the opera that he had almost come to believe that they must have written it. Incidentally, the letter contains a bitter gibe at the progressives, who, he said, had taken the wind out of his sails by condescending to attend the performances of an opera by such an old-fashioned composer.

He cautioned the president of the International Art Club against inviting him to Rome for the first performance of *Otello* in that city, as had been suggested in the newspapers, because the invitation would certainly be refused — another instance of Verdi's dislike of any public appearance without some good reason. Two years later, in 1889, he wrote an indignant letter to Ricordi about the proposal to make "important modifications" in *Otello* on the occasion of its revival at La Scala in February. The authorities at the theater were told that, if the opera really needed "modifications," they themselves would have to make them; he would prefer the opera to be performed as before, "discordant double-basses and all." Even the success of *Otello* in London in the same year, though the praises bestowed on Boïto in "the country of Shakespeare" sincerely delighted him, only served to evoke bitterness and pessimism. Faccio had written from the Lyceum Theatre, speaking of a triumph of Italian art. "You are wrong," Verdi replied; "our young Italian composers are not good patriots. If the Germans, basing themselves on Bach, have culminated in Wagner they act like good Germans, and it is well. But we, the descendants of Palestrina, commit a musical crime in imitating Wagner, and what we are doing is useless, not to say actually harmful."

There is no doubt that Verdi in the years between 1888 and 1890 was in a very black mood. One by one his few remaining friends were passing away. Arrivabene, his particular crony for more than fifty years, had died just before the production of *Otello*. In November 1890 Muzio died in Paris. Verdi, despite or because of a certain skepticism as to the extent of Muzio's musical gifts, had always felt a profound affection for him. The son of a poor shoemaker at Busseto, he had been Verdi's only pupil and had throughout his life displayed a devotion and loyalty touchingly evident in the simple letter written on his deathbed:

> MY DEAREST MASTER AND FRIEND, VERDI:
> I am afraid my will may give you a little trouble, but I beg you to do what I say. Very soon I shall leave for another world, full of affection for you and for your sweet, dear wife. I love you both, and remember, please, that from the year 1844 my faithful friendship has never failed you. Think of me sometimes, and good-by till we meet in the other world. Many kisses from your faithful and affectionate friend.
>
> E. MUZIO.

Muzio's death and letter moved Verdi deeply. He would have liked to go to Paris for the funeral and, as executor, he occupied himself in person with the carrying out of the most minute details of the will.

The disappearance of Muzio was all the more unfortunate in that he was representing Verdi's interests in a dispute that had arisen in Paris about the French version of *Il Trovatore*. The case, of which the details are exceedingly complicated and dull, need not detain us. Apparently the trouble was mainly due to the carelessness of Escudier in the first instance. The parties involved were the French publisher, Bénoit, Ricordi, and Verdi himself, who was greatly distressed and bothered by having to try to remember the details of a transaction that had taken place more than thirty years before and who, like all sensible men, viewed the law and lawyers with natural suspicion.

But in Verdi's eyes perhaps the most distasteful event of these years was a proposal to celebrate the jubilee of his first opera. He took fright immediately at the idea, which had originated with the paper *La Perseveranza* in the autumn of 1888. The most retiring of men, so fearful of being thought desirous of advertisement that he had refused, two years before, to contribute, except in the strictest anonymity, towards the cost of placing medallions of seven famous Italians on the façade of Florence Cathedral, he was truly shocked by such a proposal. He wrote at once to Ricordi, urging him to use all his influence to nip the project in the bud. "Among all the useless things in the world this is the most useless. . . . If some concession must be made, propose that this jubilee be celebrated fifty days after my death. Three days suffice to wrap men and events in oblivion. The Great Poet says: 'Oh heavens, die two months ago and not forgotten yet?'[1] My trust is in the three days. Good-by."

The project, however, was not abandoned; other papers began to associate themselves with *La Perseveranza*, so Verdi contemplated stronger measures. One of the suggestions had been a festival performance of *Otello*. Ricordi was begged on no account to permit it and told that, if he refused, the letter sent to him on the subject would be published in some foreign paper with a European circulation. Verdi then turned to Boïto, writing him a most sensible and perspicacious letter. Quite apart from his personal feelings, how could such a jubilee be celebrated in practice? By a concert of selections from his works? A commonplace and mean affair! By the performance of some operas? Why, then they would have to do at least three — the first, the last, and one other. And how would the contemporary public, with their changed tastes, enjoy sitting through the two long acts of *Oberto*? Either they would be politely bored — which would be a humiliation — or they would publicly show their disapproval, in which case the event might turn out to be a scandal rather than a festival.

And suppose that the other proposal were adopted, to open a national subscription for a fund to assist budding operatic composers? How much would they get? A small sum would only suffice for one of the usual scholarships, which help neither the scholar nor art. Only a very large sum, difficult to raise in such critical times, could provide the interest sufficient to enable a young composer to produce a first opera. Even then what guarantee was there that the opera would possess merit or, if it did, that the performance would be adequate? The whole scheme was full of difficulties and impracticable; Boïto must do his very best to discourage it.

Verdi's efforts to prevent any official celebration of the jubilee of his first opera were successful, but he was not able and perhaps did not desire to prevent the recognition of the day in some form or other. On the 17th of November, the date when, fifty years before, *Oberto* had been produced at La Scala, messages of congratulation from all over Italy poured in. There was a telegram from the King to his illustrious Senator; another from the Mayor of Milan. Best of all, the *Gazetta Musicale* published in facsimile an autographed letter from Carducci, in which the greatest poet of modern Italy paid a tribute to Verdi as artist and patriot so touching that he wrote a personal letter to express his admiration and gratitude.

[1] *Hamlet*.

If Verdi was averse to any commemoration of his own exploits he showed himself less adamantine where others were concerned. Thus, in May 1889, during the very time when he was fighting tooth and nail against the celebration of his own jubilee, he wrote to Joachim accepting the offer to associate his name with the Beethoven Festival at Bonn. Participation in such celebrations was, he wrote, against his principles but "Beethoven is in question and before his name we all bow in reverence."

Moreover, in 1892, when the centenary of the birth of Rossini was celebrated at La Scala by a performance of some of his music, Verdi consented to appear in person to conduct the prayer from *Mosé*. There had been some talk of coolness, to say the least, as regards Verdi's attitude to Rossini, and many people maintained that he would not accept the invitation to conduct. Possibly his acceptance was prompted by a desire to scotch such baseless gossip. At any rate, on the 9th of April, despite his seventy-nine years, he punctually appeared, receiving an ovation worthy of his graceful gesture. It was the last occasion, so far as we know, on which he came before the public as a conductor.

Exactly how and when the project of *Falstaff* first took definite shape is unknown. Verdi was indubitably sincere in having thought that with the production of *Otello* he had "fired off his last cartridge." But the pressure on him not to retire definitely from the field was strong. Even during the congratulatory visits in connection with the first performances of *Otello*, references were made by one of the authorities of La Scala to the comic opera he had in mind. This was possibly the work already mentioned, or it may have been an opera dealing with Don Quixote, a subject that had been suggested to him at some time or other by the Mayor of Milan. We are told, too, that Giuseppina, who, like the clever and perceptive woman that she was, had helped to break down his reluctance to undertake *Otello*, unobtrusively worked to the same end with regard to *Falstaff*. It seems almost certain, however, that Boïto himself was the principal agent in not only leading Verdi to the water but finally making him drink. Indeed, he is said to have sketched the original scenario in forty-eight hours after a conversation with the composer about comic-opera subjects in general.[2] At any rate, it is in a letter written by Verdi to Boïto from Montecatini in July 1889 that there is first definite mention of *Falstaff*.

"In tackling *Falstaff*," he wrote, "have you ever thought of the enormous number of my years? I know that you in your answer will exaggerate the robust state of my health. Well, even granted that it is as you say, you will nevertheless agree with me that in as-

[2] Barrili.

suming such a burden I may be taxed with great rashness. Suppose I could not stand the strain? Suppose I did not manage to finish the music? Then you would have wasted time and trouble for nothing. I would not have it so for all the money in the world. The idea is intolerable to me; all the more intolerable if your work on *Falstaff* should lead you, I do not even say to abandon your own *Nerone*, but to distract your mind from it or to retard the date of its production. I shall be held responsible for this delay, and the thunders of public malevolence will fall on my head."

Boïto succeeded, nevertheless, in alleviating the old man's scruples, and a year later the composition of *Falstaff* had begun. The secret was first revealed to the world in November 1890. Verdi, Boïto, and some friends were dining at Ricordi's house. When, at the end of dinner, Boïto rose to his feet, glass in hand, everybody expected him to give the toast of the veteran composer. Instead he proposed the health of "Fat-paunch." Since everyone present happened to be thin, nobody quite knew what to make of the toast until Ricordi, banging his fist on the table, shouted: "*Falstaff*" — and the riddle was solved.[3]

The news of Boïto's perhaps calculated indiscretion raced through Italy. Verdi was besieged with letters. In answer to one from his future biographer Monaldi, he wrote that he had been desirous to write a comic opera for forty years, that he had known *The Merry Wives of Windsor* for fifty years. The usual and inevitable "buts," however, had always prevented any correlation of the two facts. "Now Boïto has removed all the 'buts' and has provided me with a lyric comedy unlike any other. I am enjoying myself writing the music. I have no definite plans and I do not even know whether I shall finish it. I repeat, I am enjoying myself. Falstaff is a rogue who commits every kind of rascally action, but in an amusing way. He is a type. . . . The opera is wholly comic."

Over and over again Verdi insisted that he was writing *Falstaff* for fun, to pass the time and for no other reason. On the 1st of January 1891 he told Ricordi that, though it was true that about half the music was written, the remaining half, which included the final revision, not to mention the scoring, "which will be a very great labor," must be far the more arduous. In July of the same year he said much the same to someone at Montecatini, save that by this time the music was finished with the exception of the scoring. While as a young man he could often work ten or even twelve hours a day, whatever his state of health, he could now work only when he felt inclined. The opera would certainly not be finished in 1891; he would not guarantee any date.

Six months later he was equally adamant and half inclined, besides,

[3] Checchi.

to have the opera produced privately at Sant' Agata instead of at La Scala. We know from other sources that he worked at it for only two hours a day and, as a matter of fact, Pizzi tells us that Verdi's resolve to proceed slowly with *Falstaff* was a definite decision taken after the reading of a book on fatigue by one Mosso, who exposed the dangers of cerebral anæmia attendant on excessive exertion in old men — a statement that, apart from Pizzi's transparent if not excessively intelligent honesty, seems probable in view of the exceptional preoccupation with questions of health shown by Verdi throughout his life. Verdi feared illness and hated, without fearing, the idea of death. He hated it for the very reason that some Eastern philosophers have welcomed it: because it entails the cessation of activity.

By the summer of 1892, despite three months' interruption from work at the end of 1891 owing to his own and Peppina's indisposition, the score was finished. Verdi then turned his attention to the question of casting the opera — by no means an easy matter, for all the leading singers wanted outstanding parts, whereas Verdi considered that in *Falstaff* all the parts were and must be of equal importance. Over none of his operas did Verdi keep such a strict control as this. He would not have excessive salaries paid to the singers or payment for rehearsals; he would not even bind himself to produce *Falstaff* in any specified place; if he were dissatisfied with the *répétition générale* at La Scala, he would walk out and the opera would be withdrawn. Though he gladly chose Maurel to interpret the leading part, he refused to entertain for one moment that baritone's demand to be granted a monopoly in it for a certain number of subsequent performances. Hohenstein, the scene-designer, who had been sent to England to absorb the atmosphere of Windsor and to copy the old houses in Holborn, had proposed to place the screen in the second act against the wall. Verdi would have none of it, exposing also his own precise views as to how the garden in the second scene of the first act should be represented. In short, Verdi may be said to have treated *Falstaff* very much as a treasured private possession of his own, to be shared with the outside world only on the strictest terms imaginable.

CHAPTER XXIII

Preparations for rehearsals were well advanced in September 1892, but Verdi does not seem himself to have gone to Milan till later, for it was from Genoa at the beginning of November that he wrote to Signora Pasqua (cast for the part of Dame Quickly) certain recommendations as to her solo in the second act. Milan, though excited at the announcement of the first performance of *Falstaff* on the 9th of February 1893, was not perhaps, quite so excited as it had been about the first performance of *Otello*. So far as the public was concerned, the triumph of the earlier opera had solved once and for all any doubt as to Verdi's vitality and competence in his old age. True, there was much discussion as to what form the comic opera would take. Had Verdi consciously followed in the footsteps of the composer of *The Barber of Seville* or had he turned his eyes back to even earlier models, such as *Il Matrimonio Segreto* or *La Serva Padrona*? But these considerations were of greater moment to specialists than to the public at large. Perhaps the prevailing sentiment may best be summarized as one of intense interest rather than of excitement. There arrived, maybe, even more operatic magnates from all over Europe, especially from Germany; even more critics, whom Maurel, greatly daring or greatly hoping, entertained at lunch. Four representatives of the French press even endeavored to enlist the good offices of the composer to obtain the privilege of attending a rehearsal, but their request was met with an exceedingly firm if polite refusal. How could Verdi, the protagonist of privacy in such matters, ask the authorities to be untrue to his own principles?

Needless to say, the performance was a brilliant success. The veneration and enthusiasm of the public for Verdi would have ensured as much in any event. The packed theater, the electric atmosphere, the calls for Verdi and the principal interpreters, the acclamation of the dense crowds in the street — though on this occasion Verdi managed to avoid their attention by slipping out unobserved through a side door at the end of the performance — were but a repetition of those already described on the occasion of *Otello*. But, reading between the lines of contemporary Italian accounts, it is impossible not to realize that the audience failed to appreciate the conclusion of the last act. Indeed, the honest Monaldi openly admits that "after the fairy music and the exquisite romance for the tenor, the music, though graceful and elegant, no longer pleased. Even the final fugue, a splendid piece of music. seemed too long and in no wise beautiful.

The success of the opera, so unmistakable in the first, reaching its climax in the second, definitely waned in the third act."

The notices of the Italian critics consist so essentially of detailed accounts and analyses of each scene that it is impossible, without complete quotations, adequately to paraphrase them. Nappi, who had succeeded Filippi as the critic of *La Perseveranza*, was especially struck by the blend of "modern beauty and classical purity" in the opera. The critic of the *Corriere della Sera* was disgusted with the tenor and preferred Falstaff's second monologue to the famous monologue on honor. He of the *Lega Lombarda*, though struck by "the classical, Olympian, I would almost say Epicurean repose in the expression of the comedy, and the agreeable, pleasing, roguish titillation of the humor," did not like that famous trill of the entire orchestra in the first scene of the last act which illustrates the effect of wine on Sir John. Otherwise all practically wrote the same thing. They were overwhelmed — it is not too strong a word — by the brilliance and subtlety of the orchestration; they noted the rapid movement of the music and its extraordinary fidelity to the text. They praised everything, especially the love music of Fenton and Nannetta, the final scenes of the first and second acts, and Ford's monologue on jealousy, which, strangely enough, they agreed in finding extremely funny. They duly noted the encores that the audience, forgetful or ignorant of Verdi's views six years before, had obtained after Falstaff's "*Quand' ero paggio*"[1] and the women's quartet in the second scene of the first act. They exalted to the skies Maurel's interpretation of Falstaff, the brilliance of the orchestral playing under Mascheroni, who after the death of Faccio had succeeded to the conductor's chair at La Scala.

The French and the German criticisms were in the main but an echo of the Italian and, in the first instance at any rate, dealt principally with the performance. Indubitably the most interesting is that of Alfred Bruneau in the *Gil Blas*. "The score of *Falstaff*," he wrote, "not so much in its form as in its musical essence, derives directly from Rossini and the Italian composers who preceded him, with here and there some exquisite recollections of Mozart and Haydn. I heard people around me say that the influence of *Meistersinger* was apparent, but, frankly, I cannot see it. Neither on this nor on any other occasion does Verdi seem to have wished to assimilate the polyphonic style of Richard Wagner, and his lyrical comedy remains in the key of an extravaganza (*dans le ton de la bouffonnerie*) with snatches of poetry of which the grace, though it is delicious, has no true analogy with the luxuriant grandeur of the German work."

[1] "When I was page."

Several English papers sent representatives, whose opinions coincided on the whole with those of their foreign colleagues. The criticism in the *Athenæum* provides an interesting exception, in that the actual performance is pronounced definitely unworthy of the work and the occasion. The critic considered that none of the female singers rose above mediocrity; that Maurel's interpretation of the title part just missed greatness by reason of its overseriousness; that Signor Mascheroni was too unyielding and hard to be an ideal conductor; that the theater was in any case too large both for the work and for the singers. With regard to the work itself, however, he agreed in ranking it as a masterpiece of which the chief characteristic was "the charm that comes of absolute simplicity, having nothing in common with the comic operas of Mozart and Rossini except genius with the first and gaiety with the second."

The Times, after noting that the final fugue was a little above the heads of the ordinary public, found in the score hardly a single trace of the Verdi of the earlier operas. It emphasized the originality of the opera; "in its unrestrained gaiety and its assured mastery of effect, it is difficult to avoid calling it Beethovenish; in its dramatic force and excellence of construction it reaches a level which has not been touched since Wagner died." The *Daily Telegraph* wrote that "those who had ears more especially for the music were delighted with its beautiful clearness and unfailing charm of melody and treatment, which again and again recalled the Mozart of 'Le Nozze de Figaro.' The suggestions of Mozart are among the notable features of the opera and present a very interesting study of a manner in a composer, who, when at an extreme age, reverts to the style that extensively prevailed in his youth."

Beyond question, however, the most interesting criticism of all, whether English or foreign, came from the pen of Villiers Stanford, who had been sent to Milan on behalf of the *Daily Graphic*. Like the admirable musician and scholar that he was, Stanford seized on all the salient points of the libretto and of the score. He unreservedly praised Boïto for his mastery of Renaissance Italian; for the high order of his poetry; for the ingenuity of the situations and the ensemble verses that he had contrived. He noted the apt borrowing from *Henry IV*, such as the monologue on honor and the allusion to Bardolph's red nose; the felicitous reduction in the number of characters as well as of the scenes in which Falstaff is discomfited in one way or another.

His analysis of the score is so admirable that one regrets not to be able to reproduce it in full. He praises various details; the ensemble for nine voices in the second scene of the first act, which though "of marvellous intricacy on paper sounds as clear as a solo in performance"; the monologue on honor, "smiling sister of the *Credo* of Iago"; the whole of the second act and the fairy music of the last, "quite different from Weber's or Mendelssohn's." He characterizes the duet between Fenton and Ann Page (Nannetta) as the gem, and the great trill in the first scene of the third act, started on one instrument and taken up by the whole orchestra, as the brightest flash of genius of the whole opera.

It is especially interesting to note that Stanford went even further than the critic of *The Times* in tracing the influence of Beethoven, which he described as paramount. "The close student of the quartets and the piano sonatas was evident everywhere, but Verdi's very memories of Beethoven are tinged by his affection for Scarlatti. . . . Occasionally there are traces of Meyerbeer but cleansed of his banalities and tricks; more often there is a twinkle of 'Meistersinger' . . . with the unmistakable stamp of Verdi over all."

Stanford found something to criticize in the music after the comic torture of Falstaff in the last act, which he thought offered the only possible occasion for a cut. He also felt the lack of a central melody, considering that the music of the two young lovers, however exquisite, was too frail to provide the repose desirable in such a whirl of brilliance. He had no doubt whatever of the supreme genius of the work as a whole. "It is," he writes, "as sunny as the composer's garden at Busseto, clear as crystal in construction, tender and explosive by turns, humorous and witty without a touch of extravagance or a note of vulgarity. Each act goes as quickly as lightning, without halt, almost without slow tempi." His article ends with a charming tribute to Verdi, who "through all the excitement and triumph remained what he is, a quiet, calm, modest gentleman — one of those intellectual giants who scorn to trade upon their greatness and are content to be as other men are."

Stanford's account of *Falstaff* is so admirable in every way that there remains little further to be said about the opera in general, especially as the attitude of critical opinion during the last thirty years has not changed with regard to either the libretto or the score. Indeed, Boïto's work is, if anything, more highly considered than ever. We know nothing of the details of collaboration, though a friend of mine, who knew both men during some of the time that they were engaged on their task, Verdi living in Genoa, Boïto at Nervi, just outside, says that they used to meet on most days to discuss various points. One thing is certain: Verdi, though he subsequently made some alterations in his own score, did not ask for the alteration of even a word in the libretto once it was completed — an almost if not wholly unprecedented phenomenon.

Boïto may have viewed Sir John Falstaff and some of the other characters from an angle rather different from that of Shakspere; his work remains, nevertheless, quintessentially Shaksperian. The relations of Boïto and Verdi are discussed in detail elsewhere. Perhaps they may best be summarized here in saying that the part of intellect was played by Boïto, the part of character by Verdi. In a sense their collaboration marked a perfect fusion of masculine and feminine elements, Boïto fascinated by the strength of the old Lion of Busseto, Verdi influenced almost unconsciously by the subtle plasticity of Boïto's restless if hesitating mind. To this is due that unity between words and music in *Falstaff* which has certainly never been surpassed in the annals of opera. In one respect alone does modern opinion seem to differ somewhat from that of Verdi and his contemporaries. He himself wrote, as we have seen, that the opera was "wholly comic," and his contemporaries appear to have agreed with him. Except in the strictly classical sense, this is not the adjective that would first come to our minds in connection with *Falstaff*. There are, of course, very humorous scenes, such as the hiding of Sir John in the basket, his exit with Ford at the end of the first scene of the second act, and so on; but on the whole *Falstaff* strikes us as brilliant, graceful, witty, rather than funny. It is noteworthy, for instance, that Ford's monologue on jealousy, considered so diverting by the Italian critics of the time, has been characterized in recent years as almost too genuine, too poignant for a comic opera.

As regards the music pure and simple, Stanford has said all that generally needs saying. Readers of the detailed analyses of the operas in the second part of this book will not be surprised at his insistence on the influence of Beethoven, for that influence was noticeable in several operas previous to *Falstaff*. Moreover, Boïto, despite a certain volatility of taste, remained always primarily an admirer of Beethoven rather than of Wagner, whatever may have been said or written to the contrary.

Stanford's especial admiration for the love music of Fenton and Nannetta is also justified. Boy and girl love has never been more exquisitely, more intimately translated into music; the *Schwärmerei* of Eva and Walther seems almost gross in comparison. Further, Stanford put his finger on the weak spot in the opera when he regretted the absence of repose deriving from the lack of some central idea. The rapid tempo of *Falstaff*, wonderful though it is, is difficult for anyone but a musician to appreciate to the full. It always seems rather to bewilder the public, who on this account have rarely been able to extract from *Falstaff* the exquisite pleasure that might and should be theirs by right. Only in Germany during the last two or three years can the opera be said to have been in any way a popular

VERDI AND HIS DOGS OUTSIDE THE VILLA SANT' AGATA

Courtesy of Messrs. Ricordi

Courtesy of Messrs. Ricordi

VERDI IN THE GARDEN OF SANT' AGATA

success. The very brilliance and sparkle of the score, justly and unanimously praised by musicians of every school, but accentuates the feeling. In the whole of music there is perhaps no orchestral writing quite like this. From beginning to end the opera resembles a shimmer of light dancing before the eyes; one incomparable beauty after another is gone almost before its presence can be noted. The melodic invention, if comparatively less kaleidoscopic, is so profuse as scarcely to be apprehensible by anyone unacquainted with the details of the music. Nevertheless *Falstaff*, though it may lack that broad sweep needful to capture by storm the human heart, remains technically, perhaps æsthetically, not only Verdi's masterpiece but, it seems to me, one of the three outstanding masterpieces of comic opera. With its wit, its translucence, it remains the most exquisite flower of Mediterranean musical culture, which, as Cecil Gray has well written, would have been far better fitted than *Carmen* to provide Nietzsche with a worthy embodiment of that artistic ideal which he sought to oppose to the fundamentally Teutonic art of Bayreuth.

Two days after the first performance of *Falstaff* a notice appeared in the press to the effect that Verdi was to be created Marquis of Busseto. Feeling with justice that any such project must make him ridiculous, Verdi took the strongest possible steps to prevent it, addressing his protest direct to a member of the Ministry. This peril successfully surmounted, he felt at liberty to indulge that good humor which, in notable contrast with the melancholy attendant on the completion of *Otello*, marked the launching of *Falstaff*. True, he had parted with the score with a certain measure of sadness, for there is something very touching about the little *envoi* in imitation of a well-known passage in the libretto, recently brought to light by Toscanini and given to me by his wife:

> *Tutto e finito.*
> *Va, va, vecchio John —*
> *Cammina per la tua via*
> *Fin che tu puoi.*
> *Divertente tipo di briccone*
> *Eternamente vero sotto*
> *Maschera diversa in ogni*
> *Tempo, in ogni luogo —*
>   *Va, va,*
> *Cammina, cammina,*
>   *Addio! ! !* [2]

[2] All is finished. Go, go, old John — proceed on your way as long as you can. Diverting type of rascal that you are! Eternally true, in different guises, at every period, in every place — go, go; proceed on your way; farewell.

But there was no tinge of regret in the pleasure Verdi took in the triumphal progress of *Falstaff*, first throughout Italy, then in Europe. He himself went to Rome, whither the Milan production had been transplanted, cast, conductor, and all. The welcome prepared by the capital was a fitting climax to his career. From the time of his arrival at the station he was acclaimed by vast crowds. The performance at the theater was attended by a huge and brilliant audience that included the royal family. Thanks to a singularly happy inspiration on somebody's part, the orchestra of the theater, under the direction of Mascheroni himself, assembled at midnight in front of his hotel after the last performance to play a representative program of his works beginning with the overture to *Nabucco*.[3]

Verdi seems to have enjoyed it all, and even when his personal participation was at an end, when he had returned first to Genoa and then to Sant' Agata, he kept himself fully informed of the details of the tour organized by the authorities of La Scala. The main source of his information was Mascheroni, for whom he seems to have developed a great affection, calling him "Farfarello,"[4] and writing him the most intimate and good-humored letters. Venice! Vienna! Brescia! He wanted to know what happened at all of them, how the singers, new and old, were getting on. He even indicated one or two slight modifications in the scoring.

In April 1894 the old man actually betook himself to Paris to attend the first French performance of *Falstaff* at the Opéra Comique. This production seems to have been due in the first instance to the initiative of Maurel, and Verdi took a genuine interest in it, writing to the director of the theater, Carvalho, a letter in which he urged him to pay special attention to the part of Alice: "Of course a beautiful and very flexible voice is necessary, but above all a real actress and somebody with a bit of a devil in her." Both Carvalho and Maurel had urged him to disregard his years and come to Paris, Maurel tempting him with the information that many of the Wagnerians, notably Catulle Mendès, had become his passionate admirers.

Jealous, it appears, of the success of the Opéra Comique in launching the first performance of *Falstaff* in France, the management of the Opéra proposed to give performances of *Otello* in Italian about the same time. But Verdi would have nothing to do with the project. Perfectly aware that any performance in a foreign language was directly contrary to the traditions of the Opéra, the maneuver seemed to him ludicrously transparent. "If *Otello* is to be given at the Opéra it must be given in French," he telegraphed to Ricordi; and in French it was eventually given, with some new ballet-music and a modified

[3] Checchi. [4] Little imp.

version of the difficult ensemble in the third act, the translation being the work of du Locle and Boïto himself.

Apart from this excursion, life passed tranquilly enough for Verdi and Peppina, at Sant' Agata in the summer, at Genoa in the winter months. There were few visitors: Teresa Stolz, Boïto of course, Ricordi, and one or two others less intimate. Occasionally he suffered from a fit of depression or skepticism, as for instance in 1895, when he wrote thus to a friend: "Having been born poor in a poor village, I had no means of instructing myself in anything. They gave me a miserable spinet and a little while afterwards I began to write notes — notes, notes, nothing but notes! The trouble is that now, at the age of eighty-two, I have grave doubts as to the value of these notes — a cause of remorse and desolation to me." [5]

On the whole, however, he seems to have been more mellow, more expansive than at any other time in his career. The old feud with Busseto was finally buried. He wrote several charming letters, notably to Camille Bellaigue, whom he came, perhaps, to prefer above all other music-critics; he forgave with remarkable affability an indiscretion of Eugenio Checchi as regards himself and Mascagni. Even a request from the editor of the *Deutsche Verlags-Anstalt* that he should write his memoirs amused rather than annoyed him. "Never, never will I write my memoirs," he answered the editor, who scarcely can have been aware of the rashness of his request. "It is quite enough for the musical world to have put up with my notes for so long. . . . I will never condemn it to read my prose!"

The disaster of Adua in 1896 saddened him. Brought up in the old school, he could not appreciate the advantages of colonial enterprise. He felt that the Italians had met in Abyssinia with the fate they deserved — a fate that he thought and hoped would one day be shared by the English for their "tyranny and oppression in India." [6] Still, the problems attendant on the shouldering of the White Man's Burden did not really move him so deeply as matters nearer home, such as the presentation of two golden pheasants to the public gardens of Cremona, the question of the appointment of a local doctor, and the failure of his efforts to induce the authorities of the Parma Conservatoire to waive the age-limit in favor of the son of his coachman — a rebuff that must have awakened a sympathetic echo in his memory. Indeed, the only thing that seriously disturbed the placid uniformity of his life was the avalanche of begging letters that descended in such numbers that to deal with them he had to draw up a circular in reply.

There is no doubt that this circular was responsible for procuring him at the time a reputation for being close-fisted if not actually avaricious. That he was exceptionally careful in money matters need

[5] Bonaventura.   [6] Pizzi.

not be denied; such a trait is characteristic of the peasant strain that persisted as the basis of his personality.[7] But in the present instance he had with typical determination merely made up his mind how his money should be spent and did not propose to allow any pressure to divert him from his own pet schemes. For some years he had had in mind the construction and endowment of a home in Milan for aged musicians. As early as 1889 he had bought the site. In 1895 he was in correspondence with Camillo Boïto, the architect-brother of the composer, who had been commissioned to prepare the plans. Verdi, with characteristic caution, wondered if they were not unnecessarily ambitious, whether one door and one window would not suffice for a room for two people, and so on. He feared especially to embark on a scheme and not to be able to bring it to fruition. Eventually, however, he was satisfied, and in May 1896 paid up the money necessary for carrying out the building operations in full. Verdi was by this time a comparatively rich man, but only the elimination of secondary charities enabled him to assure the very large sum of money necessary to carry out a scheme that, as he later told the sculptor Monteverde, was the favorite of all his works, musical or otherwise.[8]

[7] A recent biographer has protested against the description of Verdi as having remained a peasant at heart. But the pride and sense of independence that he adduces as evidence to the contrary are by no means rare attributes in Italian peasantry of the best type, as I, who have the privilege of intimate acquaintance with one or two of them, can testify from personal experience. Verdi's caution and secretiveness were typical of his class. Even more so his natural reactions where money was concerned. For instance, his magnificent honesty in matters of finance was the honesty of a peasant, meticulous sometimes to a ludicrous extent. A story, told to me, of his dealings with Ricordi well illustrates the point. Verdi always insisted on receiving the interest due on payments in arrear, but on one occasion, when, at his own wish, a certain payment was delayed, he refused to accept the additional interest, saying that he was not entitled to it since the delay was of his own making. Heaven knows there is no belittlement in describing a man as a peasant at heart in a country where the peasants, apart from certain inevitable limitations, are the salt of the earth! Verdi, who all his life loved to use local dialect and referred to himself with evident relish as the *contadino* of Sant' Agata, would have been the last person to resent such a description.

[8] Checchi.

CHAPTER XXIV

On the 14th of November 1897 the curtain rose on the final act of the life-drama of Giuseppe Verdi, for on that day Giuseppina died. She had been ailing in one way or another for several years; as far back as 1891 Verdi had almost despaired of some trouble in her knee being definitely cured. Up to the end she does not seem to have realized how ill she was, for when Verdi brought her a flower to smell, she said to him: "Thank you, I can smell nothing; I have got rather a cold." A few hours later all was over.

Verdi faced the loss with typical dignity. He kissed her once in her death agony and once again as she lay dead. Then he summoned his friend and lawyer, Amilcare Martinelli, saying that he would like to see him but could not talk. Martinelli describes how he found the old man standing near a table covered with papers; the piano shut. With his chin sunk on his chest, his cheeks flushed, his hair and beard silver rather than snow-white, he gave an impression of grief all the more poignant because of its restraint. It could scarcely have been otherwise. Giuseppina was a part of his own life. As a singer she had shared his first triumph in *Nabucco;* as a companion she had watched with him his final triumph in *Falstaff*. They had scarcely ever been separated, for she accompanied him on almost all his journeys and had attended almost all the first performances of his works. Even in the last years of her life she was the first to sing over the tunes that he had composed. Her passing meant the disappearance of the last link that attached the old man to the failures and successes of his youth and middle age, to the world of Solera, Merelli, Piave, and Escudier, which had now vanished forever.

For half a century, moreover, she had as a wife watched over him with loving but never importunate care. Nor had the task always been easy, as he himself must have known full well, for in his black moods or in the fever of creation Verdi was not an easy person to deal with. Giuseppina often felt the strain. "Oh God!" she once wrote to a friend, "Oh God, grant that Verdi shall compose no more operas!" Yet it was always she, we are told, who was the first to encourage him to attempt new experiments, to adventure on new paths. One thing alone Giuseppina failed to understand in Verdi: his attitude to religion. Herself completely orthodox, she was unable to see how a man of such sterling qualities as her husband could refuse to share her own simple beliefs or appreciate her even more simple reasons for them. There was never any feeling in the matter. Verdi was not a dogmatic unbeliever and, in fact, built Giuseppina a chapel at Sant' Agata for her private use. The essential affinity between the two is well shown in the last sentence of Giuseppina's will: "And now farewell, my Verdi. As we were united in life, may God unite our spirits in heaven."

According to Martinelli, to whom we owe most of the details of Giuseppina's last days, Verdi after her death was "neither ill nor quite well." But the shock had made a permanent breach in a constitution that people had persuaded themselves to be impregnable. His heart began to trouble him, his hand to tremble. He slept so badly that in Milan, where he had taken the habit of spending a considerable part of the winter in order to avoid the old associations of Genoa, he used to stay up chatting with friends until midnight in order to make the nights seem shorter. He wrote to Mascheroni in January 1898 that *Falstaff* had quite passed out of his memory; he was not ill, merely too old. The idea of living without being able to do anything filled him with horror.

Nevertheless, at the very time he wrote these words to his favorite "Farfarello," he was planning to go to Paris to hear the performance of the *Pezzi Sacri*, which Taffanel was arranging at the Opéra. Though he much wished to undertake the journey, it was obvious by the end of March that increasing heart trouble must put any such idea out of the question. So Boïto, after having studied the score with the composer, went in his stead.

The impression is sometimes given that the *Pezzi Sacri* were written after the death of Giuseppina, if not actually composed as a posthumous homage to her religious ideals. This is not correct. The *Pezzi Sacri* consist of four independent pieces, an *Ave Maria*, a *Laudi*, a *Stabat Mater*, and a *Te Deum*, of which the first and the last at any rate can be dated with certainty before 1897. Indeed, the idea of the *Ave Maria* may be traced back to 1889, when Verdi wrote to Boïto about the "enigmatic scale" that he had discovered in the *Gazzetta Musicale* and on which the piece is founded. He had written it by the beginning of 1895, in which year he turned his attention to the *Te Deum*. With this, however, he seems to have been mainly occupied in the February of the following year, for it was at that time that he wrote to the director of the choir of Loreto to the effect that none of the interpretations of the *Te Deum* that he had heard, either old or new, seemed to him completely satisfactory. The conventional association of the *Te Deum* with occasions of pomp and thanksgiving was justified so far as the first part of the hymn was concerned, but the second part seemed to suggest a very different atmosphere. In all probability the composition of the *Laudi* and *Stabat Mater* took place about the same time.

His Life and Works

It is perhaps a pity that the four pieces were bracketed together (though doubtless all were intended as a tribute to the ideals of the Palestrina he so passionately admired), for, the *Stabat Mater* and the *Te Deum* excepted, they have little in common. Verdi's refusal to allow the *Ave Maria* to be performed in Paris shows clearly that he shared this view to some extent. He had always regarded it rather as a tour de force than a serious musical composition; it was, as he said, a typical product of second childhood, reminding him pleasantly of the days when he was set by Lavigna or Provesi to harmonize basses. Yet, with its ingenious treatment of the subject, it is an indubitably effective example of unaccompanied writing in four parts. The *Laudi alla Vergine Maria*, to give it its full title, was a setting of words from the last canto of Dante's *Paradiso*. Written for unaccompanied female voices in four parts, the essence of its beauty is mystical, ethereal. The *Stabat Mater* and the *Te Deum* on the other hand, both definitely liturgical works, were written for chorus and orchestra, the *Te Deum*, in fact, for a double chorus. Both seem to me legitimate descendants of the Requiem Mass, even if some of the vitality of their great ancestor has gone. The *Te Deum*, with its wonderful final prayer, *Dignare Domine*, and its magnificent *Sanctus*, is usually considered the masterpiece of the four compositions, but it may be doubted whether Verdi ever wrote anything more beautiful than the end of the *Stabat Mater* or the beautiful phrase ushered in by the words "*Tui nati vulnerati*." As an epilogue, so to say, to the work of a lifetime, the *Pezzi Sacri* is worthy of the composer of *Otello, Falstaff*, and the Requiem Mass.

They were played for the first time in Paris in Holy Week 1898, and introduced to Italy in May of the same year at the Turin Exposition, when they were conducted by Arturo Toscanini, already beginning to be known for his insight into the music of his great compatriot. The authorities of La Scala wished to arrange a performance at their theater in the following year, but Verdi asked Boïto to associate himself with Ricordi in preventing it. He did not think that it would be well done in the first place; in the second, as he adds with a final flash of typical sardonic humor, "my name is too old and boring — I bore myself when I mention it! Then in addition there are the remarks of the newspapers . . . though I must admit I cannot read them."

Gradually, ineluctably, the shadows began to close in on Sant' Agata, where Verdi, tended with real devotion by Maria Carrara, continued to spend his summers. Outwardly his life had changed but little. He still went to Montecatini for the cure in July, to Genoa or Milan in the winter; his sister-in-law, Barberina, still continued to come and stay; those of his friends who remained alive, Teresa Stolz,

Boïto, Ricordi, still paid their customary visits. But something had snapped and he knew it. The physical decline was bad enough. In addition to all his other troubles he could hardly see; his hearing was affected and his legs were beginning to fail him. The doctors might say, as in fact they did, that the state of his nervous system and general health was remarkable for so old a man. The trouble lay elsewhere. All the gloom, the pessimism temporarily banished by the composition and the production of *Falstaff*, came down on him again like a fog, more penetrating, more desolating than ever. He became increasingly morose and taciturn. For this the loss of Peppina was directly responsible, as is shown by a letter he wrote to a friend a month after her death: "Great grief does not demand great expression; it asks for silence, isolation, I would even say the torture of reflection. Words dull, enervate, and destroy feeling. There is something superficial (*poco sentito*) about all exteriorization; it is a profanation."

A few months later he excused himself for delay in answering a letter on the ground that he had nothing cheerful to communicate. "Life is suffering. When we are young, the exuberance of living, activity, and amusement torment and fascinate us. We shoulder our portions of good and ill as they come and we do not notice life at all." Apart from the genuine appeal of the Neapolitan proposal in 1899 to celebrate the centenary of Cimarosa, whose *Matrimonio Segreto* he considered a model of what an *opera buffa* should be, only one external event penetrated the numbness of his last years: the assassination of King Humbert in July 1900.

The horror which Verdi felt for that senseless crime quickened in him once more an interest in the world outside, and the prayer written by Queen Margherita after the murder moved him deeply. His friend the Countess Negroni Prati wished him to set it to music and he himself, though incontinently and quite rightly rejecting as unworthy of the original the rhymed version that she had had prepared for him, confessed to having entertained the same idea. "The Queen's Prayer in its simplicity might have been written by one of the early fathers of the Church. Inspired by deep religious sentiment, she has found words so true and of so primitive a color that they could not be translated into the terms of our turgid and self-conscious (*ricercata*) music. One would have to go back three centuries, to Palestrina." For this reason, as well as on the grounds that he was "half ill" and that the doctors had forbidden him any kind of effort, he refused to undertake the task; but it is characteristic of the man, with his ingrained habit of secrecy, of never committing himself prematurely, that sketches for the music were, in fact, made. They were the last notes ever written by Giuseppe Verdi.

The end came soon after. During the last months of 1900 he grew noticeably more feeble, having to be wheeled about the garden in a chair. In December he was taken, in the charge of Maria, to Milan where he spent an agreeable Christmas in the company of Teresa Stolz, Boïto, and the Ricordi family, staying in his usual apartments in the Hotel di Milano. On the 21st of January, at half past ten in the morning, while dressing himself, he had a stroke and never again recovered consciousness, though the pious say that he bestowed a feeble smile on the priest who attended him and administered extreme unction at dawn of the 24th.

The telegrams of inquiry arriving continually from the King, from ministers and deputies, from friends and admirers all over Italy, all over Europe; the crowds waiting outside the hotel as in the days of his triumphs, but now silent and anxious; the slow, losing fight waged by the unconscious master against the advance of death, provided a theatrical touch not inappropriate to the passing of such a man. Giacosa,[1] who was at his bedside during the last days, describes how he seemed in all outward appearances to be asleep; how the indications of pulse and breathing alone betrayed to the doctors the struggle that was going on within. Boïto, equally dutiful but more imaginative, realized with greater acuteness the inner significance of the drama. "The maestro is dead," he wrote immediately afterwards. "He carried away with him a great quantity of light and vital warmth. We had all basked in the sun of his Olympian old age. He died magnificently like a fighter redoubtable and mute. The silence of death fell on him a week before he died. With his head bent, his eyebrows set, he seemed to measure with half-shut eyes an unknown and formidable adversary, calculating in his mind the force that he could summon up in opposition. Thus he put up a heroic resistance. The breathing of his great chest sustained him for four days and three nights; on the fourth night the sound of his breathing still filled the room; but what a struggle, poor maestro! How magnificently he fought up to the last moment! In the course of my life I have lost persons whom I idolized, when grief was stronger than resignation. But I have never experienced such a feeling of hate against death, such loathing for its mysterious, blind, stupid, triumphant, infamous power. For such a feeling to be aroused in me I had to await the end of this old man of ninety."

Verdi died on the 27th of January at ten minutes to three in the morning, and though preparations for a great public funeral had been launched, he was buried with the greatest simplicity three days later, in accordance with an instruction contained in his will. This remarkable document, drawn up in the previous year at Busseto, was typical

[1] One of Puccini's librettists.

alike of his method and of his imagination. His estate amounted to 7,050,000 lire (approximately 1,410,000 dollars), of which half went to his residuary legatee, Maria Carrara,[2] the other half, apart from some few legacies to employees and relations—his gold repeating watch to Dr. Carrara, his guns and gold studs to Alberto Carrara—being devoted to charitable bequests. Thus various institutions in Genoa, the hospital at Villanova, the Monte di Pietà at Busseto, all received substantial sums. But the major portion, as well as all future royalties on his operas, his Erard piano, the old spinet, and other objects associated with his career, went to the home in Milan wherein a hundred destitute old musicians, sixty male, forty female, were to be housed. Here, together with Giuseppina, Verdi wished to be buried without pomp or ceremony, without music or singing, at daybreak or in the evening at the time of the Ave Maria.

In the first instance, as we have seen, Verdi's wishes were conscientiously carried out, for it was at seven o'clock in the morning that his coffin, borne on a cheap hearse and preceded by one crucifix, a couple of candles, and a priest or two, was transported to the Church of San Francesco da Paola preparatory to being interred in the cemetery. Special authorization, however, had to be procured for the burial of Verdi and his wife in the oratory of the Musicians' Home, which did not take place until a month later. This event evoked an extraordinary demonstration on the part of the citizens of Milan, who felt, perhaps, that, whereas the first funeral had rightly been celebrated in accordance with the wishes of the composer, they were now justified in seizing upon the reinterment as an opportunity to show their own feelings. More than two hundred thousand of them, it is said, lined the streets. Soldiers, representatives of national and municipal bodies, dignified ecclesiastics accompanied in formal procession Verdi and Giuseppina to their last resting place, now heaped high with wreaths and other tributes from all over the world.

Twelve years later not only Milan but the whole of Italy celebrated the centenary of Verdi's birth in much the same spirit. Almost every little commune throughout the peninsula, often devoid even of an adequate water supply, raised money to pay its tribute to the occasion. Innumerable statues and monuments were erected; demonstrations, which included such incongruous features as horseraces, aviation meets, and football matches, were organized. Performances of representative operas, from *Nabucco* to *Falstaff*, took place at La Scala. Busseto planned to present in its beautiful little theater *La Traviata* and *Falstaff* under the direction of Toscanini. Boïto published a manifesto in which he proclaimed Verdi as "the genius of our race. He revealed to the world in the divine freedom of musical

---

[2] Chop.

sounds the ardor, the dash, the affection, the force of the spirit of Italy so that the world learned to understand and love it."

Of all the manifestations of enthusiasm, some felicitous, some ridiculous, but all indubitably genuine, Verdi would probably have preferred the choral and agricultural competitions organized at Parma; for singing and agriculture were, of all human activities, perhaps the most dear to his heart. He would certainly have preferred them to the pretentious monument, with allegorical figures representing each one of his operas, erected in his honor by that city.

Doubtless it is difficult for a northerner to appreciate wholeheartedly the conscious theatricalism favored by Latins on occasions such as the second funeral and the centenary of Giuseppe Verdi. He who will look a little below the surface, however, should understand their attitude readily enough. On both occasions Italy saluted not only the composer but the representative of a past epoch, the great personality indissolubly linked with the struggle for her independence and its establishment. We of another race and culture may salute him also as the representative of a past ideal.

Verdi was the last of the great line of craftsmen-composers, the line of Mozart, Haydn, Handel, and Bach. He had none of the revolutionary genius of a Wagner, little of the experimental passion of a Beethoven. He was content, during by far the greater portion of his working life, to satisfy the current requirements of his day in the manner that seemed to him best suited to the purpose. Not being primarily of an inquiring turn of mind, not being tormented by the restlessness typical of the modern world, he displayed a tolerance, if not a definite liking, for æsthetic convention difficult of apprehension by many people at the present day. In this, as in several other ways, he showed a curious affinity with Handel. Both men accepted and enlarged the conventions of their time without seeking to destroy them; both were gifted with a taste in musical poetry irresistible on account of its very simplicity; both possessed unbounded vitality as well as the uncanny sense if "the right note in the right place," Handel to paint a picture, Verdi to express emotion in music. In their private lives both showed the same unswerving determination, the same integrity, the same practical ability in affairs. Neither has ever appealed, or ever can appeal, to the purveyor of mere romance, the lover of the abstruse for its own sake, the decadent or the effeminate. Of Verdi might be written what Edward FitzGerald wrote of Handel: "His is the music for a great active people" — to which may be added the tribute paid him in d'Annunzio's memorial ode: *"Pianse e amò per tutti."* [3]

[3] Literally, "He wept and loved for all." But the translation gives little idea of the implications of the Italian.

Those whom temperament or prejudice inclines to a liking for the experimental or the exotic will doubtless prefer to seek their pleasure in the music of other men. Perhaps the principal charm of Verdi lies in his natural simplicity, his complete sincerity. He may have had qualms and doubts, he may have asked himself at times whether his best was worth while, but he never felt, never had reason to feel, that it was not his best. Boïto said that of all the great composers he had known, Wagner, Rossini, and Meyerbeer among them, Verdi was the one that interested him the most. His tribute may well be endorsed by anyone who has felt the rugged fascination of Verdi's character both in art and in life. Verdi the farmer of Sant' Agata and Verdi the composer of *Otello* and *La Traviata* were, after all, one and the same person. It was not even a case of dual personality. His life in both instances was lived in accordance with the spirit not of the *Æneid* or the *Eclogues*, but of the *Georgics*. The conceit is justified by the Roman characteristics of a man who has been called, not without reason, the Lion of Busseto.

THE BUST OF VERDI BY GEMITO

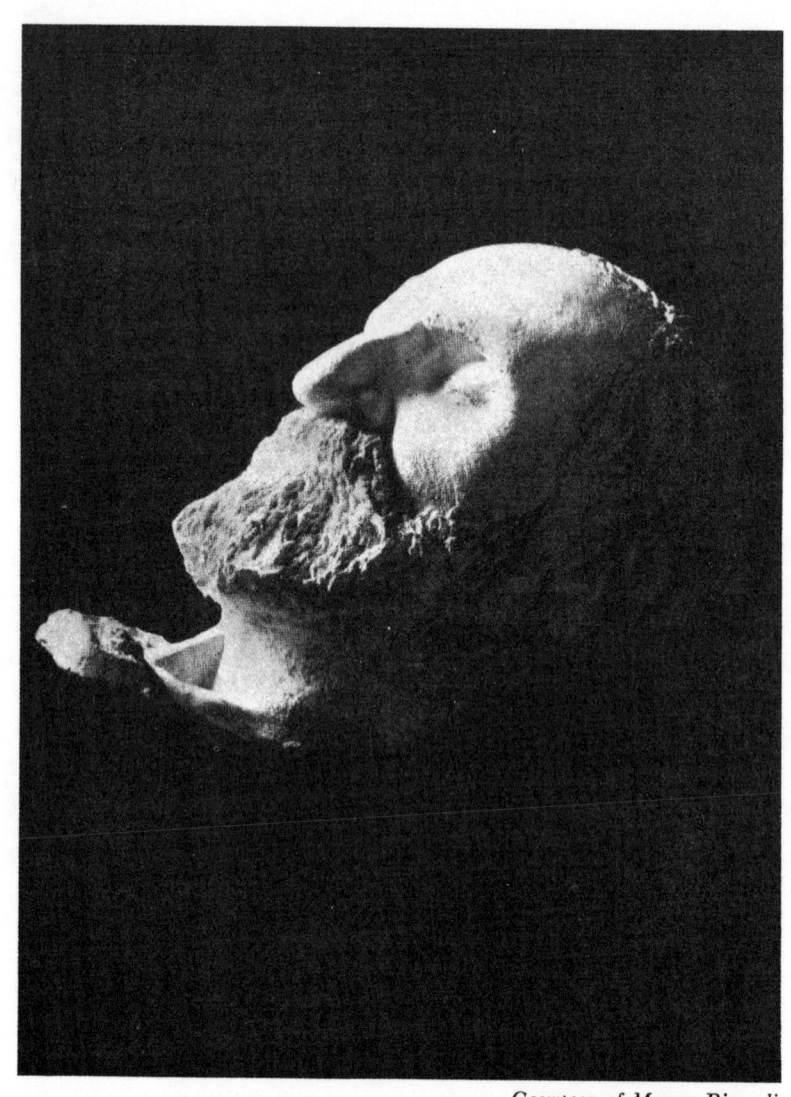

Courtesy of Messrs. Ricordi

VERDI'S DEATH-MASK

OPERAS

PART II

PART II

OPERAS

OBERTO, CONTE DI BONIFACIO

Libretto by Piazza and Solera
Production: MILAN, November 17, 1839
TWO ACTS, FOUR SCENES

LEONORA (soprano), the daughter of Oberto, Count of Bonifacio (bass), has been seduced by Riccardo, Count of Salinguerra (tenor), and both she and her exiled father, who has cast her off, have separately left the country. Riccardo in the meantime has become betrothed to Cuniza (mezzo-soprano), a noble lady who lives with her brother, Ezzelino, in his castle.

The opera opens in a "delicious countryside" near Bassano whither ladies and gentlemen in attendance on Cuniza and her brother have come to greet Riccardo, who has arrived to claim his bride. After they have all moved away, Leonora enters, tells the sad story of her betrayal by her lover and her quarrel with her father, who presently, thanks to one of those fortunate coincidences so dear to the authors of opera librettos, returns to the same place at the same time. Both are bent on vengeance. At first Oberto will have nothing to do with his daughter, but on her promise to expose and punish Riccardo he finally relents, and the two go off together.

The scene changes to an apartment in Ezzelino's castle, where Riccardo and Cuniza are confiding to each other their hopes and fears. Leonora arrives and asks to see Cuniza, Oberto remaining concealed till the propitious moment when both join forces to reveal to Cuniza the infamous conduct of Riccardo. He is sent for and confronted with Leonora and Oberto; whereupon all the characters and chorus bring the act to an end in a typical ensemble.

The second act opens with a short scene in Cuniza's private apartments, wherein she confides to her attendants her resolution to make Riccardo marry Leonora at whatever cost to herself. In the meantime, however, Oberto has sent a challenge to Riccardo, and in the second scene he is waiting for an answer in a deserted spot just outside the castle grounds. His unauthorized return has exposed him to the penalty of death, but the remission of this does not satisfy him; he thirsts for vengeance. Presently Riccardo arrives to tell Oberto that he cannot fight a duel with so old a man. Nevertheless, with one of those taunts of cowardice that no hero or villain of romantic melodrama can resist, Oberto finally provokes him, and the two men are about to fight when Cuniza enters with Leonora, announcing to Riccardo her forgiveness on the condition that he marries Leonora, who admits that she still loves him. Oberto whispers to Riccardo to feign acceptance, adding that he will await him in the wood later. Riccardo promises to come, and immediately after the women have departed in the belief that everything has been satisfactorily arranged, the duel takes place off the stage. Riccardo, returning in an agony of remorse at having killed Oberto, decides to leave Italy forever, bequeathing his property to Leonora. The body of Oberto is discovered; Leonora, bereft at once of lover and father, sees no prospect of relief but in death, and the curtain falls on her despair, accompanied by aspirations for heavenly comfort on the part of Cuniza and the chorus.

Verdi, despite many traditional, vulgar, or merely dull pages, did succeed in making this improbable story live; for the score of *Oberto* gives a general impression of personal vigor that still compels attention. For instance, the energy of the finale of the first act, at times surprisingly classical in feeling, is remarkable; and the same is true to an even greater extent of the quartet in the second act, certainly the best music in the opera and a fine piece of ensemble-writing, in which, towards the end, the curious will find an amusing reminiscence of Schubert's *"Marche Militaire."* In the overture, despite Soffredini's praise, I can find little of interest, though adumbrations of *Rigoletto* in the middle section and of *I Vespri Siciliani* in the last are worthy of note. The choruses are mostly poor and highly sententious, rather like a commonplace echo of the very worst choruses in a Greek play, commenting on the action rather than taking part in it.

There is little trace of the power of characterization so noticeable in the later operas. The personages are essentially lay figures, types rather than people, with the dubious exception of Leonora, a decidedly wooden ancestress of her great descendants in *Il Trovatore* and *La Forza del Destino*. She has, however, a few moving bars of recitative at the end of the opera when she discovers that her father has been killed by her lover. But both her first cavatina and her duet with her father are more remarkable for their effective instrumental introductions than their melodic or expressive merits. Riccardo, on the other hand, has two successful arias, the second, with its beautiful first phrase deploring the death of Oberto, being particularly good.

IL FINTO STANISLAO
(Un Giorni di Regno)

Libretto by Romani

Production: MILAN, September 5, 1840

TWO ACTS, FIVE SCENES

The Cavaliere di Belfiore (baritone), a wild young officer from Paris posing as Stanislaus, King of Poland, enjoys in that capacity the hospitality of the Baron Kelbar (buffo-bass) at his castle near Brest. When the opera opens, preparations are in progress for a double wedding, that of Giulietta di Kelbar (mezzo-soprano), the Baron's daughter, with La Rocca (buffo-baritone), Treasurer of "the States of Brittany"; and of the Marchesa del Poggio (soprano), a young widow, the Baron's niece, with Count Ivrea, Commandant of Brest. Giulietta is in reality in love with the Treasurer's nephew, Edoardo (tenor), but is being constrained by her father to marry the old man for his money.

Apparently Belfiore's escapade was undertaken to enable the real Stanislaus to reach Warsaw unperceived and win the support of the Polish Diet. For when he learns that one of the brides is the Marchesa, to whom he was engaged in Paris, he writes immediately "to court" asking to be allowed to "abdicate," lest he should lose a wife. While waiting for the answer, however, he takes a fancy to and nominates as his esquire Edoardo, who, in despair at Giulietta's marriage, has offered to follow him to Poland. More than that, he contrives by flattery of the Baron and the Treasurer to throw the lovers together and finally, dangling before his eyes the prospect of office, great estates and alliance with a Polish princess, induces the Treasurer to abandon Giulietta altogether; which so enrages the Baron, who will not hear of the impecunious Edoardo as a substitute, that the two men prepare for a comic duel.

In the meantime the Marchesa has arrived. She duly recognizes her faithless lover, but, determined to punish him, pretends to be deceived and announces her intention of proceeding with her marriage with Ivrea unless Belfiore makes his appearance within the hour. Almost the last act of the sham king is to order the Treasurer to settle an estate aand money on his nephew so that the objections of the Baron to his daughter's marriage cease to exist. He himself in the nick of time receives a dispatch from the mysterious "court" to the effect that the real Stanislaus has arrived in Warsaw and been acclaimed by the Diet, while he has been made a marshal for his services and can now quietly "abdicate." So he reveals himself as Belfiore, holds the Marchesa to her promise, and the opera ends, as it began, with the expectation of a double wedding.

Comic genius of the highest order would have been necessary to make anything like a success of this hodge-podge, which is involved without being in the least amusing. Verdi's own temperament, to say nothing of the circumstances in which the opera was composed, precluded any such possibility. At its best *Il Finto Stanislao* can be reckoned only a workmanlike essay in conventional *opera buffa* tunes and rhythms, an inferior copy of Donizetti and Rossini, without the grace of the one or the exuberant sparkle of the other. At the same time the verdict passed on it by critics has been, perhaps, excessively severe. There are several numbers in the opera worthy of regard. For instance, in the first act, the simple little trio between the Marchesa, Giulietta, and Edoardo, with its effective chromatic cadence, has real charm; while Giulietta's cavatina, "*Non san quant' io nel petto soffra mortal dolore*," has been praised with good reason. Not improbably it was inspired by a particularly acute appreciation of the appropriateness of the words.

It will be noticed, however, that in neither instance is there a question of essentially comic-opera music. For this we must go to the second act, wherein there are two duets which, if conventional, are none the less effective. The "duel" duet between the Treasurer and the Baron, particularly the concluding section in 6/8, and the *Allegro*, in three time, of the duet between the Marchesa and Belfiore, are both really gay. One thinks almost of Sullivan or Offenbach. There are points, too, in the duet between Giulietta and Edoardo, but it is in no way funny. Incidentally the occasional carelessness of Verdi in setting words is shown in the false accent given to "*se*" in the tenth bar of the *Allegro* in this duet, while the curious will find in the opening bars of the *Allegro moderato* of the *duetto-buffo* between the Baron and the Treasurer in the first act a foretaste of the march in *Aïda*.

Verdi himself in later years summed up the salient characteristics of *Il Finto Stanislao* accurately enough when he wrote that it was doubtless a bad opera but that equally bad operas had held the stage in their time. Since then dozens of similar operas, no better, no worse, have come to birth and died.

NABUCODONOSOR
(Usually known as *Nabucco*)

Libretto by Solera
Production: MILAN, March 9, 1842
FOUR ACTS, SEVEN SCENES

The priests and people of Jerusalem are assembled in the Temple to bewail their defeat by Nabucodonosor, King of Babylon (baritone), and his imminent descent on the city. The High Priest, Zaccaria (bass), strives to encourage them, reminding them of the wonders Jehovah has wrought on their behalf in the past. More than that, he holds Fenena (soprano), daughter of Nabucodonosor, as a hostage and hands her over for safe-keeping to Ismaele (tenor), nephew of the King of Judah. But in the days when Ismaele was ambassador to Babylon, Fenena, braving the anger of her people and the watchfulness of her jealous sister, Abigaille (soprano), had rescued him from prison, and the two had fallen in love. Ismaele promises to save her, but suddenly Abigaille appears at the head of Babylonian soldiers, announcing that the Temple has been captured. She threatens the lovers, whispering to Ismaele that she too loves him and that even now, if her love is returned, she can save him and his people. Ismaele refuses. The people and priests, panic-stricken at the fall of the Temple, fly at the approach of Nabucodonosor, who rides his horse to the very entrance of the Holy of Holies. Zaccaria threatens him with the wrath of Jehovah and the death of his daughter if the sanctuary is profaned. Nabucodonosor answers with taunts at the Jews and their God, and Zaccaria is about to stab Fenena to the heart when Ismaele interposes and sets her free. All impediment to his fury now removed, Nabucodonosor puts the Temple to fire and sword, and the Jews are carried away into captivity.

The second act is laid in the royal palace of Babylon, where Nabucodonosor, who is away at the wars, has left Fenena as Regent. Abigaille has discovered from a secret document that she is no daughter of the King, but slave-born. Rather than that her shame should be made public, she determines to bring ruin on Fenena, Nabucodonosor, even, if necessary, on herself. The opportunity for action soon presents itself, for the High Priest of Babylon arrives to announce Fenena's intention to free the Jews and asks her to lead those opposed to such rash clemency. In the meantime the Levites and Zaccaria are preparing to excommunicate Ismaele for his treachery, but even the fanatical Zaccaria is mollified when he learns that Fenena has been converted to Judaism and that Ismaele has therefore saved not a Gentile but a Jewess. Abigaille appears at the head of her supporters, demanding the Regent's crown from Fenena. At that moment, however, Nabucodonosor returns unexpectedly, takes the crown, and puts it on his own head. In a frenzy of excitement he dares anyone to remove it, proclaims himself God, and commands all to worship him. The Jews, including their new convert, Fenena, refuse, while Zaccaria calls down the curse of Jehovah on such impious pride. The crown is struck from the King's head by lightning and and he is seen to have become a hopeless lunatic, to the satisfaction of Abigaille, who, picking up the crown, proclaims the continued glory of Babylon.

In the third act Abigaille is reigning as Regent, supported by the priests. Nabucodonosor approaches, his wits wandering, his attire in disorder. Abigaille extorts from him a signature that authorizes the massacre of the Jews, including Fenena. With a momentary return of half sanity he realizes the import of his action and, in an effort to save his daughter, throws the slave-birth of Abigaille in her face; whereupon, before his eyes, she tears to pieces the document that attests the fact. Instead of anger he then tries supplication, but the determined Abigaille merely informs him that he is henceforward a prisoner. The scene changes to the banks of the Euphrates, where the enslaved Jews lament their lost fatherland. Zaccaria, however, chides them for their pusillanimity, bringing the act to an end with a prophecy of the utter destruction of Babylon.

At the beginning of the last act Nabucodonosor is a prisoner in the palace. From the window he sees Fenena being led to execution and prays to Jehovah to pardon his blasphemy and presumption. The prayer is granted, for when the loyal captain of the guard, Abdallo, comes with soldiers to rescue him, he is overjoyed to find the King once more in his right mind. In the meantime Fenena and the Jews are preparing for death, from which they are saved by the arrival of Nabucodonosor and his followers. The image of the god of Babylon falls, shattered, to the ground, and the King proclaims his allegiance to Jehovah, in whose honor is being sung a great chorus when the arrival of Abigaille, escorted by two soldiers, interrupts the general rejoicing. In despair at the failure of her plans she has poisoned herself and presently dies with a prayer for forgiveness on her lips, while the opera ends with Zaccaria promising Nabucodonosor unlimited glory and power as the faithful servant of Jehovah.

Solera's libretto has many defects: coincidences are too abundant, the actions of the characters are usually too sudden, and their motives are often unintelligible. For instance, Fenena's conversion and Abigail's poisoning of herself are merely narrated in one sentence apiece, of which the audience can scarcely be expected immediately to realize the great importance; while Nebuchadnezzar's comings and goings are excessively mechanical. Nevertheless, as a whole, the libretto has the undoubted merit of dramatic sincerity, enhanced by a genuine feeling for the Bible atmosphere. Verdi's score throws both into relief. The spirit of the famous and lovely chorus "*Va, pensiero, sull' ali dorate*" is very much that of certain melancholy psalms, even if translated into terms of Bellini; the fanaticism of Zaccharias is precisely the fanaticism of the Old Testament set to music.

The choruses of the first act alone would suffice to attest the dramatic sincerity of the work; they are splendid. Perhaps that which depicts the panic of the people at the capture of the Temple is the best, the triplet-figure that characterizes the accompaniment being admirably expressive. But the first chorus of all, in which the priests and people supplicate Jehovah, is scarcely less good and, for the matter of that, the solo interludes, notably Zaccharias' "*Come notte a sol fulgente*," play a worthy part in it. The construction of the concerted chorus that concludes the act is also admirable, the ingenious manner in which the fury of Nebuchadnezzar and Abigail in the *Andante* movement is depicted and, so to say, isolated by means of a rushing semiquaver figure being particularly happy. Incidentally, Zaccharias' warning to the King not to profane the Temple is almost identical with the phrase used by Rigoletto in dismissing the courtiers in the third act of the opera of that name.

In the second act the concerted finale is again most effective as regards contrast between the music allotted to soloists and chorus, while Zaccharias' Prayer is a good example of an impressive bass aria. But there can be little doubt that the gem of the act is the scene of Abigail's pact with the priests of Babylon. Herein her cabaletta, with its intense declamation punctuated by exceptionally happy and vigorous comments by the priests, is not only so good in itself as a successful essay in a form notoriously unsatisfactory but so typical of the new energy that Verdi was infusing into Italian opera that the opening theme may be quoted:

Indeed, the scene as a whole suggests in many ways the spirit of the revengeful, cruel priests in *Aïda*.

Apart from the chorus "*Va, pensiero*" and the solemn "Prophecy" of Zaccharias, with which Verdi himself replaced a duet originally planned by Solera, the third act consists almost exclusively of a duet between Abigail and her reputed father. There is a good deal to admire here, particularly the King's change of mood from rage to supplication and the instrumental conclusion, with its chromatically descending figure. The fourth act, on the other hand, is on a distinctly lower level, though attention should be called to a very simple and moving little aria for Fenena, which has unaccountably escaped the notice not only of the public but of most commentators.

To sum up, *Nabucco* is probably the most satisfactory of all the early Verdi operas. There are passages more expressive in *Macbeth* and *Luisa Miller*, but as an entity *Nabucco* stands above them both, and not till *Rigoletto* did the composer produce again an opera so satisfactory as an artistic whole. Weak points, of course, abound. The marches are bad; the chorus of Levites, effective enough when heard in the overture, is poor as choral music; some of the arias are vulgar or conventional; the recitatives often mechanical. The scoring, too, is excessively noisy. So much so that Bonaventura has preserved the following amusing (and, alas, untranslatable) epigram written when the opera was produced in Paris:

> Vraiment l'affiche est dans son tort,
> En faux on devrait la poursuivre.
> Pourquoi nous annoncer Nabucodonos — or
> Quand c'est Nabuchodonos — cuivre.

Nevertheless, I do not think that any person capable of getting beneath the imperfect surface of the score, of making allowance for the now discarded convention in which the musical ideas are presented, can fail to appreciate the vigor, the fine dramatic quality, of this music. Even the overture, as Roncaglia points out, was the first since *William Tell* to be linked with the development of the theatrical action. The contrasted moods of pathos and violence throughout the opera are admirably interpreted, while all the characters, except, perhaps, the conventional Ismael, live separate and genuine musical lives of their own. *Nabucco* is essentially a production of genius, more, not less, lovable because of certain youthful crudities, certain obvious flaws.

I LOMBARDI ALLA PRIMA CROCIATA

Libretto by Solera

Production: MILAN, February 11, 1843

(As *Jérusalem, Production:* PARIS, November 26, 1847)

FOUR ACTS, ELEVEN SCENES

The people of Milan are awaiting the return of Pagano (baritone) to his native city. Many years ago Pagano and his brother Arvino (tenor), sons of Folco, both loved the same lady, Viclinda (soprano), who preferred Arvino and married him. Whereupon Pagano, intent on revenge, had treacherously attacked his brother and had been condemned to exile, from which, thanks to Arvino's clemency, he is now allowed to return. Pagano, however still nurses plans of revenge in his heart and, after a scene of feigned reconciliation with Arvino, Viclinda, and their daughter, Giselda (soprano), proceeds to put them into execution. Assembling a band of ruffians he descends on Folco's house with the intent of killing Arvino and carrying off Viclinda. In the dark, however, it is his father, not his brother, who is murdered. Overcome with shame and remorse, Pagano then tries to kill himself, but, not suffered to find so easy an escape, he is once more banished forever amid the execrations of all.

The second act opens in the palace of Acciano (bass), tyrant of Antioch. He and a "chorus of Ambassadors" invoke the wrath of Allah on the army of Crusaders advancing against them. Giselda, by some means not disclosed, has been captured and enslaved and Oronte (tenor), Acciano's son, has fallen in love with her, to the delight of his mother, secretly a Christian, who hopes that his love will lead him to the true faith. In the second scene we are transported to the mountainous exterior of the cave of a hermit who is none other than Pagano thus expiating his sins. No one recognizes him, not even his former follower Pirro, who, in bitter remorse at having abjured his faith and become a Moslem, comes to pray for forgiveness from the holy man. As a pledge of his sincerity he offers to betray Antioch to the Crusaders who, headed by their band, are now defiling over the plain. Presently, led by Arvino, a detachment of them arrive and, after paying due homage to the hermit, join with him in a chorus proclaiming the imminent fall of Allah. Pirro, as good as his word, opens to them the gates of the city, and the last scene of the act shows the harem of Acciano, where the Crusaders penetrate just in time to prevent the suicide of Giselda, ashamed of her unholy love for the infidel Oronte. But Giselda, when she sees on her father's hands what she imagines to be the blood of her lover, is seized with pacifist fury, proclaiming war and bloodshed contrary to God's will; which so incenses the militant spirit of Arvino that he would have killed his daughter had not the hermit intervened to save her with a plea of insanity.

The first scene of the third act is laid in the valley of Jehoshaphat outside Jerusalem, "dotted with practicable hills, the Mount of Olives being the most prominent." After a processional chorus of ecstatic contemplation of the Holy City, Giselda enters and to her delight and surprise meets Oronte, who, it appears, had not, as she thought, perished in the capture of Antioch, but had escaped in disguise. She decides to fly with him despite Oronte's warning of the outlaw's life that awaits them. Their flight is discovered, to the fury of Arvino, who, in a short scene laid in his tent, laments that he should have begotten such a daughter, his anger being swollen by the further information that Pagano has been seen in the Crusaders' camp. In the last scene of the act the fugitives, Oronte mortally wounded, arrive at a grotto in the mountains. Giselda accuses the cruelty of God in destroying the love that is all she has left; but the hermit, appearing suddenly, reproves her and points out that her love is a crime unless Oronte becomes a Christian. Since Oronte had been, apparently, desirous of conversion for some time, he is immediately baptized and dies with the promise to await Giselda in heaven.

After the opening scene of the last act, in which Giselda has a vision of Oronte among the angels, we are shown the camp of the Lombards, where the Crusaders are preparing for an assault on Jerusalem. At the conclusion of an orchestral interlude the hermit, supported by Arvino and Giselda (now reconciled with her father), is led into Arvino's tent. He was the first to scale the walls and, mortally wounded, reveals his identity as Pagano, praying for forgiveness from God and man. Arvino embraces him, and the opera ends with the dying man's request for a sight of the Crusaders' flags flying over Jerusalem illuminated by the rays of the morning sun.

It may be doubted whether the annals of opera contain a more uncouth libretto than this. Solera, in a regular fury of romanticism, seems to have striven to extract from the poem by Grossi, on which he based it, every effect dear to the romantic sentiment of the time, and Verdi cannot be acquitted of the charge of overlooking glaring particular defects in favor of a certain general effectiveness as regards situations and contrasts. This love of violent contrasts is well exemplified in the first act by the juxtaposition of a nuns' chorus, a conspirators' chorus, and a chorus of horror and revenge. With the exception of the conspirators' chorus, all these are good, especially the opening pages of "*All' empio, che infrange la santa promessa*" — in which, incidentally, Verdi's passion for contrast is again illustrated by the alternation of *pianissimo* and *fortissimo* — and the chorus, "*Mostro d'Averno orribile,*" at the end of the act. There is real nobility of conception in this, particularly in the theme announced by Pagano with the words: "*Farò col nome solo il cielo inorridir,*" while the decidedly Rossinian figure and crescendo culminating in the final *Presto* are most effective. There are other interesting points in the music of the act. For instance, the quartet has been highly praised, and, as a general rule, all the elaborate writing for principals and chorus may be reckoned successful. Giselda's Prayer too (much admired by Rossini) is truly beautiful both melodically and harmonically, foreshadowing, as it does, in the opening especially, the "*Ave Maria*" of the last act of *Otello*:

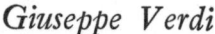

It is odd that this lovely melody should not have attracted the attention of some enterprising prima donna. Incidentally, the act is rich in hints of music to come. Thus the writing for the organ and the nuns' chorus is the obvious ancestor of all Verdi's writing in this style, while the accompaniment of a portion of Pagano's first aria is a definite forerunner of a similar figure in *Rigoletto*.

The second act has little to recommend it. Perhaps the worst feature is the alternate writing for military band and orchestra associated with the march of the Crusaders. This music, not only trivial but ridiculous, makes us feel that Verdi's youthful compositions for the Busseto military band must have been very poor stuff which he did exceedingly well to destroy. Indeed, it is remarkable how unsuccessful as a rule Verdi was in writing for the medium with which he was first associated, the march in *Aïda* being but the exception which proves the rule. Soffredini waxes enthusiastic over Oronte's cavatina and cabaletta (of which last, incidentally, Verdi not only wrote but preserved two versions), and Weissmann praises the fire of the Crusaders' chorus; but the dark contours of the recitative and *Adagio* of the hermit's scena seem to me the most interesting feature of the act. The coloratura-writing for Giselda in the last scene, too, is effective; indeed, the whole scene is not devoid of interest. Here, coupled with a slight foretaste of the ballet music in *Aïda*, we have an essay in the conventional Turkish atmosphere exemplified by the familiar "alla Turca" of Mozart. Weissmann signalizes the 6/8 tempo as something "unknown in *Nabucco*"; but this, though literally accurate, conveys a wrong impression, in that *Oberto* and *Il Finto Stanislao* contain examples of both 6/8 and 12/8 tempi. Apparently the peculiar lilt of 6/8 was often associated in Verdi's mind with "chambering and wantonness," for which the wholly robust *Nabucco* offered no such inducement as does this scene in a harem.

The third act is better, the opening of the liturgical chorus, "Jerusalem," and some of the duet between Giselda and Oronte being truly expressive, though the latter is marred by the final *Allegro*.

Undoubtedly the best music is to be found, however, in the trio that forms the climax of the act. Opening with a prelude in which the solo violin plays an important and, as regards the *cantabile* at any rate, a very effective part, it is further characterized by much writing for the harp which is used to accompany Oronte's baptism and generally to suggest celestial effects. Indeed, at one place the composer gives the actual indication: "angelico," whatever that may have conveyed to conductor or instrumentalist. More important than any orchestral effects, however, is the significant writing for the voice, whether alone or in combination. This is shown in the vigor of Giselda's accusation of God's cruelty, with its typical Verdian figure in the accompaniment; in the calm serenity of the hermit; in the broken, breathless phrases of the dying Oronte, worth quoting to show Verdi's striving for expressiveness in these early days:

ORONTE.
Andantino

Più non mi reg - go a-i - ta-mi io ti discerno ap-pe - na,

Moreover, the beautiful *cantabile* with which the trio ends is an admirable example of the fusion of three voice-parts, which, it has been well said, might almost be called an *aria a tre voci*.

The whole of Giselda's vision that opens the last act is mediocre and the famous chorus that follows it, "*O Signore dal tetto natio*," though we may admire the broad opening phrases, seems to me in no way comparable with its equally famous and far more beautiful predecessor in *Nabucco*. The Crusaders' war-chorus is the same as in the second act; so is the music for the military band that apparently accompanies them wherever they go. The most interesting feature of the act, perhaps, is some of the recitative-writing, notably Giselda's *Andante* in the last scene, which ends on a happy and unexpected modulation. The finale is quite conventional.

On the whole, the outstanding merit of *I Lombardi* may be summed up as that of uncompromising sincerity shown mainly in the choral and ensemble writing. So absolutely sincere, indeed, was the composer that much of the music, as Roncaglia acutely points out, is as absurd as the words it sets, an eloquent if unconscious tribute to Verdi's dramatic sensibility. Take the words of the conspirators' chorus in the first act:

> D'un sol colpo in paradiso
> L'alme altrui godiam mandar;
> Col pugnal di sangue intriso
> Poi sediamo a banchettar.

Which, doggerel for doggerel, may be translated thus:

> With one blow we like to send our
> Fellows' souls in heaven to shine;
> Then with gore-encrusted daggers
> We sit calmly down to dine.

If we did not know the blindness of the romantic movement to humor it would be impossible not to consider them deliberately funny. Small wonder, then, that Verdi's accompanying music is grotesque; and the example, if extreme, is typically illustrative of much of the opera. The surprising thing about *I Lombardi* is, not that it abounds in absurdities and crudities, but that it contains so much fine music.

Very little need be said about *Jérusalem*, the version of the opera produced at the Paris Opéra. The French librettists, Royer and Vaez, simplified the story somewhat by abolishing Oronte and his Christian mother and making the heroine's inevitable lover one of the original pair of brothers, who, wrongly accused of his father's murder, has been forced to fly to foreign parts. The Crusaders become French instead of Italian, and in the first scene Toulouse takes the place of Milan. Fundamentally, however, the psychological action remains identical, if different in actual detail. As regards the music, there is a good deal of rearrangement, in which, though the importance of the chorus is lessened, most of the best numbers are preserved, as a rule in a lower key so as to render the *tessitura* more acceptable to French voices. Verdi rewrote much of the recitative, added a few numbers, none of them in any way distinguished, and inserted a long ballet, which contains some of the worst music of the kind that he ever penned. In short, where *Jérusalem* differs from *I Lombardi* it differs as a general rule for the worse; nothing is gained and certain elemental rugged qualities are lost. To the best of my belief, it has, unlike *I Lombardi,* lapsed into final oblivion.

ERNANI

Libretto by Piave

Production: VENICE, March 9, 1844

FOUR ACTS, FIVE SCENES

Don Ruy Gomez de Silva (bass), an old man passionately in love with his ward and niece, Elvira (soprano), has determined to marry her. She, however, is in love with and loved by Ernani (tenor), an outlaw, who at the opening of the opera appeals to his followers for help to carry her off. The scene changes to Elvira's apartments in Silva's castle. Attendants bring her bridal gifts and congratulate her on the approaching marriage; but all her thoughts, all her longings, are for Ernani. A visitor is announced. To Elvira's shocked surprise, he is none other than Don Carlo, King of Spain (baritone), who has come to offer her his heart if not his hand. Elvira refuses him and Don Carlo, incensed at seeing an outlaw preferred to himself, is about to carry her off when Ernani appears. The two men recognize each other at once. It was Don Carlo's father who killed Ernani's father and confiscated his possessions, so Ernani defies him as the scion of the house responsible for all his woes. Don Carlo, in contemptuous pity, bids Ernani fly and save his life; but at that moment Silva enters, naturally thinks the worst at finding two men in his niece's room at night, and challenges both to a duel. Just as he is about to engage Don Carlo, Riccardo, the King's esquire, enters and proclaims his master's identity to the inexplicably unenlightened Silva, who can do nothing but apologize. The King announces his intention of staying in the castle and ensures Ernani's escape by proclaiming him as one of his followers. Ernani, however, is not moved from his plans of ultimate vengeance, and the act ends in an ensemble in which all the characters explain their various states of mind.

The second act opens an hour before the time fixed for the wedding of Elvira and Silva. A pilgrim is introduced and welcomed by Silva with the pledge of hospitality. Elvira appears in her bridal finery; whereupon the pilgrim throws off his cloak and discloses himself as Ernani, offering his life as a wedding gift. His followers have been slain and he is closely pursued by the King's men, with a price upon his head. But Silva, assuring him of protection in accordance with the Castilian traditions of hospitality, goes off to see to the defense of the castle against his pursuers. Elvira and Ernani, left alone, confess their irresistible love for each other, so that Silva on his return finds them in each other's arms and would take summary vengeance, but at that moment an attendant announces the presence of the King and his soldiers at the castle gates, demanding admission. Silva, partly mindful of his duties as a host, partly desirous of himself taking vengeance on Ernani, hides him in a secret place behind one of the ancestral portraits, and when Don Carlo, furious at finding the entrance barred, demands the fugitive under penalty of the destruction of the castle and the execution of its owner, he refuses pointblank to violate the sacred laws of hospitality by such a betrayal. His resolution is nearly broken when Elvira is taken away as a hostage, but his loyalty to tradition wins the day and he bids her follow Don Carlo. When they are gone, he fetches Ernani from his hiding-place and challenges him to a duel. Ernani refuses and, learning that Elvira has departed with the King, swears, if only a respite is granted enabling them both to be avenged on Don Carlo, that his life shall be forfeit to Silva at any time the old man blows a blast on the horn that he hands to him as a pledge.

The third act discloses Don Carlo in meditation before the subterranean tomb of Charlemagne in Aix-la-Chapelle, while the Electors are sitting to decide whether he shall succeed as Holy Roman Emperor. Aware that a band of conspirators against his life will meet in this place, he decides, by hiding in the tomb itself, to discover their identity. Presently the conspirators arrive, among them Ernani and Silva. Lots are drawn as to who shall kill the King and the lot falls on Ernani, who refuses to abandon the privilege, despite Silva's offer, if he will only retire in his favor, to give up the horn and all that it stands for. Three cannon-shots, the prearranged signal, announce that Don Carlo has been elected Emperor. He emerges from the tomb, courtiers and soldiers crowd into the vault, and the conspirators are captured. Don Carlo gives orders that the noble among them shall be executed, the rest thrown into prison. Ernani, announcing his identity as Don Juan of Aragon, claims the right of being included among the former, but Don Carlo, partly owing to the entreaties of Elvira, partly owing to a new realization of his responsibilities as the successor of Charlemagne, not only pardons all the conspirators but gives Elvira to Ernani as wife. The act ends with a chorus in honor of the humane Emperor.

Silva, however, has not absolved Ernani from his pledge and when, at the conclusion of the masked ball that forms part of the wedding festivities in the last act, the sound of a distant horn is heard, Ernani realizes with horror what it means. The sound grows nearer; whereupon Ernani, dismissing Elvira on some pretext or other, awaits the coming of Silva. No appeal suffices to soften the old man, who reminds Ernani of his oath, giving him the choice of suicide by poison or dagger. Ernani, having chosen the dagger, is about to stab himself when Elvira returns. Her prayers are equally unavailing, and the curtain falls on the death of Ernani, with Elvira prostrate and senseless on the ground.

Piave, constructing his libretto on Victor Hugo's play of the same name, may be said generally to have taken the situations and discarded the details that made them comparatively credible. For instance, the opening of Victor Hugo's *Hernani* presents Don Carlos's regal status as unknown to all the characters, while his admission to Dona Sol's (Elvira's) apartment in mistake for the brigand and their subsequent common concealment in the cupboard on Silva's entrance provide a link between the two men that makes it just possible to understand the chivalrous dismissal of his rival. Besides, in the play Don Carlos has a definite sense of humor and is not a mere puppet who, for no apparent reason, turns from a lecherous and frivolous Prince into a humane and statesmanlike Emperor. Dona Sol, too, is perhaps a trifle more human than Elvira, but Ernani seems substantially similar and Silva equally preposterous in both play and opera — a kind of romantic Dr. Bartolo. At least Piave has spared us the scene in the play where he invokes one after the other the portraits of his ancestors. Hugo's contemporaries waxed especially enthusiastic over this scene, but to us it seems the acme of absurdity, a mere foretaste of *Ruddigore*, which may possibly have been intended as a parody of it, just as Bernard Shaw's *Arms and the Man* is a perfect travesty of the first act. In both opera and play there are of course other scenes and motives that strike us as merely ludicrous, but the opera, as was so often to be the case in Piave's librettos, further suffers from an undue compression that at times makes the action scarcely intelligible. What in the play is a whole scene becomes in the opera a sentence, a mere indication. Often only a minute scrutiny of the libretto reveals the motives of the characters.

It is, then, primarily each situation as it comes that Verdi illustrates in his music, sometimes inadequately, more frequently with a kind of savage sincerity that compels admiration. The characters are types rather than human beings, Silva being the embodiment of chivalry and revenge, Don Carlo first of eroticism, then of magnanimity, Ernani of revolt, and so on. Silva is, musically, the most successful, his choleric vigor being primarily an expression of Verdi's own temperament. Don Carlo, except in the third act, is the worst. Even if we contrive to forget that he was in fact that extremely important historical personage Charles V, he remains a quite unconvincing character divided into two incompatible halves.

Viewed as music pure and simple, however, the score of *Ernani* has much to recommend it. The short prelude, ingeniously compounded of two significant themes from the opera, provides an appropriate introduction; the opening drinking chorus (towards the end a rhythmical forerunner of Iago's immortal essay on the same theme in *Otello*) is full of vigor, while the *sotto voce* chorus *à la Rigoletto* that follows, with its strong contrasts of *piano* and *forte*, is a great improvement on the somewhat similar chorus in *I Lombardi*. I have never been able to share the enthusiasm of commentators or public for Elvira's famous cavatina, "*Ernani, involami,*" which opens the second scene; it is spoiled by the second phrase and a superfluity of uninspired ornamentation. The cabaletta which follows, "*Tutto sprezzo che d'Ernani,*" with its fine opening phrase and expressive cadence, seems to me superior in every way; indeed, it is one of the best cabalettas that Verdi wrote at this time. The recognition of Ernani by Don Carlo provides a good example of declamatory writing, and the staccato, unaccompanied chorus *"Vedi come il buon vegliardo,"* is most effective, leading, further, at the entrance of the orchestra, to a smooth phrase, quite Mozartean in its loveliness, first sung by Elvira and Ernani and subsequently developed into a splendid ensemble. The actual finale, however, is very conventional.

The second act is, as a rule, dismissed as of no particular interest; wrongly, I think. True, with the exception of the pretty duet between Elvira and Ernani, and Don Carlo's fine aria *"Lo vedremo, veglio audace,"* developing later, with that characteristic alternation of major and minor thirds which became almost a mannerism with the composer, into a duet with Silva, there are few "set pieces" of note. True, the opening gallop is one of the very worst instances of "party-music" perpetrated by a composer whose idea of social festivities never passed beyond the limits of the piazza at Busseto. As regards detail, however, there are some fine things: Elvira's beautiful phrase when she confesses her unbroken love for Ernani; the bold harmonic progression in the ninth bar in the orchestral introduction to Don Carlo's entry and his subsequent scena; the impressive theme that accompanies the pledge given by Ernani. But, to my mind, the outstanding feature of the act is Silva's music throughout. Beginning with his discovery of the two lovers, it sometimes has an almost Beethovenian quality. And even where the purely musical interest is less, the theatrical impressiveness remains constant. Take the *Velocissimo,* "*No, vendetta*"; it is an extraordinary manifestation of energy, such as no other composer of the time could have achieved, carrying us off our feet with its fire and fury.

The third act is usually considered the best. For instance, Don Carlo's opening recitative and first aria, culminating in the expressive and typical Verdian phrase: *"E vincitor dei secoli il nome mio farò,"* has been deservedly praised, though, in my view, Elvira's music when she pleads for clemency is more admirable still, the long phrase with which it ends being a stroke of genius in the impression it gives of intensity and strain. Most of the act, of course, is taken up with the conspiracy. The music of this, by no means remarkable in itself, is interesting primarily as showing the skill with which Verdi led up to the famous unison chorus *"Si ridesti il Leon di Castiglia."* With the possible exception of one phrase this is a fine if crude tune, but, thanks largely to its preparation, it creates an overwhelming emotional effect, giving us the same kind of thrill as the sound of a shot from a big gun. With similar unerring instinct Verdi prepares the climax of *"A Carlo Magno sia gloria ed onor"* by previously abandoning the *legato* style in favor of a few bars of pure declamation. Indeed, the music of the whole finale is admirable and has been singled out by Basevi as one of the most effective numbers ever written by any operatic composer.

The importance of the last act is to be sought mainly in the famous trio, though in fact there is much of interest before the three characters appear simultaneously on the stage. For instance, the moment when the sound of Silva's horn first disturbs Ernani's quiet, while Elvira, all unconscious, sings a very beautiful and expressive phrase, is one of true dramatic significance. Ernani's simple cavatina is at least pretty, and the "pledge" music sounds as effective as ever. Nevertheless, it is the trio that provides the high light of the act. No composer has ever written more expressively for the human voice, the detailed nature of the indications to the singers, the soprano especially, being a sign of Verdi's ambition in this respect. Apart from any question of technical skill, however, the trio possesses great musical beauty, and the following passage, in the midst of straightforward music, seems worth quoting as an example of the composer's ability even in those days to make an effect by means of harmony and rhythm as well as counterpoint:

From the technical point of view *Ernani* possesses at least one feature of great importance: it provides the first instance of that association of a theme with a certain event or mood which Verdi was to employ frequently in later years and which some people have, perhaps maliciously, compared with the Wagnerian *Leitmotiv*. Here the music associated with Ernani's horn, after an indication in the prelude, appears both in the second and in the fourth act. It is impossible that Verdi should have known anything of Wagner's music at the time — *Tannhäuser* had not been produced — yet the fortuitous similarity of the proceeding and, incidentally, the almost Wagnerian nature of the theme itself, seem to justify a quotation:

If Ernani had maintained the level touched in its best numbers it would easily be the best of Verdi's early operas. In a sense it falls below *Nabucco* because it is more ambitious than *Nabucco*. With the exception of the conspiracy scene in the third act, the interest is entirely human. The composer cannot here rely on religion and politics to provide the unity of feeling indispensable in a work of art. Each character appears on the canvas as a splash of violent color. The music is crude, often downright brutal; there is little question of subtlety or blending. *Ernani* is in essence the projection of a personality ruthlessly sincere in both its qualities and its defects.

I DUE FOSCARI

Libretto by Piave
Production: ROME, November 3, 1844
THREE ACTS, EIGHT SCENES

In the Doge's Palace at Venice the Council of Ten is assembling to decide the fate of Jacopo Foscari (tenor), the son of the octogenarian Doge, who, having been banished for a supposed murder, has transgressed the law in returning to catch a glimpse of his beloved native city, even if he is not, as his enemies suggest, in treasonable correspondence with Milan. Loredano (bass), a member of the Council of Ten, has sworn a feud against the Foscari family, who have, he thinks, been responsible for the death of his father and uncle, and maneuvers to get Jacopo punished by either death or perpetual exile. The Council votes for the latter, and Lucrezia (soprano), Jacopo's wife, comes to the Doge, begging him to intercede with the Council, over which he himself presides. But old Foscari (baritone), spied on by the Ten, torn between his paternal feelings on the one hand and his official obligations on the other, can do nothing though in his heart he is convinced of the innocent intentions of his son.

The second act opens with Jacopo in prison. Half-delirious, he does not recognize his wife, who has come to bid him a last farewell; for the Council has decided that neither she nor their children shall be allowed to accompany him into exile. Then the Doge comes to do likewise, impressing on Jacopo the depth of his paternal love though, as Doge, he may not show it or be influenced by it. The interview is interrupted by Loredano, who enters to summon Jacopo to the Council Chamber, where his sentence will be formally handed down. In the final scene the Council is seen in session, which, after Jacopo has read his sentence, is about to be raised when Lucrezia bursts in, accompanied by her two children, hoping thus to soften the hearts of the Ten to the extent at least of allowing her and them to share Jacopo's exile. All in vain, however, and the act ends with Jacopo's departure in custody.

In the third act Venice is *en fête*, the Square of St. Mark's crowded with masked revelers, gondoliers singing a barcarole. The State galley arrives to bear away Jacopo, who departs after bidding farewell to Lucrezia. The scene then changes to the private apartments of the

I Due Foscari

Doge, who laments the unjust fate from which he could not save his last surviving son. Barbarigo (tenor), a Senator, who has throughout felt pity for Jacopo, comes to announce the joyful tidings that the perpetrator of the murder for which Jacopo was originally banished has confessed to the crime on his deathbed; but at that very moment Lucrezia enters with the news that Jacopo died when the ship set sail. She is shortly followed by members of the Council of Ten, who, after a few conventional expressions of sympathy, inform the Doge that, in view of the weight of his years and sorrows, his abdication has been decided upon. He refuses, reproaching them with ingratitude and reminding them that, years before, when he wished to abdicate, the privilege was refused him. However, he is forced to obey and hands over the insignia of office. Presently the sound of a bell is heard announcing the appointment of his successor, to the unconcealed joy of Loredano, who now sees his vengeance on the Foscari family complete. As indeed it is, for the old Doge, overwhelmed by this final blow, collapses and dies with a last despairing cry for his son.

The choice of Verdi and Piave of such an unsatisfactory play as Lord Byron's *The Two Foscari* for the basis of an opera libretto seems, to say the least, odd; all the more so since Byron himself thought little of it. Probably the reason must be sought in Jacopo Foscari's passion for Venice, which, they may well have thought, might reasonably endear the subject to an audience only too ready to snatch at any form of patriotic sentiment. Nor, perhaps, would the atmosphere of unrelieved gloom have appeared so uncongenial to them as it does to us. As a matter of fact, by the introduction of the *festa*, of the Barcarole sung by gondoliers, an attempt was made to lighten this atmosphere, which might have been successful had the accompanying music been better. Otherwise Piave followed Byron's original fairly closely, inventing only Lucrezia's attempt to soften the hearts of the judges by the introduction of her children into the Council Chamber and suppressing a torture scene *à la Tosca*. The defects of this libretto are mainly confined to his constant vice of undue compression. The death of Jacopo and the demand for the Doge's abdication are really too simultaneous for belief; Jacopo's supposedly treasonable correspondence with Milan, without which the play is incredible, is barely hinted at; Loredano's fanatical belief in the poisoning of his father and uncle is never confuted as it is in Byron's tragedy, so that the audience is left wondering whether his ruthless vengeance may not, after all, be excused. At the same time the usual summary dismissal of the libretto as devoid of all human interest seems hardly justified. True, the interest is one of tears rather than passion; but the character and the tragic situation of the old Doge, at any rate, compel sympathetic pity.

Verdi seems to have felt this for with the Doge is associated what remains undoubtedly the best music of the opera. From his first scena and aria, "*Oh vecchio cor che batti*," his music has real character, only lost temporarily in the brilliant and inapposite *Presto* that concludes the otherwise effective trio in the first scene of the second act. Some of the duet, too, between him and Lucrezia at the end of the first act is very good, while the final abdication scene, particularly where the bell of St. Mark's announces the election of a new Doge, shows a dignity and pathos worthy of the situation. To Jacopo, too, is allotted some very expressive music. The exile's appreciation of the limpid atmosphere of Venice is most successfully suggested in his first recitative and aria, while the cabaletta that follows, if dramatically inapposite, has real energy, the orchestral passage between the verses being exceptionally happy. Very expressive, too, is the passage: "*Nel tuo paterno amplesso*," which opens the D-flat movement of the trio in the second act. Indeed, the whole of this movement is good till the final *Presto*, already referred to. Moreover, the music in the finale of this act, in which Jacopo confides his children to the Doge's care, is really moving, and the finale as a whole is a good example of effective and well-contrasted concerted writing.

An interesting feature of *I Due Foscari* is the quantity of motifs linked with the characters or their actions. Thus a certain orchestral figure is associated throughout with the Council of Ten; the same holds good for the private meditations of the Doge; Lucrezia's agitation and Jacopo's despair both have themes of their own recurrent throughout the opera. Unfortunately, with the exception of the last (which, incidentally, figures in the prelude), none of these themes possesses any distinction. Another point worthy of note is the extended use of 3/4 time to express excitement or energy, a proceeding subsequently much favored by Verdi. The opening chorus of the last scene of the first act and the *Allegro prestissimo* of the duet with which the same scene ends provide typical examples of this.

In short, *I Due Foscari* is not a good opera, but it contains a certain amount of music that compels admiration as well as interest, foreshadowing in some ways its later and far more important successor, *Simon Boccanegra*.

GIOVANNA D'ARCO

Libretto by Solera

Production: MILAN, February 15, 1845

PROLOGUE AND THREE ACTS, SIX SCENES

    The French are lamenting their evil plight at the hands of the conquering English. Carlo, King of France (tenor), enters to announce his abdication, absolving all from their allegiance. He has had a vision of a maid bidding him lay down his helmet and sword in the midst of a certain forest and, hoping by his renunciation to turn the wrath of Heaven from stricken France, he asks whether such a place is known to any present. Apparently the chorus know it well, for, fearing the influence of evil spirits, they try to dissuade him from his quest. Nevertheless he sets out.

    The place seen by Carlo in his vision is precisely that where Giovanna (soprano) is wont to go to pray for strength to become the savior of France. Not even her father, Giacomo (baritone), is certain whether the power she invokes is of heaven or hell, and at the opening of the second scene we find him concealing himself in a cave near by in order to ascertain the truth. Presently Carlo approaches and lays down his helmet and sword as commanded in the vision. Giovanna, who has been conscious, on the one hand, of heavenly spirits promising the fulfillment of her prayer if only she will swear to renounce all earthly affection, on the other, of demons urging her to the delights of life and love, recognizes the King. She joyfully takes up the helmet and sword for which she has so ardently prayed and with a promise of victory departs in his company — to the dismay of her watchful father, who thus sees, as he imagines, his worst fears confirmed.

    The first act opens in the camp of the English army under Talbot, thoroughly dispirited by their defeat at the hands of Carlo and Giovanna, who, they believe, is endowed with supernatural powers. Giacomo, half-demented, comes and begs, though a Frenchman, to be allowed to fight against the King who has dishonored his daughter, promising further to hand her over to the English. The scene then changes to the court at Rheims, which Giovanna, longing for her home and countryside, has just decided to leave when Carlo enters and entreats her to stay. She has, he says, brought him victory, but, more than that, she has now taught him to love her; she must stay and crown him king in the cathedral. Giovanna, despite the warning of the heavenly voices and the exultation of the demons, which she alone hears, cannot refrain from confessing that she too loves him, though she realizes that the avowal means her own destruction.

The second act is laid outside Rheims Cathedral during the pomp of Carlo's coronation. When all have entered the church, Giacomo waits to confront his daughter, hoping by the exposure and punishment of her sins in this world to save her soul in the next. Giovanna comes out, followed by the King in his coronation robes, who, amid the applause of the people, couples her with Saint Denis as the patron saint of France. This is Giacomo's opportunity. He denounces the blasphemy, proclaims himself Giovanna's father, and declares, to the consternation of all, that her power is derived from a secret midnight pact with demons. He presses Giovanna by everything she holds most sacred to admit her guilt. She answers not a word; but a sudden thunderclap sufficiently attests the truth of her father's charge and, despite Carlo's efforts and appeals, the crowd clamor for the witch to be handed over to the English.

In the last act Giovanna, laden with chains, is imprisoned in a fortress in the English camp. The French are attacking and she prays to God for mercy and deliverance from her chains. She has, she admits, broken her covenant with Heaven by falling in love, but it was only for an instant. Giacomo, overhearing the prayer and struck by its genuine piety, suddenly realizes his mistake, strikes off her chains, and begs her forgiveness. Asking for his blessing and his sword, Giovanna rushes out once more to lead the French to victory. But in the battle she is mortally wounded and is carried back to the now captured fortress to die, her banner in her hand, a vision of the Virgin before her eyes, words of forgiveness on her lips; all prostrate themselves before her lifeless body.

Solera's libretto, supposedly based on Schiller's *The Maid of Orléans*, wanders very far from the original. Indeed, except for the scene of Charles's abdication and that in which her father comes to curse Joan for being the King's mistress, there is little detailed connection between the two. Even Joan's captivity, basically identical in both, has this difference: that Solera abandoned Joan's miraculous deliverance from her chains in favor of direct action by her father. In general, moreover, it may be said that all Schiller's historical background is wiped out. There is no sympathetic Agnes Sorel; no Isabeau, that Queen-Mother who with her implacable, historical hate for her son nicely balances Giacomo with his incredible, operatic credulity as regards his daughter. There is no Dunois. Only the English commander, Talbot, remains, a lifeless remnant of what was perhaps the best aspect of Schiller's play. Still, nobody but a German, and an exceptionally pedantic and sentimental German at that, is likely to take up the cudgels on behalf of *The Maid of Orléans*. Much has been made of Solera's "mutilation"; but what was his unforgivable sin? He transferred Joan's sudden infatuation for Lionel on the field of battle — one of the most idiotic episodes ever invented — to a momentary infatuation for Charles, which is in fact more credible. He caused Joan to be betrayed to the English by her father in place of a malevolent French leader. This is obviously less satisfactory; but, as some compensation, he showed Joan's father as convinced of her liaison with Charles from the outset, thus providing better, not worse, ground for his denunciation during the coronation scene. On the whole, then, Solera, it seems to me, has been maligned. He was concerned with Joan of Arc rather than *The Maid of Orléans*. As an opera librettist he was forced to omit the historical background, to concentrate on the personal aspect. Apart from the altered ending, his own original contributions to the story — the rival choruses of demons and angels, Giacomo's confusion between Joan's prayer to Mary and her supposed pact with the devil — are doubtless unfortunate; but the former at any rate might have been effective if Verdi had in fact provided more appropriate music for them. In short, if *Giovanna d'Arco* seems to us incredible and silly, it is only one degree more silly and incredible than *The Maid of Orléans*.

Verdi's music has been dismissed as worthless. This, too, is unjust. There is a considerable amount of purely conventional music in *Giovanna d'Arco*, and some that is downright bad, among which must be included the angelic and demoniac choruses. Verdi, never conspicuously happy in a fantastic vein, failed utterly to suggest the supernatural in either. The demons in the prologue are the worst; for they indulge in a 3/8 lilt, intended, as is so often the case with this rhythm, to be seductive, but actually suggesting comic-opera peasants and fishermen. Where, as at the end of the first act, they indulge in malignant though exceedingly diatonic comments on Joan's despair and Charles's love-making, the writing is inoffensive if not as admirable as the intention behind it. The marches, both triumphal and funeral, are negligible, though the trio of the former is noteworthy as anticipating a popular phrase in *Aïda*. The cabalettas, especially that sung by Joan at the end of the first scene of the last act and the syncopated "one-step" that concludes the prologue, are wholly uninspired.

Nevertheless, there is something to admire in every act, though it must be conceded that, speaking generally, *Giovanna d'Arco* steadily deteriorates as it goes on. Thus the first theme of the overture, decidedly reminiscent of Beethoven in character, gives the appropriate atmosphere at once, while the little concerted *Andante pastorale* for flute, oboe, and clarinets that follows is very charming. Incidentally, Weissmann writes that the overture was subsequently used for *I Vespri Siciliani*, but between the two published versions at any rate I can find no connection. The first scene of the prologue maintains the same high level. The chorus-writing throughout, whether descriptive of despair, rage, or romantic horror, is admirable, while Charles's cavatina "*Sotto una quercia*" is pretty. Moreover, the orchestral contribution to the general result cannot be summarily dismissed. The accompaniment figure of the opening is very felicitous and the eerie orchestral effect that illustrates Charles's "*Trascorrere m'intesi ignoto senso per le vene*" deserves praise; all the more so in that it serves to throw into relief the lovely placid phrase that immediately follows. Giacomo's scena, especially the atmospheric introduction, raises equally high hopes for the second scene, unfortunately destined to remain unrealized.

Perhaps the most attractive feature of the first act is Joan's little cavatina, "*O fatidica foresta.*" Nobody seems to have noticed it, but the emotion appears to me truly expressive of her longing for home and family. The English soldiers, too, at the beginning of the act have a special interest for us. They are associated with a tune that begins, probably as the result of sheer coincidence, exactly like "Hearts of Oak" and seems in any case a typical embodiment of that nonchalance characteristic, apparently, of English armies in the fifteenth as in the twentieth century. Much of the chorus-writing in the second act is skillful, particularly, perhaps, as regards the semiquaver comments on the placid tune of Joan and Charles in the finale, which, moreover, ends with an *Allegro vivo* remarkably full of life. There is, too, a very happy change of key when the trumpets introduce this same finale after Giacomo's air, in which, incidentally, may be traced the first accents of Germont in *La Traviata*. The same may be said of the duet between father and daughter, which, together with Charles's beautiful and truly elegiac cavatina, "*Quale più fido amico?*" provides the outstanding feature of an otherwise undistinguished last act.

Roncaglia is unquestionably right in his assertion that in *Giovanna d'Arco* Verdi wished to enter the lists of grand opera with Rossini and Spontini. Indeed, the influence of *William Tell* is evident in the instrumental phrase that opens the first act, even more in the *Andante* of the overture. That he must be regarded as having failed should not blind us to the fact that *Giovanna d'Arco* shows a definite striving, occasionally successful, after new harmonic and orchestral effects. Far too much has been made of the accidental circumstance that the opera was composed in three months. It was not lack of care, but lack of the necessary technique, coupled perhaps with a certain paralysis of imagination, characteristic of Verdi's work at this time, that made *Giovanna d'Arco* a comparative failure.

ALZIRA

Libretto by Cammarano

Production: NAPLES, August 12, 1845

PROLOGUE AND TWO ACTS, SIX SCENES

About the middle of the sixteenth century a band of Incas have captured Alvaro (bass), the Spanish Governor of the country, and are about to kill him when Zamoro (tenor), head of the tribe and reputed dead after his capture in battle, unexpectedly returns. With true savage magnanimity he sets Alvaro free, but, learning that his sweetheart, Alzira (soprano), and her father are prisoners in Lima, he unites his followers in a war of vengeance against the Spaniards.

The first act opens in Lima, where Alvaro is resigning his position in favor of his son Gusmano (baritone), whose first act is to sign peace between Spain and the Incas, asking from their chief, Ataliba, as a pledge of the covenant, the hand of his daughter, with whom, despite himself, he is passionately in love. She, however, is none other than Alzira, who, unable to forget her beloved Zamoro, cannot bring herself to obey her father's command to marry Gusmano. At the very moment of her final refusal there appears Zamoro, who has gained admission by a stratagem. Alzira at first thinks him a ghost, but, soon convinced of his reality, falls into his arms, where she is surprised by the untimely entrance of Gusmano. The two men at once recognize each other, for it was Gusmano who had treated Zamoro so ill in captivity and against whom the Inca had sworn vengeance. Gusmano, despite the peace signed with Ataliba and the taunts of Zamoro, summons his guards to carry the Inca off to execution and, mad with fury and jealousy, refuses to pardon him, even though Alvaro, mindful of his own experience with the Incas, begs for his life. Hearing, however, that the Incas have crossed the river Rima and are about to attack the town, Gusmano unexpectedly sets his prisoner free, vowing that they shall meet on the field of battle.

The battle is lost by the Incas, many of whom, including Zamoro, are being led as prisoners into Lima at the opening of the second act. Zamoro is sentenced to death, but Gusmano promises freedom for the rebel if Alzira will marry him; which, with considerable reluctance, she consents to do. With her aid Zamoro escapes to the mountains, joining a band of Inca warriors, from whom he hears of

Alzira's forthcoming marriage to Gusmano. Maddened by her supposed treachery, he vows vengeance and, despite the entreaties of his followers, returns once more to Lima. The town is *en fête* for the wedding ceremony. Indeed, Gusmano is about to take Alzira's hand when an unknown soldier stabs him to the heart. The soldier is none other than Zamoro, who has taken advantage of the disguise provided for his flight to pass again into the town. The bystanders are about to slay him when the dying Gusmano, by way of showing him that there are qualities superior even to the savage virtues, commands that his life be spared and that he and Alzira be married.

Essentially Cammarano's libretto is identical with Voltaire's play of the same name, on which it is founded. Only the librettist turns into a prologue an incident merely related in the play, thus giving it undue importance and eliminating as far as possible in favor of a conventional story of love and revenge that essay on the "noble savage" theme which is, perhaps, the best feature of Voltaire's otherwise dreary verses. Voltaire, unconventional and daring, maintained in his play that true Christianity, albeit the rarest of attributes, was in fact superior to the savage nobility invented, beloved, and preached by eighteenth-century philosophy. The thesis may have been conceived with his tongue in his cheek (improbable in view of the Alexandrines), as a kind of paradox *à la* Bernard Shaw. At any rate the thesis remains, a remarkable witness to one of the fallacies from which the French Revolution was subsequently to derive. Except for a line here and there, all this is passed over by Cammarano, who never forgot that Verdi had especially enjoined on him brevity. We may be thankful for it. These incredible Peruvians — both playwright and librettist amusingly call them "Americans" — and impossible Spaniards are quite devoid of any human interest. They seem to exist not as individuals at all, but as means to create dramatic situations, of which two, incidentally, are identical with situations to be found later in *Trovatore* and *Ballo in Maschera*.

This lack of characterization is faithfully reflected in the music, which consists almost entirely of a procession of uninspired essays in the conventional operatic language of the time. There is an effective *stringendo* at the end of the overture, which, incidentally, is built on a large scale; the music that orchestrally introduces the Incas both in the prologue and in the first act must have sounded duly barbaric to a contemporary audience; in the opening number of Zamoro and his followers there occurs a phrase identical with that subsequently to be immortalized in the drinking song in *Otello*. Otherwise there is nothing to excite, I will not say enthusiasm, but even interest, till the finale of the first act, where the duet between Alvaro and Gusmano beginning at "*Nella polve genuflesso*" is good, being worked up at the entrance of Alzira into a dozen pages of fine music with a spirited *Allegro* to bring the act to an end.

There is a little more in the second act. The duet between Alzira and Gusmano, if conventional, is pretty. The concluding accompaniment figure of the finale is really poignant; but probably the best feature of the opera is the orchestral introduction to Zamoro's arrival at the mountain cave. This, characterized by a clashing of sharps and naturals that looks positively frightening on paper, must have sounded most effective, the prevailing color, too, being admirable.

To my mind, *Alzira* is undoubtedly the worst of Verdi's operas, and it is satisfactory to know that he himself came cordially to dislike it. Only a few months after production he characterized the overture and the finale as the only redeeming features of the opera, and in later years he spoke of the whole as "really ugly."

ATTILA

Libretto by Solera

Production: VENICE, March 17, 1846

PROLOGUE AND THREE ACTS, SEVEN SCENES

In the middle of the fifth century Attila (bass), invading Italy at the head of his army, had sacked and destroyed Aquileia, and the opening of the prologue shows his barbarous warriors, in expectation of his trumphant arrival, singing the praises of Woden and Valhalla amid the ruins. When Attila arrives, he is displeased at seeing a band of captive women, for he had given orders that the whole population was to be put to the sword; but on learning that they had fought side by side with the men, his anger changes to admiration. To his inquiry of the reason for such Amazonian valor, Odabella (soprano), daughter of the late Lord of Aquileia, answers proudly from among the captives that the women of Italy, unlike the women in his army, know full well how to fight. Attila, pleased at this spirit, offers her any gift she may choose. She asks for a sword. Whereupon he gives her his own, with which she secretly vows to exact vengeance for the loss of all she holds most dear. Ezio (baritone), an envoy from the Roman Emperor, is then shown in. In private colloquy with Attila he offers the King the empire of the world if only he may keep Italy, pointing out that the Emperor of the East is an old dotard, the Emperor of the West a mere boy. Attila, disgusted at such treachery, refuses to listen, exclaiming that a kingdom whose most valiant soldier is capable of such treachery must be feeble indeed. Ezio, angry at the rejection of his advances, reminds the King of Châlons and, becoming again the dutiful ambassador, dares him to defy Rome at his peril.

In the meantime Foresto (tenor), a knight of Aquileia, and a band of refugees from the doomed city have sought refuge in the lagoons of the Adriatic, where the second scene shows the first miserable huts destined later to blossom into the palaces of Venice. Symbolically, perhaps, a storm at the beginning changes gradually to perfect calm and brightness, while the population praise God and join with Foresto, broken-hearted though he is at the loss of his beloved Odabella, in a prophetic vision of the future splendor of the city.

In the second act, which takes place in Attila's camp, Odabella is lamenting her father's death when she is surprised by Foresto, who has penetrated the lines in order to see her. He reproaches her bitterly with abandonment of himself and acceptance of the advances of the slayer of her father, but she manages to convince him of his mistake and reveals her determination to avenge the woes of her house and her country on the barbarian conqueror. The scene then changes to Attila's tent, wherein the King has a vision of an old man warning him against the continuation of his march on Rome. Though momentarily shaken, he determines to proceed, and his army is assembled for the purpose when there approaches a band of virgins and children headed by the same old man (in fact none other than Leo, subsequently canonized) whom he has seen in his vision, repeating the same words of warning. The coincidence is too much for the superstitious King, who, deciding to respect the will of Heaven, gives orders for the march to be stopped.

A truce is declared between Rome and the Huns, but in the third act Foresto plans to surround them with Roman troops, who at a given signal shall fall upon and massacre them. He obtains in this scheme the support of Ezio, who, baffled in his political ambitions, decides to conquer or die as the last of the Romans. In the second scene Attila, despite the warning of his "Druids," is entertaining Ezio and the Romans in honor of the truce when a sudden squall from the mountains extinguishes the torches. Everyone is horror-struck at the omen, but Attila, saying that he refuses to be frightened by the wind, bids the banquet proceed. Uldino, a young Breton slave who has apparently been won over by Foresto, offers him a cup of poisoned wine, which Odabella, imbued with other ideas of vengeance, warns him not to drink. Attila, not unnaturally annoyed, asks who is the culprit. Foresto proudly admits his guilt and would have been slain forthwith but that Odabella begs for his life as the price of her disclosure. Foresto, failing to realize Odabella's ultimate purpose,

Attila

bitterly upbraids her and departs, while Attila, bidding Ezio return to Rome to announce the termination of the truce, proclaims his forthcoming marraige with Odabella as her reward for saving his life.

Foresto and Ezio, however, have not given up their plan of massacring the Hun army, and the opening of the last act finds them discussing the final details. It is the day fixed for Odabella's wedding. Foresto is mad with jealousy and when Odabella presently appears, explaining her intentions, he is even less ready than Ezio to believe in them. But she soon has the opportunity of proving her good faith, for when Attila, wondering what has become of her, comes and discovers her in the company of his enemies, she throws away the crown and stabs him to the heart as the Roman soldiers rush in to carry out their determined plan of extermination. Attila, who has listened unmoved to the indictments of Foresto and Ezio, addresses her precisely in the words of the dying Cæsar to Brutus, and the opera ends in general rejoicing at the punishment meted out to "the Scourge of God."

This libretto, based on a forgotten tragedy by Verner, suffers from the obvious defect that the sympathies of the listener are with Attila. The contemptible Ezio, the double-faced Odabella, the incredible Foresto, are singularly unattractive instruments of divine vengeance, though doubtless a contemporary audience, in a fever of patriotic excitement, would have been unconscious of anything but the happy overthrow of the impious invader from the north. Needless to say, the King himself, with his chivalry, his Druids, and his prayers to Woden, bears no relation to the historical Attila; but that is of little importance. What matters is that Solera's construction bears every sign of haste if not of laziness. The last scene of the third act must be quite unintelligible on the stage; it is impossible, till one reads carefully the words of the concerted number, to know how the poisoned cup has been given to Attila or why Odabella prevents him from drinking it.

Verdi, who himself discovered the subject, waxed enthusiastic over its possibilities, and he was not wrong, for, treated with imagination and subtlety, it might have made a good opera libretto. We have his own original sketch, wherein the names of the characters (presumably identical with those of the Verner play) and the general lay-out of the scenes differ entirely from those of the final version. He himself suggested the invention of the character who subsequently became Foresto, and his original idea of placing the attempted poisoning of Attila at the end of the first act was worsened rather than bettered in the later version. Nevertheless, Verdi must share with Solera the responsibility of the shortcomings of the ultimate libretto, for he expressly states his satisfaction with it. Indeed, he clearly regarded *Attila* as one of his best operas, recommending it to Escudier as eminently suitable for Paris.

Yet, with the exception of the prologue, such merit as is to be found in *Attila* must be sought in details rather than in any whole. There are many beautiful phrases scattered throughout the opera. As a rule the early works of Verdi are remarkable more for brute force and ensemble-writing than for beauty of melody, but *Attila* is an exception. The Huns and Ostrogoths, who sing staccato tributes to Attila or military-band-like hymns to Woden, might for once have been more brutal with advantage. Except for the unaccompanied chorus at the end of the second act after the passing of the squall, the ensemble-writing is in no way striking. But there are some lovely and expressive tunes or fragments of tunes: for instance, the whole D-flat movement of the trio in the last act, the phrase that accompanies the meeting of Foresto and Ezio in the second act following Ezio's pretty if rather undistinguished aria. The music, too, associated with Saint Leo's warning to Attila is very fine; while certain critics have found, perhaps justly, in Foresto's "*Si, quello io son*" a forerunner of Alfredo's magnificent insult to Violetta in the finale of the second act of *La Traviata*.

Nevertheless, from the dramatic point of view all the best music of *Attila* is practically contained in the two scenes that constitute the prologue. The orchestral prelude may be simplicity itself, but it is appropriate and expressive, while Odabella's vigorous pæan on the spirit of Italian women, from her first recitative to the fine aria and cabaletta with their energetic, hate-charged coloratura, could hardly be bettered as examples of this kind of writing. Though the duet between Attila and Ezio contains the famous line: "*Avrai tu l'universo, resti l'Italia a me!*" which brought down the house over and over again all through Italy, there is little in it of purely musical interest. It is the way in which the phrase is manipulated rather than the phrase itself that is so happy.

From the musical point of view the scene of the founding of Venice is perhaps the outstanding feature of the opera, containing, as it does, one of those first essays in "nature music" connected with the psychology of the action, of which Verdi was to make such a success subsequently in *Un Ballo in Maschera*, *Rigoletto*, and *Otello*. The diminished sevenths of the storm in *Attila* may be humble precursors of these, but they are not ineffective. Even the very naïve painting of the gradual clearing of the sky, though thematically undistinguished, has a certain primitive charm, with its persistent and ever louder reiteration of a pedal G leading eventually, as it were in a burst of sunlight, to a great shout of praise to God in C major. The little figure, too, that accompanies the arrival of the boats is admirably illustrative, while Foresto's succeeding aria and cabaletta are at least adequate, so that the whole scene must be reckoned a definite success.

Doubtless *Attila* achieved popularity primarily on patriotic grounds; doubtless as a whole it is reminiscent not only of the composer himself but, at times, of his predecessors as well. Nevertheless, it can by no means be considered, like *Alzira*, an utter failure.

MACBETH

Libretto by Piave

Production: FLORENCE, March 14, 1847

Revised Version: PARIS, April 21, 1865

FOUR ACTS, TEN SCENES

The opera opens with a chorus of witches, who, on the arrival of Macbeth (baritone) and Banco (bass), greet the former as Thane of Cawdor and King of Scotland, the latter as sire of future kings. A messenger arriving from King Duncan informs Macbeth that the Thane of Cawdor has been executed for "treasons capital, confess'd and proved," and that he has been appointed thane in his stead. Banco and Macbeth, impressed by this sudden and unexpected fulfillment of the witches' prophecy, meditate diversely on the situation, Macbeth struggling against the thoughts of regicide that surge within him, Banco frightened by this manifestation of the powers of evil, while the witches conclude the scene with a dance and chorus.

In the second scene Lady Macbeth (soprano) is reading a letter from her husband telling her of the witches and their prophecy. She expresses in a soliloquy her fear of Macbeth's vacillating nature and wishes he would come that she might

> ". . . chastise with the valour of my tongue
> All that impedes thee from the golden round,
> Which fate and metaphysical aid doth seem
> To have thee crown'd withal."

An attendant announces the imminent arrival of Duncan to pass the night in the castle. She calls on the spirits of hell to assist her in the deed she would do:

> "That my keen knife see not the wound it makes,
> Nor heaven peep through the blanket of the dark. . . ."

Macbeth arrives and Lady Macbeth unveils her purpose, bidding her husband "look like the innocent flower, but be the serpent under't." After Duncan's entrance and retirement, to martial music, Macbeth, ordering a servant to bid Lady Macbeth strike on the bell when his evening drink is ready, remains alone. "Is this a dagger that I see before me?" Presently the bell is heard:

> "Hear it not, Duncan; for it is a knell
> That summons thee to heaven or to hell."

Lady Macbeth, entering, waits while Macbeth murders the sleeping King. He returns, panic- and conscience-stricken:

> "Methought I heard a voice cry: 'Sleep no more!
> Macbeth does murder sleep.' . . ."

Lady Macbeth bids him bear the bloodstained dagger back to the room that the crime be laid at the door of the two drugged attendants and, on his declaring his inability to enter the room again, herself does so. A knocking is heard, to the terror of Macbeth:

> "Will all great Neptune's ocean wash this blood
> Clean from my hand?"

Lady Macbeth chides him for his cowardice and, on the knocking being repeated, leads him to their chamber lest they be discovered near the scene of the murder. It is Macduff (tenor) who has knocked, charged by the King to wake him early, and presently, accompanied by Banco, he enters the King's room. Macduff returns, aghast at the discovery of the murder: "O horror! horror! . . . Do not bid me speak." Banco rushes into the room while Macduff rouses the house, and the act ends with a chorus and ensemble expressing the horror and dismay of all concerned.

The second act opens with a short scene between Macbeth and Lady Macbeth in which she exhorts him to forget the past — "What's done is done" — and be comforted by the thought that Duncan's son, Malcolm, by his flight to England has laid himself open to the charge of parricide. Macbeth, tortured by the thought of the prophecy concerning Banco's children, is encouraged by Lady Macbeth to decide on his immediate assassination, while she gloats over the prospect of her future royal state. The second scene shows a park in the neighborhood of Macbeth's castle, where a band of murderers have assembled to lie in wait for Banco and his son. Banco, after an aria expressing presentiment of evils to come, is killed, but the son escapes. The final scene is laid in a state room in the castle. A banquet is in progress, with Lady Macbeth giving the toast of the evening, when one of the murderers appears to inform Macbeth privily of the death of Banco and the son's escape. Macbeth, who has left the table to hear

Macbeth

the news, returns to find his seat occupied by Banco's ghost. He is completely unnerved:

> "Thou canst not say I did it: never shake
> Thy gory locks at me."

The company (to whom the ghost is invisible) marvel at his agitation; whereupon Lady Macbeth, exhorting him to be a man, assures them that it is but a familiar and passing disorder. She repeats her previous toast, this time in honor of the absent Banco, but Macbeth, who has temporarily recovered his self-possession, is once again terrified by the reappearance of the ghost:

> "Avaunt! and quit my sight! Let the earth hide thee! . . .
> What man dare, I dare;
> Approach thou like the rugged Russian bear,
> The arm'd rhinoceros, or the Hyrcan tiger;
> Take any shape but that, and my firm nerves
> Shall never tremble. . . ."

Lady Macbeth again reproaches him with cowardice, and the disturbed banquet concludes with an ensemble in which the principals express their various thoughts: Lady Macbeth her disbelief in the return of the dead; Macbeth his determination to wrest the secret of the future from the witches; Macduff his vague suspicions in general.

In the third act the witches are seated round their cauldron in a dark cave:

> "Double, double toil and trouble;
> Fire burn; and, cauldron, bubble."

In a ballet pantomime they invoke Hecate, who, in dumb show, announces the approach of Macbeth, instructing them how to deal with him that his doom be no longer delayed. She then disappears and the witches dance round the cauldron. Macbeth comes, asking what "deed without a name" is theirs, and demands to be shown the future. The first apparition conjured up is that of an "armed head." "Macbeth! Macbeth! Macbeth! beware Macduff." The second, that of a bloody child, bids him

> Be bloody, bold, and resolute; laugh to scorn
> The power of man, for none of woman born
> Shall harm Macbeth.

Then "an apparition of a child crowned, with a tree in his hand, rises."

> "Macbeth shall never vanquish'd be until
> Great Birnam wood to high Dunsinane hill
> Shall come against him."

Finally "eight kings appear and pass in order," the eighth, Banco, with a mirror in his hand. Macbeth, terror-stricken, rushes at the specters with his sword and swoons; whereupon the witches call on the spirits of the air to restore him. Lady Macbeth comes and he tells her of the apparitions, rousing her fury by his account of the vision of Banquo's descendants as future kings of Scotland. Both vow to exterminate ruthlessly all hostile to them and to their dynasty.

The fourth act opens in a deserted place "near Birnam wood," where a chorus of Scottish exiles bewail the tyranny that lies heavy on their country and Macduff laments the death of his wife and children murdered by Macbeth. The English army approaches under Malcolm, who commands that

> . . . every soldier hew him down a bough
> And bear't before him . . .

and the scene ends with a patriotic chorus.

In the second scene a doctor and a lady-in-waiting watch for Lady Macbeth, who walks in her sleep. Presently she enters, in her hand a lighted taper.

"Out, damned spot! . . . Fie, my lord, fie! a soldier and afeared? . . . All the perfumes of Arabia will not sweeten this little hand."

The scene changes to a hall in the palace, where Macbeth, comforted only by the witches' prophecy that no man born of woman shall harm him, curses his lot:

> ". . . My way of life
> Is fall'n into the sear, the yellow leaf;
> And that which should accompany old age,
> As honour, love, obedience, troops of friends.
> I must not have. . . ."

The lady-in-waiting comes to announce the death of his wife to the now indifferent Macbeth, to whom life

> . . . is a tale
> Told by an idiot, full of sound and fury,
> Signifying nothing.

The approach of the enemy is signaled and the boughs carried by each soldier give the impression that Birnam wood is moving indeed. Macbeth, sure now of his fate, calls for his armor and prepares for battle. During incidental music the scene changes to the battlefield where Malcolm's army, their "leafy screens" thrown down, engage Macbeth and his followers. Macduff and Macbeth meet face to face. Macbeth, still confident in his immunity from any man born of woman, and weary of bloodshed, urges his adversary to fly;

Macbeth

but Macduff who "was from his mother's womb untimely ripp'd," pursues and slays him, and the opera ends with a chorus of rejoicing at the liberation of Scotland from the yoke of the tyrant.

Little need be said about this libretto, for which, as has already been stated, Verdi was himself mainly responsible, the industrious Piave only supplying the verses, in two instances touched up or supplemented by Maffei. It is not Shakspere. Indeed, if the conventional view be adopted, that the principal charm of Shakspere is to be sought in the beauty of his language, it is about as far removed from Shakspere as possible, because Piave's imagination was decidedly pedestrian. Nevertheless, it has been excessively abused. When Roncaglia, for instance, belabors Piave for interpreting the mingled grotesqueness, fantasy, and vulgarity of the witches in a line like:

"*Tre volte miagola la gatta in fregola,*"

he seems to be unaware that Shakspere himself wrote:

"Thrice the brinded cat hath mewed."

Piave's translation may be uninspired, but it is not inaccurate. And as a whole this is true of the libretto all through. In my summary I have tried to indicate by the use of Shaksperian quotations those scenes in the opera which follow the tragedy more or less in detail; by the absence of them those scenes in which there are considerable or total divergencies. The former, it will be seen, are in the majority. In the process of adapting *Macbeth* to operatic purposes much was necessarily, something unnecessarily, sacrificed. The subsidiary characters such as Malcolm and Macduff become mere puppets; but the dogged, terrifying persistence of Lady Macbeth is well preserved and Macbeth himself remains, at any rate, a human being, animated by intelligible motives.

The score is full of interest. The witches' music must on the whole be dismissed as another of Verdi's failures in the domain of the fantastic; the march associated with Duncan is wholly commonplace; Banco's assassins are typically absurd. There are one or two excessively conventional set pieces, in particular Lady Macbeth's "Toast" at the banquet, of which the music is mostly of the shoddy stuff favored by the composer in the matter of social activities. But as an essay in dramatic expression *Macbeth* reaches heights never before attained by the composer. The major part of Lady Macbeth's music, for instance, is first-rate, from the opening scena, with its splendid outburst, "*Pien di misfatti è il calle della potenza,*" to the effective sleepwalking scene, of which such happy use is made in the prelude. Her aria "*La luce langue*" is one of the most beautiful things achieved by the composer, not only excellent in respect of melody, harmony, and instrumentation, but highly expressive as regards mood. Scarcely if at all inferior are the two duets between her and Macbeth in the first and third acts. Indeed, the latter is a wonderful piece of music, foreshadowing not only the passion but the vigorous declamation of *Aïda*. Macbeth's music, as is psychologically fitting, plays a secondary part. After the duet already mentioned, perhaps the best of it is to be found in the scena *"Mi si affaccia un pugnal?"* especially in the *Andante* section, where the sense of the words is admirably expressed, and during the banquet when the ghost of Banquo appears. Also the dark-colored aria *"Sangue a me,"* which immediately follows, leading to the effective finale, has real character, as has the music of his sudden decision to kill Macduff and of his joy at the prophecy concerning Birnam wood in the scene of the apparitions.

Two of the choruses, at any rate, are of the first order, that for unaccompanied voices at the end of the first act being a fine example of the kind of dramatic effect obtainable in this manner, that of the Scottish exiles in the last act showing a new and very remarkable feeling for expressiveness in choral and orchestral writing. Excellent too, if not on quite such a high plane, are Macduff's mournful aria *"Ah, la paterna mano,"* and the pretty Chopinesque waltz of the ballet music, which, except for a beautiful and decidedly Wagnerian passage associated with the appearance of Hecate, is not otherwise remarkable, though effective enough.

Macbeth is especially important, however, as containing several examples of purely orchestral passages of the highest quality. The best instance, perhaps, is to be found in the theme that ushers in the apparitions of the eight kings. In itself very distinguished:

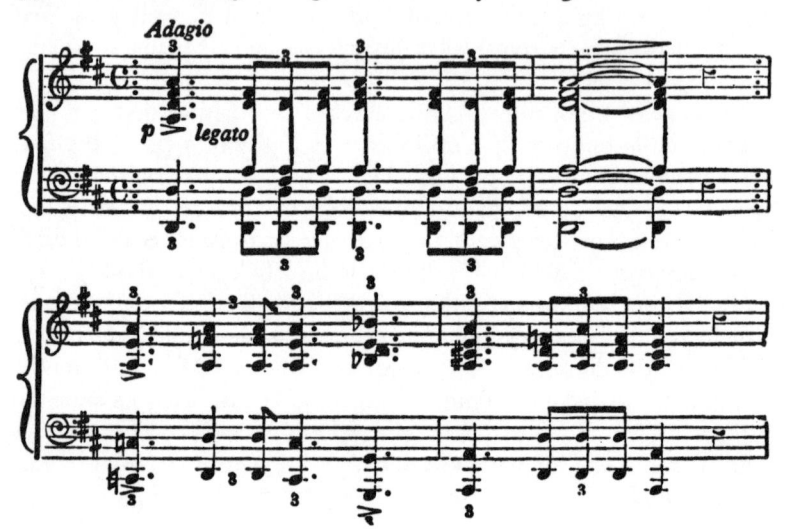

it was the object of Verdi's especial care. He had scored it for two oboes, six clarinets, two bassoons, and double-bassoon and gave especial instructions that it was to be played under the stage, just beneath an open trapdoor, "so that the sound can penetrate the theater, but in a mysterious manner and as if at a distance." The orchestral aspect of the fugue that describes the battle was also of concern to him, for he deplored to Escudier the Parisian habit of replacing valve-trumpets by key-trumpets, "which are neither fish, flesh, nor fowl" and must detract from the effect of dissonance intended to represent the clash of battle. Incidentally, the fugue itself serves its purpose admirably. Though Verdi laughed at himself for this lapse into the kind of academicism he particularly disliked, the dictates of his extraordinary dramatic instinct were sovereign. Apart from these special instances, *Macbeth* possesses many happy orchestral effects, notably in the sleepwalking scene.

A characteristic of the score is the extensive use of that wail-like figure, a descent or ascent of a minor second, so often used by Verdi to signify lamentation. The best instance of this is to be found in the chorus of Scottish exiles:

but that in the sleepwalking scene is hardly less good:

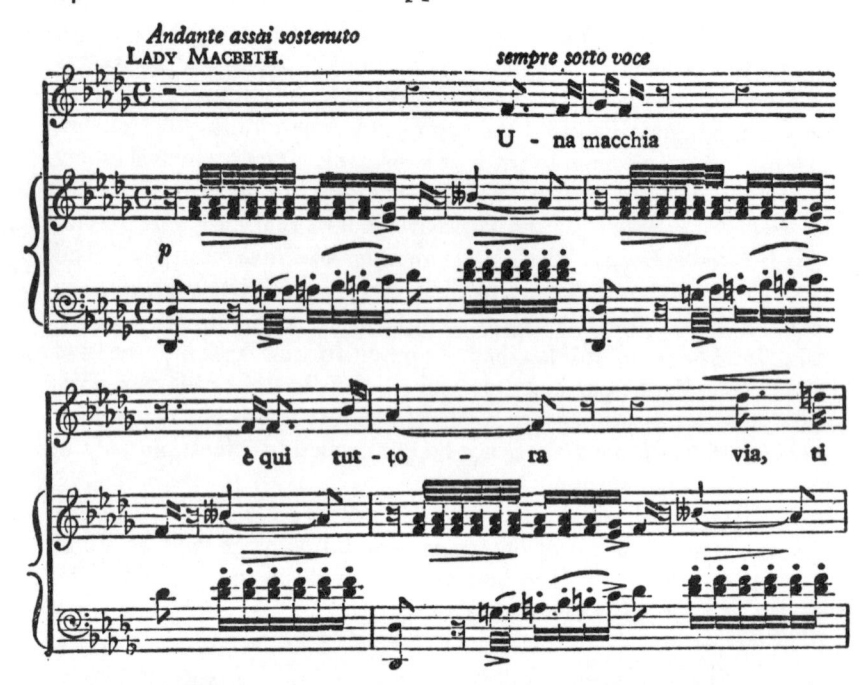

In both instances the persistency with which the figure is worked is admirable.

Another characteristic that seems to me remarkable in *Macbeth* is the classical feeling of the first act. The flavor of Beethoven in Verdi's music has been stressed on various occasions, but here it is especially strong. The accentuation off the beat in the melodic line, the first fifteen bars of the *Adagio* movement in the prelude — above all, the phrase that ushers in Lady Macbeth's first scena, which might almost have come out of the "Pathetic" Sonata — remind one inevitably of Beethoven, just as the terrible knocking at the door after Duncan's murder recalls *Don Giovanni*.

Even if we did not know that Verdi had an especial fondness for *Macbeth*, we could deduce it from the score, for no other is so rich in detailed instructions. The witches are humorously told to remember that they are witches; Macbeth and Lady Macbeth are urged to sing their first duet "darkly, *sotto voce*, except in the case of a few phrases specially marked"; Lady Macbeth's music throughout is profusely annotated with directions and marks of expression. The fact is that Verdi felt that he was here experimenting for the first time in real music drama, though he never used the term. He was working for an expressiveness, an acute delineation of the human soul, never before realized. In this he was only partially successful, but those of us who love the composer cannot help sharing his own love for an

Macbeth

opera that marks an especial striving after, and at times an especial realization of, new and noble ideals. *Macbeth*, gloomy, unequal, a mixture of perhaps incompatible styles, was never a success with the public; it is none the less the most interesting of Verdi's early operas.

The only edition of *Macbeth* available to the public is that prepared after the 1865 revision made for Paris, so that a few words as to the changes then made seem indispensable.

The two best numbers in the opera are later insertions, Lady Macbeth's aria in the second act being substituted by means of a new modulation for a very conventional, "jumpy" cabaletta, and the duet between her and Macbeth that concludes the third act being entirely new as regards both words and music. Indeed, in the original version she does not appear here at all, Macbeth contenting himself with a few bars of recitative and a poor cabaletta, with one effective passage describing "the wild-beast" passion in his heart. New, too, is the Scottish exiles' chorus in the fourth act. It supersedes a straightforward chorus, "*cantabile e melanconico*," intended, perhaps, as a kind of sequel to the famous "*Va, pensiero*" in *Nabucco*. The fugue descriptive of the battle is new, and the original ending, where Macbeth dies on the stage in a manner and spirit typically operatic, is much improved in the present version.

Otherwise, except for the ballet, the new edition is merely the old touched up. In the first act there are no changes of note; in the second the alterations, apart from the new aria already mentioned, are associated with Macbeth's music, the following being a typical and interesting instance:

OLD VERSION

Giuseppe Verdi

-lar t'è con-ces-so fa-vel-la Il se--pol-cro può render gli uc-ci-si? Fa-vel-la, Fa--vel-la. Il se-pol-cro può ren - der, può ren - der gli uc-ci - si può

etc.

Macbeth

NEW VERSION

Allegro agitato

Oh poi che le chiome scrollar t'è concesso, favella!... il sepolcro può render gli uccisi? può

In the third act the scene of the apparitions is considerably changed till the vision of the eight kings, which is merely an enriched version of the old; Macbeth's final aria before he swoons has an entirely different accompaniment figure and, except for the phrase "*E Banco! ahì vista orribile!*" a different melodic line; while the last two pages of the scene where the spirits of the air dance and the witches sing are new except for eight bars that recall the original subject.

There can be no reasonable doubt, then, that the second version of *Macbeth* is superior to the first, and one would not willingly lose the admirable music it called forth. Verdi, however, would have been better advised to rewrite the opera entirely, making use of some of his original material. The old bottle, despite its undeniable quality, despite the care bestowed on its reconditioning, was not really adapted for the new wine. As an opera, therefore, *Macbeth* must be reckoned a splendid and uncommonly interesting failure.

I MASNADIERI

Libretto by Maffei

Production: LONDON, July 22, 1847

FOUR ACTS, EIGHT SCENES

At the beginning of the eighteenth century in Germany a nobleman, Massimiliano Moor (bass), had two sons, Carlo (tenor) and Francesco (baritone). Owing to high spirits and extravagance Carlo had left home and joined a band of wild young men who subsist on brigandage, but, repenting of his evil ways, he has written to his father begging for forgiveness. Francesco, the younger son, however, seeing a chance to gain the succession for himself, has intercepted the letter and forged an answer. In the opening scene Carlo receives this

I Masnadieri

forged answer and, in despair at its harsh content, consents to become leader of the band of brigands, swearing loyally to serve them and their interests. In the second scene Amalia (soprano) is watching by the deathbed of her uncle, Massimiliano, for whom she feels deep devotion despite his responsibility for the banishment of Carlo, her plighted lover. The old man himself longs for the presence of his favorite son, but presently a certain Arminio, disguised, and suborned by Francesco, enters with a sword and a letter purporting to have come from Carlo as he lay mortally wounded on the field of battle. In the letter Carlo releases Amalia from her vows and bids her marry Francesco. Amalia cries that he never loved her; Massimiliano, breaking into bitter lamentations for the loss of his son, swoons and is to all appearances dead; Francesco exultingly proclaims himself the master at last.

The second act opens with Amalia praying before the tomb of Massimiliano while sounds of revelry are heard from the castle. Presently Arminio, repenting of the evil he has done, comes to her and confesses not only that Carlo is alive, but that Massimiliano is not dead. Her joy at the unexpected news is interrupted by Francesco, come to find out why she has left the feast. He offers her his hand and his heart, but Amalia spurns both; whereupon, saying that he will make her his servant and his mistress, Francesco is about to drag her off when Amalia, feigning submission, manages to snatch his sword, with which she effectively keeps him at a distance.

The second scene, laid in the Bohemian forest, describes the rescue by Carlo and the band of his lieutenant, who lies under sentence of death in Prague. The operation has been a brilliant success, but Carlo, left alone at last, bewails the disgraceful depths to which he has sunk, only to be roused to action again by the news that he and his band are surrounded by a thousand soldiers.

In the third act Amalia has fled from the castle to a neighboring wood, whither by chance Carlo and the survivors of his band have also come. Amalia at the sight of the brigands gives herself up for lost, but her despair turns to joy when she recognizes Carlo, to whom she relates Massimiliano's supposed death and Francesco's villainous designs on herself. Carlo, shrinking from revealing his true state, promises her safety and allows himself the momentary illusion of being in love again. When everyone is asleep, he contemplates suicide, but decides that it is his duty to live and suffer. At that moment Arminio approaches, bringing food for Massimiliano, whom, by a useful coincidence, he has hidden in a tower near by. Surprised by Carlo, whom he mistakes for Francesco, he flies, crying out that he had not the heart to carry out the pitiless orders given him. Carlo, opening the door of the tower, discovers his father wasted to a skeleton. The old man, ignorant of the identity of his son, relates the terrible story of how Francesco, having discovered that he was only in a trance, would have buried him alive but for his stealthy rescue by Arminio; whereupon Carlo, in furious indignation, summons the band to swear that they will capture his unnatural brother and bring him back alive for punishment.

The fourth act shows Francesco much frightened by a dream. He has had, he tells Arminio, a detailed vision of the Last Judgment wherein he was denied salvation. Such indeed was his terror that he has sent for Moser (bass), the local clergyman, who, in answer to his direct question, tells him that the sins of parricide and fratricide are those particularly odious in God's sight. At that very moment the band of brigands burst into the castle, while Francesco, fearing that death is near, vainly seeks absolution from the clergyman. In the last scene we are back in the wood, where Massimiliano, still ignorant of his son's identity, blesses him as his savior. The robbers return, dragging with them the panic-stricken Amalia, but Carlo is now relieved to hear that they have, after all, failed to capture Francesco. Caught, however, in the net of his oath to the band, he now reveals his identity to Massimiliano, explains the nature of his following, and with his own hands kills Amalia rather than let her share his life of shame.

Maffei's libretto, drawn from Schiller's *Die Räuber*, is a grievous disappointment. Maffei possessed literary gifts indubitably superior to those of Verdi's other librettists at this time. He was, moreover, a specialist in translation from English and German. Yet, despite some happy details in the versification and a rather ingenious fusion of Schiller's Hermann and Daniel as the character to whom Francesco confides his terror at the vision of the Last Judgment, *I Masnadieri* is in no way superior to the productions of Piave or Cammarano, the third act, indeed, being even more of a muddle than usual. For instance, it is clear from one press notice that the act has a change of scene; without such a change, indeed, Amalia's subsequent capture as well as a certain stage direction in the fourth act referring to "the last scene of the third act" are both unintelligible. But there is no indication in the score of anything of the kind. Nor is it made clear whether Francesco dies or not, much less the manner (if any) of his death.

Speaking generally, Maffei boiled down *Die Räuber* to its bones, and the operation, though not unfaithfully done — a careful reading of Maffei's text reveals most of the mainsprings of Schiller's action — deprives the original play of its principal value. For instance, the brigands themselves, who, despite their revolting wickedness, are interesting people in Schiller, became in Maffei a mere operatic chorus that might have stepped out of *Il Trovatore* or any other similar opera. The psychology of the two brothers, also, suffers considerably, while the strength of the tie forged between Carlo and his men when, hemmed in by soldiers, they refused, despite every inducement, to give him up is never explained in the opera; with the result that his reasons for killing Amalia seem decidedly inadequate. Amalia's recognition of Carlo, moreover, which in *Die Räuber* does not take place till the last act, is in the opera unfortunately and senselessly anticipated. An English commentator, however, may be grateful to the Italian for not preserving Schiller's original designation of the father as "Old Moor" — a title that would have caused him considerable embarrassment.

Verdi's music, as is not infrequently the case, seems unconsciously enslaved by the very imperfections of the libretto. That associated with Francesco provides a good example of this. Maffei's Francesco is, of course, an Iago, but an Iago of third-rate melodrama who might be expected at any moment to ejaculate in the traditional manner: "How I love her; curse her!" His music is curiously similar, the vision of the Last Judgment, obviously intended to be his great scene, being decidedly conventional and effective only in a mechanical way — chromatic harmonies (forerunners, incidentally, of those in *Rigoletto*), the sequential, semitonal rises of a phrase in the manner favored by Verdi when he wished to indicate horror or excitement, and so on. His arias are even more indicative. Alike when he is planning to hasten his father's death and declaring his love for Amalia, the music, placid and suave, is entirely inappropriate, better suited to a Sunday-school teacher than to a monster of villainy. It is clear that Francesco's character as a whole conveyed nothing to Verdi. Where he really felt the situation, as, for instance, at the end of the duet with the clergyman or in the recitative (almost prophetic of *Otello*) which leads to Francesco's first aria, his touch is unerring. The music associated with Carlo suffers in much the same way. Only in this case, even if the strength of the man is not indicated, the arias are psychologically possible. Viewed as music pure and simple, one at least, that in the second act, is a gem, the recitative being as good as the song, while that in the first act is very pretty.

There is too much coloratura in Amalia's music to make it palatable to us, but her aria in the second act seems expressive and in fact much of the coloratura is skillfully written. At times, as, for instance, when she exclaims in the first act that Carlo never loved her, she achieves phrases of real poignancy. In this respect, however, Carlo's discovery of his father must be considered perhaps the most happy moment of the opera. As an example of an expressive contour new in the composer's music the phrase seems worth quoting, all the more so since in flavor and orchestral color (soft brass) it is decidedly Wagnerian, though Verdi can scarcely have known a note of Wagner's music at the time:

[Musical notation: Carlo. Allegro — "Om- bra del Moor! che pe-na da' mor-ti a noi ti me-na?" Agitato, etc.]

Except for the decidedly Meyerbeerian chorus at the end of the third act, which is effective, the less said about the brigands' music the better, though their interposition in the admirable trio that concludes the opera is well conceived. The final quartet of the first act is good and there is one tolerable duet between Amalia and Francesco in the second act. Otherwise *I Masnadieri* is an essay in conventional patterns and rhythms in no way different from those of preceding operas.

IL CORSARO

Libretto by Piave

Production: TRIESTE, October 25, 1848

THREE ACTS, SEVEN SCENES

Amidst a band of pirates on an island in the Ægean, Corrado (tenor) is lamenting his lost honor when a message announcing his appointment to the command of the band in an immediate expedition against the Moslems rouses him and his followers to martial excite-

Il Corsaro 249

ment. He goes to bid farewell to his beloved Medora (soprano), who, full of gloomy forebodings, tries to persuade him to stay. Duty calls, however, and with the promise of a safe return he departs.

In a "delicious room" in the harem of Seid, Pasha of Coron (baritone), Gulnara (soprano), his favorite slave, bewails her lot. She detests the Pasha and spurns the gifts by which he thinks to win her love. The Pasha summons her to a banquet given in honor of his approaching victory over the pirates. Unwillingly she goes, and the feast is at its height when a dervish is announced. He is none other than Corrado in disguise, come, in reality, to spy out the land, but pretending to have escaped from the hands of the pirates. At first Seid believes his story, but presently, when the fleet in the harbor bursts into flames, he gives orders for his arrest. Corrado, throwing off his disguise and appearing in full armor, puts himself at the head of the pirates, who at that moment penetrate into the palace. Surprised at the sudden onslaught, the Moslems first give ground, but presently rallying, capture or slaughter the pirates; whereupon the Pasha taunts the now captive Corrado, vowing to put him to death amidst the most horrible tortures.

But Gulnara, struck by the chivalry of Corrado in protecting her and her female companions in the moment of his temporary triumph, has fallen in love with him. She pleads with Seid for his life, but only succeeds in arousing the Pasha's suspicion with regard to the true state of her feelings. With her hatred of the Pasha more inflamed than ever, she goes, after bribing the guards, to the cell where Corrado is confined and, giving him a dagger, suggests that he should kill the sleeping Seid. Corrado refuses to do anything so cowardly; wherefore Gulnara herself commits the murder. On her return she confesses to Corrado that it was primarily love for him that drove her to such an act though she has discovered in the meantime that he loves another. As some recompense Corrado, though reluctantly, consents to fly with her to his native land. On their return they are met by the dying Medora, who, in despair at the news of Corrado's capture brought her by the survivors of the expedition, has apparently decided to die. She conveniently survives, however, to learn the true story of Gulnara and Corrado, which, with a perspicacity rare in romantic opera, she actually believes. Nevertheless, finally she dies, and Corrado, mad with grief, jumps into the sea.

Any detailed consideration of this preposterous libretto seems superfluous. Generally speaking, it may be divided into two categories: the incredible and the unintelligible, Corrado's purposeless adventure as a spy being an instance of the former, Medora's death of the latter attribute. Byron's *The Corsair,* on which Piave based his libretto, following the story in detail, is a *bravura* essay in heroic couplets immortalized by one line. It may be doubted, however, whether one person in a thousand associates the name, "Link'd with one virtue and a thousand crimes," with that of the wooden Corrado, who, together with the other characters in the poem as in the opera, is not so much a person as a peg on which to hang verses or music. Even the dramatic situations are not remarkably effective.

The truth is that Verdi took less trouble with the libretto than usual, making, apparently, no suggestions, leaving everything to Piave for once in a way. He did not wish to write the opera at all and only did so because of a contract, which, as a matter of fact, he tried to cancel. In the circumstances the surprising feature of *Il Corsaro* is not that it is bad, but that it contains a number so exquisite as the little scena depicting Corrado in prison. Alike in the instrumental introduction, the vocal part, and the unexpected coda, the writing here could not be bettered for sincerity and expressiveness. The accompaniment figure, anticipating in a sense that of Leonora's "*Madre, pietosa Vergine*" in *La Forza del Destino*, has a distinct flavor of Beethoven, and the scena as a whole, though in no way comparable with the similar scena in *Fidelio*, possesses a certain affinity with it. Nor is the ensuing duet between Corrado and Gulnara without good points, especially towards the end, so that this scene must unquestionably be reckoned the best in the opera. The concluding pages of the final trio, too, are interesting, if only because Gulnara sings a phrase that is not so much a forerunner as a definite anticipation, both melodically and harmonically, of Gilda's duet with her father in the second act of *Rigoletto*. I cannot agree, however, with Soffredini's praise of it as "the salvation of the opera," any more than with his commendation of Gulnara's cabaletta in the second act, though this may be recommended to singers in search of an unfamiliar and exceedingly difficult exercise in coloratura. The duet between Gulnara and Seid in the second act is not ineffective, particularly where he discovers her love for the pirate, while the beginning of his hymn to Allah has a certain dignity, and the chromatics representing the "serpent of jealousy" in his song that opens the third act are at least amusing. Otherwise *Il Corsaro* is a wilderness of conventionalism, and hasty, artificial conventionalism at that. It is perhaps the only opera in which Verdi was definitely, if not deliberately, false to his fine ideals of craftsmanship. It possesses, however, the merit of extreme brevity.

LA BATTAGLIA DI LEGNANO

Libretto by Cammarano

Production: ROME, January 27, 1849

FOUR ACTS, SEVEN SCENES

In the twelfth century Frederick Barbarossa (bass) planned to invade Italy with a great army. To meet the danger the cities of Lombardy formed a league, and the opening of the first act shows the arrival of various contingents in Milan. At the head of the Verona contingent is Arrigo (tenor), greeted with enthusiasm by his old friend and comrade-in-arms Rolando (baritone), who believed that he had been killed in battle, whereas he had in fact been severely wounded and imprisoned for several years in enemy country. All swear to give their last drop of blood for the defense of the fatherland. The scene changes to "a shady spot" where, surrounded by her ladies, sits Lida (soprano), Rolando's wife, for whom Marcovaldo, a German prisoner of war generously released by Rolando, cherishes a hopeless passion. She indignantly spurns his advances, and Marcovaldo, with miraculous perspicacity, discovers from the manner in which she receives the news of the approach of her husband and Arrigo that she is in love with the latter. And in truth, when the men arrive, Arrigo and Lida look on each other with consternation, for years before they had been plighted lovers. Presently, Rolando being summoned to take part in a council of war, Arrigo, left alone with Lida, turns on her with bitter reproaches for her faithlessness in marrying another. She explains that everybody thought he was dead; but the explanation does not satisfy Arrigo, in whose view constancy should extend to the next world, and he departs in anger, having convinced Lida herself, apparently, that she was entirely to blame.

The second act takes place in Como, whither Rolando and Arrigo have come as envoys of the League to beg the authorities to put an end to their old feud with Milan and join the common cause. Como refuses, pleading a treaty with Frederick, to the indignation of Rolando and Arrigo, who point out that there are times when the obligations of patriotism are superior to those of a scrap of paper. The language of Como may be Italian, but its heart is barbarian; what answer shall they take back to Milan? It is given by the dramatic appearance in the Council Chamber of Frederick himself, who shows the delighted Comaschians and the unimpressed Lombards a huge German army encamped on the surrounding hills. He bids the envoys return to Milan with the news of approaching doom; to which Rolando and Arrigo retort that a people fighting for liberty is more than a match for a horde of mercenaries, however numerous.

The third act opens in the crypt of Milan Cathedral, where Arrigo is made a member of the Death-Riders, a select band of warriors who, under penalty of rejection by God and man if the oath be broken, swear to push the invader beyond the Alps or die on the field of battle. The scene changes to Lida's apartments. Distracted with grief and fear for the death certainly awaiting the desperate Arrigo on the field of battle, she has written him a letter, which her attendant promises to deliver. Then Rolando enters. He has returned to bid farewell to his wife and son, urging her, if he falls, to bring the boy up to fear God and honor his country above everything else in the world. Arrigo joins them and Rolando tells him in confidence that he has been chosen to lead the Death-Riders, who form the advance-guard of the army. It is the most dangerous, if honorable, post of all. Will Arrigo promise, in the probable event of his death, to watch over his wife and child? Arrigo, much moved, swears to do so and the men embrace and depart, each his own way. Just as Rolando, however, is leaving the room, he is called back by Marcovaldo, who, to revenge himself on Lida, has by means of a bribe secured her letter to Arrigo, in which she begs him by their former love to come and see her before the battle. He reads this to Rolando, who, mad with rage at the treachery of his wife and friend, swears vengeance on them both.

The last scene is laid in Arrigo's room. He is writing a farewell letter to his mother when Lida enters. Confessing that she loves him still, she says that they must part for ever, he to live for his mother, she for her child. She has come, she adds, because her letter remained unanswered. At that very moment there is a knock at the door and Rolando's voice is heard demanding admission. Arrigo pushes Lida onto the balcony, where she is discovered by Rolando, who steps out on the pretext of looking to see whether it is yet dawn and time to set forth. Rolando, disregarding all protestations of innocence, is about to kill Arrigo, who makes no defense, when suddenly he changes his mind; a better punishment than death will be a life of dishonor. So he departs, locking the door behind him. But Arrigo, overwhelmed with shame and despair at the thought of what will be said of a Death-Rider's absence from the battle, risks his life in a leap from the balcony and disappears with a shout of "Long live Italy!"

In the last act the citizens of Milan are anxiously awaiting the result of the battle that is taking place at Legnano. Gradually rumors of victory turn to certainty. The Austrian army has been completely defeated and the Emperor himself has been dragged from his horse

La Battaglia di Legnano

by Arrigo, who, mortally wounded, has asked to be carried back to die in the cathedral. He takes advantage of the situation to swear to Rolando that there has been no guilty intrigue between Lida and himself; at which Rolando, convinced by the oath of a dying hero, shakes his friend's hand as a sign of complete forgiveness and presses Lida to his heart. So Arrigo dies, kissing his country's flag, amidst the mingled lamentations and rejoicings of the crowd.

Cammarano's libretto has been abused, unjustly, I think. Doubtless the psychology is weak, if indeed it can be said to exist; doubtless Marcovaldo's suspicion and Arrigo's condemnation of Lida seem incredible to us. But the latter at any rate would not have appeared incredible to the romantic ideals of the mid-nineteenth century, and an artistic production must be judged in the first instance by contemporary standards. In any case *La Battaglia di Legnano* is not primarily concerned with human character at all, but with human action. Verdi himself, who had his own ideas as to how the Como act should be treated, recognized the secondary importance of Lida as compared with Arrigo and Rolando, suggesting to Cammarano her scena in the third act in order somewhat to enhance it; just as he suggested the subsequent pathetic farewell of Rolando to his wife and child in order to enhance what the mandarins of Fleet Street and of Hollywood call "the human interest." Nevertheless *La Battaglia di Legnano* was conceived primarily as an essay in patriotic emotion, and in that aspect Cammarano seems to me to have performed his task remarkably well. The story is clear; the verses are tolerable if somewhat bombastic; the situations well contrived and varied. Indeed, the intertwining of personal with public motives at the end of the third act is an ingenious piece of dramatic construction *à la* Sardou.

From the musical point of view *La Battaglia di Legnano* is an exact equivalent of the libretto on, so to say, a higher plane. With the exception of Barbarossa's scene in the second act where his pride and Arrigo's and Rolando's defiance, not to mention the cowardly vacillation of the Comaschians, are admirably depicted, the music is not remarkable for delineation of character. All the composer's efforts are concentrated on illustrating the dramatic situations rather than the motives of the puppets nominally responsible for them. In the result he was unquestionably successful. The combination of ecclesiastical and popular rejoicing in the last act, for instance, may be somewhat facile, but it is extremely effective, and the final trio is not only lovely as regards detail but satisfying as regards the dramatic whole. Equally good, if not better, is the musical interpretation of the situation so cunningly contrived by Cammarano as a conclusion of the third act. The admirable part-writing, the happy introduction of the

Lombards' march, the vigorous declamation, all combine to make a dozen pages positively tingling with excitement. Best of all, however, are the two great patriotic choruses in the first and third acts, especially the latter. The manner in which, after the initiation of Arrigo as a Death-Rider, the music leads up to the outburst: *"Giuriam d'Italia por fine ai danni,"* is beyond praise, while the chorus itself, except for a rather conventional passage in the middle, is worthy of the situation.

Moreover, *La Battaglia di Legnano* possesses both melodic and orchestral distinction. How expressive are both Arrigo's and Lida's cavatinas in the first act! How happy many melodic phrases throughout the opera: the orchestral introduction to the first scene of the third act is none the less effective because it is extremely simple, while the overture is one of the best Verdi wrote. It is based mainly on the march of the Lombards ingeniously treated and extended to form the last section, with an important interlude of an *Andante* consisting of a beautiful tune, somewhat reminiscent of Bellini, associated subsequently with Arrigo's letter to his mother. The instrumental use of the twittering chorus of the Comaschians as an accompaniment to Rolando's plea for peace between Como and Milan is also ingenious.

Those who wish to follow the development of the composer will find the opera particularly interesting in that here, more, perhaps, than anywhere else, may be found the meeting-place of the young and the middle-aged Verdi. Basically *La Battaglia di Legnano* belongs in its entirety to the early operas; indeed, in a sense, it is a reversion to the style of *I Lombardi* and *Ernani*. The patterns, albeit a trifle more elaborately worked, are the old patterns; the rhythms, though decidedly more extended and free, are the old rhythms. But the student cannot fail to be struck by the multitude of buds destined to blossom later in new and more familiar forms. Lida's cry:

is Violetta's *"Amami, Alfredo,"* in *La Traviata*. Arrigo's protest:

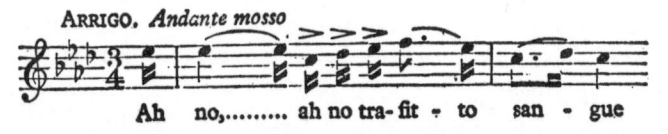

is Manrico's *"Ah che la morte ognora"* in *Il Trovatore*. In addition to these, two accompaniment-figures, one to Arrigo's dying aria, the other to Lida's opening cavatina, definitely suggest similar figures in *Aïda* and *La Forza del Destino*.

Apart from technical considerations, however, *La Battaglia di Legnano* possesses a definite charm of its own as a complete musical synthesis of Verdi's love for his country. To dismiss it, as has been too often done, as a mere *pièce d'occasion* like Beethoven's *Battle of Vittoria* is wrong. Fierce, burning patriotism is what makes this music glow with a sincerity that we can feel even today. The inspiration may only be a glorified form of the inspiration that dictated the opening phrase of *La Marseillaise*, but it is unquestionably there, manipulated, moreover, by a master craftsman, not an amateur like Rouget de L'Isle. Doubtless in previous operas Verdi had striven with varying degrees of fortune after more complex, more subtle expression. Doubtless *La Battaglia di Legnano*, like *Nabucco*, owes its success to its limitations, to the composer's readiness to concern himself only with the broadest effects. But of its kind *La Battaglia di Legnano* is an excellent opera, which, but for the prejudice aroused by the circumstances in which it was born, aggravated, not improbably, by its uninviting title, might deservedly have escaped the oblivion into which it seems to have fallen.

When the revolution which it was intended to consecrate failed, *La Battaglia di Legnano* was, of course, banned by the Austrian censorship; but it was revived (unsuccessfully) at Milan in 1861 under the title of *The Siege of Haarlem*, with characters and circumstances appropriately altered.

LUISA MILLER

Libretto by Cammarano

Production: NAPLES, December 8, 1849

THREE ACTS, SEVEN SCENES

On a spring morning during the seventeenth century the inhabitants of a "pleasant village" in the Tyrol have gathered to celebrate the birthday of Luisa (soprano), daughter of Miller (baritone), an old soldier in retirement. Father and daughter thank their fellow villagers, but Luisa anxiously awaits the arrival of a young stranger with whom, despite the misgivings of her father, she has fallen deeply in love. Presently he arrives and, to her delight, joins the others in offering her flowers, protesting the sincerity of his love. But Miller still doubts his honorable intentions, and when Wurm (bass), himself desirous of marrying Luisa, reveals the identity of the stranger as Rodolfo (tenor), son of the Count of Walter (bass), he sees his worst fears confirmed. In the second scene Wurm, slighted at what he considers the affront put on him by Luisa's rejection of his suit and Miller's refusal to exercise paternal authority in the matter, revenges himself by going to his master, Walter, with the information of Rodolfo's love-affair. The Count is furious. Ambitious and worldly, he has arranged for Rodolfo a highly advantageous marriage with his cousin Federica (contralto), the young widow of the Duke of Ostheim, who in fact is in love with him. He demands obedience from his son, who has no time to make any explanation before Federica enters with her ladies; whereupon Walter leaves the two together. Rodolfo, deciding to throw himself on the mercy of Federica, tells her the truth, but she, hurt in both her love and her pride, will not forgive him, and the two part in anger.

The third scene is laid in Miller's house, where Luisa anxiously awaits the fulfillment of Rodolfo's promise to slip away from the hunt, the sounds of which are heard in the distance. Miller comes to tell her who her lover really is; but the despair of Luisa and the rage of her father are interrupted by the entrance of Rodolfo himself, who, while admitting his identity, repeats to the distracted Miller his intention of marrying Luisa despite Walter's opposition, which he can, he hints, overcome if forced to extremes. Walter arrives and tells his son that he has come to save him from the wiles of a mercenary adventuress. Luisa faints at such an insult, which is, moreover, hotly resented not only by Rodolfo but by Miller, who threatens vengeance. Walter, despite Rodolfo's protests, orders the arrest of both father and daughter. Rodolfo tries once again to move Walter to pity, but, failing, draws his sword to defend Luisa. Then the infuriated Walter orders his arrest also. Rodolfo, seeing that the moment has come to exchange prayers for threats, departs with a whisper to his father that he can and, if necessary, will, reveal the means by which he attained to nobility and power. Walter, thunderstruck and cowed, gives orders for Luisa's immediate release and goes in search of his son.

Rodolfo's threat, though momentarily efficacious, has not sufficed to prevent the subsequent arrest of Miller, of which Luisa hears in the opening scene of the second act. He is being led in chains to the castle to be charged with threats of violence against his feudal lord, a crime punishable with death. In the meantime Wurm and Walter have concocted a villainous plan to rid themselves of Luisa. By way of working on her filial feelings they have prepared a letter, purporting to have been written by her to Wurm, in which she expressly states that her love for Rodolfo was mere venal pretense of which she is tired and that she wishes now to return to her first and genuine love, Wurm. This letter is brought by Wurm himself for her signature, the reward of which is to be her father's release. Luisa at first indignantly refuses; but subsequently, unable to face the responsibility of sending her father to death, she consents, promising not only to swear that she wrote the letter of her own free will but to come to the castle and show herself to Federica as Wurm's betrothed. In the second scene Wurm has returned to the castle to report to the Count the success of their plan. Somebody will be bribed to give the letter to Rodolfo; all will be well. But Wurm is terrified to learn from Walter that Rodolfo knows about the clandestine murder by which, with Wurm's help, Walter attained to power, though Walter assures him that they will stand or fall together. Then Federica enters and Wurm introduces Luisa, from whose own lips the Duchess wishes to hear the truth about herself and Rodolfo. Luisa, closely questioned by Federica, tortured with jealousy, contrives nevertheless to play her part to the end so that the Duchess is satisfied.

In the third scene, which takes place in the garden of the castle, Rodolfo has received from a peasant Luisa's letter, which drives him to despair and fury. He sends for Wurm and challenges him to a fatal duel with pistols, but, to summon help, Wurm fires off his weapon prematurely. Walter and attendants rush in and Rodolfo, falling at his father's feet, begs for pity in his sad plight. Walter, pretending to relent, offers to waive his objections to Luisa, but Rodolfo tells him of her faithlessness and deceit. So Walter suggests, by way of revenge, an immediate marriage with Federica, to which Rodolfo, half-dazed with despair, miserably consents.

In the third act, which takes place at night in Miller's house, Luisa is discovered writing a farewell letter to Rodolfo. Despite the entreaties of her friends she refuses to eat or drink anything, merely asking what is the reason of the illumination of the church, to which they reply in some confusion that it is in honor of Rodolfo's bride. Then Miller, released from captivity, enters, and Luisa's friends discreetly retire. Having heard the whole story from Wurm, he is filled with forebodings at the unnatural calm of his daughter and asks what letter she is writing. Obtaining a promise of its safe delivery, she gives it to him, and he, from what he reads between the lines, understands that she is contemplating suicide. With an appeal to her to consider not only the enormity of her crime but the loneliness of his own declining years, he finally succeeds in persuading her to tear up the letter and the two decide to leave the country together to pass the rest of their lives as wanderers and beggars. When her father has left, Luisa, hearing the sound of the church organ, kneels to say her prayers in the home of her childhood for the last time. A figure muffled in a cloak appears at the door. It is Rodolfo, who, after watching her for a moment, pours a flask of poison into a cup on the table and then interrupts her devotions to ask whether she in truth wrote the letter. On her affirmative reply he asks for the cup, drinks it, and then hands it to her. She also drinks. They must now, he tells her, go their several ways; but presently his forced composure breaks down, he weeps bitterly, and, when the castle clock strikes the hour, tells her that what they have both drunk is poison, asking her again for the last time if she really loved Wurm. Luisa thereupon tells him the truth, to the despair of Rodolfo, who curses the day he was born. Miller, who has heard their cries, enters the room in time to learn the meaning of the ghastly scene. Presently Walter, Wurm, and the villagers also arrive. Luisa is dead; but Rodolfo, summoning his last reserves of strength, runs Wurm through the body with his sword before he, too, falls lifeless on the ground.

Cammarano's operatic version of Schiller's *Kabale und Liebe* has been scorned and abused, but, apart from some of the verses, it seems to me an excellent piece of work, which carries conviction even today. The main differences between the characters in his libretto and those in Schiller's fine play are the new importance given to Federica, the elimination of Lady Milford and the Hofmarschall, and the change of Miller from an old musician to a retired soldier. The last is of no importance, a mere matter of detail. The ridiculous, effeminate Hofmarschall one loses with regret as a person; but Cammarano was singularly well inspired in making Wurm instead of him the recipient of Luisa's dictated love-letter in the second act. It is in fact more credible, considering that in both Schiller and Cammarano, Wurm is the unsuccessful and jealous pretender to Luisa's hand. The elimination of Lady Milford, the King's mistress, is more regrettable, if only because the scene between her and Luisa is perhaps the finest in the whole of *Kabale und Liebe*. Neither Cammarano nor Verdi sacrificed her or it willingly, but neither saw how she could be retained. So as much of the scene as possible was transferred to Federica of Ostheim (merely mentioned in the Schiller play), who also succeeded the disreputable Lady Milford as the match chosen by Walter for his son — a change for the worse because Lady Milford's fierce determination to get a husband seems more consonant with her *déclassée* condition than with Federica's irreproachable and enviable circumstances. Cammarano further eliminated all the social and political allusions that play so important a part in *Kabale und Liebe*, concentrating exclusively on the individual poignancy of the situations. His invention of the idyllic opening of the opera, devoid of any hint of tragedy to come, is a good instance of his skill in this direction and Dr. Georg Göhler has justly emphasized the ingenuity with which the chorus is employed throughout.

Luisa Miller

To Verdi himself must be given some credit for what seems to me an exceptionally good libretto. It was he who insisted on the rapid action at the end of the first act, so effective dramatically; who emphasized the importance of allowing the wicked intrigue between Walter and Wurm to dominate the opera, as in Schiller's play; who suggested improvements in the last act. In short, in *Luisa Miller* we have the fruit of probably the most happy and close collaboration hitherto experienced in the composer's career. Cammarano's singularly intelligent attitude in the matter has already been emphasized elsewhere.

The musical interest of *Luisa Miller* is evident from the outset because the overture is one of the two best ever written by the composer. It is not, as usual, in two or three sections, but consists of one theme, ingeniously worked throughout to express different moods and colors. The polyphonic treatment is admirable, the orchestration adequate; its rediscovery by some enterprising conductor seems overdue. In general form the first act is decidedly the most conventional of the opera and there are one or two examples of downright misalliances between words and music. For instance, the delicate grace of the phrase in which Rodolfo, in the second scene, asks Federica's pardon for the "bitter words" he is going to utter represents nothing in the world less than unpleasantness. Nevertheless, an occasional blemish such as this only serves to throw into relief the quality of the music as a whole. Luisa's first aria, "*Lo vidi, e'l primo palpito il cor sentì d'amore*," with its significant coloratura, Miller's address to Wurm about the free choice of a husband for his daughter, Walter's expression of his overwhelming ambition for his son in the second scene, may all be conceived in somewhat conventional forms, but the sincerity and aptness of the underlying musical idea cannot be denied. The opening chorus has no particular interest in itself, but sung *mezza voce*, as directed, it most happily suggests a pleasant Theocritean idyll. The movement marked *Andantino affettuoso* in the duet between Federica and Rodolfo is agreeable, while the distant hunting chorus (which might almost have come out of *Freischütz*) is decidedly effective. But the best music of the act is undoubtedly to be found in the finale. The *Adagio* in which Rodolfo announces his determination to marry Luisa; the *Largo*, with its fine crescendo, worked on a constant bass-figure, where he first reveals his knowledge of Walter's guilty secret; Louisa's expressive phrase, suggesting the woes of Desdemona, "*Ad immagin tua creata*"; the sharply contrasted concerted number before the final *Allegro* — all these combine to make music of a high order.

In general character the second act is like the first. There are instances of pure conventionalism such as Rodolfo's cabaletta "*L'ara o l'avello apprestami,"* and (in the opening chorus) a flagrant example of mis-accentuation. The level of the whole remains, however, higher. Luisa's aria *"Tu puniscimi, o Signore,"* is very expressive, while the dependent cabaletta, effective in any case, is noteworthy as opening, exceptionally, in the minor. Much of the duet between Wurm and Walter, too, is fine, the instrumental phrase in the accompaniment when Walter discloses Rodolfo's knowledge of the murder being particularly effective with its dark, sinister coloring. But the outstanding features of this act are undoubtedly Rodolfo's beautiful aria *"Quando le sere"* — a perfect example of mood-painting in melody, of which the general atmosphere is not unlike that of the familiar "O star of eve" in *Tannhäuser*, but, it seems to me, more truly poetical — and the unaccompanied vocal quartet at the end of the second scene. This is a truly remarkable piece of music, worthy to rank among the best examples of the kind in operatic literature. The opening may be cited as an illustration of the new intimate feeling characteristic of *Luisa Miller:*

and, after a curious unison passage, the music is most effectively worked to the end.

The third act is the best of all, not because it contains any numbers superior to those just mentioned, but on account of the consistent beauty and dramatic fitness of the music. The theme on which the overture is built, changed into 3/4 time, plays an important part in the accompaniment of the tender opening chorus, which contrasts so admirably with the long scene between Miller and Luisa immediately following. This contains music of the first class. When, after the tragic letter-scene, Luisa sings *"La tomba è un letto"* — a foretaste, by the way, of the "vaporous" music at the end of *Aïda* — the simple pathos is very moving, her momentary lapse into C major when she decides to tear up the letter expressing the drama admirably; while in the final *"Andrem, raminghi e poveri"* there is a return to pathos of quite a different kind. At the entrance of Rodolfo we are back again in the realm of pure drama, with an interlude of pity and tenderness, of which the effective simplicity is very typical of the composer's genius. Could anything be more expressive than Luisa's gentle comfort?

No less admirable is the musical picture of utter despair when Rodolfo, learning the true story, curses the day he was born. Indeed, the last half-dozen pages of the duet before Miller's entrance (itself most happily depicted by a modulation from hammer-like chords of G minor to a unison D flat very reminiscent of Beethoven's Fifth Symphony) are among the best of the opera, though perhaps such praise should in fact be reserved for the final trio, which is a model of expressiveness and beautiful concerted writing.

It is presumably this last act that led Basevi and other critics to consider *Luisa Miller* as the inauguration of a new "manner" in Verdi's composition. To divide the operas into any kind of chronological divisions of style seems to me impossible. Certain operas can be grouped as representing certain different tendencies; but the factor of their date, though implying something, is only of secondary importance. Nevertheless, there is a new quality in *Luisa Miller*, a flavor hitherto unperceived. Perhaps it may be defined as "intimate pathos." In previous operas Verdi had painted passion, hate, rage, despair; but the pathos of Luisa and her father is new, and it is this pathos that has led some people to consider *Luisa Miller* as a kind of study for *La Traviata*. Certainly the scene between father and daughter in the last act suggests the scene between Germont and Violetta, and, generally speaking, the musical characterization shows a subtlety prophetic of the later opera. Luisa, Miller, Rodolfo, even Walter at times, are human beings, not mere types.

From the technical point of view, too, *Luisa Miller* is interesting in that the vocal line is less rigid or at any rate less formal. Somewhat greater responsibility is laid on the orchestra, which, indeed, in the scene where Miller discovers Luisa writing and in a portion of the scene between Walter and Wurm in the second act, plays an almost predominant part. To some extent, then, *Luisa Miller* gives us a first taste of that perfect blend of supple vocal writing and orchestral virtuosity which is to be found in *Falstaff*. Quite apart from any questions of scholarship, however, *Luisa Miller* is worth study. It still stands, so to say, on its own feet as one of the most lovable of Verdi's operas.

RIGOLETTO

Libretto by Piave

Production: VENICE, March 11, 1851

THREE ACTS, FOUR SCENES

The Duke of Mantua (tenor), an unprincipled libertine, is giving a party, where he discusses his amorous adventures with the gentlemen of his court. He is especially interested in one that he is having with a young girl whom he, in the disguise of a simple citizen, meets in church every feast-day. But that does not prevent him from making love at this very party to the Countess of Ceprano almost before her husband's eyes. All women, he says, are alike to him provided they are pretty. In the service of the Duke is a hunchbacked jester called Rigoletto (baritone), who encourages his master in every kind of insolence and vice. In the actual presence of Ceprano he advises the Duke to imprison, exile, or even kill the Count so as to be able to court the Countess in complete freedom. Ceprano, not unnaturally, loses his temper, but Rigoletto, secure in the Duke's protection, merely laughs at the threats of vengeance uttered by him and the other courtiers. Presently Monterone (baritone), whose daughter the Duke has established as his mistress, forces his way in to denounce the Duke as a villain. Rigoletto mocks him, but Monterone, though put under arrest, has more spirit than the obsequious courtiers and, turning on the Duke and Rigoletto, he curses them both for insulting a father's grief. Rigoletto, to his horror, feels that the curse has struck home, while the others express their annoyance at the party being spoiled by such an intrusion.

The second scene shows the courtyard of Rigoletto's house and the street outside it. Rigoletto, returning from the palace, is accosted by a professional cut-throat, Sparafucile (bass), who offers his services in case of need, which, he hints, may not be so remote as Rigoletto thinks. His favorite method, using his sister Maddalena (contralto) as a decoy, is to entice the victim to his lonely house by the river and there dispose of him. Everything is carried out quietly and expeditiously; the tariff is low; the terms — half the agreed sum in advance — are easy. Rigoletto, sufficiently interested to take his name, then enters the house, railing against himself for his wickedness and his deformity, against the Duke and the courtiers for having made him what he is. And all the while Monterone's curse rings in his ears. He finds comfort, however, in the company of his daughter, Gilda (soprano), who loves him dearly and whom he loves more than anything else in the world. In an affecting scene she begs him to reveal his true name and state or, if that is impossible, to tell her at any rate the name of her mother. But Rigoletto will not answer her questions, only saying that her mother was an angel of goodness and that to Gilda, now she is gone, is devoted all his love and care. Gilda begs for a little more freedom; for three months she has not been allowed outside the house except to go to church. Rigoletto, however, is even more firm on this point. So far from going out, extra precautions must be taken to prevent anybody's knowing of her existence. He calls Giovanna, the woman in whose charge are his house and his daughter, and bids her redouble her watchfulness. But Giovanna has been bribed by a young man who has met Gilda at church (in fact, though she does not know it, none other than the Duke himself) to let him into the house, and he, overhearing the end of the scene, learns with surprised amusement that the girl is Rigoletto's daughter. Presently, when the jester has left the house, he reveals himself to the shrinking and ashamed Gilda as a poor student, by name Gualtier Maldè. The two, discreetly left alone by the venal Giovanna, exchange vows of love. Startled by a noise outside, Gilda, thinking that her father has returned, hurries her lover out by another door. Indulging in girlish dreams of love and delighted to have discovered, as she thinks, her lover's identity, she then goes to bed. But the noises she has heard were real enough, proceeding from a band of courtiers who had gathered outside the house. One of them, as we learn in the first scene, had discovered Rigoletto's house and in it a woman whom all naturally imagine to be his mistress. What a joke to carry her off! What an even better joke to make Rigoletto assist at the abduction in the belief that the lady to be abducted is the Countess of Ceprano! Favored by the darkness, the courtiers succeed in both enterprises.

Rigoletto

The wall of Rigoletto's courtyard is scaled, the door opened to the band. Rigoletto, whose eyes under pretense of masking they have in fact bandaged, stands by, ignorant of the fact that he is assisting at the rape of his own daughter. But a cry for help, a shout of triumph from the now distant courtiers, rouse his suspicions. He tears the mask-bandage from his eyes to recognize his house with the door standing open. In an anguish of terror he rushes in. Gilda is gone. Monterone's curse is indeed working.

The second act is laid in the private apartments of the Duke, who is lamenting the loss of the only woman he ever loved. Though forced to fly the house, he had later returned to find the door open, everything deserted, Gilda gone. Then the courtiers arrive, delighted with their exploit, which they retail with great relish to the Duke, telling him that they have Rigoletto's mistress in the palace at this very moment. The Duke, however, knowing her true identity, astounds them by his sudden moodiness and departs to console the frightened girl. Rigoletto appears, looking everywhere for his daughter. Under a pretense of badinage he tries to discover exactly what happened in the night, but everyone simulates complete ignorance. A page arrives from the Duchess to demand an audience with the Duke. The courtiers get rid of him on excuses so transparently ridiculous that Rigoletto understands at once where Gilda is. Turning on the courtiers, he demands, to their extreme surprise, not his mistress but his daughter. He curses them for their mercenary vileness, but presently, breaking down, makes a desperate appeal to their better nature not to deprive him of the only thing he values in the world. Then Gilda, distraught and disheveled, appears, to his infinite joy though her appearance confirms his worst fears. Endowed by the bitterness of his feelings with real nobility, the wretched hunchback shames the courtiers into departure, and father and daughter are left alone together. On hearing the story of Gualtier Maldè, Rigoletto forgives his daughter, but, despite her prayer for clemency, swears an oath that the vengeance on the Duke vainly invoked by Monterone shall be carried out by his hands.

The third act shows Sparafucile's inn both inside and out. Hoping to cure Gilda of her infatuation, Rigoletto has brought her to see with her own eyes what kind of man her lover is. For the Duke, attracted by the charms of Maddalena, has come to visit her, ordering wine and singing a gay little song about the fickleness of women. While Maddalena and the Duke are flirting inside the house, the heartbroken Gilda and the revengeful Rigoletto watch outside. Presently Rigoletto dismisses his daughter, bidding her put on boy's clothes and go to Verona. Sparafucile comes out to see him, for he has taken advantage of the bravo's proffered services and arranged for the murder of the Duke, though Sparafucile, needless to say, has no idea who the victim is.

The sound of an approaching storm is heard, so the Duke decides to occupy a room in the inn. Maddalena, who has taken a fancy to the handsome youth and knows his danger, endeavors vainly to dissuade him. When he has gone to bed, she tries to persuade her brother to spare his life; why not kill the hunchback when, as arranged, he comes back to fetch the body, and thus get the promised money all the same? Sparafucile, his professional vanity touched, indignantly refuses. What, murder his employer! However, she prevails on him to promise, in the unlikely event of a stranger coming to the house before midnight, to kill him and deliver his substituted body to Rigoletto. But Gilda, who, despite her father's commands, has felt irresistibly compelled to return to the house, has overheard the conversation. In her boy's dress and the darkness of the now raging storm she will pass as a belated wayfarer. If she knocks at the door and asks for shelter she will be killed and thus save her lover's life. The plan works. Sparafucile stabs her and puts her body in a sack, which he hands over to Rigoletto on his return at midnight. Rigoletto, gloating over his vengeance, is about to throw the sack into the river when he hears the Duke singing a fragment of his song. In a frenzy of apprehension he hastens to open the sack and discovers his daughter, still sufficiently conscious to beg his forgiveness for herself and the lover for whom she has given her life. Payment for Monterone's curse has been exacted to the uttermost farthing.

Piave's task in adapting Victor Hugo's *Le Roi s'amuse* was not a difficult one. It is a fine play which needed little change for adaptation to operatic purposes. True, the censorship, by forbidding the presentation of Francis I and the historical personages, such as M. de Saint-Vallier (Monterone in the opera), the father of Diane de Poitiers, and Clément Marot (Marullo), who surrounded him, did not help matters. Moreover, their horror at Francis's latchkey, already mentioned elsewhere, made the scene between Blanche and Francis, one of the most moving and effective in Hugo's play, impossible in the opera. We are never allowed to know what happened between Gilda (Blanche) and the Duke of Mantua (Francis) when the unfortunate girl found herself in the palace confronted by him whom she had in her innocence imagined to be a poor student. The bald fact of her seduction conveys nothing, whereas in *Le Roi s'amuse* the process that leads up to it, culminating in her taking refuge in his very room, is both significant and emotional. For this omission, however, Piave cannot be blamed, any more than he can be blamed for the ridiculous appearance and feebleness of Monterone at the end of the second act, in that they are equally reprehensible in the play. He might with advantage have preserved more of the comedy of the bribing of Bérarde (Giovanna) in the second scene of the first act, insisted more on the plebeian origin of Marot as a reason for Rigoletto turning to him in his despair in the second act, preserved more fully the venal characteristics of Hugo's courtiers; but on the whole he performed his task uncommonly well. All the salient features of the characters, even the grim humor of Saltabadil (Sparafucile), are faithfully reproduced, and in the last act — a condensation of two of *Le Roi s'amuse* — he seems to me to have effected a notable improvement by abolishing the casual personages who for no particular reason appear at the end and by substituting the recollection of Monterone's curse for Hugo's rather tame "I have killed my child" as a final curtain. In short, the libretto of *Rigoletto* is one of the best that Verdi ever set to music.

It certainly inspired him to achieve a degree of perfection never before attained. As a work of art *Rigoletto* remains even today among the finest manifestations of Verdi's genius. In unity of dramatic conception, in delineation of character, this music excels that not only of all the operas that preceded, but of most of the operas that succeeded, it. If ever there was a case of sheer inspiration, *Rigoletto* constitutes such a one, for from the technical point of view it differs but little from its brothers and sisters. There are obvious exceptions of course, such as the scene between Sparafucile and Rigoletto in the second scene of the first act and the quartet in the last act, universally acknowledged as one of the masterpieces of operatic literature. In both instances technical mastery is combined with inspiration in the highest degree. The conversation carried on by the cut-throat and the hunchback above the sinister, somber melody, given, with singular appreciation of orchestral coloring, to solo cello and double-bass, is a magnificent specimen of skill in *parlante* writing. The theme itself is remarkable enough, but the treatment is more remarkable still:

As for the quartet, one hardly knows which to admire the more, the beauty of the themes themselves or the manner in which they are blended without loss of the characteristics representative of the different personages portrayed:

GILDA. *Andante*
MADDALENA.
DUCA.
Bel - la
fi - glia dell' a - mo - - -
RIGOLETTO.
pp
In - - - fe - li - ce,
Ah! ah! rido ben di core, chè tai baje costan po-co,
- re,
Schia - vo son de' vezzi tuo -
Ch'ei men - ti - va,
pp

270   Giuseppe Verdi

cor tra - di - to,
quanto val-ga il vostro gioco, mel credete so apprezar.
- i; con un detto, un detto sol tu
che'i men - ti - va

Ah!............... no, non scoppiar,
Sono avvezza bel signore, ad un simile scherza - - re,
puo - - i le mie pene le mie pene con-so-lar,
sai si - cu - - ra,

Rigoletto

The entire quartet, from the first note to the last, is a perfect example of dynamic ensemble-writing as distinct from the static nature of, let us say, the quintet in *Meistersinger* or the trio in the last act of *Rosenkavalier*. In these, lovely as they are, the characters momentarily cease to exist, become mere mouthpieces for the musical inspiration of Wagner and Strauss. In *Rigoletto* each preserves his own identity, lives an independent musical life. Perhaps this instance is of more than particular interest; a general case might be made out for the dramatic superiority of the dynamic qualities of the Italian as contrasted with the static characteristics of the German operatic convention in this respect.

There are some weak moments in every act except the last, for the final duet between Gilda and her father, though its customary omission in English theaters may perhaps be justified on grounds of dramatic fitness, contains some beautiful music of genuine tenderness, the harmonic treatment of her farewell being particularly felicitous. But the *Allegro con brio* that plays such an important part in the first act is trite, sounding all the more so for being played on a military band "off." Nothing could suggest to us less the elegance of a court ball, but it must be admitted that Verdi's ideas of social festivity rarely rose above the popular *feste* of an Italian provincial town. Indeed, the music associated with the courtiers throughout, except when they are gathered outside Rigoletto's house in the second scene of the first act and when they leave him and his daughter together in the second act, is notably lacking in distinction compared with the rest. Neither of the Duke's two arias in the second act, *"Parmi veder le lagrime"* or, worse still, *"Possente amor,"* possesses much interest, and the *Vivacissimo* in which he and Gilda say farewell to each other in the second scene of the first act, though effective, sounds conventional, not to say coarse, after the tender music that has gone before.

But these are small blemishes in comparison with the outstanding merit of most of the score. The short prelude, adumbrating the notes but not the characteristic harmony of the splendid theme associated with Monterone's curse, which provides, as it were, the motto of the whole opera, gives the somber atmosphere at once. The Duke's first aria, *"Quest' o quella"* (in fact not an aria at all, but the beginning of a ballet) is enchanting not only for its tune but for its rhythm, though the purist might object to the accentuation of some of the words. Like the drawing of an accomplished artist, it portrays the frivolous, worthless character of the man in two or three strokes. The minuet that follows shows that Verdi, if surfeited with *Don Giovanni* in his youth, did not scorn to imitate it, and the final chorus of the scene, though in unison till the inevitable *piu mosso*, is one of the most effective examples of a style that has come in for a good deal of abuse. Probably Monterone's music is actually the best of the whole scene; the strength and sincerity of the declamation after the words *"Ah sì, a turbare,"* with the repeated semiquavers in the treble, punctuated by ejaculations in the bass of the accompaiment, are admirable.

The duet between Sparafucile and Rigoletto, already noted, that opens the second scene has never been surpassed for atmospheric suggestiveness. Victor Hugo himself, we are told, bracketed it with the quartet as one of the two places in which the opera was an improvement on his play. Rigoletto's scena that follows, with its impotent rage periodically interrupted by recollections of Monterone's curse, is only less good, while the subsequent duet between father and daughter, praiseworthy in all its moods, rises to almost equal heights in the passage where they speak of Gilda's dead mother, her *"Oh quanto dolor"* and the final episode in canon, with its exquisite end, being especially effective. With the exception of the Duke's *"E il sol dell' anima,"* whereof the insinuating, seductive charm could hardly be better, the duet between him and Gilda is less interesting. The pendant to it, the famous *"Caro nome,"* in reality a thing of genuine beauty, has been ruined by a succession of fatuous prima donnas; while the chorus of courtiers assembled to carry off Gilda, though excellent as regards music pure and simple, has become almost a parody of operatic conspiracy in general.

The second act, with the defects already noted, is undoubtedly the weakest of the opera. There are many beautiful moments in the scene between Rigoletto and his daughter, notably the last page of her *andantino*, his *"Solo per me l'infamia,"* and the passage for both together before the entrance of Monterone, with the heartrending figure for the violins and Gilda's pathetic sobs punctuating the even flow of Rigoletto's expressive melody. But the finale, though exciting when well sung, is of a caliber distinctly inferior. Rigoletto's entrance, his denunciation of the courtiers and subsequent appeal to their pity, are all of the first order, though the cello obbligato to the last, perhaps because it is extremely difficult to play, never seems to be quite as effective as it should.

For my part, I would not willingly see a note altered in the last act. Apart from the quartet, the scenes between Maddalena and Sparafucile, Sparafucile and Rigoletto, the sighing of the wind represented in the *bouche-fermée* passages for the chorus, even the translation of lightning-flashes into terms of the piccolo, seem to me incapable of improvement. Remains of course the familiar but much discussed *"La donna è mobile."* It has been said that this, not being in itself a good tune, cannot be "good music," though no one, I think, denies that either it or the treatment of it could be better from the dramatic point of view. When the tune is divided between the singer and the clarinet, even more, perhaps, in its repetition at the end, at the very moment when Rigoletto is about to throw the sack into the river, it moves, thrills the listener in an extraordinary degree. Here, if ever, is an example of the right tune in the right place. It dramatize to perfection the worthless libertine singing of the faithlessness of women at the very moment the woman he has betrayed is about to die for him. All through the act the melodrama of the action is thus raised by the music to greater heights of emotion; the spectator experiences something of the "pity and horror" considered by the Greeks indispensable to genuine tragedy. And in this music "*La donna è mobile*" plays an important if not a preponderant part. How, then, can anyone refuse to designate such a tune as a masterpiece of its kind? Inevitably, divorced from its context, transported to concert or music hall for the delectation of some tenor or other, it loses half its point, for "*La donna è mobile*" is almost as much a motif as an aria. In a different way "*Caro nome*" has suffered equally from similar treatment. It is not a show-piece intended to display the virtuosity of this or that prima donna. It represents, truly and movingly represents, a young girl's thoughts of the lover who has just left her. It should be sung quietly, without effort, with the coloratura falling into its proper place as an expressive subsidiary, not emphasized like a set-piece in a display of fireworks.

Verdi, be it remembered, once informed a singer who wished him to write another number for Gilda that he had "conceived *Rigoletto* without arias, without final tableaux, just as a long succession of duets"! Literally the statement might be challenged; but no one can hope to appreciate the dramatic significance of this great opera unless he realizes that it is substantially and practically true.

IL TROVATORE

Libretto by Cammarano

Production: ROME, January 19, 1853

FOUR ACTS, EIGHT SCENES

The scene opens in the hall of the castle of Aliaferia, half palace, half fortress, a residence of the court of Aragon. There is civil war in the land, and soldiers and attendants are keeping guard. In addition to the danger of attack, the Count of Luna (baritone) is on the lookout for a troubadour who comes by night into the garden to serenade

Leonora (soprano), the lady of his choice. To pass the time, Ferrando (bass) tells the men under his orders the story of the Count's brother. Many years ago, in the dead of night, the nurse woke up to find a gypsy-woman standing by her charge's bed. Aroused by the nurse's cries, servants arrived and seized the woman, who, despite her protests that she only wished to cast the child's horoscope, was condemned to be burned to death for witchcraft, for from that time the child became pale and sickly. The witch, however, left a daughter, who, to avenge her mother's death, stole the child and burned him to death on the very same spot. Despite every effort this woman could never be traced and eventually the old Count died, refusing to the last to believe the boy was dead and charging his son never to relax the search for his brother. The old witch, too, in the shape of various animals, continued to haunt the neighborhood; one serving-man, who had seen her in the guise of an owl, had died of fright. Horrified and frightened, the soldiers and attendants as the clock strikes twelve conclude the scene by invoking the curse of Heaven on such devilish sorcery.

In the second scene Leonora is waiting in the garden of the castle with her attendant, Ines (soprano), hoping against hope for the arrival of the troubadour. In answer to Ines's exhortations to prudence she tells how, before the outbreak of civil war, she gave her heart to this knight whom she thought to have lost forever, till one beautiful moonlit night his song was heard under her window; her love for him is inexpressible, irreplaceable. The women then enter the house. But in the silence of the night the Count, his heart consumed by passion, watches outside Leonora's apartments. Presently the song of the troubadour is heard and Leonora descends to meet her lover. At first in the darkness she mistakes the Count for the troubadour but when she finds two men instead of one, she throws herself between them, protesting her eternal love for the troubadour. The outraged Count bids him raise his vizor, to discover that he is none other than Manrico (tenor), a freebooter in the service of the Pretender of Urgel, with a price upon his head. Manrico tauntingly bids the Count call the guard so that by arresting a rebel he may rid himself of a rival. But the Count wishes for private, not public, vengeance, and the act ends with the two men about to fight a duel while Leonora falls fainting to the ground.

The second act shows an encampment of gypsies in the mountains. With them are Azucena (mezzo-soprano) and Manrico, who has come to visit her whom he believes to be his mother. The gypsies begin to work on their anvils and the crackling of the fire reminds Azucena of that terrible scene many years ago when her mother was burned at the stake, for she is no other than the daughter of the

Il Trovatore

gypsy-woman. Twitted by the gypsies with the sadness of her song, she replies that it is no more sad than the incident that gave it birth. Then, glancing at Manrico, she murmurs to herself that he will be the instrument of her vengeance. Left alone, Azucena at Manrico's request describes to him the scene of the burning of her mother and how she herself kidnapped the Count's child. After a momentary impulse of pity, stifled by the recollection of her mother's last agonized cry for vengeance, she had in truth burned the child alive, only to discover that in her mad frenzy the baby she had murdered was not the Count's but her own. Manrico, horrified and surprised, asks whose son he is if he is not hers; whereupon the half-crazy Azucena, realizing that she has unguardedly revealed her secret, corrects herself and bids him pay no attention to her ravings. Has she not proved by her devotion that she is indeed his mother? Manrico gratefully acknowledges her care, especially now when she has nursed him back to health after a battle in which he had been left for dead. Azucena reminds him bitterly of the single combat when he spared the Count of Luna's life, urging him, should the opportunity present itself, never again to be guilty of such weakness; to which Manrico replies that the impulse that prompted him to spare his enemy's life was inexplicable even to himself and that she need fear nothing of the kind in the future. A messenger arrives to inform Manrico that the forces of Urgel have captured Castellor and that he has been put in command. Not only that; Leonora, misled by the news of his death, proposes to enter a convent that very night. So Manrico, dispatching the messenger for a horse, prepares to depart immediately, disregarding the pleas of Azucena, who seeks by every means to detain him.

The Count, however, who has also been informed of Leonora's determination to take the veil, has decided to carry her off from the very steps of the altar. At the opening of the next scene he, accompanied by some of his men, lies in wait in the garden of the convent, protesting that not God Himself shall come between him and Leonora now that Manrico is dead. The chant of the nuns is heard, interrupted by the comments of the Count and his men, and presently Leonora appears, bidding a sad farewell to the faithful Ines; since the death of Manrico earth holds no further joy for her. As she is about to cross the threshold the Count steps out from his hiding-place to stop her, but at that moment Manrico arrives. Neither Leonora nor the Count can believe their eyes, the one in an ecstasy of delight, the other mad with anger. The Count bids Manrico go if he does not wish to be put to death, but Manrico calls on his hidden followers, who, thanks to superior numbers, soon disarm the Count and his men. Leonora, now abandoning all thoughts of the convent, says that she will follow

Manrico anywhere, and the act ends with the characters commenting on the situation from their different points of view.

In the first scene of the third act the army of Aragon, under the command of the Count of Luna, is preparing to assault Castellor, where Leonora and Manrico are besieged. The Count, his soldierly ambitions reinforced by personal jealousy, anxiously awaits the dawn to give the signal for attack. Presently Ferrando comes to announce the capture of a spy discovered wandering on the outskirts of the camp. It is Azucena, who, as she tells the Count, has come to look for the ungrateful son who has deserted her. Questioned as to her origin, she says she is a gypsy from the mountains of Biscay; whereupon the Count asks if she has ever heard tell of his stolen brother. Azucena, realizing his identity, shows signs of perturbation, and Ferrando, who has been observing her for some time, proclaims his recognition of her as the woman who stole and burned the child, the daughter of the sorceress. The Count thereupon bids the soldiers draw her bonds tighter while Azucena in her despair and agony calls for aid on her son Manrico. The Count is delighted to be able to combine vengeance on his rival with justice on the murderess of his brother; Azucena, invoking the curses of Heaven on the "worse son of an impious father," is dragged off to be burned at the stake.

The scene changes to the interior of the castle, where Leonora and Manrico await the assault. He tells her that the danger is great, but that the thought of her will give him double strength to win the coming fight or, should he fall, comfort his last moments. Suddenly Ruiz comes to say that the old gypsy-woman is being dragged to the stake in full view of the castle. So Manrico, crying to Leonora that his first duty is to her as she is his mother, prepares to head a desperate sortie to save Azucena or perish in the attempt.

At the opening of the last act Leonora and Ruiz come to that part of the Castle of Aliaferia which serves as a prison. Leonora, sending Ruiz away, remains alone in the hope of saving her lover from the death to which he has been condemned after the capture of Castellor. The chant of the "*Miserere*" for those about to die strikes terror to her heart, and presently the voice of Manrico is heard singing from the prison a final farewell to Leonora, who, moved by his adjuration not to forget him, exclaims that her love will prove stronger than anything in the world. The Count enters and, though conscious that he is probably exceeding his powers, gives orders that at dawn Manrico is to be executed and Azucena (also imprisoned in the castle) burned at the stake. He mourns the disappearance of Leonora, who could not be found when Castellor was taken. She reveals herself to him, rousing his fury by her prayers for Manrico's life; but eventually she gains her point by offering herself as the price of clemency. This promise obtained, she sucks poison from a ring on her finger so that her bargain may be fulfilled in the letter, not the spirit, and both rejoicing, she for her success in saving Manrico's life, he for his anticipated possession of the woman he loves, enter the castle.

The last scene shows the dungeon where Azucena and Manrico are confined. She is half-delirious with terror at her approaching doom, but he succeeds in calming her and presently she falls asleep, soothed by a waking dream of their returning together to the peace of their native mountains. Leonora enters, to Manrico's inexpressible joy, which, however, turns to anger when she tells him that he is free to depart, but that she must stay behind. Guessing at once the nature of her bargain with the Count, Manrico refuses to accept his life on such terms, overwhelming her with reproaches. But he soon discovers how unjust are his suspicions, for, the poison taking effect more quickly than she anticipated, she dies in his arms. The Count enters and, furious at the deception, gives orders for Manrico's instant execution. As he is being led away, Azucena wakes and asks for her son. Disregarding her prayer for a moment's respite, the Count drags her to the window so that she may see the end. With a cry that he has killed his own brother and that her vengeance is now complete, Azucena sinks lifeless to the ground, leaving the Count horror-struck at the loss of everything he has lived for.

Cammarano's libretto is often dismissed as preposterous and unintelligible; it is neither. Doubtless we cannot appreciate the wholly unrestrained passions of the protagonists, to which everything — religion, honor, humanity, even life itself — must be sacrificed. But that they were credible enough to patrons of the romantic drama is proved by the popularity of Gutierrez's *El Trovador*.

In one respect the opera is less extreme than the play, for in the latter Leonora has actually taken her vows as a nun when she runs away with Manrico. Otherwise Cammarano followed the original as closely as he could. True, he eliminated Leonora's scheming brother Guillen, but the loss is not felt. More important is the whittling down of the historical and political aspects of the action, which, as Prime-Stevenson has pointed out in his excellent and witty essay on the opera, is difficult to follow unless we realize that the country was in a state of civil war. Prime-Stevenson even claims a historical basis not only for all the characters with the exception of Azucena but for the love-drama of de Luna, Manrico, and Leonora. In the play this lady occupies a less equivocal position than in the opera, where her presence in the Castle of Aliaferia (usually accepted as the residence of the Count of Luna, whereas it was of course the residence of the court of Aragon, to which de Luna is attached as general in command and Leonora as lady-in-waiting) arouses the gravest suspicions from the outset. Throughout the story Cammarano and Verdi pay penalties of this kind for their exclusive preoccupation with the "human interest" of the action. Further, their passion for compression makes the plot very difficult to follow at times. Difficulty, however, is not synonymous with impossibility. If we realize that Azucena, who, be it remembered, must be regarded as the real pivot of the drama, is half-mad, or rather, like Hamlet, oscillates between madness and sanity; that her version of the story of her burning of the child told to Manrico in the second act is the true version, though she subsequently denies it; that belief in witches and witchcraft was a very real thing in medieval Europe — then the plot becomes clear enough. Doubtless it is difficult to believe that a woman would have burned one child in mistake for another, but a woman crazy with fear and hate, especially a fourteenth-century outcast, might have done so. Certain details are obscure in play and opera. Why was Azucena not burned in the third act? Presumably the sortie was successful and Castellor captured only subsequently; but we are never told so. The fact, pointed out by Prime-Stevenson, that the actual geography of Aliaferia makes Leonora's movements in the last act impossible seems to me of no importance. From the constructional point of view three such long narrations of previous events as those given by Ferrando, Leonora, and Azucena are regrettable. Nevertheless, though some of Cammarano's verses are bombastic and turgid, his presentation of the dramatic incidents is as a rule admirably vivid. Moreover, the placing of the arias is singularly happy in most instances; they seem to come precisely where they will intensify rather than detract from the significance of the action. "*Di quella pira*" and, needless to say, the duet between Leonora and Manrico in the "*Miserere*" scene are good examples. To sum up, then, the libretto of *Trovatore* is the quintessence of conventional romanticism, first cousin if not twin brother to that of *Ernani;* but, within the limits of the convention, the characters are credible enough and well contrasted from the theatrical point of view, Azucena, especially, being an interesting study of maternal and filial devotion.

The very essence of the music of *Il Trovatore* precludes any necessity for much detailed analysis. Fundamentally the passion of the opera, wild and unrestrained, is expressed in melodies so well known that quotation seems superfluous. In a sense Ferrando's narration in the first scene sums up the good and bad characteristics of most of the music. Here we find the profusion of 3/4 rhythm, the prevalence of minor tonality, the often superficial triviality, the underlying, respect-compelling sincerity, the contrasts violent to the point of brutality, typical of the opera as a whole. Moreover, the final shout on

Il Trovatore

the chord of A major after the succession of pages in the minor provides a characteristic instance of the kind of thrill in which Verdi here so excelled. The means are of the simplest; the result is irresistible.

In the second scene there is little but Leonora's *"Tacea la notte placida,"* a beautiful and expressive aria, well prepared, moreover, by the preceding recitative, especially the lovely nine bars of *Andante* where the change of key most happily illustrates her change of mood. The less said about the succeeding cabaletta the better; it is, exceptionally, a mere excuse for virtuosity. Manrico's first snatch of song to harp accompaniment is principally interesting as containing a phrase that plays an important part not only in the famous *"Ah che la morte ognora"* in the fourth act but in Aïda's *"O patria mia"*; it has been praised as possessing character, but seems to me indeterminate. The best parts of the final trio, one of those facile melodies in unison that abound in the earlier operas, are the orchestral accompaniment of the opening, and the *stretto* of the conclusion, which, if not remarkable in itself, is extraordinarily effective in performance.

Both scenes of the second act reach a higher level. Apart from the virility of the remarkably industrious chorus of gypsies, with their hammers and anvils, and Azucena's narration, with its mixture of madness and horror, in the first scene, the charm of the Count of Luna's popular melody, *"Il balen del suo sorriso,"* in the second, and Leonora's joy at the unexpected appearance of Manrico, are admirable specimens of dramatic music. Leonora's breathless semiquavers to the words: *"E deggio e posso crederlo,"* worked through the ensuing ensemble to the emotional climax: *"Sei tu dal ciel disceso"* (in the version made for the Paris Opéra given to the tenor as well), represent to perfection her state of mind. Azucena's music, beginning with the familiar *"Stride la vampa,"* used as a kind of motif not only here but in the last act and continuing through the description of her mother's death, could hardly be better of its kind. Even the orchestral effects, elementary though they may seem, produce a real atmosphere, while the vocal writing, of course, remains of the first class, the unaccompanied simplicity of her *"Strana pietà"* just after Manrico's account of how he spared the Count's life being a typical instance.

The most interesting feature of the first scene of the third act is the important ballet music composed for the Paris Opéra and printed only in the French score. Verdi wrote so little good ballet music that the unfamiliarity of this seems curious. There are some poor movements, notably the final gallop; but the Gitanilla is one of the best pieces of dance music he ever wrote. The Sevillana, too, is effective, and there are two charming numbers in 3/4 and 3/8 time, surprisingly delicate and graceful. A point worthy of note is that Verdi introduced two themes from the gypsies' chorus into this ballet music, one in the opening number, the other in the ensemble. It is, I think, the only instance of such a proceeding, Verdi's ballet music being as a rule a wholly separate entity.

The ballet is danced by gypsies after the famous soldiers' chorus, which, for this or some other reason, is in the French version transposed into E major, the music that precedes it being appropriately altered and the end of the chorus itself changed to *fortissimo*, presumably because the chorus remain on the stage instead of going off as in the ordinary version.

In my opinion full justice has never been done to the second scene of this act, usually dismissed with a few casual words of praise for "*Di quella pira.*" Everybody agrees that this is a splendid example of a formal cabaletta, perhaps the only one of the tribe that, when properly sung, can still cause a modern audience to vibrate with something of the excitement felt by its first admirers. Sketches in existence at Sant' Agata show that Verdi originally planned it in common time like the rest of the movement; the present 3/4, however, with its nervous intensity, is an undoubted improvement. But apart from the lovely almost Mozartean tenderness of Manrico's "*Ah si, ben mio*" that opens the scene, the music that immediately precedes and succeeds "*Di quella pira*" is worthy of note. There is a touch of Beethoven about the orchestral accompaniment to Manrico's reception of the news of his mother's doom, about the music of the soldiers gathering for the sortie, that is very remarkable. For sheer virility these are some of the best pages of the whole opera.

Both the scenes that together constitute the fourth act are admitted masterpieces. Indeed, with the exception of Leonora's *Allegro* (often omitted) and the cabaletta for her and the Count that concludes the first scene, scarcely a note could be changed with advantage. Moreover, even these are by no means bad examples of their kind; it is the kind that has become outmoded. The very familiarity of numbers such as the "*Miserere*" or "*Ai nostri monti*" obscures the genius that inspired them. If we could hear the "*Miserere*" for the first time today we should be overwhelmed by its effectivenes, which, on analysis, can be seen to depend on contrasts — the contrast between the somber, full orchestra accompanying Leonora and the clear tones of Manrico's harp, the contrast between the thoughts of heaven put forward by the chorus and the purely amorous regrets of Manrico, both linked together in Leonora's impassioned sobs. The nostalgia of Azucena's "*Ai nostri monti,*" so right, so moving, is evident to all. What may not be so evident is the skill with which it is introduced into the last trio, bringing the half-conscious Azucena into proper perspective, as it were, without interruption to the scene between Manrico and Leonora. Apart from such salient features, however, there are other points that need emphasis. Such, for instance, are the quality of Leonora's "*D'amor sull'ali rosee*," the happy use of clarinets and bassoons that introduce the preceding recitative, not to mention the somber beauty of the recitative itself. Both *parlanti* between Leonora and the Count in the first and Leonora and Manrico in the second scene are first-rate, the characteristic broken rhythm of her "*Prima che d'altri vivere*" in the last trio being also singularly happy. Azucena's horror at her approaching doom, Manrico's attempts to soothe her, and the rugged strength of the final *Allegro* with her terrible cry: "*Sei vendicata, o madre*," are no less good. No one in Europe today possesses the secret of achieving such effects with such simple means.

Which is true of *Il Trovatore* as a whole. It may be crude, unequal, devoid of technical, especially rhythmical, interest. It may lack depth of insight and subtlety of characterization, though Azucena wholly, Leonora and Manrico in part, come to life in the music if not in the action. As a work of art inferior to *Rigoletto* and *La Traviata*, it is perhaps the nearest approach to a purely "singers' opera" that Verdi ever wrote. Some of the effects, since repeatedly copied by many other composers, may strike us as commonplace. Nevertheless, there is quality in *Il Trovatore*, democratic, if you will, rather than aristocratic, but none the less impressive. It is this, in conjunction, of course, with its extraordinary wealth of melody, that has assured the triumph of the opera. Periodically, after a succession of conventional or trivial pages, something emerges and hits you, as it were, between the eyes, something elemental, furious, wholly true. *Il Trovatore* has been reproached with vulgarity, and the reproach is not unfounded. But this vulgarity is the vulgarity of greatness, a by-product of the vitality and passion without which there can be no great art. Is Shakspere never vulgar? Or Beethoven?

LA TRAVIATA

Libretto by Piave

Production: VENICE, March 6, 1853

THREE ACTS, FOUR SCENES

Violetta (soprano), a Parisian demi-mondaine, is giving a supper party. A young man, Alfredo (tenor), is introduced by Gaston, a friend of both, who whispers to Violetta that Alfredo is in love with her and every day during her recent illness came to inquire after her. Violetta, though a little touched, refuses to take the matter seriously. As her professional admirer, Baron Douphol (baritone), is unwilling, she calls on Alfredo for a song and he sings a toast in praise of pleasure, in which she too joins. Dancing begins in a neighboring room, whither Violetta is about to accompany her guests when she suddenly feels faint. Begging the others to proceed without her, she promises to join them in a minute. Alfredo, however, has stayed behind to warn her that care for her health is imperative. Violetta asks bitterly who there is to care for her; to which Alfredo responds with a declaration of his love. At first she is inclined to laugh, but when he tells her that he has been in love ever since he first saw her years ago, she bids him leave and forget her except as a friend. Coquettishly, however, she gives him a flower, telling him that he can come back when it is withered. Alfredo departs in an ecstasy of delight and the other guests return to take their leave. Left alone, Violetta muses on the unfamiliar joy of truly loving and being loved, but puts away the thought as an idle dream; her destiny is to tread the round of pleasure to the end, though the sound of Alfredo's voice singing outside the balcony suggests that her resolution will soon be broken down.

The second act is laid in a country house outside Paris where Violetta and Alfredo have been living together for three months. Alfredo's exuberant happiness is interrupted by the chance discovery that Annina, Violetta's maid, has been to Paris to sell what remains of her mistress's possessions to meet the expenses of the house. Overwhelmed by shame and remorse, he declares his intention of raising the necessary money on his own account, charging Annina to say nothing of their conversation. When he has gone, Violetta returns and a visitor is announced. Thinking it to be the lawyer she is expecting, she bids him be shown in. It is, however, Alfredo's father, Germont (baritone), come to rescue his son from the clutches of a woman who, he thinks, is ruining him. Violetta, from the documents prepared for the lawyer, has no difficulty in convincing the astonished Germont that it is her money, not Alfredo's, that is being used to pay for the house; but the old man, though satisfied as to her generosity and real love for Alfredo, asks for a further and greater sacrifice; Alfredo's sister is engaged to a young man who will not marry her unless her brother breaks off such a disreputable liaison. Violetta, thinking that this only entails a temporary separation, is prepared to consent, but Germont tells her frankly that the separation must be permanent. She replies that she cannot give up her newfound happiness, that death would be preferable. Germont, however, bids her reflect on what will happen to her and Alfredo when age has cooled their passion. How can a union such as theirs be blessed by Heaven? Violetta, struck by the truth of his words, consents to do as he wishes, only begging Germont to let Alfredo know some day the extent of her sacrifice. Much moved, the old man kisses her and goes out into the garden to await his son. Violetta sits down to write a parting letter, but is interrupted by Alfredo himself, who has heard of his father's arrival and proposes that they meet him together. Violetta in great agitation pretends to wish that Alfredo should see Germont first and with a tragic cry of insistence on her love makes as if to go out into the garden. In reality, however, she joins her maid, whom she has instructed to have a carriage in readiness to drive to Paris. Alfredo, suspecting nothing, even though told by a servant that Violetta is gone, sits down to read a book. A letter is brought to him. It is Violetta's farewell, handed to a messenger at the very moment she set out for Paris. Germont enters just in time to catch Alfredo as he reels from the shock into his arms. By calling up memories of their native Provence and promising complete forgiveness and the loving care of his family, the old man seeks to console his son, but Alfredo, mad with grief and jealousy, can think of nothing except that Violetta has left him for Douphol. An invitation to a party, which Violetta had received earlier in the day from her friend Flora, lies on the table. Reading it, he finds his suspicions confirmed and, followed by Germont, rushes from the house, intent on revenge.

The second scene is Flora's party in Paris, opening with a masked ball. Presently the guests take off their masks; some continue dancing, others sit down to gamble. Rumors of the separation of Violetta and Alfredo have reached Paris, soon confirmed by the entrance of Alfredo alone. Almost immediately afterwards Violetta arrives, accompanied by Douphol. Flora tells them that Alfredo is there, to Violetta's great distress and to the annoyance of Douphol, who commands her not to speak to him. Alfredo, who is having a phenomenal run of luck at the gaming-table, proclaims that he will use his winnings to buy Violetta's return with him to the country. Everybody notes the insult and Douphol, irritated beyond measure, takes his seat at the table. Fortune, however, still favors Alfredo, but the announcement of supper temporarily interrupts the game. Violetta returns to have an interview with Alfredo, whom she begs to leave the party at once lest a fatal quarrel with Douphol ensue. Alfredo, after taunting her, says he will consent only if she will promise to follow him wherever he goes. This she refuses to do, giving Alfredo to understand that she loves Douphol and has promised never to see him again. Alfredo, mad with jealousy and anger, calls in the guests from the supper-room and in the presence of them all throws the purse containing his winnings at Violetta, calling upon them to witness that he has now paid his debt in full. Amid the general consternation,

Violetta in a faint, the others horrified, Germont enters and reproaches his son for behaving thus to a woman; whereupon, after a short ensemble in which everyone expresses his or her point of view, the act ends with Germont leading away Alfredo, now thoroughly ashamed of himself.

The third act shows Violetta's bedroom, where she lies dying of consumption, watched over by the faithful Annina. The doctor enters and, though he pretends to her that she is better, whispers to Annina that she has only a few hours to live. It is Carnival time and Violetta sends Annina out to give ten of her remaining twenty louis to the poor, profiting by the maid's absence to read once again a letter she has received from Germont in which he tells her that Alfredo has left the country as the result of his duel with Douphol, but that he has now been told the truth and will return to ask her pardon. Realizing, despite the doctor's comforting assurances, that her doom is sealed, she laments the end of her once lovely dreams, above all the absence of her lover; she will die in a nameless grave, without a friend to mourn her. The sound of revelry outside breaks in on her meditation; then Annina returns in a great state of excitement to prepare her for the news that Alfredo has come. He throws himself at her feet, begging forgiveness for himself and his father; no power on earth can ever separate him from her any more. The lovers plan to leave Paris, but first, Violetta says, let them go to church to render thanks for his return. When, however, she attempts to rise and dress, the effort is beyond her strength and she falls back exhausted into a chair. While Alfredo attempts to comfort her, she bewails the cruel fate that dooms her to die at the very moment happiness is in her grasp. Germont and the doctor arrive, the former much grieved at the sight of what she has become as the result of keeping her promise to him. Violetta kisses the old man, gives Alfredo a portrait of herself when she was still beautiful, telling him to show it to the girl he will marry one day, and quietly sinks back, happy to die in the presence of the only people she has ever really loved.

Piave could not go far wrong in his treatment of a play as well constructed as *La Dame aux camélias*, for, with the main lines so clearly indicated, all he had to do was to produce tolerable verses and not to interfere with Dumas's action. He made two mistakes: the introduction of Germont in the gambling scene and the ambiguous note on which the first act ends. The latter, though psychologically inferior to the original, in which Marguérite's capitulation to Armand provides a clearer climax, is perhaps justified on musical grounds; the former, probably due to a desire for an ensemble of all the principal characters, cannot be defended. Germont could and would never have come to Flora's party. In some minor details, too, the book of the opera is inferior to the play. Douphol, for instance, has none of the personality of de Varville; Gaston, in the play rather a touching figure, has no real existence in the opera. We miss the grasping, parasitical Prudence, the attractive if sentimental pair of lovers, Nichette and Gustave. Nevertheless, there are some deft touches, such as Flora's invitation, not to mention the elimination of Dumas's unnecessary second act, and the main features of the story are so well preserved that any discussion of the libretto of *La Traviata* amounts in practice to a discussion of *La Dame aux camélias*, which is perhaps unnecessary.

Still, one or two things may usefully be said. Though Dumas, as he himself tells us, wrote his play in eight days and primarily to make money, its effect on contemporary opinion proves that it seemed only too true to life. How deeply it shocked current prejudices has already been related, but nobody, I think, ventured to deny that Dumas had painted an accurate picture of a world with which he was clearly well acquainted. Moreover, from the psychological point of view, the clash between the aspirations of Marguérite (Violetta) and the conventions of society is a fundamental one. Doubtless a certain section of society nowadays would rather welcome her as an interesting addition to the family, but translated into other terms and deprived of the romantic glamour attaching to the demi-mondaine, she must always appear equally impossible as a wife for Armand (Alfredo). The attitude of Duval (Germont) is difficult for an English audience to appreciate, the impediment to Armand's sister's marriage perhaps impossible. Both, however, not only were, but are, absolutely true to French provincial life. The effect of the death-scene is of course heightened by every theatrical artifice known to the author, but life, in Latin countries especially, is often surprisingly true to the theater. The gist of the whole matter is that all the characters in this drama are acting even to themselves. Marguérite sees herself in this or that situation; Armand, though sincerely in love, perpetually externalizes his emotions; not for nothing does Duval retain his hat and gloves on his first visit to his son's mistress. This, however, does not make of them shallow or incredible people, for such behavior, though less common, perhaps, than it used to be, is by no means unknown even among intelligent people in the modern world. Fundamentally, then, the emotions of *La Dame aux camélias* seem to me true; they are certainly moving. Far too much has been made of the sentimentality of the drama. When drama ceases to be sentimental, it loses its hold on the public, for the appeal of drama rests primarily on emotional, not intellectual foundations. "In trying to be more clever than the rest of the world you sometimes become less so," once wrote an exceptionally wise Frenchman. *La Traviata* remains essentially an opera for "the rest"; which is the reason why it has lived.

Few, however, will deny that Verdi in his music raised the rather obvious effectiveness of *La Dame aux camélias* to a higher plane altogether. There is no question of "exteriorization" in the pathos or the passion expressed in the score of *La Traviata;* they could scarcely be more genuine, more intimate. Never before, except momentarily and in comparison tentatively in the last act of *Luisa Miller*, had Verdi attempted anything of the kind. Indeed, the novelty of the conception, as well as the realism of the subject that is in fact bound up with it, was one of the causes contributory to the failure of the opera in the first instance.

Further, *La Traviata* is characterized by a technical skill unapproached in any of the previous operas. Instances of this are so many that only the most striking can be adduced. The division of the violins in the preludes to the first and third acts is one of them. Though not new, it seems to have been considered daring at the time and is of importance as the forerunner of the same proceeding in that prelude to *Aïda* which was later accused of being an imitation of the prelude to *Lohengrin*. Possibly Verdi took the idea from Berlioz; it certainly owed nothing to Wagner.

The gaming scene in the last portion of the second act is another, the use of the clarinets, later reinforced by oboes and flutes, in the significant orchestral figure that runs through it like an *idée fixe* being most expressive:

The three interruptions by Violetta in eight bars of poignant misery, the manner in which the conversation continues throughout in an almost nonchalant manner, make of the whole scene a most interesting example of technical skill. The treatment of the dialogue in the first act, as well as in the scene between Violetta and Germont in the second, is also most ingenious. In the latter, especially, it is often difficult to say where the recitative ends and the aria begins, so imperceptibly does one merge with the other. But perhaps the passage in the whole opera most remarkable for a blend of technical mastery and emotion is that which leads up to Violetta's *"Amami Alfredo"* in the second act when, unknown to him, she is saying a final farewell. Her broken, ejaculatory phrases; the somber minims of clarinet and bassoon; the rhythmical insistence of the violins repeating a trill from G to F; the harmonic poignancy of the entrance of the cellos, each is simple enough in itself, but the combination of them that prepares the diatonic climax when her anguish, bursting through like a flood, sweeps every restaint aside, seems to me one of the most deft pieces of construction in operatic literature.

Turning to the acts in detail, we are confronted at once in the first by an atmosphere not only of brilliance but of genuine gaiety rare in Verdi's operas. The prelude, made up of the passage for divided strings already quoted and the theme of Violetta's parting adjuration to Alfredo, skillfully embroidered with a counterpoint from which springs an exquisite pendant, has summed up admirably the pathos of the opera in general; but the opening of the act bids us momentarily forget it. Both subjects associated with Violetta's party are singularly happy, perhaps the best example in all Verdi's operas of a kind of music in which he was not as a rule successful. The first, which consists in fact of two themes, recurs at intervals almost till the end of the act, the second, a waltz notable for charm and variety, coming in the middle. The admirable manner in which the general conversation is carried on during the entire act has already been noted, but particular attention should be drawn to the psychological insight shown by Verdi in not allowing, as a lesser composer might have done, Violetta's first premonition of illness to interrupt the waltz. Even Alfredo's first intimation of love is hardly distinguishable from the general revelry; it is not till the *Andantino* of *"Un dì felice"* that the love theme, which subsequently plays so important a part, stands, so to say, on its own feet. Violetta's final scena, with the famous aria *"Ah fors' è lui"* and its brilliant pendant, *"Sempre libera degg' io folleggiare,"* has been ruined for many in a succession of hackneyed interpretations by vain prima donnas; it is in fact not only skillful but truly poetical. Properly sung and in its right place, the coloratura which has so unfortunately endeared it to these ladies is truly expressive of the feverish desire for excitement characteristic of the demi-mondaine, just as the coloratura in her preceding duet suggests the frivolity and indecision of her mind. No one who heard Mme Ponselle sing this music will need to be convinced further that coloratura of this nature can play a definite part in musical expression.

Apart from the perfection of the parting between Violetta and Alfredo already indicated, there can be no doubt that the interview between Violetta and Germont contains the best music in the first part of the second act. The scene that precedes it is in practice confined to Alfredo's *"De' miei bollenti spiriti"* and its succeeding cabaletta, *"Oh mio rimorso,"* though it is perhaps unfair to pass over in silence the effectiveness of the rapidly moving bass in the *Allegro* that divides them. Both aria and cabaletta are good examples of their kind, especially the coda of the latter, but they remain conventional in comparison with what comes after. For with the entry of Germont the music at once rises to another plane and, with the possible exception of *"Un dì quando le veneri,"* remains there. The beauty of the familiar *"Pura siccome un angelo"* and *"Dite alla giovine,"* so well expressing the new factor of Alfredo's young sister, needs no emphasis. Violetta's *"Così alla misera"* that precedes the latter, and, even more, her *"Non sapete quale affetto,"* with its breathless rhythm and the poignant harmonic progression at the end, will perhaps be of more significance to the student.

Unfortunately the concluding scene between father and son is not of the same quality. Apart from the often and not undeservedly pilloried *"Di Provenza il mar,"* with its conventional structure and intolerable repetitions, there is the downright triteness of the final

"*No non udrai rimproveri.*" The only musical interest of the scene lies in the succession of chords on a pedal A flat when Alfredo learns that Violetta has gone; they are of great beauty.

Verdi himself seems to have felt that all was not well with this scene, for in the French version of the opera the musical sequence is completely changed. Thus, "*Di Provenza*" comes immediately on the entrance of Germont, and the discovery of Violetta's departure is reserved till the last page. This has the advantage not only of keeping the best music and the climax of the drama till the end but of providing the purist with the satisfaction of knowing that the scene concludes in the same key as it began. Unfortunately the proceeding entails a repetition by the orchestra of the "*Amami Alfredo*" passage, which seems dangerously like an anticlimax. Could this be avoided, the Paris version would be preferable from every point of view.

The second part of the act is undoubtedly the weakest portion of the opera. True, there are some fine passages: the wholly admirable gaming scene, the ensuing interview between Violetta and Alfredo, introduced by that upward rush of violins suggesting so effectively breathless excitement; Alfredo's denunciation, which, though in conventional cabaletta rhythm, conveys admirably his scorn and brutality. Excellent, too, is the music that accompanies Germont's entry, as is that of Violetta's "*Alfredo, Alfredo*" (marked with typical care to be sung passionately but with the weakest possible tone), which interrupts the final ensemble. But the ensemble itself, though effective enough, harks back to an earlier and more rigid style, the characters, moreover, with the possible exception of Alfredo, being less happily delineated than usual. A more serious defect is the conventionality of the opening scenes, for the music associated with the "gypsies" and the "Spanish matadors," especially, is unsatisfactory as regards both the quantity, which is excessive, and the quality, which is poor.

As in *Rigoletto* and *Il Trovatore* the last act is the best — an accident or a quality that perhaps partially explains the popularity of all three operas. In a sense it is the poetry of the music in general that is chiefly remarkable; a mere technical analysis of the act as a whole would explain its beauty as little as a similar analysis of the prelude, which, with the exquisite simplicity of its main theme, is a veritable masterpiece of pathos. One or two points, however, are worthy of notice. The raising of the curtain on the first bars of the prelude, showing Violetta on her bed of sickness, was a singularly happy innovation. So was the use of the spoken word in the two most emotional moments of the act, when Violetta, to the accompaniment of the love theme, reads Germont's letter, and again just before her death. The Bacchanale, though dramatically suggesting the spirit of a Parisian carnival, is, as music, quite undistinguished. The treatment of the modulation linking "*Parigi, o cara*" to the music that precedes it is rather clumsy — which is true, incidentally, of similar modulations before one or two other arias in the opera — but these defects are at least outweighed by the felicitous change of key in Violetta's reference to the young girl whom Alfredo will one day marry; the working up of excitement in the insistent figure for the violins before Alfredo's long-awaited return; the happy division of the melody between the voice and the oboe in "*Addio del passato.*"

Still, the outstanding merits of the act lie not so much in any technical treatment as in the inspiration of the musical ideas themselves; the pathos of "*Addio del passato*"; the wistfulness of "*Parigi, o cara*," first cousin to "*Ai nostri monti*" in *Il Trovatore;* the emotional quality of the final pages. The last act of *La Traviata* is the feminine counterpart of the last act of *Rigoletto*, different in essence but almost, if not quite, equal in merit. The proportion of weak passages in the opera as a whole is, perhaps, greater but the emotion is finer, more intimate. Of no opera written by Verdi before that time could it be said, as was said in 1930 by a distinguished man of letters leaving Covent Garden after a well-nigh perfect performance: "What taste the man had!"

I VESPRI SICILIANI

Libretto by Scribe and Duveyrier
Production: PARIS, June 13, 1855
FIVE ACTS, SIX SCENES

In the thirteenth century the French held Sicily, and the opening of the opera shows Palermo occupied by their troops. The inhabitants are cowed and sullen, the soldiers truculent. Presently Elena (soprano), sister of Frederic of Austria, comes out of her palace, mourning her brother, who has been executed for treason against the sovereign power. She is accosted by an intoxicated French soldier who bids her sing a song for the delight of himself and his comrades. Elena consents to sing; but her song, far from being the kind he expected, is an incitement to the brave seafaring Sicilians to lay aside fear and, strong in their trust in God, to rise against their oppressors. The song has such an effect on the populace that they are about to fall on the soldiers when Monforte (baritone), the French Governor of Sicily, appears. Though alone and unarmed, his mere presence puts the crowd to flight, Elena and her attendants remaining alone in the square. Arrigo (tenor) joins Elena, who is delighted

I Vespri Siciliani

to hear that, despite Monforte (as he thinks), he has been acquitted by his judges on a charge of treason. Elena departs, but Monforte, bidding him remain, asks him his name and history and, notwithstanding his defiant answers, offers him fame and fortune in the service of France. Arrigo indignantly refuses; whereupon Monforte, though angry at the spurning of his clemency, gives him a final warning to avoid at all costs communication with the rebel Elena. Even when the warning is turned into a command, Arrigo refuses to heed it, and the act ends with his defiant entrance into Elena's palace.

The second act is laid in a valley outside the city, where Procida (bass), a Sicilian patriot, sings a song in praise of Palermo while awaiting his followers. Elena and Arrigo, whom he has sent for, presently arrive, and when the three are left alone, he tells them that foreign support will be forthcoming provided the whole of Sicily rises against the French. He proposes to find some means to bring this about and departs, emphasizing his reliance on Arrigo. Arrigo tells Elena of his overwhelming love for her despite their difference in station and she promises to be his if he will constitute himself the avenger of her brother. A messenger from Monforte arrives with an invitation to Arrigo to attend a ball. He again indignantly refuses, but is surrounded and led away by soldiers. Procida returns and, at the sight of the young men and maidens of the city approaching to celebrate in accordance with their custom their betrothals by a dance in this particular place, is struck by the possibility of using this opportunity to create the popular feeling he so much desires. He will suggest to the French soldiers that they carry off the girls, and the men will then be filled with irresistible fury against them. The plan works well. The approach of a boat filled with elegant Frenchmen and Frenchwomen serves further to enrage the Sicilians, already infuriated by the loss of their women, and the act ends with their chorus of vengeance punctuating the Barcarole sung by those on the French boat.

In the third act Monforte is discovered alone in his study, a prey to gloomy reflections. He has everything that ambition could desire; but he is deprived of what he most longs for: the love of his son, who, as we learn, is none other than Arrigo. Arrigo is shown in and Monforte tells him that he is indeed his son, whom it will be his delight to honor and favor in every way. But the discovery horrifies Arrigo, who thinks more of the barrier now erected between him and Elena than of the prospects of riches and power. Besides, Monforte is odious to him for the wrong done to his mother, and the scene ends with Monforte's vain appeal for filial love and Arrigo's despair at the situation in which he finds himself. The scene changes to the ballroom where the Ballet of the Four Seasons is given for the entertainment of Monforte and his guests. At the end of the ballet Elena and Procida, both masked, are seen among the guests, some of whom have silk ribbons fastened to their breasts. These, as Procida explains in a whisper to Arrigo, are signs distinguishing the conspirators against Monforte's life. He fastens one on Arrigo, who, torn between filial instinct and loyalty to his friends, does not know what to do. He tries to warn Monforte, begging him to leave the ball, but is met with a refusal. Arrigo goes further, half explains the meaning of the ribbon on his breast. Monforte contemptuously tears it off and at that moment the conspirators, headed by Elena, surround him and attempt to strike him dead. But Monforte is too quick for them. Calling on his officers, he orders the arrest of all wearing the ribbon except Arrigo, whom he proclaims as his savior, and the act ends in an ensemble expressing the various emotions of the characters, the Sicilians uniting in execration of Arrigo's treachery to their cause.

In the fourth act the miserable Arrigo, having obtained a pass from Monforte, comes to visit the prisoners in the fortress. His heart is with them, but he feels apprehension as to whether any will listen to the explanation of his conduct. Elena is ushered in by an officer. At first she expresses nothing but disgust at Arrigo. When he reveals to her that Monforte is his father, however, her determination is shaken, and on Arrigo's saying that his debt is now paid and that he considers himself free to rejoin the conspiracy, she confesses that the duty of hating him was the most cruel blow of all. The lovers then vow eternal fidelity; but presently Procida, led in by soldiers, contrives to whisper to Elena the news that a ship from Aragon, laden with weapons for the insurgents, lies off the port. His only regret is not to be able to profit by it. Then, noticing Arrigo, he refuses to believe his repentance to be anything but another treacherous maneuver. Monforte enters and orders the immediate execution of the prisoners. Arrigo begs for their lives, saying that he will die with them, to which Procida retorts that he is unworthy of the honor. Monforte bids him pay no attention to such insults but to remember that he is his son, which unexpected revelation completes the discomfiture of Procida, who now sees no hope either in the present or in the future. Arrigo again begs for clemency, but Monforte answers that the price of clemency is Arrigo's recognition of him as his father. Arrigo at first refuses, but at the sight of the block and Elena entering the execution chamber his determination gives way. Monforte thereupon stops the execution, announcing the immediate wedding of Elena and his son as a sign of the reconciliation of the two races. Procida whispers to the hesitating Elena that she must comply for the sake of her country and her brother, and Monforte announces to the delighted populace a general pardon in celebration of his joy at the recovery of a son. The act then ends in a scene of fraternization between the French and the Sicilians.

In the fifth act, which takes place in the gardens of Monforte's palace, a crowd is gathered to do honor to the wedding of Arrigo and Elena, who, presently approaching in bridal attire, sings a song expressive of her happiness. On the departure of the chorus Arrigo joins her in a love duet, at the conclusion of which Procida comes to tell Elena that the moment of vengeance is near; when the bells ring to announce the conclusion of the marriage ceremony, the population will fall on the unarmed and unsuspecting Frenchmen. Elena, aghast at such inhuman treachery, tries in vain to mollify the fanatical patriot, but, inflexible, he merely dares her to denounce him. This she cannot bring herself to do; so, to the bewilderment and despair of Arrigo, she refuses to proceed with the marriage, hoping thus to avert the dreaded signal. But Monforte, informed of her resolve though not of its cause, brushes aside all objections and, placing her hand in Arrigo's, orders the bells to be rung in honor of their union. Immediately the Sicilians, armed with swords and daggers, pour into the garden and massacre the French to the last man.

This libretto, a typical product of the "Scribe factory," so amusingly and maliciously described by Wagner in one of his most genial essays, was clearly regarded by the author as entirely suited to the idiosyncrasies of the composer. There were conspirators, massacres, patriotic songs and choruses, all the ingredients that had played so important a part in Verdi's earlier operas. By every rule it should have been a success. Yet we know that Verdi disliked it, firstly because he thought the construction mechanical, secondly because he considered it offensive to Italy and the Italians. His first impulse was to cancel his contract with the Opéra altogether, and he only consented to write the music on the condition that many changes were made. One wonders what they were, for *I Vespri Siciliani* as we know it today is characterized by precisely the defects of which Verdi complained. The Sicilians, headed by Giovanni di Procida, are a treacherous crew; the action is clumsy and excessively protracted. Above all, it seems to me, Scribe's libretto is transparently insincere. Whether it is true or not, as has been stated, that the plot was taken from an earlier play on the subject of the Duke of Alva, the result is equally unfortunate. Neither Sicilians nor Frenchmen are real human beings; they are merely mechanical puppets on whom depend a succession of more or less effective theatrical incidents. A minor but striking incongruity is the retention of the historical title, derived from the fact that the bells ringing for vespers were to be the signal for the uprising, whereas in the opera, it will be noticed, the bells ring for a marriage.

Scribe's artificiality seems to have paralyzed Verdi, in whom complete, unabashed sincerity was a primary virtue. The patriots and conspirators of *I Vespri Siciliani*, though interpreted at times with greater musical ingenuity than their predecessors in *Ernani*, *Attila*, or *La Battaglia di Legnano*, do not carry the same conviction for the excellent reason that Verdi himself obviously did not believe in them. Even Procida's invocation of Palermo, pretty as it is, cannot for genuine emotion be compared with similar songs in previous operas. Doubtless the composer was further handicapped by having to adapt his music to the rhythms and contours of a language not his own. Certainly, even in the Italian version of the opera, which is alone remembered today, the general impression is one of a rigidity quite alien to the composer.

There is, then, little of musical interest in *I Vespri Siciliani*. Undoubtedly the best thing about it is the overture, perhaps the most successful written by the composer, which is both vigorous and ingenious. In it figure three themes from the opera, the beginning of the *Allegro* being the tune associated with the massacre of the French, the beautiful *pianissimo* subject with tremolando strings that of the farewell scene when Procida and Elena prepare to die. In both these instances the rhythms are changed; but the most prominent theme of all is alike rhythmically and harmonically identical with the fine tune that forms the climax of the duet between Monforte and Arrigo. It is hardly too much to say that nearly all the music of *I Vespri Siciliani* worth preserving is to be found in the overture, which represents, moreover, better than the opera itself, the gloom, the fury, and the pathos of the dramatic idea.

Nevertheless, there are isolated examples of genuine inspiration. The unaccompanied quartet, for instance, at the entrance of Monforte is an oasis in the otherwise barren first act; while the conclusion of the second act, with the impotent rage of the Sicilians punctuating the self-satisfied Barcarole of the French, is effective as an idea, even though the themes themselves are in no way remarkable. The first scene of the third act is better, containing, as it does, the important duet between Monforte and Arrigo, which deserves its popularity, for not only the main tune but the subsidiary movements and the dramatic writing generally are good. Monforte's aria that precedes it is also effective, the chromatic passage before the *meno mosso* being especially admirable. The four pages of *adagio* in the finale of the next scene are excellent; but most of the scene is taken up with the Ballet of the Seasons, which, unlike some of my colleagues, I am unable to admire. There are one or two agreeable movements — the

Allegro giusto of the Winter scene, amusingly reminiscent of Violetta's toast in *La Traviata*, the final gallop, which will cause some to remember, and more to regret, a similar movement in *La Boutique fantasque;* best of all, the 6/8 *Allegretto* that ushers in Summer, a pleasant, pastoral-like tune. Furthermore, the scoring is effective, sometimes remarkably so. But on the whole the general effect is decidedly mechanical. Verdi was very rarely happy in his ballet music; he did not think naturally in terms of the dance, which suggested to him no musical ideas. It was not primarily a question of temperament. Tchaikovsky, more melancholy, more pessimistic, composed some of the best ballet music ever written. Verdi needed the stimulus of words or, at any rate, the stimulus of a definite dramatic situation to call forth the music that was in him.

The fourth act begins well, the duet between Arrigo and Elena being at least effective and her *Andante* aria in the middle, with its chromatic *mezza-voce* cadence, something more. The execution scene, too, is moving, while the ensemble, which contains the lovely phrase "*Addio, mia patria*," is further remarkable as possessing a bar in 5/4 time, a very rare phenomenon in these operas. Elena's bolero in the last act has been much admired, but I prefer Arrigo's melody "*La brezza aleggia*," a delicious little tune providing a welcome interlude in this "night of carnage," as Wagner not inaptly christened *I Vespri Siciliani*. The trio between Elena, Arrigo, and Procida, especially in the *Largo* section, is also effective.

Nevertheless, it would take more than these isolated details to make the opera palatable as a whole. An admirable striving after a new technique, a greater pretentiousness of manner, do not suffice to mask a conventionalism more marked than in several earlier works. With *I Vespri Siciliani* Verdi was attempting to beat Meyerbeer on his own ground, at his own game. He was unsuccessful.

SIMON BOCCANEGRA

Libretto by Piave

Production: VENICE, March 12, 1857

Revised Version: MILAN, March 24, 1881

PROLOGUE AND THREE ACTS, FIVE SCENES

In the fifteenth century, Simon Boccanegra (baritone), a freebooter in the employ of the Genoese Republic, has rendered great service by freeing the seas from African pirates. The question of electing a doge has arisen and a faction, headed by Paolo Albiani (baritone), is in favor of choosing Boccanegra, partly because of his services to the State, partly because his election will humble the pride of the patrician party, represented in the opera by Fiesco (bass), and open up possibilities of wealth and power to plebeians such as Paolo himself. Boccanegra, at first reluctant, consents to stand for the office when Paolo reminds him that as doge he will be able to marry Maria, the daughter of Fiesco, whom he loves and by whom he has had a child. For the moment she is thought to be rigorously confined in the palace of her father, who presently appears, lamenting Maria's death and calling down Heaven's vengeance on her betrayer. Outraged, he recognizes Boccanegra, who pleads for pardon, offering his life as satisfaction. The proud Fiesco refuses, however, to stoop to assassination. If Boccanegra will hand over the baby girl born to him and Maria, pardon shall be granted; not otherwise. This, however, Boccanegra is unable to do. The old woman to whose care the baby was entrusted has been murdered, the baby herself stolen, and in spite of arduous searches he has been unable to find her. When Fiesco departs, abruptly telling him that, if this is so, there can never be peace between them, Boccanegra decides to see Maria at all costs. Knocking at the door of the Fieschi Palace, he finds it open, the house deserted. So he enters and presently, when he discovers the corpse of Maria, his cry of anguish is heard. While Fiesco, who has been watching the scene unobserved, grimly remarks that the hour of punishment has struck, the heartbroken Boccanegra comes out of the house, to be greeted by the shouts of the excited populace. He has been elected Doge.

The first act, which takes place twenty-five years later, opens in the gardens of the Grimaldi palace outside Genoa. Amelia (soprano), looking at the sea, waits for the dawn to break and her lover Gabriele (tenor) to arrive. She confides her fears to him. At night she has seen him and old Fiesco (whom she and the world now know as Andrea) wandering about together in a suspicious manner. So many patricians have been proscribed and exiled; will he not abandon politics? A messenger announces the imminent arrival of Boccanegra, who, as Amelia knows full well, has come to ask her to bestow her hand on his favorite and supporter, Paolo. She begs Gabriele to marry her at once. The lovers are delighted at the thought. She goes into the house and, on Fiesco's opportune appearance, Gabriele asks him whether, as a kind of self-constituted guardian of the girl, he will consent to the marriage. Fiesco tells him that he must first know that Amelia is not in reality a Grimaldi at all, but a foundling who was given the family name to save the property of the exiled young Grimaldis from the confiscatory vengeance of the Doge. Gabriele replies that her humble origin is of no consequence; whereupon the two men express their affection for each other. The Doge is announced. He has brought with him the pardon of Amelia's two supposed brothers, and, by his expression of surprise at Amelia's retirement from the world, is obviously leading up to the question of her marriage when she informs him that she would be quite happy in her love were she not pursued by a villain — Boccanegra guesses at once that she means Paolo — who wishes to marry her for her wealth. She then confesses to him that she is not really a Grimaldi but an orphan brought up in Pisa by an old woman who left with her a picture of a lady said to be her mother. Boccanegra, greatly excited at the story, draws a picture from his breast and shows it to her. It is the same. Amelia is not Amelia at all, but Maria, daughter of the Maria Fiesco whom he has mourned for twenty-five years. Father and daughter, though vowing to keep it secret, rejoice in their discovery of each other, and later, when Paolo asks how his suit is progressing, the Doge curtly tells him to dismiss all ideas of the marriage from his mind. Wherefore the disappointed Paolo makes arrangements for the abduction of the lady.

The second scene is laid in the Council Chamber, where State business is being transacted. Among other things, consideration is given to a letter from Petrarch pleading for peace with Venice. Boccanegra urges the Council to remember that Venice and Genoa have one common fatherland, Italy, but, headed by Paolo, they shout that the only fatherland they recognize is Genoa. The noise of riot is heard outside. Gabriele and Fiesco, followed by the mob, are fighting for their lives. The old feud between patricians and plebeians has broken out again; it extends even to the members of the Council. Cries are heard threatening death to the Doge. Unperturbed, he proclaims any fugitive a traitor — thus preventing the disappearance of Paolo, who realizes that his scheme to abduct Amelia is responsible for the disturbance — opens the door of the palace and sends out a herald to tell the crowd that he is waiting for them. There is silence while the herald speaks. Presently, to Boccanegra's scorn, the rage of the mob against him changes to shouts of acclamation. They pour into the Chamber, dragging Gabriele and Fiesco with them, clamoring for their death. Gabriele has killed Lorenzino, who, as he tells the horrified Doge, was trying to abduct Amelia. But Lorenzino, he shouts, was not the real culprit; behind him stood some person of high importance — no less than Boccanegra himself. He thereupon attacks the Doge with a dagger, but Amelia (who has come in with the rest) interposes, first saving Boccanegra, then successfully interceding for the life of Gabriele. At the Doge's request she tells the story of her abduction. She knows, she says, looking straight at Paolo, who was really responsible. The hatred between patrician and plebeian breaks out again in mob and Council, each faction crying out that the unknown criminal belongs to the other. Boccanegra, after again reproaching them with their fratricidal passions, puts Gabriele under arrest. He has guessed, however, Paolo's guilty secret and, in terrible anger, calls on him, by virtue of the high office he holds, to curse the malefactor. Paolo cannot do otherwise; then, overcome with shame and terror, he rushes from the room.

In the second act, laid in the palace, Paolo, overwhelmed by the weight of his own curse, is waiting for Fiesco and Gabriele, whom he has summoned from prison. Furious at what he considers the ingratitude of the man who owes him everything, he prepares a cup of poison, a last act of vengeance before his departure from Genoa for ever. The prisoners enter and Fiesco is offered liberty if he will kill Boccanegra in his sleep. The aristocrat, saying he is not an assassin, indignantly refuses and returns to prison, whither Gabriele prepares to follow him when Paolo intervenes. Does he not know that Amelia is in the palace, the object of the Doge's lecherous caresses? Will he not do the deed rather than submit to lifelong imprisonment? Gabriele, left alone, bursts into imprecations against Boccanegra, first the slayer of his father, now the ravisher of his mistress. His fury changes to despair at the thought of Amelia's faithlessness, and he overwhelms her with reproaches when she presently enters, disregarding her protestations of innocence. On the arrival of the Doge she conceals him on the balcony outside, begging her father, once they are alone, to consent to their marriage. The Doge tells her that Gabriele is his enemy, a conspirator in league with the Guelphs, but finally he yields to her pleading on the condition that Gabriele recants. He then bids her leave him, as he wishes to remain alone till morning. After drinking from the cup into which Paolo has poured poison, he goes to sleep. Gabriele creeps in from the balcony and is about to stab the sleeping Doge when Amelia, who has been watching, again flings herself between the two men. Boccanegra, after a first outburst of anger, sorrowfully tells Gabriele that by stealing the heart of his daughter he has indeed avenged his own father. Gabriele, overwhelmed by the discovery of the relationship, reviles himself as a common assassin unworthy of Amelia's or Boccanegra's forgiveness. Shouts are heard outside. It is the Guelph party preparing to attack the palace. The Doge bids Gabriele go and join his friends. He refuses; he will never raise his hand against Boccanegra. Then the Doge, promising him Amelia as a reward, bids him go as a messenger of peace, and the act ends with Gabriele swearing that he will return to fight by the Doge's side if the conspirators are not disarmed by such clemency.

In the third act, also laid in the palace, Genoa is illuminated in honor of the crushing of the rebellion. Fiesco is led in, also Paolo, who has been captured in the ranks of the rebels. He tells the horrified and disgusted Fiesco that Boccanegra's triumph will be short, as the slow poison he has prepared means certain death. After Paolo has been led off to execution, Fiesco hides in order once more to meet the Doge face to face. Boccanegra enters, orders the illuminations to be extinguished as offensive to the brave dead, and, looking at the sea, recalls regretfully the days of his old exploits. It had been better, he says, had he then died. Fiesco, stepping from his place of concealment, agrees, revealing his true identity to Boccanegra, who had thought him long since dead. Boccanegra tells him that the condition of peace demanded by Fiesco twenty-five years previously can now be fulfilled because Amelia is his granddaughter. Fiesco, dismissing all thoughts of vengeance, bewails the sad fate that kept him so long in ignorance of the truth and tells Boccanegra of the poisoned draught prepared by Paolo. The Doge, who has already felt strange discomfort, realizes that his last hour has come. He tells Amelia of her noble descent, proclaims Gabriele his successor and dies as the last of the illuminations in the city is extinguished.

Piave's libretto was founded on a play by Gutierrez, the author of *El Trovador*, who, with his weakness for the changing of babies in their cradles, may be regarded as the original target at which W. S. Gilbert aimed the arrow of his popular satires. *Il Trovatore* is a notoriously difficult maze to thread, but *Simon Boccanegra* seems more tangled still. Amelia, who is not Amelia at all but Maria, the daughter of yet another Maria; Fiesco, who begins and ends his operatic life as himself, but passes most of his career as Andrea; Gabriele, a sworn enemy of the Doge for a reason that is not made clear till the second act — these people, themselves ignorant of each other's or even of their own identities, leave in a state of blank bewilderment those who have to follow them. In short, the ramifications of the plot are unintelligible without careful study and are not always clear then. To take but one instance, why was Fiesco so interested in his as yet undiscovered granddaughter?

Yet underneath the jumble there is a noble, a well-nigh Shaksperian conception that justifies Verdi's affection for the subject. Piave, who followed Gutierrez's original play only too faithfully, cannot be blamed overmuch for failing to emphasize this better, for when Boïto, incomparably more gifted and skillful, attempted the task later, he can scarcely be said to have made a success of it. True, he judged it impossible from the outset and yielded reluctantly to Verdi's insistence in the matter. What he did, however, he did uncommonly well. Verdi must have the credit for suggesting the

Petrarch letter and the ideas that derive from it in the new finale of the first act; but Boïto's handling of the scene as a whole is masterly. He further brought Paolo's preparation of the poisoned cup, only mentioned in the Piave version, on to the stage, thus making the cause of the Doge's death intelligible; he suppressed a superfluous change of scene in the first act; he changed a phrase here, a few lines of dialogue there, almost invariably for the better. With the exception of the first-act finale, then, Boïto's contribution to *Simon Boccanegra* is more remarkable for quantity than quality. He did little or nothing to lighten the atmosphere of unrelieved gloom, which, reinforcing the muddle of the action, has always militated against the success of the opera. He could not be expected to do away with a defect inherent in the subject-matter.

Verdi's revision of the music, on the other hand, was far more radical. He may be said to have subjected the score to the process known in building-operations as "grouting." Here was no question, as in *Macbeth*, of substituting a few new numbers for old, or otherwise minor alterations. Definitely new ideas were added or substituted, of course, and these will be indicated presently; but throughout the score we find the orchestration changed, sometimes only for a page, the vocal line or key altered, the harmony enriched, the accompaniment-figures reworked, for anything from half a dozen to a couple of hundred bars. It is obviously impossible to indicate here such minute details, as to the nature of which two examples, taken from the prologue, will give some idea. They represent the reception by the crowd of Paolo's suggestion that Boccanegra be elected Doge:

OLD EDITION

NEW EDITION

The greater subtlety of the later version, in expressing by means of a *pianissimo* the shocked surprise of the people at having an ex-pirate as Doge, is typical of the improvements made by the composer.

It is as a rule impossible even to indicate the orchestral changes (among the most important in fact) because it was Verdi's habit when he had changed anything in a score to obliterate or destroy the original. But I was able to gather one characteristic instance where the original scoring was decipherable through the erasure-marks. Nothing could illustrate better than this one bar either the general nature of the alterations or the progress made by the master in orchestration in twenty-four years:

302 Giuseppe Verdi

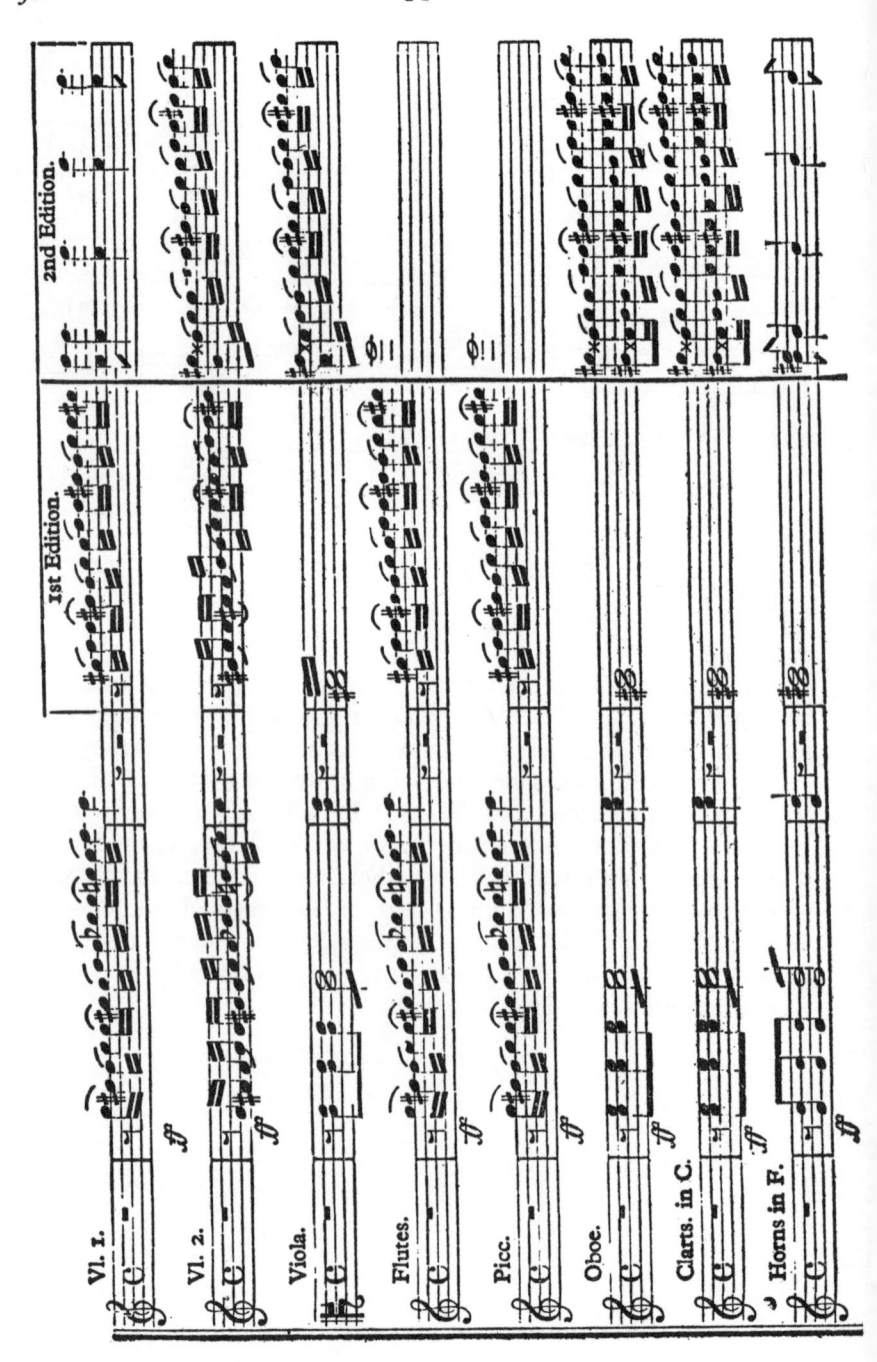

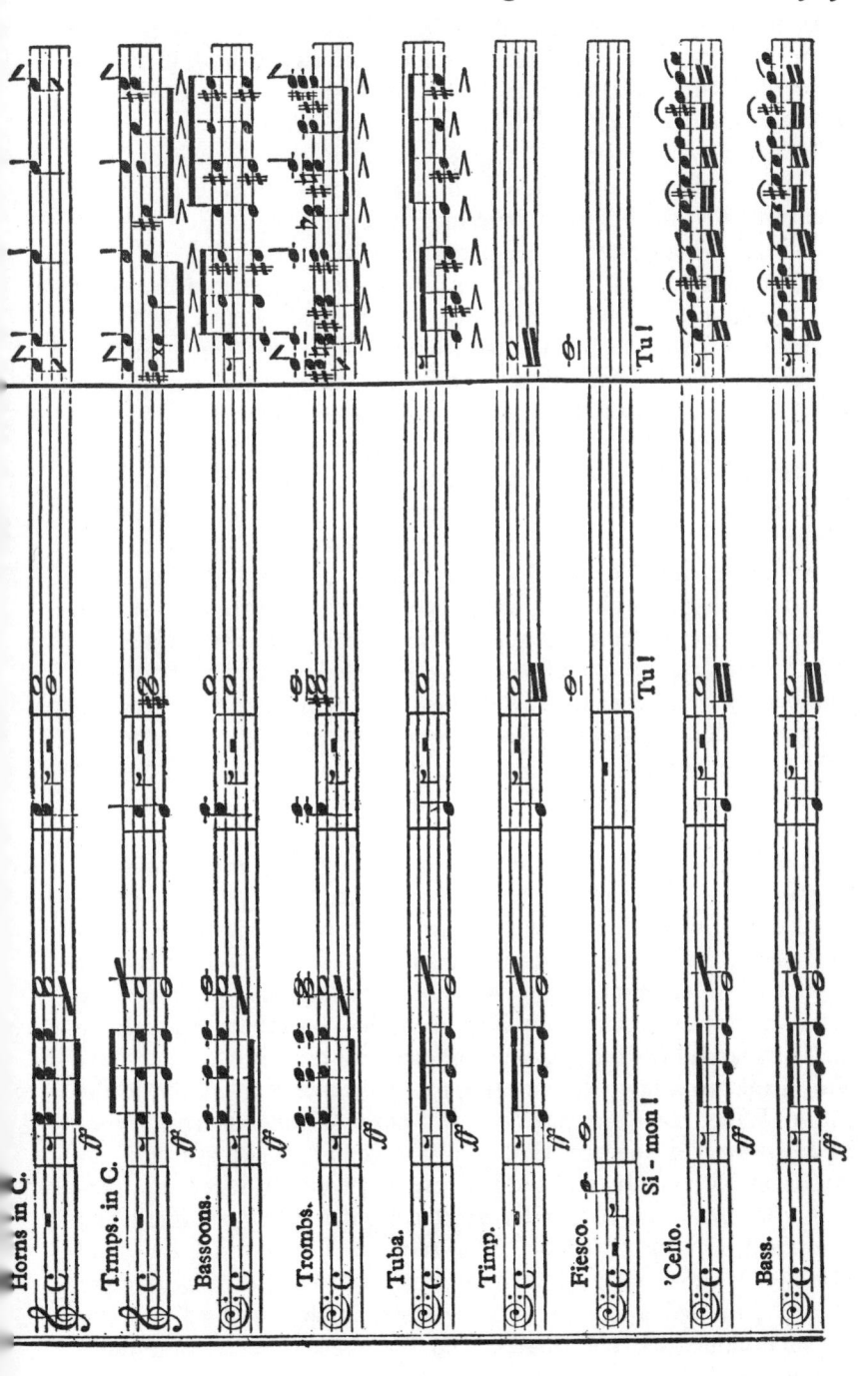

Simon Boccanegra

Incidentally, this curious, old-fashioned method of arranging the score was practiced by Verdi till the day of his death as, it may be parenthetically observed, was the old method of writing for singers in the soprano and tenor clefs.

When one considers that the revision of *Simon Boccanegra* preceded the composition of *Otello* by only a few years, it is scarcely surprising that the opera contains much excellent music. For instance, the placid yet somber-colored prelude, replacing a "full-dress" overture, merges admirably, almost imperceptibly, into the dialogue of the opening scene, wherein the orchestral writing, all new, is admirable, as is the vocal line throughout. Indeed, the whole scene is new except Paolo's "*L'atra magion,*" and this has been put down a tone, perhaps to provide greater contrast with Fiesco's familiar "*Il lacerato spirito*" that follows. Preceded by some admirable recitative, this lament, with the poignant sighs of the women and the whispered "*Miserere*" of the men breaking through, not to mention the lovely orchestral ending, possesses great merit. Those who, like me, have heard it in English concert-halls, badly sung, deprived of its essential chorus, with the orchestral parts mechanically or wrongly played, will find some difficulty in appreciating its great beauty. Nevertheless, the beauty is there, all the more remarkable because the whole number remains unchanged from the first version. The duet between Fiesco and Simon, also unchanged except in certain details, is an excellent example of free declamation, but the final chorus, untouched in the revision, is poor, and clashes, moreover, with the style of the preceding music.

The first act opens with a charming — and new — orchestral introduction, descriptive of daybreak, very prettily scored for woodwind and strings, which leads into Amelia's aria. This is rather undistinguished, the accompaniment remaining perhaps the best feature of it. The subsequent duet between the lovers does not become really interesting until Amelia leads Gabriele to look at the sea, though we may be grateful for the previous displacement of a tiresome cabaletta and, thanks to a few deft changes, of a welcome acceleration in the action. Effective as is Amelia's "*Vieni mirar la cerula marina,*" with its *stornello*-like cadence, Gabriele's succeeding phrase — a new importation — is even better, and the rest of their duet, especially, perhaps, the little canon, a relic of the original version altered and shortened, is very charming. The grave duet between Fiesco and Gabriele is new and a great improvement from the musical point of view, though I am not sure whether, in this instance and this instance alone, the old number did not explain the action more clearly. Here in the original version the scene changed, the duet between Boccanegra and Amelia being substantially the same till the words "*Ah se la speme*" when, beginning with a new cello-figure in the accompaniment, there are considerable alterations; indeed, many passages of entirely new music. The duet as a whole is most effective, particularly in the last half-dozen pages that culminate in the soft climax (new) when Boccanegra dwells on the delight of having found a daughter. No less effective, however, is the exceedingly apt dialogue between Pietro and Paolo that brings the scene to an end, and this remains unaltered from the old version.

The second scene, with the exception of Amelia's narration, which, though much altered, is based on the same idea as in the original version, is new in every particular, as regards both words and music. Originally this was merely a conventional scene of festivity with a ballet of African pirates and lusty choruses working up to a violent old-style demand for vengeance on the unknown villain. There were no politics, no patricians and plebeians, few indications of the clash of human interests and passions that make the present scene of such absorbing interest. In my opinion this long finale — for that is what it is from the technical point of view — is one of the most splendid of Verdi's achievements, worthy to rank among the best pages of *Otello*. One hardly knows which to admire most: the orchestral turmoil of the opening (or, for the matter of that, the orchestral writing throughout); the splendid declamatory music of Boccanegra, culminating in his noble plea to the Genoese to forget their feuds; the impressive silence when the herald is sent out to the mob; the dramatic handling of the chorus; the lovely ensemble worked up from "*Il suo commosso accento*," with Amelia's poignant prayer for peace dominating the whole; the sinister, muttered curse on the evil-doer at the end, where the theme (cello and double-bassoon) irresistibly recalls Fafner in his cave. All these are in their several ways first-rate. From the beginning to the end there is scarcely a weak page and I can only hope that this necessarily inadequate analysis will lead the curious to rediscover for themselves what is undoubtedly a masterpiece of construction and inspiration.

The second act comes, almost inevitably, as an anticlimax, all the more noticeable as it is probably the weakest portion of the entire opera in any case. Such lyrical music as there is — Gabriele's second aria, his duet with Amelia, and so on — hardly reaches even standard merit, and the concluding chorus is definitely bad. On the other hand the trio between the principal characters, liberally refurbished, is effective, especially at the end; and some passages in Boccanegra's soliloquy show real somber grandeur, the *Andante* movement (new), when he is first left alone, being perhaps the most striking. Gabriele's first scena and aria and the duet between Paolo and Fiesco, both to be found in the original version, are excellent; before the *Allegro sostenuto* of the former the curious will find a unison passage prophetic of that which introduces the final fugue in *Falstaff*. But the best music of all is to be found in the couple of new pages written for Paolo at the beginning. Spiritually, as well as in one instance (the curse theme) literally, reminiscent of the previous scene, it is a fine example of declamatory writing, worthy of what has gone before.

The level of the last act is distinctly higher, though in general style it retains the characteristics of the earlier rather than the later version. The opening pages up to Boccanegra's entrance are new and the distant wedding chorus for female voices and the unison passage accompanying the entrance of the captain charged to put out the illuminations, effective enough in themselves, are doubly welcome when one knows the victory and wedding choruses of the original. The use of the 6/8 rhythm in Boccanegra's contemplation of the sea is very felicitous; it suggests, while preserving a tinge of melancholy, just the kind of reminiscence of past happiness familiar to us all. The duet between the Doge and Fiesco, untouched except for a few changes in the scoring, is, however, the best thing in the act. From Fiesco's sinister opening phrase, through the *Allegro assai* in vigorous, typical 3/4 rhythm, to the moving pathos of the last section, it represents three distinct varieties of emotion, all with conspicuous success, and deserves a high place among the many fine duets for men written by the composer. The final quartet for solo voices was largely rewritten, mainly, it appears, with a view to giving greater prominence to the phrase *"non morrai,"* certainly the most striking feature of the music; while the ensuing concerted ensemble, though preserving the old idiom, is considerably changed in details of the part-writing, with regard to the soprano in particular. Both quartet and ensemble are very effective and moving music, gaining rather than losing from the *parlato* and tiny choral fragments that bring the opera to an abrupt close immediately afterwards.

Verdi was definitely dissatisfied with the first version of *Simon Boccanegra*, which he described to Escudier as "monotonous and cold." Many critics have since applied the same adjectives to the opera in its final form. I am unable to agree. Gloomy *Simon Boccanegra* certainly is throughout, and to that extent monotonous. But that an opera characterized by such sincere, forceful dramatic writing should be called cold seems to me preposterous, all the more so in view of the interest attaching to the character of Boccanegra himself. Verdi told Boïto that both Boccanegra and Fiesco offered considerable scope. He was wrong in the latter and right in the former respect. Boccanegra is the only interesting person in the opera, but he fortunately dominates it from beginning to end. Perhaps the strong feeling, latent throughout, for the sea-atmosphere and traditions of Genoa can only be appreciated fully by one who, like myself, happens to share it. Nobody, however, can fail to appreciate the dark turbulence of much of the dramatic action. It is this that the music so faithfully reflects; there are few, too few, moments of lyrical beauty. In short *Simon Boccanegra* is never likely to be a very popular opera; but of all the lesser-known operas by the composer, it is perhaps the one most worthy and most susceptible of resurrection.

Indeed, in 1930, thanks to the indefatigable and enthusiastic Werfel, to whom every lover of Verdi owes a deep debt of gratitude, the opera was successfully revived in Vienna and Berlin. Werfel's German version of the libretto serves by stage indications and several alterations in the text to elucidate some obscure points, notably in connection with Fiesco's masquerading as Andrea; but there is no rearrangement of scenes, as in his version of *La Forza del Destino*. His verbal alterations, however, were all to the good.

AROLDO

(Originally *Stiffelio*)

Libretto by Piave

Production: RIMINI, August 16, 1857

As *Stiffelio*, Production: TRIESTE, November 16, 1850

FOUR ACTS, FIVE SCENES

Aroldo (tenor), a knight, is being entertained on his return from the Crusades by his father-in-law, Egberto (baritone), at the latter's castle "near Kenth." During his absence his wife, Mina (soprano), has been seduced by Godvino (tenor), a knight adventurer who is also staying in the castle, and when the banquet is over, she prays for her involuntary sin to be forgiven. Aroldo enters with Briano (bass), a hermit, whom he introduces to her as having saved his life at Ascalon. The two have been together on a pilgrimage and have sworn not to be separated for the rest of their lives. Left alone with his wife, Aroldo is moved by her sorrowful appearance; but her discomfiture is increased when he discovers that she no longer has his mother's ring, the loss of which, he insists, will be fatal to their happiness. Mina (who has in fact given the ring to Godvino), overwhelmed by this final catastrophe, is writing a letter to her husband in which she tells him the whole truth when she is surprised by Egberto, who urges her not to jeopardize the happiness and perhaps the very life of Aroldo. For Aroldo's sake she must put a brave face on her suffering, he on his dishonor. The scene then changes to another part of the castle, where Godvino comes and leaves a letter for Mina in a locked book of which he has the key. But, unnoticed, Briano has been watching, and presently, when the guests troop in for a reception, he discloses everything to Aroldo. Only, owing to similarity of costume, he indicates Enrico, Mina's cousin, as the culprit instead of Godvino. Aroldo, on the pretext of recounting the adventures of King Richard in Palestine, tells to the assembled company the story of the book and the letter. Then he seizes the actual book lying on the table, asks Mina for the key, and, on her being unable to produce it, himself breaks the lock. The letter falls out; he is about to read it when Egberto picks it up and, despite threats of violence, refuses to give it to him. During the final chorus, through which all the characters give vent to the various emotions aroused in them by the incident, Egberto orders Godvino to meet him later in the graveyard of the castle, and the act ends amid general perturbation.

The second act opens in the graveyard, whither Mina has come to pray at the tomb of her mother. She is surprised by Godvino, who refuses to leave despite her entreaties and disgust at the profanation of such a place by their unholy love, which she now curses to his face. Egberto, still intent on keeping the secret from Aroldo, enters with two dueling swords, offering the choice of one to Godvino, who refuses to engage in unequal combat with an old man. Goaded to fury, however, by Egberto's taunt that he is not only a coward but the son of an unknown father, he finally consents, and the two men fight a duel, interrupted presently by the arrival of Aroldo, who bids them put up their swords. Egberto, outraged at the sight of his guest and friend shaking the hand of his betrayer, blurts out the truth. Aroldo appeals to Mina, who cannot deny it; whereupon, snatching Egberto's sword, he is about to continue the duel on his own account with the unwilling Godvino when the sound of pious chants is heard and Briano appears, reminding him of his Christian duty to forgive all sinners, even his faithless wife and her betrayer.

Egberto, however, thinks otherwise, for in the third act we find him resolved to commit suicide at the intolerable thought of having failed to exact the vengeance due to his honor. He is indeed about to swallow the contents of a poisoned ring when Briano enters with the news that the fugitive Godvino will presently return. With an oath that one of them shall not leave the house alive, Egberto retires, leaving the coast clear for an interview between Godvino and Aroldo, who, mastering himself with an effort, asks Godvino which he values more, freedom or the future of the woman he has wronged. He is then shut up in the next room that he may overhear what passes between Mina and her husband. Aroldo tells Mina that the time has come for them to separate and presents her with a bill of divorce, which, to his surprise, Mina signs without protest. She then, heartbroken, tells him that she has always loved and still loves him, that Godvino took advantage of her. Aroldo vows vengeance on the seducer, but at that moment Egberto enters from the next room with a bloodstained sword, having killed Godvino. Aroldo is led away by Briano to seek religious consolation, while the unfortunate Mina again implores Heaven's pardon for her involuntary sin.

The last act takes place on the banks of Loch Lomond. Harvesters, shepherds, and huntsmen descend from the hills as night falls, their joyful songs arousing envy in the tortured breast of Aroldo, who, together with Briano, has come to live as a hermit in those parts. Presently there arises a great storm and all rush to the water's edge to help to bring to shore a half-wrecked boat in which are Mina and Egberto. They ask for shelter at the hut where Aroldo and Briano live. Aroldo, recognizing Mina with astonishment, would drive her away, but Egberto, explaining that she has voluntarily shared the exile necessitated by the killing of Godvino, begs him to have mercy on his friend's daughter even if he cannot pity his own wife. Then Briano intervenes once more, recalling the instance of the woman taken in adultery, and urges Aroldo to listen to Mina's agonized prayers for forgiveness. Aroldo, who in his heart still loves her, is won over, and the opera ends with a tribute to the "divine law of love."

The absurdity of this libretto is too patent to need emphasis. Why did Mina, not really in love with Godvino, give him Aroldo's ring? What is the point of Briano's confusion between Enrico and Godvino? The coincidences in the action are incredible. None of the characters has any personality and Briano, in particular, is a mere god from the machine. The trouble doubtless originated in the change of libretto. *Stiffelio*, originally extracted by Piave from a forgotten French play by Souvestre and Bourgeois, dealt primarily with the conflict between jealousy and Christian forgiveness in the breast of a mystic evangelical clergyman called Müller living in Germany at the beginning of the nineteenth century. To turn such a person into a medieval Crusader, with a tame hermit on whom are fathered his religious sentiments, was nothing less than an invitation to psychological disaster, and, as a matter of fact, we know from a letter to Piave that the change was made against Verdi's better judgment. That the action should have been diverted to Kent and Loch Lomond is an accident that strikes an Englishman as especially unfortunate. But it has no real importance; the action might as well take place in the moon for any relation it bears to time or place. Which, it may be remarked in passing, is by no means true of the original *Stiffelio*, handicapped though it was by a married clergyman as protagonist, and a tenor at that!

The music, unlike the libretto, gained in the revision. For instance, the whole of the last act is new and it contains the best music in the opera. The storm may not rise to the heights of its successor in *Otello* or its predecessor in *Rigoletto* — which it closely resembles in the use of vocalization and the figure intended to represent lightning — but it is extremely effective. Also its kinship to the storm in Beethoven's "Pastoral" Symphony has been noted. The concluding trio and quartet are better still. The dramatic poignancy of Mina's dialogue with her father; Aroldo's fine, broad phrase, very much in the *Forza del Destino* idiom, culminating in an almost Wagnerian frenzy; the melody of Egberto's plea for his daughter that immediately follows it, similar in style and at least equal in inspiration — all these are worthy of the composer at his best. Indeed, it is a pity that, with such material, the finale of the opera is not a little longer, for the end comes almost as a surprise. In the first act, too, Mina's opening scena, a powerful piece of dramatic writing, and the subsequent prayer, suggesting the flavor if not the notes of a well-known passage in *Aïda*, are new; while the music that accompanies Aroldo's command to Mina to open the book in which lies the concealed letter is more expressive and concise than in *Stiffelio*, rising almost to a forecast of the terrible jealousy of Otello. Moreover, we should be thankful for the replacement of an uncommonly poor coloratura aria for Mina in the second act by a cabaletta that, as regards the minor section in particular, is a model of vigorous writing in this manner. Her preceding scena and aria, on the other hand, date from *Stiffelio* and are first-rate, the orchestral figures in both instances being entirely individual and beautifully worked. The excellent ensemble at the end of the act, which contains some fine dramatic writing, is also to be found in the original version, as, except for a few alterations in detail, is the duet between Aroldo and Mina in the second act, an effective number in which the musical interpretation of Mina's sobs is especially worthy of note. The sextet and chorus that end the first act, however, are treated with notably greater freedom in *Aroldo* than in *Stiffelio*, though the basic ideas remain the same.

I am unable to share the enthusiasm of some of my predecessors for the overture, which, though comparatively elaborate, seems to me uninspired — an adjective that might, not inappropriately, be applied to *Aroldo* as a whole, with the few exceptions indicated above. A great deal of the dramatic writing throughout bears evident traces

Un Ballo in Maschera 311

of a master's hand, but as an entity the opera seems to miss fire altogether. It is not contemptible; it is dull, and the "purple patches" do not suffice to make us forget that distressing quality.

UN BALLO IN MASCHERA

Libretto by Somma

Production: ROME, February 17, 1859

THREE ACTS, SIX SCENES

A crowd of deputies, noblemen, and officers are awaiting, in the anterooms of his residence, the appearance of Riccardo (tenor), an English Governor of Boston in the eighteenth century. Most of them are devoted to him, but a faction headed by Samuel and Tom (basses) await the opportunity to assassinate him for private reasons as well as for the losses that his military ardor has inflicted on the country. Riccardo enters, ready to dispense justice and receive petitions as his duty demands. Oscar (soprano), a page in attendance, hands him a list of invitations for a forthcoming ball. Riccardo, seeing among them the name of Amelia (soprano), the wife of his friend and adviser Renato (baritone), falls into a reverie, for, despite himself, he loves her. When the audience is finished and while Riccardo is still buried in his thoughts of Amelia, Renato enters, expressing surprise to see the Governor so moody. Riccardo says the reason is a secret one, and Renato, to Riccardo's horror, replies that he knows it. But Renato has only discovered the conspiracy against Riccardo's life, which leaves the Governor unmoved. Indeed, he will not even allow the names of the conspirators to be read to him lest he should have to punish them, unheeding Renato's protest that his life is too valuable to the country to be exposed to such danger. The Chief Justice enters to demand Riccardo's signature to a decree of banishment against a certain Negress, a fortune-teller called Ulrica (contralto), who has acquired a considerable following in the neighborhood. Riccardo, disinclined to acquiesce, asks Oscar what he thinks. Oscar frivolously but effectively defends her, and Riccardo determines, as a joke, that he himself, disguised as a fisherman, accompanied by all those in attendance on him (also disguised), shall pay a visit to the sorceress that afternoon at three — to the dismay of Renato, who fears the risk, to the delight of Oscar, who wants his fortune told, to the satisfaction of Tom and Samuel, who see a possible opportunity to carry out their plans.

The second scene shows Ulrica's habitation, with a magic caldron smoking on a tripod and such-like appurtenances of her calling. She is holding a crowd of women and children spellbound with her efforts, eventually successful, to call up the spirit who enables her to tell the future. Riccardo arrives in his fisherman's dress and watches his sailor, Silvano, have his fortune told by Ulrica, who reads in his hand the promise of money and promotion. Riccardo slips into his pocket a nomination to the rank of officer, the discovery of which fills Silvano with surprised delight and the crowd with enthusiastic wonder at the rapid fulfillment of the prophecy. Amelia's servant arrives by the secret entrance to arrange a private audience for her mistress; whereupon Ulrica, on the pretense of a confidential consultation with Satan, gets rid of the crowd, Riccardo, however, remaining behind in hiding to discover the purport of Amelia's visit. Amelia has come for a potion to eradicate the love that, as Riccardo learns with delight, she feels for him. Ulrica knows how such a potion should be brewed, but an essential condition is that the herbs of which it is made should be gathered by the user at night in the place of execution outside the city. Amelia nerves herself to carry out the plan, while Ulrica encourages her to be brave and Riccardo, from his hiding-place, gives vent to his sympathy and joy, determined, moreover, that she shall not go alone to such a gruesome spot. Immediately Amelia has gone, Oscar, Samuel, Tom, and the other participants in the first scene arrive by the main entrance, while Riccardo, in his capacity as a fisherman, sings a gay ditty expressing courageous defiance of death and fate. Ulrica rebukes his presumption and he gives his hand for her to read the future. She rightly classes him as a person of importance who has seen much fighting, but suddenly refuses to say anything further. Pressed, however, she foretells his imminent death at the hand of a friend. Riccardo laughs at, while the others comment on, her prophecy according to their several wishes and characters. Then Riccardo asks who shall kill him; to which she replies: the man with whom he first shakes hands. Riccardo, taking up the challenge at once, vainly tries to persuade those present to oblige him. When, however, Renato enters, ignorant of what has taken place, Riccardo shakes his hand, to the relief of Samuel and Tom, who feared the discovery of their plot. Riccardo then proclaims the folly of the whole affair. Renato is his best friend; Ulrica's powers of divination had not even revealed to her his identity or the fact that her banishment was being discussed that very morning. Throwing her a purse of gold, he bids her rest in peace, but Ulrica earnestly warns him once more against treachery, and the act ends with a chorus led by Silvano in his praise, though Renato and Ulrica are full of forebodings and the conspirators resent such a manifestation of popularity.

In the second act Amelia is seen coming to the place of execution in a lonely field outside Boston in order to gather the herb indicated by Ulrica. It is midnight and, terrified by the gruesome associations of the place, she thinks she sees a head rise from the ground and fix her with an angry stare. Falling on her knees, she prays to God for help, when Riccardo appears. Full of pity for her distress, he cannot refrain from declaring his love, but she reminds him that she is the wife of his most trusted friend, begs him to have pity and leave her. Riccardo, carried away by passion, entreats her at least to say whether she loves him or not and she confesses that she does, begging him to help save her from herself. Half in ecstasy, half in despair, the lovers are interrupted by the arrival of Renato, who has come to warn Riccardo that the conspirators, hearing of his assignation, have surrounded the place with the intent to kill him. Amelia, at her husband's approach, has veiled herself, and Riccardo, though loath to leave her, finally yields to her whispered entreaties and Renato's reiterated adjurations to escape by disguising himself in his cloak. Before he goes, however, he extorts a promise from Renato to escort the unknown lady back to the city without addressing a word to her or looking on her face. Renato gives his word and, after Riccardo's departure, the two move off together. They fall in, however, with the conspirators, who, in their disappointment at finding Renato instead of the Governor, insist on discovering at any rate the identity of the veiled lady. Renato, drawing his sword, threatens to kill any who touches her; whereupon Amelia, to avoid bloodshed, herself lifts the veil, to the great amusement of the conspirators, who enjoy the joke of this midnight rendezvous of husband and wife; to the fury of Renato, who thinks himself betrayed by the man for whom he was prepared to lay down his life. In accordance with his oath he again prepares to conduct Amelia back to the city, but, before he goes, asks Tom and Samuel to come and see him in the morning; which, though mystified, they consent to do. So, with the laughter of the conspirators growing more and more faint in the distance, the act ends.

In the first scene of the third act, laid in the study of Renato's house, Renato tells Amelia that such infidelity can only be punished with death. Admitting that appearances are against her, even that she did in fact love Riccardo, Amelia protests her actual innocence; but Renato is adamant, his sole concession to her being a final interview with their son. When she has gone, however, the portrait of the Governor on the wall reminds him who is the real culprit; Riccardo, not the frail Amelia, should be punished for the destruction of his happiness, the insult to his honor. When Samuel and Tom arrive to keep their appointment, Renato tells them that he knows every detail of their conspiracy, but bids them have no fear as he now wishes to join it, overcoming their incredulity at such a sudden change by the offer of his son as a hostage. Since each of the three wishes to have the honor of killing Riccardo, they decide to settle the matter by drawing lots. The opportune entrance of Amelia, announcing the arrival of Oscar with the invitation to the masked ball at the Governor's house, enables Renato, with terrible sarcasm, to suggest that her innocent hand shall be the one to extract one of the three pieces of paper that have been placed in a vase. The trembling Amelia obeys and the lot falls upon Renato, to his savage joy. Oscar is then admitted, with his customary lightheartedness forecasting the splendor of the ball, which the conspirators hail as a heaven-sent opportunity for the execution of their plot; while Amelia, who has guessed the object of the drawing of lots, despairingly wonders how Riccardo can be put on his guard.

At the opening of the second scene Riccardo is in this room. Now convinced that honor and duty demand his separation from Amelia, he is in the act of signing an order for Renato to return immediately to England, though the prospect of never seeing Amelia again, except perhaps at the dance, fills him with despair. The scene changes to the ballroom, where Oscar hands him a note from an unknown woman warning him that there will be an attempt on his life, but, unwilling to be thought a coward, he decides to pay no attention. In the throng of masked dancers the conspirators, distinguishable by their blue dominoes with scarlet sashes, are unable to discover the identity of the Governor or even to be certain that he is present. Oscar, approaching Renato, mischievously announces that he has penetrated his disguise; whereupon Renato seizes the occasion to ask where Riccardo is and what he is wearing. At first Oscar refuses to tell, but on Renato's saying that important business is in question, finally describes Riccardo's disguise. Amelia approaches Riccardo and, at first unrecognized, urges him to leave the ball at once. Soon, however, she is identified by Riccardo, who, amid her fervent entreaties to fly while there is yet time, bids her farewell forever. At that moment Renato, who has overheard their final words of parting, stabs him to the heart. Everything is in confusion; Renato is seized by soldiers and guests; tearing off his mask, they furiously demand his death as a traitor. Riccardo, however, bidding them let him go, calls Renato to his side, affirms on his dying oath that Amelia is innocent, and, as further proof of the fact, shows the order for the immediate return of both husband and wife to England. He then pardons all who may have been concerned in the conspiracy, bids a sad farewell to America, and dies, amid the remorseful lamentations of Renato and the shocked horror of the general assembly.

Un Ballo in Maschera

As the story appears in the opera it strikes us as exceedingly silly. This incredible English colonial Governor and his "Creole" adviser, the Negress, Ulrica, and, above all, those ludicrous personages Samuel and Tom, all seem like parodies rather than human beings. There is, too, something deliciously incongruous in the chaste and austere Boston being selected as the locale of an action possible only at the dissipated court of an absolute monarch in eighteenth-century Europe. For all this, however, as we have already seen, Somma cannot be held responsible. The vagaries of two censorships and the weariness of Verdi provide the explanation if not the excuse. As a matter of fact Somma closely followed the original libretto written for Auber by Scribe under the title of *Gustave III, ou Le Bal masqué*, altering little except the names. True, the artistic side of Gustavus of Sweden (Riccardo), emphasized in the first act of Scribe's libretto, is completely omitted, as is the attempt on the King's life actually about to be made by Counts Horn and Warting (Tom and Samuel) after the scene with the fortune-teller Arvedson (Ulrica), and foiled by the opportune entrance of the enthusiastic populace. The end too is changed. According to Scribe only the Countess Ankarstroem (Amelia) knows that she is to accompany her husband on his nomination to the government of Finland (Renato's dispatch to England in the opera is a singularly unhappy equivalent. What would a Creole have done there?), and Gustavus does not live long enough after his assassination to ensure the definite pardon of his assassin, though it is in fact indicated.

Still, these are comparatively unimportant details, and Somma (or Verdi) may at the least be credited with the invention of the very effective end of the gibbet scene, the planning of *"Eri tu"* and the abolition of an unnecessary formal ballet in the final act. Moreover, he contrived to preserve successfully the characteristics of the page, Oscar, the most attractive and successful figure in the opera, and the half-fraudulent, half-genuine attributes of the fortune-teller. The wooden nature of the other characters is equally noticeable in the original though their historical background makes them less absurd. Somma's most obvious weakness lay not in his construction but in his versification; many of the lines of *Un Ballo in Maschera* are sheer doggerel and were always so regarded, even in the earliest days. One is not altogether surprised that the librettist preferred for some time to remain anonymous.

The manner in which Verdi contrived to infuse life into the personages of this drama is remarkable. Ulrica may remain in essence a conventional operatic soothsayer, with music deriving in part from Azucena, in part from the witches in *Macbeth*, but she is a striking and effective figure. Amelia may lack salient personal characteristics, but in the lyricism of her music she becomes a genuine embodiment of passion and tenderness. Riccardo is even more successful. The subtle difference between his music and that of the Duke in *Rigoletto* should be noted. Though of the same kin, Riccardo is not a mere libertine, and his music tells us so. In detail, moreover, the differentiation between his moods of seriousness and high spirits, as exemplified, for instance, in the sentimental "*La rivedrà nell' estasì*" on the one hand and the mischievous "*Ogni cura si doni al diletto*" on the other, is admirable. Even greater subtlety is observable, perhaps, in the difference between the songs, "*Di' tu se fedele*," which he sings in his fisherman's disguise, and "*E scherzo od è follia*," in which he is again himself; the flavor of the one is essentially plebeian, the skeptical dash of the other aristocratic. Again, Renato, quite characterless in the libretto, comes to musical life in the most surprising manner. Even before the hackneyed but splendid "*Eri tu*" he never becomes a bore — the fate that awaits the majority of loyal operatic friends.

The modern listener, however, will probably agree with Verdi himself in giving his especial affection to Oscar, a figure who might have stepped out of a drawing-room not only of the eighteenth but of the twentieth century. The gay frivolity of the page — totally unlike that of his master, be it observed — is perfectly reproduced in the sparkle and the lightheartedness of his music. Moreover, these qualities appeared for the first time in an opera by Verdi, since the ill-fated *Un Giorno di Regno* at any rate. When Oscar makes his entrance and sings:

Un Ballo in Maschera 317

we are conscious of a new and unfamiliar flavor, confirmed later by numbers such as "*Di che fulgor*" in the first, and "*Saper vorreste*" in the last, scene of the third act. It is this that in the main makes *Ballo* such an important opera, for here we catch a first glimpse of the plant which, budding again in the music of Fra Melitone in *La Forza del Destino*, was to blossom fully in *Falstaff*. Further, to Oscar's musical lightness of heart must be added the humorous sarcasm of the conspirators as they depart after the discovery of Renato's apparent assignation with his own wife:

> E che bac-ca-no sul ca-so strano, e che commenti per la cit-tà
>
> E che bac-ca-no sul ca-so strano, e che commenti per la cit-tà

As an innovation in Verdi's style this is as important as the music of Oscar. The conspirators remain our old friends of *Ernani,* but they have learned how to laugh.

Another point of technical interest in the opera is the greater elaboration of the orchestral writing. This is evident at once in the prelude, which in fact consists of the two motto themes of the opera: the first a figure, usually associated with the bassoons, representative of the conspiracy, the second expressive of Riccardo's love for Amelia. The treatment of both is more full, more "conscientious," than hitherto, the former indeed becoming a regular *fugato*, which provides the first instance of Verdi's use of the fugal form to express a definite idea — in this case the idea of the tortuous working of the plans of the conspirators. The accompaniment to Ulrica's incantation is equally remarkable; not only is there a new richness of texture, but the instrumental color is more adventurous. In the very first bars of the introduction, with the low notes of the C clarinet joined to the strings, we are conscious of the magic, sinister atmosphere. The second act, too, is admirably orchestrated throughout, the introduction and the felicitous use in Amelia's first aria of the cor anglais, which takes from her the melody of the second verse, being especially good. Again, Oscar's music is interpreted as happily in the orchestra as in the vocal line; there is in it a suggestion of irresponsible frivolity definitely new in Verdi's scoring. The skillful use of the piccolo in his first number may be quoted as a typical example. Finally, a word must be said of the wonderful characterization of the ensemble-writing at the end of the first act and of the quintet that closes the opening scene of the third. The quality itself, of course, was not new, for Verdi always excelled in this respect. But as examples of it these two ensembles would be difficult to surpass, for, despite great elaboration, the individuality of all the characters concerned is maintained throughout. The first, built round the staccato laugh of "*E scherzo*," is remarkable enough, but the second is

Un Ballo in Maschera

perhaps even more remarkable, for here Verdi was confronted with the task of differentiating Oscar and Amelia, both sopranos, a problem that he solved with complete success.

This comparatively detailed consideration of the most striking merits of *Ballo* as a whole leaves little to be said about the individual scenes, but one or two points are worth noting. For instance, the ingenious may like to find in the appointment for three o'clock at Ulrica's cave, made by Riccardo in the first scene, a definite adumbration of Sir John Falstaff's rendezvous. The figure that accompanies Amelia's entrance in the second act is sister rather than cousin to the figure associated with Leonora's anguish in *La Forza del Destino*, as, incidentally, the "*O qual soave brivido*" movement at the end of her duet with Riccardo is akin to Leonora's "*Tua grazia, o Dio*" in the same opera. Ulrica's invocation is conventional descriptive music, if you will, but, for reasons already given, highly effective. From the musical aspect perhaps the most interesting passage is the crescendo worked up on a phrase of decidedly Wagnerian flavor to the climax when she proclaims the success of her magic. The passage, too, where she examines Riccardo's hand, prophetic of a well-known motif in Humperdinck's *The Miracle*, is truly expressive of foreboding. No praise can be too high for either of Riccardo's tunes; "*E scherzo od è follia*," in particular, is a masterpiece of its kind, as anyone who ever heard it sung by an artist like Bonci can scarcely fail to realize, the modulation to D flat before the coda being singularly happy. The weak feature of this scene is the final apostrophe to Riccardo as the "Son of England"; it has an effective *stretto* at the end and the middle section is well marked, but as a tune it possesses no distinction, suggesting, moreover, anything in the world rather than Anglo-Saxon enthusiasm.

Most of the success of the second act, apart from the final scene already commented upon, can be traced to the sheer inspiration of the melodies. For instance, Amelia's first aria and both the main subjects in the ensuing duet between her and Riccardo are so lovely that they would make their effect however handled. In fact, all are treated with great skill. Thus, in the duet, the beautiful "*Non sai tu*" is well set off by the alternation of major and minor in the preceding section, while the hesitation of the *Più Lento* passage that follows, wherein Amelia fearfully admits her love, is an admirable preparation for the final broad tune in C major, "*Oh qual soave brivido*," in which the surrender to love is complete on both sides. As an entity this duet seems to me to be the high-water mark of Verdi's expression of passionate love up to this time.

The orchestral introduction to the act, in which Verdi, mindful perhaps of the success of a similar proceeding in the last act of *La*

Traviata, wished to convey the atmosphere by raising the curtain immediately, is technically admirable, the use of the tune associated with Amelia's fears in the trio of the first act being very apt. Excellent, too, is the suggestion of breathlessness conveyed by the figure in the accompaniment when Renato arrives on the scene. Unfortunately the final tune of the trio, effective enough in itself, is spoilt for Anglo-Saxon ears by the affinity of the opening bars with a Gilbert and Sullivan patter-song.

For most people, perhaps, the interest of the third act lies exclusively in Renato's "*Eri tu*" and Oscar's "*Saper vorreste*." Doubtless both must be considered the outstanding numbers, not only because they are of superior merit as music but because they express so admirably the dramatic situation. "*Eri tu*," needless to say, should in reality never be divorced from its context; it loses half its force, half its poignancy. The effect of the simplicity of the concluding passage, "*Oh dolcezze perdute*," for instance, is scarcely realizable by anyone who has not heard it in the opera. Prepared not only by the vindictiveness of the first part of the aria but by the whole preceding scene of inflexible rage and the subtlety of modulation that indicates the turning of Renato's fury against Riccardo, it stands out as the very embodiment of the anguish of a broken heart.

Still, there is more than these; first and foremost, of course, the quintet, already noted, at the end of the first scene. Then the opening duet, especially the passage in rising semitones, is extremely effective, while Amelia's pathetic air of supplication, with its tragic little coda, is something more. As an essay in what may be called refined Meyerbeer, the scene of the drawing of lots as to who shall kill Riccardo is very successful, though the tune in A flat, representing the climax of the conspiracy, may strike the purist as incongruous.

The dance music of the final scene has been highly praised, but I find myself unable to concur. Wholly admirable, however, is the manner in which the duet between Amelia and Riccardo is carried on over a mazurka rhythm; his final phrase, stopping in the middle of a word, is also effective. But there can be little doubt that the last scene as a whole is the weakest in the opera. Equally, there can be no doubt that the opera as a whole, not only as regards technical skill but as regards range of expression, registers a marked advance on anything accomplished by Verdi up to that time. It will always remain particularly dear to the discriminating student of the composer's development.

LA FORZA DEL DESTINO

Libretto by Piave
Production: ST. PÉTERSBURG, November 10, 1862
Revised Version: MILAN, February 20, 1869
FOUR ACTS, EIGHT SCENES

In his palace in Seville the Marquis of Calatrava (bass) is bidding good-night to his daughter, Leonora (soprano), who, unknown to him, has prepared that very night to elope with her forbidden lover, Don Alvaro (tenor). When the Marquis has gone, her maid, Curra, begins to assemble her things, but, overcome with remorse at deceiving the father she loves so dearly and with grief at leaving her home and country, Leonora hesitates, to the disgust of Curra, who bids her remember the risks to which Don Alvaro is exposing himself for her sake. Leonora sings a song expressive of her grief and, looking at the clock, announces with something like relief that the hour is too late for Don Alvaro now to come. At that very moment the sound of horses' hoofs is heard and Don Alvaro enters by the balcony. Many unexpected obstacles have detained him, but now at last, strong in his pure love, he is here to take her away. Horses are in readiness; a priest waits to marry them; at the rising of the sun they will be man and wife. Leonora, however, still hesitates. Will he not wait till tomorrow? Though her heart is full of love for him, she longs to see her father once more. Don Alvaro, not unnaturally misinterpreting her vacillation, bids her take back her promise if she does not love him as he loves her. Leonora, her last scruples overcome, protests passionately that she will follow him to the end of the world, while he assures her that no power on earth can henceforward separate them.

But the delay has proved fatal. The noise of the opening and shutting of doors is heard; Curra announces that people are coming up the stairs. Leonora bids Don Alvaro hide, but this he refuses to do, drawing out his pistol, which, in answer to Leonora's horrified protest, he explains is for use against himself, not her father. The Marquis, attended by two servants, rushes in with drawn sword, refusing, despite Don Alvaro's protestations of Leonora's innocence and his own sole responsibility, to listen to a word of excuse. Leonora is no longer his daughter; Don Alvaro's conduct betrays only too clearly the lowliness of his origin. Don Alvaro urges the Marquis to kill him as he stands, but the Marquis, exclaiming that such as he should perish at the hands of the executioner, not of a gentleman of rank, bids the servants arrest him. Don Alvaro, raising his pistol, refuses to allow them to approach; he will only surrender to the Marquis, offering his life as a proof of Leonora's innocence. He then throws away the pistol, which, as it strikes the ground, goes off and mortally wounds the Marquis. With a curse on his daughter, the old man collapses in the arms of his servants, and the curtain falls on Don Alvaro carrying the distraught Leonora to the balcony.

The first scene of the second act is laid in the kitchen of an inn in the village of Hornachuelos, where, waiting for the evening meal, mulateers and villagers dance. There are also present the Mayor and a student, who, though calling himself Pereda, is none other than Don Carlo (baritone), the son of the dead Marquis, intent, as ever, on executing vengeance on his father's murderer. The hostess serves dinner and all take their places at the table. At that moment Leonora, who, disguised as a young man, is also lodging at the inn, opens the door. Recognizing her brother, she immediately withdraws, and the meal goes merrily on with appropriate comments and compliments. A young gypsy girl, Preziosilla (mezzo-soprano), enters, announcing that war has broken out and that all should hasten to Italy to fight the Germans. She sings a song in praise of war and reads Pereda's palm, from which, as she tells him confidentially, she learns that he is not the student he pretends to be. A band of pilgrims, bound for the jubilee celebrations at the neighboring Franciscan monastery, pass by outside, and all leave the table to join in their prayers; Leonora, too, makes a furtive appearance, when she prays to be delivered from the vengeance of her brother. After the pilgrims have gone their way, Pereda begins to ply the mulateer Trabuco with questions about the young stranger whom he brought to the inn. Is it a man or a woman? Did it ride astride or side-saddle? Trabuco retorts that the affairs of his clients concern no one but themselves and that, as for him, he is tired and prefers to sleep among his mules, who, though they may be ignorant of Latin and have no university degree, do not at any rate pester him with questions. Pereda then says it would be a good joke, as the stranger is beardless, to endow him with whiskers and mustache by means of blacking — a proposal welcomed by some of the company, but discountenanced by the Mayor, who says that his duty is to protect strangers. Since the student is so curious, it might be as well if he told them something about himself. Pereda, nothing loth, says that he is a Bachelor of Arts of Salamanca University, but that he gave up his studies to follow to Seville his friend Vargas, who had sworn vengeance on a man, the seducer of his sister and the murderer of his father. Together they followed his tracks to Cadiz, where they learned that the sister had perished in the fight between the followers of the father

La Forza del Destino

and of the murderer, who, incidentally, had fled to South America, whither Vargas then followed him. At the end of the story the Mayor says that it is time to go to bed, and after a final dance all retire.

In the second scene Leonora, still in man's clothes, is discovered outside the Church of the Madonna degli Angeli, forming part of the Franciscan monastery. From the story told by her brother in the inn she now knows that Don Alvaro, who she thought had been killed on the fatal night of their elopement, is still alive. In utter anguish she prays to the Virgin that she may root out all memory of him from her heart and expiate her sins in this holy place. To the sound of the friars singing early matins she entreats God to have pity on her. She rings the convent bell, but through his grating the porter, Brother Melitone (baritone), tells the stranger to come back at five, when the church will be open for the jubilee. She begs to see the Father Superior at once, saying that she has been sent by Father Cleto. Impressed by the name of such a holy man, Melitone bids the stranger enter and wait. This, however, Leonora refuses to do, saying that she prefers to remain outside. So Melitone, half suspecting a case of excommunication, replies that he will announce her, and if he does not return, she must go away. Presently, accompanied by Melitone, the Father Superior appears, asking who it is that wishes to speak with him. Leonora says that the matter is secret; whereupon, to the curious Melitone's muttered disgust, the Father Superior dismisses him. She then reveals her identity as a woman and begs help to save her soul. At her mention of a message sent by Father Cleto, the Father Superior immediately recognizes her as Leonora di Vargas and bids her lay her sins and troubles at the foot of the cross. Already more tranquil in her mind, she requests to be allowed to pass the rest of her days in the cave where, as she had learned from Father Cleto, another penitent had once before expiated her sins. He urges her not to take such a grave step without deep reflection, suggesting a convent as an alternative. Leonora, however, scouts the idea. If he turns her away, she will wander as an outcast in the hills till the very beasts take pity on her. The Father Superior, now convinced of her resolve, accedes to her desire. Clad as a monk, she shall live the life of a hermit in the cave; no one shall know her name or station; he himself will bring her food. Then, summoning Melitone, he bids him call the monks together in the church. When they are assembled, the Father Superior announces that the cave of the hermit will again be occupied, that no one is to approach it or endeavor to discover the identity of the occupant. He then asks them to join in a curse on any who may transgress his orders. This they do, and Leonora, after a general prayer to the Virgin for protection, departs alone to the hermit's cave. In the case of extreme peril, or at the hour of death, there is a bell in it that she may strike; otherwise she will never again set eyes on a human being.

The second act opens in a wood near Velletri, in Italy, where the Spanish army has come to fight the Germans. Off the stage there are sounds of gambling; on the stage is Don Alvaro, dressed as a captain of grenadiers. He bewails his sad fate: Leonora and his sole chance of happiness taken from him in a single night, the miserable failure of his father to establish an independent kingdom in South America, the hardships of his youth, spent first in prison, then in the wilderness. Nameless and an exile, he wishes he might die, calling upon Leonora to look down from heaven and take pity on him. A cry for help and the clashing of swords are heard. He runs to see what is the matter, presently returning with Don Carlo, who tells him that the gambling had led to a brawl and a pack of ruffians had set on him. He would gladly know to whom he owes his life; he is Don Felice di Bornos, adjutant to the general. Don Alvaro answers that he is Don Frederico Herreros, a name Don Carlo recognizes as that of the bravest soldier in the army. The two men then swear friendship and, as a summons to arms is heard, go off together into the battle.

The scene then changes to a room near Velletri, whence a military surgeon and his attendants watch the progress of the battle. Finally, after a shout from the allied Spaniards and Italians proclaiming victory, the grievously wounded Don Alvaro is brought in on a stretcher. Don Carlo tells him that as a reward for his valor he will receive the Order of Calatrava, but the mention of the name elicits from the wounded man, though only half-conscious, a protest that startles Don Carlo. Don Alvaro then asks to be left alone with his friend, indicates a key in his bosom, which unlocks a box containing a packet that Don Carlo must swear to burn unopened if he dies. This Don Carlo promises to do; but when the wounded man has been carried away, he is tempted to open the package. The horror shown by Don Alvaro at the name of Calatrava suggests his possible identification with "the cursed Indian" of whom he is in search. The memory of his oath, however, restrains him and he examines the box for other proof, which is soon forthcoming in the shape of a portrait of Leonora. At that moment the surgeon enters with the news that Don Alvaro's recovery seems assured — to the delight of Don Carlo, who exults in the prospect of being able to execute vengeance on him whom he now identifies with certainty as his father's murderer.

The scene changes to a military camp near Velletri just before dawn. A patrol passes and, as day begins to break, Don Alvaro enters, immersed in gloomy thoughts. Don Carlo joins him and asks whether he is completely cured. Don Alvaro replies that, thanks to his tender care, he is now as well as ever. When Don Carlo goes on to ask whether he is well enough to fight a duel he remains completely mystified until Don Carlo, with a suggestion that Don Alvaro, the Indian, might have sent him a message, challenges him to fight. Don Alvaro, loth to fight a man who was his friend, refuses, protesting the innocence of his intentions with regard to both the Marquis and Leonora; after recovery from the wounds received on the fatal night, he sought her for a year, only to learn that she was dead. Don Carlo brands him as a liar; Leonora is not dead, only a fugitive. In a transport of delight at the news, Don Alvaro begs Don Carlo to join him in search of her. His race and name are noble; there is no real obstacle to their marriage. Don Carlo, however, is inexorable. First he will kill Don Alvaro; then, having found her, Leonora. Maddened by the thought of the danger to his beloved, Don Alvaro swears that her brother shall die first, and the two men engage in a duel, interrupted by the entrance of the patrol, who, despite his furious protests, arrest Don Carlo, while Don Alvaro, throwing away his sword, exclaims that nothing but the peace and forgetfulness of a monastic life can now serve him.

At sunrise the camp becomes animated. Soldiers polish their accouterments; vivandières sell food and wine. A peddler offers his wares; Preziosilla offers to tell fortunes. Presently some recruits arrive, rather depressed. To raise their spirits the vivandières make them join in a tarantella, interrupted by the arrival of Melitone, who treats the assembly to a kind of punning sermon on their vices, which so exasperates them that they turn on him. Preziosilla, however, bids them not make war on a monk and concludes the act with a brilliant "Rataplan" song in which all join.

The last act shows the courtyard inside the Franciscan monastery, where Melitone is distributing soup to a crowd of beggars. They quarrel among themselves and with him, regretting the absence of Father Raffaele, whom they cite as a model of generosity and goodness. Finally Melitone, exasperated, kicks over the caldron of soup and turns them out. The Father Superior reproaches him with his lack of patience, his dislike of being compared unfavorably with Father Raffaele. Melitone professes friendly feelings for Raffaele, but owns to an inability to understand him; he looks so strange, behaves so often in an odd manner. Is he perhaps some kind of devil who, as in days of old, has taken the habit of a monk? The Father Superior reproves him for his fancies; it is the sorrows of the world and his many fastings and penances that have made Raffaele appear strange. Then, as the doorbell rings, he departs, leaving Melitone, however, only half convinced. The visitor, who is none other than Don Carlo, asks for Father Raffaele. Melitone says there are two of that name, but Don Carlo, satisfied from the description of one that Raffaele is in reality Don Alvaro, asks to be announced merely as "a gentleman" and, while waiting for the monk to come, muses on the vengeance soon to be exacted from his enemy. Immediately on the appearance of the astonished Don Alvaro he demands a duel, for which he has thoughtfully provided two swords. Don Alvaro, despite taunts of cowardice, refuses. Affirming once again his own and Leonora's innocence, he begs Don Carlo to have pity on him and not to seek to provoke him to an action so inconsistent with his present life and habit. If the austerity of his penance and the extent of his sufferings do not suffice to carry conviction, he will degrade himself to kneel for mercy. Don Carlo retorts that the ignominy of the action attests the baseness of his birth; he must be a mulatto. Don Alvaro, stung by the insult, impulsively seizes one of the swords, but, with a final effort at self-control, throws it on the ground. Don Carlo then strikes him in the face; whereupon, mad with rage, Don Alvaro snatches it again and the two men rush off to fight to the death.

The scene changes to the exterior of Leonora's cave whence she emerges to pray God for peace and forgetfulness. Hearing the clash of swords, she hurriedly retires again, and presently a cry for a confessor is heard from Don Carlo. Don Alvaro, with sword still drawn, enters in an agony of remorse; once again he has killed a Vargas. He beats on the door of the supposed hermit with a fervent entreaty that he will come and shrive a dying man. Leonora's voice is heard protesting that such a thing is impossible. Don Alvaro beats on the door with redoubled insistence; at which she rings the bell for assistance and comes out to invoke the wrath of Heaven on those who have ventured to disturb the sanctity of her retreat. Don Alvaro is unable to believe his eyes when he sees that the hermit is not only a woman but Leonora; she, recognizing Don Alvaro, thinks he must be a ghost. When he rapidly explains what has happened, she rushes off to comfort her dying brother as best she may. A shriek is heard and she reappears, wounded, her faltering steps sustained by the Father Superior, whom the sound of the bell has summoned to the spot. Even at the moment of death Don Carlo could not forgive and, recognizing his sister, stabbed her with his dagger. Don Alvaro curses the blind vengeance of Fate, but is reproved by the Father Superior, while Leonora with her last breath promises him God's forgiveness. Don Alvaro, convinced at last of such a possibility, throws himself at her feet. "She is dead," he cries. "She has gone to God," replies the Father Superior.

The main features of Rivas's remarkable play *Don Alvaro* have already been discussed. It possesses a certain somber fascination, and the vivid portraiture of the scenes depicting popular life in Spain can still be appreciated. Unfortunately the psychology of the characters in the main drama is unintelligible to us without an effort of constructive imagination. To us Don Alvaro seems merely unfortunate, in that all through the play he does everything possible to avoid shedding the blood of the father and brother of Leonora. But in an age when the principle of the blood-feud was accepted, facts, not intentions, were what mattered, and the facts remained undeniable. It is possible that Rivas, who started life with radical opinions, intended in his play to do something more than tell what to his audience, at any rate, seemed a most thrilling and effective story, wishing perhaps to suggest that there were things in the world even more important than the honor of noble Spanish families. Christian charity, for instance, and forgiveness of sins. Such speculation, however, is profitless. Not only *La Forza del Destino* but *Don Alvaro* must always remain for us typical examples of "blood-and-thunder" romantic drama, though that is no reason for refusing to take them seriously. But whatever excuses we may find, there remain many weak points as regards both action and characterization. Coincidences of time and place throughout the play are too frequent; Leonora is not so much a person as an embodiment first of vacillation, then of demented misery. On the other hand there is genuine movement and atmosphere in most of the scenes, while the characterization of Brother Melitone and some of the minor personages is admirable. The two brothers (embodied as one in the opera) may seem mechanical, but Don Alvaro's is a truly tragic figure.

Piave was confronted with a perhaps impossible task in his attempt to turn the "five days" of Rivas's play into a consistent and intelligible four-act opera. By omitting some scenes altogether and abridging others, he contrived to reduce the whole to manageable proportions, though in the process he inevitably sacrificed many of the most striking details of the play, and the action became even more confused. These people, who appear in various guises and under various names, are difficult enough for an audience to apprehend in the most favorable circumstances. When their motives or the revelation of their identities are compressed into a single line or a whispered aside, they become scarcely recognizable. Don Carlo, masquerading as a student, provides an appropriate instance. The audience cannot recognize him from the personality of the actor because this is his first appearance, while the emphasis of the whole scene is laid on a description of precisely what he is not!

On the other hand Piave has no responsibility for two of the worst blots on the libretto: the position of the duet between Don Alvaro and Don Carlo in the third act, and the fact that the duel between them at the end of the opera and the subsequent stabbing of Leonora both take place off the stage. These defects were introduced in the revision made by Ghislanzoni and Verdi for the Milan production in 1869. The reason for the first seems evident. Verdi, we know, felt that the atmosphere of the opera as a whole was excessively gloomy and hoped, by concluding his act with a succession of light brilliant numbers, to take some emphasis off the tragedy. But the result is disastrous. Not only is the main action held up at the worst possible moment, but the duet, which contains some of the best music in the opera, is deprived of its natural and rightful position as the climax of the act. With regard to the second, the collaborators probably had the same object in view. We know at any rate that for this very reason they eliminated Don Alvaro's original suicide. Nevertheless, the mere fact that the audience do not see Leonora stabbed or Don Carlo die would hardly seem to make any material difference, and nothing can palliate the weakness of two events of such major importance being heard and not seen.

Werfel, in his admirable German version of the opera, has, I am glad to see, returned to Piave's original so far as lay in his power. In view of the beauty and importance of the music written for the new ending of the opera, little could be done here, but Don Alvaro and Don Carlo are at least seen fighting amid the rocks in the manner of Siegmund and Hunding. The duet is restored to its original position. In my view the opera should henceforward never be given without these indispensable adjustments.

The music of *La Forza del Destino* is not such as lends itself to detailed analysis; in the ultimate resort the charm of the opera lies in the profusion and quality of its melodies, which either appeal to the listener or not. There is little of technical interest — a probable explanation of the disfavor with which the opera has been regarded by all critics and many connoisseurs. The overture, originally a prelude, built on themes from the opera, notably the beautiful "motto" tune and the figure associated with the idea of fate, was much lengthened and rescored for the 1869 revision. It is effective, but, lacking the constructive ability, shown, for instance, in the prelude to *Ballo*, remains something of a hodge-podge. The working of the poignant accompaniment to Leonora's "*Madre, pietosa Vergine*" in the second act, the treatment of the panting figure in the great duet between Don Carlo and Don Alvaro in the third act, are both admirable. The scene where the pilgrims pass outside the inn, singing in the minor while the rest of the characters, divided into eight distinct parts, sing in the major, is a wonderful example of skill in choral writing; as, indeed, is the effective "*Rataplan*" number, so popular in Italy, though I am unable to admire it as music. Further, the instrumentation throughout, but especially in the last act, as well as much of the harmonic scheme, register decided progress. It may be doubted, for instance, whether a passage like that quoted could be paralleled in previous operas:

DON CARLO. *Agitato*

El - la vi - - ve, ma in bre - ve

Nor should we overlook the flexibility and expressiveness of much of the accompanied recitative. The scenes between the Father Superior and Leonora in the second, and Don Alvaro and Don Carlo in the third, act, to take but two examples, are carried through with a command of effect so certain that its very ease may lead us to overlook it; while the final scene and trio (incidentally dating from the revision) are in this respect, as well as regards melodic inspiration, a miniature masterpiece. Nobody but a master could have penned that wonderful passage where, to the accompaniment of the flute, oboe, and clarinet repeating with almost brutal insistence first the high, then the middle G against the rhythmic throb of the brass and strings, the wounded Leonora enters to describe how Don Carlo stabbed her.

From the technical point of view, however, there can be no doubt that the main interest of *La Forza del Destino* lies in the music of Brother Melitone. This typical gross and humorous friar is admirably portrayed from the outset, while in his characteristic punning sermon in the third act, suggested, it is said, by a similar sermon in Schiller's *Wallenstein*, both the rhythms and the color of the music inform us at once that we are in the presence of a personage wholly different from any who has yet appeared in a Verdi opera. Here is not the sardonic wit of the conspirators or the elegant gaiety of Oscar in *Ballo;* his is plebeian humor, of the Leporello variety. Even more interesting is the music of the scene where he distributes food to the poor. Up to now Melitone has remained a character who might have stepped out of a classical *opera buffa*, but at the end of this scene he becomes the direct ancestor of Falstaff, a relationship emphasized by the new scoring of the second half of the scene for the 1869 version:

MELITONE. *Allegro vivo*

Pez-zen-ti piu di Laz-za-ro, Sac-chi di pra-vi-tà via, via, bricco-ni, al dia-vo-lo, to-glie-te-vi di qua.

Indeed, the whole scene, with the differentiation of the music of the Father Superior, and the contrast between the whining beggars clamoring for Father Raffaele and the jovial impatience of Melitone, is of the first order throughout, an example of consummate craftsmanship as well as of inspiration.

Nevertheless, in the ultimate resort we come back to tunes for the outstanding feature of *La Forza del Destino*. The mere profusion of them, making detailed enumeration impossible, is remarkable enough. Neither before nor after, perhaps, was Verdi more lavish with his incomparable gift of melody. And with one important exception the quality of it is almost as remarkable as the quantity. The exception is to be found in the triviality of the popular music, the songs of the student and the peddler, the choruses and dances in the camp, and so on. Preziosilla's numbers, notably the brilliant *Venite all' indovina*, are better, but remain in a class definitely inferior to the serious portions of the score.

There is little love music, for the good reason that the action of the play prevents the lovers being together or declaring their passion except in the first act where we may admire the lyricism of "*Pronti destieri*" and the impetuosity of "*Seguirti fino agli ultimi*." The purely dramatic music, in addition to the somber simplicity of Don Alvaro's "*Solenne in quest' ora*" and Don Carlo's "*Urna fatale*," contains that extended duet between the two men which is not only one of the best numbers in the opera but one of the best numbers ever penned by the composer. For variety of invention the music is remarkable enough, but those who heard Caruso and Scotti sing it will know that the duet can evoke a thrill of excitement inexplicable in terms of mere analysis.

It is in the numbers associated in one way or another with religious emotion, however, that the great strength of *La Forza del Destino* lies. Such are Leonora's prayer to the Virgin and her subsequent duet with the Father Superior, leading eventually, through that spirited passage where the curse of Heaven is invoked on any who dares profane her sanctuary, to the final "*La Vergine degli angeli*," one of the most simple examples of writing for soprano and bass chorus imaginable, yet so exactly right that the beauty of it is overwhelming. Again, her "*Pace, pace*" in the last act, with its quite Mozartean purity, and the final trio, wholly exquisite from the first flowing phrase of the Father Superior to the ethereal passage at the end, possess a beauty greater, so to say, than seems to be contained in the notes.

La Forza del Destino, then, is an opera unequal in merit and, from the technical point of view, inferior to several of its predecessors, in that it is a collection of numbers rather than a dramatic unity. But the undeniable fact remains that it makes an appeal of its own which to many of us is irresistible, though we may be as alive as are the most severe critics to its æsthetic shortcomings. If *La Forza del Destino* inspires love at all, it is perhaps the instinctive tenderness and worship given by a lover to his mistress rather than the reasoned affection of friend for friend or husband for wife.

DON CARLO

Libretto by Méry and du Locle
Production: PARIS, March 11, 1867
Revised Version: MILAN, January 10, 1884

FIVE ACTS, EIGHT SCENES

The scene opens in the forest of Fontainebleau, where Elisabetta di Valois (soprano), escorted by her page, Tebaldo, is riding. A hunt is in progress and Don Carlo (tenor), hidden in the wood, watches the scene. Braving the anger of his father, Filippo, he has come incognito from Spain to see with his own eyes the Princess to whom he is betrothed and with whom he has fallen in love at first sight. Presently Elisabetta and Tebaldo return, having lost their way in the growing darkness. Don Carlo introduces himself to the Princess as one of the suite of the Spanish envoy; whereupon she dismisses Tebaldo, who has caught a glimpse of the lights of Fontainebleau in the distance, and entrusts herself to the protection of the noble stranger.

When Tebaldo is gone, Don Carlo lights a fire, symbol of his growing love for Elisabetta, and it transpires, as they talk, that the war between France and Spain is about to be concluded, that one of the conditions of peace is the betrothal of Elisabetta, daughter of the French King, to Don Carlo, heir to the Spanish throne. Elisabetta plies the stranger with questions about him. She is nervous at the prospect of leaving her country; will he love her as she is prepared to love him? The seeming stranger, replying that he can vouch for the sincerity of Don Carlo's love, says that he has brought for her a portrait of her betrothed. On seeing it, Elizabetta immediately realizes that the stranger is none other than Don Carlo himself; whereupon he falls at her feet with a declaration of his devotion. The new-found happiness of the lovers, for whom the darkness of the wood has become a joy in place of a menace, is interrupted by the return of Tebaldo and pages carrying torches. Prostrating himself, he salutes Elisabetta as Queen; the King of Spain has asked for her hand in marriage and her father has consented. She protests that she is promised to Don Carlo, not Filippo, but presently a crowd arrives, escorting the Spanish envoy, who, while leaving her full liberty of choice, formally repeats the demand on behalf of his master. Pressed by the crowd to accept and thus put an end to the war, Elisabetta reluctantly consents amid the blessings of the crowd, but

Don Carlo

to the despair of Don Carlo, who sees his dream of happiness gone forever.

The second act opens with the monks chanting before the tomb of Charles V in the Convent of San Giusto, whither Don Carlo, in imitation of his grandfather, has come to forget, if possible, the sorrows of the world. When the voice of a monk is heard proclaiming the uselessness of expecting peace in this life, Don Carlo, terrified, imagines he hears and sees his grandfather. Rodrigo, Marquis of Posa (baritone), arrives, to the delight of Don Carlo, overjoyed to see once more his dearest friend. Rodrigo tells him that the Flemings are in dire need of his help; then, struck by the anguish in the expression of his face, begs him in the name of their friendship to declare the reason of his sorrow. Don Carlo, confessing that he loves his stepmother, asks whether even a friend like Rodrigo will not turn away from him in horror. Rodrigo affirms the contrary and, on learning that the King is still ignorant of the matter, advises Don Carlo to solicit for himself the governorship of Flanders in order to forget his private woes in the relief of an oppressed people. King Filippo (bass) arrives, accompanied by Elisabetta, much moved at the unexpected presence of Don Carlo. Presently, after a brief pause before the tomb, they pass on, leaving the two friends to swear a pact of eternal friendship and a readiness to die, if need be, in the cause of liberty.

In the second scene, a garden outside the gates of the monastery, the pages and ladies in attendance on the Queen await her return. To pass the time, one of them, Princess Eboli (mezzo-soprano), bids Tebaldo fetch his mandolin that she and they may sing the song of the veil, a Moorish love-romance. At its conclusion Elisabetta returns from the convent and almost immediately Rodrigo is announced. He is the bearer of a letter from her mother in Paris, but with it he slips into her hand another note that, in a whisper, he earnestly begs her to read. Elisabetta, who guesses at once that the note is from Don Carlo, hesitates, while Rodrigo and Eboli chat about the latest news from the French court. When she decides to open it, she reads a message from Don Carlo adjuring her to put complete trust in the bearer. She bids Rodrigo ask some favor, to which he replies that he will do so, but not on his own behalf: Don Carlo, hurt at the hostility of his father, begs an audience; a word of affection would do much to comfort him. Eboli, who is in love with Don Carlo, begins to wonder whether he, too, does not love her; Elisabetta, understanding better the purport of the note, asks herself whether she can bear to see him again. Finally she decides to send a message to the effect that the mother will be glad to receive her son. Thanks to the maneuvers of Rodrigo, the ladies-in-waiting are kept at a distance when Don Carlo enters, so that he is able to speak with the Queen alone. At first their attitude is restrained. He begs her to use her influence to cause the King to send him to Flanders; she, careful to speak as mother to son, promises all the assistance in her power. Her insistence on their relationship, however, so maddens Don Carlo that his reserve breaks down and he begs for one word of pity as a human being. Much moved, she replies that her seeming indifference is a matter of duty. With increasing fervor he entreats her once more to open her heart to him; whereat, to his inexpressible delight, she confesses that, though they must say good-by, she still loves him. Carried away by his passion, exclaiming that even should the earth open and swallow him up he will continue to love her, he takes Elisabetta in his arms, but she shakes herself free, asking, with deadly sarcasm, whether he proposes first to kill his father and then lead his mother to the altar. The shaft strikes home, for, with a cry that he is accursed, Don Carlo rushes away, while Elisabetta, falling on her knees, thanks God for watching over them. Furious at discovering the Queen unattended contrary to his express orders, the King on his entrance dismisses the lady-in-waiting who should have been on duty. The Queen, bidding her a tender farewell, asks her to keep silence with regard to the insult and goes out, accompanied by the ladies and courtiers. The King, noticing Rodrigo, tells him to remain; despite his conspicuous service, he has never asked for an audience, never made any request on his own behalf. Rodrigo protests that he wants nothing; the honor and ordered civilization of Spain provide him with sufficient reward. On the King's pressing him again to ask some favor, he repeats that he desires nothing for himself, but that he would like, if he might, to ask a favor on behalf of others. He has just returned from Flanders, which persecution has turned into a land of desolation and mourning. Will not the King have pity? Filippo replies that only through bloodshed can the world have peace. Are not the prosperity and contentment of Spain the best proof? Rodrigo retorts that this kind of peace is the peace of the dead; the kind of peace that Nero gave to the world; Filippo should give it liberty. The King concludes the conversation by telling Rodrigo that he dreams strange dreams, but that he need have no fear; only let him beware of the Grand Inquisitor. He then confides to him his anxiety about the Queen and Don Carlo; it shall be the duty of Rodrigo, as his loyal friend, to watch them, with the privilege of access to the Queen at any time. Rodrigo is overjoyed at the opportunity that chance has given him, and Filippo, with a final warning to beware of the Inquisition, expresses the hope that he himself may at last find peace of mind.

The third act opens at midnight in the Queen's gardens in Madrid, where Don Carlo is discovered rereading a letter of assignation for that hour. He imagines it has been sent by Elisabetta, though actually the sender was the Princess Eboli, who presently enters, heavily veiled. In the belief that she is the Queen he makes love to her, but when she unveils he is so taken aback, so profuse with excuses, that she realizes at once that he mistook her for another — in fact, the Queen. Indeed, Don Carlo has practically admitted as much when the watchful Rodrigo comes forward, ordering her to pay no attention to his mad words. But the jealous woman, her vanity mortally hurt, proclaims her knowledge of the truth and tells Rodrigo that, however powerful he may think himself as the King's confidant, he will find her no insignificant enemy. To think that she had quailed before a woman who under the mask of virtue was prepared to go to such lengths to satisfy her love! Rodrigo threatens to kill her. Eboli then turns on Don Carlo, bidding him beware of her vengeance, and departs in a frenzy of rage. When the two men are left together, Rodrigo asks Don Carlo to hand over to him all compromising documents that may be in his possession. Don Carlo at first hesitates to trust one who has become the King's intimate, but Rodrigo soon succeeds in persuading him of his continued loyalty to himself, and the scene ends with both protesting their mutual trust and affection.

The second scene is laid in the great square, where a number of heretics are to be burned at the stake. It is full of people; the bells are ringing. While the people sing the glories of Filippo and of Spain and monks lead to the stake those condemned to die, the Queen and the court enter, taking up their position on the steps of a church, of which the doors presently open to disclose the approach of Filippo with the crown upon his head as a symbol of the solemnity of the *auto-da-fé*. As he comes down the steps of the church, six deputies from Flanders, introduced by Don Carlo, prostrate themselves at his feet imploring mercy for their oppressed country. Filippo, branding them as traitors and heretics, orders their removal by the guard, and, in a great ensemble, the crowd and some of the court second their plea for mercy while Filippo and the monks insist on the fact that they are rebels. Don Carlo then begs to be entrusted with the administration of Flanders, a request summarily refused by Filippo, who asks whether he is likely to put in the hands of his son a weapon that could be turned against himself. Don Carlo, drawing his sword, swears to avenge the Flemings; Filippo commands the guards to disarm him. No one ventures to do so till Rodrigo comes forward and to him the dumbfounded Don Carlo gives up his sword. The King, after bestowing on Rodrigo the title of Duke, moves away; the rejoicings continue; the fires that consume the heretics grow ever brighter, a voice from heaven promising the sufferers peace in the next world.

At the opening of the fourth act Filippo is alone in his study, a prey to the gloomiest reflections; Elisabetta has never loved him, he is doomed always to be alone. The Grand Inquisitor (bass) arrives, summoned by Filippo to discuss Don Carlo's punishment. The King, determined either to absolve his son entirely or to punish him with extreme rigor, asks whether, in the latter alternative, he would have the support of the Inquisition. The Grand Inquisitor replies that God did not hesitate to sacrifice His Son; what is the life of one man in comparison with the maintenance of the true faith? Then, saying that it is now his turn to speak, he demands from the King the sacrifice of Rodrigo, a culprit far greater than the merely impetuous Don Carlo. Filippo angrily refuses; Rodrigo is the only man about him whom he can trust. The Grand Inquisitor, retorting that he should have no need of any confidant outside the Church, hints that, but for this interview, he himself might have been haled before the Inquisition. The Inquisitor takes his leave, the King expressing the hope that there may be peace between them, but, when alone, remarking bitterly to himself that as usual the throne must give precedence to the altar. Elisabetta enters with an indignant demand for justice; the casket wherein she keeps her jewels and other precious possessions has been stolen. Filippo, in whose possession it is, bids her open it and, on her refusal, himself does so, discovering the portrait of Don Carlo. He turns on her in a fury, but she calmly replies that he seems to have forgotten that she was in the first instance betrothed to Don Carlo; she is innocent. His anger increasing, he then openly taxes her with infidelity, threatens her with death. She faints. At the King's call for help Eboli and Rodrigo enter, she overcome with remorse at the sight of a catastrophe for which, it appears, she is mainly responsible, he convinced that the moment has come when he must sacrifice himself for the good of his country. Elisabetta, recovering consciousness, laments her isolation in a foreign land; Filippo, now ashamed of his suspicions, curses the demon that prompted them. When the two men have retired, Eboli throws herself at the Queen's feet, begging forgiveness for her treachery. It was she who, out of jealousy, stole the casket, prompted the charge of infidelity. Worse still, she herself has been guilty of the very crime of which she accused the Queen, for she allowed Filippo to seduce her. Elisabetta, giving her the choice between exile and a cloister, departs, leaving Eboli to curse the fatal gift of beauty that has been her ruin. For the rest of her life she will repent her sins in a convent, but one day of freedom still remains for her to devote to the salvation of Don Carlo.

In the second scene Rodrigo visits the unhappy Don Carlo in prison with an assurance not only of friendship but of a determination to save him. He has come to say farewell, for the hour of death is at hand. Don Carlo's treasonable correspondence has been found in his possession; henceforward he, not Don Carlo, is associated with the Flanders rebellion. When Don Carlo refuses such a sacrifice, saying that he will reveal everything to the King, Rodrigo insists that it is Don Carlo's duty to live for the redemption of Flanders, as it is his to die for his friend. At that moment a man who has come unnoticed on to the stairs leading to the cell discharges his arquebus at Rodrigo, who falls, mortally wounded, his last words being a renewed insistence on their mutual duty and a message that the Queen awaits Don Carlo at the Convent of San Giusto. The King arrives to restore to Don Carlo the sword that has been taken from him. Don Carlo, however, draws back in horror; he is no longer the son of a man who has murdered his most loyal friend. Filippo, too, is much moved by the sight of the dead body of a man who, he realizes, is irreplaceable. A clamor is heard outside. It is the populace attacking the prison and demanding the heir to the throne. Despite the protests of the attendants, the King orders the gates to be opened, and the crowd, intent on vengeance, rush in. Among them is Eboli, in disguise, who urges Don Carlo to take advantage of the opportunity to escape. At that moment the Grand Inquisitor enters and bids the crowd prostrate themselves before a King who is under God's protection. Cowed by the old man, all sink on their knees, while King and Inquisitor advance to meet each other. The altar has saved the throne.

The last act takes place at night in the Convent of San Giusto, where Elisabetta is discovered praying before the tomb of Charles V. She, too, has learned the vanity of the world, the momentary duration of the joys that once, in her dear native country of France, she had thought would last forever. And now, in accordance with her promise to Rodrigo, she is to bid an eternal farewell to Don Carlo, whose life must be devoted to the cause of Flanders and of liberty. Don Carlo arrives for a final interview. At last, he tells her, he is strong enough to do his duty in a manner worthy of his friend's sacrifice and their love for each other; he can now embrace her without a tremor of remorse. Elisabetta, though she weeps, expresses her admiration for his resolve and the lovers resign themselves to the knowledge that their hopes and desires can only be satisfied in the next world. When, however, as mother to son and son to mother, they are taking their last leave of each other, the King enters, seizes the Queen by the arm, and bids the attendants on the Grand Inquisitor hold Don Carlo. At that moment a monk in the habit of Charles

V emerges from the tomb; the attendants, thinking, like the King and the Inquisitor themselves, that they are confronted with an apparition, loose their grasp on Don Carlo, who, half conscious, is spirited away by the seeming ghost into the interior of the convent.

If Schiller's admirable play had to be adapted to operatic purposes at all, it is difficult to see how Méry and du Locle could have treated the main outlines in a manner fundamentally different. To preserve all the interesting subsidiary characters, such as the Dukes of Alva and Medina Sidonia, was clearly impossible, the canvas remaining in fact overcrowded as it is. The action, if at times slow, moves with comparative smoothness; the characters live and are well differentiated, though both Philip and the Princess Eboli have necessarily lost something of their subtlety. If Rodrigo, Marquis of Posa, is an anachronism, as Verdi himself thought, Schiller must be held responsible. True, his is a more wooden figure in the opera, but in essentials he differs little from the original concept. Philip, Elisabeth, Don Carlos himself, remain much as they were, subject to the drawbacks of inevitable condensation. In fact, the play is too rich in characters and incidents to lend itself satisfactorily to operatic treatment, but, granting the choice, it might have been worse handled. Méry and du Locle's libretto is, generally speaking, workmanlike in what may be called the *Les Huguenots* tradition, of which excessive length was one of the worst characteristics.

The collaborators committed one major and several minor sins. Their alteration of the end of Schiller's play is as unnecessary as it is ludicrous; this dressing-up of a monk as Charles V and spiriting away of Don Carlos heaven knows whither being a miserable substitute for Schiller's manly climax, when Philip, with icy calm, hands over his only son to the Inquisition. Further, Eboli's passion for Don Carlos, her attempt at seduction, her own intrigue with Philip, are dealt with far too casually in the opera. More unsatisfactory still is her attempted revenge on the Queen, linked in the play with Alva's political ambitions in Flanders and hatred for Don Carlos. The audience scarcely realize its existence and certainly fail to appreciate its importance. Again, the actual invasion of the palace by the crowd, instead of their rioting in the streets as in Schiller's play, is historically incredible. On the other hand the introduction of the *auto-da-fé* scene and the showing of the incident at Fontainebleau where Don Carlos first sees Elisabeth (only indicated by Schiller) both seem justifiable additions; they certainly provide two of the most effective scenes in the opera, even though the elimination of the latter was the main object of the revision later undertaken by Ghislanzoni and Verdi.

Don Carlo

Perhaps the most marked characteristic of the score of *Don Carlo* is its inequality of merit as well as of style. The best passages of the opera, such as the duets between Elisabetta and Don Carlo in the second and last acts, the scenes between Filippo and Rodrigo in the second and Filippo and the Grand Inquisitor in the fourth act, Filippo's famous soliloquy, *"Ella giammai m'amò,"* rise to great heights. The worst, such as the tune that serves as a kind of motif for the friendship of Don Carlo and Rodrigo, Rodrigo's final aria, the *Marziale* passage that is almost the only serious blot on the last act, are not so much conventional as downright bad. It can scarcely be mere coincidence that the first at any rate preserves a genuine Meyerbeerian flavor. As we have seen, *Don Carlo* marked a conscious approximation to the style of *Les Huguenots* and *Le Prophète*, the favorite operas of the intelligentsia at the time, and the nearer the approximation, the worse as a whole the result. Doubtless Verdi, like Wagner, learned much from Meyerbeer; it would be unfair to overlook his influence with regard to the richer scoring and the greater harmonic freedom that generally characterize *Don Carlo*. But the exigencies of the Paris Opéra, that apotheosis of Meyerbeerism, always seem to have exerted a paralyzing effect on the more spontaneous qualities of Verdi's genius. For this reason, perhaps, *Don Carlo*, despite great merits in detail, sometimes gives an impression of strain, of self-consciousness.

This, however, is not true of the first act, of which, exceptionally, the outstanding feature is lyrical beauty. There is no prelude, and neither the first hunting scene nor the final pages after and including the unaccompanied chorus are of particular interest. But Don Carlo's aria *"Io la vidi,"* very classical in feeling, though the accompaniment before the words *"Tanta gioia"* possesses an indubitable flavor of Wagner, is an exquisite love-lyric, with the following duet between him and Elisabetta at least equally good. This opens with an orchestral phrase, noteworthy not only for its melting tenderness but for the novelty of its contours:

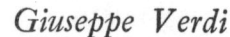

which leads eventually to the lovely flowing melody that is the principal subject of the number. The *poco più mosso* section between the two statements of this is worth attention for the manner in which the lovers' excitement at the illumination of the castle is suggested, the subsequent interpolation of a passionate 3/4 passage in the midst of the general four-time rhythm being particularly happy. Incidentally, this duet, as well as the preceding aria, provides two of the motifs that play so important a part in the opera, the latter being used to symbolize Don Carlo's love for Elisabetta, the former her longing, amid the misery of her life in Spain, for the happiness associated with Fontainebleau and France.

The first scene of the second act opens with another motif, a solemn phrase in alternate minor and major thirds chanted by the monks before the tomb of Charles V and subsequently associated with that defunct potentate. Though the least used, it is of all the themes probably the best adapted to its purpose, just as the climax of the duet between Don Carlo and Rodrigo that concludes the scene is the worst. A trivial tune in any case, it sounds all the more so for coming after the fine somber music in which Don Carlo has revealed to his friend his secret passion for the Queen.

Though the opening female chorus is pretty and the popular "*Canzone del velo*," with its flattened leading note and its conventional Oriental flavor, reminiscent of portions of Mozart's *Entführung*, is effective enough, there is nothing of importance in the second scene till the duet between Elisabetta and Don Carlo. The variety of moods here is remarkable, each being admirably translated into terms of music; but perhaps the most successful is the wistful phrase for three flutes and clarinet which, though similar to a tune in the last act of *Simon Boccanegra*, extends the new flavor already noticed in their duet in the first act:

[Musical excerpt: Don Carlo. Meno mosso (Con voce morente) — "Perduto ben, mio sol tesor, ah! tu splendor di mia vita." Markings: dolce espressivo, perdendosi, morendo.]

The sweep of the phrase immediately preceding it and the poignancy of the final passage where Elisabetta thanks God for watching over them are scarcely, if at all, less happy. Her farewell to the disgraced lady-in-waiting, if very simple, is a well-nigh perfect example of a pathetic aria, the orchestral introduction and conclusion that center on the cor anglais — indeed, the accompaniment throughout — being as good as the melody itself. But it is when we come to the elaborate duet between Filippo and Rodrigo that we are conscious of notable technical progress alike in the harmonic scheme and in the orchestration. The *più animato* passage that leads to Rodrigo's noble "*Ah, sia benedetto Iddio*"; the pages that immediately follow it; the vacillating triplets that accompany Filippo's designation of Rodrigo as a dreamer of strange dreams; the skillful use of the figure introduced at the *Allegro moderato:* all these show a hand both more skillful and more ambitious. Moreover, the characterization is admirable. Rodrigo, especially in his aria earlier in the act, has hitherto been distinctly wooden, but here he really comes to life, his idealistic enthusiasm being unmistakably differentiated from the gloom of the morose Filippo.

The beautiful prelude to the third act, built on Don Carlo's love theme, is one of the gems of the opera, the boldness of the harmonic progression in the concluding bars being unmistakably new. Since these date from the revised version of 1884, however, they cannot be quoted as evidence of progress. None of the music that follows attains to such a poetical level, though the duet between Eboli and Don Carlo is charming, especially as regards modulation, and the final trio is not only vigorous but notable for its highly skillful differentiation of the moods of the various characters.

More notable still in this respect is the great ensemble that constitutes the second scene of the act. Viewed as music pure and simple it is unequal, the festal march, a poor ancestor of that in *Aïda*, being as trivial as the funeral march associated with the monks leading the victims of the Inquisition to the stake is impressive. Nor, despite the almost fanatical admiration of Soffredini, can I think that the music of the Heavenly Voice at the end, derived from what may be called the trio of the funeral march, really rises to the occasion; while the reference to the friendship motif, when Don Carlo is disarmed by Rodrigo, only serves to illustrate once more the inadequacy of that miserable tune. Nevertheless the scene as a whole is an undoubted masterpiece, first and foremost because of the manner in which the characterization of everybody concerned is preserved in the exceedingly elaborate ensemble-writing. Elisabetta, Rodrigo, Filippo, Don Carlo, never lose their individualities, while the differentiation from the crowd of the fanatical monks and the homely Flemish suppliants, with their distinctive theme that plays so important a part in the musical structure, is beyond praise. Nor is this all. In his handling of soloists, choruses, semi-choruses, orchestra, and band on the stage Verdi showed a mastery and a certainty of effect that can assuredly not be matched in any previous opera. The variety and brilliance of the result are extraordinary, superior, if one may say so, to anything suggested by the mere notes — a phenomenon not uncommon in Verdi's music.

The first part of the fourth act is, perhaps, the best in the whole opera, containing two, if not three, important numbers of the first order and nothing unworthy or inharmonious. It opens with Filippo's famous *"Ella giammai m'amò,"* a most difficult soliloquy to interpret adequately, as the innumerable basses who have transported it to the concert platform should have discovered long since. Apart from the technical excellence of the orchestral introduction and accompaniment, the originality of its structure, the expressiveness of its melody, it is interesting as giving us a first glimpse of Filippo the man as distinct from Filippo the King, who has hitherto remained paramount, even in the fine duet with Rodrigo already mentioned. His loneliness, his despair, the gloomy atmosphere of his nocturnal vigil, are perfectly reproduced in the music. No less successful is the scene that follows between him and the Grand Inquisitor. Based largely on a theme in the bass that admirably suggests the implacable

Don Carlo

determination of the Inquisition, it has not undeservedly been described as "hewn out of granite." Even when the Inquisitor sings what is very nearly an aria, we never forget that he is a ninety-year-old fanatic with a will-power that dominates the King throughout the scene. Indeed, the manner in which Verdi has solved the difficult technical problem of sustaining the interest in a long duet between two basses is perhaps the most remarkable feature of a number that at first sight would seem to lend itself but ill to musical expression. In this respect attention should be drawn to the passage where the Inquisitor reproaches the King for his dalliance with new-fangled ideas, culminating in a demand for the sacrifice of Rodrigo; few composers would have imagined such expressive music in such a context. The quartet after the Queen has fainted is perhaps too conventional in its general outline to be ranked in the same category, but it is very effective, especially Filippo's broad phrase to the words "*No, non macchiò la fè giurata.*" Eboli's final scene with the Queen, culminating in the popular "*O don fatale,*" is admirable, particularly the passage where she confesses her misconduct with the King, the aria itself being decidedly improved when not wrenched from its proper position. Only thus, after the passionate regret of the opening *Allegro*, can the portrayal of her changing moods, remorse at her treatment of the Queen, determination to save Don Carlo, preserve its full value, the whole point of the number being that it is an essay in contrasted emotions.

Several commentators have found much to admire in the choral writing and Rodrigo's music in the second part of this act, but I am unable to share their enthusiasm. Both Rodrigo's arias seem to me conventional. The music of the mob is spirited, but mainly interesting, I think, as illustrative of a rather new kind of treatment of the chorus, to be perfected later in *Otello*. The best music of the scene is to be found, perhaps, in the suggestive chords of the orchestral introduction, with the Fontainebleau motif as a particularly happy interpolation.

The last act is almost wholly Elisabetta's, first alone, then in a duet with Don Carlo. Her scena, after an orchestral introduction where the soft bars announce the Charles V motif, opens with a fine unaccompanied phrase leading to the aria proper, both being repeated at the end. It is the music in between, however, that is the most attractive, the Fontainebleau motif being charmingly introduced and the *Allegro agitato* passage, with its insistent figure, prophetic of *Aïda*, where she bids a final farewell to her dreams of happiness, striking the right note at once. The duet is even better. Here Verdi had the happy idea of making use of the phrase that plays so important a part in the lovers' duet in the second act, enriching it with a pendant of exceptional orchestral and harmonic lusciousness that, more than anything else in the opera, might reasonably be termed Wagnerian.

The last section, beginning with the words: *"Ma lassù ci vedremo,"* though less "progressive" in style, contains what is, perhaps, the most moving music of the whole duet, if not of the whole opera. The quality and treatment of the accompaniment figure, the poignancy of the last page, with the dying away of all passion, provide an ideal climax to a duet which, except for the unfortunate *Marziale* section, is one of the most beautiful penned by the composer. The principal merit of the final scene immediately following is its extreme brevity.

To avoid misunderstanding, it should be stated that this account of *Don Carlo* is based on the so-called "Third Edition" of the opera — that is to say, the edition that incorporates the alterations made in the 1884 revision — but restores the first act then eliminated by Verdi and Ghislanzoni. On the whole this revision cannot be accounted an unqualified success. True, certain important improvements were effected, but something of value was sacrificed. Thus, the opera can ill spare the lyricism of the first act, and if Verdi managed to preserve Don Carlo's aria by transporting it in a new and by no means wholly improved form to what had been the second act, he abandoned completely the charming duet with Elisabetta — a loss all the more felt because the duet contains, as we have seen, one of the main motifs of the opera. Incredible as it may seem, the *Marziale* section of the final duet is a product of the revision, the only instance, perhaps, of a definitely bad afterthought, for otherwise all the alterations in detail were for the better. Thus we owe to the revision the welcome shortening of the final scene, the insertion in the farewell duet between Elisabetta and Don Carlo of the reminiscence of their former duet, including the lovely development already noted, an entirely new and improved version of the scene where the mob breaks into the palace prison. The duet between Rodrigo and Filippo at the end of the second act was also drastically altered; indeed, from the words *"Ah, sia benedetto Iddio"* both music and text were entirely rewritten, which implies that all the best music in it dates from the revision, though the original version, straightforward and short, was not devoid of merit. Undoubtedly the most important alteration, however, was the substitution of the present prelude to the third act for a scene containing music for Eboli and Elisabetta, a chorus, mainly unaccompanied, and a ballet. In view of the merit of the prelude, not to mention the saving of time, the alteration seems advantageous. Nevertheless, some of the music sacrificed deserved a better fare. For instance, the unaccompanied chorus in imitation of mandolins is charming, as are Eboli's song in conjunction with it and the delicate poignancy of the orchestral introduction, all of which provided relief from the intense seriousness of the opera as a whole. The ballet music, which consists of five numbers, contains some of Verdi's more successful essays in the form. It is, however, effective rather than important. There is a graceful waltz and an amusing final *prestissimo* not unlike Mendelssohn's *Rondo Capriccioso*, while the middle section of the solo dance of the White Pearl — it is a "Pearl" ballet — sounds decidedly prophetic of a well-known passage in Tchaikovsky's *Nutcracker*. Incidentally, the insertion of a slur at the beginning of this dance was, according to Monaldi, one of those flagrant liberties taken by Mariani in his Bologna performance which started the estrangement between the two friends described in the first portion of this book.

To present *Don Carlo* in a form worthy to rank with, let us say, *Aïda*, is doubtless impossible, because some, though not much, of the weakest music must remain in any event; but I cannot help feeling that of all Verdi's operas this offers the most fruitful field for an intelligent new version. Even in its present form the opera is adequately carried by the excellence of its best music, though, as already stated, it lacks charm and unity. In a sense *Don Carlo* is the antithesis to *La Forza del Destino*, in that it commands respect rather than love. As a landmark in the evolution of the composer, however, it is of indubitably greater importance, for, without the orchestral and harmonic experiments, to say nothing of the conscientious endeavor to blend more intimately words and music characteristic of the best pages of the score, Verdi could hardly have risen to the heights of *Aïda*, *Otello*, and *Falstaff*.

AÏDA

Libretto by Ghislanzoni
Production: CAIRO, December 24, 1871
FOUR ACTS, SEVEN SCENES

In the hall of the King's palace at Memphis, Radames (tenor) and Ramfis (bass), chief of the priests of Isis, are discussing the rumor that the forces of Ethiopia threaten Thebes and the valley of the Nile. Ramfis significantly informs Radames that the oracle of Isis has been consulted and has indicated a young warrior as commander of the Egyptian troops. On Ramfis's departure to inform the King of this fact, Radames wonders whether perchance he has not been chosen. If so, not only will his dreams of victory and glory be fulfilled, but he will be able to marry Aïda (soprano) and free her from the slavery to which she has been condemned by the fortunes of war. His musing on the charms of his love is interrupted by the entrance of Amneris (mezzo-soprano), the King's daughter, who asks the reason of the joyful expression on his face. Radames, anxious above all things to preserve the secret of his love, mentions only the elation caused by his possible appointment as general. Amneris, who herself passionately loves Radames, is not deceived however, and when, on Aïda's entrance, she notes the perturbation of Radames, her suspicions grow stronger. Aïda, too, shows much agitation, asserting, however, that it is only due to the rumor of war with her own countrymen. Amneris, who has always treated her more like a sister than a slave, feigns sympathy, despite her jealous fury at scenting a rival in her subordinate, while Radames remains in deadly apprehension lest she shall find out the whole truth.

The King (bass), accompanied by Ramfis, the captains, and officers of state, enters and, informing them that they have been assembled to hear precise news of the invasion, summons to his presence the messenger who has brought it. The Ethiopians, led by their King, Amonasro, have indeed invaded Egypt and threaten Thebes. All except Aïda, who is amazed and saddened to hear that her father is in personal command of the invading army, enthusiastically acclaim the King's summons to war. Then, designating Radames as the man indicated by Isis as general, the King bids him proceed to the Temple of Vulcan to be invested with the insignia of authority. In a great ensemble Radames is sped on his mission, all, even the distraught Aïda, joining in fervent expressions of hope for his victorious return. But when Aïda is left alone she feels ashamed of her sentiments. The victory of Radames means the defeat of the father, intent on saving her, the death of her brothers and fellow countrymen. Yet she cannot bring herself to pray that Radames may lose the battle; she loves him too well. Torn between her love for her father and her passion for Radames, she can only pray Heaven to take pity on her misery and let her die.

The second scene is laid in the interior of the Temple of Vulcan, where the priests, headed by Ramfis, and the priestesses invoke the aid of Phtha, the creator of heaven and earth. During a sacred dance of the priestesses Radames enters, unarmed. Led to the altar with a silver veil on his head, he is then consecrated to the service of the god and Egypt, and the scene concludes with renewed appeals to Phtha by Ramfis, Radames, the priests and priestesses, that victory be granted to the Egyptian arms.

Aïda 347

At the beginning of the second act Amneris is in her apartments, surrounded by female slaves who are attiring her for the festal reception of the victorious army and its leader. While they are thus engaged and after little Moorish slaves have danced for her, Amneris muses to herself on the thrill of hearing once more the voice of him she loves. But noticing the approach of Aïda, she bids the slaves be silent and depart in consideration for the grief that the captive Princess must feel on account of the defeat of her fellow countrymen. Amneris, however, unable to stifle the jealous doubts that the sight of Aïda revives in her, determines to learn the truth once and for all. Expressing her sympathy and affection, she bids Aïda remember that time is a healer of suffering, that in addition to time there is always the possibility of love. The obvious agitation of Aïda gives her an opening to invite further confidences. Perhaps Aïda loves someone in the army; not all have shared the sad fate of Radames, who has fallen in the battle. Aïda, overcome by the news, says that she will mourn him forever. Then Amneris turns on her, saying that her secret is a secret no longer; Radames's death was an invention. Aïda, unable to restrain her joy, gives thanks to Heaven; whereupon Amneris, bidding her dissemble no more, asks how she, a slave, dares to set herself up as a rival to a daughter of the Pharaohs. After a momentary outburst of pride Aïda falls at Amneris's feet with a prayer for forgiveness. It is true that she loves Radames; will not Amneris, so powerful, so blessed by fortune, leave her what is her only possession? Amneris, consumed with jealousy, abuses and threatens her. Like the slave that she is, she shall attend her mistress at the formal welcome to Radames, of which warlike cries outside proclaim the imminence. All Aïda's prayers for pity, first to her, then to Heaven, cannot suffice to alter her inexorable determination.

The second scene shows the great avenue of the city, which Radames and his troops are to enter through a triumphal arch. The King, surrounded by the priests and great officers of state, takes his seat on the throne, with Amneris on his left hand. The place is thronged with crowds singing the glories of Egypt and of Isis while the priests urge them to render thanks to the gods. Presently the first column of the army appears, succeeded by dancing-girls bearing the spoils of the conquered. Then come more soldiers, war-chariots, banners, images of the gods of Egypt, followed at last by Radames, borne aloft in triumph. The King, after greeting him and bidding him approach that Amneris may place the crown of victory on his head, swears to grant him whatever he may ask. Radames's first request is that the prisoners may be brought in. When they enter, Aïda recognizes among them her father, King Amonasro (baritone), dressed as an ordinary officer. To the amazement of everybody, she rushes towards him, but Amonasro whispers to her not to betray him and, questioned as to his identity, proclaims himself merely as Aïda's father, an officer who has done his duty in the service of his country and his King, now lying dead on the field of battle. Will not the King of Egypt have mercy on him and his fellow prisoners? The priests vindictively cry that all must be put to death; the crowd plead for mercy; in a great ensemble all the principal characters express the emotions aroused in them by the situation. Finally Radames, who has observed the distress of Aïda, asks the King that the lives of the prisoners may be the boon promised to him. Once again the priests, headed by Ramfis, demand their execution, the most sure means of preventing a war of revenge. Radames retorts that, now the warrior King Amonasro is dead, the Ethiopians can entertain no such hope. Ramfis then urges that at least Aïda's father be kept as a hostage. The King on this condition grants Radames's request, announcing at the same time the bestowal on him of the hand of Amneris and, consequently, of the future sovereignty of Egypt. The act ends with general rejoicing except for the wretched Aïda, whom Amonasro, in a whisper, bids be of good cheer; the day of vengeance will soon dawn for her and her country.

The third act shows a moonlit night on the banks of the Nile. In the distance priestesses are heard chanting in the Temple of Isis, to which Amneris comes, escorted by Ramfis, to pass in supplication to the goddess the vigil of her marriage with Radames. When they have entered the temple, Aïda, veiled and apprehensive, arrives to keep tryst with Radames. She wonders what he has to say to her; if he comes to bid her farewell she will throw herself into the Nile and find peace at last, though the remembrance of the home and country that she will never see again fills her with regretful longing. Amonasro, however, to whom the love of Aïda and Radames suggests possibilities of revenge, has followed his daughter and now proposes to her a plan by which not only may her haughty rival be humbled but her country be saved. He recalls all that Ethiopia has suffered at the hands of the Egyptians, portrays her ability to win at one blow a lover, a throne, and the delights of home. He knows that the Ethiopians have taken up arms to fight again. Radames will once more command the Egyptian army. If she can but coax him to tell her the route to be followed, the Ethiopians will fall upon them and victory be assured. Aïda refuses to lend herself to such a plan; so Amonasro turns on her in fury, saying that she is no longer his daughter, only an Egyptian slave. Disregarding her supplications for pity, he at last overcomes her scruples with a picture of the terrible fate that will otherwise await Ethiopia, and she consents despairingly to sacrifice the honor of her lover to the salvation of her country. Radames arrives in an ecstasy of delight at seeing Aïda, but she, reminding him of his betrothal to Amneris and the hopelessness of their position, bids him not try to deceive her. Again he protests his unalterable love. War with the Ethiopians has broken out again; once more he will be put in command of the army, and as the reward of victory he will then ask the King for her hand. Aïda replies that, even so, the vengeance of Amneris will not spare her and her father; the only way is for them to fly and love each other in the freedom of her native land. Radames, mindful of his honor, of the ties that bind him to his country, recoils at the idea. Aïda retorts that he does not love her; let him go to Amneris, abandoning her and Amonasro to their fate. Radames, unable to resist her despair, then consents to fly with her. She asks him how they can avoid the paths taken by the army, to which he replies that the army is going to advance through the gorge of Napata, but that the way will be clear until the next day. Amonasro, who has remained in hiding and overheard everything, exultingly proclaims his intention to see that the forces of Ethiopia are duly stationed at Napata. Radames, hardly able to believe his ears and realizing that he has betrayed a military secret of the highest importance to no less a person than the Ethiopian King, whom he believed dead, bitterly reproaches himself for his involuntary treachery. Aïda and Amonasro attempt to calm him, and, with a promise of future happiness, Amonasro is about to drag him away when Amneris appears, denouncing him as a traitor. Amonasro advances on her with a dagger, but Radames throws himself between them, bidding Aïda and Amonasro fly for their lives. Ramfis sends soldiers in pursuit of them while Radames, making no attempt at resistance, gives up his sword.

At the opening of the fourth act Amneris is discovered alone in a hall of the palace, a prey to bitter despair. Torn between fury at Radames's consent to fly with Aïda and her own love for him, she scarcely knows whether to abandon him to the vengeance of the priests or to try to save him for herself. She bids the guards bring him to her and, when they are left alone, offers to do everything possible to save him if he will be hers; country, throne, life itself she is ready to sacrifice for his love. Radames, though asserting the innocence of his intentions, replies that he, too, has sacrificed everything for love. Now that Amneris has removed and probably killed Aïda, there is nothing left in life for him; he prefers by a brave death to expiate his guilty indiscretion. Amneris protests her innocence with regard to Aïda. In fact, though Amonasro was killed on the fatal night, Aïda vanished and has not since been seen. Overjoyed by the news, Radames utters a prayer that she may reach her home in safety. Once more Amneris offers him life and liberty if he will promise never to see Aïda again. Her love turned to hatred by his refusal, she abandons him to his fate; he then tells her that he desires death and that her compassion is the only thing he now fears. When Radames has returned to his cell, Ramfis and the priests in solemn procession cross the stage on their way to the subterranean hall of judgment, while Amneris bitterly reproaches herself for the jealousy that has given over her lover to priestly vengeance. Presently, as Radames is led into the judgment hall, Amneris, uttering distraught prayers that the innocence of his intention may be established, listens to what is taking place below. The voice of Ramfis is heard indicting Radames on three separate charges. Thrice he bids him clear himself; thrice, as Radames remains silent, the priests proclaim him a traitor, Amneris continuing the while her broken-hearted prayers for his safety. When, after sentencing him to be immured alive under the altar of the god he has insulted, the priests again pass in procession across the stage, Amneris turns on them like a tiger; they have outraged both divine and human justice in their condemnation of an innocent man. Finally, as they pass on, coldly replying that Radames is a traitor and must die, she invokes the curse of Heaven on them for their cruelty and impiety.

The last scene shows the crypt in which Radames has been immured. Above, in the temple, two priests are in the act of letting down the stone that gives access to it, and Radames is bidding farewell to life and to Aïda, when he becomes conscious that there is someone else in the crypt. It is Aïda herself, who, guessing his fate, has hidden there so that they may die together. Radames, horrified at the idea of her death, tries to displace the stone that seals the entrance. All his efforts, however, prove useless. The lovers sing a last ethereal farewell to earth and to each other while, above, the priestesses chant their invocation to Phtha, and the grief-stricken Amneris comes to weep on the tomb of her beloved, praying that Isis may grant him peace in heaven.

Doubtless the precise value to be attached to this libretto will depend primarily on the importance given to theatrical effectiveness for its own sake. As already stated, the characters do not lack humanity; they are real enough — in the case of Amneris, at any rate, exceptionally so. There is little pretense, however, of subtle psychology; the emotions portrayed are broad, elementary, usually dependent on violent conflict. Thus Aïda is torn between her love for Radames and her obligations to her father and her country; Radames has to choose between his love for Aïda and his duty as a soldier; Amneris passes from moods of ardent love, in which no sacrifice seems too great, to moods of jealousy in which everything seems permissible, the passion of both culminating in the scene where she pours the concentrated fury of her remorse on the impassive priests — incidentally another, if somewhat different, study in conflicts.

Granted, however, the full importance of the human factors in the drama, it remains first and foremost an expression of theatricalism, generally, though not always, objective rather than subjective. The spectacular element, the local color, the insistence throughout on violent contrasts, sufficiently attest the fundamental nature of *Aïda*. This is the libretto of a grand rather than a tragic opera. Only it possesses the supreme advantage that nobody concerned felt anything but sincere pride in its manufacture. Least of all Verdi himself.

The extent of Verdi's share in the construction of this libretto is not generally realized. Without actually inventing and writing all of it, he could scarcely have been more responsible. An account of Mariette Bey's original scenario and of the activities of du Locle and Ghislanzoni has already been given, but this seems the place to trace the main features of Verdi's share in the proceedings.

From the time that du Locle's prose version passed to Ghislanzoni for versification he may be said to have taken supreme command. He indicated the exact psychology of Aïda, Amneris, and Radames in the concerted number at the end of the first scene of the first act. He criticized the dramatic effectiveness of the text in the consecration scene, noting especially that the priests were not priestlike enough. The beautiful chant of the priestesses (Mariette had told him he could have as many as he liked without being guilty of an anachronism) and their sacred dance; the solemn answer of the priests; Ramfis's short invocation to the god — all were his own ideas. In the second act he exerted himself to make the first scene dramatically effective despite the lack of action. It was he who invented the dance of young Moorish slaves and Amneris's extraordinarily effective soliloquy in the midst of the female chorus, even indicating the metrical nature of the verses that he desired. In the following duet between Aïda and Amneris he suggested almost the very words of the text at the moment where Amneris and Aïda discover that they are rivals for the love of Radames. The important thing, he urged, was to express the action in the most clear-cut manner possible without excessive preoccupation with literary perfection, for "in the theater it is sometimes necessary for poets and composers to be clever enough to know when to jettison both poetry and music," a true but hard saying which may be commended to the excessively purist opera composers of our own time. In the scene of triumph that concludes the act he commended to Ghislanzoni's notice the typical mixture of piety and jingoism in the telegram sent by the Emperor William after the Battle of Sedan (which had taken place a week previously) as a model for the final utterances of the priests. The prisoners must say something distinctive; so must Ramfis. The passage where Aïda and Amonasro recognize each other, though rewritten eight times, was still not satisfactory. The first eight verses of the chorus were to be changed; the whole scene culminating in the triumphant appearance of Radames should be considered as one great, complex march.

As Verdi became increasingly absorbed in his task, his demands became more and more exacting. After praising the third act in general and Ghislanzoni's verses in particular, he began to tear them both to pieces. The poet was told that his version of the scene between Aïda and her father was far less theatrically effective than that of the scenario. No cabalettas were wanted; Aïda should remain half-dazed by the insults of Amonasro. The words "*O patria mia, quanto, quanto mi costi*," like, in Aïda's preceding aria, her idea of drowning herself in the Nile, must be preserved at all costs. Verdi's treatment of the duet between Aïda and Radames can only be compared with a dog worrying a bone. Day after day, week after week he returned to it, suggesting the sense of several passages and even several actual phrases which now appear in the text, notably at the moment when Aïda reproaches her lover with failing her. As for the discovery of Radames's plan by Amonasro and the final scene, Verdi outlined them almost exactly as they now stand. It is clear that he saw from the beginning the full possibilities of an act which, as he himself says of the opening, must be impregnated with the "smell of Egypt." To obtain this and a succession of rapid and vivid dramatic effects was the main object of all his suggestions and improvements. He was equally careful about the last act, suggesting that the duet between Amneris and Radames should begin not in recitative but in lyrical form, though of a more declamatory nature than the old-fashioned cavatina. He found the cabaletta at the end too long. "Ah! these damned cabalettas! They have always the same shape and are always alike." It was Verdi's idea, after Amneris's soliloquy (which in its original form he found cold) and the judgment scene, to bring the priests back on the stage so that she could turn and curse them. In the final scene he found less to alter, only emphasizing the fact that it should be first and foremost of a lyrical character. Otherwise his suggestions were mainly confined to questions of meter, in which he had, in fact, manifested the greatest interest throughout this and the preceding act.

It will be noted that all Verdi's efforts were concentrated on obtaining simple and direct effects, on the finding of *le mot juste* which should portray a situation in a nutshell. The sense of theatrical effectiveness was always uppermost in his mind. In view of the extent of Verdi's contribution, the libretto of *Aïda* remains, then, perhaps the best evidence of the kind of qualities to which he attached supreme importance. If subtlety and intellectual depth are not among them, they include, at least equally important in a writer for the theater, vivid imagination, simple directness, and a just appreciation of the value of contrasts. An admirer of the opera has found in this libretto "something of Greek tragedy as of Biblical simplicity." The praise may be too high, but from personal experience I can testify to the relief it has been to turn to the terse, straightforward clarity of the libretto of *Aïda* after the intricate maze of *La Forza del Destino* and the rhetorical prolixity of *Don Carlo*. There are blemishes. For instance, the continued concealment of Amonasro's identity after Aïda has recognized him as her father seems scarcely credible, while nobody has ever explained how or when Aïda found her way into the crypt where Radames was to be buried alive. But, as a whole, the libretto of *Aïda* is a very fine piece of work if not actually the best specimen extant of its period and class.

Prime-Stevenson in his book, *Long-Haired Iopas*, has written such an admirable account of the music of *Aïda* that no subsequent writer can avoid treading frequently in his footsteps. He gives, for instance, the authority of Boïto for stating that the present prelude was intended as an entr'acte. We have already seen that Verdi experimented unsuccessfully with a full-dress overture — which, in fact, seems called for in an opera of this character — but, this apart, the prelude would undoubtedly gain from being heard in the course of the opera, when the audience could appreciate readily its great beauty and perhaps realize better the significance of the themes from which it is constructed. The latter point, however, should not be overemphasized. In the heyday of Wagnerism, when theme-hunting was a fashionable sport, Verdi's admirers insisted much on his use of motifs in this opera. As we have seen, such motifs abound in other operas also. But they are not as a rule of the first importance nor have they in fact any connection with Wagnerian procedure. It is possible to find some half a dozen motifs in *Aïda:* two representing the love or jealousy of Amneris, another — a fanfare — the military prowess of Radames, another the appeal to Phtha. In this prelude, however, appear the two most important, Aïda's love theme, as Prime-Stevenson calls it, and a theme associated, according to various authorities, with the priests, Radames's consecration, or both, the very indefiniteness suggesting the futility of such labels. How far taste has changed in the matter is shown by the fact that at one time Verdi is said actually to have been criticized for not linking Amonasro with a definite theme, whereas everybody now realizes that the King's music in the third act is some of the most expressive and personal in the opera. Similarly, the ultimate merit of the prelude lies not in the fact that it is ingeniously built on two themes associated with the action, but in the inherent excellence of the themes themselves, as of their contrapuntal manipulation into an exquisite little unity of symphonic music. Since, after *Aïda*, Verdi made less, not more frequent use of recurrent themes, consideration of the point seems apposite here.

Possibly the outstanding features of the score of *Aïda* are its wealth of melodic invention, its vivid contrasts, its luscious harmonic and orchestral coloring. All three are in evidence at once. The effect of the trumpets and trombones associated with Radames's military ambitions is electrifying after the short, quiet dialogue between him and Ramfis, which, to the accompaniment of divided cellos, opens the opera. And we have scarcely recovered from our surprise when Radames glides almost imperceptibly into thoughts of love — the beautiful melody "*Celeste Aïda.*" It is usually spoiled by the tenor's singing the conclusion *fortissimo* instead of *pianissimo* and *morendo* as marked, the effect of a daydream intended by Verdi thus being effectually ruined. Moreover, an interesting point about "*Celeste Aïda,*" often overlooked, is the subtle manner in which the low register of the flutes is used to suggest the tropical fragrance of Ethiopia when Radames expresses the wish that he might restore Aïda to her native country. Thus early, then, appears that felicitous writing for wood-wind so remarkable in the opera as a whole. The main interest of the duet and trio that follow lies in the quality and treatment of the theme associated with Amneris's jealousy. There are other points, in particular the scarcely definable manner in which the falseness of Amneris's solicitude for Aïda is suggested; but the character of the theme in question, a distant relation, by the way, of an important theme in *Nabucco*, remains so strong in its turbulence that it dominates the whole. Associated almost exclusively with the strings, it is certainly one of the best themes ever imagined by the composer and is treated, moreover, with unwonted freedom. In the same manner the scene of the King's entrance, though the opening fanfares, the terse "*Ed osan tanto,*" and, above all, the savage cry for immediate war could not, in fact, be bettered, is dominated by the great, four-square tune: "*Su! del Nilo.*" This is, I suppose, one of the tunes pilloried by a recent critic in a contemptuous reference to the "Salvation Army rhythms" of *Aïda*. As an expression of the kind of patriotic fervor in evidence at the outbreak of war it seems to me not only right but inspired. Doubtless, it will never appeal to those who would like to see *La Marseillaise* rewritten in the style of Bach, but to anyone capable of appreciating more primitive emotions the

Aïda

sheer virility of it can, and usually does, give an unforgettable thrill. Nor is the manipulation so straightforward as is sometimes supposed. The contrapuntal anguish of Aïda when Radames takes up the tune in C major, the return to the clamor for war as a kind of coda, the unsuspected retardation of the climax on the chord of the seventh, which provoked such excitement at the dress rehearsal in Cairo — all these are instances of technical ingenuity often overlooked in the excitement produced by the number as a whole. Aïda's famous soliloquy, which follows, explores a great variety of rhythms possible within the general scheme of common time, but its interest is primarily harmonic and emotional though the dramatic effect of the opening *"Ritorna vincitor,"* a repetition of the last phrase of the preceding chorus, is a stroke of genius necessarily lost in concert performance. Nothing, however, can detract from the somber despair of *"Vincitor de' miei fratelli,"* with the cellos, oboe and bassoon playing a chromatic passage identical with a phrase in the last act of *Rigoletto;* from the agitation of the writings for strings as well as the melody of the *"I sacri nomi"* section; above all, from the poignancy of the final *"Numi pietà"* with its expressive cadence dying away into sobs of anguish.

The scene of Radames's consecration is built up on three main musical ideas, with the dance of the priestesses as a kind of intermezzo. This delicious number, entrusted mainly to three flutes, which, with their trills and sinuous triplets, admirably suggest the East without being in any way Eastern, is perhaps the best piece of dance music ever written by Verdi. Akin to it in feeling, though more consciously Oriental and definitely hieratic, is the first of the main subjects, the priestesses' chant to Phtha. With its modal character, its undulating rhythm and simple harp accompaniment, it might well pass for genuine Egyptian music did we not know that it was invented by Verdi himself. It alternates for some time with the solemn mystical invocation of the priests, giving place presently to the broad theme of Ramfis's *"Nume, custode e vindice,"* built up into an ensemble at the end of which all three ideas are pressed into service. The whole scene, essentially theatrical, may be called an apotheosis of musical objectivity.

The first scene of the second act, on the other hand, except for a touch of theatricalism at the beginning and the end, is essentially subjective, the varying moods of Amneris and Aïda being interpreted with a skill and an insight that are beyond praise. A revelatory point about it is that, though Aïda's love theme plays an important part in her music, neither of the two themes associated with Amneris earlier and later in the opera is heard at all. Her various emotions are translated into entirely new terms, all of them admirable. What could be better than the languorous passion of the invocation to her lover while the slaves are attiring her for his reception? The insinuating falseness of her attempts to gain the confidence of Aïda; the jealousy when she proclaims her rivalry; the hatred and contempt when she reminds Aïda of her servitude? The wealth of musical invention by which these feelings are conveyed is as striking as the technical skill shown in the handling of it. Aïda's music, with its theme and reference to the *"Numi pietà"* of the last act, is not so remarkable in this respect, though the beautiful melody and expressive accompaniment on bassoon, clarinet, and flutes of her appeal for mercy, *"Ah pietà ti prenda,"* is one of the gems of the scene. Incidentally, a point worth noticing is the difference in character between the song of the slaves attiring Amneris and the chant of the priestesses in the first act though the rhythm and the use of the harp are not dissimilar in both. Also, the dance of the little Moorish slaves is charming alike from the standpoint of harmony and orchestration.

The second scene is, of course, purely theatrical, great choruses supported by a brass band on the stage, the famous march for the long trumpets when the troops enter, and a full-dress ballet. Such psychological interest as there is lies in the typical utterances of the priests, Amneris's exultation at what she imagines to be her definite triumph over Aïda, and the manner in which the characters are differentiated in the great final ensemble, one of the most masterly specimens of this kind of writing ever penned. Amonasro scarcely comes to musical life in this act, though associated with *"Ma tu Re,"* perhaps its most beautiful tune; even Radames is little but the embodiment of martial glory. Nevertheless, to dismiss the music as of small value on account of its preoccupation with external trappings would be a mistake. For my part, I could well dispense with the stage band and I am not especially enamored of the *"Gloria all' Egitto"* chorus, even though it was chosen as the Egyptian National Anthem. But the handling of the material, the deft use of the introduction of the Ethiopian prisoners as an occasion for musical repose, are evidences of exceptional constructive ability. There is also the ballet music, remarkable alike for variety and orchestral skill. Never quite losing a flavor of Orientalism, it remains admirably differentiated from the sacred dance music in the same idiom. As a rule Verdi was not successful in his ballets, but all such music in *Aïda* must be regarded as a brilliant exception. Hard words have been said about the long trumpets by those who have never tried to write a tune for the open notes of such an instrument or have failed to realize that the resulting brilliance is due to Verdi's success in this respect. The electric shock of the change from the A-flat to the B-natural trumpets is familiar to all who have heard the opera, but the ingenuity, first pointed out to me by Malcolm Sargent, of treating the D-sharp harmonic of the latter as E flat and thus effecting a combination of the two at the climax, has never, I think, been emphasized. At any rate, whatever precise value be attached to the music as music, the whole scene never fails to achieve its effect, especially when the crowd is dynamically handled and not allowed to stand wearily waving palm leaves, as if watching a Lord Mayor's show on a wet day!

The third act, though the suggestion of atmosphere has an important share in it, is wholly personal, even the "local color" of Egypt or Ethiopia being used to reinforce the emotional values of this or that situation. For instance, the opening, miraculously suggestive of a hot starlit night, blends imperceptibly with Aïda's homesickness; just as the musical painting of the tropical charm of her native country plays its part in her seduction of Radames from his duty as a soldier. In the wonderful scoring throughout, Verdi was not merely being picturesque — an orchestral ambition which, as he explicitly said, he eschewed on principle. Nevertheless, full justice has perhaps never been done to the technical virtuosity shown here in this respect. Has any other composer ever written quite in this way for the wood-wind, achieved quite this expressive smoothness in his handling of the instruments? The writing for the flutes throughout, nearly always used to depict some exotic sensation or other, is perhaps the most remarkable feature of all, but the treatment of the oboe, clarinets, and bassoon in the "*O patria mia*" section is equally expressive in its way. Nor does the merit of the scoring cease here. The opening passage for strings, with those harmonics on the cellos that are the product of sheer inspiration; the soft trumpets associated with Radames's description of the imminent war; the fiery turbulence of brass and strings in Amonasro's denunciation of his daughter — all are models of what may be called psychological orchestration. The musical material itself is also of the first order. The distant chant of priestesses and priests; the poignant melodic and orchestral themes interpreting Aïda's longing for home; first the promises, then the fury, of Amonasro culminating in that great "*Su dunque, sorgete*" which is a veritable epitome of primitive passions; the varying moods of the duet between father and daughter — these show a certainty of touch, a power of imagination never hitherto attained by the composer. Perhaps the music becomes a trifle more conventional at the entrance of Radames, the *Allegro assai vivo* at the end of the duet between him and Aïda being very nearly a cabaletta. But what a cabaletta! Here, moreover, we have that "*Là, tra foreste vergini*" section which is one of the high lights of the opera. The end of the act, too, with its short, incisive strokes, provides the only possible climax to music that has never ceased to be dramatic even in its most lyrical, its most pictorial moments.

Amneris dominates the first scene of the last act, the music interpreting with hitherto unexampled flexibility every shade of her passion, hatred, and remorse. Prime-Stevenson is right, I think, in tracing here a certain affinity with Racine; the scene definitely suggests one of the great monologues of French classical tragedy. The musical invention displayed throughout is remarkable. Both themes associated with her in the first act are jettisoned almost at once, and after the entrance of Radames to eight bars of wonderful music, decidedly Wagnerian in flavor, all the material of this duet is new. Excepting that passage of haunting beauty where Radames prays that Aïda may have reached her native land, it consists essentially in a gradual working up of intensity. The somber music of the "*Già i sacerdoti adunansi*" section is full of foreboding, which, with the music at the words "*Ah tu dei vivere*" (exceptionally, it may be noticed, bearing the stamp of Bizet and Gounod), changes to the breaking down of all Amneris's reserve. Then comes the excitement of the passage, again somewhat Wagnerian, descriptive of the flight of Aïda and her father, culminating in the now utter despair of Amneris and that lovely phrase of Radames: "*E la morte un ben supremo*" which might have been suggested to Verdi by *Tristan and Isolde* had he known the opera at the time. The ensuing scene of the trial and condemnation continues the crescendo of emotion, Amneris with her "*Ah pietà! Ah lo salvate, Numi*" (a phrase that descends directly from the Leonoras of *La Forza del Destino* and *Il Trovatore*, growing more and more hysterical in her grief and remorse till the climax of her wild outburst against the priests. The whole of this scene, with its blend of subjective emotion in Amneris and objective theatricalism embodied first in the different chants of the priests, then in the scarcely audible drum-pulsation that follows each charge against Radames, is a masterpiece, the only flaw being the comparative weakness of the harmony in Amneris's final "*Empia razza*," which, however, is immediately atoned for by the magnificent orchestral passage that brings the agony to an end.

Though the happy repetition of the priestesses' chant to Phtha lends a touch of drama to the final scene, it is not dramatic, not even, in the active sense, emotional. With unerring instinct Verdi felt that the conclusion of the opera, after the turbulence and passion, the brilliance and color that had gone before, must be quiet and lyrical. And essentially the whole scene remains a lyrical duet between the doomed lovers. The lyricism, however, has a peculiar quality of its own. It is ethereal, vaporous, in the "*Vedi? di morte l'angelo*" section almost light-headed. Verdi was so uncertain of the effect of the novel orchestration here — six muted violins *legato* in the upper register, the other desks dividing an alternate *arco* and *pizzicato* accompaniment, the second violins and violas sometimes *pizzicato*, sometimes *tremolando*, harp, flute, and two clarinets, with an occasional horn or bassoon — that he wrote especially to Bottesini at Cairo to know how it sounded. Certainly this orchestration and the lovely tune that it accompanies combine to produce a transcendental effect justifying, perhaps, Soffredini's description of the music as "not so much notes as tears." In any case it may be doubted whether the composer ever achieved anything more truly poetical.

Verdi once wrote, with reference to Shakspere, that to copy reality was good, but to invent it even better. Bonaventura has happily applied the saying to the effects of local color in *Aïda*. I am not sure that he might not have gone a step further and applied it to the opera as a whole. The libretto is a copy — an excellent, if conventional, copy — of reality; but the music invents it.

OTELLO

Libretto by Boïto

Production: MILAN, February 5, 1887

FOUR ACTS, FOUR SCENES

A terrific storm is raging over Cyprus, where the inhabitants anxiously await the arrival of Otello (tenor), the Moorish general dispatched by Venice to engage the Turkish fleet that has been threatening the island. Amid the thunder, the lightning, and the hurricane they pray that Otello's ship, which has just been sighted, may safely make port. To the secret disappointment of Iago (baritone), Otello's "ancient" or ensign, she eventually does so after narrowly escaping wreck on the rocks and Otello steps ashore, bidding all rejoice, for the defeat of the Turkish fleet has been turned by the storm into absolute destruction. While Otello, followed by Cassio (tenor), his second-in-command, and Montano (bass), the former Governor of the island, enters the fortress, the populace indulge in rejoicings, and the storm gradually subsides. Iago is left alone with Roderigo (tenor), a young Venetian gentleman, who, in despair at the hopelessness of his passion for Otello's newly wedded bride, Desdemona (soprano), says that he has a mind to drown himself. Iago bids him take heart; she will grow tired of her husband with his thick lips and savage ways and he shall yet win her, helped by Iago himself, who, though he simulates love, in fact hates the

Moor for having promoted Cassio over him despite his long service at the wars. The townspeople light a bonfire and sing round it; the arbor outside the fortress is illuminated; Iago, Roderigo, and Cassio sit at a table to drink. Iago, who knows that Cassio has "very unhappy brains for drinking," keeps filling up his cup. Cassio at first protests, but allows himself to be persuaded to drink one more toast to the wedding of Otello and Desdemona, whose beauty and charms he extols. Iago then calls for more wine, fills up the cups, and sings a song in praise of drinking, during which he urges Roderigo in a whisper to find some pretext or other to pick a quarrel with Cassio, who is now completely drunk. Montano, entering to tell Cassio that the guard awaits his orders, is shocked to observe the lieutenant's condition. As Cassio rises to go, Roderigo laughs at him. Cassio resents the insult and the two men come to blows. Montano endeavors to separate them; whereupon Cassio threatens to break his head if he interferes. Montano characterizes the words as those of a drunkard, to the fury of Cassio, who draws his sword. Montano does likewise and they fight, while Iago, though pretending to try to make peace, whispers to Roderigo to go and rouse the town. The crowd disperse with cries of alarm, and presently Otello, aroused by the tumult, enters with an imperative command to put up their swords.

> "Are we turned Turks and to ourselves do that
> Which heaven hath forbid the Ottomites? . . .
> Honest Iago, that look'st dead with grieving,
> Speak, who began this? On thy love I charge thee."

Iago professes ignorance; all were good friends —

> ". . . and then but now —
> As if some planet had unwitted men —
> Swords out, and tilting one at other's breast,
> In opposition bloody. I cannot speak
> Any beginning to this peevish odds;
> And would in action glorious I had lost
> Those legs that brought me to a part of it!"

Otello first rebukes Cassio for so far forgetting himself; then, further incensed by the discovery that Montano is wounded, as well as by the arrival of Desdemona, whose repose has been disturbed by the din, deprives him of his command. The secretly delighted Iago is sent to restore order in the town while Otello himself remains behind with Desdemona to see that all disperse quietly to their several quarters. So they are left alone in the now silent night to enjoy the memories of their love, the sweetness of murmuring together:

"Do you remember?" They recall once again the stories of adventure and suffering with which he first won her heart:

> "She lov'd me for the dangers I had pass'd
> And I lov'd her that she did pity them."

Then, as the sky finally clears and the moon and stars begin to come out, they kiss before retiring together to the castle.

The second act is laid in a ground-floor room of the castle. Iago tells Cassio not to disquiet himself. In a short time he will recover his rank and take up as gaily as before his love-affair with Monna Bianca; only let him secure on his behalf the intercession of Desdemona, to whom Otello can refuse nothing, and all will be well. Moreover, an opportunity will soon occur, for it is her habit to walk in the garden at this hour. As Cassio moves away to await her on the veranda, Iago flings malevolent gibes at his retreating form. He is but Iago's puppet, just as Iago himself is but the puppet and sport of the ruthless God who has created him in His own image; the essence of human nature is evil, virtue only hypocrisy; from the cradle to the grave man remains the plaything of an unjust Fate. And after the grave — what? Nothing!

When Cassio, informed by Iago of her approach, has left the veranda to join Desdemona in the garden, Iago muses how he can bring Otello to see them talking together and thus awaken jealousy. Otello's entrance gives him the opportunity he desires. Standing motionless on the veranda, he carefully times an expression of disgust so that Otello may overhear it, and to Otello's question as to what he said, replies with an evasion. Otello then asks whether it was not Cassio who had just taken leave of Desdemona. Iago feigns incredulity:

> "Cassio, my lord? No sure I cannot think it
> That he would steal away so guilty-like,
> Seeing you coming."

Otello, though convinced that it was Cassio, pays little attention till Iago asks whether Cassio knew Desdemona well in the past, whether he is certain that Cassio is an honest man. Otello, his suspicions aroused by Iago's simulated reticence, bids him speak openly. Iago, protesting his devotion, replies that his thoughts are his own; only let Otello beware of jealousy:

> "It is the green-ey'd monster which doth mock
> The meat it feeds on."

Otello, still maintaining self-control, refuses to give way to vain suspicions:

> "I'll see before I doubt; when I doubt, prove;
> And, on the proof, there is no more but this, —
> Away at once with love or jealousy!"

Iago pretends to be delighted that he is now free to speak openly and bids Otello, though there is as yet no question of proof, watch Desdemona well. While he speaks the last words, Desdemona reappears, surrounded by inhabitants of the island who have come to serenade her and give her flowers. The charming scene, which only spurs Iago on to greater malignity, restores to Otello confidence in his wife, a confidence, however, that is of short duration; for when, after the departure of the islanders, Desdemona, followed by Iago's wife, Emilia (mezzo-soprano), her lady-in-waiting, comes to plead with him for Cassio, all his suspicions return with renewed force. Desdemona, noticing though not understanding his perturbation, takes out her handkerchief to wipe his heated brow. Otello throws it to the ground, ordering her to leave him. She craves his pardon if she has unwillingly offended him, and, in the course of the ensuing quartet, Iago commands Emilia to pick up and give to him the handkerchief, which, as she shows great reluctance, he eventually snatches from her hand. When the women have gone, Iago, who has also pretended to go but has in reality remained in the doorway to gloat over the Moor's agony, comes with simulated joviality to bid Otello dismiss the matter from his mind. Otello turns on him with a curse for having disturbed his blissful ignorance:

> "Farewell the tranquil mind! farewell content! . . .
> Farewell the neighing steed, and the shrill trump,
> The spirit-stirring drum, the ear-piercing fife,
> The royal banner, and all quality,
> Pride, pomp and circumstance of glorious war! . . .
> Farewell! Othello's occupation's gone."

When Iago attempts consolation, he turns on him again more furiously than ever, taking him by the throat and swearing that, if he cannot substantiate his insinuations, a storm of fury shall descend upon his head. Iago, feigning deep resentment at such a slight on his honesty and loyalty, makes as if to go, but Otello bids him stay and help to dissipate the doubt:

> "I think my wife be honest and think she is not.
> I think that thou art just and think thou art not.
> I'll have some proof."

Iago with fiendish cunning asks if he expects "ocular proof," thus driving Otello to madness; or, since actual demonstration is out of the question, would he be satisfied with reasonable certainty? Iago proceeds to describe a dream that Cassio once had:

> "In sleep I heard him say: 'Sweet Desdemona,
> Let us be wary, let us hide our loves' . . .
> . . . 'Cursed fate that gave thee to the Moor!' "

The dream almost suffices to convince Otello, but Iago, as one who would be scrupulously fair, insists that further corroborative proof is necessary; does he know if Desdemona possessed a fine embroidered handkerchief? On Otello replying that he gave her such a one as a first love-gift, Iago affirms that he has seen it in the hands of Cassio. Otello's fury now knows no bounds:

> "O, that the slave had forty thousand lives!
> One is too poor, too weak for my revenge.
> Now do I see 'tis true."

He then kneels down and "by yond marble heaven" swears implacable revenge; whereupon Iago also, kneeling at his side, vows to devote

> "The execution of his wit, hands, heart
> To wrong'd Otello's service."

In the third act Otello and Iago are conversing in the great hall of the castle when a messenger announces the imminent arrival of envoys from Venice. Paying but scant attention, Otello bids Iago continue to outline his plan, which is to engage Cassio in conversation and try to extract from him some word or gesture sufficiently compromising to carry conviction of his guilt. As Desdemona enters, Iago departs with a parting injunction to Otello to bear in mind the handkerchief. Otello, dissembling his feelings, asks Desdemona to give him her hand, which he says requires

> "A sequester from liberty, fasting and prayer,
> Much castigation, exercise devout;
> For here's a young and sweating devil here
> That commonly rebels."

Desdemona replies that, be that as it may, it was with this hand she gave him her heart, and then begins to plead again for Cassio. Otello pays no heed, merely bidding her wipe his fevered brow with her handkerchief. She does so, but he exclaims that the handkerchief he needs is the one that he once gave her. Let her beware if she has lost it; the handkerchief possessed magical properties:

> "To lose't or give't away, were such perdition
> As nothing else could match."

Desdemona, rather frightened, replies that she will presently look for it. Otello orders her to do so at once; whereupon, in her candor, she says that all this irritation is but a ruse to prevent her pleading the cause of Cassio. She then proceeds to do so, to the ever rising anger of Otello, who vouchsafes no reply except reiterated demands for the handkerchief. Finally he forces her to look him in the face and swear to her innocence and chastity. Which when she does, he shouts that she has sworn her own damnation. Once more the now terrified Desdemona proclaims her innocence; so Otello, after loading her with foul insults, says with bitter sarcasm that he must have been mistaken:

> "I cry you mercy, then:
> I took you for that cunning whore of Venice
> That married with Othello."

After forcing her to leave him, he remains alone for a while, a prey to successive emotions of shame, misery, and fury. Iago comes to say that Cassio is at hand. If Otello will conceal himself, he may from their conversation gather that definite proof of guilt which he so ardently desires. Iago, then, encouraging the reluctant Cassio to enter, artfully inveigles him into a conversation about his love-affair with Bianca, which Otello, from mention of the name of Desdemona at the outset, imagines has reference to his wife. Every gesture, every laugh, confirms his suspicions. Finally, when Cassio produces and jokes about the handkerchief, which he has found in his lodging, suspicion changes to certainty; though his words are inaudible, Cassio's attitude and possession of the handkerchief appear to indicate their drift only too clearly. A trumpet-call from the castle, announcing the arrival of the Venetian galley, puts an end to the conversation. Otello emerges from his hiding-place, the sole question now in his mind being how he shall kill Desdemona. He bids Iago bring poison, but Iago suggests that it were better to "strangle her in her bed, even the bed she hath contaminated"; he himself will see to the removal of Cassio. Both ideas please Otello, who then and there promotes Iago to the vacant command. Amid the acclamations of the crowd the Venetian envoys enter, accompanied by Desdemona, whom, to avoid suspicion, Iago has hastily summoned. The principal envoy, Ludovico (bass), hands Otello a dispatch from the Doge and Senate of Venice and, while he reads it, engages Desdemona and Iago in conversation, expressing astonishment at the absence of Cassio. Iago explains the situation; Desdemona ventures to say that she hopes he will soon be pardoned, for the love she bears Cassio is very real — a sentiment that lashes Otello to such fury that, but for the intervention of Ludovico, he would strike her. Cassio is

Otello 365

summoned to hear the reading of the dispatch, while Ludovico expresses to Iago his surprise at the change in Otello. On Cassio's arrival Otello reads out the dispatch, which, to his own chagrin and the disappointment of Iago, who sees his plans thwarted at the very moment of their fruition, orders the appointment of Cassio as Governor in his stead and his own immediate return to Venice. All through the reading he has in malevolent asides taunted the weeping Desdemona with hypocrisy — "O well-painted passion" — and at the conclusion he throws her brutally to the ground. There follows a long ensemble. Desdemona gives vent to her misery; Iago urges Otello not to delay his revenge and Roderigo immediately to dispose of Cassio if he would not lose Desdemona, while all the rest of the characters express various emotions of pity or horror. Finally Otello in terrible anger bids them all depart, turning with a curse on Desdemona, who would comfort him. Left alone, Iago's insinuations recur to his now quite delirious memory and he falls to the ground in a faint. From outside are heard the jubilant trumpet-calls, the acclamations of the crowd proclaiming the glories of the Lion of Venice. Iago listens to the shouts and, putting his foot on the head of the senseless Otello, emphasizes with hideous sarcasm the humiliation of the much vaunted Lion.

The last act shows Desdemona's bedchamber. Sick at heart, she prepares to retire for the night and await Otello as he has ordered her to do, telling Emilia that she is haunted by the memory of her mother's maid, Barbara:

> "She was in love, and he she lov'd proved mad
> And did forsake her; she had a song of 'Willow' . . .
> And she died singing it; that song to-night
> Will not go from my mind."

While Emilia lets down her hair Desdemona sings the song to herself, at the end calling to Emilia to give her a farewell kiss. With a prayer to the Virgin she goes to bed, when Otello almost immediately enters by a secret door. For a while he gazes on the sleeping Desdemona, then kisses her three times. She wakens and he asks her if she has said her prayers, if there are any sins for which she should ask Heaven's pardon:

> "I would not kill thy unprepared spirit,
> No; heaven forfend! I would not kill thy soul."

Desdemona, with a gradual realization of her peril, begs for mercy, asking what her fault may be. Otello tells her of the handkerchief and accuses her of loving Cassio. Despite her denials, her request to be spared till Cassio has the opportunity to prove the charge a lie,

Otello pays no heed, informing her that Cassio is dead. Desdemona's lament: "Alas, he is betrayed and I undone!" only serves to inflame his wrath. He smothers her, but, before she is quite dead, a knock is heard at the door. It is Emilia urgently demanding admission; Cassio has killed Roderigo. A groan from the bed leads to the discovery of Desdemona, still able to murmur that she is innocent though no one but herself is responsible for her death. Otello brands her a liar; he killed her because she was Cassio's lover; let Emilia ask Iago. Emilia, cursing him for a fool, shouts for help. Ludovico, Cassio, and Iago enter. Emilia bids Iago give the lie to such a foul murderer and say whether he thought Desdemona faithless or no. Iago replies that he thought her guilty and Otello instances the handkerchief; whereupon Emilia, despite Iago's whispered command to be silent, reveals how the handkerchief was snatched from her hand, while Cassio tells of his finding it in his lodging. At that moment Montano enters with the news that Roderigo in his last moments has revealed the whole story of Iago's machinations. As Otello bids him clear himself, Iago, with a curt refusal, rushes out, pursued by some of Montano's soldiers. Otello, who has snatched a sword to kill him, tells the others not to be afraid:

> "Though you do see me weapon'd,
> Here is my journey's end."

Then, throwing the sword to the ground, he goes to Desdemona's bedside to look his last on her pale, cold loveliness. Suddenly he draws a concealed dagger and stabs himself, falling upon Desdemona:

> "I kiss'd thee ere I killed thee; no way but this,
> Killing myself to die upon a kiss."

Boïto's libretto is a masterpiece, a masterpiece of condensation in particular. Possibly, in his determination to prune Shakspere's play of every conceivable redundancy, he sacrificed one or two points that had better been retained—Iago's suspicion of an intrigue between Emilia and Othello, for instance, and the deadly deduction drawn from Desdemona's deception of her father to the likelihood of the deception of her husband. The awakening of Othello's jealousy is, moreover, excessively rapid in the opera, though subsequently it follows much the same course as in the play, its persistent growth being indeed more rather than less logically demonstrated. Nevertheless, as already suggested, his total elimination of the first act, except for two lines introduced into the love duet, was a master stroke, and his rearrangement of certain scenes in the third and fourth acts of Shakspere's *Othello*, not to mention the combination of an exterior and an interior scene in the second act of the opera, was singularly happy. What is more, the deliberate filching of the handkerchief from Emilia seems an improvement, while few will regret the suppression of the excessively protracted end of the tragedy as Shakspere wrote it, in particular the unnecessary murder of Emilia and the promised torture of Iago. Indeed, the curt refusal of Iago to answer Othello's question and his rapid flight dispose of him in a very satisfactory manner, the condensation of the action here permitting the librettist previously to provide lyrical opportunities for Desdemona and in general to concentrate our attention on her and the Moor.

Desdemona's stubborn and inappropriate insistence on Cassio's reinstatement produces, owing to the elimination of intervening material, an effect even more artificial and tiresome than in Shakspere; but fundamentally there is no difference between play and opera in this respect. Some commentators, notably in Germany, have designated Boïto's Iago as a more deliberate villain than Shakspere's, but I am unable to follow them. Iago, as befits an operatic character, is drawn by Boïto in perhaps more crude colors; the cause of his hatred for Othello is reduced to envy of Cassio alone. But his essential delight in wickedness for its own sake seems to me equally implicit in Shakspere. Possibly the famous "*Credo*," suggested to Boïto, it is said, by isolated passages in *Othello* itself, *Timon of Athens*, and perhaps *Titus Andronicus*, provides an explanation of the criticism. Shakspere's Iago never expresses himself so openly. He does not, but in the first act he very nearly does. It is conceivable that Boïto, the Goethe-enthusiast, the author as well as the composer of *Mefistofele*, was unconsciously tempted to overstress the affinity between Othello's ancient and "the spirit that ever denies." The affinity, however, is there.

Consideration even of such criticisms should not obscure the fact that Boïto's libretto has met with well-nigh universal praise. It could not be otherwise. The skill he displayed in providing occasions for lyrical expression, notably the love duet in the first act, will be obvious to everybody. Those familiar with Italian will further appreciate the great beauty of his verses; alike where they translate or supplement Shakspere, they are not unworthy of the original.

As we have already seen, Verdi's definite ideal in setting this libretto to music was to give to Boïto's verses "the most true and significant accents possible." There was nothing new in the ideal itself, but the nature of the subject and the literary quality necessitated rather different handling. The extent of the difference has, on the whole, been exaggerated, though Verdi himself seems to have been conscious of a certain sense of experiment. Some critics have written as if *Otello* were, *sui generis*, in a category apart from any of its predecessors; which seems to me true only of its merits, not of its general characteristics. *Otello* marks the culmination of an existing ideal, the perfection of an already established procedure rather than a revolutionary departure. Because we find in it a complete mastery of passion expressing an ideal fusion of voice and orchestra, a superior power and flexibility of dramatic declaration, a perfect blend of aria and recitative, we are not obliged to define these qualities as in themselves new. Pages of *Aïda*, even of *Don Carlo*, *Boccanegra*, *Rigoletto*, *La Traviata*, *Macbeth*, are there to show that harmonic expressiveness, effective fusion of voice and orchestra, powerful and flexible dramatic declamation, successful blending of aria and recitative, existed before *Otello*. Only they were never before displayed so consistently, in such masterly guise. Much has been made of the absence of set numbers in *Otello*, but this is due to circumstances arising from the nature of the subject as much as to deliberate design. Shakspere's *Othello* has appeared to at least one critic, not altogether without reason, as very unpromising material for music owing to the scant opportunities for lyrical expression. Thanks to Boïto's skill, these are emphasized and notably increased in the opera libretto, and Verdi, we may observe, fastened on them with satisfaction. Where Shakspere or Boïto allows him to write an aria, such as Desdemona's "*Salce*" in the last, or Iago's drinking-song in the first, act; where he can contrive a formal duet like that between Otello and Desdemona or Otello and Iago; where he can justify a regular ensemble or a set chorus — he does so without shame or hesitation. But the rapidity and subtlety of the action mainly prevented such indulgence. Led by his unerring instinct, he knew he had to concentrate on achieving the maximum of expression in the setting of the dialogue, and to this he devoted the accumulated experience of a lifetime, bending his unparalleled melodic gift to the service of perfect declamation, forcing his comparatively new-found mastery of the orchestra to rival, though never to supersede, his lifelong insight into the potentialities of the human voice.

As in the best passages of *Aïda*, he used natural phenomena or theatrical effectiveness to reinforce the inner psychology of the drama. This is evident at once in the great storm with which the opera immediately opens. The culmination of many storms in previous operas — does not the piccolo repeat for us the very lightning of *Rigoletto*? — this stupendous outburst, in which all available instruments, including the pedals of the organ, are employed, interprets not only the fury of the elements but the anxiety of the spectators. As an example of musical construction it is magnificent. These rushing semiquavers and staccato quaver-triplets, interrupted from time to time by a broad vocal phrase such as that of the basses in the

"*Fende l'etra*" passage; the harsh insistence of the brass before "*Dio, fulgor della bufera*"; the occasional lulls contrasting with the din that precedes and follows them — all these are welded into a whole that keeps us agog with excitement until Otello's entrance on the shout of "*Esultate*" that announces his safety and the destruction of the Turkish fleet. Even then the storm is not over, the breathless "*Vittoria! Sterminio!*" chorus — except for the choral writing in the "Revolt" scene in *Don Carlo* a new kind of treatment on Verdi's part — and the pages that follow serving as a kind of extended coda.

The musical portraiture of Iago, the most vivid as well as the most subtle characterization in the opera, begins at once in the dialogue with Roderigo, the phrase that sets the word "*Ed io rimango di sua Moresca Signoria l'alfiere*" translating his smooth cynicism, the quick leap down of an octave in the orchestra at the conclusion of a remark (used profusely throughout) illustrating perhaps his sarcastic nonchalance. The so-called "Fire Chorus" is essentially an intermezzo, which might almost be termed an orchestral scherzo, in that the principal interest lies in the orchestra rather than the chorus. After the *Sturm und Drang* that has gone before, its delicate freshness is doubly welcome, enhanced by the writing for the wood-wind, the *pianissimo* passage for violins that accompanies the words "*E son fanciulle dai lieti canti*," the lyrical grace of all the orchestration from the E-major section to the end of the number. The famous drinking song, though in itself one of the best examples of its kind, is something more than it appears to be, in that here for the first time, in the chromatic cadence, we catch a glimpse of that definite Mephistophelian quality which has been singled out as the main difference between the Iagos of Shakspere and Boïto. In fact, though probably a coincidence, the affinity of the song with some of Mephistopheles's music in Berlioz's *Faust* seems obvious. The duet between Otello and Desdemona, which, after the admirably succinct duel between Cassio and Montano, occupies the rest of the act, is the high-water mark of Verdi's love music. It has everything: perfection of melody, harmony, orchestration, and construction. The student should notice how the classical placidity of the preceding page insensibly, with the same orchestral figure, dissolves into the atmosphere of sentiment when husband and wife are left alone. Then, with the change of key and the new figure given to divided cellos, comes that mood of melting tenderness which persists throughout, now interpreted by the orchestra, as in the theme associated with the kiss of Otello; now by the voice, as in the melody that sets the words "*E tu m'amavi per le mie sventure*" or in Otello's "*Scendean sulle mie tenebre*"; now by harmonic effect, such as that at the miraculous moment when Desdemona says how sweet it is to whisper together: "Do you remember? . . ." Had Verdi written nothing else, these pages would almost have sufficed to rank him with Mozart and Wagner as one of the three supreme opera composers. They are the ideal interpretation of true love in music, possibly too ethereal for lovers so physical as Otello and Desdemona must have been. Nevertheless, it is in the spoiling of this beautiful thing that lies the real tragedy we know is coming, and the reference to it in the music of the last act, when the tragedy has taken place, is of a poignancy that could never be conveyed by mere words.

The second act belongs almost entirely to Otello and Iago — especially Iago, now, in the famous *"Credo,"* openly Mephistopheles, just as the seemingly innocuous turn that has played so important a part in the accompaniment of the opening scene with Cassio here first stands revealed in all its blatant malignity. The *"Credo"* has always been exceptionally popular, partly because of the militant wickedness of its sentiments, partly because of the opportunities it offers to a fine singer. But it is less subtle than most of the music in *Otello*, being in fact little more than an apotheosis of melodramatic villainy. Technically, needless to say, it is beyond praise. To set these words at all must have been very difficult. To find such potent musical phrases for them, set off by such striking orchestration as that, for instance, of the opening shake or the passage that illustrates the worm that is man's ultimate destiny, argues supreme craftsmanship. Nevertheless, the succeeding duet between Otello and Iago seems to me more interesting. Apart from what may be called its high lights, such as the passage in which Iago paints the monstrosity of jealousy, its plasticity throughout, alike in the vocal and orchestral writing, is extraordinary, every change of mood, every subtlety of idea, being exactly followed. The serenade to Desdemona, with its scoring for pipes, mandolins, and guitars, though pretty and effctive, is as music perhaps the least inspired thing in the opera; it serves its purpose little more. Wholly admirable, however, is the manner in which Iago's repeated admonition to Otello, *"Vigilate,"* is, so to say, carried over into the opening phrases, while the principal accompaniment figure is worked at its conclusion into a long, delicate cadence for violins not unlike a well-known passage at the end of the second act of *Die Meistersinger*.

In the music preceding the quartet during which Iago snatches the handkerchief, Desdemona's first premonition of her fate at the words *"Perchè torbida suona la voce tua?"* immediately attracts attention, while in the quartet itself Verdi shows something more than his usual mastery in differentiating the emotions of the characters: the pathetic humility of Desdemona, the reluctance of Emilia, the suspiciousness of Otello, the insistence of Iago. Despite the orchestral effectiveness of the C-flat passage describing his farewell to arms in the popular *"Ora e per sempre addio"* section, Otello's music is perhaps most remarkable in the previous *"M'hai legato alla croce,"* whereof the sense is translated almost realistically into sound, and in the subsequent crescendo on the strings, *"staccato e tremolo,"* worked up to a climax of the full orchestra as he throws Iago to the ground. Iago's revenge, first prepared in the significant *"Avvinti vederli forse?"* to the accompaniment of two quavering flutes, reaches its zenith in the description of Cassio's dream. This is a wonderful piece of music, the voluptuous atmosphere being unmistakably suggested by the orchestra while the vocal line, beautiful in itself, delicately stresses every shade of insinuation in the text, differentiates unmistakably Iago's story and Cassio's talk in his sleep. So marvelously is it all done that when, after the words, *"Il rio destino impreco che al Moro ti donò,"* the strings enter *dolcissimo,* we know at once by the changed feeling that the dream is over, even before the text tells us so. It may be doubted whether any fusion of voice, orchestra, and text has ever been more perfect than this. The next few pages are in essence a preparation for the great final duet in which the composer of *Otello* showed, perhaps deliberately, that he was not ashamed of the composer of *Rigoletto* or even of *Attila* and *Ernani.* Fundamentally, its æsthetic is identical, provoking the same kind of thrill in the same kind of way. Only the tune in which Otello and Iago vow vengeance has a new nobility and is reinforced by an orchestral sonority, not to say tumult, that would have driven a mid-nineteenth-century audience out of the theater.

Whereas the second act, as Bellaigue has well said, is fundamentally a struggle not only between Otello and Iago but between two tendencies in Otello himself, the third act shows Iago triumphant, Otello convinced. We do not realize it at once. The short prelude, based on the fine theme that fortunately did not become a "jealousy motif," still suggests only dark suspicions. In the duet between Desdemona and Otello he answers the tender phrases that so exquisitely convey her innocence in a tone of what may be called polite skepticism, only the orchestra revealing at times his latent fury. It is not till Desdemona's constant (and rather maddening) reiterations of her plea for Cassio, met by his repeated demands for the handkerchief, that Otello finally abandons all resistance to his jealousy. Perhaps the moment may be precisely indicated in the passage beginning *"Alza quegli occhi,"* when the violins and violas play a chromatic, descending scale similar to that which accompanies Rigoletto's denunciation of the courtiers. At the words *"Giura e ti danna"* any pretense of control is gone; Otello is as good as mad; Iago, though absent, remains the undisputed master of the situation. In the anguish of *"Esterrefatta fisso,*" with its somber pulsating accompaniment on bassoons, horns, and trombones borrowed from the last act of *La Traviata*, in the simple pathos of "*Io prego il cielo*" Desdemona still pleads; in the furious, highly expressive "*Dio mi potessi scagliar,*" scored in so original and effective a fashion, working up through the poignant phrase that accompanies the words "*Tu alfin, Clemenza,*" to the hysteria of his cries for proof and confession, Otello still writhes. But we do not need Iago's entrance, announcing Cassio, to know that the victory is his. He immediately takes command musically as well as dramatically, for he is the pivot of the scene when the concealed Otello listens to his conversation with Cassio. As an essay in characterization the whole scene is admirable. First, we sense the false good-fellowship of Iago, then his false gaiety when he begins to question Cassio about his amours with Bianca. Next, in the section based on a 6/8 theme redolent of the early eighteenth century (which, incidentally, when it modulates into C-flat major, furnishes two of the most delightful pages in the whole score), we feel the fatuous complacency of Cassio, the anguish of Otello, the delight of Iago, who brings his devilish work to an end in a lighthearted *Allegro brillante* definitely prophetic of *Falstaff*.

The trumpet-call that interrupts the trio may be considered the foundation-stone of the great edifice of sound that brings the act to a close. As the calls grow in number and intensity the dialogue moves swiftly on, sometimes to orchestral accompaniment, sometimes to the accompaniment of the stage-calls themselves. After the pomp and circumstance of the entry of the Venetian envoys and chorus there should be noted the charm of the music built on Desdemona's naïve "*Credo che in grazia tornerà,*" the blind fury of Otello's fine declamation, half addressed to the crowd, half, aside, to Desdemona, culminating in the rush of violins when he throws her to the ground. Then the final ensemble begins with a significant *pizzicato* on the lower strings, over which the oboes, clarinets, bassoon, and horn present a *cantabile* theme identical with the opening of the first subject in the last movement of Mozart's "Jupiter" Symphony. Out of these and Desdemona's subsequent "*E un dì sul mio sorriso,*" the complicated structure is fashioned with marvelous skill, practically all the music except a short unaccompanied quartet being ultimately referable to them. Study of the score reveals the fact that the personalities of the different characters, Iago especially, are faithfully reproduced throughout but in performance such details are apt to be lost in the overwhelming effect of the whole. After the ensemble Otello, now completely out of his mind, curses Desdemona, the three trombones holding E flat against the shake of cornets and trumpets in F-sharp major; the full orchestra paints his delirium as the horrified spectators leave him alone; in broken, panting rhythms alike of voice and instruments he falls fainting to the ground. With the sinister trill that has played so important a part in the vocal characterization, Iago, now visibly as well as psychologically the master, indicates scornfully the prostrate embodiment of the "Lion of Venice" whom the fanfares and chorus in the castle continue to acclaim. It is the one touch of undiluted musical theatricalism in *Otello*. Heaven be praised for the intuitive genius that prevented Verdi and Boïto from being ashamed of it!

In the French version of the opera this third act ensemble is altered in several respects. For instance, the bass figure at the opening is treated rather differently, the harmony varied, and the whole considerably curtailed, the unaccompanied quartet and all the very intricate contrapuntal writing that follows it being omitted. Speaking generally — though in fact there exist divergencies of detail — the versions correspond up to the eighth bar after letter K in the vocal score, and from letter O to the end of the number. The change was possibly due to Verdi's distrust of the capacity of the choristers at the Paris Opéra to tackle successfully the great vocal difficulties of the music. Outside Italy the ensemble is often much curtailed in any event, so that the alterations made in the Paris version deserve attention. Ballet music was also written for Paris, being inserted before the entrance of the Venetian envoys; in fact, five bars before letter C. It consists of four numbers, a Turkish dance, an Arab dance, a Greek dance, and a dance for Venetian sailors called "La Muranese," none of which seems quite worthy of the rest of the opera, though there is an amusing experiment in Oriental scales in the Turkish, and an attractive grace in the Greek, dance. All, it must be added, are delightfully scored. I cannot think, however, that the general merits of the ballet are such as to justify the holding up of the action at this point.

To write about the fourth act is difficult. There are certain technical points that may be stressed, such as the lovely use of the cor anglais at the beginning, one of the comparatively few occasions when that instrument, unaccompanied, does not remind the listener of the last act of *Tristan*. The curious recourse to the then exceptional four-stringed double-basses, too, in that recitative which first introduces the theme associated with Otello's contemplation of the sleeping Desdemona; the admirable conciseness with which the action is translated into music; the simplicity and clarity of the scoring throughout; above all, perhaps, the insight shown in leaving the climax of the dialogue between Emilia and Otello unaccompanied — all these may be adduced as evidence of craftsmanship. Nor should the apparent simplicity of the familiar "*Salce*" lead us to overlook the consummate skill with which Verdi therein differentiated Desdemona, Barbara, and the refrain. Indeed, he himself wrote that the necessity for such differentiation made the composition as well as the interpretation of the song exceptionally difficult.

But it is the poetry of the whole conception that is in reality the keynote of the act, a poetry lovely in itself and made lovelier still by contrast with the brutality and horror that have gone before. Heard anywhere, Desdemona's *"Salce"* and *"Ave Maria"* are beautiful; heard in their proper position in the opera, their beauty becomes uncanny, just as her outburst when she bids farewell to Emilia acquires from its situation a scarcely bearable poignancy. Nor is the final scene inferior in this respect. The suggestion conveyed to a sensitive imagination by the repetition of the theme in which was embodied all Otello's and Desdemona's happiness has already been emphasized. To my mind, however, the most beautiful, the most moving passage of the opera is when Otello cries to the dead Desdemona: *"E tu . . . Come sei pallida! E stanca, e muta e bella!"* In this single line of music, half sung, half sobbed, without accompaniment of any kind, lies the kernel of the whole tragedy.

In my view *Otello* is the greatest of Verdi's operas. Owing to its wonderful sense of form, its unparalleled technical skill, musicians have as a rule ranked *Falstaff* first. There exist, however, qualities in a work of art more important than what may be called its professional attributes. All things said and done, the greater nobility of the theme of *Otello* must be taken into account. Have the love, the anguish, the passion, and the hatred of human beings ever been presented to an audience with deeper insight or poignancy than in this music? I think not. Shakspere himself did not do, could not have done, better.

FALSTAFF

Libretto by Boïto

Production: MILAN, February 9, 1893

THREE ACTS, SIX SCENES

In a room of the Garter Inn at Windsor Sir John Falstaff (baritone) sits drinking with his minions, Bardolfo and Pistola. Dr. Caius (tenor) enters and threateningly asks Falstaff whether it was he who broke into his house and beat his servants. Falstaff, at first taking no notice, eventually condescends to reply airily that it was, but that Dr. Caius, if he values his skin, would be well advised to do nothing in the matter. Dr. Caius then complains that on the previous night

Falstaff

Bardolfo and Pistola made him drunk and then rifled his pockets. Falstaff, after pretending to inquire seriously into the facts, strenuously denied by both rascals, with mock solemnity dismisses both the case and Dr. Caius, who departs vowing that he will never be drunk again "but in honest, civil, godly company." When he has gone, Falstaff rates his followers for their bad artistry and turns to considerations of finance. There is no money left; Bardolfo and Pistola cost too much. True, Bardolfo's red nose has saved "a thousand marks in links and torches," but the sack he has drunk more than counterbalances the economy. If Falstaff grows thin he is no longer himself; the situation must be dealt with. There are two women in Windsor, one, Alice (soprano), the wife of Ford (baritone), the other, Meg (mezzo-soprano), the wife of Page, who have bestowed admiring glances on his great body; both have the keys of their husbands' coffers; two profitable love-affairs seem indicated, so Bardolfo and Pistola are to take to Meg and Alice two letters that he has written. To Falstaff's disgust, both refuse, pretending that such a commission is incompatible with their honor. Then Falstaff, dispatching the letters by the page of the inn, treats them to a discourse on so-called honor. What have such as they to do with honor? What is honor anyhow "Can honor set to a leg? No." Or "take away the grief of a wound? No. What is that word, 'honor'? Air. Honor is a mere scutcheon" of no interest to him. At last, turning on the knaves, he angrily chases them from the room.

In the second scene, outside Ford's house, Alice and Meg have received the letters, which under a pledge of secrecy they compare and find identical except for the names. Alice's daughter, Nannetta (soprano), and Mistress Quickly (mezzo-soprano) are taken into their confidence; whereupon all determine to join in making a fool of the fat knight. As they move away, Ford enters, accompanied by Bardolfo, Pistola, Dr. Caius, and Fenton (tenor). All are talking to him at once about the iniquities of Falstaff, for Bardolfo and Pistola have told the story of the letter which as men of honor they refused to convey to Alice. Pistola in particular emphasizes Falstaff's indiscriminate gallantry — "he loves the gallimaufry" — and bids Ford "have open eye" with regard to his wife, which Ford, incurably jealous in any case, savagely vows to do. The women return for a moment, passing out one way, while the men go another. Nannetta and Fenton, however, stay behind to snatch a kiss under the trees. Alice, Meg, and Mistress Quickly come back, their plans made. Mistress Quickly shall go to Falstaff to make an appointment for him to pay Alice a visit, when they will teach him a lesson. Perceiving Fenton in the distance and afraid that they are being spied upon, they depart; whereupon Fenton seizes the opportunity to make love again to his Nannetta. But their charming flirtation is soon interrupted by the return of the other men. Ford has arranged with Bardolfo and Pistola to present himself under a false name to Falstaff so as to discover the true state of affairs and lay a trap for the old knight. The women, too, return to take part in an ensemble wherein all the characters express their points of view, and, after the men have withdrawn, the act ends with the dispatch of Mistress Quickly on her mission, a parody of the ridiculous declarations of love in Falstaff's letter, and a general laugh as the women take leave of one another.

The second act shows the return of the ostensibly penitent Bardolfo and Pistola to their master as he sits drinking at the Garter. Falstaff pays little attention to them, but on their saying that a woman waits to see him, bids them show her in. Mistress Quickly, apparently the very embodiment of humility and respect, enters, bearing messages from Alice and Meg. Sick with love for him, Alice wishes Sir John to be told that her husband is always absent from two to three, when she will be glad to receive him; Meg, no less lovesick, regrets to inform him that her husband is rarely away from home. Falstaff asks Mistress Quickly whether the two women have not perchance confided in each other, but she, by a vivid portrayal of their charms and judicious flattery of his own irresistible physical attractions, allays all suspicions. Dismissing her with a reward and a promise not to fail in his duty as a man, Falstaff exults in his success. "Old Jack, go thy ways. Good body, I thank thee!" Bardolfo then returns to announce a certain Fontana, who would be glad to make his acquaintance and offers a demijohn of Cyprus wine for his refreshment. Falstaff, replying that "such Brooks are welcome that o'erflow such liquor," bids him be shown in. Fontana, who is none other than Ford disguised, enters escorted by Bardolfo and Pistola, proclaims himself a man of substance desirous to secure Falstaff's assistance in a private matter of great delicacy. Falstaff, dismissing his followers, who have with secret merriment been watching him fall into the trap, then informs Ford that he can tell his story. Ford, with much parade of a bag of money placed at Falstaff's disposal, relates how there lives at Windsor a certain lady called Alice Ford with whom he is passionately but hopelessly in love. Whatever gifts he lavishes upon her, whatever money he spends, she will pay no heed to him; he is left outside to sing a madrigal. Falstaff chaffingly takes the cue:

"Love like a shadow flies when substance love pursues
Pursuing that that flies, and flying what pursues."

Ford repeats the song, which Falstaff interrupts to ask if he has "received no promise of satisfaction at her hands." Ford says that he has not, which is in fact the reason why he has come to ask for help. Falstaff is a great gentleman, a soldier and a man of the world; let him spend all the money he will on condition he promises to "lay an amiable siege" to Alice. When she has once fallen, his opportunity will come; she will no longer be able to use her virtue as a defense. Falstaff takes the money with an assurance that Fontana shall win Ford's wife. Will not he himself be with her, "by her own appointment," in half an hour? As for Ford, Fontana soon "shall know him for a knave and a cuckold." He then goes out to don his finery while Ford, distraught with jealousy, gives vent to his bitterness, cursing marriage and the whole race of women. "Cuckold! The devil himself hath not such a name. . . . I will rather trust a Fleming with my butter, an Irishman with my aqua-vitæ bottle, than my wife with herself. . . . God be praised for my jealousy!" Falstaff returns in his finest clothes; Ford offers to put him on his way, and the scene ends with the ceremonious refusal of each of the two men to take precedence over the other by passing first through the door — a problem eventually solved by both going out together.

The second scene is laid in Ford's house, where Alice and Meg await the return of Quickly, who arrives almost at once to tell the tale of her successful mission. Alice, hearing that Falstaff may arrive at any moment, bids her servants bring in the linen-basket. Suddenly aware that Nannetta is crying instead of sharing in the general fun, she asks what is the matter. Nannetta replies that her father wishes her to marry Dr. Caius and that she would rather be stoned to death. Comforted, however, by the assurance of help from her mother and the other women, she has quite recovered her spirits when the servants bring in the basket, and all proceed gaily to arrange the scene for the reception of Sir John, with Alice's lute on the table, the screen opened to its fullest extent, the servants outside awaiting Alice's summons to enter, take the basket, and throw it in the ditch. Presently, on the approach of Falstaff, the women run to their arranged positions, Alice remaining alone in the room and playing on the lute. Falstaff enters. "Have I caught my heavenly jewel? Why, now let me die, for I have lived long enough." He then proceeds to court her. How gladly would he see Ford dead and her his lady, loaded with rich jewels! Alice with mock coquetry answers that she prefers a simple flower in her hair to jewelry; he sins in loving her. Falstaff, trying to kiss her, replies that he cannot help himself; there is no sin in following an irresistible vocation. He was not always fat; in his youth, as page to the Duke of Norfolk, he was so slender and supple that he could have passed through a ring. Then Alice, changing her tactics, charges him with deceiving her and being in reality in love with Meg. Falstaff, with a protest that he loathes her very face, proceeds to bolder love-making; but at that moment Mistress Quickly, in a state of simulated agitation, enters to say that Meg wishes most urgently to speak with Alice. Falstaff hides himself behind the screen, while Meg, as previously arranged, informs Alice that Ford has raised a hue and cry throughout Windsor and, with fury in his heart and curses on his lips, is running to the house to discover the lover whom he believes to be concealed there. Then Quickly returns, genuinely agitated this time, to say that Ford, followed by a crowd of men, is already in the garden. Alice is not sure at first whether to believe her or not, but the sound of Ford's voice outside puts an end to all doubt, and Falstaff, who has made a move to escape, is again concealed behind the screen. Ford and the men enter. While he dispatches the others to search the house and guard the doors, he himself, suspecting that Falstaff may be hidden in the basket, scatters the dirty linen on the floor. Finding nothing, he rushes off to join in the general search. Alice and Meg take advantage of the respite to suggest that Falstaff shall get into the basket. Alice is doubtful whether his great bulk will permit of it, but Falstaff in terror insists on his ability to do so and eventually succeeds, even finding occasion, when Alice has gone to call the servants, to whisper to the reproachful Meg that he loves her alone. As the women cover him with the "foul linen," Fenton and Nannetta steal in. They have taken advantage of the hurly-burly to snatch a few moments together and disappear behind the screen. Ford and the men return, looking in the chimney, forcing open the cupboard. During a lull in the hubbub the noise of a kiss is heard from behind the screen. Ford, noting the absence of Alice, jumps to the conclusion that she is concealed there with Falstaff. He bids all the men make ready, and after a rapid ensemble for everybody — even Falstaff in his basket and the lovers in their hiding-place — he upsets the screen to discover, to his fury, Nannetta and her forbidden lover. They separate, covered with confusion, but at that moment Bardolfo and Pistola, mistaking the retreating Fenton for Falstaff, cry out that the knight is on the stairs; whereupon all the men rush in pursuit of him. Alice, who has returned in time for the discovery of Fenton and Nannetta, calls in the servants and bids them empty the basket and its contents from the window into the ditch. Then, sending for Ford and taking his arm, she leads him to the window to enjoy the ridiculous spectacle below; jealousy finally vanishes in a general burst of laughter.

When the curtain rises on the third act, Falstaff, much dejected, is discovered outside the Garter, calling for mulled wine. He reviles the world and his misfortune. "Have I lived to be carried in a basket and to be thrown into the Thames?" His spirits revive, however, as he drinks the wine and he starts a veritable pæan in praise of it, interrupted by the arrival of Mistress Quickly, who states that she bears a message from Alice. The very mention of the name throws Falstaff into a rage. He recalls all his discomfort, but Quickly, with a vivid description of Alice's despair, soon manages to convince him of her innocence in the matter and gives him a letter to read wherein she asks Falstaff to meet her at midnight in the Great Park by Herne's Oak, disguised as the Black Hunter. Quickly explains that Alice, in order to see him, is taking advantage of the popular legend about Herne and the oak, so Falstaff leads her into the inn to discuss the matter further — to the joy of Ford and the others who have crept in during the interview to watch the progress of their plot. When the coast is clear and Ford has been plainly told by Alice that his jealous suspicions deserve a very different reward, she proceeds to arrange the details of Falstaff's punishment, suggesting that all appear to him in the guise of the characters associated with the legend of Herne's Oak. Nannetta shall be Queen of the Fairies, Meg a woodland nymph, Quickly a witch; she herself will collect children to play the parts of fairies, sprites, imps, and so on, who at a given signal must set on Falstaff and torment him till he confesses his sins. While the women are giving each other final injunctions, Ford whispers to Dr. Caius that this will be an admirable opportunity to solve the problem of Nannetta's marriage. Let Dr. Caius remember her disguise, and then at the end of the fun they can both appear before him with their faces masked and he will declare them man and wife. The plan, however, has been overheard by Mistress Quickly, who, as night falls on the now deserted street, hastens away to reveal it to Alice.

The second act shows Windsor Forest at night with the moon slowly rising. Fenton, who has arrived in advance of the other conspirators, muses on the mystery of love. Hearing Nannetta's voice, he hastens to meet her, but is stopped by Alice, who bids him immediately change his disguise and put on the monk's gown and mask she has brought with her. The bewildered Fenton obeys, Alice merely explaining that Ford's double-dealing will now turn against himself, Quickly adding that the sham bride has been arranged for. Meg arrives to report that the children are hidden in the ditch, and at the sound of Falstaff's approach all scatter to their respective positions. Midnight strikes as Sir John enters, dressed as Herne, a pair of antlers on his head. He implores the aid of Jupiter, who, for love's sake, also suffered himself to be changed into a beast. Alice enters and he makes love to her, but she tells him that they are not alone! Meg has followed her. Falstaff is delighted at the double adventure. "Why, now is Cupid a child of conscience; he makes restitution." Meg's voice is heard crying that the fairy rout approaches; whereupon Alice, simulating terror and praying that her sins may be forgiven, runs away while Falstaff, comforted only by the conviction that "the devil will not have him damned," flattens himself as best he may against the trunk of the oak. Nannetta's voice is heard summoning the fairies. This completes the discomfiture of Falstaff, who prostrates himself face downwards on the ground, moaning that death awaits anyone who sees the fairies. Nannetta appears with her attendants. She sings the Fairy Queen's song that she has learned; the fairies dance. Presently, in various disguises, the other characters enter, pretending horror at the presence of such an impure monster. Alice finds occasion to whisper to Nannetta to keep away from Dr. Caius and to remain in hiding with Fenton till she calls her. Then, while the men preform rites of exorcism over Falstaff's body, the children pinch him, tickle him, climb over and dance on him till he is well-nigh distraught. Bardolfo and Pistola take the opportunity to give their master a good beating; the women chant a mock litany for his repentance, but eventually Falstaff recognizes Bardolfo, whose hood has fallen off in the excitement, and gives furious chase to him. Quickly whisks him away behind a tree, saying that she will conceal him under a white veil. Everybody present unmasks, when Falstaff delightedly greets Ford, whom he still imagines to be Fontana. Alice, however, at once undeceives him, while Quickly asks how he could think two women so foolish as to imperil their souls and bodies for such a dirty, fat old man. Falstaff admits that he has been "made an ass," but recovers his spirits and self-esteem by pointing out that without him and his nimble wit the joke could never have taken place. Ford then proposes that the revelry shall be crowned with the wedding of the Fairy Queen, while Alice asks that another pair of lovers may also take advantage of the occasion. Ford willingly consents and pronounces both couples man and wife. But when, at his order, the couples unmask, Dr. Caius's bride is found to be Bardolfo, and the other pair none other than his daughter and her forbidden lover. It is now Falstaff's turn to laugh at Ford, who, seeing that there is nothing for it but to make the best of a bad business, forgives Nannetta and Fenton and proposes that they shall all go home to supper. So the opera ends with a formal fugue on the theme that man is born a jester in a world that is one great jest; he laughs best who laughs last.

Little need be added to what has been said previously about Boïto's amazing ingenious libretto, which, as will be obvious to every reader familiar with Shakspere, shows considerable divergence from *The Merry Wives of Windsor*. Apart from the monologue on honor, the description of Bardolph's nose, and other borrowings from the Falstaff of *Henry IV*, there are many changes, mostly in the way of omission, but partly of invention as well. For instance, the number of characters as of incidents is considerably reduced. Thus, Page goes altogether, as do Evans and Shallow. Dr. Caius in the opera is a kind of amalgam of Dr. Caius and Slender in the play; Falstaff pays one visit instead of two to Alice's house, the searching of the basket being an addition from the omitted episode; Ford, masquerading as Brook, comes only once to see Falstaff, and so on. The most important inventions are to be found in the comedy of Falstaff and Ford at the end of their interview; in the charming love-passages of Nannetta and Fenton, which scarcely exist in Shakspere in all the business with the screen in the second act; in many details of the final scene.

All Boïto's changes may not be improvements. It would be unwise, for instance, to inquire too closely into the legality of the double marriage at the end of the opera, whereas in *The Merry Wives* Slender, Dr. Caius, and Fenton all go to Eton or Windsor to get married. Nor can any Anglo-Saxon help regretting "Sweet Anne Page," not so much because of her change into Ann Ford as of the long association of the phrase with the ridiculous Slender. Nevertheless, on the whole, *Falstaff* is a better comedy than *The Merry Wives of Windsor*, in that the action sprawls less, the intrigue is more tidy and concentrated. Moreover, the character of Falstaff, though perhaps somewhat Latinized, possesses greater interest. He may remain a buffoon but he is not a mere buffoon like the Falstaff of *The Merry Wives*, for Boïto, in his desire to provide Verdi with a "type" (in the French sense of the word), drew nearer to the Falstaff of *Henry IV*. The literary quality of the dialogue has been universally commended and the profusion of recondite words or expressions will only disturb those exceptionally familiar with current Italian.

It may seem a paradox, it is none the less a fact, that *Falstaff*, indubitably Verdi's technical masterpiece, is the most difficult of all his operas to write about from the technical point of view. Yet the explanation is simple enough: There is so much to discuss — structure, melodic, harmonic, contrapuntal, and rhythmical inventions, orchestration, an intimate wedding of words and music never surpassed in the annals of music — that any adequate analysis seems inseparable from excessive length, from preoccupation with a mass of detail tending to obscure the outlines of the whole. Treatment similar to that of *Don Carlo*, for instance, would imply the indication of points of interest on almost every page. The sole method, therefore, is that of rigid self-control, based on a determination to emphasize only the most salient characteristics. In this opera, constructed essentially out of fragments, little notice can be taken of fragmentary beauties; otherwise there would be no end.

The music of the opening scene with Dr. Caius, Bardolph, and Pistol bears, as Stanford truly pointed out, the imprint of Beethoven. The boisterous main figure itself, with the last quaver accented, is decidedly Beethovenian in character; so is much of its treatment. It should be noted here at once that this theme, though associated with Falstaff's revelry, is never used as a motif. In *Falstaff*, compared with *Otello*, the repetition of themes embodying certain ideas is more marked — for instance Fenton and Nannetta's love, Falstaff's rendezvous with Alice between two and three o'clock, Mistress Quickly's greeting, all have themes — but Falstaff himself has no label except perhaps a constant predilection for the key of C major. Or rather he is constantly changing his labels in accordance with his varying moods. Thus his first theme, after throwing various offshoots — a particularly delightful one should be noted when Bardolph makes Dr. Caius feel his pulse — eventually vanishes for good to give place to another, equally characteristic, that culminates in the acclamation of "*Immenso Falstaff*." The phrase associated with Alice is so tender, especially in that lovely modulation after the passage where, in a glorious ascending sequence, Falstaff preens himself on his irresistible physical charms, that it comes almost as a shock to be reminded by his falsetto phrase, as well as by the twittering music referring to Meg, that it is all nothing but cupboard love. Then, after the delicious scoring when the page is sent off with the letters, comes the famous monologue on honor. Roncaglia has well labeled this the humorous counterpart of Iago's "*Credo*"; the two trills on bass and wood-wind, the grunts on clarinet, bassoon, and *pizzicato* double-bass after each one of Falstaff's queries as to the practical advantages of honor, are sufficient warning for us not to take it seriously. The scene ends with a passage so reminiscent of Rossini that I like to think of it as a deliberate and sly reminder to the spirit of "Signor Crescendo" that Verdi, after all, had succeeded in writing a comic opera.

The gaiety of the wood-wind that ushers in the second part indicates the change of atmosphere at once — a typical instance of that orchestral characterization which is so noticeable a feature of the opera as a whole. We sense the mischievous laughter of the Merry Wives, their chatter, their sense of fun, associated generally with a 6/8 rhythm in which Verdi here achieves a distinction and a variety particularly rare. Perhaps the gem of this scene is the unaccompanied quartet, a miracle of light-heartedness, but, with the exception of the figure (possibly derived from the opening theme) to which Falstaff's letters are read and that amusing passage where to the words *"E il viso tuo su me risplenderà"* Verdi parodies himself, making Alice a caricature of all his tragic heroines, the music throughout just trips and sparkles alike in voice and orchestra. With the entrance of the men the predominant rhythm changes to 2/2, though the women still cling to their 6/8, the resulting nonet being not only one of the most brilliant things in the opera but one of the most brilliant things ever written. Generically a descendant of the ensembles of Cimarosa and Pergolese, it looks exceedingly complicated on paper, but in performance it sounds crystal-clear. The love duet between Fenton and Nannetta comes as a kind of interlude. This exquisite music consists essentially of two themes; the first, *"Labbra di foco,"* richly harmonized *à la* Wagner, the second, *"Bocca baciata non perde ventura,"* unaccompanied. As an embodiment of tenderness and the charm of youth it is worthy to stand beside the love music of *Otello.* There is, too, a delicious flavor of wistfulness, enhanced by the manner in which the lovers, during the bustle, seize every opportunity to repeat it. This is perhaps the only operatic music in which the love of boy and girl is adequately interpreted in accordance not only with Latin but with Anglo-Saxon ideals. Lovely though it is, the music of Eva and Walther in *Meistersinger,* of Oktavian and Sophie in *Rosenkavalier,* appears too Teutonic, too lush in sentiment. Next comes a repetition of the nonet (Fenton, however, maintaining his sentimental mood), which is worked up to a new climax with some wonderful scoring for the brass; Alice, now joined by the other women, repeats her parodical phrase, and the act comes to an end in a burst of laughter.

In the scene between Falstaff and Mistress Quickly in the first part of the second act the subtle humor depends mainly on three musical phrases associated with certain ideas: first, Quickly's obsequious *"Reverenza,"* decidedly Rossinian, always accompanied by the strings; then the two triplets that set *"Dalle due alle tre,"* an inspiration of genius if ever there was one, for after hearing it we can never think of the music without the words, while its thematic value is such that in development it makes an admirable accompaniment to the *agitato* section of Falstaff's subsequent speech to Ford. Less important, perhaps, are the notes in which Quickly exclaims *"povera donna"* whenever she is bewailing to Falstaff the parlous condition of Alice or Meg. Like the others, however, though in a lesser degree, it becomes increasingly funny on repetition. Moreover, the sham poignancy of the music that accompanies the words *"Le angoscie sue son crudeli,"* the sham lovesickness of the description of Meg, are altogether admirable. So is Falstaff's ensuing soliloquy, *"Va vecchio John,"* with its intense physical self-satisfaction embedded in the gross insistence of the staccato brass but translated even more emphatically, perhaps, in the flaring passage for full orchestra that introduces and closes it, of which both the scoring and the harmony are beyond praise. The scene with Ford hardly rises to such heights, though many of the details are delightful, as, for instance, the manner in which the orchestra suggests a placidly flowing river when Ford appears under the assumed name of Brook, or the jingling of money when he offers Falstaff his purse. Quite charming, too, are Ford's *"C'è a Windsor una donna"* and the madrigal *"L'amor, l'amor,"* which the two men sing together; while the whole section before Falstaff goes out "to make himself beautiful," culminating in the significant phrase *"Te lo cornifico,"* is a masterpiece of writing in what may be called the tradition of classical Italian comic opera. Another point, sometimes overlooked, is that Ford, too, appears to parody his emotional predecessors at the words *"Per te sprecai tesori"*; more obviously, indeed, it seems to me, than in the great ensuing "jealousy" monologue, though the commentators seem to find no difficulty in discovering here humorous reminiscences of *Otello*. It may be so. Passages like *"Le corna! Bue! Capron! Le fusa torte!"* or *"Affiderei la mia birra a un Tedesco"* would doubtless not have been found in an essay in serious declamation, and the fact that the phrase before *"L'ora è fissata"* is played on the horns, with a commentary on bassoon and cellos reminding us of *"Dalle due alle tre,"* suggests that its somber, mysterious quality is not to be taken at face value. Divorced from the words, however, the magnificent concluding phrase is about as little humorous as can well be imagined, either in itself or in its accompaniment; while the same is true of *"O matrimonio: Inferno!"* and several other passages. One is inclined to guess that, in setting the words, Verdi found his old instincts taking the bit between their teeth and had to pull them up with a jerk from time to time. Besides, was not the subject cuckoldry, to Latins, as to Elizabethans, funny in any circumstances? Apart from any question of humorous appropriateness, the monologue is of the first order as music; words were never set with more power or incisiveness, with more vivid orchestral comment. After this fierceness, real or sham, the grace of the melody that accompanies the re-entrance of Falstaff in his best clothes is sheer delight; and as to the humor of the music as well as of the situation when the two men bow themselves out of the door together, there can be no doubt whatever.

In the second scene of the act we are back again in the realm of *Il Matrimonio Segreto* and *Così fan Tutte*. Cimarosa and Mozart would have hailed as their own legitimate descendant this bubbling, chattering music wherein the three wives discuss their plan for the discomfiture of Falstaff. The rapid flow is interrupted only by

Quickly's account of her interview (with musical quotations) and a moment of genuine distress on the oboe when Nannetta cries at the prospect of being forced to marry Dr. Caius. The whole scene between Falstaff and Alice, introduced by a few chords on the guitar suggestive of a serenade, is of the first order, his wooing to the words "*T'immagino fregiata del mio stemma*" is ludicrous in itself without the accompanying bassoons; her sham coyness and coquetry are perfectly reflected in the music. But the gem of the scene is, of course, "*Quand'ero paggio*," one of the most exquisite and delicate things ever imagined by any composer; almost too delicate, too exquisite, perhaps, for a sensualist like Falstaff, the contrast between the song and the singer being so striking as to arouse a sense of pity that I can scarcely believe was intended by either composer or librettist. It is all over in a minute and almost at once we hear in the bass a theme of repeated semiquavers, at the same time bustling and ominous, which announces the approach of Ford and his men. Except for a couple of isolated episodes and a brief moment snatched by Fenton and Nannetta for their love-making, practically the whole of the concluding scene is constructed from this, another *staccato* semiquaver theme worked into a regular *moto perpetuo* and a theme in a rhythm that amounts in practice, though not in theory, to 12/8. Every device of tonality, scoring, contrast, or blending is used to achieve a brilliance of effect, a rapidity of movement, exactly suited to artificial comedy; the music flashes past us at the pace of a cinematograph farce till the climax is reached on a great chord of C major when Falstaff is bundled into the river, leaving the listener well-nigh as breathless as the singers themselves.

This ensemble, it should be noted, contains one of the two major alterations made in the score after completion, the music having been rewritten from (63) to three bars before (65), to quote the indications given in the standard vocal score. Verdi, as was his custom, obliterated all traces of the original version.

When we come to the first part of the third act, we feel a kind of *détente*, inevitable in view of the situation, of what has gone before as well as what is going to come after. Indeed, the avoidance of even a suspicion of dullness here is one of the great, if least obvious, strokes of genius in the score. First, we have to thank the effective prelude — incidentally, the only one in the opera — based on the repeated semiquaver theme of the former act; next, Falstaff's declamation, throughout so expressive of the text; the new theme that admirably translates his black mood into music; the happy references in both his monologue and the interview with Mistress Quickly to themes in preceding acts. Moreover, as the opportunity occurs, we have essays in orchestral brilliance such as that so highly praised by

Stanford, when the gradually expanding effect of wine is illustrated by a trill progressively taken up by the whole orchestra, including trombones, trumpets, with big drum *tremolando* — an astonishing piece of virtuosity. The transition to the scene where the other women and men enter is most adroitly carried through in Alice's imitation of Quickly, the scene itself being in the main built round the charming tune: *"Fandonie che ai bamboli"* in 3/4 and the tripping *"Avrò con me dei putti"* in common time. Moreover, towards the end of the scene the orchestra has a descending passage, based on the first of these, which contains what is probably the most lovely harmonic sequence in the opera. In a sense all this scene may be regarded as a parody, delicate as filigree, light as thistledown, of the conspiracies in *Rigoletto* or *Ballo in Maschera*. Here is the second of the alterations already referred to, the music having been revised from Quickly's exit from the inn (20) to the end of the act.

In the last part a distant horn-call suggests at once the eerie atmosphere that serves to frame the beauty of Fenton's love-song, the only aria in the score. It is typical of Verdi's lavishness of melody that, except for a fleeting reference in the introduction, the musical material is wholly new till, at the end, the song glides imperceptibly into the *"Bocca baciata"* theme, now harmonized for the first time. With the entrance of Falstaff, to a suggestive subject on the strings, with the heart-searching harmonies that accompany the striking of midnight, the atmosphere of mystery and fantasy takes first place, hardly disturbed by the piquancy of the brief and breathless wooing of Alice. Up to Falstaff's discovery of the joke played on him all the subsequent music has won universal praise — the call that summons the elves and nymphs, the dance of the little fairies, the accompaniment on divided violins to which Nannetta sings her song as Fairy Queen, above all, perhaps, the *"Pizzica, pizzica"* section, surely one of the most delicious essays in innocent malice ever penned. A charming tune in any case, it is scored with an inventive imagination that is beyond praise. The commentators, headed by Stanford, have rightly emphasized the absolute originality of this music as distinct from the fairy music of Weber and Mendelssohn, but it is worth pointing out, perhaps, that we have here in reality the music not so much of fairies as of pure fancy. Windsor Park might equally well have been the garden at Busseto; the whole conception is one of deliberate artificiality, related more nearly, despite its setting, to the Commedia dell' Arte than to any dramatic product of romanticism. For this reason the final fugue, which has been pilloried as pedantic, is not only justified but wholly, magnificently right, the last breath of living, natural classicism in music as distinct from the self-conscious variety that has now become fashionable. Like all Verdi's fugues it is definitely expressive. Readers of the first part of this book may remember that Giuseppina once wrote of his "great laugh." This is what the music, bubbling with vitality and humor, expresses. The main subject is said to have been suggested to the composer by a tune that a child sang in his garden. Is it too fanciful to imagine the simplicity of extreme age and extreme youth here joining hands to instill in us that sense of divine gaiety which is the best medicine of the soul? In any case one is glad that Verdi finished his operatic career on such a note. Bellaigue most happily illustrates the point when he writes that Verdi precisely reversed the crime of Adam, whom Dante describes as having "changed honest laughter and sweet playfulness into tears and misery."

Nevertheless, *Falstaff* has never captured the heart of the masses and possibly never will. Æsthetically it is too aristocratic; it is wanting in that emotional quality which the public seeks first and foremost in music that does not just titillate the senses. It moves so rapidly that the manifold subtlety of the score, the amazing fertility of ideas, pass almost unnoticed by the layman. *Falstaff* remains, then, among Verdi's operas predominantly the musicians' favorite. Even so, according to J. W. Klein, some musicians have failed to appreciate it. Grieg thought that Verdi's fancy here no longer soared as before; Hanslick considered it more a work of talent than of genius. Such opinions, however, are exceptional. The vast majority of musicians agree with Richard Strauss in his definition of the opera as "one of the greatest masterpieces of all time." It is, moreover, especially important as a link between the early classical opera based on Monteverdi, to which it shows a marked kinship as regards general æsthetic, and the chamber opera that seems likely to establish itself as the main musico-dramatic form of our own time. Inevitably it lacks the humanity of *Otello*, but for characterization within the limits of its convention it could scarcely be bettered. Falstaff's music paints the man to perfection; all the women are admirably differentiated; even the unpleasant Ford possesses a musical personality rare in comic opera. Tribute has already been paid to its superlative technical skill in every department. Only one comic opera by Mozart, one by Rossini, and one by Wagner can rank with it — and, of all these great works, it is certainly not the least in stature.

ECCLESIASTICAL WORKS

A REQUIEM MASS

First Performance: MILAN, May 22, 1874

IT IS of the first importance when approaching the Mass to leave behind certain preconceived opinions as to what is or is not music suitable for ecclesiastical purposes. If a man judges such music by the canons that obtain, for instance, in Anglican cathedrals, he will, *ipso facto*, be repelled by this work. He will, moreover, not be helped by exchanging Westminster Abbey for Westminster Cathedral, where, in accordance with the deliberate cult of the archaic at present in vogue, the contrapuntal austerity of Palestrina and his compeers sets the fashion. The point is not whether this or that school is superior. Verdi himself, be it remembered, showed something like fanaticism in his admiration of Palestrina, proclaiming over and over again his supremacy, his right to occupy in Italian music the position occupied by Bach in Germany.

In my opinion as well as that of many other people, the English cathedral school of music is one of the glories of England though attention is too often concentrated exclusively on the composers of the sixteenth and seventeenth centuries, to the detriment of men like the Wesleys, who possessed genius, and of many isolated compositions by other truly gifted composers. The music of all periods heard in most English cathedrals is not only as a rule good in itself but wholly characteristic and individual, different from anything else in any other country. It is not, therefore, with any desire to belittle traditions, one of which I admire and the other I love greatly, that I venture to assert the right of a composer to write in a style rejected in this country by Anglicans and Catholics alike.

The dramatic setting of liturgical words, then, is alien to us though we show a marked preference for the dramatic setting of sacred subjects in the form of oratorios. It is not, however, alien to other nations. The Requiem Masses of Cherubini and Mozart, the Beethoven Mass in D, even portions of Bach's B Minor Mass, sufficiently attest the fact. The words of the Requiem Mass, in particular when the *Dies Iræ* is included, appeal inevitably to the dramatic sense; otherwise a composer such as Berlioz, who was primarily interested in emotion and color, would never have set them to music. How could they be interpreted in any other way by a man like Verdi, to whom theatrical expression was second nature? As already stated elsewhere, any other kind of setting would have been a proof, not of deep sincerity, but of insincerity, at least of self-conscious pedantry on his part. To worship Palestrina as a master in one particular style was one thing; to copy him deliberately quite another. True, Verdi's familiarity with his music has left its traces on one or two pages of the score, but as a whole the Mass is undiluted Verdi from the first note to the last. And, all things said and done, this is the quality that matters. Molds (which may be taken as synonymous with styles, romantic or classical, descriptive or non-descriptive) change, become unfashionable, and, not infrequently, fashionable again. It is what an artist has poured into the mold that remains of importance.

Perhaps the best way for an Anglo-Saxon to approach the Mass is to think of it as a kind of oratorio, a sacred opera if you will, on the subject of the Last Judgment, with Alessandro Manzoni's soul as the objective theme of the drama, much as the soul of Gerontius is the subjective theme of *The Dream of Gerontius*. It is surprising how readily the music lends itself to visual interpretation. In the opening bars we can imagine the chorus kneeling in whispered prayer for the repose of the soul; the *Kyrie* is a definite appeal for mercy. Directly the *Dies Iræ* begins, we can visualize the scene as vividly as the storm in *Otello*. These great chords, with the big drum punctuating the unaccented beats, the shouting chorus, the rush of strings, the typical piccolo trills, irresistibly suggest darkness and despair. Then, as the first climax passes, the broad rush of the strings is changed to fragmentary runs on the wood-wind, the piccolo to low notes on the flutes and the chorus is left shivering in terror with the words: "*Quantus tremor est futurus.*" Suddenly trumpets sound, first in the orchestra, then from afar (an idea not improbably suggested to Verdi by Berlioz's Mass), growing always in intensity till the chorus basses — we can almost see them rise from the ground! — acclaim the Last Trump on a particularly felicitous chord. The rest of the chorus join them, the trumpet-calls cutting through the while. Then the bass soloist declaims that curious "*Mors stupebit,*" which Verdi himself described as particularly difficult to do well and which possesses more significance than the notes seem to suggest, the soloist not only acting the surprise of death but commenting on it. The mezzo-soprano soloist describes the bringing out of the book wherein the good and evil deeds of men are recorded, the chorus muttering "*Dies iræ*" from time to time. Again the avalanche of terror descends, presently to give place to the lovely trio in 6/8 in which the soloists, with the exception of the bass, lament their unworthiness and apprehension, reinforced by a poignant wail repeatedly insisted upon by the clarinets. The Judge takes his seat, greeted by that magnificent phrase: "*Rex tremendæ majestatis,*" into which Verdi seems to have distilled the very essence of the sound of the words. The basses thunder it, the tenors repeat the words (but not the music) very softly; the soloists beg for salvation, as later do all the chorus with the exception of the basses, who continue their acclamation to the King of Heaven. Particularly interesting here is the manner in which Verdi has dramatized two aspects of the prayer for salvation, the one purely piteous, the other fearful. The soprano and mezzo-soprano appeal to the Redeemer to be mindful of His sacrifice in behalf of mankind, succeeded by the tenor, who sings what can only be called a set aria in the same sense, wherein the wistful beauty of the phrase "*Inter oves locum præsta*," shared by the oboe to the accompaniment of divided violins, is irresistible. The bass soloist, more virile, not afraid to recall the sufferings of the damned, continues the invocation, of which the beautiful "*Ora supplex et acclinis*," with its open fifths and even more, perhaps, the masterly writing for the wood-wind, in which Verdi here achieved, as in *Aïda*, an effort of smoothness all his own, are the outstanding features. Once more the "*Dies Iræ*" cataclysm descends, to give place this time to the mezzo-soprano's *Lacrymosa*, an essay in what may be called the pathos of resignation, but punctuated later, when the bass takes up the theme, by poignant sobs precisely similar to those associated with Violetta in *La Traviata* or Leonora in *La Forza del Destino*. The oboe and the clarinet (directed to play "*come un lamento*") participate in them; even the big drum (*ppp*) takes part in the orchestral lament, which presently merges into an unaccompanied passage of great beauty for the quartet of soloists, one of the few passages in the work where the character is definitely ecclesiastical. The movement ends in the liturgical, devotional atmosphere of the opening: "*Dona eis requiem*." An "*Amen*" on the chord of G major marvelously interrupts for two bars the prevalent tonality of B-flat major, re-established at once by the soft brass, which gives a somber color wholly appropriate and satisfying. The first scene of the drama is at an end.

It is unnecessary to labor the conceit, despite the vivid enthusiasm of the *Sanctus* double chorus, almost as visual in conception as the "Hallelujah Chorus" itself, despite the changing moods of the *Libera me*, with that splendid fugue so dynamic and insistent that one seems to sense the clamor of a multitude intent on achieving salvation by violence. Indeed, it is hardly an exaggeration to say that, by treating the *Offertorium* and perhaps the *Lux Æterna* as meditative entr'actes, an imaginative producer might almost stage the entire Mass, so consistently does the character of the music suggest dramatic action. Little need be written about the *Offertorium*. Apart from four bars of undiluted opera at the words: "*Fac eas, Domine*," it shares with the *Agnus Dei* the distinction of containing the most ecclesiastical music of the score. The beautiful harmonic change at the first entrance of the soprano after the trio, the ethereal ending, when the muted violins hark back to the original subject, exceptionally suggest mysticism. Even the other main subject, "*Quam olim Abrahæ,*" treated canonically, is definitely liturgical. Both movements seem to me to attain something little short of perfection, for the mystical beauty of the *Agnus Dei* has also found fervent admirers and no one could deny its effectiveness after the brilliance of the *Sanctus*. This last has always been one of the movements that the purists have found difficult to digest. To me it seems a masterpiece. Not only is the writing for double chorus superb, with the middle section, "*Pleni sunt cœli,*" in admirable contrast, but the scoring throughout is remarkable. For instance, the working up from a little delicate violin figure at the end of the middle section to the impetuous chromatic scale in quavers, where the whole orchestra accompanies the sustained minims of the choral "*Hosanna*" at the climax, is one of Verdi's master strokes. Played and sung with the requisite fire, the sound evokes a thrill not often experienced in listening to music.

Though the *Lux Æterna* opens rather operatically, with the changing harmonies of the much divided violins suggesting a shimmer of light, the words "*Requiem æternam dona eis*" preserve throughout a distinctly Gregorian flavor, and none of the rest of the music is as theatrical as usual. A notable feature of the movement is again the extremely skillful writing for the wood-wind. There is a notable use of the piccolo in association with the first violins when the theme that sets the words "*Et lux perpetua*" first appears, and the wood-wind embroidery on the repetition of the theme by the bass soloist, not to mention the lovely flute and clarinet figure at the end of the movement, are beautiful examples of workmanship. With the *Libera Me*, a survival, be it remembered, from the original Rossini Requiem, we are back again in the atmosphere of drama. The opening expresses a vague terror that becomes quite precise with the words "*Tremens factus sum,*" culminating in two bars prophetic of the broken-hearted Desdemona. Even the "*Dies Iræ*" phrases are reintroduced to heighten the horror, eventually dying away in a most effective low passage for the basses in alliance with the trombones and bassoons. Then, after the soprano soloist with unaccompanied chorus has recalled to us the opening pages of the work and the introductory recitative has been repeated, we are at the fugue, which is the most important feature of the number. This has received, as it deserves, unstinted admiration from the technical point of view. Perhaps the most remarkable point about it is the poignant effect achieved when the soprano soloist first enters in augmentation, with notes of twice the preceding value; but the whole fugue is charged with an emotional intensity not usually associated with the form, the final section that begins with the words *"Dum veneris"* suggesting almost a threat of conspiracy. Finally, as if to denote the futility of passion and resentment, the mood subsides into one of quiet supplication. Again, as at the opening of the work, the soloists and the chorus are on their knees, whispering the words: *"Libera me, Domine, de morte æterna."* Force has failed; only the appeal to mercy remains, now so abject that it is spoken rather than sung.

Doubtless the Requiem Mass will appear naïve to some people. A phrase, even a word, often suffices to dictate to Verdi the emotional contour of the music. Let those who may be inclined to scoff remember that the same is true of Bach, Handel, and Haydn. Like most great composers Verdi was a simple man, intent on the expression of feeling rather than of abstract thought. If the qualities of intellect and emotion can in reality by separated in music, his Mass shows the latter rather than the former. Acutely sensitive to the drama and color of the words he had to set, animated by a passionate desire to honor the memory of Manzoni, whom he idolized, Verdi here produced a work that may leave something to be desired as an expression in music of ecclesiasticism or even of spirituality, but that, as an interpretation of the hopes and fears of mortal men, could scarcely be more poignant and certainly not more sincere.

AVE MARIA

PATER NOSTER

Words by Dante

Production: MILAN, April 18, 1880

These settings of Italian paraphrases by Dante of the Ave Maria and the Lord's Prayer are not of great importance, though each is skillful and effective in its very diverse way.

The *Ave Maria*, for soprano solo with accompaniment for string orchestra, is "sacred music" of a style more popular in the nineteenth century than now, a style essentially emotional, sentimental if you will. It might almost serve as an aria in an opera and, in fact, is definitely akin in feeling to the *"Ave Maria"* of *Otello* and the *"Salve Maria"* of *I Lombardi*. The construction is of the simplest: an opening in B minor, with the voice-part mainly in monotone, passing through a *cantabile* section in B major back to the original material and tonality. In view of the graceful writing for the voice and the effective harmony of the accompaniment, its infrequent performance

Ecclesiastical Works

is rather surprising, all the more so as it is better suited to concert purposes than the arias usually selected.

The *Pater Noster*, written for two sopranos, contralto, tenor, and bass, unaccompanied, is of more solid workmanship, more definitely ecclesiastical in character. Indeed, after the opening phrase the main subject is treated for a little while in a fugal manner, and some of the modulations are reminiscent of early church music. On the whole, however, the music here also aims primarily at emotional expression, as is sufficiently attested by outbursts like "*E laude e grazia di ciò che ci fai*" or "*Dell'infernal nemico*," the latter, incidentally, being introduced in a very effective manner by the successive entrances of the voices with the original subject. Supplicatory passages, such as that first heard to the words "*Padre, padre, dà oggi a noi pane*," passages indicative of desolation, such as that which sets "*E che noi perdoniam*," work to the same end. But the best music of all, perhaps, is contained in the last two pages, especially where the "*Amen*" is ushered in on a chord of F in the midst of a G-major tonality, a procedure recalling that wonderful "*Amen*" at the conclusion of the *Lacrymosa* in the Requiem Mass. Needless to say, the actual part-writing is beyond criticism

QUATTRO PEZZI SACRI

1. *Ave Maria*
2. *Stabat Mater*
3. *Laudi alla Vergine Maria*
4. *Te Deum*

First Performance: PARIS, April 7, 1898

These, the last compositions completed by Verdi, must be regarded at least as much as an expression of æsthetic as of religious faith, for in different degrees they represent an attempt, perhaps conscious, to adapt some characteristics of the Palestrina and Marcello he so greatly admired to the requirements of contemporary taste. At the same time they are in no sense mere copies of the antique, the harmony, in particular, being intensely individual throughout, the "*Stabat Mater*" and portions of the "*Te Deum*" showing a sensitiveness to the dramatic significance of the words akin to that manifested in the Requiem Mass.

The "*Ave Maria*" and the "*Laudi*," both written for unaccompanied voices, may be taken together. The former is in essence little but an experiment in harmonizing a so-called "enigmatic scale":

that an anonymous contributor had sent to the *Gazzetta Musicale*, originally, it appears, discussed with Boïto, but subsequently carried through by Verdi alone. This scale is entrusted as a *canto fermo* (if the term may be allowed in an essentially harmonic essay) to all four voices in succession, first to the bass and tenor, then, with the key changed to the subdominant, to the alto and soprano, the treatment being different on each occasion. Though Verdi himself attached so little importance to the experiment that he preferred the remaining pieces to be performed in Paris without it, the result is something more than a mere essay in ingenuity. Apart from the undoubted interest and originality of the harmonic treatment, the last section in particular is definitely a thing of beauty.

The *"Laudi,"* a setting of words from the last canto of Dante's *Paradiso* for two sopranos and two altos, is simplicity itself, mainly built on harmonic rather than contrapuntal lines. There is an ethereal beauty in this music that makes one wonder why it does not figure more often in the limited repertory of compositions for unaccompanied female voices. Probably the last two pages, beginning with the expressive *cantabile*, *"La tua benignità,"* which leads to the fine climax of *"In te s'aduna,"* to die away again almost at once in the final *"Ave,"* contain the most notable music; but the whole composition is an admirable expression of tenderness and mystical reverence.

When we turn to the *"Stabat Mater"* and the *"Te Deum,"* we are in the presence of compositions of a very different caliber, not merely owing to the fact that they are written for full orchestra as well as voices. The *"Stabat Mater,"* for instance, is a definite picture in music of the scene wherein the mother watches and shares the agony of her Son hanging on the cross. In contrast with many settings of the same subject, the words are never repeated; they are used once and once only, Verdi's desire for directness being further indicated by a note at the beginning of the score in which he insists on the maintenance of one tempo throughout and warns the interpreters against taking liberties with the time except in so far as they can momentarily be justified by considerations of expression. The result possesses the distinction and charm of a drawing executed with a minimum of lines. The somber opening subject, given out by the chorus in unison (and, incidentally, only again referred to in the four bars that bring the work to a close), produces the appropriate atmosphere at once.

Passages such as the "*Cujus animam,*" with the soblike syncopation of clarinets and violins so typical of the composer, the plaintive "*Quæ mœrebat,*" wherein the accompaniment figure, rising in semitones, gradually develops into a passage of truly celestial beauty, the broken-hearted "*Vidit suum dulcem natum,*" with its tragic silences emphasized by the soft big drum as in the Mass or *Aïda* — all these, in but a dozen pages, paint a vivid emotional picture.

With the "*Eja Mater,*" a beautiful piece of writing for unaccompanied voices, the mood becomes more subjective until, after the four bars of vocal and orchestral drama suggested by the word *crucifixi*, we come to the lyrical contemplation of the "*Tui Nati*" section, as regards melody and harmony one of the most lovely things imagined by the composer. With the prayer that Christ's death and sufferings may bring salvation to humanity there is a return to more pictorial music, which culminates, as regards drama, in the soft trumpet-calls suggesting the Day of Judgment in the "*Per te, Virgo*" passage and, as regards sonority pure and simple, in the fine crescendo for voices and orchestra that represents longing for the joys of paradise.

Admirably scored and possessing throughout a harmonic flavor in particular that is truly individual, the "*Stabat Mater,*" without rivaling the glories of the Requiem Mass, remains a pendant not unworthy of them, a miniature that retains a charm of its own, though lacking the vitality and significance of the full-sized canvas.

The "*Te Deum,*" written for double chorus and scored for a large orchestra that includes a cor anglais, is perhaps the most ecclesiastical of all Verdi's compositions. This is scarcely surprising in view of the fact that the music is in the main derived from two themes of liturgical character and origin:

The former opens the work, and the subject derived from it, which first makes its appearance on the wood-wind after the final "*Sanctus,*" is much used in the subsequent choral writing. The latter, introduced by the trumpets before the words "*Tu Rex gloriæ*," provides the main foundation for the intricate eight-part writing that follows. In both these sections, which in fact constitute the bulk of the work, the interest is contrapuntal rather than harmonic, though the exceptionally vivid and elaborate orchestral coloring also plays an important part. It is in the beautiful passage for unaccompanied voices, to the words "*Salvum fac populum*," that harmony first enjoys and maintains predominance, even the principal subject, when it reappears, being subsequently treated in a series of effective harmonic progressions.

What may be called the high lights of the "*Te Deum*" are undoubtedly the "*Sanctus*" outburst, with the word insistently repeated by the second chorus during the ensuing sentences till finally it dies away *pianissimo* in the distance; the wonderful choral and orchestral writing based on the second subject; and the "*Salvum fac populum*" section already referred to; the somber unison passage, "*Dignare, Domine*"; the final "*In Te, Domine, speravi*," punctuated by the three successive E's on the trumpet, each louder than the last, which lead up to the final climax. These are the most striking points, but, in fact, the whole of the "*Te Deum*" maintains a very high level in every respect. Verdi allowed himself slightly more latitude in the matter of word-repetition and word-arrangement than in the case of the "*Stabat Mater*," but he unquestionably achieved his object, noted in the first portion of this book, of giving to the text the most accurate musical interpretation possible. Moreover, the score — headed, it should be noted, by the same instructions as figure in the "*Stabat Mater*" — is not only a model of directness but a model of felicitous and economical use of musical material. Alike in formal construction and treatment of chorus and orchestra, the "*Te Deum*" is certainly the most important of the *Pezzi Sacri*; it alone shows almost, if not quite, the same vitality as the Requiem Mass.

MISCELLANEOUS WORKS

Except for the summary indications already given, no attention need be paid to the works of Verdi's adolescence: the *Stabat Mater* and other ecclesiastical music, the marches and overtures written at Busseto, the cantata composed for Count Borromeo, and the like. The attitude of the composer towards them is best summed up in the fact that, wherever possible, he destroyed them. He might with advantage also have destroyed the setting of Mameli's *Suona la Tromba* (1848), but one is curious to know why, if Perosio is correct, he made an exception in favor of his settings of Manzoni's *Cinque Maggio* and *Cori delle Tragedie*. The explanation may lie in his almost mystical veneration for the author.

SONGS

Two Albums

I (1838)

"Non t'accostare all' urna"
"More, Elisa, lo stanco poeta"
"In solitaria stanza"

"Nell'orror di notte oscura"
"Perduta ho la pace"
"Deh pietosa oh Adolorata"

II (1845)

"Il Tramonto"
"La Zingara"
"Ad Una Stella"

"Lo Spazzacammino"
"Il Mistero"
"Brindisi"

Miscellaneous

L'Esule (1839)
La Seduzione (1839)

Il Poveretto (1847)
Tu dici che non m'ami (1869)

Notturno a tre voci: "Guarda che bianca Luna" (1839)

Most of these songs, it will be seen, date from the period of Verdi's second sojourn in Milan, though the probability is that some of them at any rate were actually written earlier. The explanation of the late date of "*Tu dici che non m'ami*" may be found in the fact that it was composed, according to Neisser (to whom I owe the precise dates of composition), for the Piave Album mentioned in the first part of this book. Though only a few of the songs are procurable at the present time, I have had access to nearly all of them in one way or another and cannot pretend that their disappearance has left the world appreciably poorer.

They are written in the conventional idiom of the time, and, generally speaking, the less ambitious, the more pleasing they are. Thus, in the first album there is a certain *stornello*-like charm about "*More, Elisa*" and "*Perduta ho la pace*," the latter, incidentally, anticipating a well-known phrase of Gilda's in *Rigoletto*, just as "*Brindisi*" in the second album anticipates the rhythm and one phrase of the famous "*Brindisi*" in *La Traviata*. Another song of merit is "*Deh pietosa*," divided, as are many of the longer songs, into minor and major sections, the latter of which anticipated the doubtless unconscious Saint-Saëns in the first two bars of the refrain of "*Mon cœur s'ouvre à ta voix*." The songs in the second album are, as a rule, rather more elaborate, with some attempt at atmosphere-painting in the accompaniment; that of "*Il Mistero*," for instance, suggests a definite if primitive impression of a lake. "*Il Tramonto*" is pretty, but perhaps "*Lo Spazzacammino*" is the most successful of the collection; with its recurring waltz-refrain it is at least amusing in a rather obvious way. The less said about would-be descriptive or dramatic songs such as "*L'Esule*," the better; neither in form nor in idea have they anything to recommend them.

INNO DELLE NAZIONI

Words by Boïto

Production: LONDON, May 24, 1862

There is nothing here to detain us for long. Boïto's poem, the kind of panegyric on the supersession of war by commerce and the arts typical of international gatherings, and usually (as in this case) the prelude to fresh hostilities, is pompous and, it seems to me, wholly insincere. Verdi's music, equally pompous and little more sincere, doubtless achieved the purpose for which it was brought into being: the adequate representation of Italy and the creation of immediate effect.

It opens with a chorus apostrophizing the glory of nothing very definite, which contains a fine passage distinctly prophetic of the priests in the second act of *Aïda*. Then the soloist, in the guise of a bard, rhapsodizes on the splendor and delight of the scene in an uncommonly poor recitative, which leads to a broad, not unattractive tune very typical of the composer at his second best, accompanied by the harp and repeated by the chorus. Finally comes the most important section of all, wherein the bard, later reinforced by the chorus, describes the more glorious attributes of England, France, and Italy. Verdi took advantage of this, after presenting successively *God Save the Queen*, *La Marseillaise*, and the "*Inno di Mameli*," to work a decidedly ingenious combination of the three tunes, the soloist representing Italy, the chorus England, and the orchestra France. It must have sounded effective, though an English audience may have wondered why the national anthem should all of a sudden be presented in common time, with the words at the end decidedly askew. The cantata ends with a return to Verdi's own broad tune, in choral unison this time, and (after a momentary pale orchestral reminiscence of *God Save the Queen* restored again to 3/4 time) shouts of exultation accompanied by a fanfare on the orchestra.

Verdi in later years thought little of this work and repented of having written it. Few will be found to disagree with his judgment.

STRING QUARTET IN E MINOR

First Performance: NAPLES, April 1, 1873

Though Verdi himself attached so little importance to this quartet that he would not allow it to be printed or performed in public for some time, it has on the whole been under- rather than overrated. It contains obvious defects. For instance, the third movement, *Prestissimo*, is practically negligible and the abundance of fast passages in every movement is so marked as to lead to definite monotony. On the other hand, it cannot be dismissed airily as a mere by-product, least of all on the ground that it does not follow the lines of the ordinary classical quartet. Doubtless, no German composer would have written the *Andantino* but this minuet-like melody, with its wistful grace and unaffected simplicity, is none the less charming on that account. The movement is interesting, moreover, in that it contains three bars definitely prophetic of a well-known passage in the first act of *Falstaff*; it is marred by a semiquaver episode particularly unnecessary here as well as by a poor return to the original subject.

Undoubtedly the first and the last movements are the outstanding feature of the quartet. The kinship of the main subject of the first movement, *Allegro*, to a figure associated with Amneris is perhaps not accidental in view of the fact that we owe the quartet to a postponement of the production of *Aïda* at Naples. However that may be, it makes an uncommonly good subject for chamber-music, and the treatment of it, coupled with the very pretty second subject, which forms a charming contrast, provides the most satisfactory music in a movement that is otherwise inclined to degenerate into something of a scramble. The last movement, *Allegro assai mosso*, is usually considered the best. In essence it consists of a single idea, treated and developed with marked ingenuity, which unmistakably suggests the rapid chatter of the women in *Falstaff*. Only it is even more rapid, and the twitter of birds rather than the chatter of women might better define the general characteristics of the music. There is a good deal of individuality, not only in the subject itself but in several details of its handling, notably when the first violin holds a long E against the bustle of the other instruments, as well as in the effective final coda marked *Poco più presto* — an instruction that in practice, I fancy, must be seen rather than heard, for the pace of the whole movement is unconscionable.

VERDI THE MUSICIAN

THE preceding analyses as well as certain passages in the first part of this book will have thrown into relief the most salient characteristics of Verdi as a musician. There remain, however, some details of his attitude towards his art and of his relations with other composers that should be emphasized.

Perhaps the basis of Verdi's æsthetic creed is best shown in his views on musical education. They were eminently practical. First and foremost, he believed in rigid discipline and hard work. He did not believe in theories or systems. He thought a general literary and, especially, a historical culture more important than concern with abstract questions of æsthetics; the acquisition of fluency by means of assiduous practice in strict counterpoint and the writing of fugues more desirable than conscious stimulation of the imaginative faculties. "The student with genius," he once wrote, "who has been well initiated into the mysteries of the art will end by accomplishing that which no master could ever have taught him."

He did not consider it advisable that a student should be largely preoccupied with contemporary music, because of the danger of such preoccupation developing an idolatrous enthusiasm for some composer or other liable to stifle individuality. In the ultimate resort he certainly regarded the fearless expression of personality as the cardinal virtue in a composer and the lack of it as the outstanding defect in the music of his younger contemporaries. A letter to Arrivabene written in 1875 gives his point of view in a nutshell:

> I am unable to say what will emerge from the present musical ferment. Some want to specialize in melody like Bellini, others in harmony like Meyerbeer. I am not in favor of either. I should like a young man, when he begins to write, never to think about being a melodist or a futurist or any other of the devils created by this kind of pedantry. Melody and harmony should only be means to make music in the hands of the artist. If the day ever comes when we cease to talk of melody or harmony; of Italian or German schools; of past or future, etc., etc. — then perhaps the kingdom of art will be established.
>
> Another calamity of the present time is that all the works of these young men are the products of *fear*. Everybody is excessively self-conscious in his writing and when these young men sit down to compose, their predominant idea is to avoid antagonizing the public and to enter into the good graces of the critics.

You tell me that my success is due to a fusion of the two schools. I never gave either of them a thought . . .

Verdi was undoubtedly justified in claiming that he had never given a thought to the theoretical advantage of this or that school. In some respects it might have been better if he had, but in others he was the gainer. The essential practicality of his mind was to a large extent responsible for the individuality and the sincerity of his music. His creed coincided with the injunction of the Preacher to do with his might whatever his hand found to do. That is not to say that he was unconscious of the shortcomings of his own cultural limitations. On the contrary, he often deplored the circumstances of his upbringing and asked with true, not affected, modesty what the judgment of a peasant like himself could be worth. Nevertheless, in his heart he did not believe in judgments at all, either his own or those of other composers, however eminent. He believed in personal taste. Towards the end of his life, in 1893, when a fellow composer submitted a sonata for his opinion, he answered as follows: "Everybody has and should have his own way of feeling; wherefore judgments are always diverse and useless, sometimes false. Boïto (who was there) joined with me in admiring your composition, especially the very beautiful and expressive phrase at the beginning. If I told you that the composition in general seemed to me too much based on dissonance, you could answer: 'Why not? Dissonance as well as consonance is an element of music; I prefer the former, etc.' And you would be right. On the other hand, why should I necessarily be wrong?"

Two years later, writing to the same musician, he insisted that "judgments have no value even when they are sincere. Everybody judges according to his personal feelings, and the public interprets the judgment of others in exactly the same way." Other instances of his emphatic views in this sense have already been given elsewhere. In short, though Verdi doubtless believed as firmly as Rossini that music could be divided only into two categories, the good and the bad, he did not pretend to know any infallible method of distinguishing the two, except perhaps a definite insistence that music of one kind should never pretend to be of another. For himself, he recognized as valid the claims of every school and of every period. "I admit the past and the present," he wrote to Arrivabene in 1882, "and I would admit the future, too, if I knew it and found it good."

Verdi never pretended to an intellectual outlook in which he did not, in fact, believe. He scarcely ever consulted the scores of other men and he was not ashamed to admit that music on a merely visual acquaintance meant nothing to him. As late as 1880 he avowed that in his opinion a good cabaletta was preferable to all the harmonic and orchestral ingenuities at present in vogue. Indeed, anticipating the extreme moderns of our own day, he thought that much of the vaunted progress in music was in reality a step backwards, not forwards, because "Art devoid of spontaneity, naturalness, and simplicity ceases to be Art." "In the Arts," he wrote in 1884, "excessive (I say, excessive) reflection stifles inspiration." To sincerity he was prepared to sacrifice everything, even those attributes of contemporary music which, as he wrote to Bellaigue in 1893, he recognized as genuine improvements and admirable in themselves. It must not be imagined from this that Verdi was ever a mere *laudator temporis acti*. On the contrary, he once summed up his views with typical simplicity and conciseness thus: "One must belong to one's own epoch." Though enthusiastic for celebrations in honor of Palestrina and Cimarosa, he poked fun at those who made an excessive cult of the past, suggesting on one occasion, when some commemoration or other was mooted, that it might be a good idea to start a movement for an erection of a statue to Pythagoras and, if that were a success, to Jubal as well. He frequently commented adversely on the tendency of the public never to honor the living equally with the dead, on their readiness to turn against a composer who had achieved success while still young.

Indeed, the ignorance, the stupidity and, above all, the fickleness of the public were constant themes with him and he preached rigid indifference to them as necessary to the true artist. The finest day in an artist's life, he thought, was when he could turn round and say: "Fools, you were wrong!" Yet his letters show him as fully recognizing the truth of the apparent paradox that in the ultimate result the judgment of the public is the sole true criterion of values. At the very end of his life he did not even hesitate to say, with an admission of his prosaic outlook in certain respects, that the takings of the box office provided the "only infallible thermometer" of success or failure, though he did not think that such a test was necessarily applicable immediately.

To the opinions of professional criticism, on the other hand, he paid little attention, despite personal respect for individual critics such as Filippi and, even more, Bellaigue. Somewhere or other he makes the odd statement that, whereas the artist should look into the future, it is not only the right but the duty of the critic to judge according to established standards; which seems to imply that he did not even expect exceptional insight or flair in that quarter. The truth of the matter is that Verdi could never forget that critics were also journalists — that is to say, members of a tribe especially obnoxious to him as being connected with what he probably hated more than anything else in the world: publicity.

Though Verdi was conscious of musical claims superior to considerations of nationality and environment, he was throughout his life an ardent apostle of what we now should call musical nationalism. During the seventies and the eighties he was exceedingly distressed, as we have seen, by what he considered the excessive Germanization of Italian music. He wished the Germans to remain German and the Italians Italian, emphasizing the fact that the music of the former was primarily instrumental, that of the latter, vocal. He never ceased to urge on his countrymen the importance of regarding Palestrina as the basis of their national music. It would be interesting to know precisely the time when Verdi developed this enthusiasm for Palestrina. Did it date from his student days or did it come later? The sole certainty is that it existed at the time of the composition of *Aïda;* in fact, one of the choruses in that opera was originally planned as an essay in the manner of Palestrina.

When Boïto, in 1887, asked Verdi's opinion as to the best six composers to study for the purposes of choral singing, he answered in a letter so interesting that it deserves quotation:

I send you some names, the first that come into my mind. They are more than six, but there were so many excellent men in the period you mention that it is difficult to know whom to choose.

1500
* Palestrina (*in primis et ante omnia*)
Victoria
Luca Marenzio (a very pure writer)
Allegri (he who wrote the *Miserere*)

And the many other excellent composers in that century, except Monteverdi, whose part-writing was poor.

1600 Beginning
* Carissimi
Cavalli

Later
Lotti
* Scarlatti, A. (who is full of harmonic treasures also)
* Marcello
Leo

1800 Beginning
* Pergolesi
Jomelli

Later * Piccini (the first, I believe, to write quintets, sextets etc. Composer of the first genuine *opera buffa, Cecchina*).

If you are really limited to six, those marked * seem to me entitled to preference.

The list is interesting for many reasons, not least because there figures in it Piccini, often summarily dismissed by people totally ignorant of his music as a mere worthless antagonist of Gluck; for whom, incidentally, Verdi entertained by no means the conventional reverence, describing him as "not much superior to the best men of his time despite his powerful dramatic sense, and definitely inferior to Handel as a musician."

Verdi also wished to see vocal rather than string quartets popular in Italy, reiterating, even at the time when he himself had written a string quartet, his belief in their greater conformity with Italian musical traditions. In 1879, when the Scala orchestra began giving concerts in Milan under Mancinelli, he was pleased at their success but skeptical as to their utility. "I do not know," he wrote to the Countess Maffei, "how it can help *our* art. Let us be frank; *our* art is not instrumental." A year before he had not been at all enthusiastic about the visit of the same orchestra to Paris under Faccio, though on this occasion the remarkable triumph of the enterprise led him to say that his advice was probably bad, as usual.

His whole attitude with regard to nationalism in general and Germany and Italy in particular is well illustrated by his correspondence with Hans von Bülow. Von Bülow had in the heyday of his Wagnerian enthusiasm written a scathing criticism of the Requiem Mass after one of the original performances at La Scala. Prompted, it is said, by Brahms, he subsequently recanted and with typical impetuosity wrote, in 1892, a letter to Verdi so apposite that a portion of it must be quoted:

> I began with the study of your last works, *Aïda, Otello,* and the Requiem, of which a recent performance, though quite mediocre, moved me to tears. I have studied them not only according to the letter that killeth but the spirit that giveth life. Let me say, illustrious Master, that now I admire, I love you! . . . And, faithful to the Prussian motto: *Suum Cuique,* I exclaim with enthusiasm: Long live Verdi, the Wagner of our Allies!

It may be doubted whether Verdi, who had little love for the Triple Alliance, altogether relished this peroration, but the letter caused him real joy. Perhaps he found in it some compensation for the defection of Mariani twenty years before. He answered with charm and dignity, writing among other things: "If the artists of north and south have different tendencies, it is well that these should be different. Everybody should preserve the characteristics of his own nation, as Wagner so rightly observed. You are fortunate in that you are still the sons of Bach. And we? We too, sons of Palestrina, once had a great school of our own, but it has become bastard and looks like perishing utterly."

Much emphasis has been laid on Verdi's independent evolution both in the first part of this book and in the analyses of the various works. Such emphasis is not meant to imply that Verdi differed in this respect from other composers — for instance, the genesis of Wagner's mature works is often discernible in his earlier operas — but an uncompromising assertion of the fact was necessary, since, up to recent times at any rate, it has been customary to admit Verdi as a great composer only after he came within the orbit of Teutonic influence. The fallacy is complete, because there was always a quality of greatness in Verdi's music and he never in any real sense came within the orbit of Teutonic influence.

Nevertheless, like every composer, Verdi was influenced by the work of other men. At the outset of his career the contours of his melody owed much to Bellini, for whom three years before his death he had not lost his admiration. He found Bellini's orchestration and harmony poor, but the sentiment and the melancholy of his music as a whole entirely individual. Above all, he admired the length of his melodies, describing the *lento a piacere* phrase in the introduction to *Norma* as one of the most beautiful things ever written. To Rossini his debt was greater or at any rate more definite. For instance, the theme of the "*Sì, Vendetta*" duet in *Rigoletto* is strikingly akin to a passage in Rossini's *Otello*, while the accompaniment of the "*Miserere*" in *Il Trovatore* is almost identical with that of "*Qual mesto gemito*" in *Semiramide*. There never was a composer so utterly devoid of snobbery as Verdi, who, despite his profound reverence for Beethoven in general and the Ninth Symphony in particular, did not hesitate to say that the workmanship of the last movement of that symphony was very bad and was not ashamed to own that he found some of Bach's B minor Mass arid, and classical music occasionally dull. Wherefore he did not judge it necessary to claim perfection for everything Rossini had written though he admired him wholeheartedly not only for his music but for his mental capacity. He thought that *The Barber of Seville* was the best comic opera ever written, that *William Tell* was a great masterpiece, and that other operas contained passages of sublime beauty. Rossini, it may be remarked, returned a portion at least of the admiration, for he once described Verdi as the most original and robust of contemporary composers and paid tribute to his character as a rare example of private and public virtue.

In later life Verdi was influenced, like every other opera composer of the generation, by Meyerbeer. So many instances of this influence have been given in preceding pages that it is unnecessary to go into the matter further. Except, possibly, in the case of *I Vespri Siciliani*, Verdi never capitulated to it, but traces of Meyerbeerian procedure may be found in most of his operas, even, according to Stanford, in *Falstaff*, though completely assimilated and individualized. Pizzi tells us that Verdi entertained a genuine admiration for Meyerbeer's intellectual qualities despite the fact that he was repelled by "the banker's" intrigues and journalistic maneuvers in pursuit of success. He praised warmly the blend of fantasy and realism in *Robert le diable*, the dramatic power of *Le Prophète*, and, like everybody else, Wagner included, he raved over the fourth act of *Les Huguenots* though he found the opera as a whole heavy and long.

Verdi's relations with Berlioz were more cordial — on both sides. Berlioz describes Verdi in his *Mémoires* as a "noble and honorable artist." Verdi, writing to Escudier, bids him salute Berlioz, "whom I love as a man and respect as an artist." Again, in a letter to Arrivabene written in 1882, Verdi summed up Berlioz as follows:

> Berlioz was a poor sick fellow, full of fury against the world at large, bitter and spiteful. His intellect was vast and keen. He had a natural flair for scoring and anticipated Wagner in many orchestral effects. (The Wagnerians will not admit this, but it is so.) He did not know the meaning of moderation and was deficient in that calm, that balance, let us say, which produces complete works of art. Even when he did praiseworthy things he exaggerated. . . .

One would gladly know more of the relations between these two remarkable men, so utterly different yet obviously sympathetic one to the other. Verdi must have learnt much from Berlioz as regards scoring, a notable instance being the use of the echoing trumpets in the *Dies Iræ* section of the Mass, whereof the *Kyrie*, it should be noted in passing, also shows unmistakable traces of the influence of Cherubini's fine Masses.

A certain amount has already been written about the relations of Verdi and Wagner, but something must be added. First of all, with reference to Wagner's attitude to Verdi — a slight task, for it can scarcely be said to have existed. Wagner just ignored his greatest operatic contemporary. So far as I am aware, Verdi is not once mentioned by name in the whole course of Wagner's letters and writings. There is a contemptuous reference to "the new *furia* of modern operas as exemplified in *I Vespri Siciliani* and other nights of carnage." There is an equally contemptuous expression of sympathy for a favorite singer who had to abandon *The Flying Dutchman* for *Il Trovatore*. Otherwise, Verdi is casually included in such a label as "Donizetti and Co."; nothing more. The omission is perhaps more striking than surprising. Wagner, who, according to J. W. Klein, would not even read Berlioz's operas though urged to do so by no less a person than Liszt, was notoriously indifferent to the music of his contemporaries. In view of his own wonderful achievements his indifference and egotism were justified, for, all things said and done, the music written by a composer is the only thing that ultimately matters. This is Wagner's real justification. The justification sometimes put forward, to the effect that Verdi had written nothing worthy of his attention before his death in 1883. will not hold water. Even granted — and few people nowadays would grant it — that there was nothing in the earlier operas up to and including *Don Carlo* to awaken interest and admiration, both *Aïda* and the Requiem Mass were composed and performed everywhere before Wagner wrote the last of his innumerable pages of prose. His neglect is all the more remarkable because (again according to Klein) Wagner's devoted disciple Cornelius greatly admired *Aïda*, while the Requiem had been the subject of much comment in the musical world. The presumable explanation of the matter is that Wagner had early in life made up his mind about Verdi and never troubled to examine the facts anew. To him, Verdi was only one of the Italian composers who wrote for the opera public as distinct from that nebulous abstraction which he christened "the Folk." As if in Italy, at any rate, they were not one and the same thing!

The extent to which Verdi's music was actually or probably influenced by Wagner has been indicated in the main body of this book. Most apparent, perhaps, in *Don Carlo* (an opera characterized by so fervent an admirer as Bizet as pretentious owing to its Wagnerian tendencies), this influence was never anything more than a result of that desire to keep abreast of the times which, as we have seen, Verdi considered to be the duty of a composer. Even so, some of the similarities are probably fortuitous. Verdi, however, unlike Wagner, was curious about his rival's music. He deplored the celebrated fiasco of *Tannhäuser* in Paris, because it deprived him of the opportunity of hearing the opera. Radiciotti says that he first heard the overture at a concert at the Paris Opéra in 1865 and, like Berlioz on a first hearing of the first act of *Tristan*, found it "mad." If, as seems likely, this was the first occasion on which Verdi heard Wagner's music, the case for any conscious imitation in *Don Carlo* becomes very slender. It is certain that he heard one of the Bologna performances of *Lohengrin* in November 1871.

There exists at Busseto a vocal score of *Lohengrin*, with pencil annotations made by Verdi during some actual performance. Many of these notes are criticism, mainly unfavorable, of the performance; which creates a difficulty in reconciling it with the Bologna production, usually considered by everybody, including Wagner himself, to have been of the first class. Verdi also attended a performance of *Lohengrin* in Vienna some time or other, for he mentioned the fact to Pizzi, and it is conceivable, therefore, that this was the performance in question, though Lualdi, who has carefully examined and described the notes on the score, does not even suggest such a possibility.

I was fortunate enough myself to look at these notes, which are often scarcely legible. Some are profoundly interesting. For instance, Verdi found all the Swan music ugly; he did not like, or at any rate did not understand, the first scene of the second act, but praised the end of the third; while his previous study of the score is attested by the remark that the wedding march did not sound so effective as he thought it would. His general impression, noted at the end, was that the reflective music was better than the music of action, that there were too many words moving too slowly, that there was abuse of organ-like effects in the writing for the wood-wind. Except for some criticism of the string-writing he generally admired the orchestration and found the music as a whole beautiful when the underlying thought was clear.

It should be noticed how scrupulously fair Verdi was in all this to the music of a man who was being used as a kind of cudgel to beat him to the ground, in the midst, possibly, of all the bitterness caused by the defection of a valued friend. He never made any secret of his admiration for Wagner's genius. Writing late in life, he summed up his music as "music where there is life, blood, and nerves; music, therefore, that is entitled to survive. Wagner shows artistic patriotism to an exceptional degree. He pushed his passion so far in this respect as to write in accordance with a preconceived artistic idea. This preconceived idea did him harm; but most of the harm came not so much from himself as from his imitators." Nevertheless, admiration for Wagner as a composer was a very different matter from acceptance of the dogmatic tenets of Wagnerism, which he found ridiculous and pretentious. Indeed, it is not too much to say that Verdi hated Wagnerism and all that it stood for, while he was always ready to poke fun at the "Music of the Future," expressly stating on one occasion that he saw no reason to fear it.

Both as men and as artists Wagner and Verdi stood at opposite poles. Verdi always remained conscious and proud of his Latin birth and characteristics. He held in abomination the uncouth heroes of the Nibelung saga, Siegfried in particular. He disliked the great length of Wagner's operas almost as much as the total darkness accompanying their performance, which, he said, induced a torpor in everybody, the Germans included; though his prophecy that they would on that account never become popular in Italy has been falsified by events. As Monaldi truly wrote, Verdi was always primarily an instinctive artist, bent only on improving his artistry; he was never a philosopher or an æsthetic speculator like Wagner. Moreover, unlike Wagner, whose object was the concentration of all the arts in the theater, Verdi sought first and foremost the greatest possible musical perfection. Even in the realm of music pure and simple their ideals were fundamentally different, for Wagner had symphonic aspirations, while Verdi believed (to quote his own words) that opera was opera and a symphony a symphony. Verdi stated in so many words his conviction that a theatrical composer must be prepared on occasions to sacrifice portions of his music, however admirable, in the interests of succinctness; Wagner's prolixity, though perhaps inseparable from his resourcefulness and inventive fertility, has been singled out as his most obvious weakness. As regards intellectual speculation Wagner was of course Verdi's superior; as regards inflexibility of determination there was nothing to choose between them. Perhaps Wagner's most remarkable achievement was that he invented an idiom that became for more than fifty years the musical language of the world. One of Verdi's greatest feats was that, almost alone among Wagner's contemporaries and immediate successors in western Europe, he successfully avoided speaking that language.

In a sense the influence of Boïto on Verdi was the most fruitful of all, but only in a strictly limited sense. The once prevalent idea to the effect that Verdi absorbed Wagnerian ideas and aspirations through the medium of Boïto is not true. To begin with, Boïto was in no sense a Wagnerite though he passionately admired Wagner's music. His judgment on Wagner, contained in a letter to Bellaigue, deserves to be better known: "Hybrid and monstrous, half-man and half-brute, fawn, satyr, centaur, or triton; or, better perhaps, half-god and half-ass, Dionysus in the divine frenzy of his inspiration, Bottom in his stupid obstinacy — how can we ever love him unreservedly?" Boïto was far more a Verdian than a Wagnerian, for he preferred Verdi's outlook in every respect, æsthetic as well as social, even though he might have admitted the superiority of Wagner's intellectual equipment in most, and his musical equipment in some, respects. Second, Boïto, whether a Wagnerite or not, seems to have had no direct musical influence on Verdi at all. What he did influence was his cultural outlook. Verdi always possessed an instinctive, uncultivated *flair* for what was great — for Shakspere, Michelangelo, and Beethoven. Boïto made it more conscious. He instilled into him a new respect for the literary value of a phrase as distinct from its dramatic value; he made him see more clearly, perhaps, that it was not enough for a situation as a whole to be effective, but that the details of it as expressed in words must be of themselves worthy of their context. This is the most that can be claimed for him, and even here, remembering the libretto of *Aïda* or even of *King Lear*, it behooves us to walk warily. Boïto's great and undeniable merit was to have made himself so beloved by Verdi that the composer accepted with enthusiasm from his hands incomparably the two best librettos in the history of Italian opera. His inquiring, restless mind may have stimulated Verdi's imagination, just as his wonderful, loyal devotion, amounting to real self-abnegation, may have been more responsible than we know or guess for encouraging the old man not to cease from his labors. But nothing can alter the fact that in the Verdi-Boïto partnership Verdi remained always the dominant partner, the masculine element. May one venture to sum up the situation by suggesting that Boïto became to Verdi in the æsthetic sense very much what Giuseppina Strepponi was in the life of every day?

In any attempt to sum up Verdi's characteristics as a musician due regard must be paid to the circumstances and the environment in which the major part of his working life was spent. Franz Werfel, in the introduction to his collection of Verdi's letters, has very justly emphasized the extraordinary pressure exercised on an Italian composer by the demands of the public in the first half of the nineteenth century. This pressure not only determined the enormous size of the output expected from a composer but rigorously dictated what he might and might not do. There is no parallel in modern music to such a state of things; perhaps the nearest analogy to it in England was the musical-comedy stage in the days of George Edwardes. New operas were expected at regular and frequent intervals, written in conformity with conventions that could not be defied with impunity. Verdi, though first subordinating himself to these conventions, eventually, thanks to his iron will, did not so much defy as change them. But the process was arduous. He succeeded at the outset in adapting the prescribed mold to the expression of his new personal vigor. Thus, he curtailed the length of the operatic form — Mercadante, for instance, when he first heard *Nabucco* is said to have remarked that it was all over by the time he himself would have got to the end of the first act — and restricted the license of vocal embellishments which, despite the greater discipline already imposed by Rossini, still stood in the way of the unfettered presentation of the composer's intentions. In the main, however, he conformed to the conventional patterns strictly and, up to the time of *Rigoletto* at any rate, readily enough.

Inevitably such conditions affected the quality of Verdi's early output. Between March 1842 and March 1851 he wrote fourteen operas, one of them twice over! How could it be expected that he should always give of his best? The amazing thing is that these operas include not only *Nabucco* and *Ernani* and such "progressive" works as *Macbeth* and *Luisa Miller*, but *Rigoletto* itself. There was, however, a good as well as a bad side to this operatic tyranny. It developed a standard of craftsmanship scarcely realized in the world of music today. The treadmill was undoubtedly responsible for much worthless music, but it left Verdi with an unrivaled capacity "to bend the notes" (his favorite phrase) to the service of his meaning. Moreover, the very exclusivism of the system worked in the end to his advantage. Italy neither knew nor cared anything about the music of other countries. The harmonic language of her composers might be a quarter of a century behind that of the rest of Europe; the standard of her orchestral performances infinitely lower. Provided her singers maintained their world-wide supremacy, she remained indifferent. This state of things undoubtedly explains the backwardness of Verdi's harmony in comparison with that of several of his contemporaries in other countries. It probably explains also his very tentative experiments in orchestral effects; for what was the use of making experiments if there were no orchestras capable of carrying them out? But mark the result! He never was lured into that overindulgence in harmonic or orchestral ingenuity which has proved a refuge to so many second-rate composers in distress. He was forced to concentrate on the intrinsic value of the bare musical idea ungarnished by any more or less adventitious trappings. The way in which he laughed at himself and all his colleagues for overworking the chord of the diminished seventh is very revelatory in this respect. When, however, the musical ideas he had to express demanded greater harmonic freedom, he did not, like so many composers, take other people's ideas ready-made, but gradually and laboriously evolved a genuine idiom of his own. His attitude to orchestration followed a precisely similar orbit, with the result that alike in middle life, when they were comparatively backward, and in late life, when they were comparatively advanced, both his harmony and his orchestration remained entirely individual, indissolubly part and parcel of what he had to say. It was largely, then, this habit of self-reliance and self-containedness that enabled him to achieve the almost unique distinction, already noted, of withstanding the potent magic of the Wizard of Bayreuth, because, with insignificant exceptions, he never borrowed anything from anybody that could not be assimilated and individualized.

Doubtless, he was further assisted by another aspect of his musical psychology: lack of a sense of shame. Attaching little value to cleverness for its own sake, Verdi never hesitated to write down his musical ideas as he really felt them without a thought, so it seems, as to whether they were original, refined, calculated to elicit admiration or the reverse. Beyond question this was responsible for occasional vulgarities, but they were always the vulgarities produced by exuberance of vitality or sentiment. Many lesser composers have been possessed of better taste, for a certain kind of good taste has always been the hereditary enemy of genius. Verdi's unswerving search for truth, alike in music and life, was not a cold but a passionate quest, forming the nucleus of that compelling sincerity which has often been stressed as the outstanding feature of his art, and which, by a curious paradox, is perhaps more, not less, indispensable to a writer for the artificial medium of the theater than to any other.

But, in a sense, the whole character of this apparently so simple man was a paradox. With an unsurpassed instinct for the theater he hated everything the theater stood for, just as he despised the race of singers while rating the human voice as the most potent means of musical expression. His haughty contempt of the public was only equaled by the humility with which he bowed to the ultimate validity of their judgment. A believer in tradition, he persistently protested against belittlement of the present; an exponent of nationalism in practice, he preached the importance in theory of considerations superior to nationalism. He was a skeptic and an enthusiast, a pessimist who never capitulated to pessimism. The most proud and secretive of men, he remained the most modest and expansive of musicians. No one ever lived a more practical or a better-balanced life, yet the soul of his music was romance, expressed in violent contrasts and quivering emotion. Most paradoxical of all, as has been truly observed, this man to whom the world owes some of its most passionate love-songs has not, to my knowledge, left behind him a single love-letter.

Verdi's unbounded vitality, his fundamental simplicity and integrity, fused these incompatibilities, more apparent of course than real, into a personality of such force that still today the music in which it was expressed can thrill and stimulate us in a manner peculiar to great art and, in some measure, to itself. Boïto defined Verdi's predominant quality alike in his music and his life as that of putting "the right note in the right place." No praise could be higher, for, in art as in letters, that quality is the monopoly of the true poet, the supreme master. Perhaps one who has devoted several hours almost daily during nearly three years to the study of the man and his works may be allowed in all humility to endorse it. He did not expect greater familiarity with Giuseppe Verdi to breed the proverbial contempt but, to be frank, he was not prepared for the ever deeper, ever more certain love and admiration which that familiarity has in fact called forth.

INDEX

Adam, Adolphe, 83
Albert Hall (London), 149
Alberto, Carlo, 47
Alboni, Marietta (Contessa Pepoli), 79
Alexander II, Czar of Russia, 113
Allegri, Gregorio, 404
  Miserere, 404
Angeleri, examines Verdi at Milan Conservatoire, 11
Apollo Theater (Rome), 70, 94
Argentina Theater (Rome), 34-5, 54
Ariosto, Attilio, 77
Arrivabene, Conte Giovanni, 153-4, 162, 164, 175, 401-02, 407
Asquith, Antony, 172
Assemblée Nationale, 83
Athenæum, The, 48-9, 110, 182
Auber, Daniel François Esprit, 74, 80, 91, 109-12, 126, 315
  Gustave III, 111, 315
  Robert le diable, 80

Bach, Johann Sebastian, 25, 26, 148, 174, 195, 388, 392, 406
  B Minor Mass, 148, 406
Bagier, Director of Théâtre Italien, 119, 134
Baistrocchi, organist and Verdi's first teacher, 6
Balfe, Michael William, 50
  Bohemian Girl, The, 50
Balzac, Honoré de, 23 n
Barbarossa, Frederick, 54
Barberina, Verdi's sister-in-law, 191
Barbieri-Nini, in *Macbeth*, 45, 46
Bardare, 70
  Libretto of *Il Trovatore*, 70
Barezzi, Antonio, 7-10, 14, 16, 20, 35, 42, 47, 90, 125, 126
Barezzi, Giovanni, 58
Barezzi, Margherita, 8, 15, 19
Barnby, Sir Joseph, 149
Barrili, Antonio Giulio, 15 n, 79 n, 177 n
Basevi, on *Luisa Miller*, 59, 262; on *Le Roi s'amuse*, 62; on *La Traviata*, 75; on *Ernani*, 217
Basily, of Milan Conservatoire, 11-13

Beaumarchais, Pierre Augustin Caron de, 94
Beaumont, translator of *Macbeth*, 118
Beethoven, Ludwig van, 3, 25, 80, 146, 148, 150, 177, 182-4, 195, 216, 225, 240, 250, 262, 281, 382, 388, 406, 410
  Battle of Vittoria, The, 255
  Eroica Symphony, 3
  Fidelio, 250
  Mass in D, 148, 388
  "Pastoral" Symphony, 310
  "Pathetic" Sonata, 240
  Symphonies
    3rd (*Eroica*), 3
    5th, 262
    6th ("Pastoral"), 310
    9th, 406
Bellaigue, Camille, 58, 160, 168, 187, 371, 387, 403, 410
Bellini, Vincenzo, 13, 16-17, 24-28, 46, 83, 85, 111, 205, 254, 401, 406
  I Montecchi ed i Capuletti, 27
  Norma, 24-5, 27, 406
  Sonnambula, La, 85
Belviglieri, journalist for *Il Lavoro*, 132
Bennett, Sir William Sterndale, 109, 111, 168, 170
Bénoît, Pierre Léonard Léopold, 175
Berliner Tageblatt, 167 n
Berlioz, Louis Hector, 44, 55, 80, 82-3, 123 n, 138, 158, 286, 369, 388-9, 407-08
  Faust, 369
  Mémoires, 83, 407
  Requiem Mass, 148, 388-9
Bertani, Prospero, 142-3
Bizet, Georges (Alexandre César Léopold), 185, 358, 408
  Boutique Fantasque, La, 295
  Carmen, 185
Boïeldieu, François Adrien, 25
Boïto, Arrigo, 16 n, 58, 88, 112-13, 158-62, 164-8, 171, 174, 176, 182-4, 186-7, 190-4, 196, 299-300, 306, 359-69, 373-81, 394, 398, 402, 404, 410-11, 413
  Hero and Leander, 159

Index

Inno delle Nazioni, 112–13, 158–9, 398
Libretto of *Falstaff*, 176–8, 182, 184, 374–81
Libretto of *Falstaff*, translated into French with du Locle, 186–7
Libretto of *Otello*, 158, 167, 171, 359–69, 373
Libretto of *Simon Boccanegra*, revised, 88, 161–3, 299–300, 353
Mefistofele, 159, 164, 367
Nerone, 178
Boïto, Camillo, 188
Bonaventura, 60 n, 167 n, 187 n, 206, 359
Bonavia, on Verdi's politics, 31; 122
Bonci, Alessandro, 319
Bononcini, Giovanni Battista, 15
Borri, Carlo, 145
Borromeo, Count Renato, 14
Bottesini, Giovanni, 136–7, 139, 359
Bourgeois and Souvestre, 60, 309
  Stiffelio based on a play by, 60, 309
Bragagnolo-Bettazzi, 154 n
Brahms, Johannes, 405
Bruneau, Alfred, 181
Bülow, Hans von, 34, 148, 405
Byron, George Noel Gordon, Baron, 34, 36, 221, 249–50
  Corsair, The, 249–50
  Two Foscari, The, 34, 221

Calzado, Director of Théâtre Italien (Paris), 85, 86
Cammarano, Salvatore, 34, 38–9, 54, 56, 59–61, 69–70, 72, 77, 227–8, 246, 251–3, 255–9, 273–8
  Libretto of *Alzira*, 38–9, 227–8
  Libretto of *Battaglia di Legnano, La*, 54, 251–3
  Libretto of *Lucia di Lammermoor*, 38
  Libretto of *Luisa Miller*, 56, 255–9
  Libretto of *Trovatore, Il*, 69, 273–8
Capecelatro, 58
Caponi, letter from Verdi to, on refusal by Milan Conservatoire, 11
Capponi, in the Manzoni Requiem, 146
Carcano, Giulio, 61, 163
  Libretto of *Hamlet*, 61
Carducci, Giosuè, 176
Carissimi, Giacomo, 404

Carlo Felice Theater (Genoa), 89
Carrara, Alberto, 194
Carrara, Dr., 106, 141, 194
Carrara, Maria, 191, 193–4
Caruso, Enrico, in *La Forza del Destino*, 115, 331
Carvalho, Léon, 166, 186
Cavaletti, Stefano, 5
Cavalli, Francesco (Pietro Francesco Caletti-Bruni), 404
Cavour, Conte Camillo Bensodi, 16, 47, 98–103, 145, 154
Cellini, Benvenuto, 68 n
Cesari, editor of Verdi's correspondence, 35
Chaliapin, Fyodor Ivanovich, 86 n
Checchi, Eugenio, 90 n, 164, 166 n, 178 n, 186 n, 187, 188 n
Cherubini, Maria Luigi Carlo Zenobio Salvatore, 25, 141, 146, 148, 388, 407
  Requiem Mass, 148, 388
Chop, 194 n
Chopin, Frédéric François, 27, 238
Chorley, Henry Fothergill, 18, 28, 48–50, 85 n, 89, 97, 110–11, 128
  Reminiscences, 111
Ciccarese, 75 n
Cimarosa, Domenico, 180, 192, 383–4, 403
  Matrimonio Segreto, Il, 180, 192, 384
Cornelius, Peter, 408
Correnti, Cesare, 141
Corriere della Sera, 168–9, 181
Corriere di Milano, 146
Costa, Sir Michael, 50, 112, 123
Court Theater (Copenhagen), 89
Covent Garden (London), 50, 112, 149
Cromwell, Oliver, 31
Crosnier, Director of Paris Opéra, 82
Crowest, F. J., 149
Cruvelli, Johanne Sophie Charlotte (Crüwell), 81
Crystal Palace, 151

Daily Graphic, 182
Daily Telegraph, 150, 170, 182
d'Annunzio, Gabriele, 195
  "Pianse e amò per tutti," 195
Dante Alighieri, 157, 191, 387, 392
  Paradiso, 191, 394

Index

Paraphrase of *Ave Maria*, 157, 392
Paraphrase of *Pater Noster*, 157, 392
Davison, James, 48–9, 110–11
Delfico, caricatures by, 153
Delle Sedie, Enrico, 79
Derivis, basso, as Zaccharias in *Nabucco*, 22
Deutsche Verlags-Anstalt, 187
Directory (Government of France), 3
Disraeli, Benjamin, 100
Donizetti, Gaetano, 13, 22, 26–7, 31, 34, 36, 46, 51, 69 n, 183, 202, 408
  Don Pasquale, 27
  Elisir d'Amore, 27
  Lucia di Lammermoor, 25, 27
  Maria di Rohan, 22
Draneht Bey, director of Cairo Opera, 136
Drury Lane Theater (London), 110
du Locle, Camille, 119, 122, 130, 134–6, 156, 186–7, 332–8
  Libretto of *Aïda*, translated into French, Nuitter, 156, 345
  Libretto of *Don Carlo*, with Méry, 119, 122, 332–8
  Libretto of *Falstaff*, translated into French, with Boïto, 186–87
Dumas, Alexandre (père), 62, 103
  Kean, 62
Dumas, Alexandre (fils), 72, 73, 75, 284–6
  Dame aux camélias, La, 72, 73, 75, 284–6
Duplessis, Marie, 75
Dupré, Giovanni, 45, 156
Durante, Francesco, 141
Duveyrier, Anne Honoré Joseph, 79, 290–4
  Libretto of *I Vespri Siciliani*, with Scribe, 79, 290–4

Edwardes, George, 411
Escudier brothers, 55, 73, 80, 117
Escudier, Léon, 87, 90, 107–08, 116–17, 119, 121, 123–6, 149, 151, 155–6, 161, 175, 189, 232, 239, 306, 407
Eugene, Prince, 4
Eugénie, Empress of the French, 123

Faccio, Franco, 138, 147, 158–60, 164, 168, 170, 172, 174, 181, 405
Fama, La, 17, 139

Fancelli, tenor in *Aïda*, 139
Farini, Luigi Carlo, 99
Fava, Angelo, 145
Fedeli, Doctor, 167
Fenice Theater, La (Venice), 31–2, 40, 62, 70, 72–3, 87
Ferdinand II, King of Naples, 93
Ferdinand VII, King of Spain, 108
Ferrari, Giovanni, 14, 15
Fétis, François Joseph, 11, 12
Figaro, 17, 19, 23, 30
Filippi, Filippo, 129, 137, 146, 157, 159, 162, 181, 403
FitzGerald, Edward, 195
Flauto, of Teatro San Carlo (Naples), 38, 42, 43, 57
Florimo, Francesco, 140–1
Fortis, 139, 162
France, La, 121
France Musicale, 30
Francis I, King of France, 91
Frezzolini, in *I Lombardi*, 30; in *Giovanna d'Arco*, 37

Gaisruk, Cardinal, Archbishop of Milan, 29
Galeazzo, Count, 153
Gallo, Antonio, 74
García Gutiérrez, Antonio, 69, 71–2, 87, 91, 277–8, 299–300
  Tesorero del Rey Don Pedro, El, 91
  Trovador, El, 62, 69, 71, 277–8, 299
Gardoni, 49, 79
Garibaldi, F. T., passport description of Verdi cited by, 10
Garibaldi, Giuseppe, 100, 103, 120, 159
Gautier, Théophile, 121
Gazzetta di Milano, 23, 30
Gazzetta di Venezia, 33, 65, 74, 87–8
Gazzetta Musicale, 23, 30, 39, 40, 46, 58, 61, 71, 74, 88–9, 95, 114, 146, 155–6, 176, 190, 394
Ghislanzoni, Antonio, 104, 122, 128, 135, 139, 159, 162, 328, 338, 344–53
  Art of Making Debts, The, 129
  Libretto of *Aïda*, 135, 345–53
  Libretto of *Don Carlo*, revision, 162, 338, 344
  Libretto of *Forza del Destino, La*, revision, 129, 328
  Ugly Women, 129

Index

Giacosa, Giuseppe, 193
Gibbon, Edward, 146 n
   Decline and Fall of the Roman Empire, The, 146 n
Gilbert, W. S., 72, 299, 320
   Ruddigore, 215
Gil Blas, 181
Gioberti, Vincenzo, 29, 34
   Moral and Civil Primacy of the Italians, The, 29
Giusti, Giuseppe, 30, 45, 47
Glinka, Mikhail Ivanovich, 146
Gluck, Christoph Willibald, 15, 121, 141, 405
God Save the Queen, 113, 399
Goethe, Johann Wolfgang von, 159, 367
   Faust, 159
Göhler, Dr. Georg, 258
Gounod, Charles François, 138, 358
Grey, Cecil, 185
Grieg, Edvard Hagerup, 387
Grossi, Tommaso, 29, 209
Grove, Sir George, 11
   Dictionary of Music and Musicians, article on Verdi in, 11
Guasco, tenor in *Ernani*, 33
Gustavus III, King of Sweden, 91
Gutiérrez, Antonio García, *see:* Garcia Gutiérrez, Antonio
Gye, producer at Drury Lane, 110, 149
Gyrowetz, Adalbert, 18
   Il Finto Stanislao, 18

Habeneck, François Antoine, 80
Halanzier, director of the Paris Opéra, 156
Halévy (Jacques Fromental Élie Lévy), 80, 114, 130
   Frou-Frou, 130
Handel, George Frideric, 15, 151, 194, 392, 405
   Messiah, The, 63
Hanslick, Eduard, 387
Haydn, Joseph, 9, 13, 25, 150, 181, 195, 392
   Creation, The, 13, 16
Hearts of Oak, 226
Her Majesty's Theatre (London), 112
Hohenstein, designer for *Falstaff*, 179
Hudson, Sir James, 100–01

Hueffer, Francis, 168, 170
Hugo, Victor, 31, 33, 62, 64, 66, 72, 91, 214, 266–7, 272
   Hernani, 31, 214
   Roi s'amuse, Le, 62, 64, 266–7, 272
Humbert, King of Italy, 176, 192
Hummel, Johan Nepomuk, 15
Humperdinck, Engelbert, 319
   Miracle, The, 319

Illustrated London News, 48, 110
Imperial Italian Theater (Moscow), 113
Imperial Theater (St. Petersburg), 108
Imperial Theater (Vienna), 17
International Art Club (Rome), 174
Ismail Pasha, Khedive of Egypt, 134, 138

Jacovacci, Director of Apollo Theater, 94–5, 97, 116
Joachim, Joseph, 177
Jomelli, Niccolò, 404
Journal des Débats (Paris), 83, 169

Kalkbrenner, Christian, 15
King Lear, 31, 61, 77, 81, 85, 91, 119, 160, 411
Klein, J. W., 387, 408

Lablache, in *I Masnadieri*, 49; in *Cinderella*, 80
Lamartine, Alphonse Marie Louis de Prat de, 25
Lambertini, report on *Nabucco* in *Gazzetta di Milano*, 23; report on *Giovanna d'Arco*, 37
Lanari, of Pergola Theater (Florence), 43, 44, 46
Lauzières, de, 117, 129
Lavigna, teacher of Verdi, 11–14, 16, 191
Lavoro, Il, 132 n
Leduc, 165
Lega Lombarda, 181
Leo, Leonardo, 141, 404
Leoncavallo, Ruggiero,
   I Pagliacci, 20
Levi, of Soragna, 55
Levrini, of Rimini, 89
Lind, Jenny, 48; in *I Masnadieri*, 49
Lissa, 127

Index

Liszt, Franz von, 23 *n*, 408
Loewe, in *Ernani*, 32; in *Giovanna d'Arco*, 40; in *Attila*, 41
Lombard League, 54
Lotti, Antonio, 404
Louis XIV, King of France, 92
Louis Napoleon, Prince, 49; *see also* Napoleon III
Louis Philippe, King of France, 53
Lualdi, *quoted* on Verdi, 27, 28, 409
Lucca, publisher (Milan), 42, 50–2
Luccardi, sculptor, 41, 68, 70, 73, 94, 95, 116
Lumley, director of Her Majesty's Theatre (London), 42–3, 47, 49, 50; director of Théâtre Italien (Paris), 69; 87
Luzio, editor of Verdi's correspondence, 35
Lyceum Theatre (London), 174

Maffei, Andrea, 23 *n*, 39, 45, 47, 237, 244
  Libretto of *Macbeth*, extra verses for, 47, 237
  Libretto of *Masnadieri, I*, 48, 244–7
Maffei, Countess Clara, 23, 40, 48, 55, 68 *n*, 73, 79, 94, 98, 125, 127, 131, 142, 152, 154, 158, 163, 167, 405
Maini, in the Manzoni Requiem, 146
Malmesbury, Lord, 100
Mameli, Marchese Goffredo, 55, 397
  Fratelli d'Italia, 55
  Suona la Tromba, 55, 397
Mancinelli, conductor, 132, 405
Mancinelli, Signora, 132
Manzoni, Alessandro, 45, 126–7, 145, 147–9, 154, 163, 389, 392
  Cinque Maggio, 397
  Cori delle Tragedie, 397
  Promessi Sposi, I, 145, 163
Mapleson, James Henry, 112
Marcello, Benedetto, 12, 393, 404
Marenzio, Luca, 404
Margherita, Queen of Italy, 192
Maria Louisa, Duchess, 101, 105
Mariani, Angelo, 81, 89, 101, 103–04, 119, 123–5, 128, 130–4, 136, 345, 405
Mariette Bey, Auguste Édouard, 134, 351

Mario, tenor in *Un Ballo in Maschera*, 97
Marseillaise, La (Rouget de Lisle), 112, 113, 255, 354, 399
Martello, censorship official in Venice, 64
Martinelli, Amilcare, 189–90
Martini, Giovanni Battista, 141
Mascagni, Pietro, 187
Mascheroni, conductor of La Scala, 181–2, 186, 190
Masini, 13, 14, 16
Masini, Angelo, 149
Maurel, Victor, 162, 164, 166–7, 170, 179, 181, 186
Mazzini, Giuseppe, 31, 55, 100, 154
Mazzucato, of Milan Conservatoire, 145
Medini, bass in Manzoni Requiem, 149
Meilhac, Henri, 130
  Frou-Frou, 130
Mendelssohn-Bartholdy, Felix, 5, 26, 183, 345, 386
  Rondo Capriccioso, 345
Mendès, Catulle, 186
Mercadante, Saverio, 31, 91, 140, 411
Merelli, 17, 20–4, 29, 31, 189
Merli, 55
Méry, 119, 122, 332–8
  Libretto of *Don Carlo*, 119, 122, 332–8
Meyerbeer, Giacomo (Jakob Liebmann Beer), 48–9, 74, 79, 84, 109–10, 112, 114, 119, 121–3, 138, 156, 196, 248, 295, 320, 338–9, 401, 407
  Etoile du Nord, 79
  Feldlager in Schlesien, 48
  Huguenots, Les, 81–82, 84, 338–9, 407
  Prophète, Le, 339, 407
  Robert le diable, 407
Michelangelo, 45, 410
Milan Conservatoire, 11, 24, 145, 158
Mocenigo, Count, Director of La Fenice, 31–2
Monaldi, 13, 36 *n*, 41, 54, 67 *n*, 69 *n*, 124 *n*, 168, 180, 345, 410
Moniteur, 121
Monte di Pietà e d'Abbondanza, Busseto, 9, 14–15, 105, 194
Monteverde, Giulio, 188
Monteverdi, Claudio, 387
Morelli, Domenico, 160, 164

Morning Post, the (London), 49, 112, 150
Mosso, Angelo, 179
Mozart, Wolfgang Amadeus, 5, 12, 25–6, 111, 141, 146, 149, 181–2, 195, 210, 216, 240, 331, 370, 372, 384, 387–8
  "Alla Turca," 210
  Così fan Tutte, 384
  Don Giovanni, 240, 271
  Entführung, 240
  "Jupiter" Symphony, 372
  Nozze de Figaro, Le, 182
  Requiem, D Minor, 149, 388
Mugnone, performance of *Nabucco* in 1913, 24
Musella, director of San Carlo, 143
Musset, Alfred de, 25
Mussolini, Benito, 99, 154
Mussorgsky, Modest Petrovich, 121 *n*
  Boris Godunov, 86 *n*
Muzio, Emanuele, 42, 45, 73, 134, 136, 155–6, 175

Naples Conservatoire, 140
Napoleon I, Emperor of the French, 3, 108
Napoleon III, Emperor of the French, 68 *n*, 93, 98–99, 120, 142
Nappi, critic of *La Perseveranza*, 181
Negroni Prati, Countess, 39, 192
Neisser, 14 *n*, 16 *n*, 106, 157 *n*, 397
Nicholas I, Czar of Russia, 40
Nicolai, Otto, 21
Nietzsche, Friedrich Wilhelm, 185
Nievo, 3 *n*
Nord, 114
Novaro, Michele, 55
  Fratelli d'Italia, 55
Novello, Messrs., 149
Nuitter (Charles Louis Etienne Truinet), 118, 156
  Translation into French of *Aïda*, with du Locle, 156
  Translation into French of *Macbeth*, with Beaumont, 118
  Translation into French of *Tannhäuser*, with Beaumont, 118
Nuova Antologia, 169

Offenbach, Jacques, 202
Opéra (Paris), 51, 55, 67, 80–1, 86, 119–20, 122–5, 156, 190, 279, 293, 339, 373, 408
Opéra Comique (Paris), 149, 166, 186
Origen, 146 and *n*
Orsini, Felice, 93, 98–9

Pacini, Giovanni, 31
Palestrina, Giovanni Perluigi da, 12, 25–6, 143, 148, 174, 192, 388–9, 393, 403–04, 406
Pallade (Rome), 54
Pallavicino, Marchese, 105
Pall Mall Gazette, 149
Pantaleoni, Signora, in *Otello*, 170, 172
Paris Conservatoire, 141
Parma Conservatoire, 187
Pasqua, Signora, 180
Patti, Adelina, 79, 117, 149
Pélissier, Mlle Olympe (Mme Rossini), 127–8
Pergola Theater (Florence), 43, 45
Pergolesi, Giovanni Battista, 143, 383, 404
  Serva Padrona, La, 180
Perinello, 16 *n*
Perosio, 15 *n*, 397
Perrin, Director of Paris Opéra, 119
Perseveranza, La, 175–6
Petrarch (Francesco Petrarca), 161, 299–300
Piantanida, hears Verdi at Milan Conservatoire, 11
Piave, Francesco, 31–3, 35–6, 39–40, 44, 46, 52, 60–6, 69, 73, 75, 87–9, 109, 114–16, 118, 125, 128, 135, 161, 189, 212, 214–15, 220–1, 233–7, 246, 248–50, 263–7, 281–6, 295–300, 307–10, 321–8
  Libretto of *Aroldo*, 61, 85, 89, 307–10
  Libretto of *Attila*, 40
  Libretto of *Corsaro, Il*, 52, 248–50
  Libretto of *Due Foscari, Il*, 35–6, 220–1
  Libretto of *Ernani*, 31–3, 212, 214–15, 278
  Libretto of *Forza del Destino, La*, 109, 114, 321–28
  Libretto of *Macbeth*, 44, 233–7
  Libretto of *Rigoletto*, 63–64, 66, 263–7

Index

Libretto of *Simon Boccanegra*, 87–8, 161, 295–300
Libretto of *Stiffelio*, 60, 309–10
Libretto of *Traviata, La*, 75, 281–6
Piazza, 14, 16 n, 199
Libretto of *Oberto*, with Solera, 14, 199
Libretto of *Rocester*, 16 n
Piccini, Niccolò, 15, 404–05
Cecchina, 404
Piccolomini, in *Traviata*, 85, 110
Pinetti, double-bass player, 105 n
Piroli, 120, 141
Pius IX, Pope, 47, 54, 108, 154
Pizzi, Italo, 23 n, 40, 58 n, 105 n, 106, 122, 140 n, 179, 187 n, 407, 409
Ponselle, Rosa Melba (Ponzillo), 288
Porpora, Niccolo, 9
Pougin, Arthur (François Auguste Arthur Paroisse-Pougin), 15, 73, 138, 157 n
Presse, La (Paris), 83
Prime-Stevenson, Edward, 69 n, 277–8, 353, 358
 Long-Haired Iopas, 353
Provesi, Ferdinando, 8, 9, 11, 14, 191
Puccini, Giacomo, 121 n, 193 n
 Tosca, 221
 Turandot, 121 n
Pungolo, Il, 146

Racine, Jean Baptiste, 358
Radiciotti, on Verdi and Rossini, 23; biography of Rossini, 26; 79 n, 408
Reszke, Edouard de, in *Aïda*, 155; in revised *Simon Boccanegra*, 162
Reyer, Louis Étienne Ernest, 137, 139, 168–9
 Sigurd, 138
Ricci, 160 n
Ricordi, Giovanni, 17, 38, 42, 55, 60, 62, 69
Ricordi, Giulio, 81, 85, 94, 114, 117, 127, 129, 134–5, 138–9, 142, 156, 158–61, 164, 166, 167 n, 168–9, 174–6, 178, 186–7, 188 n, 191–3
Ricordi, Tito, 20, 88, 148–9, 154–5
Riemann, Hugo, 55
Rivas, Angel de Saavedra, Duque de, 72, 108, 109, 114, 115, 129, 326–7

Don Alvaro, o La Fuerza del Sino, 72, 108, 109, 326–7
Rivista di Roma, 36
Rolla, advice *quoted* by Verdi, 11; 12
Roman Republic, 54
Romani, 18, 23, 35, 201
Libretto of *Il Finto Stanislao*, 18, 201
Roncaglia, 206, 211, 237, 382
Ronconi, baritone, as Nebuchadnezzar in *Nabucco*, 22
Roqueplan, Director of Paris Grand Opera, 62, 69, 82
Rossi, 18
Libretto of *Il Proscritto*, 18, 21
Rossini, Gioacchino Antonio, 9, 13, 16–17, 23–6, 31, 46, 63, 67, 74, 79–80, 89, 109–12, 121, 123, 126–7, 130, 146, 154, 156, 160, 167, 177, 180–2, 196, 202, 209, 226, 382–3, 387, 401, 406, 411
 Barber of Seville, The, 9, 26, 63, 112, 180, 406
 Cinderella, 9, 80
 L'Italiana in Algeri, 26
 Mosé, 24, 26, 177
 Otello, 25, 160, 167, 406
 Semiramide, 25–6, 406
 Tancrede, 24
 William Tell, 15–16, 26, 206, 226, 406
Rossini Mass, 127–28, 131–32, 134, 145, 148, 159, 391
Rouget de Lisle, Claude Joseph, 255
 Marseillaise, La, 112, 113, 255, 354, 399
Royer and Vaez, 51, 62, 112
Libretto of *Jérusalem*, 51, 112
Rubini, Giovanni Battista, in *Cinderella*, 80
Ruddigore (Gilbert and Sullivan), 215

Saint-Saëns, Charles-Camille, 84 n
 "Mon cœur s'ouvre à ta voix," 398
San Benedetto Theater (Venice), 74
San Carlo Theater (Naples), 34, 53, 60, 85, 91, 142
Sant'Agata, Villa, 56–60, 68, 77, 85, 90, 94, 98, 101, 103, 107, 116–19, 125–6, 130–1, 134, 138, 140, 143, 145, 151–2, 156, 168, 173–4, 178, 186–7, 190–1, 196, 280

Index

Sardou, Victorien, 253
Sargent, Malcolm, 357
Sassaroli, Vincenzo, 154
Sax, Adolphe, 123–4
Scala, La (Milan), 16–18, 19, 22, 29, 37, 44, 51, 60, 88, 94, 105 n, 118, 125, 128, 131, 136, 147, 149, 159, 161, 167–8, 174, 177–9, 186, 191, 194, 405
Scalaberni, director of the Opera (Bologna), 128
Scarlatti, Alessandro, 141, 143, 183, 404
Schiller, Johann Christoph Friedrich von, 37, 45, 48, 56, 62, 119, 122, 224–5, 246–7, 258–9, 329, 338
  Don Carlos, 62, 119, 122, 338
  Kabale und Liebe, 56, 59, 258–9
  Maid of Orleans, 37, 224–5
  Räuber, Die, 45, 48, 246–7
  Wallenstein, 329
Schröder-Devrient, Wilhelmine, performance in I Montecchi ed i Capuletti, 27
Schubert, Franz Peter, 11 n, 16, 26, 129, 200
  "Ave Maria," 129
  "Marche Militaire," 200
Scott, Sir Walter, 108
Scotti, Antonio, 115, 331
Scribe, Augustin Eugene, 69, 78–80, 82, 84, 91, 94, 96, 290–94
  Gustave III, ou Le Bal masqué, 91, 94, 96, 315
  Libretto of I Vespri Siciliani, with Duveyrier, 69, 79–80, 82, 84, 290–4
Scudo, 81–3
Secolo, 169
Seletti, Pietro, 8, 9, 12
Sella, Quintino, 102
Shakspere, William, 44, 61, 77–8, 114, 118–19, 126, 157–8, 160, 163–4, 171–2, 174, 176, 184, 233–7, 281, 299, 359–69, 374–81, 410
  Hamlet, 61, 126, 163, 176
  Henry IV, 182, 381
  King Lear, 31, 61, 77, 81, 85, 91, 119, 160, 411
  Macbeth, 44, 118, 233–7
  Merry Wives of Windsor, The, 178, 381
  Othello, 158, 160, 164, 171–2, 360–9, 374
  Timon of Athens, 367
  Titus Andronicus, 367
Shaw, George Bernard, 215, 228
  Arms and the Man, 215
Shaw, Miss, responsible for first English interest in Verdi, 18
Società Orchestrale (Milan), 157
Soffredini, 25, 200, 210, 250, 342, 359
Sole, Il, 147
Solera, Themistocles, 14, 18, 21–3, 29, 32, 37, 40–1, 68, 189, 199, 203–08, 223–5, 229–32
  Libretto of Attila, 40, 229–32
  Libretto of Giovanna d'Arco, 37, 223–5
  Libretto of Lombardi alla Prima Crociata, I, 29, 207–09
  Libretto of Nabucodonosor (Nabucco), 21–3, 203, 205
  Libretto of Oberto, with Piazza, 14, 199
  Melody, 18
Somma, Antonio, 77–9, 91–2, 94–7, 311–15
  Libretto of Ballo in Maschera, Un, translated from the French, 91–2, 94–7, 311–15
  Libretto of King Lear, 77–9
Soragna, 9, 55
Souvestre and Bourgeois, 60, 309
  Stiffelio based on a play by, 60, 309
Spontini, Gasparo Luigi Pacifico, 226
Staël, Mme de, 40
Stainer, Sir John, 149
Stanford, Villiers, 182–4, 382, 386, 407
Stendhal (Marie-Henri Beyle), 17, 24 n, 25, 26
Stolz, Teresa, 38, 125, 131–2, 136, 138, 143, 146–7, 149, 155, 168, 187, 191, 193
Strand Theatre (London), 81
Straus, Richard, 271, 383, 387
  Rosenkavalier, Der, 271, 383
Strepponi, Felice, 24
Strepponi, Giuseppina, see Verdi, Giuseppina (Strepponi)
Sullivan, Sir Arthur Seymour, 60 n, 202, 320
  Ruddigore, 215
Syracuse, Count of, 93

Index

Taffanel, 190
Tamagno, Francesco, 162, 166, 170
Tamberlik, 127 and *n*
Tasso, Torquato, 77
Tchaikovsky, Piotr Ilyich, 295, 345
  Nutcracker Suite, 345
Temps, Le, 121
Tennyson, Alfred Lord, 109
Théâtre Italien (Paris), 42, 70, 82, 85–6, 116, 119, 134, 155
Théâtre Lyrique (Paris), 117–18
Theocritus, 259
Thomas, Ambroise, 126
  Hamlet, 126
Times, The (London), 48–9, 100, 110, 112–13, 149, 170, 182–3
Titiens, Mme, 112
Torelli, director of San Carlo Theater, 92
Torlonia, Don Alessandro, 35
Torresani, Chief of Police, Milan, 29
Toscanini, Arturo, 24–5, 185, 191, 194
Trilby (du Maurier), 23

Uttini, Luigia, wife of Carlo Verdi, 4, 69

Vaez and Royer, 51, 62, 112
  Libretto of *Jérusalem,* 51, 112
Vaini, Minghelli, 101
Valori, Prince de, 25
Varesi, baritone, in *Macbeth,* 46; in *Rigoletto,* 67
Vaucorbeil, director of the Paris Opéra, 156–7
Ventignano, Duke of, 57, 93
Verdi, Carlo, 3, 120, 126
Verdi, Giuseppe Fortunino Francesco: —
  Career — birth and parentage, 3–4; early musical sensibility, 4–5; first lessons from Baistrocchi, 6; organist at Le Roncole, 6; sent to Busseto, 6; befriended by Antonio Barezzi, 7; first directs and composes music, 8; grant from Monte di Pietà, 9; sent to Milan, 10; personal description of, 10; refused by Milan Conservatoire, 11–12; studies with Lavigna, 12–13; conducts at Filodrammatici Theater, 13–14; marriage to Margherita Barezzi, 16; moves with family to Milan, 16; contract with Merelli, 17; first association with Ricordi, 17; production and press opinion of *Oberto,* 17; first association with Strepponi, 17; death of wife and children, 19 (*see also* Introduction); composition and production of *Nabucco,* 21–5; becomes fashionable, 23; meets Countess Clara Maffei, 23; first meeting with Piave, 31; first contacts with England, 41; negotiations with Lumley, 42–3; visit to England, 43; visit to Paris, 50; effect of political events of 1848, 53; begins close association with Strepponi, 55; buys Sant'Agata, 56; considers *Hamlet* and *King Lear,* 61; writes and produces *Rigoletto,* 62–8; his mother's death, 69; writes and produces *Il Trovatore,* 69–73; *La Traviata,* 72–6; visits Rossini, 79; meets Mariani, 89; life with Peppina, 90; effect of political events of 1859–60, 98; elected to Italian Parliament, 102; marries Giuseppina, 103; goes to St. Petersburg, 109; chosen as musical representative of Italy at Great Exhibition, London, 1862, 110; in Moscow, 113; decorated by Czar, 113; in Madrid, 116; elected foreign member of French Academy, 117; resigns from Italian Parliament, 118; effects of Italy's hostility with Austria, 119–20; his father's death, 120; makes headquarters in Genoa, 125; death of father-in-law, 125; generosity to Piave, 125–6; visits Manzoni, 126; death of Rossini, 126; efforts on Rossini Mass, 127; coolness with Mariani, 128; friendship with Ghislanzoni, 128–9; created Knight of the Order of Civil Merit of Savoy, 130; death of Mariani, 132; negotiations with Cairo over *Aïda,* 134; effect of Franco-Prussian war, 135; *Aïda* performed in Cairo, 138; asked to be director of Naples Conservatoire, 140; member of Naples Philharmonic Society, 141; president of Florentine commission on Conservatoires, 141; String Quartet, 143; death of Manzoni and Requiem, 145–6; Commander of the Legion of Honor, 149; retires to Sant' Agata, 152; elected Senator, 153; Grand Officer of the Legion of Hon-

or, Paris, 156; begins collaboration with Boïto, 158; reception of *Otello*, 168; hospital at Villanova, 174; deaths of Muzio and Arrivabene, 175; proposed Jubilee, 175-7; Beethoven festival, 177; production of *Falstaff*, 180; proposal that he be made Marquis of Busseto, 185; Paris, 186; endows home for aged musicians, Milan, 188; death of Giuseppina, 188; death of Verdi, 193; will, 193-4; funeral, 194

Operas:

Adelia degli Adimari, 93

Aïda, 21, 123, 132-44, 154-5, 160-1, 172, 202, 206, 210, 225, 238, 254, 261, 279, 286, 310, 342-3, 345-9, 368, 395, 398-9, 404-05, 408, 410

"*Ah pietà! Ah lo salvate, Numi*," 358
"*Ah pietà ti prenda*," 356
"*Ah tu dei vivere*," 358
"*Celeste Aïda*," 354
"*Ed osan tanto*," 354
"*E la morte un ben supremo*," 358
"*Empia razza*," 358
"*Già i sacerdoti adunansi*," 358
"*Gloria all' Egitto*," 356
"*I sacri nomi*," 355
"*Là, tra foreste vergini*," 357
"*Ma tu Re*," 356
"*Nume, custode e vindice*," 355
"*Numi pietà*," 355-6
"*O Patria mia*," 279, 352, 357
"*Ritorna vincitor*," 355
"*Si dunque, sorgete*," 357
"*Su! del Nilo*," 354
"*Vedi? di morte l'angelo*," 358
"*Vincitor de' miei fratelli*," 355

Alzira, 34, 37-40, 51, 58, 227-9
"*Nella polve genuflesso*," 229

Aroldo, 85, 87-9, 91, 307-11

Attila, 37, 40-2, 129, 229-33, 294, 371
"*Avria tu l'universo, resti l'Italia a me*," 41, 232
"*Si, quello io son*," 232

Ballo in Maschera, Un, 91-8, 102, 111, 123, 226, 232, 311-20, 328-9, 386
"*Ah! ah! ah!*" 317-18

Verdi, Giuseppe (continued)

Operas:

"*Ah, è con Lucifero d'accordo ognor*," 316-17
"*Di che fulgor*," 317
"*Di' tu se fedele*," 316
"*Eri tu*," 315-16, 320
"*E scherzo od è follia*," 316, 318-19
"*La rivedrà nell' estasì*," 316
"*Non sai tu*," 319
"*O qual soave brivido*," 319
"*Ogni cura si doni al diletto*," 316
"*Oh dolcezze perdute*," 320
"*Saper vorreste*," 317, 320

Battaglia di Legnano, La, 54-6, 60, 91, 251-5, 294
"*Ah no, ah no trafitto sangue*," 254
"*Giuriam d'Italia por fine ai danni*," 254
"*Ma Dio mi volle*," 254

Corsaro, Il, 31, 47, 51-2, 248-50

Don Carlo, 119-24, 128, 130, 162, 332-5, 353, 368-9, 381, 408
"*Ah, sia benedetto Iddio*," 341, 344
"*Canzone del velo*," 340
"*Ella giammai m'amo*," 123, 339, 343
"*Io la vidi*," 339
"*Ma lassù ci vedremo*," 344
"*No, non macchiò la fè giurata*," 343
"*O don fatale*," 123, 343
"*Perduto ben, mio sol tesor*," 341

Due Foscari, I, 31, 34-6, 39, 48, 77, 107, 220-2
"*Nel tuo paterno amplesso*," 222
"*Oh vecchio cor che batti*," 222

Ernani, 32-4, 36, 40-2, 48, 72, 74, 81, 85, 107, 117, 121, 212-20, 254, 278, 294, 318, 371, 412
"*A Carlo Quinto sia gloria e onor*," 34, 216
"*Ernani, involami*," 215
"*Evincitor dei secoli il nome mio farò*," 216
"*Lo vedremo, veglio audace*," 216

Verdi, Giuseppe (continued)
  Operas:
    "Nel momento in che Ernani vorrai spento," 219
    "No, vendetta," 216
    "Si ridesti il Leon di Castiglia," 34, 216
    "Tutto sprezzo che d'Ernani," 215
    "Vedi come il buon vegliardo," 216
  Falstaff, 7, 24, 79, 107, 113, 157, 171, 176–86, 189–92, 194, 263, 306, 317, 319, 329, 345, 372, 374–87, 399–400, 407
    "Affiderai la mia birra a un Tedesco," 384
    "Bocca baciata non perde ventura," 383, 386
    "C'è a Windsor una donna," 384
    "Dalle due alle tre," 383–4
    "E il viso tuo su me risplenderà," 383
    "Fandonie che ai bamboli," 386
    "Immenso Falstaff," 382
    "Labbra di foco," 383
    "L'amor, l'amor," 384
    "Le angoscie sue son crudeli," 383
    "Le corna! Bue! Capron! Le fusa torte!" 384
    "L'ora è fissata," 384
    "O matrimonio: Inferno!" 384
    "Per te sprecai tesori," 384
    "Pizzica, pizzica," 386
    "povera donna," 383
    "Quand' ero paggio," 181, 385
    "Reverenza," 383
    "Te lo cornifico," 384
    "T'immagino fregiata del mio stemma," 385
    "Va vecchio John," 383
  Finto Stanislao, Il, see Giorno di Regno, Un
  Forza del Destino, La, 72, 109, 113–17, 119, 128–30, 156, 200, 250, 254, 306, 310, 317, 319, 321–31, 345, 353, 358, 390
    "Ella vive, ma in breve," 329
    "La Vergine degli angeli," 331
    "Madre, pietosa Vergine," 129, 250, 328
    "Pace, pace," 331

Verdi, Giuseppe (continued)
  Operas:
    "Pezzenti più di Lazzaro," 330
    "Pronti destieri," 331
    "Rataplan," 114, 328
    "Seguirti fino agli ultimi," 331
    "Solenne in quest' ora," 331
    "Tua grazia, O Dio," 319
    "Urna fatale," 331
    "Venite all' indovina," 331
  Giorno di Regno, Un, 18–20, 42, 201–02, 210, 316
    "Non san quant' io nel petto soffra mortal dolore," 202
  Giovanna d'Arco, 37–38, 40, 223–7
    "O fatidica foresta," 226
    "Quale più fido amico," 226
    "Sotta una quercia," 226
    "Trascorrere m'intesi ignoto senso per le vene," 226
  Giovanna di Guzman, 84
  Jérusalem, 51, 80, 82, 212
  Lombardi alla Prima Crociata, I, 20, 29–31, 33–4, 38, 42, 48, 51, 207–12, 254, 392
    "All' empio, che infrange la santa promessa," 209
    "D'un sol colpo in paradiso," 211
    "Farò col nome solo il cielo inorridir," 209
    "Jérusalem," 210
    "Mostro d'Averno orribile," 209
    "O Signore, dal tetto nation," 30, 211
    "Più non mi reggoaitaimi," 211
    "Salve Maria," 209, 392
  Luisa Miller, 56–9, 61, 69, 73, 82, 87, 106 n, 110, 206, 255–63, 286, 412
    "Ad immagin tua creata," 259
    "Andrem, raminghi e poveri," 261
    "Come celar le smanie del mio geloso amore?" 260
    "L'ara o l'avello apprestami," 259–60
    "La tomba è un letto," 261
    "Lo vidi, e'l primo palpito il cor senti d'amore," 259
    "Piangi, piangi," 262
    "Quando le sere," 58, 160, 260
    "Tu puniscimi, O Signore," 260

Verdi, Giuseppe (continued)
Operas:
Macbeth, 44–7, 88, 117–18, 121, 206, 233–44, 300, 315, 368, 412
"Ah, la paterna mano," 238
"D'orfanellie di piangenti," 239
"E Banco! ahi vista orribile!" 244
"Fatal, mia donna," 46
"La luce langue," 237
"La patria tradita," 47
"Mi si afficcia un pugnal?" 238
"Oh poi che le chiome scrollar," 241–4
"Pien di misfatti è il calle della potenza," 237
"Sangue a me," 238
"Una macchia è qui tuttora via," 240
Masnadieri, I, 47–50, 110, 244–8
"Carlo vive," 50
"Ombra del Moor!" 248
Nabucodonosor (Nabucco), 15, 21–5, 28, 30–1, 33–4, 42, 48, 74, 77, 94, 125, 186, 189, 194, 203–07, 210–11, 219, 241, 255, 354, 411–12
"Come notte a sol fulgente," 205
"Salgo già del trono aurato," 205
"Va, pensiero, sull'ali dorate," 21, 23, 25, 28, 125, 205, 241
Nino, 42, 48
Oberto, Conte di Bonifacio, 14–18, 22, 24–5, 176, 199–201, 210
Orietta of Lesbos, 38
Otello, 67, 107, 113, 158–9, 162, 164–7, 174–6, 180, 185–6, 191, 196, 215, 226, 232, 247, 304–05, 310, 343, 345, 359–74, 382, 384, 387, 389, 392, 405
"Alza quegli occhi," 371
"Ave Maria," 209, 374, 392
"Avvinti vederli forse?" 371
"Credo," 367, 370, 382
"Credo che in grazia tornerà," 372
"Dio fulgor della bufera," 369
"Dio mi potessi scagliar," 372
"Ed io rimango di sua Moresca Signoria l'alfiere," 369
"E son fanciulle dai lieti canti," 369

Verdi, Giuseppe (continued)
Operas:
"Esterefatta fisso," 371–2
"Esultate," 369
"E tu . . . Come sei pallida! E stanca, e muta e bella!" 374
"E tu m'amavi per le mie eventure," 369
"E un dì sul mio sorriso," 372
"Fende l'etra," 369
"Fire Chorus," 369
"Giura e ti danna," 371
"Il rio destino impreco che al Moro ti dono," 371
"Io prego il cielo," 372
"La Muranese," 373
"M'hai legato alle croce," 371
"Ora e per sempre addio," 371
"Perche torbida suona la voce tua?" 370
"Salce," 368, 373–4
"Scendean sulle mie tenebre," 369
"Tu alfin, Clemenza," 372
"Vigilate," 370
"Vittoria! Sterminio!" 369
Rigoletto, 60, 62–8, 70, 74, 76–7, 79, 92, 102, 110–11, 114, 116, 123, 200, 205–06, 210, 215, 232, 247, 250, 263–73, 281, 289–90, 310, 316, 355, 368, 371, 386, 397, 406
"Ah sì, a turbare," 272
"Bella figlia dell'amore," 269–70
"Caro nome," 272–3
"E come in casa?" 268
"E il sol dell' anima," 272
"La donna è mobile," 65–6, 272–3
"O quanto dolor," 272
"Parmi veder le lagrime," 271
"Possente amor," 271
"Quest' o quella," 271
"Sì, Vendetta," 406
"Solo per me l'infamia," 272
Rocester, 16 n
Siege of Haarlem, The, 255
Simon Boccanegra, 87–9, 91, 93, 95, 116, 118, 153, 161–3, 222, 295–307, 340, 368
"Ah se la speme," 305
"Il lacerato spirito," 304
"Il suo commosso accento," 305

Verdi, Giuseppe (continued)
  Operas:
    "L'atra magion," 304
    "Miserere," 304
    "Simon! Tu! Tu!" 302–03
    "Simone? il corsaro?" 300–01
    "Vieni mirar la cerula marina," 304
  Stiffelio, 60–3, 85, 87, 89, 91, 309–10
  Traviata, La, 72–6, 82, 85–86, 110, 116–17, 123, 150, 194, 196, 226, 232, 254, 262, 281–90, 295, 319–20, 368, 372, 390, 397
    "Addio del passato," 290
    "Ah, fors'è lui," 74
    "Alfredo, Alfredo," 289
    "Amami, Alfredo," 254, 287, 289
    "Brindisi," 397
    "Così alla misera," 288
    "De' mei bollenti spiriti," 288
    "Di Provenza il mar," 76, 288–9
    "Dite alla giovine," 288
    "No non udrai rimproveri," 289
    "Non sapete quale affetto," 288
    "Oh mia rimorso," 288
    "Parigi, o cara," 290
    "Pura siccome un angelo," 288
    "Sempre libera degg' io folleggiare," 288
    "Un dì felice," 288
    "Un dì quando le veneri," 288
  Trovatore, Il, 69–73, 85–87, 110–11, 113, 116, 121, 162, 172, 175, 200, 226, 247, 254, 273–81, 289–90, 358, 406–08
    "Ah che la morte ognora," 254, 279
    "Ai nostri monti," 280, 290
    "Di quella pira," 100, 278, 280
    "D'amor sull'ali rosee," 281
    "E deggio e posso crederlo," 279
    "Il balen del suo sorriso," 279
    "Miserere," 71, 280, 406
    "Prima che d'altri vivere," 280
    "Sei tu dal ciel disceso," 279
    "Sei vendicata, o madre," 280
    "Strana pietà," 279
    "Stride la vampa," 279
    "Tacea la notte placida," 279
  Vendetta in Domino, Una, 92

Verdi, Giuseppe (continued)
  Operas:
    Vespri Siciliani, I, 69, 79, 81–5, 111, 123, 200, 226, 290–5, 407
    "Addio, mia patria," 295
    "La brezza aleggia," 295
  Other works
    Ave Maria, 157, 392–3
    Capriccio for horn, 15
    Cinque Maggio, 397
    Copialettere, 35, 37, 102, 132, 161
    Cori delle Tragedie, 397
    Duetto Buffo, 15
    Inno delle Nazioni, 112, 158–9, 398–9
    Inno di Mameli, 55, 113, 397, 399
    Suona la Tromba, 55, 397
    Pater Noster, 157, 392–3
      "Dell'infernal nemico," 393
      "E che noi perdoniam," 393
      "E laude e grazie di ciò che ci fai," 393
      "Padre, padre, da oggi a noi pane," 393
    Pezzi Sacri, 190–1, 393–6
      Ave Maria, 190–1, 393–4
      Laudi alla Vergine Maria, 190–1, 393–4
        "Ave," 394
        "In te s'aduna," 394
        "La tua benignità," 394
      Stabat Mater, 190–1, 393–6
        "Cujus animam," 395
        "Eja Mater," 395
        "Per te, Virgo," 395
        "Quæ mœrebat," 395
        "Tui nati vulnerati," 191, 394–5
        "Vidit suum dulcem natum," 395
      Te Deum, 190–1, 393, 395–6
        "Dignare dominum," 191, 396
        "In te, Domine, speravi," 396
        "Salvum fac populum," 396
        "Sanctus," 191, 395–6
        "Te Deum laudamus," 395
        "Tu Rex gloriæ," 396
    Requiem Mass, 145–52, 154, 160, 191, 388–93, 395–6, 405, 407–8
      Agnus Dei, 147–8, 390–1
      Dies Iræ, 146, 148, 150, 389–90, 407

Verdi, Giuseppe (continued)
  Other works:
    Kyrie, 389, 407
    Lacrymosa, 150, 390, 393
    Libera Me, 127 n, 145, 148, 150, 390-2
    Liber Scriptus, 150
    Lux Æterna, 148, 390-1
    Mors Stupebit, 150, 389
    Offertorium, 147, 390
    Pleni Sunt Cœli, 146, 391
    Recordare, 150
    Sanctus, 147, 390-1
    Tuba Mirum, 148, 150
  Songs, 397-8
    "Ad Una Stella," 397
    "Brindisi," 397-8
    "Deh pietoso oh Adolorata," 397-8
    "Il Mistero," 397-8
    Il Poveretto, 397
    "Il Tramonto," 397-8
    "In solitaria stanza," 397
    La Seduzione, 397
    "La Zingara," 397
    L'Esule, 397-8
    "Lo Spazzacammino," 397-8
    "More, Elisa, lo stanco poeta," 397-8
    "Nell'orror di notte oscura," 397
    "Non t'accostare all'urna," 397
    Notturno a tre voci: "Guarda che bianca Luna," 397
    "Perduta ho la pace," 397-8
    Tu dici che non m'ami, 397
    Stabat Mater (youthful), 15, 397; see also under Pezzi Sacri
    String Quartet in E Minor, 143-4, 399-400
Verdi, Giuseppina (Strepponi), 17-18, 22, 24, 51, 55, 68, 87-8, 90, 98, 101, 103, 106-07, 113, 116-18, 131, 153, 168, 177-8, 187, 189-90, 192, 194, 387, 411
Verdi, Icilio, 16, 19
Verdi, Virginia, 16, 19
Verner, Attila based on a play by, 40, 231
Victor Emmanuel II, King of Italy, 98-103, 119, 120
Victor Emmanuel III, King of Italy, 193

Victoria, Queen of England, 49, 111
Victoria, Tomás Luis de, 404
Vigier, Baron, 81
Virgil (Publius Virgilius Maro), 196
  Æneid, 196
  Eclogues, 196
  Georgics, 196
Vitali, report on I Lombardi in Gazzetta Musicale, 30; portrait of Verdi in 1843, 31
Voltaire (François Marie Arouet), 34, 38, 228
  Alzira, 34, 37, 38, 228

Wagner, Richard, 5, 26-8, 37, 48, 52-3, 56, 66, 80, 84 n, 110-11, 118, 121, 132, 138-40, 142, 146, 153, 160, 163, 169-70, 174, 181-2, 184, 186, 195-6, 218-19, 238, 248, 260, 271, 286, 293, 295, 319, 339, 344, 353, 358, 370, 373, 383, 387, 405-10, 412
  Flying Dutchman, The, 408
  Lohengrin, 132, 286, 408-09
  Meistersinger, Die, 66, 181, 184, 271, 370, 383
  "Parisian Fatalities," 80, 293
  Parsifal, 170
  Tannhäuser, 118, 140, 218, 260, 408
  Tristan und Isolde, 75, 172, 358, 373, 408
Waldmann, Maria, 138, 145-7, 149, 151, 153, 155
Washington, George, 99
Weber, Carl Maria von, 150, 183, 259, 386
  Freischütz, Der, 259
Weissmann, 34 n, 70 n, 73 n, 87 n, 144, 210, 226
Wellington, Duke of, 49
Werfel, Franz, 79, 115, 142, 162, 167 n, 306, 328, 411
  German version of Forza del Destino, La, 328
  German version of Simon Boccanegra, 162, 306
  Verdi, 79, 142
Wesley, Charles, 388
Wiener Zeitung, 170
William I, King of Prussia, 119, 352